A HISTORY OF THE
NORTHUMBERLAND FUSILIERS

A HISTORY
OF THE
NORTHUMBERLAND FUSILIERS

1674–1902

BY H. M. WALKER

WITH MAPS AND ILLUSTRATIONS

LONDON
JOHN MURRAY, ALBEMARLE STREET, W. 1
1919

All rights reserved

PREFACE

I HOPE the Northumberland Fusiliers will forgive me for attempting a history of their regiment, and that this book may be of some use in outlining the past.

The Army Lists in the Appendix are intended to illustrate the state of the Fifth during a particular period or campaign; the original spelling has been followed, but in the text the modern form has been generally used. The lists for 1799 and 1812 are from the collection of the late Sir David Smith, preserved at Alnwick Castle, the current official Army List making no distinction of battalions.

The " History of the British Army " has been closely followed for the period covered by Vols. I.-VIII., and I am also indebted to Mr. Fortescue for permitting the reproduction of the battle plan of Wilhelmsthal and the map showing Whitelocke's march to Buenos Ayres. For the Peninsular War much use has been made of Professor Oman's History; and I have also to thank Professor Oman for allowing reproductions to be used of the plans of Ciudad Rodrigo, Badajos, and Salamanca.

I also wish to record my obligation to Colonel Dashwood and other officers of the Northumberland Fusiliers for their kind help; to the late Duke of Northumberland for allowing me access to the collection of Sir David Smith; to the present Duke for the illustrations of Lord Percy, Fort Niagara, and the map of St. Lucia; Mr. J. C. Hodgson, F.S.A., for much valuable advice and assistance; to Mr. Alfred Brewis for his generosity in allowing the use of his collection of books and pamphlets for the illustrations facing pages 16, 22, 130, 190, 198, and 366, and for the two coloured sketches by the late Captain Leaske; and to Captain Caleb Whitefoord for allowing the portrait of Colonel Whitefoord to appear.

Historians of the Fifth must always be grateful to Colonel Leather, and many others who have collected and added to the literature of the regiment. The pages of the *St. George's Gazette* bear witness to their work.

I have throughout the book adopted the spelling Wilhelmstahl, instead of the more correct form Wilhelmsthal, as the name is thus inscribed on the Colours of the Regiment and in the record of Battle honours in the Army List.

H. M. W.

October, 1919.

FOREWORD

By MAJOR-GENERAL SIR PERCIVAL WILKINSON, K.C.M.G., C.B.,
COLONEL NORTHUMBERLAND FUSILIERS

IT is somewhat surprising that a really full and reliable History of such an old and distinguished regiment as the Northumberland Fusiliers has not been written in the past.

We have Wood's History of the regiment, Fortescue's "History of the British Army," and other works in which the actions of the regiment are referred to in general terms, but it has remained for Miss Walker to write a full and authentic account of the regiment and its achievements.

The time of its appearance is most opportune. During the late war nearly fifty additional battalions were raised—a greater contribution to the armed forces of the Crown than that made by any other purely county unit. These battalions represented the regiment on nearly all the battle fronts. It will, therefore, be impossible in the future to write a History of the regiment as a whole, and future historians will have to confine themselves to a record of the part played by individual battalions.

The demand for a reliable History of the regiment is great at the present time among the many thousands whose sons and relatives have recently served in its many battalions, and I feel sure that they will welcome the appearance of the present volume.

The individuality of a regiment is a very real thing, which is hardly recognized outside the Service. It has seldom been more clearly explained than by Major

Pattison, who, writing in 1840, expresses himself as follows:

"There is something in the appearance of many corps not easily defined, but which at once gives to the most experienced eye the impression that is usually understood among military men by the term 'crack regiment.' This may be distinguished by an offhanded way of doing things, a smartness of their trim, a neatness and particularity, even to the very polish of their buttons, a sharp lively step of confidence, a sort of pride in one another expressed upon their countenance, all of which, both as regards officers and men, informs you, whatever it is, that their *tout ensemble* breathes the very life and essence of a soldier. . . . These regiments seem to be handed down from one clever officer to another. . . . Perhaps none could be said to verify these remarks more strictly than the Old Fifth, or Northumberlands. . . . There was an air of warlike spirit about them, retained from past experience, when, under Ridge, Mackenzie, Eames, Pratt, and many more, they preserved a reputation acquired in other fields."

It is this spirit which enables a battalion to tide over bad times, which in the Service are represented by bad commanding officers (and all battalions must get them at some time or another), unhealthy stations, and the stress of hard fighting and heavy losses. It is carefully instilled into the recruit, officer, and man, and becomes part of the bone and blood of the older members.

This spirit is fully recognized and carefully fostered by the higher authorities, and no changes are permitted which are likely to affect it adversely. The wearing of the Flash by the Royal Welsh Fusiliers, and the Red and White Plume of the Northumberland Fusiliers, are instances of treasured distinctions which help to keep alive regimental *esprit de corps*; whilst anniversaries, such as St. George's Day and Minden Day, are observed for the same reason.

Regimental Histories tell us how these distinctions were won, and why certain festivals are kept.

In writing this History Miss Walker has had the great advantage of free access to the papers belonging to the Duke of Northumberland, and has drawn from them much new material. The work has been a labour of love, written within sight of the Castle of Alnwick, the home of one of the regiment's greatest Colonels, from whom it gets its name.

I congratulate the regiment on now having a History worthy of its fame, and congratulate Miss Walker on the results of her patient and unselfish work.

CONTENTS

CHAPTER I
1673-1676
FORMATION OF REGIMENT

Disbanding of Charles II.'s army—Early adventures of John Bernardi—Formation of an English brigade in Flanders—Lord Clare's regiment—Fenwick succeeds Clare—Motto and badge   1-8

CHAPTER II
1676-1677
MAESTRICHT

Sir John Fenwick—The siege of Maestricht—Assault of the Dauphin Bastion—Further adventures of John Bernardi—Wisely succeeds Fenwick—Lieut.-Colonel Anselmne   -   -   9-18

CHAPTER III
1677-1689
THE REVOLUTION

The campaign of 1677—Battle of St. Dennis—Monk succeeds Wisely—Monmouth's rebellion—Regiment goes to England—Fifth of the Line—Returns to Holland—Tollemache succeeds Monk—The Revolution   -   -   -   -   -   -   19-27

CHAPTER IV
1689-1702
THE WARS OF KING WILLIAM

James II. lands in Ireland—Lloyd succeeds Tollemache—Fifth in Ireland—Battle of the Boyne—Dublin—Sieges of Athlone and Limerick—Flanders and back—On board the Grand Fleet—Fairfax succeeds Lloyd—Namur—Execution of Sir John Fenwick 28-44

CHAPTER V
1701-1712
THE WAR OF THE SPANISH SUCCESSION

Pearce succeeds Fairfax—The Fifth in Portugal—Battle of the Caya—Treaty of Utrecht—Clothing—Drill   -   -   -   45-51

CONTENTS

CHAPTER VI
1713-1728
GIBRALTAR

Garrison duty—Provisioning a garrison—Besieged by a Spanish army—Lord Portmore—The siege raised—Fifth return to Ireland   52-61

CHAPTER VII
1713-1728
PATRONAGE

Ireland in 1729—Purchase and patronage—Cope succeeds Pearce—Irwin succeeds Cope—Lord Chesterfield and John Irwin—Charles Whitefoord at Preston Pans—Lord George Sackville—Recruits and reviews—Whitefoord succeeds Irwin—His death -   62-76

CHAPTER VIII
1750-1760
"DISCIPLINE AND ŒCONOMY"

Discipline—Colours and uniform regulated—Bennet Cuthbertson's book—Bentinck made Colonel - - - - 77-83

CHAPTER IX
1754-1757
THE FIRST RAID

The Seven Years' War—Fifth return to England—Inspections and recruiting marches—Expedition sails for Rochefort, and returns 84-91

CHAPTER X
1758-1759
ST. MALO

Preparations for further raids—St. Malo—George Sackville's courage—Destruction of Cherbourg harbour—St. Malo again attempted—The army retreats—Disaster at St. Cas—Hodgson succeeds Bentinck - - - - - - - 92-104

CHAPTER XI
1759-1760
GERMANY

The war in Germany—Ferdinand of Brunswick—Fifth at Sachsenhausen Warburg—Zierenberg—Kloster Kampen—Losses in the campaign - - - - - - - 105-114

CONTENTS

CHAPTER XII
1761-1763
THE FIRST HONOUR

John Irwin leaves the Fifth—Campaign of 1761—Kirchdunkern—Lord Granby—Wilhelmstahl—The third Colour and the snuff-box—End of the war—Ensign George Harris - - - 115-126

CHAPTER XIII
1763-1774
IRELAND

A march through England—Corporal Stubbs—Ireland in 1764—Dubin—Adventure of Mrs. John Smith—The Medal of Merit—George Harris and Captain Bell—Lord Percy succeeds Hodgson—Letters of Junius—Rebellion in North America—The Fifth sail 127-138

CHAPTER XIV
1774-1775
REBELLION

Trade Laws and the Colonies—The army outside Boston—Percy and his regiment—A court-martial—Lieut.-Colonel Walcott - 139-146

CHAPTER XV
1775
BUNKER'S HILL

War—Lexington—The Blockade of Boston—Bunker's Hill—Harris wounded—Lord Rawdon—Howe and Washington - 147-157

CHAPTER XVI
1776-1778
INDEPENDENCE

Evacuation of Boston—Halifax—Invasion of Long Island—Brooklyn—Whiteplains—Fort Washington—Trenton—Invasion of Pennsylvania—Brandywine—Germantown—Death of Walcott—Occupation of Philadelphia—Medows commands the Fifth—France declares war—Evacuation of Philadelphia—Freehold—The raid on Little Egg Harbour - - - - 158-175

CHAPTER XVII
1778-1780
ST. LUCIA

The West Indies—Capture of Morne Fortuné—Medows at La Vigie—George Harris and Benjamin Hill—The French retreat—Sickness among the troops—A sea-fight—War with Spain—Fifth return to England—Medows leaves the Fifth—Adventures of George Harris - - - - - - - 176-190

CONTENTS

CHAPTER XVIII
1781-1787
IRELAND
PAGES

Sir John Irwin commander-in-chief—Lieutenant Hickson fights a duel—The Order of St. Patrick—Recruiting Acts—The "Northumberland Regiment"—Stopford succeeds Percy—David Smith cheated of his company—Harris leaves the Fifth—Sail for Canada - - - - - - - 191-200

CHAPTER XIX
1787-1797
CANADA

Canada in 1787—Thomas Carleton—Quebec—Prince William Henry—Montreal—Surgeon Holmes fights a duel—Major John Smith commands a district—Fort Niagara—General Simcoe—Clarke succeeds Stopford—Personnel - - - - 201-213

CHAPTER XX
1793-1798
AFFAIRS AT HOME AND ABROAD

War with France—Pay and discipline in the Army—Joining a regiment—Uniform—Duke of York as commander-in-chief - 214-220

CHAPTER XXI
1797-1799
HOLLAND

The Fifth recruit in Lincolnshire—Norman Cross—A second battalion raised—Campaign in Holland—Russian allies—Fifth storm Schoorldam—Failure of expedition—Withdrawal—Rear-guard action at Winkel - - - - - - 221-236

CHAPTER XXII
1799-1806
GARRISON DUTY

Gibraltar in 1800—A naval battle—Fifth repair ship—Treaty of Amiens—Second battalion disbanded—England succeeds Clarke—Guernsey—The war renewed—Stephen Morley joins—Second battalion raised—Abortive expedition to Hanover—Wreck of the *Helder* - - - - - - - 237-252

CHAPTER XXIII
1806-1807
BUENOS AYRES

Sir Hume Popham captures Buenos Ayres—Spaniards retake the town—Reinforcements sent from England—Whitelocke attempts to retake the town—Fifth capture St. Catalina—Whitelocke withdraws—The expedition returns to England - - 253-266

CONTENTS

CHAPTER XXIV
1808
PORTUGAL

An army sent to Portugal—Lieut.-Colonel Mackenzie — Rolica — Vimeira—The Convention of Cintra - - - 267-273

CHAPTER XXV
1808-1809
CORUNNA

Sir John Moore leads an army into Spain—Conflicting rumours—Napoleon at Madrid—Moore retreats—Stragglers and plunder—Morley taken prisoner—The heights of Palavea—Death of Mackenzie—Corunna - - - - - - 274-284

CHAPTER XXVI
1809
WALCHEREN

Situation in Europe—A diversion planned—Island of Walcheren—Siege of Flushing—Walcheren fever—Evacuation - - 285-291

CHAPTER XXVII
1804-1810
SPAIN AND PORTUGAL

The second battalion—Henry King—Detachments in Spain—Stephen Morley rejoin—Passage of the Douro—Talavera—2nd Fifth land in Portugal—The Third Division—King and Picton—Guarding the frontier—Busaco—Lines of Torres Vedras - - - 292-304

CHAPTER XXVIII
1811
THE CAMPAIGN OF 1811

Massena retreats—Third Division in pursuit—Sabugal—Fuentes de Onoro—Badajos—" Wellington's Bodyguard "—El Boden 305-316

CHAPTER XXIX
1812
CIUDAD RODRIGO AND BADAJOS

Ciudad Rodrigo invested—Ridge commands the 2nd Fifth—Assault and capture—Badajos invested—The attack on the Castle—Death of Ridge—Storming of Badajos—Escape of Marmont's army - - - - - - 317-328

CONTENTS

CHAPTER XXX
1812
SALAMANCA CAMPAIGN

The 1st Fifth after Walcheren—In Ireland—Join 2nd Fifth in Portugal—Wellington invades Spain—The Third Division at Salamanca—2nd Fifth ordered home—Madrid—Wellington retreats into Portugal - - - - - - - 329-335

CHAPTER XXXI
1813-1814
THE LAST CAMPAIGN

Wellington turns the French flank—Vittoria—Wellington crosses the Pyrenees—Nivelle—Orthes—Toulouse—Napoleon abdicates 336-342

CHAPTER XXXII
1814-1818
AMERICA AND FRANCE

War with United States—1st Fifth sent to Canada—Plattsburg—Garrisoning the frontier—Escape of Napoleon—1st Fifth return to France—Paris after Waterloo—Army of occupation—Disbanding of 2nd Fifth—Wynyard succeeds England - - 343-350

CHAPTER XXXIII
1817-1856
THE YEARS OF PEACE

Reduction of the army—Discipline—Health—Clothing and arms—Fifth garrison West Indies—Lieut.-Colonel Emes—England—Ireland—William Sutherland—Gibraltar—Loss of Third Colour—Malta—Colville succeeds Johnson—The Ionian Islands—Gibraltar—Ireland—England—Nichols succeeds Colville—Mauritius—Grey succeeds Nichols—Order of Merit abolished - 351-367

CHAPTER XXXIV
1857
THE INDIAN MUTINY

The beginning of the Mutiny—Lucknow invested—Fifth at Dinapore—Relief of Arrah—Outram and Havelock—Havelock's march to Lucknow—Dhooly Square—Sorties from the Residency—Besieged - - - - - - - 368-386

CHAPTER XXXV
1857-1860
THE INDIAN MUTINY (*continued*)

Colin Campbell's march—Relief of the Residency—Withdrawal of the garrison—Outram holds the Alum Bagh—Fight at Guilee—Pat M'Hale—Campbell captures Lucknow—Subjugation of Oudh—End of the Mutiny - - - - - 387-399

CONTENTS

CHAPTER XXXVI
1857-1899
THE SECOND BATTALION

Second Battalion raised—Mauritius—South Africa—Aldershot—Glasgow—Dublin—England and India—The Black Mountain Campaign—Chaila Crag—England and Northumberland - 400-406

CHAPTER XXXVII
1862-1899
THE FIRST BATTALION

1st Fifth at Aldershot—Duke of Cambridge—Life in the army—Ireland—India—Russian menace in Afghanistan—Peshawar Valley Field Force—Third Afghan war—Lines of communication—Return to England—Ireland—*St. George's Gazette*—The Sudan—Omdurman—Khartoum—Crete - - - - - 407-422

CHAPTER XXXVIII
1899
SOUTH AFRICA

The Cape and the Transvaal—Opposing armies, Briton and Boer—War declared—1st Fifth with Methuen—Belmont—Graspan—Modder River—Magersfontein—2nd Fifth with Gatacre—Stormberg 423-435

CHAPTER XXXIX
1899-1900
SOUTH AFRICA (*continued*)

Roberts takes command—1st Fifth Mounted Infantry with French—Bloemfontein occupied—Sannah's Post—2nd Fifth Mounted Infantry at Reddersburg—Roberts' march to Pretoria—Methuen's "salvation army"—First De Wet hunt—Transvaal annexed 436-447

CHAPTER XL
1900-1902
SOUTH AFRICA (*continued*)

De Wet and De la Rey—2nd Fifth at Nooitgedacht—1st Fifth at Lichtenberg—Kleinfontein—2nd Fifth Mounted Infantry with Benson—1st Fifth at Jagd Spruit—Tweebosch—Blockhouses—End of the war - - - - - 448-458

APPENDICES

I. Extracts from Army Lists - - - - 460
II. Phœbe Hessel - - - - - 485
III. Holland Campaign, 1799 - - - - 485
IV. The Affair of El Bodon, September 25, 1811 - - 487
V. Letter Written after the Capture of Ciudad Rodrigo by Lieut.-Colonel Ridge - - - - 488
VI. An Extract from "Camp and Quarters" (1840) - - 490
Bibliography - - - - - - 491
Index - - - - - - - 493

LIST OF ILLUSTRATIONS

UNIFORM OF 5TH FOOT, 1768, GRENADIER. By J. C. Leask - - - - - -
    Captain J. C. Leask, M.C., 5th (Territorial Battalion) Northumberland Fusiliers, reported "wounded and missing" since March 30, 1918.

SIR JOHN FENWICK - - - - - -

MAJOR JOHN BERNARDI. Engraved by General Vander Gucht - - - - - - -

COLONEL CHARLES WHITEFOORD - - - -
    From a portrait in the possession of Captain Caleb Whitefoord.

THE ORDER OF MERIT - - - - - -
    From the collection of Mr. Alfred Brewis.

HUGH, LORD PERCY, AFTERWARDS 2ND DUKE OF NORTHUMBERLAND, K.G. - - - - -

GENERAL SIR WILLIAM MEDOWS, K.B. - - -

LIEUT.-GENERAL LORD HARRIS. Engraved by J. Chapman

FORT NIAGARA IN 1794 - - - -
    From a water-colour sketch belonging to the late Sir David William Smith.

LIEUT.-COLONEL RIDGE, KILLED AT THE SIEGE OF BADAJOS
    From a miniature in the possession of the Officers' Mess, 1st Battalion Northumberland Fusiliers.

UNIFORM OF 5TH FOOT OFFICER (BATTALION COMPANY), 1814. By J. C. Leask - - - -

UNIFORM OF 5TH NORTHUMBERLAND FUSILIERS, 1846 -
    From a print by A. M. Hayes. Published by G. Spooner.

LIST OF MAPS

	FACING PAGE
WILHELMSTHAL	122
GERMANY	126
ST. LUCIA	182
HOLLAND	236
WHITELOCKE'S MARCH	260
CIUDAD RODRIGO	322
BADAJOS	326
SALAMANCA	332
LUCKNOW	390
INDIA	406
FLANDERS	End of book
NORTH AMERICA	,,
PENINSULA	,,
SOUTH AFRICA	,,

A HISTORY OF THE NORTHUMBERLAND FUSILIERS
1674–1902

CHAPTER I
1673–1674
CHARLES II.

FORMATION OF REGIMENT—SIEGE OF GRAVE

THE VISCOUNT CLARE—SIR JOHN FENWICK

IN the early years of the Restoration the professional soldier had a prodigality of choice in deciding where to tender his services. He could learn his trade under Turenne, Condé, or Luxemburg; he could fight in Portugal, under brave Colonel Hunt, to defend Lisbon against Don John of Austria; he could join the fleet as a volunteer, and fight with Rupert and Albemarle and other soldiers turned sailors; he could join an expedition to curb the insolent Dutch, and to wrest from them their colonies in the New World; or he could take and defend that unhappy dowry, Tangiers. For twelve years fighting was continuous and not without glory.

The power of the Dutch navy was broken in 1666, and, our colonial jealousy at an end, France grew too powerful for an ally, and Spain too weak to be feared. In February, 1674, a Treaty with the Dutch was concluded which brought the wars of Charles II. to an end. For the second time in his reign, the disbandment of the standing army was begun. The companies in the garrison towns were reduced; the main army, encamped at Blackheath under command of Marshal Schomberg, was first reviewed by the King, and then partially reduced. A large number of professional soldiers were set free to carry their swords to other countries and other quarrels.

During the next fourteen years England stood aloof from the wars of Europe—probably at no other time in her history did her honour as a nation sink so low. The last two Stewart kings were content to exist, the one as the pensioner of France, the other as the weak but obstinate servant of Rome.

Though England as a nation sank so low, individual Englishmen there were in plenty to uphold her old traditions, and to show that the sons of the New Army were worthy of their fathers.

The professional soldier was often a cadet of family; his sword was his capital, his pay was always in arrears, and in peace time his trade was a matter for contempt to those who were the first to seek his aid at the sound of the enemies' guns.

Charles was too deeply bound to France openly to sanction an offensive alliance with Holland, but he yielded to the undoubted wish of his people, and, though not withdrawing his regiments in the French service, he allowed the enlisting of his disbanded battalions in the Dutch army.

The sleeping chivalry of England had been roused by the gallant defence of the young Stadtholder against the might of France. In 1672 Turenne, Condé, and Luxemburg swept over the United Provinces with 150,000 men, and England at the same time harried the Dutch colonies and fleet; 6,000 Englishmen, Marlborough among them, fought under Turenne. The Prince of Orange had ships lying in the Texel, and his people were ready to flee to New Holland and the Indies rather than yield to France. They opened the dykes, and the sea accomplished what their soldiers could not; the French retreated; Austria and Spain made an effort to retake the Spanish Provinces; England made a separate peace, and William was no longer alone in defying the power of France.

One of the first officers of the future Fifth Regiment has left a record of these times. In the reign of Elizabeth Count Philip Bernardi came to England as the accredited agent of the Republic of Genoa; his son Francis, though English born, in his turn represented Genoa at St. James's. In 1653 Francis Bernardi was superseded, but chose to remain in his adopted country, and settled in Worcestershire, where he cultivated his garden and brought up his children with such severity that, according to his son's account, his behaviour was the subject of comment and remonstrance by their country neighbours. In 1670 his son John, then fourteen years old, ran away from home.[1] The first day he covered some sixteen miles, and took refuge for the night in a wheelwright's house, his father hot on his heels; just escaped capture, and next day made across country to Sir Clement Fisher's house. Lady Fisher had befriended him, as once she had befriended the fugitive King Charles. The boy found the house deserted—Sir Clement and his wife had gone to town. Nothing daunted, he followed to London to their lodgings in Whitehall, and there he found Lady Fisher most kind. She did not attempt to dissuade the boy or force him to return, but sent him to her kinsman, Captain Littleton Clent,[2] who commanded a garrison company at Portsmouth. There young Bernardi learnt his drill and spent three happy years, treated as a brother, and making many friends among the surrounding gentry. In the winter of 1673–74 the first rumours of peace came to Portsmouth, and the reduction of the garrisons was begun. Bernardi was sent off to seek fortune anew. He went first to London, with £20 in his pocket, and

[1] See "History of John Bernardi," printed for J. Newcombe in the Strand, 1729.

[2] Littleton Clent, son of John Clent, of Knightwick, and Lettice, daughter of Sir Edward Littleton, M.P. for Staffordshire, who married Mary, daughter of Sir Clement Fisher. Clent was captain of a company in Colonel Lawes's regiment of Foot, June 13th, 1667. This regiment was disbanded the same year. In 1672 he had a company in Fitzgerald's Foot.

there in lodgings in Covent Garden fell ill of the smallpox. A Hampshire young lady, Mrs. Gardener, took pity on him; he was sent out to nurse, and she made him a present of twenty shillings a week. When convalescent he found his friends shunned him for fear of infection, and in his loneliness he bethought him of his godfather, Colonel Anselmne, who was living at Kingstead, three miles from London. Anselmne, a soldier of fortune, had fought with distinction in the Spanish army, and had risen to be colonel of a regiment and a major-general. After Rocroy and Lans he had left the Spanish service and returned to England, and now, though close on seventy, was eager to carry his sword to fresh fields.

He offered to take Bernardi with him, gave him money to buy necessaries, and, three days after the first interview, they embarked from Billingsgate for Holland.

They landed at Brill, and found there twelve English captains and as many men as these could persuade to serve with the Dutch. These companies remained at Brill learning their drill and getting into some sort of order; Bernardi was left under the care of one Captain Creanols, while Anselmne went forward to meet the Prince of Orange and learn the conditions of service. The Prince was preparing for the summer campaign; with him were Sir Walter Vane and many English volunteers, and a treaty was concluded to bring 8,000 or 10,000 of the King's subjects into the Dutch service.

France had four armies in the field—one on the German frontier, one in Flanders, one on the borders of Roussillon, and one, with the King himself in command, had opened the campaign by taking Besançon and subduing Franch Comté.

The army of Flanders was under Condé, and the Prince of Orange hoped to create a diversion by defeating him and invading France.

Colonel Anselmne returned to Brill for his godson, who, fearing himself forgotten,[1] was much delighted at the old soldier's return. With other Englishmen they

[1] Bernardi feared his godfather had sold him. Recruits fetched £3 a head (*vide* his History).

joined the Prince's army only a day or two before the fierce fight of Seneffe (August 11th).

Condé chose his moment well, attacked the rear of the confederates, and threw them into confusion. The Prince of Orange, always at his best when threatened with disaster, rallied his army, and led them again to charge, pushing back the veterans of France. The fight went on all day, and for some hours by moonlight; 12,000 men were left dead on the field, among them Sir Walter Vane.[1] Both sides claimed the victory. The advantage appears to have lain with the French, but their army was too exhausted to follow it up. In retreating, the Prince laid siege to Oudenarde, but on the approach of Condé he fell back to Grave, the last town of the seven Provinces remaining in French hands. There word came to the Prince that ten companies of English were at Bois-le-Duc, well equipped, and in good order. The Prince sent for them. In two days they arrived, and were at once ordered to the trenches; young Bernardi went with them as a volunteer.

Among these captains were Sir Henry Bellasis,[2] Thomas Monk,[3] Sir John Morgan,[4] Philip Savage, and Hugh Mackay of Scoury. Mackay was made senior to the other captains, which caused much jealousy. Savage in consequence attacked one night without orders, was repulsed, and lost heavily. Bernardi was a volunteer in his company, and earned some distinction.

The fall of Grave on October 29th ended the year's campaign. Turenne and the army of Germany had swept the Imperial forces aside, possessed the Palatinate, and forced the German Princes over the Neckar and the Maine; only in Holland had Louis' soldiers met with a semblance of defeat.

The English brigade went into winter quarters at

---

[1] Fourth son of Sir Harry Vane the elder; born 1619.
[2] Sir Henry Bellasis, son of Sir Richard Bellasis, of Ludworth and Ounton in Durham, M.P. for Morpeth in 1696.
[3] Afterwards lieutenant-colonel of the Sixth Foot, and in 1680 colonel of the Fifth.
[4] Sir John Morgan, afterwards Governor of Chester.

Bois-le-Duc. Out of the ten companies and other
English recruits, four regiments were formed; two
English, commanded by Colonels Disney and Lillingston;
one Scottish, under Colonel Graham; and an Irish one,
commanded by the Viscount Clare. Added to these
were two Scottish regiments, who had been so long in
the Dutch service that they beat the Dutch march
until a campaign with their countrymen revived old
traditions.

Lord Clare[1] was a descendant of the O'Briens, Earls
of Thomond, king's men for many generations. As a
young man he had attended Charles II. in exile, and
through his influence his grandfather had been given his
viscounty. He did not continue long in command of
his regiment. Charges of conspiracy were brought
against him; and it is quite probable that, with other
disaffected Irishmen, he was in the pay, or at any rate
the confidence, of the Duke of York. The King's
brother had been in exile since the passing of the Test
Act, and it was to his interest that the Prince of Orange
should be defeated and discredited.

Lord Clare fled the country, and Colonel Anselmne
was given temporary command of the regiment, with
rank of lieutenant-colonel.

In the spring a dispute as to seniority arose among
the officers—Captain Roger McElligot quarrelled with
Captain Patrick Lavallain;[2] Major John McElligot[3]
espoused his brother's cause; and also Captains Mc-
Gillicuddy and Lee.

Lavallain charged them with conspiracy, and with
being implicated with their late colonel; they were put
under arrest and in irons, not knowing why or wherefore,

[1] Daniel, son of Connor, second Viscount Clare, who died in
1670, and Honora, daughter of Daniel O'Brien; date of birth un-
certain; married Philadelphia, daughter of Francis, Lord Dacre.
Lord Clare fought at the Boyne for King James, and was outlawed
May 11th, 1691. He appears to have died that same year. (*New
Peerage.*)

[2] The Irish families of Browne (Kenmare) and Roche (Fermoy)
intermarried with the Lavallains about this date.

[3] A Captain John McElligot appears in Roger McElligot's regiment in 1688, but not in any subsequent list.

and were forbidden to hold communication or write letters. During the summer campaign of 1675 they were marched, under a strong guard, in the rear of the army. In the autumn the four miserable gentlemen appealed for a court-martial before the army should break up and go into winter quarters. Captain Lavallain was ordered to produce his witnesses, but he failed to substantiate the charge. He fled; the others were released. Lavallain was declared a villain and a deserter by beat of drum, and his name on an iron plate was nailed to the gallows.

The regiment subscribed funds to send the four officers to England to plead their cause before Charles. He received them graciously, and gave them £400. Major John McElligot did not return to his regiment, but retired with a pension. Roger McElligot[1] was promoted to be lieutenant-colonel in the Earl of Pembroke's Foot, and in after years he was commissioned to raise a regiment of his own. Lee[2] and McGillicuddy returned to Holland.

The campaign of 1675 was uneventful for the Prince's army; William was opposed by Condé and Louis in person, but neither commander would hazard a general engagement. French action was paralyzed by the death of Turenne,[3] which necessitated the transference of Condé to the west.

Lord Clare's late regiment was ordered to winter in Utrecht.

In August Sir John Fenwick was appointed colonel; the regiment lost the designation of Irish; many Englishmen joined, and presently Fenwick's took rank as the first English regiment at The Hague.

The drummers beat the English march; and tradition says that for badge they wore St. George and the Dragon, their motto the same as that the banner of the Sidneys

---

[1] Colonel of a regiment of Foot in the pay of the King of France in 1688, which regiment came to England at the Revolution and was quartered at Portsmouth, and was broken 1689. Roger McElligot was afterwards Governor of Cork.

[2] Killed at the Siege of Maestricht.

[3] July 27th.

bore—" Quo fata vocant "—while their coats were lined with gosling green.[1]

[1] *Badge, Motto, Facings.*—There appears to be no record of the origins of the badge, facings, and motto. " St. George and the Dragon," the emblem of the Garter, was probably a Royal mark of favour, and may have been conferred by James II. in 1685, when he reviewed the regiments at Hounslow; or given by him at The Hague, when there in exile as Duke of York; or it may have been a legacy of one of the old disbanded regiments, and adopted with the motto. In 1892 the then Secretary of State for War is quoted as stating that the Fifth had kept St. George's Day since 1674. No authority is given for Sir Henry Campbell-Bannerman's pronouncement. Cannon gives it as his opinion that the badge and motto were assumed in 1675, when Sir John Fenwick became colonel; but he also mentions a tradition that they were conferred for gallant conduct during the " German War or the War of the Spanish Succession." " Quo fata vocant " was the motto of the Sidneys; and among the officers who took service with Fenwick there may have been some who had served in Lord Leicester's or Lord Lisle's own regiment. Henry Sidney, afterwards Lord Romney, 1641-1704, after long service in the Hollands Regiment, commanded the English Brigade at The Hague in 1681. At one time there seems to have been some idea that Sidney should become colonel of the Fifth, but in 1688 he became honorary colonel of Cutts's Regiment, afterwards disbanded. The Depôt Record gives the facings in 1688 as yellow, and dates the green from 1742. The Royal Warrants of 1751 and 1768 confirm the " Ancient Badge." On the first " Medals of Merit "—March, 1767—the motto surmounted the badge.

CHAPTER II

1676–1677

CHARLES II.

MAESTRICHT

"I saw the Prince's armèd men come down
By troops by thousands to besiege the town.
I saw the Captains, heard the trumpets sound,
And how his forces covered all the ground—
Yea, how they set themselves in battel-ray
I shall remember to my dying day.
I saw the colours waving in the wind,
I saw the mounds cast up against the town,
And how the slings were placed to beat it down—
I heard the stones fly whizzing by mine ears."
BUNYAN: *The Holy War.*

FENWICK

SIR JOHN FENWICK, Baronet, of Fenwick and Wallington, in Northumberland, was born in 1654. He married Lady Mary Howard, and was closely connected with the Royalist and Catholic North. In 1667 he got his company in Sir John Sayers' Foot; then, after a year or two of Court life, he joined the Queen's troop of Guards as cornet, with the rank of major (1672). Monmouth was his colonel, and together they fought for Louis under Turenne. In 1675 Fenwick, Guidon of " our dearest Consort the Queen's troop of our Guard," obtained leave to proceed to Holland and offer his services to the Prince of Orange and try if change of sides would bring him fortune. The Prince, recognizing in him a soldier who had seen service, and one who was in favour at his uncle's court, gave him Clare's late regiment. Shortly after Henry Wisely was made lieutenant-colonel, *vice*

Anselmne, who, however, still retained his company, and remained on with captain's rank.

Louis opened the campaign in Flanders. Early in April he laid siege to Condé, and took it by storm; Bouchain also fell into his hands. The Prince of Orange, ill-supported by his allies, dared not force a general engagement. However when Louis returned to Versailles William attempted a blow at one of the vital links in the fortress chain.

The English brigade[1] had been sent to Bois-le-Duc from Utrecht, and before long marching orders came. Towards the end of June, at midnight, a lieutenant-general came galloping with urgent commands. Two hours later the drums beat, and, leaving on guard only one newly raised regiment, the brigade marched away. Other companies and troops joined each day as they marched through Utrecht Province, and there were many speculations as to their destination until, five days later, they halted before Maestricht.[2]

This fortress commanding the upper reaches of the Meuse could, in the hands of the Prince, threaten the left flank of the army of Germany and the right flank of the army of Flanders, and would cover a force within striking distance of Liège, Tongres, Linburg, and Namur.

The town was well built, about four miles in circumference, the greater part on the left bank; but the village of Wyck, on the right bank, was also enclosed in the fortifications. Maestricht was an adventurous town, taken and retaken by Orange and Spain and France, until, in 1673, Louis and Turenne captured it for France, and Vauban set himself to make recapture impossible. The walls, reconstructed by the greatest engineer of the century, were strengthened by seven bastions—Le Roi, La Reine, Le Dolphin or Dauphin, Monmouth, Turenne, Condé, and Créqui. The garrison numbered about 900.

---

[1] Foot, 4,500; horse, 2,000; dragooners, 500; artillery and grenadiers (Newsletter).

[2] Sir John Fenwick, while serving with Monmouth, had been one of the successful besiegers in 1673, and also possibly one of those who, in August, 1675, in the meadows at Windsor, replayed the scene in pantomime.

The Governor, Marshal d'Estrade, was at the Congress at Nimeguen as plenipotentiary of the French King; in his place a Catalonian, Don Calvo, a man of experience and courage, had command.

The attacking party made up a total of about 24,000 men, for, besides the Dutch, were the Brandenburgers, the Prince of Offenbach, and other allies, and the four regiments of the English brigade, commanded by Fenwick, Widdrington, Astly, and Collier.

A council of war was held on July 1st, regiments were posted, and all orders given. The three English regiments " prayed that they might be encamped together, and share any enterprise, that the praise or blame might be theirs alone." To this the Prince agreed, and they were given a post of honour next the Prince's own guard. Colonel Fenwick, as eldest colonel, acted as brigadier. The three regiments numbered about 2,600 effective men, excluding volunteers.

The prince issued an order that no " Leaguer " should pay or exact any duty on provisions. This wise measure brought the country folk flocking in to join the League and benefit by the cheapened food; the men were at once set to work trench-digging.

The Prince's bad luck dogged his footsteps; it was all to his advantage to strike quickly and fiercely before the French could hurry up reinforcements; but his siege guns and battery trains had to come by river, and, owing to the dry season, they were much delayed, and did not arrive until the 17th.

Meanwhile sundry skirmishes were going on under the walls, the besieged attempting to feed their cattle, the besiegers making dashing forays. The trenching parties were much harried, but after the arrival of the train the French were so " galled by the field pieces that they came no more with their cattle."[1]

Captain Archer, of Fenwick's, was severely wounded on reconnaissance duty; he was shot through and through with a brace of bullets, but managed to return bringing

[1] " A Letter written out of Holland by a Friend to a Person of Quality," printed by G. Keenholt at the King's Head, etc., 1676.

a prisoner—" some say two "—with him. He appears to have been a most gallant and efficient officer.

The Prince himself did not hesitate to lead any enterprise; he was always the first in any hard or difficult task, and was only exceeded in daring by the young Rhinegrave, who led the volunteers in any desperate work.

On July 18th the ground was broken for an approach. The task was given to the Dutch guards, the Rhinegrave in command; with him went Captains Lee and Roger McElligot, and other volunteers. With the English regiments in support the guards made progress close to the wall of the Dauphin Bastion, but not without many casualties; the Rhinegrave was wounded, and the Prince had a bullet through his clothes. A ball went through Sir John Fenwick's kitchen, whereupon his French cook left for The Hague, saying his bargain had been not to come within cannon-shot.

On the 29th the English were ordered to assault the Dauphin Bastion.[1] A small party was picked from the three regiments, armed with snaphances, halberds, and pikes, supported by men carrying woolsacks, and led by " two bold Britons, Sergeants Powel and Pinder." The defenders were taken by surprise, and after a brief hand-to-hand fight the French broke, and the Bastion fell into English hands. Among the volunteers was a young man, George Villiers Carleton,[2] who by his gallant conduct won for himself an ensigncy in Fenwick's Foot

If courage was not lacking on the Prince's side the advantage of skill lay with the French; the engineering train was much neglected, especially by the English; no attempt was made to strengthen the Bastion against a

---

[1] " To encourage them the Prince gave each company two sheep and an ox " (Newsletter).

Other authorities state that it was given as a reward after the second and successful assault and that this gift roused the jealousy of the Dutch.

[2] George Villiers Carleton, great-nephew of Lord Dudley Carleton, present at the Battle of St. Dennis; left the regiment in 1685 (see his Memoirs).

counter-attack. The curtain wall on the town side was very slight, and cannon were so arranged as to command the Bastion should it fall into enemy hands.

The English stood manfully to their posts for over an hour, under an ever-increasing fire, their colonels asking that others of their own regiments might be sent to relieve them. Reinforcements were sent, but of the Dutch guards; the redcoats began to file sullenly away, their departure gladdening the hearts of the besieged. The bluecoats had hardly got to their station when some powder in the approach trench exploded. This added to the confusion; Dutch and English fell back together, fearing a mine. The French suddenly counter-attacked, and gallantly retook the Bastion.

The next day the Dutch made another attack, but were repulsed with loss.

Early in August the English took their turn in the trenches. On the 2nd Colonel Fenwick was wounded in the cheek; Widdrington was killed in the approach, and Colonel Dolman succeeded to the command of his regiment. There was no moon, and to guard against a night attack the French hung their walls with torches of pitch and tar.

On the 4th the English were ordered to retake the Bastion.[1] Again the assaulting party was chosen from the brigade, with Captain Barnewell[2] of Fenwick's as major in command, *vice* Archer, wounded. The little party paraded at 3 in the afternoon in front of the brigade. This time a detachment was told off in support to act as engineers in strengthening the defences of the Bastion when won, and also to discover any mines that might be concealed.

---

[1] 2 sergeants, 10 firelocks; 1 sergeant, 12 grenadiers; 1 officer, 1 sergeant, 12 grenadiers; 1 sergeant, 12 men half pike; 1 captain, 1 lieutenant, 2 sergeants, 50 firelocks; 1 sergeant, 12 men half pike; 1 captain, 1 lieutenant, 1 sergeant, 28 men with spades and shovels Reserve: 1 captain, 1 sergeant, 56 men (*London Gazette*, cited by Cannon).

[2] Anthony Barnewell, third son of Sir Richard Barnewell, of Crickstown, Castle Meath, and his second wife, Julia, daughter of Sir Gerald Aylmer. One of Barnewell's sisters married John Archer of Riverstown.

The orders were that if the English should fail the Dutch guards were to make the attempt, and failing them two other parties were held in readiness; but the English led the van.

Captain Barnewell marched at the head of his men. He had stuck a white feather in his cap; he adjured them "to remember they were English, their enemies were French, who never yet had made the English run!" Then, with a shout, "Fall on, brave boys!" he dashed up the Bastion, followed by the eager men.

Within "a little quarter of an hour" the French gave way; Barnewell, ahead of his men, shot the commander of the Swiss, crying, "They run! they run!" only to fall himself with a hundred wounds, "sealing the victory and the possession of the Bastion with his life."

Captain Savage, now the senior officer, marched his men in without difficulty. Secure for the moment, an attempt was made to remove the wounded and some fifty dead, and Savage and an engineer officer made search for any trace of mines, but found nothing. The reliefs marched in, sentries were placed, and all appeared tranquil.

Suddenly a mine was sprung in the very centre of the Bastion. Profiting by the confusion, and by the neglect of a sentry, the French made their way back. Fully armed, they sprang in with scythes in their hands, crying "Tue! Tue!" A second explosion killed and wounded some of the Scottish officers who had reinforced the English; the reserve was insufficient, and English and Scottish alike were swept out of the Bastion. In the first fury no quarter was given to the half-buried men, but Captain Savage called out in French, asking for his life as an officer. They were then stripped of all they possessed, and on another alarm more of the men were killed.

The Dauphin Bastion was not allowed to remain long in French hands; a third vigorous assault drove out the besieged, and this time it was made secure from all counter-attacks. The unhappy wounded were dug out; though much burned and severely wounded they quickly recovered, and were soon fit for the field. Captain Savage had eleven wounds.

The next day the English kept quarters, and the colonels ordered every care to be taken of the wounded and the many sick. There was much illness in the camp, which added to the Prince's difficulties. The three regiments could only raise 300 men fit for duty; nevertheless, they never failed to take their turn in the trenches, and many a volunteer went with the Rhinegrave on deeds of daring. In one of these Patrick Lee was killed and Roger McElligot wounded dangerously.

The garrison also suffered, and, being much reduced, was on the point of surrender, when, by a ruse, messengers managed to get into the town with news of Schomberg's approach to their relief.

Heavy casualties, sickness, and defection of his allies had reduced the Prince's force, and left the Leaguers too weak to offer battle to the veterans of Louis. No man could have worked harder or spread himself less; but, with a heterogeneous army weakened by intrigue, a second in command incapacitated, and many senior officers fallen, the Prince realized that he must retreat. First the horse and then the cannon were drawn off, and on August 28th the siege was raised.

The work of the English brigade was not yet completed —they had the honour to act as rearguard to the army. A false alarm of the near approach of Schomberg spread through the camp; there was some undue haste in leaving the trenches, and the English were left unsupported. The garrison first bombarded them, then attacked vigorously, nearly capturing Sir John Fenwick, who, with Colonel Salisbury, lay sick in a farmhouse. The camp and baggage fell into the hands of the French. The greater part of the English fought their way through and rejoined the Prince; the remainder, mostly sick and wounded, were treated with great generosity by the enemy.

Ensign Bernardi took part in the second assault on the Dauphin Bastion, and lost the sight of an eye in the retaking of the counterscarp; another shot splintered his arm; taking it into his lap he crawled back to the breach, and fell down to the bottom among the dead. One of his men, seeing him fall, leapt after him, and carried him to the trenches where the surgeons were, and saved him from bleeding to death. The sick and wounded were sent forward to Bois-le-Duc, but Bernardi could not stand the jolting of the rough carts, and he had to be taken back to the camp hospital.

Bernardi states that most of the sick and wounded were got away at the raising of the siege. He got into a pontoon boat and lay with the guns, a ten days' voyage to Grave, with rags stuffed in his wounds for want of medicines. With much pain he was carried overland to Bois-le-Duc, where he spent the next six months, until the following March, in the hands of two noted surgeons, who managed to save his arm.[1]

Bernardi rejoined his regiment in Utrecht, and not being fit for duty, he courted and married a lady of more than double his age, but of considerable fortune. She was connected with the most notable families in Utrecht, and they lived happily together for eleven years.

Meanwhile Sir John Fenwick had thrown up his command and returned to England. The Prince of Orange has been accused of ingratitude in his dealings with Sir John, who, it is said, saved the Prince's life during the late siege; but it must not be forgotten that Fenwick came direct from Whitehall, and that Charles and his brother were secret allies of the Prince's arch-enemy, and that the Prince had already found it necessary to dismiss or cashier several officers of the English brigade on account of Stewart intrigues. A slighter, but more natural, reason for Sir John's departure might be traced to the ever-increasing jealousy between the Dutch and the English. There were faults on both

---

[1] The casualties to Fenwick's Regiment included Sir John Fenwick, cheekbone; Captain Barnewell, killed; Captain Lee, died of wounds; Major Archer, severely wounded; Lieutenant McGillicuddy, wounded; Ensign Bernardi, lost one eye, wounded in arm; Ensign G. V. Carleton, bullet wound in hand, halberd stroke in collar-bone.

SIR JOHN FENWICK,

To face page 16.

sides, and probably, as in later years, the Dutch proved themselves slow, selfish, and ungrateful, and the English ill-disciplined and overbearing; they claimed the place of honour in the camp and in the field, and their words were as bombastic as their courage was high.

When the Prince favoured the English, even at the expense of his own Blue Guards, the English took his courtesy as a right. The officers resented any criticism, even when their lack of technical skill threw away the advantage their courage had won.

Lieutenant-Colonel Wisely was given the regiment on Fenwick's departure. Bernardi was appointed lieutenant to Savage's company, whereupon Savage's ensign demanded compensation because Bernardi had been promoted over his head. On Savage's refusal his ensign called him out and killed him. Captain Plunkett was then made major and given Savage's late company; but he too died shortly after, and Captain Hales[1] was promoted in his place.

Among Sir William Temple's correspondence is the following letter to the Prince:

October 31st, 1676. N.S.

" I send your Highness enclosed a letter I received from Mr. Sidney, which came not sooner because, as I found by another, he had great disputes with his Father before he could give this answer. I am very sorry for it, but since you found the Lieutenant-Colonel so very capable, I hope it will be no loss. In case he has the regiment Major Archer has begged of me to mention him to your Highness for the Lieutenant-Colonel's place, which I should not do but that I remember your Highness expressed a very good opinion of him, and I find by him, that he cannot (as he says) possibly live on in the Regiment with Fenwick and Weasly. I hear

[1] John Hales, second son of Sir Edward Hales, secretary to the Duke of York, and a Commissioner to The Hague. Hales left the regiment in December, 1688, and was then commissioned by James II. to command a regiment of foot in the pay of the King of France. After the Revolution this regiment gave their allegiance to King William; it was finally disbanded on March 31st, 1697. John Hales was appointed Governor of Chelsea Hospital November 11th, 1702, and died March 31st, 1726, aged seventy-four (Dalton).

this last is endeavouring to turn out one Captain Knight for having been a friend to Captain Archer in some of their quarrels."

However, Fenwick left, and Archer remained on in the regiment, becoming lieutenant-colonel on Wisely's promotion.

Bernardi accuses Fenwick of having misrepresented his godfather, colonel Anselmne, to the Prince as a " sottish and most hateful character," which caused the Prince, first, to deprive Anselmne of the lieutenant-colonelcy of the regiment, and afterwards of his company, reducing him to serve as a private soldier. It is quite probable that the veteran did not prove very amenable to strict discipline, and Fenwick was a great disciplinarian; in any case, his age, for he was over seventy, gave ample excuse for retiring him. His fate, like that of many soldiers of fortune, was a hard one. After Bernardi got his company he was able to allow his godfather double pay; but when Bernardi left the regiment Anselmne was destitute. Somehow he managed to live until 1693, and then, being about ninety years old, he died, and was handsomely buried by Sir William Basset.

" He was a man of a great deal of wit, much honour and good sense, and a most agreable companion, a true and tried friend, and always much respected and beloved."

CHAPTER III

1677–1689

CHARLES II.—JAMES II.

WISELY, September 11th, 1676—MONK, December 10th, 1680—TOLLEMACHE, October 9th, 1688

LOUIS opened the campaign of 1677 by an åttack on Flanders. Before the end of March Valenciennes and Cambrai had fallen, and St. Omer was closely invested. Although these disasters were not unforeseen, they spread consternation in Europe, and especially in England; more pressure was brought to bear on Charles to induce him to declare himself on the side of the Allies.

The Prince of Orange hurried his scattered army from their winter quarters, and marched to the relief of St. Omer. The besiegers were covered by a large force under Luxemburg, "Upholsterer of Notre Dame." The Prince, tried by a sudden attack at Cassel, to raise the siege. In his first line, dividing the redcoats and the blue guards, were two regiments of marines. At the first charge of the French the marines broke, and the battle was lost. The Prince with his own hands tried to force the broken men to make a stand, and, with the help of the English brigade, which behaved with great gallantry, he managed to turn disaster to retreat, but lost 1,500 men, a loss he could ill afford.

St. Omer fell, the Allies were defeated in Germany and Alsace, in Catalonia and in Sicily; the interminable Congress of Nimeguen still dragged on, and the Dutch people were sorely tempted to conclude a separate peace.

The Prince, however, had no thought of peace, and, after a short rest, invested Charleroi. Condé moved forward; the Prince offered battle; Condé refused, but making a rapid march north threatened the Dutch lines of communication. The Prince divined his purpose and forestalled him. For three weeks the armies stood watching for any moment of weakness; then the campaign ended, leaving France mistress of Europe, and the Dutch exhausted and discontented.

William crossed to England, and on November 4th, to the infinite joy of the English people, he married his cousin, Mary Stewart, daughter of the Duke of York. On his return to Holland, James, Duke of Monmouth, the King's son, and 10,000 men went with him. With Monmouth, John Fenwick and John Churchill went as brigadiers, and the gallant Ossory[1] followed them to command the English brigade.

Louis, while pretending to consider terms of peace, made all preparations for the coming campaign. As usual, first in the field, he captured Ghent and Ypres, at the same time threatening Mons and Namur. He then considered himself to be in a position to dictate terms. Spain refused to consider a truce, but Van Beverning, the Dutch Minister, was weak enough to acquiesce to a separate treaty allowing France to retain Cambrai, Aire, St. Omer, Valenciennes, Ypres, and Charleroi, only Maestricht being restored to Holland. Monmouth and his army were recalled. Furious at this treaty, which was without his sanction, the Prince resolved on one last blow at Luxemburg.

Wisely's regiment had spent the spring encamped near Brussels; the Prince, who hoped for great things, had ordered his army to march out of the garrisons, and for some weeks to live well in the villages round. Rumours of the transactions at Nimeguen caused the greatest depression, but Wisely's were in August somewhat heartened by orders to march. They left Brussels,

[1] The Earl of Ossory, son of James, first Duke of Ormonde; born 1634; d.v.p. 1680.

and in four long marches came in sight of the enemy on the 13th, a Sunday.

Luxemburg was encamped on the River Senne, his right wing resting on the abbey of St. Dennis, and his left wing at Mamoy St. Pierre. The French were in a strong position, strongly entrenched, but in view of the new treaty discipline was somewhat relaxed.

The Prince's army halted in sight of the enemy, and, to the joy of Wisely's and the other regiments, orders came to distribute ammunition at once. This was done in half an hour, every regiment having their ammunition-waggon in the rear of the battalion.

Without more ado, the Prince's cannon opened on the trenches, and under cover of the bombardment the Prince's dragoons attempted to turn the enemy's right, charging on even into the alley where Luxemburg had lately been feasting with his staff. The dragoons were beaten back, and Waldeck and two battalions of foot were sent in support.

Meanwhile, Ossory's brigade and the Dutch guards were ordered to attack the enemy left, resting on the heights of Chastau, and in front well protected by difficult country. Not without loss the troops made their way to the foot of the hill; then the grenadiers sprang forward, and, throwing their grenades,[1] did a considerable amount of damage. The musketeers followed, and after they had fired the pikemen charged. In their turn the musketeers drew their swords and charged. A desperate hand-to-hand fight ensued, but the English rallied, and charged again and again until the heights were won. Orange himself fought on foot among his men. The Prince ordered the best refreshment to be given to the troops, hoping the next day to

[1] The grenade, a small shell thrown by hand, was first used by the French in 1667; its use quickly became general. Grenadier companies were first formed in the English army in 1678, but prior to that date a small number of men were attached to each company, usually the tallest and strongest men in the regiment. In addition to the grenade the grenadiers were armed with firelocks and hatchets. To distinguish them they at first wore fur hats, but these soon gave way to the pointed grenadier hat.

renew the fight, but when morning came Luxemburg had stolen away.

Wisely's regiment lost heavily; Lieutenant-Colonel Archer and Lieutenant Charlton and 50 men were killed, and 10 officers[1] and 100 men wounded.

The victory was a barren one: the Prince was forced to acknowledge the treaty that the Minister of the States-general had signed.

The Dutch army was much reduced, but the Prince would not part with his English regiments. Ossory's brigade went into garrison in Grave and other towns.

The Duke of York had been living in retirement at Brussels until recalled to England by the serious illness of the King—August, 1679. A month later Monmouth, too successful at Bothwell Brig, was exiled to The Hague, where he was received with every kindness by Orange and the Princess Mary; but at the end of November he returned to England without orders, to be met with rapture by the people of London—a forecast of how the wind would blow. But Charles had yet five more years to live.

Wisely's appears to have remained in garrison at Grave for the next three years. Lord Ossory died in 1680, and Lord Pembroke was nominated to succeed him. Bernardi was attached to his staff, and had the use of his equipages, but the matter came to nothing, and the following year Henry Sidney was given the appointment.

Colonel Wisely was drowned crossing to England in November or December, and on December 10th Thomas Monk was given the regiment.

In 1684, when Monk's marched to Brussels, war with France appeared imminent, and the regiment was ordered west to the banks of the Dender, and later to Malines.[2] Monk had made Bernardi his captain-lieutenant, but,

---

[1] Major Hales, shot through the leg; Captains Charlton, Floyd, Coleman, and du Puy; Lieutenants Augeune, Marchant, and Wilson; Ensigns Barnewell and Armsby, wounded (Cannon).

[2] Cannon.

in 1685, Captain Gaspard Paston died of smallpox, and Bernardi got his company.

Charles II. died at Whitehall on February 6th, and James succeeded quietly to the throne. Argyle was the first to raise the standard of revolt; in May he sailed from The Hague to arm the Highlands; but the time was not ripe, and he quickly paid the penalty. Then, on June 11th, Monmouth landed at Lyme Regis, and marched through Dorset and Somerset as the Protestant Duke, his army collecting round him as he marched upon Bristol.

James seized this opportunity to recall his regiments in foreign service, and to establish an efficient standing army. Three Scottish and three English regiments came over from Holland, too late to fight their own countrymen, but in time for two of them to take rank in the British army, Colonel Monk's as the Fifth, and Sir Henry Bellasis' as the Sixth of the Line.[1]

The Fifth, with other regiments, was encamped at Hounslow, ready to march on London should the city show any signs of sympathy for her one-time favourite. Monmouth, defeated at Sedgemoor, was beheaded July 15th.

On July 14th Francis Say, clerk, was appointed " Chaplain to our three English regiments, come out to Holland."[2] In August James inspected his army at Hounslow, and afterwards wrote to his son-in-law to express his satisfaction at their efficiency. The people of England did not regard the army with equal satisfaction; the machinations of Titus Oates, the terror of Jesuit plots and the Revocation of the Edict of Nantes, had stamped in them a very real fear of a Roman Catholic dynasty if backed by a powerful army. Many of the returned regiments were officered by Catholics, thus making the Test Act a dead letter, and it was common knowledge that attempts were being made to convert the soldier to the old faith. A wooden

---

[1] Fortescue, " History of British Army," vol. i., p. 302.
[2] Dalton's Army Lists.

chapel was erected in the lines at Hounslow, and the men were urged to attend services.

James was not allowed to retain his foreign service regiments, and in 1686 the Fifth returned to the camp near Brussels.

In 1687 James again demanded his brigade, making excuse of an old colonial wrangle, but the States-general were agreed that Holland stood in greater danger of attack than England, and kept the regiments. At the same time any of the officers who wished to return to England and swear allegiance to James were allowed to do so. Six officers of Monk's regiment[1] availed themselves of this permission; James sent a yacht for them, giving to each three months' pay. Altogether some 60 of the 240 English officers left the Prince's service.[2]

William had seen one rival rush to his doom. He saw the temper of the English people was running dangerously high, and that his father-in-law in his weak obstinacy was every day strengthening the revolutionary party. William's plans were nearly ripe, and he wanted neither Stewart intriguer nor Jesuit plotter in the army that was to go to England with him. Making an excuse of the dispute caused by the death of the Elector of Cologne, he assembled an army of men between Grave and Nimeguen, and at the same time made great naval preparations. James, deluded by Sunderland, did not realize until late in the autumn that a revolution threatened his throne. Then he offered to make concessions, but the time was past for compromise; Whigs and Tories united in inviting the Prince of Orange to save them from a Papal domination.

And the Fates were propitious; Louis diverted the armies of France, which had been threatening the Netherlands, and attacked the Empire, and so, safe from French invasion, William made his venture.

[1] Lieutenant-Colonel John Hales, Major Edward Wilson, Captains du Puy, William Saxby, John Skelton, and John Bernardi (Bernardi).
[2] Bernardi.

The fleet assembled at Brill, and the transports, 300 ships, took on board the army and equipment. Hugh Mackay and the English brigade hoisted a red flag; Solmes, with the Dutch guard and the Brandenburgers, a white; and Nassau, with the French Huguenots, a blue.

Thomas Monk did not live to return with his regiment; he died October 9th, and the Honourable Thomas Tollemache[1] was appointed to succeed him. Tollemache, who had seen service in Flanders, and had held commissions in both the Coldstream and Grenadier Guards, with other malcontents had gone to The Hague and openly joined William. His appointment to command the Fifth did honour to them both. It was under no swashbuckler or common adventurer that the regiment came back to England, but they returned led by a chivalrous and brave gentleman, who, had things gone amiss, would have stood by the Orange standard and died rather than run, as in later years he was to do.

The Fleet sailed November 1st, "the Trumpets sounding, the Hautboys playing, the soldiers and seamen shouting, and a crowd of spectators on the shore breathing their good wishes after them."

They were sighted past Dover on the 3rd, steering a Channel course westward. The wind kept the English fleet inactive, and, without adventure, the army disembarked near Torquay, November 5th, Tollemache's landing near Brixham Quay, two miles from Dartmouth. The weather was so stormy the baggage had to be left on board. The men had a sorry welcome home, provisionless, without quarters, and drenched by the rain.

The next day, the 6th, the ships were able to land the stores, and the Prince's march began. The rain still came down in torrents; the roads, mere tracks at

[1] Thomas Tollemache, second son of Elizabeth, Countess of Dysart, and Sir Lionel Tollemache. Served in Flanders in the summer of 1678 as a captain in Lord Alington's regiment, afterwards disbanded. He then joined the Coldstream Guards as captain, and in May, 1679, was gazetted captain and lieutenant-colonel in the Grenadiers.

the best of times, were knee-deep in mud and slush. The country folk hung back, and as the little army marched on they saw good reason for caution; no need for landmarks to show the way, for all along in the little towns, on every hill, and thick where the tracks crossed, stood the scaffolds and gibbets that marked Monmouth's fall. The magistrates barred themselves in and the clergy fled, not to be implicated in another rising. Along the ill-lighted lanes the soldiers found only grinning skulls hanging in chains. The discipline of the army was very high, and by the time Exeter was reached the timorous had gained a little courage, and many came flocking in to see the strange company. Travel-stained and worn as the men were they made a brave show. First Macclesfield and his volunteers, shining like knights of old, each with his black page; then the Swedes, with their black armour and fur; next the Prince's banner, borne with much pomp. After forty running footmen the Prince rode on a great white horse, and near him Schomberg, who had fought for France until he had to choose between his country and his faith, and, having made his choice, had come to fight for England and the Prince's banner.

After the Swiss regiments came the veteran redcoats, Tollemache, Babbington, Ramsey, and Mackay, followed by the cannon, the movable smithy, and the bridge of boats.[1]

The townsfolk of Exeter were much impressed, and volunteers began slowly to come in. Many soldiers, deprived of their commissions to make room for Roman Catholics, hastened to the Prince when they had news of his coming; one of these, George Burston, son of an Irish clergyman, and educated at Trinity College, Dublin, attached himself to Tollemache's for a brief period. He had trailed a pike in the Royal Regiment of Foot in 1677, and afterwards purchased an ensigncy in Fairfax's; this was taken from him for being a Protestant, and so he came marching to Honiton to

[1] Macaulay.

join the Prince. He was a gallant officer, and not lacking in wit.¹

William began his march on London. James had hurriedly raised an army of 40,000 men to resist the threatened invasion, but the temper of the troops was not to be trusted—his nephews, Grafton and Cornbury, and his generals, Churchill, Trelawny, and Kirk,² all deserted to William—Churchill to be greeted by blunt old Schomberg, " the first general to desert that he had ever known."

One by one they stole away: even his daughter Anne left him. An order to disband the army was signed December 11th, and James fled the capital.

Five days later, in a moment of courage, he returned, only to meet the Prince's army marching on Whitehall. Old Lord Craven and the Grenadiers were for resistance, but the King forbade them. A Dutch regiment mounted guard at the Palace—the reign of William III. had begun.

¹ Lieutenant-Colonel Burston's balance-sheet (Dalton's Army Lists, vol. v.):

" To hard usage, small pay, and no preferment, but an Ensign's commission, bought for £230, and taken away for being a Protestant.

" To a Lieut. and Captain's commission, this last after three juniors had been preferred before him.

" To thirteen wounds at St. Esteven, besides being cured at his own expence.

" To a Major's commission with the like Hardships as before.

" To a Brevet of Colonel made good at the siege of Lerida.

" By three years' service à la Cadet and four years an Ensign under Col. Fairfax.

" By thirteen years' faithful service in Flanders, under King Wm. to the Peace of Ryswick.

" By twelve years' service on board the Fleet and in Catalonia, to the time of disbanding the Marines.

" By preserving the whole garrison of Lerida.

" Balance due from Col. Burston: Nothing."

² Kirk approached the new regiments officered by the men from Flanders, but to their honour they refused to desert their King, and the greater number joined James at St. Germains.

CHAPTER IV

1689–1702

WILLIAM AND MARY—WILLIAM III.

IRELAND—AT SEA—FLANDERS

LLOYD, 1689—FAIRFAX, November 6th, 1694

OF the captains who, fifteen years before, had assembled at Brill some were dead and some were in exile. Claverhouse was raising the Highlands for King James; Hugh Mackay was leading Dutch veterans to that hunt which ended in victory in defeat at Killiecrankie; Roger McElligot was holding Cork for the Stewarts; and the men of Connaught were rallying round Lord Clare, who had returned from conveying his Queen and Prince to safety in France.

On March 12th James landed at Kinsale, relying on the arms and gold of France and loyalty of the Roman Catholic Irish.

One month before, William and Mary had been proclaimed King and Queen—February 13th. At last the forces of England and the Netherlands were united under one ruler, and William hoped to realize his dreams of humbling France. His position was not an enviable one: he had left his country open to attack, and the men who had given him the throne of England had it in their power to nullify their work. Not one of the men in office was above bribery with foreign gold; Ireland and Scotland had risen for their legitimate king; half the army was disaffected—two regiments broke out in open mutiny; it was doubtful if the fleet would fight against their old admiral and for the hated Dutch; every department of the State was corrupt.

The Prince of Waldeck and Marlborough were sent to Flanders, and old Schomberg to Ireland. War against France was declared May 8th.

With James there had landed in Ireland the Duke of Berwick and numerous exiles and adventurers, and the King was presently joined by Lauzaun and 5,000 seasoned French troops. The landing met with no opposition from the Navy. Save for Londonderry, Enniskillen, and a small part of the northern counties, all Ireland was in possession of Tyrconnel's men.

" The keys of Dublin are in French hands. The bomb carts and carriages painted with Flower de Luces."

Schomberg's force consisted mainly of newly raised regiments, ill-officered, ill-equipped, and untrained. The rising in Scotland and the fear of French invasion forbade the weakening of the few trustworthy battalions in England: among these was the Fifth.

On May 1st their colonel, Tollemache, was sent to Flanders with the expeditionary force under Marlborough, and at the Battle of Walcourt, which his general won for the Allies, he greatly distinguished himself at the head of the Coldstream Guards. For his services he was made their colonel and governor of Portsmouth.

Major Edward Lloyd who had served many years in the Fifth, was given the regiment on May 1st, 1689. Tollemache's had spent the winter billeted in the country; in June Lloyd's marched to London, and spent the summer there. October found them at Southwark, and shortly afterwards they embarked at Greenwich and Deptford for Plymouth They wintered in Devonshire, with companies in Cornwall.[1]

The rebellion in Scotland had died with the death of Dundee, and William resolved to end the deadlock in Ireland where Schomberg's army was melting away from disease and indiscipline. Marlborough was left in England as commander-in-chief, with the Queen and

[1] Cannon.

a council to carry on the government, while William went to command in Ireland, taking with him some troops on whom he could depend.

The Fifth were warned for service. Marching to Bristol, they embarked there, and landed at Belfast. In June they joined the great camp at Armagh.

William arrived at Carrickfergus June 14th, and went to Schomberg's headquarters at Lisburn. The actual army at Armagh probably numbered about 36,000, largely composed of raw levies. The men were confident of success. William was thankful to be away from the intrigues of the Court and once more in the field.

James's army, about 26,000 strong, lay covering Dublin, behind the River Boyne, " the ould Rubicon of the Pale and frontiere of the corn country."

A decisive action was necessary; half the officers in England were ready to mutiny and turn Jacobite; the French fleet commanded the Channel, and at any time French reinforcements might arrive.

On July 1st, a hot clear day, in the beautiful valley of the Boyne, two Kings of England fought for the last time; while in England a Queen sat waiting to know if husband or father was victor, and if either had died in defeat.

James had chosen a strong position; the river covered his front, his right was protected by rising ground and his left by a morass.

William reconnoitred the ground himself, and while doing so was wounded. His orders for battle were very simple. The centre, his main body of infantry, were to force a passage at Old Bridge; at the same time the right wing of infantry, under Lieutenant-General Douglas, was ordered to turn the enemy's left, crossing the river at Slane Bridge; and the left wing was ordered to envelop the enemy right by attacking the forces which lay between James's camp and Drogheda. William's army wore green boughs in their hats to prevent confusion.

At 6 a.m. Douglas marched off, and crossed Slane Bridge without difficulty; as soon as the attack on the right developed the main action began. The Dutch guards, Huguenots, and the English battalions plunged into the river, the water waist high, and under musket fire from skirmishers well placed behind fences and barricades. They struggled through without wavering, but before they could reform they were charged by Hamilton's Horse. The men were forced back into the water and all was confusion. Then Schomberg rode down to the Boyne, put himself at the head of the Huguenots, " Those are your persecutors, gentlemen !" and pointed to the French. Back they went again, with the old soldier to lead them. A body of Irish horse had broken through one of the regiments, and now returning was mistaken for English, and allowed to pass close to the Duke; realizing their advantage they charged and wounded him in the head. At the same time a Huguenot regiment opened fire, and Schomberg fell, shot by his own men.

This accident nearly won the day for James; his infantry rallied, and was about to fall on the broken battalions of the English centre, when William, leading the Danish, Dutch, and Enniskillen horse, attacked them on the right.

This flank attack was totally unexpected, and in panic the undisciplined Irish gave way. The retreat was gallantly covered by Lauzaun and his French troops, but the battle, which had lasted barely two hours, was lost. For good reasons the pursuit was not pressed— the heat of the day, the death of Schomberg, William's wound, and the rawness of the new regiments; but the most probable explanation lay in William's own moderation—he had no wish to punish the unhappy Irish for their loyalty; his sole object was to defeat the Stewarts, behind whom stood the armies of France.

James saw the day was lost, and galloped from the field. From Dublin he fled to Kinsale, and re-embarked for France. Had he won the battle he might have rewon his throne; had he died in defeat his son might have come to his own by the remorse of a people; but, thinking only of his own life, he lost England, and for ever.

Before the news of victory could reach England, Parliament had learnt of the defeats at Beachy Head[1] and Fleurus. The fear of a French invasion grew stronger. Fortunately, Louis would not listen to James's importunities nor lend him further troops; the moment passed, and Louis failed to grasp it.

In Ireland, Drogheda surrendered and William began his march on Dublin. His wise proclamations were somewhat counteracted by the news of the French naval victory. Very few Irish laid down their arms and the French army stayed in the country. Cork and Kinsale were for all purposes French ports, and their reduction, with that of Limerick and of Athlone, became affairs of great military importance.

William marched to Limerick and summoned the garrison, but the Governor, Boisseleau, refused to surrender. Sarsfield and Berwick were among his officers, and the former, by a daring raid, captured a great part of the English artillery train. An attempt to carry the town by assault failed, and the lateness of the season compelled William to raise the siege. He returned to England, and the command of the army devolved on the hated Count Solmes. He also shortly crossed to England, and left Ginkel, a more pleasing though very inefficient officer, in his place.

Marlborough made a flying expedition to the south of Ireland and brilliantly captured Cork and Kinsale.[2] Then the campaign came to an end, and the army went to winter quarters.

From the time of their landing at Belfast the movements of Lloyd's regiment are somewhat obscure. They

---

[1] "The Dutch gott the honour, the French the advantage, and the English the shame" (Newsletter, quoted by Lord Wolseley).

[2] Roger McElligot was Governor of Cork, and it was through his negligence to garrison a fort commanding the eastern lines that the town was able to make so brief a resistance. McElligot was sent to the Tower. Bernardi says that he escaped after eight years' imprisonment. In after years he was colonel of a regiment in France. Pike describes him as "rude and boisterous." but Lauzaun wrote of him to Louvois as "one of the best men we have in Ireland" (see Wolseley's "Life of Marlborough," vol. ii., p. 174, in which he refers to him as Macgillicuddy).

were present in Ireland in June, 652 strong, and there is good reason to suppose that they were present at the Boyne, although the regiment does not appear in the Battle Orders.[1]

There is a legend that the Fifth were the first English regiment to occupy Dublin; Ormonde, with cavalry, was sent forward on July 3rd to take possession; and possibly Lloyd's Foot have taken the credit due to Lloyd's Enniskillen Horse.

During the winter of 1690–91 the Fifth lay at Dublin.

Early in the year Louis sent large supplies of ammunition and provisions to Limerick, and a great number of French officers under St. Ruth. Ireland was infested by independent troops and companies of Rapparees,[2] and these irregulars added greatly to Ginkel's task; before undertaking a siege he had first to secure his lines of communication.

All the English regiments were accused, rightly or wrongly, of gross cruelty and ill-discipline. During the winter of 1690–91 the soldiers suffered much from sickness, want of clothing, money, and even food. The atrocities committed by the Irish led to reprisals, and often the innocent suffered. The discipline of the Dutch regiments was far higher and their sickness proportionately less. Few of the English officers chose to stay in winter quarters with their men and share their hardships.

Tollemache was recalled from Flanders to command a brigade, Mackay came from Scotland with his troops, and in June the army marched west to drive the French and Jacobites out of Connaught.

Ballymore quickly surrendered, and, leaving a small garrison, Ginkel pushed on to Athlone. The River Shannon divided the town; the west, or English, side was taken by assault, the Irish breaking down the bridge

---

[1] See Cannon, Dalton, etc.
[2] The Rapparee was a peasant who lived like a savage. His food was potatoes and milk, and he went about half naked. His cunning nearly equalled his cruelty to man and beast. He relentlessly murdered men, women, and children, and he maimed cattle with all the ferocity of the lowest order of savage (Wolseley, citing Dalrymple).

as they retired. Batteries were then raised against the Irish town, and several attempts were made to repair the bridge and force a passage. The defenders made so brave a resistance that all attacks failed. The besiegers then discovered a ford a little to the left of the bridge, and after a council of war it was decided that a detachment should endeavour to effect a crossing; but even at the ford the river ran breast high, the current was swift, the bottom foul and stony, and the further bank protected by a ravelin.

On June 30th, at six in the evening, the Forlorn Hope[1] made their way down to the river. They were dressed in armour, and marched twenty abreast. Led by their officers, they plunged into the water and made their way across under a hail of balls and grenades. The supporting party, another detachment of grenadiers and six battalions of infantry, eighty choice men out of each regiment, followed quickly by pontoons and over planks laid along the broken arch of the now deserted bridge. Completely surprised, the Irish had fled, and the town was secured to the English with the loss of only fifty men.[2] Mackay and Tollemache both showed the highest courage. The wounded soldiers were well treated. " Many large tents drawn up in a quadrangle, with quilts

[1] Captain Sandys, 2 lieutenants, and 60 grenadiers (Cannon).
[2] The English lost 12 men killed, 5 officers and 30 men wounded (Cannon).

Story estimates the losses of the Irish campaigns as follows:

Irish officers	617
,, soldiers	12,676
Rapparees killed by army or militia	1,928
,, hanged by law or order of court martial	112
,, hanged by soldiers	600
English officers	140
,, soldiers (in battle or of wounds)	2,037
,, ,, (murdered)	800
Total of English and foreign officers in the three campaigns	320
Soldiers dead in the English army since landing	7,000

(This includes Schomberg's disastrous campaign, in which the Fifth had no part.)

Troops engaged: 23 regiments of horse, 5 of dragoons, 2 of horse guards, and 46 regiments of foot.

and other conveniencies for every soldier; and the surgeons did their best with much better conveniencies than heretofore."[1]

St. Ruth, thinking the town impregnable, would not believe the reports of the assault, and when, at last convinced, his reinforcements marched to Athlone, it was to find the guns of the town turned upon them. The French general then took up his position at Aughrim, and resolved to give battle.

Before marching against St. Ruth, Ginkel put Athlone in a state of defence; Colonel Lloyd was made governor, and the Fifth, with Lieutenant-General Douglas and the battering train, were left to garrison the town. On July 12th Ginkel attacked St. Ruth in his chosen position. The Fifth took no part in the battle; it was to have been posted between the regiments of Nassau and Hesse. Good news flies fast, and they soon heard how St. Ruth was dead, with a vast number of his men; how the baggage and 600 prisoners had been taken; and how the remainder had fled to Limerick, the last stronghold of the Stewart cause. And if they wished they could go to the battlefield for evidence, to see the hills white with dead, for " the rest of the Irish remained still unburied, no inhabitants being left in that part of the country to perform it."[2]

Galway and other places quickly fell, and the English army concentrated before Limerick. On August 12th a train of nine 24-pounders, nine 18-pounders, and three mortars, with ammunition and other utensils of war, left Athlone for Limerick, under convoy of Lloyd's regiment and some militia.

On August 25th the outposts were driven in; Captain Cole and an English squadron sailed up the Shannon, cutting off all hope of relief by sea. The next day batteries were opened, and the town was bombarded until September 5th. The town lay almost in ruins, and there were great breaches in the walls; but the enemy were shouting for joy, for the English were dismounting

[1] See G. W. Story, " History of the Wars in Ireland."
[2] *Ibid.*

their guns, evacuating their outer forts, and giving every indication that the siege was about to be raised. The joy of the Irish was shortlived for, in the night, a mile north of the camp, a pontoon was thrown across the river, and early the next morning a large body of horse and foot crossed over and utterly surprised the enemy.

The Irish outposts were driven into the inner town, and in their haste they left their standard, arms and two cannon. The pontoon bridge was moved nearer the town and fortified, and again the batteries opened fire. On the 22nd Ginkel with a division crossed over, and in the afternoon the Grenadiers attacked, and carried the forts guarding the Thomond Bridge. The garrison made a sally, but were so vigorously driven back that the French officer in command of the sally-port had the gates shut for fear the English would force a way in. The refugees from the forts and the sally party thus had their retreat cut off, and lost heavily—600 killed, 200 prisoners, and many drowned.

The outer town was now in the hands of the English; the position of the garrison was hopeless, and negotiations for surrender were begun. On October 4th Limerick capitulated, and this submission extended to all the places in Ireland still in the hands of the Stewarts.

Sarsfield, with some 12,000 gallant men, went to France to fight for King Louis; others accepted the generous terms offered by King William; and Ireland, for a short time, ceased to be " the enemy within the gates."

The Fifth were ordered to England. They landed at Hoylake in Cheshire, December 29th,[1] and marched to Nottingham and Derby on a recruiting expedition, and were then ordered to London.

The health of the army in Ireland in the campaigns of the Boyne and of Limerick had been good; very few men had died except of wounds.

" The establishment of his authority over the British Isles enabled William in the third year of his reign to lead the British troops across the sea."

[1] Cannon.

The Jacobites in Ireland were crushed, and the last flicker of Scottish rebellion had died in the valley of Glencoe.

France was possessed of the finest and strongest army in Europe with the King in supreme command; she had extended her frontiers on all sides, and her soldiers garrisoned a line of posts from Dunkirk to the Meuse.

The campaign of 1691 had discovered the weakness and divided interests of the Allies, and had resulted in the loss of Mons and a cavalry defeat at Leuse. Great preparations were made for the following year; the war was still popular, and Parliament voted increased supplies and men. Early in February 2,500 English troops were sent across the Channel; with them went Lloyd's regiment and their old comrades, the 6th Foot.

Louis, not content with his vast operations in Flanders and the Empire, seized this opportunity to attempt a Stewart restoration. James and the Duke of Berwick, with 20,000 Irish and French soldiers, were encamped between Cherbourg and La Hogue; transports were assembled, and a vast fleet lay ready for escort. The threat of this invasion necessitated the recall of some of the expeditionary force; the Fifth no sooner landed in Flanders than they re-embarked and returned to England.[1] The complete destruction of the French fleet by the English and Dutch navy at La Hogue removed any immediate cause for fear; but it was then too late for the Fifth to return to Holland, and they took no part in the campaign which brought to the Allies defeat at Steinkirk and the loss of Namur. The regiment remained on garrison duty in and near Portsmouth.

Mackay fell at Steinkirk. William asked him before the battle why he wore no armour. "Your Majesty's cause is sufficient armour for me." Very large in his person, Bernardi says of him, and calls him a turncoat and renegade for deserting the Stewarts; but the old captain of Brill died well. Before the attack he sent

[1] With the 2nd and 14th.

word to Solmes that the assault ordered would lead to useless waste of life; the order was repeated; "God's will be done," he said, and fell at the head of his men.

In England, Marlborough was a suspect in the Tower, and the King, doubtful of any single Englishman's loyalty, had appointed a council of three—Killigrew, Delaval, and Cloudesley Shovel—to command the Navy. They were ordered to get the fleet to sea as soon as possible and blockade the French ships in harbour. This they failed to do, for the fleet was not ready until May, much to the disgust of the merchant ships awaiting convoy. Two squadrons were detached from the Grand Fleet, one with Sir Francis Wheeler[1] to the West Indies, the other, under Sir George Rooke, to convoy the Mediterranean Fleet. A raid on the French coast was contemplated and five regiments of foot, one of them Lloyd's, were put on board the Grand Fleet. When the English and Dutch squadrons sailed they made a fine appearance, and everybody expected that something very considerable would be performed. However, their cruisers failed to get in touch with the enemy; the council of three showed weakness and hesitation, and the advantage of the campaign lay with the French, who managed to evade the Grand Fleet and cut off several ships of Sir George Rooke's convoy.

In July the fleet were ordered forty leagues south-west of Ushant in hopes of cutting off the victorious French on their return from the Mediterranean. On July 11th they put to sea, but were so terribly ruffled by a storm that they had to put back to Torquay. Their light ships still failed to bring intelligence; provisions were running very short, for they had sailed with a small supply under promise of more being immediately sent. Fifty ships laden with provisions had sailed from the Thames, but missed the Grand Fleet and also lost their convoy. Fortunately they fell in with Rooke's squadron, and Sir George brought them safe to the

[1] With Wheeler went Lloyd's Regiment of Foot; but this was not the Fifth but a new regiment lately commanded by the Duke of Bolton, and now under command of Colonel Godfrey Lloyd, late of the Fifth.

fleet, who by now were on very short rations. Later in the month the fleet were ordered back to St. Helens to disembark the troops, " and then the Fleet dispersed, having done as little for the honour of the English nation as any fleet that was ever fitted out."[1]

Lloyd's regiment were overjoyed to be on land again, free from the hectoring sea officers, the cramped quarters, the salt beef, and the stale water. After landing they marched northwards through the eastern counties, and returning in the autumn were reviewed by the King in Hyde Park. They were again under orders for Flanders, and shortly after the review embarked on the river. In December the Fifth landed in Holland, and went into winter quarters at Sluys. Thomas Burroughs left the regiment, and William Parsons got his majority, December 10th.[2]

In Flanders Luxemburg had been more than a match for the Allies: William was outmanœuvred; Huy fell; and the Battle of Landen, July 19th, was a hard-won but very complete victory for the French. Tollemache, late colonel of the Fifth, brought off his brigade in good order. The Allies lost about 12,000 men, and it was to make good this loss that the Fifth and other regiments had been sent from England. The campaign had closed with the surrender of Charleroi.

Again, in 1694, William and Luxemburg were pitted together, and for the last time. The troops marched and counter-marched, but no decisive action took place. The Fifth lay at Ghent, Tirlemont, and Bruges. Huy surrendered to the Allies; but the summer passed without accomplishing anything of importance.

In August Edward Lloyd died, and in his place Colonel Fairfax was given the regiment.

Thomas Fairfax was the second son of Sir William Fairfax, of Steeton, in Yorkshire, " a soldier, a traveller, an excellent musician, a good-natured, well-bred gentleman."[3] Prior to the Revolution he had commanded a regiment of foot in Ireland, and since March, 1689,

[1] Campbell's " Lives of the Admirals," vol. iii., p. 137.
[2] See appendix, Army List, for 1693.   [3] Evelyn's Diary.

he had been lieutenant-colonel of Viscount Castleton's Foot; he was appointed to command the Fifth, November 4th, 1694.

In an unfortunate expedition to Brest in this summer Tollemache, who was in command, lost his life. It is doubtful if the expedition could under any circumstances have been successful; but by treachery the French were given full warning, and Tollemache lacked the moral courage to abandon the attack. His force was repulsed with great loss, and he himself, a good soldier and a brave man, died of wounds.

The French armies were not so early in the field; their enormous lines of outposts were becoming a serious drain on their resources; the War Department, after the death of Louvois, rapidly deteriorated, and the death of Luxemburg (on January 4th) was an irreparable loss. William at last had an opportunity of turning defence into attack. The loss of Namur in 1691 had been a bitter blow, and he resolved on a desperate effort to retake the fortress.

At the opening of the campaign the Elector of Bavaria and the German princes lay before Brussels, the Brandenburghers and Spaniards at Huy, and the English and Dutch, under William, were encamped near Ghent. The initiative lay with the Allies; Villeroy was not Luxemburg, and Boufflers was in doubt as to where the blow would fall. William threatened Ypres and Dunkirk, marched and counter-marched, until at the end of June the three armies made a quick concerted movement straight on Namur. Boufflers had barely time to throw his army into the fortress before the three divisions closed round him.

Namur, a masterpiece of Cohorn, perfected by Vauban, was deemed impregnable by the French, who had fixed a flaunting message to the gates. The fortress lies at the junction of the Meuse and the Sambre, the citadel in the angle between the two rivers. To the north earthworks had been thrown up on the heights of Bouge, and against these works William made his first attack. Ground was broken on July 3rd, and three days later an

assault was delivered, the outworks were captured,
and shortly after the British troops captured St. Nicholas'
Gate, though with heavy losses. On the 23rd the town
capitulated, Boufflers and the garrison retiring into
the citadel.

In the meantime, Villeroy, with 80,000 troops, was
marching to the relief of Namur. Vaudement and his
corps had joined the Allies, and they were ready to give
battle. On August 15th Villeroy fired a mighty salute,
a promise of relief to Boufflers, who each night burned
fire signals to urge him to his rescue.

On the 19th, at dawn, William reviewed his army,
and sent his picked regiments, the Fifth among them,
to offer battle to Villeroy. All day the great armies
faced each other; but when night came Villeroy stole
away not daring to risk his fate. Boufflers refused to
surrender until another assault forced him to make
terms. The Fifth had no part in the final assault,
the wild-goose hunt for Villeroy had taken them too far
afield; but one of their old comrade battalions, now
Cutt's regiment, covered themselves with glory. Namur
surrendered on August 22nd; Boufflers was held a
prisoner until the garrisons of Dixmude and Deyn were
released. The Fifth marched away to Nieuport and
encamped on the Dunes.

William returned to England to be welcomed by the
city of London, and to tell the English Parliament,
" That without the concurrence of the valour and power
of England it were impossible to put a stop to the
ambition and greatness of France."

In October the Fifth went into winter quarters at
Bruges. William Parsons had succeeded Brudenel as
lieutenant-colonel, and Lawers, after seven years' service,
became major. Captains Ashly and Atcherly left, and
Godfrey Lloyd, son of the one-time lieutenant-colonel,
had joined his father's old regiment, making the sixth
of the name of Lloyd serving that year. In 1696 a very
young ensign was gazetted—Carey Godby, son of Captain
Peter Godby; but the scandal of children's commissions
was already attracting attention, and little Godby left

the regiment before 1697, being regazetted twelve years later.

Martin Bladen,[1] a nephew of Colonel Fairfax, appointed ensign to Captain Godby *vice* Carey Godby, deserves some notice. He left the Fifth in March, 1705, for a company in Hotham's Foot, and saw service in Spain in that regiment, and as aide-de-camp to Galway. He was not only a soldier, though he rose to the rank of lieutenant-colonel in the army, but also a writer of some distinction. He was the editor of "Cæsar's Commentaries," Comptroller of the Mint, and a Lord of Trade.

France made one more attempt at invasion in 1696, but with no more success than in previous years, and in 1697 the war came to an end with the Peace of Ryswick.

The Fifth spent the last two years of the war between Bruges and Brussels. In April 1697, they were, with eleven other infantry battalions under the Count de Noyelles, in the Forest of Soigne. In December they returned to England, and landed, two companies at Dover and ten at Greenwich, and went into winter quarters.[2]

France was utterly exhausted by the long war, years of famine, and bad harvests; Louis gave up Luxemburg and Lorraine, and acknowledged William as King of England; but the balance was not restored, and the peace could only be regarded as a truce, and not as a lasting settlement.

The English Parliament, profoundly ignorant of foreign affairs, insisted on an immediate reduction of the standing army, which they cut down to 7,000 men. They added a further insult to the King by forcing him to dismiss his Dutch guards.

Early in 1697 another colonel of the Fifth met a

[1] Martin Blayden, son of Nat. Bladen of Lincoln's Inn and his wife ......, daughter of Sir Wm. Fairfax of Steeton. He was M.P. for Stockbridge, Hants, 1715-1734; and for Malden, Essex, 1734-1741; and for Portsmouth, 1741 until his death February 15, 1746. He purchased Barnmoor, Northumberland, *circa* 1720. His widow left property to the Middletons of Belsay, Northumberland (see paper by J. C. Hodgson, *Berwick Naturalist*, vol. xxii., pp. 111-112).
[2] Cannon.

violent death. Sir John Fenwick, after a lengthy trial, was condemned for high treason, and executed, January 28th. There seems to be no doubt that he intrigued with St. Germains, though probably in a less degree than many men in higher stations, whose offences were condoned. Sir John possibly suffered as much for his insolence and ill manners as for his politics.

For reducing his regiment Brigadier-General Fairfax was paid £205 8s. od.;[1] and in March, 1698, he, with two other colonels, received the sum of £350 for his expenses in disbanding.

Daniel Sherrard, an engineer officer of considerable merit, joined as a captain in February. He had served at the defence of Londonderry, 1689, and was afterwards in the Flanders train of artillery. He came to the Fifth from Sir Matthew Bridges's regiment, and retained his company until 1705.

The reduced regiment marched to Chester, where they embarked for Ireland. In August they were quartered in Dublin.

The strength of the regiment in 1699 was 41 officers, 68 non-commissioned officers, 54 servants, and 466 men.[2] The fact that the regiment was on the strength of the Irish establishment had saved them from the wholesale reduction of their comrades in England.[3] An order, dated Dublin, August 3rd, 1699, gives them " 242 Snaphance Musquetts, whereof 60 with strings, 80 pikes, and 16 collars of bandoleers in lieu of the like number of muskets, and 57 pikes repairable."

After three uneventful years the War of the Spanish Succession burst on the English people.

On the death of Charles II. of Spain, Louis broke the Partition Treaty: William, a dying man, saw his lifework all undone. The Tories were in power, and Anne and the Churchills were content that England should stand on one side, clear of another Continental war. Then Louis made his last and greatest mistake, and

[1] House of Commons Journal.   [2] *Ibid.*
[3] This was evaded by placing the army in Ireland on a separate establishment, not exceeding 11,367 men.

recognized the son of James II. as King of England, and threatened to send an army to put him on the throne.

All England rose at the word; William made vast preparation, until one day, as he rode on a pony in the park at Hampton Court, the horse stumbled with him, and the accident put an end to his frail life. This pony " Sorrel " had once belonged to Sir John Fenwick, who thus managed to play traitor after his death more successfully than when alive.

William was not a great general; all his life he had the misfortune to be pitted against the greatest men of the age. It was no disgrace to be beaten by Luxemburg, Condé, and Turenne. And if defeat followed defeat, yet in the end it was William who dictated terms, and France who asked for peace. He was not a great commander-in-chief; the administration of the army was disgraceful, full of corruption—that Stewart legacy—and marked by lack of consideration and gross ingratitude for the private soldier. In spite of his coldness to the men who saved him from disaster or won his hard-earned battles, he was popular with the army, and all would follow where he led.

His was a hard school, but the Fifth could not have chosen a better one to learn their trade, and lay the foundations of that reputation they still hold after more than two hundred years.

CHAPTER V

1701–1712

ANNE

WAR OF SPANISH SUCCESSION

FAIRFAX—PEARCE

IN most English minds the War of the Spanish Succession is identified with the victories of Marlborough, the glories of Blenheim, Ramillies, Oudenarde, and Malplaquet, and in this struggle of giants the Fifth had only a very little part to play—one fight, and that a defeat, when an incompetent general left them to be forsaken by their allies and confronted by greatly superior numbers.

Although the principal theatre of war was in Flanders, descents were made on the French and Spanish coasts; an army was maintained in the Peninsula, and the French and Spanish colonies were attacked overseas. At the same time it was necessary to guard against invasion, especially in Ireland, where there was, as usual, much disaffection.

The army of 7,000 men was found hardly adequate for these various tasks.

Without a formal declaration of war Louis surrounded the barrier towns of Holland, and securely locked up 15,000 of the best Dutch troops. English regiments were hurriedly recalled from Ireland, and, under Marlborough, sent to Flanders. All the home regiments were increased to war strength.

The Fifth took no part in the glorious campaigns

that followed; the regiment was retained for home defence; once or twice on the point of embarkation the orders were cancelled, and they remained in Ireland until 1707.

About 1703 General Fairfax was made Governor of Limerick—£1 per diem, in addition to brigadier-general's pay, £547 10s. 0d. per annum. In 1704 he was removed from his regiment, and Colonel Thomas Pearce was appointed in his place.

Fairfax died in 1710, a major-general and Governor of Limerick.

Pearce had served in Cutts's regiment, and, as captain of the grenadier company of the Coldstream Guards, he had stormed the covered way at Namur in 1695, and there had been wounded and taken prisoner. In 1702 he had served under the Duke of Ormonde in the attack that failed so disgracefully at Cadiz, but met with more success in Vigo Bay. At Vigo he had led the storming-party of grenadiers, was wounded, but gained much praise. He came home to become colonel of a new regiment, afterwards disbanded, and on February 4th, 1704, he was gazetted colonel of the Fifth.

In this year the French thrust for Vienna received its death-blow at Blenheim, and all Bavaria fell to the Allies. To Versailles there came other disastrous news, for the English had taken Gibraltar. The campaign of 1705 was ruined by the inactivity of Prince Louis of Baden, and the "fairest chance in the world" was lost to Marlborough; but the next year he redeemed his fortune, and broke the French army at Ramillies.

In 1703 Portugal had joined the Allies, and Lisbon became the base of operations in the Peninsula.

The Allies met with varying fortune, and when, early in 1707, reinforcements arrived from England, Marlborough recommended, and Peterborough urged, that the army in Spain should confine itself to the defensive. King Charles of Spain and the Council of War would not agree; Peterborough was overruled, and recalled to England; Charles withdrew his army in Catalonia, and

Galway[1] and Das Minas, with more courage than wisdom, set out to brave Berwick and burn his magazines at Murcia. On April 25th was fought the Battle of Almanza; Galway lost 4,000 killed and wounded and 3,000 prisoners, and all hope of the allied offensive was at an end.

The Portuguese had raised a force to protect their frontier, the Marquis of Fronteira in command. In June four British battalions, one of them the Fifth, arrived from Cork; they formed a division under General de Montandre.[2] The Fifth had embarked at Cork May 22nd; with a fair wind and good passage they landed at Lisbon, June 8th. They were cantoned for the summer at Estremos, and they, with the rest of the Anglo-Portuguese army, remained strictly on the defensive. The British division was increased by the recruited 13th Foot, and the newly raised Paston's regiment.

The Portuguese army contented itself with acting as a corps of observation. The English division, now under command of Galway, was cantoned near Elvas, in the valley of the Caya. The Fifth, 20th, 39th, and Paston's were brigaded under De Montandre, the remaining battalions, three in number, under Sankey. The command of the army remained with De Fronteira.

In 1709 a Spanish force under the Marquis de Bay advanced to the plain of Gudina, on the left bank of the Caya, in the hopes of enticing Fronteira across the river. The device at once met with success. Against Galway's advice, and despite his entreaties, Fronteira sent all his horse and Montandre's English brigade across the Caya, and had them drawn up in line of battle. De

[1] De Ruvigny, Earl of Galway, 1648-1720. Served in the French army; aide-de-camp to Turenne 1673-1675. Emigrated to England in 1685, and entered the English army as a major of horse in 1690. "He was one of the first gentlemen in the army, with a head fitted for the Cabinet as well as for the camp; is very modest, vigilant, and sincere; a man of honour and honesty, without pride or affectation; wears his own hair; is plain in his dress and manners. The grave never closed on a braver or more modest soldier" (Hist. Dict. Nat. Biog.).
[2] De Montandre, a good officer, afterwards Governor of Guernsey, and Master-General of Ordnance in Ireland. He became a field-marshal, and died in 1739.

Bay ordered up his infantry in support, and with his horse attacked the Portuguese cavalry on Fronteira's right wing. Before the Spanish horse could reach them the Portuguese turned and fled, leaving the British flank uncovered. The four regiments stood firm; three times the Spaniards swept down upon them, but, rallied by their officers, they formed a hollow square, and, ably commanded by Montandre, beat an orderly retreat. Sankey, with his brigade, was sent in support; but before they could reach their comrades another charge by de Bay had swept the left wing of Portuguese horse. Without support, in the act of changing front, Sankey's brigade was surrounded by de Bay's full force, and after a short fierce fight laid down their arms.

Galway had his horse shot under him, and narrowly escaped capture. Colonels Pearce[1] and Barrymore were not so fortunate; they, with 80 officers, 5 guns, and 900 men, fell into the enemy's hands. The losses in killed and wounded were about 500 on either side. Ensign Francis O'Farrel of the Fifth was taken prisoner. The steadiness of the Fifth and their fellow-battalions[2] saved Fronteira from the worst consequences of his folly.

Two days after the battle Fronteira retired to Elvas, and, taking Galway's advice, was able to make skilful dispositions for his defence.

The hot weather came, and the armies went into summer quarters—none too soon for Galway, who vowed that his soldiers should never again fight with the Portuguese.

On July 9th thirteen officers of the Fifth[3] were sent over to recruit for their regiment, with orders to return by the next convoy.

[1] Pearce was exchanged for a French brigadier-general.
[2] Dalton's "English Army Lists," vol. vi., Introduction, p. xix. Cannon.
[3] Lieutenant-Colonel Peter Godby, Major Edward Johnston, Captain Robert Brudenell, Captain Thomas Giles, Captain Nicholas Fenwick, Captain-Lieutenant Henry Owens, Lieutenant Job Elrington, Lieutenant John Elrington, Lieutenant John Parry, Lieutenant Robert Caxton, Ensign Edward Griffith, Ensign Purdon, Ensign Green ("English Army Lists," vol. vi., p. 382).

In Catalonia Von Starenberg had been joined by General Stanhope with reinforcements. He carried the war into Aragon, and although he defeated the Spaniards with great loss at Almenara and Saragoza these victories were the undoing of the Allies. Vendôme was sent to command in Spain, and to him, after a hopeless struggle, Stanhope was forced to surrender. After this disaster the war in the Peninsula flickered out. Nothing of note had occurred in Portugal since the fight on the Caya. Galway was recalled at his own request, and Portmore succeeded him in command of the English divisions. After one uneventful campaign he too obtained leave and went home.

The Portuguese had proved themselves faithless Allies; the Spaniards were inclined to a Bourbon king; and, above all, the little English army was exhausted by operations so far from its base.

The politicians at St. Stephen's were thinking more of party gains than national losses. Treachery and intrigue dogged Marlborough's footsteps; at the end of 1711 he was dismissed from all his employments, and in January, 1712, Ormonde was made commander-in-chief in his place. Thus the road was made easy for the Ministry, and negotiations were opened with Louis. In shame and humiliation the British troops were withdrawn from Flanders, and the glorious campaigns of Marlborough ended in the miserable and memorable Treaty of Utrecht.

The English regiments in Portugal were sent to garrisons in the Mediterranean—the Fifth to Gibraltar, where they remained fifteen years.

In 1706 a meeting of general officers was held in the Great Room at the Horse Guards, and regulations for the quantity and quality of clothing for the foot were discussed and agreed.

For the first year: " A good cloth coat, well lined, which may serve for the waistcoat the second year; a pair of good thick kersey breeches; a pair of good strong shoes; a good shirt; a neckcloth; a good strong hat, well laced." For the second year: " A good cloth coat, well lined, as for the first year's coat; a pair of strong kersey new breeches; a pair of good strong stockings; a pair of good strong shoes; a good shirt and neckcloth; a good strong hat, well laced. That all accoutrements, as swords, belts, patroutashes, and drum carriages be made good as they are wanted. That the recruits be supplied with a new waistcoat and one shirt and neckcloth more than the old soldiers who have some linen beforehand."

" That sergeants and drummers be clothed after the same manner, everything of its kind better."

Colonel Richard Kane, of the Royal Irish—whose acquaintance the Fifth had made at sea in 1693, and whom they were to meet again at Gibraltar—was the advocate of a new system of military discipline.

A battalion of 800 or 1,000 men, drawn up in battle order, should stand, he says,[1] " Three deep, their bayonets fix'd on their muzzles, the grenadiers divided on the flanks, the officers ranged in the front, and the Colonel, or, in his absence, the Lieutenant-Colonel (who, I suppose, fights the Battalion) on foot, with his sword drawn in his hand, about eight or ten paces in the Front, opposite the centre, with an expert drummer by him. He should appear with a cheerful countenance, never in a hurry, or by any means ruffled, and to deliver his orders with great calmness and presence of mind.

" The first thing a colonel should do, is to order the Major and Adjutant to divide the battalion into four grand divisions. . . . thus we form our platoons, our subdivisions in all our marching, and from them we form our hollow square, as well standing as marching. . . .

" When Pikes were in use, our Battalions were composed but of three Grand Divisions, viz., Pikes in the centre, and divisions of Musketeers on the Right and Left of them. Each division to be divided into four platoons, which with the Grenadiers will make up eighteen.

" The eighteen platoons are to be divided into three

[1] Colonel Richard Kane, " Campaigns of King William and Queen Anne " (1745), p. 111.

firings so that there will be six in each. And as it is absolutely necessary to have a fire in reserve, the Front rank is to be reserve for that purpose, which on occasion will make a fourth firing."

Kane advises the colonel and his drummer to be careful to step on one side when it is the turn of the centre platoon to fire; and he insists upon the necessity of recognized command by drum-beat or other signal. Should the battalion retreat, " The Lieutenant-Colonel and officers in the rear are to carry their Pikes under hand. Platoon officers carry their Pikes upright."

CHAPTER VI

1713–1728

ANNE, 1702-1714—GEORGE I., 1714-1727—GEORGE II., 1727-1760

GIBRALTAR

PEARCE

THE Treaty of Utrecht brought five years' peace, then the machinations of Cardinal Alberoni involved England and Spain in another war.

Louis XIV. had died in 1715, leaving a baby to govern France. Philip of Spain by his second marriage had gained a foothold in Parma and Tuscany; he had visions of a mighty realm and intrigued to supersede Philip of Orleans as Regent of France. The authority of Orleans was far from secure, and should he be deposed, it was only a short step to the uniting of the French and Spanish crowns. Orleans threw over the Stewarts, and in 1716 an alliance was concluded between England, Holland, France, and the Empire, against the ambitions of Spain.

Matters came to a climax in 1718. Before war was actually declared Byng had met the Spanish fleet, and, off Passaro, had inflicted a severe defeat. Philip, supporting the Stewarts, attempted an invasion commanded by Ormonde, who, on the death of Queen Anne, had changed his colours. The winds fought for the English, and the enterprise was stillborn. Vigo surrendered to England; Philip opened negotiations, gave way to the Allies, and, in 1720, a treaty was signed. Three years later the Regent Orleans died; but France continued her pacific policy, and England had but to watch her old enemy Spain.

Gibraltar had been won in 1704, one more outpost of Britain to need a permanent garrison.

Garrison duty was very unpopular; only too often the moneys which should have gone to provide food, clothing, and pay, dwindled very considerably in its passage through many hands. Officers with private means could retire to England or exchange with some worthless broken man, but the private soldier was condemned to remain for long years, often forgotten, always neglected, until that welcome day when at last the transports would come and the battalions, weakened by disease and semi-starvation, would be sent back to England. Then, discharged from further service, the men had leave to tramp the highway, to point a moral to the country yokel and encourage the youth of England to follow the flag.

Until 1720 the authorities did not realize that the victualling of such an exposed fortress as Gibraltar was at the mercy of the winds, and that in time of war everything must be convoyed by the fleet, for fear of privateers and enemy squadrons. Until 1720 the fear of starvation was a very real one; after that date it was ordered that Gibraltar should always be provisioned with two months' supply in advance. A short time before the arrival of the Fifth the garrison had been forced to burn their huts for fuel.

One English general gave it as his opinion that service at Mahon should be equivalent to a punishment, and he wondered that troops had not mutinied both at Minorca and Gibraltar.

After 1720 drafts of pensioners were sent out to make up the strength of the garrison regiments—a reward from grateful England to her veterans! When the relieving battalions did arrive they were frequently at low strength, many men deserting when their destination became known. Failing volunteers from the garrison, the orders were to select by lot as many as were required. " The inevitable result was that the garrison was composed mainly of discontented men, ready to desert at the first opportunity, with an infusion of lazy cunning old soldiers who had contracted an attachment to the wine or the women of the country."[1]

In 1713 the Fifth, 500 strong, arrived at Gibraltar[2] to find their quarters had been burned for fuel, and during their fifteen years' duty things were not much bettered, for in 1730 the troops were still without a roof over their heads, and suffering much from exposure and dysentery.

Besides the garrison,[3] the victualling of the civilian population was an important matter; a large number of these were Jews, Spaniards, and Moors. These latter were a constant source of danger when England was at war, but the Jews, by hard and honest work, earned security, if not immunity, from harsh treatment. William Shearer,[4] of the Victualling Office, records the following regulations:

" Every Monday morning the regiments receive all their provisions except bread, except in winter time, when one regiment is served in the afternoon, by reason of the days being short, and they take it by turns in being served. The Biskett taking up more time, it is

---

[1] Fortescue, " History of British Army," vol. ii., p. 47.
[2] With the Fifth at Gibraltar were the 13th and the 20th; both regiments had fought at the Caya.
[3] Garrison at Gibraltar (1715):

Governor	David, Earl of Portmore.
Lieutenant-Governor ..	Colonel Ralph Congreve.
Town Adjutant.. ..	Hugh Montgomery.
Surgeon	James Penman.
Commissary of Stores and Provisions ..	Thomas Medlycott.
Artillery officers ..	Major John Nanway, chief engineer. Jonas Moore, sub-engineer.
Captain of gunners and matrosses	Charles Briscoe.
His Lieutenant	Samuel Little.
Store-Keeper and Paymaster	Thomas Musgrave, Esq.
Barrack-Master.. ..	James Barques.
Fireworker	John Forbes.

(Dalton, " George I.'s Army.")

[4] William Shearer, Victualling Office, August 3rd, 1726. See Introduction to " George I.'s Army."

served out every Tuesday morning, and when soft bread is issued out it is every fourth day, except to officers every second day.

" The gunners, ordinance, and the severall odd mess's receive their provisions on Monday after the regiments are served in ye afternoon.

" The Spaniards receive their provisions twice a week . . . when soft bread is issued they receive it every fourth day as the regiments does. I presume the reason of serving the Spaniards only twice a week was in regard to their having better conveniencys for preserving, or securing the provision than the soldiers has in their Barracks."

Arrangements were made in case some of the contracted allowance failed. " The allowance per week for one man as per contract is 7 lbs. Biskett, $2\frac{1}{2}$ lbs. of beef, 1 lb. of pork, 4 pts. of pease, 3 pts. oatmeal, 6 oz. of butter, 8 oz. of cheese. There is no deduction in weight or measure for waste, etc."

When the convoys were late, the winds contrary, and the enemy privateers vigilant, " Other species were issued in lieu of some others specified in the contract, viz., by the last contract Oyle was issuable in lieu of butter or cheese, as it is now, except you disapprove, ye proportion being one pint in lieu of a lb. of butter or 2 lbs. of cheese. When in want of pease or oatmeal, rise is issu'd in lieu, one pint in lieu of four pints of pease and halfe a pint in lieu of 3 pints of oatmeale. Flower has also been issued in lieu of these two species. . . ."

" It has sometimes happened that a larger quantity of beefe has been in the Stores than of pork, in such case there has sometimes been an issue of all beefe, . . . the proportions being about equal, and is frequently practised in the Navy."

Lord Portmore, who, as David Collyer, had served in Flanders in the pre-Revolution days, was Governor of Gibraltar; but he, with the majority of the senior officers, spent much time in England.

In 1720, when war was very near, only two field officers were with the garrison; one of these was William

Elrington of the Fifth, who, as senior officer present, was acting as commandant. The lieutenant-governor of Minorca, Colonel Richard Kane, was hurriedly ordered to embark some troops from his garrison and send them to reinforce the three weak battalions at Gibraltar. This order he anticipated, and going himself to the Rock, by a show of strength induced the Spaniards to withdraw. He remained for a short time as lieutenant-governor.

After this brief excitement the garrison relapsed into its old monotony, the younger officers seeking distraction in high play. Duels were very frequent. Of eight officers—five ensigns, two lieutenants, and a surgeon—gazetted to the Fifth in 1718,[1] only the surgeon and Ensign Ralph Urwin returned to England in 1728. General Pearce had been made Governor of Limerick in 1715, and naturally remained in Ireland, where he was major-general on the Irish establishment. In December, 1724, he was given an addition of 6s. 8¾d. per diem, " as he has distinguished himself by his vigilance and care."

In 1715 Titchbourne sold his major's commission to William Elrington; and when Peter Godby left, in August, 1722, Elrington became lieutenant-colonel after thirty years' service. Titchbourne went back to Ireland as Governor of Charlemont. Thomas Giles had joined before 1696, and in 1722 was senior captain, but Charles William Pearce, probably son of the colonel, who had joined as captain in 1708, succeeded Elrington as major, purchasing over Giles. Two other officers had served with the regiment, Captain Job Elrington, who joined in 1696, and Captain-Lieutenant Henry Owens, who joined in 1695. By this seasoning of experienced officers discipline was maintained and when, five years later, the garrison was hardly pressed, Pearce's regiment stood firm, though of the other regiments fourteen desertions are recorded.

The years of inaction at last had an end. In 1725 the Emperor and King Philip of Spain came to a secret

[1] " George I.'s Army," vol. i., p. 298.

understanding, which resulted in the Treaty of Vienna.
The northern kingdoms, justly alarmed, replied by an
alliance, confirmed at Hanover. England fitted out
three squadrons, sending one to harry the Spanish
colonies in the West Indies. Philip collected his forces
for a counter-attack.

Admiral Sir Charles Wager, cruising in the Straits,
became suspicious, and sent a fast frigate to warn the
Cabinet that stores and cannon and men were being
collected, and that the blow threatened Gibraltar. In
reply, Colonel Dunbar was sent out from England with
dispatches to the lieutenant-governor at Gibraltar.
His ship was seized by the Spaniards, and he was thrown
into prison, but somehow the dispatches escaped capture. Kane was again ordered to reinforce the Rock.
The greatest excitement reigned. Colonel Jasper Clayton[1]
had been appointed lieutenant-governor a short time
before, September 20th, 1726, and in the absence of
Lord Portmore he was in sole command. His task was
a difficult and delicate one. Neither Spain nor England
had committed themselves to an open declaration of
war, and the responsibility of such a declaration was
one to be avoided.

Early in the new year Sir Charles Wager arrived with
six ships bringing reinforcements, increasing the garrison
to about 1,500 men.[2]

A month later, 20,000 Spaniards marched into encampments on San Roque, the Count de las Torres in chief
command.

On February 22nd, ground was broken, whereupon
Clayton sent a note of remonstrance; this was ignored,
and the work proceeded. Clayton then ordered the
Fifth and their fellow-battalions to fire on the enemy;
the men-of-war opened fire too, and the Spaniards
withdrew to their own lines.

Clayton found that the daily guards and pickets

[1] Jasper Clayton. Ensign's commission dated April 23rd, 1696.
Afterwards Governor of Dunkirk, etc. Attained rank of lieutenant-general. Killed at Battle of Dettingen, 1743.
[2] Three companies of the 26th, eight of the 29th, and six of the
39th (January 14th).

absorbed nearly the whole strength of the garrison. Wager sailed west in the hope of hitting off a convoy, and by good luck found a transport with two companies of the 34th, who were put on board a man-of-war and sent into Gibraltar, together with a prize of twenty-four guns, laden with oil, wine, brandy, and iron. Such prizes were welcome; the garrison had salt food in plenty, but it made the men ill; fresh mutton that came from the Barbary coast was poor thin stuff, and cost 8d. a pound. During the siege a lean goose would fetch 13s. 6d. or 14s., and a chicken as much as 10s. Peas rose to 5s. 8d. a peck, and beans were 8d. a pound. Small beer fetched 8d. a quart, but beer of Bristol cost 1s. 4d. for a half-pint bottle. Country wine was plentiful but poor in quality; charcoal was scarce and expensive.[1]

In May further reinforcements came; first the *Prince Frederick*, with Lord Portmore on board, and many volunteers, followed by ten companies of the regiments of Guards. Lord Portmore, though now over eighty, insisted on being at his post when danger threatened. John Mackay described him in 1702 as " one of the best officers in the world; is very brave and bold, hath a great deal of wit, very much a man of honour and nice that way, yet married to the Countess of Dorset, and had by her a good estate, pretty, well-shaped, dresses clean, has but one eye, towards fifty years old."

Further reinforcements came in by the middle of May, and a prize, a frigate of 42 guns, captured by the *Royal Oak*.

Meanwhile, on March 3rd, the second parallel had been completed by the besiegers, and a forty-two gun battery unmasked, directed against the Landport Curtain. Three hundred yards from the King's lines a powerful mortar battery was placed. The Spanish musketry fire did small harm to the garrison, and the English cannon, with the loss of one artillery officer, maintaining a steady fire, did great damage to the enemy's place d'armes.

---

[1] " An Impartial Account of the Late Siege," by an Officer (1728), p. 22 *et seq*.

Heavy rains made the besiegers' work slow and difficult, and they suffered greatly from sickness and desertion. Las Torres attempted an impossible feat and tried to mine the rock, only to do hurt to his own engineers. The English reinforcements[1] arrived just in time. Early in May the Spaniards completed four gigantic batteries, and a terrific fire opened all along the line.

Heavier armament was used in this than in any previous campaign. For fourteen days, from 92 guns and 72 mortars, 700 shots per hour were thrown into the fortress. " For some time we seemed to live in flames," wrote an officer. The garrison had only 60 guns,[2] and of these 23 were dismounted in seven days. There were also 135 mortars and cohorns, but only a portion of these commanded the landside or could be brought to bear on the enemy's lines.

The garrison showed a bold front. Clayton had won the affection and trust of his men, and Portmore could be seen strolling wherever the fire was hottest. Money was plentiful; the soldiers off duty could earn 1s. a day by helping to rebuild the walls. The Jews too, and the civilians, worked hard, and the breaches were quickly repaired. Dead men were expeditiously buried for fear of infection; those who died in the morning were buried at night, and those who died in the night were carried to the sands in the early morning. A private of Clayton's regiment fell on his way to quarters and seemed dead, and a few hours later, rolled up in his blanket, was about to be buried. In the words of an eyewitness: " We had dug the hole and were just tumbling him in, when he fell agrumbling, upon which we gave him air and lugged him back to the hospital." This unfortunate lived twenty-four hours, " when, being sure of him, we reconveyed him back to his former appartment, and heard no more of him." Another soldier saved up 20s. to buy a coffin, and this was got for 17s. 6d., his officer giving the other 2s. 6d. to the man's comrades.

---

[1] One company and half of the 34th and 26th.
[2] Twenty-one on the Grand Battery, 23 in Old Mole, 9 in Willis', and 5 near the Moorish Castle.

This one had " Prayers said over him, and by a Parson too, being a man of substance. Had he been a poor rogue, he might have slipt in without, or at most been obliged to an Amen-man for it, as was often the case."[1]

With the coming of summer the enemy's fire slackened; they had burst their guns, wasted their ammunition, shot their bolt. The English were heartened by deserters from the Spanish lines all telling the same story, which was confirmed in the correspondence they were able to capture. " The day before yesterday the Duke of Wharton insisted on going to a Battery to show his Garter-Riband, crying out a thousand times, Long live the Pretender ! and using a quantity of bad language. They represented repeatedly to him that he ought to withdraw, but he refused to do so. At last he was struck by a piece of shell in the toe. He had been drinking brandy otherwise he would have been wiser. . . . If the English do not take pity on us soon, we shall have our beards grey before Gibraltar is taken."

Las Torres wrote to his master that without reinforcements of 25,000 men the fortress could not be taken; for the bombardment had made no practical breach, the garrison was hardly weakened, and his force was not strong enough to attempt an assault.

When the troops were refused, nothing remained to Las Torres but to withdraw. Notwithstanding their losses in men and guns they must still have outnumbered the garrison by three to one.

The siege began on February 11th, and came to an end in the middle of June. England and Spain were not at war, and that diplomatic peace was maintained reflects the greatest credit on Brigadier Clayton, who, forcing Spain to be the aggressor, so well upheld the honour of his country.

The garrison had 3 officers and 72 men killed, and 202 men wounded. Of these the Fifth lost 4 men killed and 9 wounded.

One other excitement they had; two Moors had been caught intriguing with the Spaniards; they were killed,

[1] " An Impartial Account of the Late Siege."

and then flayed, and their skins nailed to the gates of the town. After the siege these skins, hardened by the sun and weather, were much cut up for souvenirs. The next year the Fifth were ordered home, and in their knapsacks many bits of the Moors' hides must have found their way to Cork.

The regiment had sailed away from Cork in May, 1707, and in April, 1728, on board, and escorted by the *Revenge, Royal Oak, Grafton, Kingston,* and *Assistance,* they came back, after twenty-one years of exile.

Major-General Pearce was still colonel, Elrington lieutenant-colonel. Captains Giles, Napier, and Elrington were still serving, and among the lieutenants was Carey Godby, son of the late lieutenant-colonel. And there were two ensigns to carry on the names of Fenwick and Vanriel.

CHAPTER VII

1728–1753

GEORGE II.

"PATRONAGE"

"Hey, Johnie Cope, are ye wauking yet?
Or are your drums a-beating yet?
If ye were marching, I wad wait
To gang to the coals i' the morning."

"O! faith, quo' Johnie, I got sic flegs
Wi' their claymores and their philabegs;
If I face them again, deil break my legs—
So I wish you a' gude morning."
ADAM SKIRVING.

PEARCE, 1704—COPE, December 15th, 1732—IRWIN, June 27th, 1737—C. WHITEFOORD, November 25th, 1752

THE greater part of the inhabitants of Ireland were in a condition which would now be regarded as little differing from slavery. The Government was in the hands of a small Protestant minority, who had control of the resources of the country. The tide of emigration was at its flood, and the Catholic Irish who remained in the country lived in a state of ignorance and poverty. Their natural leaders had suffered banishment, or had died for the Stewarts. The old English families of the Pale revenged themselves for Tyrconnel's brief reign by continued absenteeism; the ruling class were thinly scattered, and there was nothing to efface old memories and old passions.

The poverty of the country was appalling. England, by her jealous folly, had choked the young Irish trade;

In 1729 three years of famine had reduced the people to the last extremities; there were tumults in Limerick, Waterford, Cork, and Clonmel; many hundreds perished. It was said that there was no work for the young; and the old and sick died and rotted away " of cold and famine, filth, and vermin."

This was the Ireland that the Fifth came back to, and where they were to remain for twenty-four years.[1]

Possibly the misery was less great in Cork than in the inland towns, and the new barracks, built ten years before, were a great improvement on the insanitary huts of Gibraltar. The extreme poverty of Ireland and the scarcity of inns had made the building of barracks a necessity.

The rebuilding of the cathedral was going on, and since 1716 Cork had established a press, and could lay claim to follow in the wake of the capital. The roads throughout the country were good and well kept, and, another asset to the foot-soldier, the cost of living was very small.[2]

Since the Treaty of Utrecht things had gone badly with the British army; many politicians of note would have rejoiced over the disappearance of the redcoat. Discipline was made subservient to party politics; the Mutiny Act was more than once in danger; commanding officers were left without power to enforce orders. The reaction following Marlborough's victories had set in; regiments were compelled to draw their recruits from

[1] *Pay—English Establishment. Irish Establishment.*

	£	s.	d.	£	s.	d.	
Colonel	1	4	0	1	4	6	per diem.
Lieutenant-Colonel	0	17	0	0	16	6	,,
Major	0	15	0	0	13	6	,,
Captain	0	10	0	0	9	6	,,
Lieutenant	0	4	8	0	4	6	,,
Ensign	0	3	8	0	3	6	,,

Surgeon, about 10s. Chaplain, 6s. 8d. Surgeon's mate, 8s.
(Dalton.)

DUBLIN, 1739.—" Beef, 1d. a lb. Butter, 3d. a lb. Coal, 14s. a ton. Turkey, 1s.; Geese, 10d. each. Candles, 3½d. a lb. Everything about 50 per cent. cheaper than in London. In Cork, in 1776, a man haveing £500 a year kept 4 horses, 3 men, 3 maids, a good table, a wife, 3 children, and a nurse " (see Arthur Young's " Tour ").

the lowest class; and, to diminish the crime and desertion which ensued, brutal punishments were employed. The sale and purchase of commissions[1] was abused, and the command of a regiment was a great temptation to the colonel to make what moneys he could out of the pay, clothing, and allowances of his men.

King George I. set his face against the spread of dishonesty and indiscipline, and in 1719 a price was fixed for the sale of commissions.[2]

It would appear from the army lists that the majority of the officers of the Fifth were not men of wealth. Many of them served long years in junior ranks without the means to purchase their step, and this lack of money kept them to duty; and so for a time, in this debased period, the regiment still maintained its old tradition of order and discipline, until the long years of inaction relaxed authority and lowered the moral of officers and men.

In 1732 Major-General Pearce was given command of the Fifth Horse (4th Dragoon Guards). He lived until 1739, having a seat in Parliament as Member for Melcombe Regis.

The appointment of officers to regiments on the Irish Establishment was practically in the hands of the Lord Lieutenant. Unless the Sovereign or the Minister in power had any candidate the recommendation of the Irish Viceroy was accepted. In 1731 Lionel, first Duke

---

[1] *Order dated* 1705. *Children's Commissions.*—" In future children will be restricted to two in any regiment at a time, and those to be the children of officers slain or suffered extremely in the service, and when any regiment is ordered abroad the children are to be removed into other regiments."

[2] Prices of infantry commissions, February 27th, 1719:

	Home.	Abroad.
Colonel and Captain	£6,000	£5,000
Lieutenant-Colonel and Captain	£2,400	£2,000
Major and Captain	£1,800	£1,500
Captain	£1,000	£840
Captain-Lieutenant	£450	£380
Lieutenant	£300	£250
Ensign	£200	£170
Quarter-Master	£150	£125
Adjutant	£150	£125

(Dalton, " George I.'s Army," vol. ii., p. 109.)

of Dorset,[1] became Lord Lieutenant of Ireland. He was a wealthy and dignified man, with very good manners. In the words of Shelburne, he was " a perfect English courtier and nothing else. He never had an opinion about public matters." He was now about forty-three, and he and his wife, niece of Lord Portmore, had made themselves popular at Dublin Castle, where their youngest son, Lord George Sackville,[2] a boy of sixteen, was already attracting attention as a young man of promise. Dorset gave the Fifth regiment to his friend John Cope, a protégé of Lord Strafford. Cope had entered the cavalry as cornet in 1707, and as captain had joined the 3rd Foot Guards in 1710. In 1730 he had been given the 39th Foot, and on December 15th, 1732, he was gazetted to the Fifth.

In 1735, the regiment, 815 strong, went to England for two years. In 1736, James Smollet was gazetted ensign in " Cope's." This was afterwards cancelled, and he was appointed to " Lanoes." His commission in the Fifth probably did not take effect; had the gazette stood, Tobias Smollet might have chronicled the doings of his brother's regiment.

On their return to Ireland, in 1737, Colonel Cope was given the 7th Foot, a Royal regiment with certain ancient privileges, which took precedence of the Fifth. Dorset was still at Dublin Castle, and again he gave the regiment to a friend of his. On June 27th, 1737, Major-General Alexander Irwin became colonel of the Fifth.

General Irwin had a son John, now about nine years old. Dorset had a great affection for this boy, with his good looks and charm of manner. When seven years old little Irwin had been made page of honour, given his ensign's commission a year later, July 8th, 1736, and in January, 1737, became a full lieutenant in his father's new regiment, and being a tall, graceful lad, doubtless found the regimentals very becoming. Be-

[1] Dorset, 1688-1765. Son of Charles Sackville, sixth Earl of Dorset. Lord-Lieutenant of Ireland, 1731-1737 and 1751-1754.
[2] Lord George Sackville, afterwards Lord George Germaine, third son of the Duke of Dorset. Born January, 1716, died August 26th, 1785.

sides the Duke, Lord George Sackville took a great interest in the boy. Lord George was now twenty-one, he spoke little, thought much, and showed some force of character and leanings to a soldier's career. He had just left Cambridge, where a young man, a future parson, Harris by name, had earned his gratitude by defending him against an assault of a notorious pugilist. Sackville had the merit of not forgetting his friends, and, many years later, he paid his debt to the orphan son of his undergraduate friend.

In July, " Ligoniere " was appointed lieutenant-colonel to the Fifth; this may have been in error. Major Pearce succeeded Elrington; his commission dates from January 1st, 1736, and he served as lieutenant-colonel until 1751. Possibly the raising of a second battalion was contemplated, for at this time two majors were serving—James Pattinson (January, 1736) and Paul Malide (July, 1737).

War with Spain was not declared until 1739, so there does not appear to have been any necessity for doubling the battalion. Malide was out of the regiment before 1740, and, after twenty years' service, Daniel Pecqueur was promoted major. Pecqueur had joined as captain in 1721, from half-pay of the 13th Foot.

In 1737 the Duke of Devonshire succeeded the Duke of Dorset. The Fifth continued the yearly routine—winter quarters, recruiting, review, summer quarters, and then the winter barracks again.

In 1744, France declared war on England. An army was sent to Flanders, and the next year suffered defeat at Fontenoy. Fear of invasion kept the Fifth and other regiments in Great Britain; but Ireland remained quiet, and it was the Highlands of Scotland that rose to follow Charles Edward. The rebellion came to an end at Culloden. In 1748 a treaty was signed at Aix-la-Chapelle between England, France, Holland, Spain, and the Emperor. By the terms of this treaty England gave up all she had fought for during the last eight years. In 1749 the Fifth was ordered to be reduced, and 200 men were discharged at Dublin.

In 1745, Philip Dormer, Lord Chesterfield,[1] succeeded
Devonshire in Ireland, and under his liberal rule Dublin
eclipsed her old traditions. Chesterfield's interest and
patronage was extended to any encouragement of art
or learning. The Dublin Society found him a powerful
protector; he was generous and fair-minded to Catholic
and Protestant alike, and did all that a high-minded
autocrat could effect for a nation which would have preferred liberty to govern itself.

In 1747 his too short reign in Ireland came to an
end. He was succeeded by another Stanhope, William,
Earl of Harrington; but to the end of his life Chesterfield retained his deep interest in Irish affairs, and kept
up a correspondence with his many Irish friends. Dorset
had bequeathed to him his interest in the Irwins, and
in 1747 John, now aged nineteen and a full captain,
obtained a hold on his affections which he never lost.
The graceful boy, with his charm of appearance and
manner, was all that he hoped the unhappy Philip
Stanhope would become.

Chesterfield urged on General Irwin the necessity of
travel as a means of education, and in 1748 John Irwin
took a year's leave and set out to see the world. His
patron gave him letters of introduction, and wrote
from London, December 6th (O.S.), 1748, to his friend,
Solomon Dayrolles, the newly appointed envoy at The
Hague:

" Captain Irwin, whom I believe you know, son to
the old General, goes by the next packet to Holland;
he has got a furloe from his Father for a year, during
which time he intends to see as much as he can abroad.
I think him a good pretty young fellow, and, considering
that he has never yet been out of his native country,
much more presentable than one could expect. Pray
carry him to court, and into some companies, where I
think you will not be ashamed of him, which will seldom
be your case with my country men."

John Irwin travelled on to Paris, there to visit " my

[1] Philip, Earl of Chesterfield, born 1694, died 1773. Ambassador
to Holland, 1728; Lord-Lieutenant of Ireland 1745-1747.

young accademition and his Governor "; and Chesterfield urged him to travel to Rome and see the Jubilee festivities there.

His year's leave up, Captain Irwin returned to Ireland and to his regiment. Chesterfield remonstrated with him, urging that he could easily obtain more leave from his indulgent father, and that travel was worth two years' delay of promotion. Young John settled matters for himself by marrying,[1] and when, in the following April, his young wife died, he began to give the regiment his serious attention.

The colonel of the Fifth was now an old man, who spent a great part of each year at Bath, in the happy society of a coterie of old friends, among them Chesterfield and the Sackvilles, powerful interest for a regiment to have, but no great guarantee of its efficiency.

Pearce, the lieutenant-colonel, was no longer young, and probably in the long years of peace his interest in the Fifth had grown less and family ties stronger; several of the senior officers had left; many of the subalterns were old men who had failed to find purchase money, and had lost heart and interest. John Irwin, with no qualifications save his social ones, was eldest captain for purchase, and, with the influence behind him, there was little doubt that the majority, when vacant, would be his. The time was a critical one; Pearce talked of leaving; the fate of the regiment hung in the balance.

In a roundabout way the late colonel, Sir John Cope, came to the rescue. In 1742 Sir John, now K.C.B., was one of the generals appointed to command troops sent to the assistance of the Queen of Hungary. The rebellion of 1745 found him commander-in-chief of the King's troops in Scotland. When the first outburst took place, a half-pay lieutenant-colonel was visiting his friends in the Lowlands after many years abroad. Charles Whitefoord was the third son of Sir Adam Whitefoord, the first baronet of Blaquhar, and his wife Margaret, only daughter of Alan, seventh Baron Cathcart. Charles was born about 1700, and grew up to find himself

[1] Eliza, daughter of Hugh Henry of Straffan, in Kildare.

one of a large family with small means. Like his elder brother Adam, Charles was " very proud to be in the Military, but Sir Adam having many children, cannot be brought to purchase for him, commissions now running so high."[1] This being the case, Charles entered the navy, and passed for lieutenant; then, his hopes vanishing with the reduction of the service, he joined the Inniskilling Dragoons, probably as troop quartermaster, where a man of some education was required. In 1728 he purchased an ensign's commission in the 31st. In 1733 he was promoted lieutenant, and got his company in 1737. He saw service abroad in various regiments, and at one time acted as aide-de-camp to his uncle, Lord Cathcart. In April, 1741, he was made lieutenant-colonel of a marine regiment, and in 1745 came home for well-earned leave. When Charles Edward landed Whitefoord at once offered his services to Cope, who was badly in need of experienced officers. At the Battle of Preston Pans he acted as engineer, or, rather, as artillery officer, though in all his varied service he had never before fought the guns.

When the infantry broke and the cavalry galloped away, Cope still saw Whitefoord's battery holding its ground while the battle swept up to and round it. At last the four guns were stormed and carried by the Camerons and the Stewarts of Apine. Sword in hand, Whitefoord was left, his raw artillery men had gone down before the dirks and claymores. Stewart of Invernahyle called to him to surrender; Whitefoord cut at him, his sword breaking on the Highlander's target; as he stood helpless, one of the clan flung up his battle-axe to brain him; Invernahyle ordered him back, and persuaded Whitefoord to surrender his broken sword.

He was rescued by the Angus Militia, and the tables were turned at Culloden. Invernahyle, his family and house, were proscribed, and Whitefoord repaid his debt. He did his utmost to procure pardon for the chivalrous Stewart, going at last to Cumberland, commission in hand, asking leave to retire if mercy was

[1] Lady Cathcart to the Earl of Stair (see " Whitefoord Papers ").

not shown to the man who had given him his life at Preston Pans.

Cumberland had his merits, and Whitefoord's persistence did him no disfavour. Cope, acquitted by the Court of Inquiry of all blame, "his courage without reproach," was eager to serve his friend and lieutenant, and began a discreet wirepulling on his behalf.

So it was that, in September, 1751, Charles Whitefoord was gazetted lieutenant-colonel of the Fifth, where John Irwin was now a major of six months' standing.

On October 5th Sir John Cope wrote from Bath, in reply to Whitefoord's letter of thanks:

"Your obligation for this small favour . . . is entirely owing to Lord George[1] [Sackville], whose protection and friendship is well worth cultivating. He is able, and the most likely to be very considerable of any young man in the army. Don't let your usual *mauvaise honte* hinder his being acquainted with your merit and I'll answer for his kindness to you and to himself not stopping here. I shall be extremely glad to hear from you.

"I am most truly, my dear Charles,
"Your much obliged and most faithful humble servant,
"JOHN COPE."

Whitefoord was a hardbitten Scotsman of fifty-one, who had seen service in every part of the globe; he had expended his health and the best years of his life in an uphill fight; every step in the service had been bought at its dearest price. His second in command was a young man of twenty-three, with money enough and to spare; such charm of manner that all men were friends with him;[2] such fortune that, without a day's real service

[1] "If Lord George Sackville is sincerely in your interest, your affair will certainly do, as he has not only a great deal to say with his father, but also he is the Duke of Cumberland's Military man of confidence in Ireland" (Chesterfield, September 1st, 1751).

[2] Lord Chesterfield to Major John Irwin, September 1st, 1751: 'Should you ever be miserable enough to want my assistance, or I unexpectedly happy enough to be able to give you any, your commands will want no preamble to introduce, nor excuses to attend them. My friendship and esteem for you will sufficiently

or an hour's work, he was now high up in the army list with all his life before him. The commander-in-chief in Ireland[1] was his very good friend, and had attached him to his staff. Dorset was again at Dublin Castle, and Major Irwin always found a welcome there.

Two strange brother officers, and yet the combination worked wonders, and in the next two years the old regiment was pulled together and set in order, the old traditions revived, and new ones worthy of the old were established. From the date of Whitefoord's commission there was set up that high standard of regimental officer and man which, though shaken, has never yet fallen. To Whitefoord and the officers that he trained and encouraged the regiment owes those after-records of discipline and order which have carried the Fifth triumphant through disaster.

That his task was no easy one the fragments of correspondence that have come down to us make very evident; but the young enthusiasm of John Irwin and the promise of one or two of the younger officers kept him in good heart.

The first business was to rid the regiment of some of the old stumbling-blocks to discipline and reform. On February 10th Irwin wrote from Dublin:[2]

---

incline, though your situation will not sufficiently enable me to serve you."

May 7th, 1754: " Are there no hopes of seeing you in England this summer?"

Bath, November 27th, 1768: " I thank you heartily for your letter which I received yesterday, and though I know you flatter me, I am extremely pleased with your thinking me worth your flattery...."

Blackheath, August 6th, 1769: " Pray, how have I deserved some compliments in your letter? I cannot recollect that I have offended you; I never made you any compliments, and I am sure that I do not make you one now, when I assure you that I am, with the truest esteem and friendship, your most faithful, humble servant."

On June 20th, 1768, Chesterfield wrote from London to Madame de Tencin: " Je ne crois pas que vous me reprochiez de vous avoir endossé M. le Général Irwin: car pour un Anglois il a de manières, ce qu'il faut avouer, est assez rara dans ce pais ici...."

[1] John, tenth Earl of Rothes; died 1767. Major-general in army 1743; lieutenant-general on Irish Staff 1751.
[2] " Whitefoord Papers."

"My dear Colonel,

"Your not coming has been a great disappointment to me on many accounts. . . . But that I expected to see you I would have wrote you word that our quondam scheme for Cuthbertson would not do, nor will that where our friend Vanriel[1] is comprehended do at all, an absolute negation being put on him and on every other Courtmartial man in the Regiment. . . . I go down the latter end of next week with Lord George to the Primate's, and from there go round the quarters of the Carrabineers[2] with his Lordship, so pray let me see you before that, and bring Cuthbertson's[3] resignation with you; that you know will hold good in all events. Bourne has sent over three recruits, good ones; they set out to-morrow. I have been out all the morning with Lord George, with whom I am to dine, and have no more time than to assure you that I am most affectionately and with respect, my dear Whitefoord,

"Yours,
"John Irwin."

The winter of 1751–52 was a gay one, and the regiment had its share in the festivities. Chesterfield wrote in April from London to his dear Irwin in Dublin: "I

---

[1] Vanriel: Lambert Van Riel, Junr., Ensign, November 24th, 1722; lieutenant, May, 1739; adjutant, April, 1749. Son of Lambert Vanriel, who served in the Fifth. Ensign, June 1st, 1695; lieutenant, April, 1707; S., 1715; O.B., 1723.

Lambert Vanriel, Junr., was gazetted captain-lieutenant of a company of Invalids stationed with three others at Berwick.

William Brown, major, November 3rd, 1755.
Lambert Vanriel, Captain-lieutenant, October 13th, 1755.
Peter P. Foubert, ensign, October 13th, 1755.

In 1758 the Berwick "Invalids" appear as a regiment, mentioned for a short time as the 81st Foot.

Alexander, Lord Lindores, colonel.
Richard Bowles, lieutenant-colonel.
Lambert Vanriel, captain-lieutenant.

He apparently died or retired in 1761 (Dalton).

[2] Carabineers, commanded by Colonel Chenevix, brother to the Bishop of Waterford. Colonel Chenevix and another officer were appointed by Chesterfield when Lord-Lieutenant to inspect and control the purchase of arms, formerly left entirely to the contractors.

[3] Robert Cuthbertson.

COLONEL CHARLES WHITEFOORD.
From a portrait in the possession of Captain Caleb Whitefoord.

find that Dublin this winter has been the seat of pleasure as well as of war. We have heard of the magnificence of your balls and entertainments." And once again he urges the value of travel on the young man: " You have attended your post as Major long enough, I should think, to be allowed a furlough for next winter, and I take it for granted that your whole Regiment is very perfect now in the roundabout way of doing things." But Irwin stuck to his men and to Whitefoord, and took his duties as seriously as his colonel could desire. The annual inspection, or review as it was called, engrossed both their minds. Whitefoord wrote:[1]

" I have the honour of the Earl of Rothes's commands, transmitted by you. . . . If they are as punctually obeyed as they are judiciously given, we shall merit his lordship's approbation, which I'm sure he'll not prostitute to any that don't deserve it, having the politeness of the Frenchman, corrected by the integrity of the Roman." And, in another letter: " I have the pleasure of yours with one from Lieutenant M'Laughlin[2] which gives me a great deal of concern. He says men are very hard to get, and has sent over but six, whereof two have been in the service. I have fatally experienced the bad consequences of giving the recruiting officer a latitude, and must have a very good opinion of the man to whom I give a discretionary power. To change low men for others no better is folly, and not to be compleat in Aprille is dangerous, therefore lads under eighteen of 5 feet 7[3] I consent to take, but would alter these instructions no further. . . . Now I must reveal to you my secret in order to make you easy, and procure the General's approbation, whose will shall always be to me a law. Our drummers are sightly fellows; I propose turning as many of them into the ranks as will

[1] " Whitefoord Papers."
[2] Peter M'Laughlin joined in 1745. In October, 1755, he and Ensign William Reade went to an Independent Company at Bristol. In 1715 twenty-five companies of Chelsea pensioners were formed to take over garrison duty; they were known as Independent Companies of Invalids. The pay was less than in the regular army.
[3] The minimum height for marching regiments was 5 feet 8 inches, while for the foot-guards it was 5 feet 9 inches.

compleat us, and 'listing boys in their roome. That saves us with the commissary, and does not exhaust the exchequer. After the Review I discharge the boys, and then shall have a fine sum in the Stock purse. At the same time, the General saves the cloathing. When winter comes we will send a greater number of officers, by which method we will save to the General, put money in the Captain's pockets, and effectuate our scheme of not haveing (at least) the worst Regiment in Ireland. I have a plot for making our sergeants fine at a small expense. You see their coats are now lapell'd. That I shall propose to alter, and have them looped like the men's with a half silver lace, which you must buy in England. By this means we shall make a show with economy, for the cloath saved will near purchase the lace, and as I have communicated this to nobody I hope you will keep it to yourself."

Major Irwin had gone to England to see his father, who was now seriously ill and a permanent invalid, at Bath.

The great day of the review came and went. Irwin on the staff had opportunities of seeing other regiments, but, " I have seen nothing to equal our review, taking one thing with another." And on June 6th Sir John Whitefoord wrote to his brother:

" My dear Charles,

" I give you joy of the fine appearance as well as of the performance of your Regiment at the Review, of which the Earl of Rothes informed Lord George Sackville from Waterford, who was pleased to communicate his lordship's sentiments to me. This I hope will do you great service, as the Earl of Rothes will do you justice in his report to H.R.H., which will be made sometime next month. Honest Masterson says you did their Regiment much service, which occasioned their making a better appearance at the Review than they would have done."

But the lieutenant-colonel had not been satisfied; something had gone wrong, and the matter was of great importance to him, for clearly General Irwin had not long to live and Whiteford's services entitled him to hope to succeed him. Much depended on the commander-in-chief's report. John Irwin tried to soothe him, writing from Dublin on June 9th:

" You say . . . ' the cursed mistake of our men preys upon me, and has robbed me of rest.' I beg to know what you mean by it, as, to the best of my recollections, I know nothing of the matter. At least, I have never heard him speak ill of either officers or soldiers (except Smith the day of the Review), but, on the contrary, has flattered both extreamly, and has more than once made my Father and me happy on the subject."

Whiteford was not to be consoled; his brother was sent to Rothes with an explanation, and the molehill mountain collapsed. On June 27th Sir John wrote from Dublin : " I made the explanation to the Earl of Rothes as you desired, which diverted him much, as he thought you too delicate upon that point, and was perfectly satisfied that the Fireing was not spoiled by any fault of yours. Had the adjutants given the proper information the thing could not have happened."[1] And then he adds : " Last Tuesday General Irwin died. . . . Lord Rothes has recommended you to succeed him, and Major Irwin to be your successor . . . (and) wrote to Lord George, ' Whiteford stand fast.' " At the same time, Sir John begged his brother not to resent it if another was given the regiment over him, and ends his letter, " Your slave, John Whiteford."

The wirepulling was hard at work again. Dorset and Rothes were both strongly in Whiteford's favour; but the settlement lay with the Horse Guards, and from London Major Irwin wrote despondingly. The regiment would probably be given to some Court man, for by strange chance this was the third time that the colonelcy of the Fifth had become vacant during Dorset's term of office. However, for once merit won the day,

[1] Irwin's reply of June 6th, 1752, may refer to this: " The General desires his compliments to you, and that you will do as you judge most proper in relation to the changes you propose among the Non-commissioned Officers."

and Whitefoord was made colonel and Major Irwin got his step.

Whitefoord was gazetted November 25th, and in that month he set his house in order and made his will. Worn out by hardships and the long struggle, he felt himself a sick man, and he knew that the regiment he had grown to love would be his for only a short time.

" Colonel Whitefoord begs that Captain Rawson will accept of his regimentals and Captain Dering of his mare and furniture, etc.; to Dr. Herbert Gibson one dozen of Holland shirts marked with blue silk; and I do further beg that Captain Dering will take charge of all my effects."

And to Chudleigh Dering he left his last written wishes:

" The favour of Captain Dering that he will take the direction of his Funeral, who desires to be buried out of consecrated ground,[1] and without Military honours. But begs that Captain Dering will inform the Garrison that such as pleases will meet where he appoints, and drink a hearty glass to his journey."

Whitefoord lived over the New Year, but on January 2nd, 1753, the brave and chivalrous soldier set out on his " journey," and John Irwin and the Fifth lost their best friend.

Like his second in command he had the power of winning hearts; his brother " rejoiced to hear from Heathcote[2] how agreeable you are to your corps, a thing I never doubted of "; and Sir John's landlady asks leave " to send you compliments and ten thousand good wishes for your prosperity." General Irwin begs " if he has a horse to run at grass he will turn him out in some fields of his."

Cumberland, Sackville, Cope, Dorset, and Rothes all fought his invincible modesty and proclaimed his true worth. Health and opportunity failed him, and he died with half his work undone.

[1] Colonel Whitefoord was probably a Presbyterian.
[2] Heathcote, a friend of Chesterfield. " I am extremely obliged to you for your kindness to your Lieutenant Heathcote, in which I think I have some share, though I hope and believe he deserves it personally " (see letter of September 1st, 1751).

CHAPTER VIII

1750–1760

"DISCIPLINE AND THE INTERIOR ŒCONOMY OF A BATTALION."

A REGIMENT cannot be put to rights in a twelvemonth even though commanded by a Whitefoord, and there were still black sheep among the officers of the Fifth. In 1752 complaints had been made when, after the Review, the regiment split up for summer quarters and the subaltern officers were removed from their colonel's influence.

One detachment, under Captain Keene,[1] marched into Limerick, where the 44th were quartered, but neglected to report to the colonel, Sir Peter Halkett. Keene did not go near him nor send word of his arrival or marching orders. Fortunately, Captain William Eustace behaved better, and made excuses for his senior; but the next day Keene had the men beat to arms and "alarumed the whole garrison." Another division marched in the next day, and also failed to report themselves. Halkett was inclined to excuse the captain in command, even though he had transgressed by riding through the streets, "because he met him drunk in the evening." This came to Rothes's ears, and he ordered Irwin to report the matter to his colonel. Rothes advised that Keene should be made to sell; but Irwin pleaded for the other offender, Mitchell, writing, "I know Mitchell intends well, and I really love him. Pray make him easy."

[1] Gilbert Keene. Joined as ensign, 1710; lieutenant, April 22nd, 1722; captain, June, 1739; resigned, March, 1754. Possibly father of Whitshed Keene, who joined as ensign, June, 1750.

Not until September, 1754, did Keene resign, and Mitchell one year later. Dering, Eustace,[1] Rawson, and Nugent[2] were good men; Irwin had special confidence in Eustace and Nugent, " whose division was well taken care of, as I am told " (June 9th, 1752). On Irwin's promotion John Mompesson, from half-pay in Boscawen's Foot (29th), was appointed major. Although his late regiment was no recommendation to his new commanding officer, who earlier in the year had severely condemned it—" Boscawen's marched abominably . . . the colonel and the major forced to be told every moment what to do, they knew nothing "—Mompesson appears to have been a good soldier, for in January, 1756, he left the Fifth to command the 52nd, and six months later was gazetted lieutenant-colonel of the 8th Foot.

In 1754 Dorset's second viceroyalty came to an end; the second term of office had not been as successful as the first, for the Lord Lieutenant was entirely under the influence of the Primate Stone and of his youngest son, who acted as first secretary.

Chesterfield wrote in April, 1752: " As well as I can judge at this distance, from the various accounts I have had of your squabbles and quarrels in Ireland, C'est tout comme chez nous. The great point is, who shall govern the government ? . . . What an effusion of claret must all this have occasioned ! . . .[3] I make no doubt but that there has more claret been drunk over the Barracks this winter than will be drunk in them these ten years. . . . I not only hope, but am persuaded, that you do not give way to this *cochonnerie*, which ungentlemans every body."[4]

[1] William Eustace. Ensign, May, 1744; lieutenant, October, 1745; captain, June, 1750; major, November, 1757; lieutenant-colonel, October, 1761.
[2] George James Nugent. Ensign, April, 1749; lieutenant, June, 1750; captain, January, 1752.
[3] Chesterfield, on March 7th, 1754, wrote: " If it would but please God by his lightening to blast all the vines in the world, and by his thunder to turn all the wines now in Ireland sour, as I most sincerely wish he would, Ireland would enjoy a degree of quiet and plenty that it has never yet known."
[4] In after years King George III. became very fond of John Irwin, and one day he turned to him, " They tell me, Sir John, that

Lord Hartington, afterwards the fourth Duke of Devonshire, succeeded Dorset, and by his judicious rule did much towards soothing the troubled water. Unfortunately, his term of office only lasted a year.

With the Hanoverian kings something of the Prussian spirit was adopted into the English army. The height of a grenadier's hat became a matter of great importance, and regiments lost half their former picturesque variety of facings and dress.

On July 1, 1751, George II. issued a warrant regulating the standards, clothing, and rank of the regiments of the standing army, and by this warrant much initiative was wrested from the hands of the colonel. No longer might his device, or arms, or livery appear on any part of the appointment of his regiment; the clothing was regulated, and might not be altered without the Captain-General's permission. The Colours were standardized, the King's, or first Colour, to be the Great Union throughout. The second Colour to be of the facing of the regiment (except for the regiments faced red or white), with the union in the upper canton.

" In the centre of each Colour is to be painted or embroidered in gold, Roman characters, the number of the Regiment within a border of Roses and Thistles . . . except those Regiments which are allowed to wear any Royal Devices or Ancient Badges, on whose Colours the rank of the Regiment is to be painted towards the upper corner." The size of the Colours and the length of the Pikes were regulated by those of the foot-guards. The drummers of all the regiments, other than Royal, were ordered to be clothed in the colour of the facing, lined, faced, and lapelled on the breast with red, and laced in such a manner as the colonel shall think fit, for distinction's sake, but the lace must be of the same colour as that on the soldiers' coats.

The forepart of the drums was ordered to be painted the colour of the facings, and the Fifth were allowed to

---

you love a glass of good wine?" "Those who have so reputed of me to your Majesty have done me great injustice, they should have said a bottle!"

blazon their George and Dragon on the drums and bells of arms. On the Grenadiers' hats, as well as St. George killing the Dragon, the White Horse of Hanover was to be worn, with the motto " Nec Aspera Terrent " over it on the flap; and the Fifth, being one of the old corps, had their ancient badge embroidered in the centre of their Colour; and in the three corners, the rose and the crown.

The gosling green drummers were somewhat inconvenient to clothe, and many years later the drummers of all the foot were dressed in white.

The discipline of the army benefited from these regulations, much as they were resented by autocratic commanding officers. Bennet Cuthbertson (possibly a son of the captain-lieutenant whose departure from the regiment in 1752 was hailed with joy by Whitefoord and Irwin) joined the Fifth as ensign in 1749, and became adjutant in August and lieutenant in October, 1755. He devoted much time to writing a book, which he dedicated to Studholm Hodgson, who was made colonel of the Fifth in 1756.

" The first step necessary for the Establishment of Regularity and Œconomy in a Battalion, is undoubtedly by the most exact subordination and obedience throughout the whole; yet in the enforcing these, a high degree of judgement, coolness, and affability is absolutely requisite from the superior to the other officers, else that harmony with which every individual should engage most chearfully in the work can never be obtained, and without it experience daily proves, Perfection cannot easily be established in a British Corps."[1]

Cuthbertson had very definite ideas of the qualifications of suitable officers, and it is not difficult to trace in his book the influence of John Irwin and his Chesterfieldian education.

" A good figure (at least, a genteel one) is a circumstance to be also considered in the young gentleman who offers himself for a pair of Colours. . . . From

[1] " A System of Œconomy of a Battalion," by Adjutant Bennet Cuthbertson, London, 1779.

16–19 is the best age for entering on the military profession, lads being then in general strong enough to bear any sort of fatigue, and may by that time be supposed to have acquired some branches of polite and useful knowledge, particularly French, Drawing, and Fortification."

Cuthbertson was a great advocate of a regimental "Mess." This was more possible in barrack life in Ireland than under the pernicious billeting system in England and Scotland. He urged that if the mess had of necessity to be divided, an equal number of officers of field rank should be allotted to each division, and that the subalterns should on no account be left to form one of their own.

"A Sergeant Major . . . ought to be sensible, sedate, and have a good address;" and for good sergeants and corporals, "Honesty, Sobriety, and a remarkable attention to points of Duty, with a neatness in their dress," should be looked for, and they also "should be able to write in a tolerable manner."

"A drum-major can never be too great a coxcomb;" but he must also be very honest, as he was so frequently employed to carry the officers' mails to and from the post.

"A handsome set of Drummers, who perform their beatings well, being one of the ornaments in the shew of a Battalion, care must be taken to enlist none but such as promise a genteel figure when arrived at maturity." He recommends that soldiers' children be employed, but "boys much under fourteen are rather an encumberance to a Regiment, especially on active service." To the recruiting-officer Cuthbertson also gave good advice: "Sailors and Colliers never make good soldiers, . . . and in-knee'd and splayfooted men should not be enlisted." With all his care for the appearance of the corps he had also thought for the comfort of the men.

"It will contribute very much to the comfort and cleanliness of the soldier if the commanding officer of the company will order towels to be fixed on rollers behind the door of every barrack room to prevent the men from wiping their hands on the sheets;" and " a careful experienced woman must be constantly employed to attend in the Regimental Hospital as a nurse, whose wages should be paid either by the surgeon or from the savings of the sick men's pay."

On the Irish establishment an allowance was made to the surgeon of each regiment of 13s. 3¾d. per month for a nurse.

" When a man dies or is dismissed, the straw he lay on should be burnt, and all bedding washed and properly aired;" and he recommends that there should be a fund for the sick, so that broth and wine, and such things that they could not afford from their pay, would be provided for them.

All non-commissioned officers and men had to obtain permission before marrying; and Cuthbertson urges them to choose women of good character and strong constitution, who could earn a little money by doing the soldiers' washing, or in other ways. But all-important to the adjutant was the detail of uniform. The men's coats must not be too long; two buttons at the breeches-knee should show. The coat should be tight, but without constraint across the breast; the buttons should be of good metal, never of pewter. White breeches of good fit could not be bettered, and as the allowance of one pair per annum was insufficient, he suggests a pair of white soft ticking for summer use. New cloth should be given out to the tailors a month before the review, that the regiment might appear in new clothes with last year's coats as waistcoats. Black stocks were more serviceable than white ones. The men were allowed no wigs. " Even short hair looks more military than a peasant's wig," and the hair must be combed morning and night, and every care taken that it should not grow thin. A fine head of hair was a strong recommendation to a new recruit.

The men must change their linen twice a week, and officers are enjoined to see that this is done.

The adjutant also took care of their souls. " From the natural profligacy of the lower classe of men, and in general their total ignorance in religious matters, it very much behoves officers to insist on the non-commissioned officers, drummers, and private men constantly attending at Divine Worship."[1]

In August, 1754, Lord George Bentinck,[2] from the 1st Regiment of Foot Guards, was gazetted colonel. He was the second son of the first Duke of Portland, a man of thirty-nine, with nineteen years' service to his credit, and, as captain, he had fought at Dettingen.

John Irwin's interest in the Fifth was somewhat lessened, for in 1753 he married again[3] and both he and his wife discovered a nice taste for entertaining and society. No man, as Lady George Sackville said, had such good taste in lace.

[1] Dissenters were allowed to attend their own chapel.
[2] Lord George Bentinck; born 1715, died 1759. Entered the army as ensign 1735; in 1752 made aide-de-camp to the King; in 1753 married Mary Davies.
[3] Anne, daughter of Sir Edward Barry, not Chesterfield's choice. " We have married you here to the daughter of Lady . . ., but that is no proof that you have married yourself to her in Ireland. If you have, I heartily wish you joy, for it is possible that there may be joy in Marriage " (April 25th, 1752).

CHAPTER IX
1754-1757

GEORGE II., 1727-1760

ROCHEFORT—THE FIRST RAID

Lord George Bentinck

On January 16th, 1756, the Peace of Aix-la-Chapelle came to an end, and war was formally declared. In the far east and the far west the truce had never been observed, and war had ensued wherever the settlers from France and England met; but now Germany became once more a battlefield; ostensibly because Frederick of Prussia and the Pompadour had said bitter words.

In 1754 the war clouds were gathering, and a year later the storm was seen to be inevitable. An England governed by a Newcastle depended on treaties and foreign aid; the army was not substantially increased, and the navy was neglected. The other side of the Channel there were vast preparations. In Toulon and Dunkirk men worked day and night; the English Ministry chose to believe that the invasion of England was the goal.

Then came the loss of Minorca, and " Byng was shot because Newcastle deserved to be hanged."[1]

From America news of Braddock's disaster had reached England, and Loudoun was sent to retrieve the English fortunes. He alienated the Provincials, and lost Oswego; Montcalm threatened New York.

Newcastle's sins were coming home to roost. Fox deserted him; each fresh disaster gave new zest to the

[1] Fortescue.

opposition; and before the New Year he resigned to make way for William Pitt.

In Europe, Frederick had roused all the nations against him; France, Austria, Russia, Sweden, and Saxony were leagued together; England and France were at war on the seas; and now, to protect Hanover, England must fight on land.

The Militia Bill was introduced; the Electorial troops and Hessians were returned to Germany; England was henceforth to fight her own battles. The whole country responded to the demands of the new Prime Minister, eager to wipe out the defeats and humiliations of the last years.

Four months later King George nearly shipwrecked the State by dismissing the Minister he hated and reinstating Newcastle; but the temper of the country was shown, stocks fell, the people clamoured for Pitt and overwhelmed him with gifts and golden caskets. In July the King was forced to recall him as Secretary of State, with full control of the war and foreign affairs.

In July the Duke of Cumberland was defeated at Hastenbruch, and compelled to evacuate Hanover; the year ended with further ill news from New England—the loss of Fort Lake George.

Pitt, with his vast dreams of empire, did not lose heart, but was determined to retain the initiative and force France to fight, where and with what weapons he chose. Louis hoped that New England and the Indies might be conquered in Germany, and laid his plans to that end; Frederick seconded him by calling loudly for help. Pitt kept the fleet in the Channel, realizing that the first step towards colonial empire was to establish and maintain an overwhelming superiority at sea. To relieve the pressure on Frederick and to divert the armies of France, he entered upon a series of raids on the French coast, and in three of these raids the Fifth regiment was engaged.

While the storm was gathering, Bentinck's, with the regiments of Bertie, York, Jordan, Folliot, Howe, Anstruther, and Loudoun, were ordered to England, to recruit as soon as possible, and augment their usual complement of twenty-nine private men per company to a war strength of seventy. Edward Barry and Henry Reddish were recalled from half-pay to command additional companies. Chudleigh Dering, the senior captain, resigned; Mompesson went to command the 52nd Foot, and John Mackay, from lieutenant of the 2nd Foot Guards, was appointed major in his place.

The Fifth landed at Bristol in March, 1755, and through Worcester, Gloucester, and Salisbury they marched,[1] drums beating and colours flying. Then on through Fisherton, Hilford and Harnham, Chelmsford, Bonsham, Broomfield, Wattle, Widford, Great Haddon, and Springfield.

When at Salisbury, on May 3rd, they were inspected by Sir John Mordaunt. "Bentinck's regiment" then contained seven English and twenty-three Irish officers. He reported that the officers were properly armed, saluted well, and were ready in their exercises; that the men were a tall body, and clean under arms, though many seemed old and the accoutrements were too bad to be fixed.[2] The regiment marched and drilled well, though most of the sergeants were away recruiting. The arms were mostly bad or wanting; but the firings—eighteen rounds by platoons standing, advancing, and retreating; again by subdivisions; street fire and general fire—were " most of them good." The accounts were well kept; the clothing was good; there were no complaints —" a regiment properly appointed but too full of recruits to be as yet fit for service."

At Chelmsford, the Adjutant-General Robert Napier signified to Lord George that as the King would pass through " on his way from Harwich to London, a Captain's guard of 100 men with the King's Colours was to be posted at the place where H.M. changed horses." The rest of the regiment, with the second Colour (the

[1] Sir D. W. Smith. See also Cannon.
[2] Uniform: Red, lapel faced and lined with green, looped and bound into a white binding; red waistcoat and breeches. In October the green is called "pale," and the regiment is mentioned as having fifes (see *St. George's Gazette*, August, 1899).

third was not yet won), were ordered to line the streets as the King passed through. A return of the regiment was ordered to be given to Lord Delamere, who was with the King.

In the next month they were again inspected. At Chelmsford, on October 28th, Sir James Stewart reported the officers perfect in their duty, the men very clean, steady and attentive under arms, the sergeants expert in their duties, the drummers perfect in their beatings, the firing all close and well. " The Regiment is well clothed and well appointed, and, considering the great number of new men, they are well disciplined and fit for service."

In the estimates the strength is given as 1,041 men, and expenses £18,955 15s. od.[1]

Lieutenant-Colonel Irwin went off to stay at Bath, and while there dined with Lord Chesterfield almost every day. His host showed him the last number of the *World* and his own contribution therein, and Irwin suggested as the subject for another essay, " Good Breeding as apart from mere Civility "; and so, on October 30th, a paper appeared, ever afterwards called General Irwin's Paper, " Good Breeding, like Charity, not only covers a multitude of Faults, but, to a certain degree, supplies the want of some Virtues."

The recruiting marches continued throughout the next year, and the Fifth had some experience of billeting, which the shadow of war made rather easier for the military officer. There was a wholesome fear of invasion in the country; collisions with civil authority grew rarer, and discharged soldiers were safe for the moment from being whipped as vagrants through the streets. The lack of barracks militated against discipline, and the inevitable separation of the companies was not the best preparation for active service.

In June the Fifth marched from Chelmsford and

[1] From the papers of Sir D. W. Smith. The estimates asked for 30,000 men for Great Britain and 19,000 for the Colonies, and 2,000 artillery and engineers (" History of British Army," vol. ii., p. 305).

other quarters to Gravesend and Rochester, then to Chatham Camp; and in the autumn through Ipswich and St. Edmundsbury to Canterbury, where they wintered.

Here, October 12th, Sackville came down to inspect his friend's regiment, and reported " a good Regiment, well appointed and fit for service, the firing especially to be commended."

Early in the new year companies were sent out to Margate, Ramsgate, and St. Lawrence and St. Peter's in Thanet, but by June the regiment was concentrated in camp on Barnham Downs.

Irwin and his wife spent much time in London. George Sackville had won a reputation as the most brilliant speaker in the House of Commons, and through him Irwin was well acquainted with all the schemes then afoot. That an expeditionary force of no mean strength was shortly to set out was common knowledge, but in the spring of 1757 London knew as little as did Versailles where the blow would fall. Hanover clamoured loudly for help; a raid in the Baltic was suggested or one on the nearer coast of France. Then a soldier brought home a report that Rochefort was ill-armed and unready, and would fall an easy prey. Pitt, driving Newcastle on, decided for Rochefort, the Home Fleet to convoy the troops, with Admiral Hawke in the flagship.

Sackville was approached, but refused to general the expedition. The command was given to Sir John Mordaunt, a veteran of sixty who had lost his nerve, with Conway, a self-contained, studious young man without much decision of character, as second in command; with them went James Wolfe as chief of the staff. The Fifth and nine other battalions of foot[1] were warned for service and ordered to the Isle of Wight; and there all through July and August they remained. The transports were collecting, but Hawke demanded more accommodation for the troops than the Ministers

---

[1] The 3rd, Fifth, 8th, 15th, 20th, 24th, 25th, 30th, 50th, and 51st.

were accustomed to allow in the cross-channel service, and it was with difficulty that he had his way.

Early in September the troops embarked. The transports lay a good mile out to sea, and the soldiers had a weary pull in the open boats. On the 8th the fleet sailed, sixteen ships of the line and the convoy making a brave show. However, those in command set out with no great goodwill. For some time past the senior officers and members of the staff had openly discussed and derided the expedition; all Portsmouth learnt that a raid conceived and planned by a civilian Minister had no chance of success, and, with preconceived determination to risk nothing of their reputations the general officers put to sea.

Foul winds and calms prolonged the voyage, and each day the courage of the generals grew less. They were convinced that the French had ample warning and adequate means of defence; they were aware, as Hawke said, of " our almost total ignorance of the coast we were to attack "; and they had been urged by Hardwicke not to delay their return beyond the end of the month.

On the 19th the fleet came in sight of their objective. Then a French two-decker hove in view; after her went the *Magnamine* and other ships of the line and chased her out of sight. Hawke with his transports kept on his course, and the next day came to the mouth of the Basque Roads, and then, for want of a pilot, he lay to. The *Magnamine* was not back from her chase, and she had the Huguenot pilot on board. Hawke waited for her return, convinced that there must be batteries to defend the Roads. When the *Magnamine* rejoined the wind dropped, and another day was lost; not until nine in the evening of the 22nd did the ships enter the Roads. The next morning Hawke found the Roads far wider than he expected, and the fleet under no danger from any batteries; but before further reconnaissance the admiral resolved on the reduction of the Isle d'Aix. Five ships of the line, Howe in the *Magnamine* leading, slowly bore down on the little island. By noon Howe was within range; the fort opened fire, but the ships made no reply until the French pilot had laid the *Magnamine* within forty yards. By then the French gunners were lying flat by their guns from fright, and before two o'clock the island had surrendered. At once Wolfe went ashore, and convinced himself that a determined assault on the town would achieve success; but the generals were obsessed by the fear of a vast French army, and remained inactive. By the following day the navy had found a landing-place where the troops could march ashore without getting their feet wet; but, instead of at once ordering a disembarkation, the generals ordered a council of war for the next day. At the council many things were discussed, and finally, after forcing Hawke to own that in case of a heavy storm or surf he could not promise to bring off all the troops, they had sufficient courage to abandon the idea of a landing. However, feeling in the two services ran so high that the generals took refuge in another council. This took place on the 27th, and it was then decided to land that very night, Mordaunt claiming the right to lead the first division.

The transports lay some way from the shore, but Hawke was not allowed to bring them farther in for fear of lessening the chance of surprise. This was unfortunate, as there were only sufficient boats to land half the troops at a time. After sunset the soldiers took their places in the boats.

" About one o'clock," Mordaunt says, " the grenadiers and a great part of the troops who were to land with me in the first embarkation were on board, when a strong wind blowing from the shore, the officers of the Navy appointed to conduct the landing represented that it was with difficulty the longboats could make way, that it would be day before the first embarkation could get ashore, that it would be five or six hours more before the troops first landed could be supported by a second embarkation. Add to this that the boats belonging to the transports could scarce be able to get ashore at all. For these reasons the generals found the forces could not be landed that night "—or any other night, for Hawke lost patience, and vowed he would take his fleet elsewhere; this brought about another council of war and the generals resolved to go home again.

So ended the first expedition against the coast of France. Of two men who did their part well, Wolfe the Fifth saw for the first and last time, but Howe of the *Magnamine*, " undaunted as a rock and as silent,"[1] they were to meet again.

[1] Horace Walpole.

CHAPTER X

1758-1759

GEORGE II., 1727-1760

ST. MALO—CHERBOURG—ST. CAS

BENTINCK—HODGSON

IN India, France, and England, Lally and Clive were fighting a death struggle which was to last another three years; in North America the French were hard put to it to hold their own, for the campaigns in Europe absorbed all their strength. Before the end of April, Coree and the Senegal Settlements flew the Union flag; and, later, in the West Indies Guadeloupe fell to the Allies after a hard fight, and a notorious nest of pirates was destroyed.

Pitt, not content with these colonial enterprises, nor dismayed by the Rochefort fiasco, issued orders for another descent on the coast of France. Regiments[1] were warned for service, and ordered by the middle of May to repair to the Isle of Wight. The expedition was to be on a large scale. All through the winter preparations in camp and dockyard had gone on, highest hopes were entertained, and from their southern quarters the finest troops in England marched to St. Helens, bands playing, colours flying. The Guards were there under General Drury. The Fifth were brigaded with the regiments of Manners, Talbot, and Howe, under

[1] One battalion of each regiment of guards, 5th, 8th, 20th, 23rd, 24th, 25th, 30th, 33rd, 34th, and 36th. The light troops of nine dragoon regiments, and a large siege train ("History of British Army," vol. ii., p. 347). The Fifth embarked 863 men.

STAFF PREPARATIONS

General Mostyn. The remaining six battalions of foot were in two brigades under Generals Boscawen and Elliot. The division was completed by three regiments of artillery and the light troops of nine dragoon regiments. The young Duke of Marlborough, not unworthy of his name, was, with Lord George Sackville, in chief command; they were surrounded by a brilliant staff and many volunteers.[1]

The Grand Fleet, Anson and Hawke, were ordered to act as escort, with a special squadron under Commodore Howe to be detached as convoy. The soldiers talked and dreamed of plunder and gold, and the nation was confident that much glory and honour was to be won.

Elaborate staff work was employed to attend to the details of equipment, hospital, and commissariat. The sick of the regiments were to be left in the regimental hospital " unless some more convenient place could be found for them." A careful non-commissioned officer was to be left in charge, with a month's pay in advance. A captain and lieutenant of Talbot's were left in command of the whole. The surgeon of each ship was ordered to provide a nurse for the hospital ship, a " sober woman that had no child to carry with her." Each nurse was provided with a complete set of bedding, the King's allowance of diet, 6d. a day for wage, 5s. to be advanced before they embarked.[2]

No officer was allowed to be absent without leave from the general. The evening before the embarkation the troops marched to the magazine at Newport and blankets were served out, and before the ships sailed regulations were issued for the preservation of health. The men were to keep on deck as much as possible, change their linen twice a week, and comb their hair every day. The decks were to be regularly swabbed, and the berths swept out every morning. No dogs were to be allowed on board.

According to the latest intelligence from Paris, the French had decided to organize a coast defence army of

[1] Captain Calcraft of the Fifth was aide-de-camp to Marlborough
[2] See " A Journal of the Late Campaign into France," 1758.

80,000 men of regulars and militia, stationed in four camps—the first between Calais and Dunkirk; the second at Havre; the third in Brittany, within reach of St. Malo, L'Orient, and Brest; and the fourth to protect Rochefort.

That year of 1758 all along the northern coast of France men looked out towards England, watching for the white sails, and wondering where the blow would fall. The wretched peasants, hastily armed and uniformed, were herded in the four camps and forced to leave their fields to grow rank with neglect. No French ships could keep the seas.

The summer was very late that year; there was much cold wind and rain; with the continual breeze off shore the people took courage, until one day word came down the coast that a great fleet was standing out to sea, and that a large convoy was steering for the Brittany coast. Scared by the white sails the remaining inhabitants fled inland, destroying or carrying off all provisions.

For all one day the big ships clustered off the Channel Islands, as if deliberating where to strike. The Bretons made hasty preparations; the militia were warned, and here and there small batteries erected. On June 5th the fleet came sailing into Cancale Bay, and while the transports anchored Howe and Marlborough, in a fast cutter, made inspection and resolved to land at once in the harbour of La Houle.

One battery on shore opened fire; a shot from one of the ships silenced it, and at nine in the evening the signal was made;[1] the grenadiers were all ready in the ships' boats, and, as if on parade, they came ashore, and quickly seized the landing-place and every point of importance. Mostyn, landing at the head of the grenadier companies, found a deserted coast and one dismounted gun in a broken barricade manned by a dead peasant and his lame son.

Lord Down, with twenty of the guards, pushing on up a narrow path, met the Intendant of the coast, the

---

[1] Troops ordered for first disembarkation: Drury with the 3rd Battalion Guards, and Mostyn with the Fifth and the ten oldest companies of grenadiers. Sackville landed with the grenadiers.

Marquis of Landal, riding with his servant following him. They called to him to surrender; this he scorned to do, and one volley killed him and his man.

The drums were beat again, and the whole Brigade of Guards pushed off and landed in perfect order. Cancale was occupied and entrenched against surprise. The French militia, supported by three troops of dragoons, came in sight but offered no resistance.

The following day the remainder of the force, men, cavalry, and guns, disembarked, and the army advanced across the peninsula that separated them from St. Malo and camped on the heights of Paramé.

Marlborough rode forward to reconnoitre. St. Malo was a famous privateer harbour; the town and fortress was built on a rock, connected with the land by a causeway, and protected the mouth of the Rance. From the sea the town was impregnable, but Marlborough had hopes of a turning movement by land. From the hills of Paramé he saw below him, south of St. Malo, the little port of St. Servan, the quays and slips busy with shipping. As well as he could judge the little port was out of range of the St. Malo guns. That night the light horse, with infantry in support, each trooper armed with a torch, raided the little place. Privateers, King's ships, worn-out hulks, and maiden frigates on the stocks, rope, timber, and stores, were destroyed in one great bonfire; of all the little fleet, only one privateer out at anchor escaped.[1]

Though this operation had been most successful the destruction of St. Malo was no nearer, and the staff argued that attack from the land was as difficult as from the sea. To a summons to surrender the governor returned a contemptuous answer. The nearest practical road for artillery was by Dol; but from the battalion outpost there came rumours of French activity, and Marlborough feared to send the guns into a trap. Howe, with his frigates, attempted to force the mouth of the Rance and to land at St. Servan, but found it impossible,

[1] Four men-of-war, 50-18 on the stocks; 62 merchantmen; 8 privateers; and 12 others in harbour, besides fishing craft.

the tides running very strong, the navigation intricate, and the channel commanded by the St. Malo cannon. Marlborough, if the matter had rested with himself and Howe, might have made some daring attempt, but Lord George Sackville had great ascendancy over him, and was in reality the true commander of the expedition. Sackville owed his reputation for courage to his intrepid charge at Fontenoy, but already whispers were beginning to be heard. Walpole gives the troops credit for saying, " Lord George was not among the first to court danger;" and in after years his aide-de-camp, Cartwright, sums him up as " a damned chicken-hearted soldier." Howe, bravest of men, held him in great contempt, but was forced to yield to the wishes of the generals, who determined to re-embark. French troops were assuredly gathering, but the danger was not yet imminent; probably the weather was made the excuse, for the coast was not an easy one, and a favourable wind was necessary for the transports to lie in close. The troops were marched back to Cancale Bay, June 12th, and, owing to Howe's admirable arrangements, re-embarked with the utmost precision, and there in the bay, held by contrary winds for a whole week, they remained. Granville was reconnoitred, and engineers were sent there, but acting on their report no attack was made.

At last the wind veered round and the fleet sailed away, making first for Caen, then, driven off by the wind, to Havre, where the boats were got out with every appearance of a serious landing. Whether the generals did not care to land in face of the opposing force assembled, or whether merely a demonstration was intended, it suffices to say that the boats were taken on board again, and on the 28th the fleet had vanished. M. de Harcourt, the governor, boasted that he had frightened them away, and he sent warnings to Brest and Rochefort to be ready for their coming. However, on June 30th the English ships came sailing into Cherbourg—a small place of some 6,000 inhabitants—where extensive works had been in progress for some years, and the great basin, some jetties, and several forts were nearly completed.

The ships anchored, and again the troops prepared to land, and again the wind rose and the boats had hurriedly to be recalled. The next day the fleet put to sea; forage and provisions were running short; the beef was old, hard, fat, and disagreeable; bad weather and cramped quarters were making the men sick; it was resolved to return to England for fresh stores.

The expeditionary force had suffered few casualties, but for all the vast preparation there was very small result. Irwin was soldier enough to feel doubts of the wisdom and courage of his generals, and on him and his regiment the disappointment must have fallen heavily, for no battalion had set out with fairer prospects.

Good news came from Germany; Ferdinand of Brunswick was conducting a brilliant campaign, and the raid on the French coast had helped him by causing vacillations at Versailles. Pitt, fearing the withdrawal of Marlborough's force would hearten France to greater efforts for the Allies' destruction in Germany, at once gave orders for another raid, and, at the same time, proposed to send help to Ferdinand, the force to be commanded by General Bligh, then serving in Ireland. The proposal roused great enthusiasm; all the young bloods were anxious to serve in a real campaign, and Ferdinand was the hero of the hour. Marlborough and Sackville urged their claims, and finally orders were given that Marlborough should have command of the army for Germany, and Sackville, in command of the cavalry, was to go with him. General Bligh on his arrival in England was told, much to his disgust, that he was to have charge of the next raid. The old veteran, now over seventy, had little heart for the task, but Pitt's imperious will carried all before him. By July 11th all arrangements were made; Howe was back with his squadron from a flying visit to London to give his candid opinion of Lord George, and a week later General Bligh received his orders. The Emden force sailed first; with it went Marlborough, to die of low fever before he had time to prove his mettle, and Sackville, who at Minden was to lose everything except his life.

On August 1st the twelve battalions sailed again. The grenadier companies were separated from their regiments[1] and on board different ships; they came under the direct command of the general, and their adjutant was warned to attend for orders when the brigade-major should make signal. For three days the fleet hung threateningly in sight, baffled by contrary winds, giving the French ample warning. M. de Raymond rightly judged the objective to be Cherbourg. He gathered in the town three battalions of regulars, three more of militia, and two hundred and fifty dragoons. On the 6th Bligh and Howe came close inshore to reconnoitre, and on the 7th the fleet came to anchor in Marias Bay, and preparations for landing went forward.

Some four miles of coast was entrenched, and batteries had been erected. The fire of the fleet kept the French behind their lines; bomb ketches were posted close inshore, and used ball mortar with great effect. The Guards, and Fifth and the grenadier companies were then rowed ashore, landing in good order and without opposition,[2] and established themselves at the village of Enville, 3,000 Frenchmen retreating before them. Then the remainder of the troops landed, and finding the lines deserted marched in two columns to Cherbourg. The town made no resistance, the brave show of troops melted away, the gates were open, and the invaders met with every civility, which they repaid with riot and plundering, not only legitimately destroying the defences and shipping, but scouring the country, robbing and burning. General Bligh tried to control the disorder, but the soldiers were out of hand, and they needed a stronger man to maintain discipline. Bligh was already showing himself unfit for the command, and his quartermaster-general was even less capable. Fortunately, the French showed no inclination to counter-attack, and the junior

[1] It was becoming customary while campaigning to mass the grenadier companies of the battalions in one or more division, the senior grenadier officer in command.

[2] "We encamped on ground near the town that the Quartermaster-General never saw till next day, without straw, and if the enemy had any spirit might have been cut to pieces" (Irwin to Sackville: Stopford-Sackville MSS.).

brigadier, Colonel Elliott, took matters into his own hands, and had the troops properly encamped on a site of his own choosing. Howe, realizing the incapacity of the old general and his improvised staff, took upon himself to draw up a scheme for safely and effectually destroying the place. Bligh meekly acquiesced, and the work was well and thoroughly done. Two hundred iron guns, with quantities of ammunition, were destroyed, and two vessels laden with spoils were towed away. Twenty-four brass cannon were sent to England, and about £3,000 was exacted from the town. The splendid harbour works, the basin and surrounding forts were destroyed. Reports that the enemy had been reinforced and were advancing hurried the departure; but the embarkation, which began at three in the morning on August 16th, met with no interference from the enemy. Luxemburg, military governor of Normandy, was at Valognes, only twenty miles away, with ten regular battalions and six of militia, besides horse and dragoons, but the French were not yet ready to avenge the poor town. The contemporary historian, Pajol, wrote: " The memory of this descent will cause a shudder to the end of time to all those to whom History shall tell what we saw and suffered."[1]

The fleet then sailed north, anchoring near Weymouth, and hoping to rest on their laurels. Pitt promptly ordered them to sea again, and taking in fresh provisions they sailed on the 31st, and on September 3rd came to anchor in St. Lunaire Bay, about twelve miles west of St. Malo. The anchorage was a dangerous one, and it was with some difficulty that the men were landed. The operation took two days; a boat with a company of the Fifth was upset, and several men were drowned and the entire arms lost. Bligh's instructions gave him great latitude, and possibly Howe, who disliked being defeated, had urged him to this renewed attack on St. Malo. An attempt to force the Rance by bomb ketches proved unpractical, and the general made plans

[1] Pajol, cited by Corbett, "England and the Seven Years' War," vol. i., p. 296.

for another attack by land. The general's staff was very inefficient, and most of the scanty information brought to headquarters was found to be false. Sir William Boothby was sent with 300 grenadiers to burn 150 ships, which, from good intelligence, they hoped to find in St. Briac Bay; but " to the surprise of everybody, they dwindled into fifteen fishing-boats." One result of this raid was to decide that St. Malo was impracticable of attack, and the idea was abandoned, " so that attempt for the destruction of a parcel of naked, starved, sick soldiers failed."[1]

The weather had grown steadily worse, and, to secure the fleet, Howe was obliged to take it round under the lee of Cape Fréhel. Land operations were abandoned, and a misunderstanding seems to have arisen between the commodore and the army. Sir John Irwin wrote to Lord George Sackville: " As soon as the ships were safe the commodore wrote to the general to let him know that he could not answer for the safety of the ships in such doubtful weather, and therefore if he did not choose to proceed towards St. Malo by land or had no other object in view, he desired to know where he would embark the troops. The general returned for answer that he was ready to embark immediately. The commodore proposed our marching to an island near us, which we could get to at low water, and from whence we could embark with the greatest safety to the ships and troops. This we all understood was to be executed, but, to our great astonishment, when we began to march we found ourselves going from the coast into the country. The generals began to enquire into this, and were told that the best place to embark at was a bay about four leagues off, which this was the best road to."

The rendezvous appointed was the little Bay of St. Cas, where Howe and his ships were lying. Bligh had a twelve-mile march before him, and with ordinary precautions his task was easy, although to cross the Equernon it was necessary to leave the coast and strike inland. On September 9th the army set out for St. Guildo,

[1] Sir John Irwin, Stopford-Sackville MSS.

a nine-mile march in a southward direction, but the nearest point where the crossing of the Equernon could be attempted. Emboldened by the departure of the fleet and the near approach of the French army, the peasants came creeping back, and in small companies dogged the retreating English. Through the long summer day the redcoats limped on, ill-shod and short of food; discipline vanished to the winds; and from the hedgerows and frequent copses the Bretons picked off the stragglers. By nightfall the army had barely covered the nine miles. Orders were issued to ford the river at six o'clock the next morning, but so ill had the staff work been carried out that only at the last moment was it discovered that the river was then at high tide. The crossing was of necessity delayed; it was evident that the French were at no great distance; the peasants became bolder. At last a priest was seized and sent as envoy with a threat to burn down the houses and farms if the firing continued. This threat was carried out and a respite gained.

At three in the afternoon the soldiers began to cross; the water was then waist deep; some men lost their firelocks, and had themselves to be rescued by tent-poles. The troops came in touch with skirmishers of the French van, who kept up a brisk fire while the English were crossing.

The other side of the Equernon, Bligh camped for the night. The next day they reached Mantignon, only three miles from St. Cas; but instead of pushing on, Bligh allowed his foolish quartermaster-general to camp for the night, only sending engineers to reconnoitre the coast. Bligh's position was not an enviable one—his staff was incompetent, his army not far removed from a rabble, provisions were scanty, the country actively hostile, and his spirits were not raised by the news brought in by a deserter that d'Aiguillon was at Lamball, with twelve line battalions, two or three thousand militia, six squadrons of cavalry, and eighteen guns.

Foul winds might disable the fleet, and very favourable circumstances were necessary for a safe embarkation.

On the night of the 11th guards were doubled, and it was evident from the alarms and skirmishes that the main body of the French was close at hand. At three in the morning the English broke camp and marched to the sea. Had this been done quietly Bligh might still have escaped, but at two o'clock he had the drums beat, and the enemy were instantly on the alert.

The English marched in single column, and, weak from starvation and sickness, took nearly six hours to cover the three miles. When the leading battalions reached the beach about nine o'clock they found that some of the transports were lying a long way out; Howe, not realizing the need for haste, had the embarkation conducted in the same orderly manner as before: each regiment was rowed to its respective troopship.

When two-thirds of the men were safely on board the enemy appeared in considerable force. For a short time the guns of the fleet kept them at a distance, but they quickly found shelter among the sandhills, and opening a battery of ten cannon and eight mortars did considerable damage among the English. The French infantry, covered by a hill and hollow way, made their way down and suddenly charged across the beach. A rearguard under General Drury, consisting of half the 1st Regiment of Guards and all the Grenadiers commanded by Colonel Griffin, in all about 1,400 men, remained on shore. Drury ordered his men to form up, intending to charge while the French were still in extended formation. Some of the men had to be recalled from the boats, the company orders were contradictory, there was much confusion, and it was the French who charged first. They were met by a scattered fire, for most of the ammunition was in the boats; then, as they came on, the redcoats, confused and helpless, broke and ran. The officers did all that brave men could to keep the men together, but there was a rush for the boats. The French artillery hurried down and opened fire at close range. Drury ran into the sea, and there he was drowned with other officers and many men. The fire of the cannon destroyed many of the boats, and for a moment the sailors hung back until Howe himself set the example, and the sailors held to their task. One small party of grenadiers retired in good order to the left, and under slight cover fired away all their ammunition and were then forced to surrender. Among this gallant little band were the grenadiers of the Fifth; the captain, Charles Heathcote, and the lieutenant, Robert Shearing, were taken prisoner. Seventy-five in all, chiefly of the grenadier company, were returned as killed, wounded, and missing.[1] The sum of £280 11s. 1d. was claimed by the colonel to replace the swords and accoutrements lost on the coast of France.

The French treated their prisoners with great humanity. The Duc d'Aiguillon sent to the general and commodore a list of the prisoners, and an assurance that the wounded should receive every care. These matters being arranged, the fleet sailed for home and anchored near Spithead.

The disaster of St. Cas had become widely known, and many tales were abroad. A Court of Enquiry was ordered, and before this could take place a primitive censorship was invoked, and many mothers must have waited anxiously for news. On September 21st, John Irwin wrote from the Isle of Wight: "We have for some time past been treated like people guilty of high treason. We have not only been confined, but in effect debarred of the use of pen, ink, and paper. For the last two expresses that left the Fleet carried only the General's and Commodore's letters, notwithstanding people gave their assurances that their letters contained no news, only accounts of their health. Yet their assurance had no weight. I do not say the caution of our leaders was wrong."[2]

Later in September there was a great review in Hyde Park, the captured cannon and mortars came past

[1] 750 Officers and men were killed and wounded, and about 250 taken prisoner. Sir John Irwin stated that he had 20 wounded not mentioned in the return. He gives the losses as: 1 captain, 1 lieutenant, 2 sergeants, and 21 men prisoners; 29 were killed or missing; 1 lieutenant and 20 wounded.
[2] Stopford-Sackville Hist. MSS. Com., 9, 3, 72*b*.

His Majesty, and set out from the Park and came through the City in grand procession, with drums beating and pipes playing, all the way to the Tower.

It was a gallant victory, but the honours lay with France! Even if both expeditions had succeeded in the highest possible degree, the moral of the troops employed would still have suffered. Crowded in transports where order in small matters was quickly lost, the soldiers grew negligent and slovenly. Regiments were split up, two or three companies at most being together; the sailors did not hesitate to show contempt of the redcoat, and added to his confusion by orders and advice which he could not understand.

The commissariat was deficient; many were the complaints against Quartermaster-General Clerk, who provided well for his own family but starved the soldiers. " Provisions we had none, cloathes we had none, the men worn out and dispirited, and our numbers lessening every day."[1]

The temptations to plunder were great. Under the weak rule of General Bligh the conduct of the troops was disgraceful; and in disgrace the raid ended, part of the force owing its safety to the moderation and generosity of the enemy.

In 1759 the Fifth was quartered at Exeter, Sandyheath, Reading, and Henley, and in this year Lord George Bentinck died at Bath, and Studholm Hodgson from the 50th Foot was appointed in his place on October 24th.

Major-General Hodgson had commanded a company in the 1st Foot Guards, and had acted as aide-de-camp to Cumberland, and seen service at Fontenoy and Culloden.

The strength was returned at 1,034 men; estimates for expenses at £18,415 18s. 0d.[2]

Major-General Cornwallis inspected the Fifth on September 14th at Sandyheath, and commented that it was " a good Regiment."

[1] Sir John Irwin.   [2] Papers of Sir D. W. Smith.

CHAPTER XI

1759–1760

GEORGE II.—GEORGE III.

WARBURG

HODGSON

IN the gigantic scheme of empire inaugurated by Pitt each regiment could only bear a small part. In 1759 the redcoats were fighting victoriously in North America, India, Africa, and the Indies; but the colonial possessions so vital to Britain were then merely adjuncts to the power of France, and her overseas defeats only urged her to fresh efforts in Europe. Louis prepared to invade England with 65,000 men; and at Dunkirk, Brest, and Havre were collected the transports and convoys.

The British establishment was set down at 85,000 men, and few of the regulars were left in the country. In May the Militia were called up, and later in the year new regiments were raised.

England was full of alarms and conjecture. In London that November they burned Hawke in effigy for letting Conflans and Bompart join forces in the Channel; then came the news of Quiberon Bay, and the bells rang for another victory and the certainty that the fear of invasion was past.

On the Continent Frederick was fighting Russia, Austria, and Saxony on the east; while Prince Ferdinand of Brunswick protected his western flank from France.

After the recall of Cumberland, Prince Ferdinand, the brother of the Duke of Brunswick, was appointed commander-in-chief of the Hanoverian army, and ordered to resume the war. To this end he detained the troops from Brunswick, notwithstanding the remonstrances of his brother, the Duke, who wished to find favour with Louis, and doubted the power of England to protect his dominion. Not only were the Duke's soldiers detained, but also his son, the young Hereditary Prince, elected to serve under his uncle.

Prince Ferdinand commanded an army of mixed nationality, chiefly German mercenaries in the pay of England—Hanoverians, Hessians, and Brunswickers, with an added element of disturbance in 10,000 English troops. The strife in the Colonies was absorbing all the military talent of the nation; no general of distinction was available for continental warfare; and once again the Fifth fought under a foreign leader. Ferdinand had won his soldiers' confidence; honest and upright, fearing no man, seeking no man's favour, courteous, patient, and tactful, filled with one single purpose—the downfall of France—he deserved all the devotion his soldiers gave him. For three campaigns he had marched and counter-marched, confronted by a superior force, yet effecting his purpose and protecting the weaker States.

Among his generals the Hereditary Prince had won a prominent place; although lacking experience, and with all the faults of impetuous youth, he had more than the ordinary courage of his race, and showed himself cool and collected when danger threatened, and capable of conceiving and carrying out a daring attack.

The campaign of 1759 was prolonged, and it was not until January that the armies went into winter quarters. Ferdinand's two divisions, the army of Westphalia, extended through Paderborn from Münster to the Wesel, and the army of Hesse lay from Marburgh eastward to the Weser. The French army of the Rhine, under St. Germain,[1] lay between Coblentz and Wesel, and the army of the Maine, under de Broglie,[2] was cantoned near Frankfort.

[1] St. Germain (1707-1778), War Minister to Louis XVI.
[2] Maréchal de Broglie (1718-1804); commanded the emigrés in 1792.

Ferdinand had been obliged to detach 12,000 men to the aid of Frederick, who was hardly pressed by the Russians and for the new campaign he asked help from England.

Under Pitt there was no delay; on May 1st the Fifth and five other regiments of foot[1] were warned for service, and on May 12th the embarkation began. On the 15th the transports dropped down the Nore, and with a fair wind they arrived in the Weser on May 22nd. On June 17th the regiments of Hodgson, Bockland, and Griffin came into camp, and were received by Prince Ferdinand, who expressed himself as well pleased with their condition. Three days later the other regiments marched in, making the strength of the English twelve regiments of foot and eleven of horse.

Sundry skirmishes had enlivened the spring, but the main French force remained quiescent until June 16th, when St. Germain's army assembled at Dusseldorf, and, crossing the Rhine, advanced to Dortmund. Broglie collected his army near Giessen, and began to march north. Ferdinand, with the army of Hesse, marched south, hoping to force a battle on Broglie before he could obtain assistance from St. Germain.

When the Fifth marched into camp they heard much of the great battle that was to be fought, and by June 24th Broglie's great army could be seen at Neustadt encamped in the face of Ferdinand. For a fortnight the two armies lay watching each other. The French made the first move; orders were sent to St. Germain to march south-east on July 4th; three days later Broglie broke camp and turned north, intending to effect a juncture with St. Germain at Corbach.

Ferdinand followed him with all speed. The Hereditary Prince, with a small force, was sent ahead with orders to delay Broglie. He marched on July 8th, and with him went the Fifth, the 24th, 50th, and 51st. Meanwhile, St. Germain had hurried his men by forced marches, and when the Allies swung into the plains of

[1] Fifth, 8th, 11th, 24th, 33rd, 50th. The 1st, 12th, 20th, 23rd, 25th, 37th, and 51st were in Germany, and the 7th and 15th were sent in June ("History of British Army," vol. ii., p. 510).

Sachsenhausen it was to find the van of the army of the Rhine already in possession. The Hereditary Prince at once attacked, but could make no headway against superior numbers. Broglie, hurrying from the south, heard the sound of guns, and saw before him St. Germain forming in order of battle. Ferdinand sent to warn his nephew that he had Broglie to deal with as well as St. Germain, and ordered him to rejoin the main army—which had now reached Sachsenhausen—as best he could, and with all possible speed. The Hereditary Prince extricated himself with skill; but at first the retreat was attended by some confusion. The enemy's cannon was in position, and opened fire, and the Prince was hardly pressed. The four regiments of British infantry were called on to cover the retreat, and were in danger of being outflanked and overwhelmed until the desperate charges of some squadrons of Dragoon Guards, with the Prince at their head, enabled them to escape.[1]

The French did not pursue their victory, but encamped on the heights of Corbach, the Allies remaining at Sachsenhausen, " their left not above half a league from the enemy's right."

The Fifth only lost five men.[2]

On July 12th General Spörcke, a Hanoverian, joined the main Allied army, bringing their numbers up to 66,000. Broglie had some 130,000 men under him. De Muy replaced St. Germain, and was detached with 35,000 men to cut off the Allies at Warburg; Broglie himself moved on Sachsenhausen.

Ferdinand resolved to attack de Muy; Spörcke and the Hereditary Prince advised that their divisions should turn the French left while Ferdinand marched to a frontal attack.

The battalion companies of the Fifth were with Ferdinand, while the grenadier company was in the massed battalion commanded by Maxwell, with the Hereditary Prince.

[1] The Hereditary Prince's casualties were about 500; seventeen guns were lost ("History of British Army," vol. ii., p. 512).
[2] Cannon, citing *London Gazette*.

At nine in the evening of July 30th the main army marched from Kalle. The men were all eagerness, and needed no urging; but the crossing of the Diemal caused some delay, and when, at six in the morning, the head of the army arrived on the heights above Corbeke there was no sign of Spörcke or the Hereditary Prince.

All the long hot day they marched on, guessing that the other division was ahead of them, and anxiously listening for the sound of guns.

The Fifth were in the van, for Waldegrave and the British infantry led the way. No troops could have shown more eagerness; many men, over-straining themselves in the morasses and deep ground, dropped on the march. At half-past one in the afternoon they heard the sound of cannon, and Ferdinand then knew that it was impossible for his wearied infantry to arrive in time. He therefore ordered Granby with the British cavalry and the British artillery to go forward alone, the tired foot-soldiers cheering them as they went.

Meanwhile, the Hereditary Prince, fearing to wait any longer for the main army, had left Corbeke at an early hour and, dividing his army of 14,000 men into two columns, marched upon Warburg.

De Muy held a high ridge on the north bank of the Diemal; his right rested on Warburg, and his left upon the hill and tower of Ochsendorf, his front covering between three and four miles.

The grenadier company of the Fifth marched with the northern column; Maxwell's battalion led the infantry, while the Royal Dragoons headed the column, marching by the villages of Klein Eider and Ochsendorf to envelop the tower. The southern column diverged at Poppenheim. The artillery of the northern column was posted in the village and outskirts of Ochsendorf, and at half-past one in the afternoon the guns opened fire and the British Grenadiers began to defile through the village. The southern column had already been perceived by the French, who began to retire eastward without firing, until the burst of cannon and sight of the grenadiers warned them of the threatened envelopment. One battalion of the Regiment Bourbonnois faced about and marched to occupy the hill. Colonel Beckwith and ten grenadiers, keeping under cover, raced up to be before them; the Hereditary Prince followed with twenty more; and, breathless and panting, this handful of men lay on the crest to await the enemy. Thus the Bourbonnois, to their surprise, were met by a brisk fire, and, unable to ascertain the numbers of the English in possession, they waited for their second battalion to come in support. This gave Daulhatt's battalion of Hanoverian Grenadiers time to join the little band, and then the French, discovering the weakness of the defence, attacked in good earnest. The odds were still two to one, and the English were slowly giving way when Maxwell's Grenadiers came hurrying up, and for the moment the hill was safe. The situation was critical: the supporting artillery was held up in a defile near the village, and blocked the way to the rest of the northern column, and de Muy was sending reinforcements to the hill. At last the guns were extricated and were speedily in action, and the southern column, hurrying forward, caught the French reinforcements in flank.

The hard-pressed grenadiers fighting round the tower and hill saw far away a cloud of dust, and out of the dust swung two lines of scarlet and blue; two hours' hard riding had brought Granby and his men to the fight. For a moment the pace checked as the squadrons formed into line; facing them stood the French cavalry, Warburg on their right, infantry on their left. Granby, sword in hand, his bald head shining in the sun, placed himself well in front of the squadrons, and gave the order to charge. They broke into a trot, then, forgetting the weary day, into a gallop, and with the shame of Minden before them made for the enemy. Only three squadrons awaited their coming, the others broke and fled, and, wheeling to the right, Granby cut the French infantry in pieces.

Charged upon flank and rear the foot-soldiers broke and fled down the slope, their retreat cut off by the

Diemal. Then the English guns came thundering up
and completed their disaster. Granby pursued the flying
men; the victory was beyond question. The French
losses were heavy, about 12 guns and 7,000 men. Of
the Allies the Grenadiers bore the brunt. Of the Fifth,
4 men were killed, and Captain Ross and Lieutenant
Baker and 26 men were wounded.[1] After the battle
the Fifth remained quartered near Warburg.[2]

Ferdinand held the line of the Diemal from Tredelburg
to Stadtbergen. Opposite him, on the southern bank,
lay the French until August 21st, when Broglie broke
camp and marched to join Prince Xavier of Saxony,
and menace Hanover and Brunswick. The Hereditary
Prince followed hard on his heels, crossed the Diemal
on the 22nd, and, gaining the left flank of the enemy,
engaged the rearguard near Zierenberg. The French,
taken by surprise, retreated, or rather fled, to Zierenberg,
and shut the gates of the town.

A fortnight later the Hereditary Prince, with five
battalions of foot, 150 Highlanders, and eight squadrons
of dragoons, marched for Zierenberg. At eight o'clock
in the evening, on September 5th, leaving their tents
standing, the little force set out; they crossed the Diemal
near Warburg, Maxwell's Grenadiers, the Highlanders,
and Kingsly's regiment leading the column, followed
by two more Grenadier battalions and Block's
regiment.

The town was defended by volunteers of Clermont
and Dauphin, 600 horse and 600 foot. They kept ill
watch, and the surprise was complete. The English
Grenadiers came up quietly and in perfect order; with
firelocks unloaded and bayonets fixed, pushed back the
enemy picquets, ran on to the town and killed the gunner
at the gate. The affair was quickly over; at two o'clock
in the morning the town was taken; by three o'clock the

---

[1] Cannon. Total loss 1,200; of these, 590 were English, 240
being of Maxwell's battalion (" History of British Army," vol. ii.,
521).

[2] Lieutenant John Smith had the picquet at Warburg, Saturday,
August 16th (Papers of Sir D. W. Smith).

Hereditary Prince, fearing to be cut off, was retreating with 400 prisoners, including a brigadier, a colonel, and many officers. The Allies lost about 10 men, the enemy some 500 men and officers, killed, wounded, and prisoners.

The French despatch gave high praise to the British Grenadiers, and also to the humanity which the English officers charged with the enterprise showed both during the action and afterwards, to their prisoners.

The grenadier company of the Fifth suffered no casualties. Ferdinand, seeing that the Wesel garrison was reduced to increase the army invading Hanover, determined to strike at this fortress, the base of the army of the Rhine. The artillery marched away on September 25th, followed two days later by the Hereditary Prince with about 10,000 Hanoverians and Hessians, with orders to cover the siege. The flank companies of the Fifth were detached for duty with the Hereditary Prince, and on the 30th passed Schirmbeck on the march to Wesel.

Broglie replied by sending an army under De Castries[1] in pursuit. Waldegrave was ordered to reinforce the Hereditary Prince. The rest of the army, including the Fifth, save for its flank companies, remained on the Diemal, and were presently ordered to build huts for the winter. Before the huts were built the officers made chimneys of sods inside their tents, with a proper " funnil " higher than the ridge-pole, and with a good fire and a pretty deep trench round the outside of the tent, managed to keep themselves tolerably warm. The men erected rough shelters round the camp kitchens and crowded round for warmth, only going to their tents the last thing at night.[2]

The flank companies of the Fifth marched towards Wesel with the Hereditary Prince; on September 29th they crossed the Rhine; on the 30th the fortress was invested. The autumn rains set in and the besiegers made slow progress. Hard on their heels came De

---

[1] De Castries, Maréchal de France (1727-1801).
[2] Bennet Cuthbertson.

Castries, strong in horse and foot. Work in the trenches had diminished the Hereditary Prince's covering army; he had only twenty battalions and twenty-two squadrons to meet De Castries with thirty battalions and thirty-eight squadrons; however, he must fight or retreat, and, scorning to raise the siege, he attempted a surprise attack.

At eleven o'clock on the night of the 15th the troops marched out; at three o'clock the next morning they came on the enemy outposts at Kloster Kampen, and, notwithstanding strict orders, some shots were fired and the enemy became on the alert; the surprise had failed, and after a hard fight the Allies were forced to retire. The siege was raised; the Hereditary Prince, retreating south,[1] wintered in Westphalia.

The campaign ended with the advantage on the side of France—she held Hesse, Göttingen, and the defiles of Münden; Hanover and Brunswick lay open to attack; Ferdinand and his nephew were divided.

On November 14th, when the news came of the death of King George II., the allied army were ordered to drape their Colours, drums, and banners in crape, the officers to cover their swords, knots, and sashes, and to wear crape round their arms and plain hats with crape hatbands.

In the past campaign the Fifth had lost heavily; between May and December 149 men had died, and in addition 79 men, 7 non-commissioned officers, and 2 officers were taken prisoner while in hospital at Wesel.[2] The conditions of service were severe; the army was far from its base, and the whole country, swept by opposing armies, and bereft of all tillers of the soil, was relapsing into a poverty-stricken wilderness. The surgeons attached to the army were inadequate, and medical stores were scarce. It is not surprising that the English regiments lost a quarter of their strength during these long and hard campaigns; but worse than

---

[1] Cannon says that the grenadier company of the Fifth lost several men.
[2] Papers of Sir D. W. Smith.

the men's sufferings were the hardships endured by the soldiers' wives. Six women were allowed to each company, and these drew their rations and shared their husbands' bivouac. The unfortunate women who followed unauthorized depended on the generosity of the soldiers for their subsistence. The Fifth appears to have had no other servants beyond the soldiers and their wives.

CHAPTER XII

1761–1763

GEORGE III., 1760-1820

KIRCHDUNKERN—WILHELMSTAHL

Hodgson

MAJOR-GENERAL HODGSON was not serving in Germany, and early in 1761 he was chosen for special service, and given command of an expeditionary force against Belleisle. After a gallant defence the French surrendered, and Belleisle became an important base for the British fleet.

In March the Fifth lost their lieutenant-colonel, and Major Marly, of the 23rd—a gallant regiment, and their comrades in the late campaign and at St. Malo—was gazetted in his place. John Irwin was made full colonel, and given the 74th regiment, then in Jamaica. Irwin went back to London, where he dined with Chesterfield and supped with his many friends, kept Sackville informed of political affairs, and joined him in abuse of Pitt and Prince Ferdinand. By July of the next year Irwin was a major-general, and in November, 1762, became a member for one of Dorset's boroughs, East Grinstead, which seat he retained for many years, though his attendance in the House was irregular.

One lieutenant, Robert Palmer, joined in January; and later in the year Lieutenant Thomas Robinson and Ensigns Baron and Carfrae were gazetted.

The armies were not left late in their winter quarters. In February Ferdinand made the first move. The snow was breast high; dead horses and broken waggons alone marked the roads. Affairs went badly, Broglie concentrated his troops on the Main, and struck north to Giessen, forcing Ferdinand to fall back from the Ohm. The Hereditary Prince was attacked at Grünberg and lost 2,000 prisoners; the Allies fell back behind the Diemal, raising the siege of Cassel, and again leaving Hesse open to the French. Both armies were exhausted by the winter struggle; the Allies had suffered very severely, and for two months the troops remained in quarters.

Versailles, tired of the war, and fearing, with just reason, the terms that Pitt might demand, resolved on one vast attempt to crush the Allies. The Prince of Soubise was sent to the Rhine, and his army was increased to 100,000 men, while Broglie had in the army of the Maine some 60,000. Soubise was ordered to march against Ferdinand before his troops could recover, and force him to retreat or give battle against overwhelming odds. Fortunately, Soubise showed no alacrity to obey his orders; he did not move until June, and then, instead of attacking from the north-west and forcing Ferdinand to abandon Westphalia, he diverged to the south, and entrenched himself a little to the north of Dortmund.

The Hereditary Prince, who had retreated with the main army, lay covering Lippstadt. Ferdinand had lent him some troops, among them the Fifth, and the least exhausted of his soldiers were sent forward, to watch the movements of Soubise. The Fifth lay at Rietberg, and from there Lieutenant John Smith was sent to Bremen to collect camp equipage.[1] The country round Münster was laid waste and all the herds driven in; Soubise, travelling with a vast train, found his movements much impeded. The Fifth and other battalions acted as eyes to the main army, and Ferdinand was able to follow every move of the French. He left Spörcke to watch Broglie and concentrated his army at Paderborn. By the 19th the Fifth were far out on the west at Soest, and Soubise, moving slowly south, lay over against them. On the 28th the Fifth were

[1] Papers of Sir D. W. Smith.

joined by the main army, and Ferdinand hoped to bring about an action before Soubise and Broglie could join forces, but the French position defied attack. Nothing daunted, Ferdinand struck north, and, after a thirty-mile march, appeared at Dortmund, right across the French line of communication.

Meanwhile, Broglie had crossed the Diemal and obliged Spörcke to abandon Warburg and leave the way clear. Soubise moved east, Ferdinand after him. Spörcke, by forced marches, rejoined the main army, but even then the Allies did not exceed 60,000, while, after allowing for all deductions, the French must have numbered 100,000.

The Allies would not abandon Lippstadt without a struggle, but the French generals were chary of attack. Near Kirchdunckern Ferdinand took up a strong position, the left covered by the Lippe, the right resting on the village of Hilbeck. A little river, the Ase, cut the position, but a good road ran behind the lines, with a bridge across the stream; a swampy burn, the Salzbach, covered the whole of the right wing; the extreme right was held by the Hereditary Prince's army. The Fifth were back in the main army. Granby's corps was posted on the left, with Wutgenau's German corps on their left and Anhalt's German corps on their right. Wutgenau and Granby held the ground between the Lippe and the Ase. Between the two rivers the ground rose, and on the Dünckerberg heights the soldiers entrenched themselves.

By July 11th the Allies were in position; two days later, a stir in the French camp called the battalions to arms; but the two French generals were not on the best terms, and for some reason the attack was postponed. Ferdinand's weary soldiers rested again; Granby's corps and the Germans held their front lines lightly while the main force camped on the western slopes, Wutgenau a thousand yards behind his trenches.

Suddenly, on the evening of the 15th, the alarm was given; the Fifth had only time to turn out, leaving all standing (the Highland regiments were caught by gunfire before they could get clear of their tents); but Granby's corps moved to their posts in excellent order, and managed to hold their own until Wutgenau could come up.

All the long summer evening the two corps fought on, Granby's bearing the brunt; short of ammunition, they were forced to give ground, especially on the right, where the land fell away to the Ase; and when with darkness the attack died away, Nordel, a little village east of Kirchdunckern, was left in French hands.

While Broglie attacked the heights Soubise was to have demonstrated in force against Scheidingen. Broglie was before time, and Soubise hung back; the assault in consequence was not pressed.

All night the ammunition-waggons plied from Hamm, and all night the Fifth had little rest, for skirmishing on Granby's front never ceased. Reinforcements came from Anhalt, and all the British in Howard's corps were hurried across the Ase; Broglie was the enemy to be feared, and he, too, was hurrying up fresh troops for the second attack.

The short summer night was quickly past; at early dawn the French advanced; the English were ready for them; every puff of smoke brought an answering shot; strict order of battle was lost, the men fought as they could, disputing every inch of the broken and difficult ground. At eight in the morning, from sheer exhaustion, the fire slackened, neither side giving way.

Soubise had moved forward and made a half-hearted attack on Scheidingen, but his feeble efforts were easily repulsed, and Ferdinand was not deceived. Spörcke, with 8,000 men, had been posted north of the Lippe; hearing the guns he sent six battalions to succour Wutgenau, and with the arrival of these fresh troops the battle broke out anew. Broglie sent two batteries to a hill opposite the Dünckerberg from which they could command Granby's entire corps. Ferdinand ordered the hill to be stormed; two Highland regiments and four foreign battalions sprang forward, led by Maxwell and his Grenadiers; the French did not wait on their coming, but, leaving their wounded and their guns, fled down the slope, many falling prisoner to the triumphant Grenadiers.[1]

The Régiment Rouge, their cannon and colours, surrendered to the grenadiers of the Fifth.[2]

The battalion companies, too, had won their battle, for Broglie had no longer any hope of assistance from Soubise, and began to withdraw his troops. This he accomplished with little loss, the ground being too enclosed for cavalry. The French losses are reckoned about 5,500, those of the Allies at 1,600. Granby's corps suffered the most heavily.

The Fifth lost Lieutenant Robert Littlewood,[3] 2 sergeants and 9 men killed, and 2 officers, 5 sergeants, and 12 men wounded.[4]

Broglie and Soubise never ceased to reproach each other for the loss of the battle; they again separated, Broglie with 40,000 marching on Paderborn, while Soubise struck west to Wesel to threaten Westphalia. The Hereditary Prince was sent after Soubise, while Ferdinand marched east to protect Hesse and threaten Broglie's communications with Frankfort. Granby's corps was sent back to the Diemal. Then followed manœuvre and counter-manœuvre all through the autumn until November, when Broglie went into winter quarters along the Leine; the Allies lay along the Lippe and Diemal from Münster to Hildesheim, where Ferdinand had his headquarters.

During the autumn campaign the Fifth were still in Granby's corps, under an ideal brigadier. Always cheerful, minding no hardships or privations, Lord Granby was as generous as he was brave, and soldiers of all ranks adored him. Deaf to no appeal, his pockets were quickly emptied, and he had then to make recourse to the purses of his staff. Once stopped by a soldier's widow, with a piteous tale, he, to the staff's astonishment, sent to change a ducat; this obtained, he continued his

[1] The Grenadiers took four battalions prisoner.
[2] Cannon.
[3] Robert Littlewood, ensign in 1755; lieutenant, 1757
[4] Cannon.

questions, changing the money from hand to hand; then, as he rode away, he pressed the whole sum into the woman's hands—the first and last time he ever asked for change!

In September the Fifth were at Willenstadt, and on the 26th helped to drive Stainville back to Cassel. In October they were in Or Camp, but the following month they took part in sundry skirmishes. At Eschershausen they again came in collision with Stainville, and the grenadier company fought at Foorwohle, both sides knee deep in snow. For winter quarters the regiment went north into the Bishopric of Osnabrück, where they were on the main lines of supplies from England. This year the Fifth lost 233 dead,[1] bringing their losses since they landed to close on 400. The wastage of the long marches was appalling; the Allies had lost 25,000 out of 95,000, chiefly from disease and hardship; but at the end of the campaign the French could claim no material gain of territory, and the one pitched battle had brought them defeat.

For one cause only had the French to rejoice: Bute had the young King's favour—Pitt was no longer in power.

Ferdinand suffered from the loss of Pitt. His English battalions were very weak, and recruits slow in coming in; the government took no steps to hasten matters.

From November to April the armies remained in their winter quarters; for the English, accustomed to the dry warm barracks of Ireland or the comfortable inns of England, the long winter in hovels or rough wooden huts called for no little endurance. Some of the officers of the Fifth could escape to England on recruiting service; the more honour to those who remained with their men.

Towards the end of May both armies began to concentrate. Broglie was recalled to Versailles, the army on the Main was raised to 80,000 and the command given to Soubise and d'Estrees. The army of the Rhine was reduced to 30,000, and put under command of the

[1] Papers of Sir D. W. Smith.

Prince of Condé. In view of the negotiations for peace, the French generals were ordered not to press matters, but merely to hold the conquered towns, Cassel and Göttingen, to husband their supplies, and to destroy the country on which the Allies depended. Ferdinand commanded an army nominally 90,000 strong, but of these many were sick men or raw recruits.

The Hereditary Prince was detached to watch Condé, and Ferdinand took up his old position on the Diemal, his main army near Corbeke, with Granby to the west round Warburg.

Soubise and d'Estrees moved from Cassel on June 22nd and marched north, part of the army reaching Gröbenstein, with headquarters at Wilhelmstahl. Their intelligence was at fault, and they did not realize how far Ferdinand's preparations had advanced. The French main army at Gröbenstein was directly opposite, and only eight miles distant from, the Allies; the Diemal lay between, but the bridges and fords had been secured by Ferdinand.

On the right of the French, but the other side of the Weser, lay Lückner and his corps. The Diemal, Weser, and the Warburg-Cassel road form a rough triangle with rounded corners; the country is hilly and enclosed and, between the Weser and Gröbenstein, heavily wooded. This forest, known as the Reinhardswald, covered the French right; they failed, however, to make it secure, allowing the Zappaburg, a hill which commanded all the forest roads, to fall into Ferdinand's hands. As a further temptation to the Allies De Castries was sent some five miles to the north, and there remained isolated from the main army.

Ferdinand quickly grasped the situation, and, wasting no time, sent word to Lückner to recross the Weser. Spörcke was ordered away to the left, and, after crossing the Diemal, was to fall upon De Castries' right flank. Lückner, from Göttesbuhren, was to march by the Zappaburg, and, extending the line beyond Spörcke, was to come up in rear of De Castries; while another force under Riedesel, was to march from the Zappaburg to

Hohenkirchen, Ferdinand himself advancing in five columns upon the main French army, while Granby was sent south from Warburg to attack the left flank.

Riedesel and Lückner were punctually in their places at 7 o'clock in the morning of June 24th. Spörcke, meeting with little opposition, climbed the heights, but, not seeing De Castries, who was hidden from him by a wood, he swung to the left and struck right across the front of the main army. The sound of shots in his rear startled De Castries, who, screened by cavalry, began to retreat; Lückner should have cut him off, but his column followed Spörcke in the wrong road, and De Castries slipped past.

In the camp at Gröbenstein there was great confusion. With the utmost rapidity the French broke camp and hurried the baggage away towards Cassel, and then fell back on Wilhelmstahl before Ferdinand's slow advance. Suddenly on their left came shots, and through the trees they saw the redcoats coming down the road. Then, realizing to the full their peril, De Stainville, with the Grenadiers of France, the Royal Grenadiers, and the Regiment of Aquitaine, turned to protect the left flank and to cover the retreat. Stainville placed his men in a wood, and, going forward himself at the head of a battalion, determined to strike first.

Down the road from Warburg came three battalions of Guards, three battalions of Grenadiers, the Fifth and the 8th Foot, " some of the finest troops in the British Army."[1] Stainville fell on the head of the column, the Englishmen deployed, and from cover poured in a steady fire. In the wood a hand-to-hand fight went on, and the cannon in the road were taken and retaken. Granby surrounded the wood on two sides, but still the French fought. At last, Ferdinand's troops coming up took them in the rear, and the battle was over. Only two battalions of the brave enemy escaped, about 1,500 were killed and wounded, and to the Fifth alone

---

[1] " History of British Army," vol. ii., p. 560.

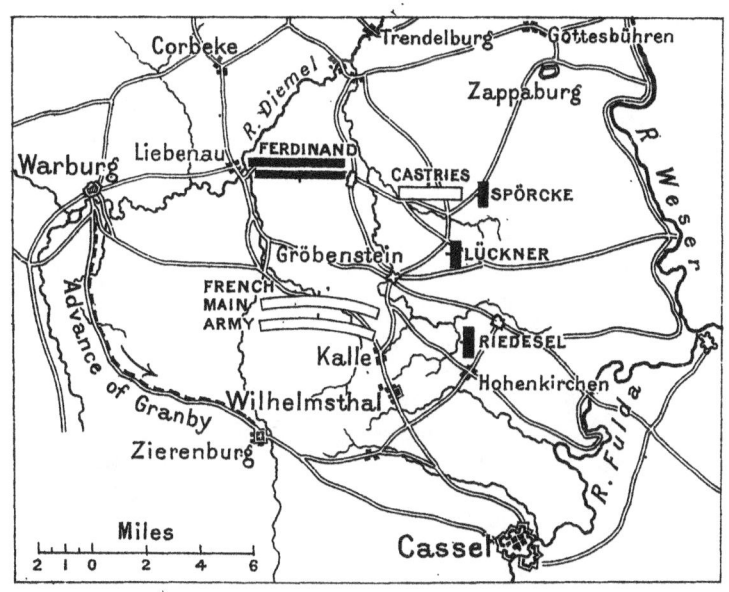

Battle of Wilhelmstahl

3,000 surrendered.[1] Lieutenant Robinson of the Fifth went forward to receive the Colours, and as he laid hands on them the French sergeant standing by shot him dead, to fall himself the moment after.[2] This was the only officer casualty the Fifth suffered, and for such a fight their losses were small, 1 sergeant and 11 men wounded,[3] 6 men captured.[4]

Ferdinand complimented Lieutenant-Colonel Marly on the behaviour of the Fifth, and as a small token gave him a snuff-box;[5] the men for their gallant conduct were granted the privilege of wearing a grenadier cap fashioned like those worn by the captured French; and tradition says that the third Colour, carried so proudly for many years, dates from the victory at Wilhelmstahl.

For the Allies the action was in part a failure; the French army was not defeated or in any sense destroyed. Soubise had been forced back, but he retreated undisturbed; Granby was sent forward to Cassel, Soubise retired behind the Fulda, and for some weeks matters were at a deadlock. In September Ferdinand offered battle, but Soubise declined, and camped along the line of the Ohm, with his left at Warburg and his right opposite Homburg. Ferdinand placed himself on the western bank, barring the way to Cassel. One important outpost was overlooked; on the French, or eastern, side there was a hill, the Amöneberg, which commanded a stone bridge crossing the river; by the stone bridge was an old castle and mill garrisoned by a mere handful of men. The French, realizing the importance of the command of the bridge, invested the castle so closely that no man could

[1] Cannon. Besides the 3,000, another French prisoner surrendered himself, not unwillingly. A black poodle left his dead master and attached himself to Lieutenant John Smith, and remained with him and the regiment for the rest of a long and honoured life.
[2] The Allies lost about 700; of these Granby's corps lost 450 (Fortescue).
The French owned to 900 killed and wounded, but their loss was probably double. The prisoners included 162 officers. The standard, six colours, and two cannon were also captured.
[3] Papers of Sir D. W. Smith. [4] Cannon.
[5] This snuff-box is now the property of the officers' mess of the 1st Battalion. The box is of tortoise shell, with a miniature painting on the lid, representing an encounter between a dog and a swan.

escape with the alarm. This was done at night, and the next day they opened a heavy fire on the bridge and on an unfinished redoubt manned by Hanoverians, afterwards relieved by Hessian and British troops.[1] After some hours' hard fighting Granby's corps was ordered up in support. The French made desperate attacks, and were met with an heroic resistance, until, on the 22nd, after repeated assaults, the little garrison was forced to surrender. The Allies lost about 750, a third being English.[2]

In October the siege of Cassel was begun; the Fifth formed part of the covering army; they were at Rodenau in November when the news came of the surrender of Cassel and the close of the war. Though hostilities ceased the terms of peace were not yet signed, and the British troops wintered in Germany. The Fifth marched from Rodenburg to Lingen.[3] In December four companies were at Ottenstein, three at Allstadt, and two at Wesel, and there they remained until January, when part of the British troops began their march through Guelderland to Wilhelmstadt, where transports were waiting to convey them to England. The army marched in four divisions, the Fifth being in the first; in February they reached Nimeguen, and from there went by water to Wilhelmstadt; on the 22nd they embarked on board the *Hawke* and the *King of Prussia*.[4]

[1] Three Regiments of Guards, three of Grenadiers, Highlanders, Blues, and one Dragoon Guards. Only the grenadier company of the Fifth engaged. Cannon states that they lost many men.
[2] "History of British Army," vol. ii., p. 565.
[3] Papers of Sir D. W. Smith.
[4] FIRST DIVISION.

	Officers.	Men.	Servants.	Women.	Horses.
Blues	27	434	55	21	508
Carabineers	12	285	38	36	358
Honeywood's.. ..	9	291	32	44	394
1 Regiment Guards ..	18	727	15	45	102
Coldstream Guards ..	17	717	8	49	105
3 Regiments Guards ..	11	745	13	43	101
Hodson's (Fifth) ..	27	692	0	54	67
Barrington's	34	642	2	86	110
	155	4,533	163	378	1,745

Ninety years had passed since the Fifth had first set out to fight on the Continent; the long coat and wide-brimmed hat were gone, the snaphance and the trailing pike; black stocks were worn in place of Steinkirk cravats, and a queue of powdered hair instead of the brown locks of the Stewarts. It was a strange country but the same enemy, with strange allies but the same quarrel, and Hodgson's Regiment came home with much the same reputation that Tollemache's had won in Flanders long ago. In a fight and on the march soldiers that any general would envy; admirable in their fire-discipline and accuracy of aim; ready to stand fast against any odds, or charge any position of unknown strength; ready to march any distance over the bad roads loaded with some sixty odd pounds; grumbling and swearing, it is true, but only needing the sound of guns to burst into cheers; heedless and careless in camp, utterly despising all foreigners; then, as always, claiming the place of honour.

On the other hand, few of the English officers looked upon soldiering as a profession, and they affected to despise what they would not condescend to learn, openly flouting the Prussian and Hanoverian captains of experience.

So much does a regiment depend on its officers that it may be hoped, from the evidence of the Army Lists, that the Fifth did not deserve the strictures that soldiers of other nations called down on their British allies. Lieutenant-Colonel Marly had served a long apprenticeship in a fine regiment; as a captain he had defended Minorca when the garrison were forced to an honourable surrender; as major he had served in the St. Malo expedition, and the next year his regiment, more fortunate than the Fifth, had won honour for itself at Minden. The second in command, Major Eustace, and the two senior captains were all Whitefoord's men. There was a leaven of experienced officers to temper the young blood. Of the subalterns, Smith and Baker showed great promise.

In men the Fifth had lost heavily, more from disease[1]

---

[1] The Fifth had 367 men in hospital in 1761 (D. W. S.).

than from battle casualties; but they had won their spurs, and shown that the long years of peace followed by episodic raids had not dulled in them the ardour of war.[1]

In July of this year a young ensign was gazetted to the regiment, George Harris, one of the seven children of Mr. Harris, a clergyman, who, thirty years before, had rescued Lord George Sackville from a Cambridge bully. George Harris was sent to Westminster School, and from there, in 1759, he had gone, by Sackville's favour, to the Royal Military Academy, being then thirteen years old. His father died that same year. In 1760 the boy passed out of the Academy as lieutenant fireworker, and for two years served in the artillery. On the reduction of his battalion young Harris was, through the kindness of Lord Granby, given an ensigncy in the Fifth; he was then a veteran of seventeen with three years' service to his credit.

[1] Hodson's (*sic*) Regiment—Claims for expenses (December 25th, 1761—October 31st, 1762):

	£	s.	d.
Camp repairs	399	1	8
To replace swords, etc., lost in 1760	248	2	6
Do. Do. in 1761	172	14	2
To replace horses, swords, etc., lost in 1760, 1761, and 1762	396	11	0
For Scout Services and sending Expresses to London	98	15	0

(W.O. Return, February 21st, 1764.)

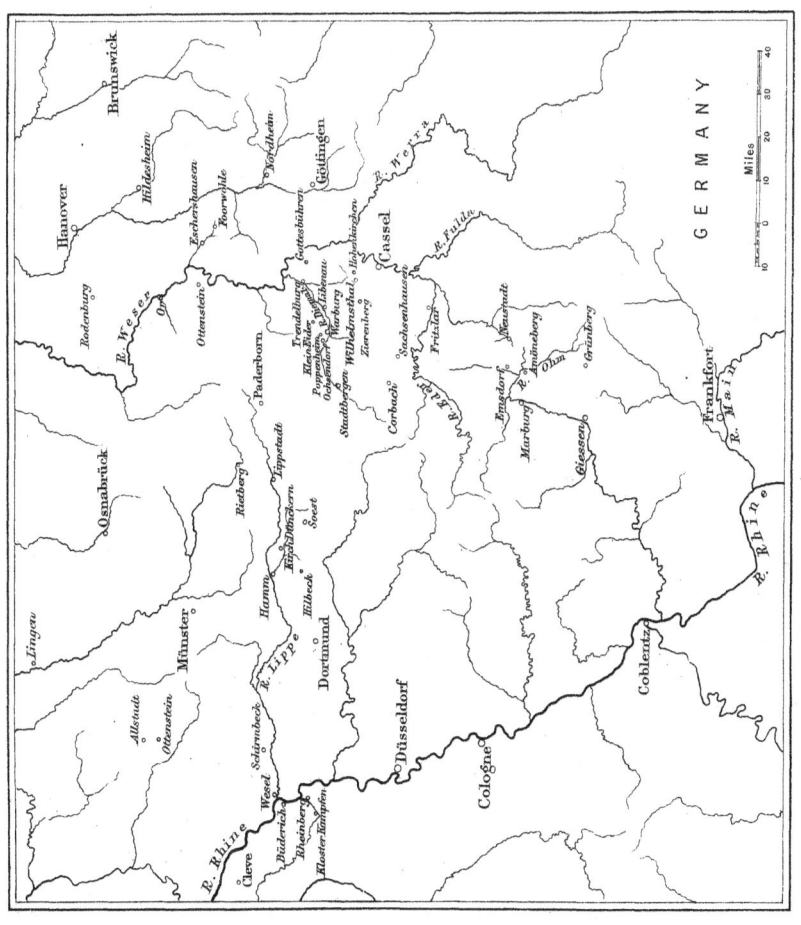

CHAPTER XIII

1763-1774

GEORGE III., 1760-1820

IRELAND

HODGSON—LORD PERCY

ON landing the Fifth marched to Norwich, and then went west through the pleasant English country to Bedford, Biggleswade, and Ampthill. Except to combat the Militia Bill the countryside had scarcely heard of the war.[1] The Fifth marched gaily with their new grenadier hats and their flaunting third Colour. Orders had come for Ireland, where most of the old soldiers had their homes. On the march to Bedford one of the corporals, Stubbs, an Englishman, who had served with great gallantry both in the St. Malo expedition and in Germany, came to his officer and asked for leave to go and see his friends who lived close by. Leave was refused, and that night Stubbs deserted.[2] He was never caught; perhaps both officers and men may not have looked too closely for fear of seeing a brave comrade disgraced and shot.

During this march across England, Ensign Harris, who joined at Bedford, saved, at great risk to himself, Ensign Bagot from drowning in the River Ouse.

From Bedford and Barnet the Fifth marched west,

---

[1] The spheres of war were so remote from both capitals that there was little bitterness between the two nations. It was quite possible for Englishmen to stay in Paris and accept hospitality from the French during the closing years of the war (see Sterne's Letters, etc.).

[2] Papers of Sir D. W. Smith.

and on May 30th embarked at Bristol for Ireland. During this year all regiments were reduced and the additional lieutenants placed on half-pay.[1]

On June 2nd the regiment landed near Waterford, where they spent the next few weeks. During their stay the bridges of the town were swept away in a heavy flood; the Suir rose twenty feet, and in the destruction of the main bridge many spectators lost their lives.

In 1764 an Englishman who went on a tour through Ireland made the following observations: " I never saw such scenes of misery and oppression. What with the severe exactions of rent, even before the corn is housed, of the Landlord, of the Parish Priest, and of the Catholic Priest, the poor reduced wretches have hardly the skin of a potato left them. The high roads throughout the south and west are lined with beggars, who live in cabins of such shocking material and construction that through hundreds of them you may see the smoke ascending through every inch of the roof."[2]

The brilliance of Dublin society formed a great contrast to the squalor of the countryside. While Halifax at the Castle encouraged native industries and tried to put new life into agriculture, the Whiteboys first made their appearance. Ireland had wrongs enough, but she now placed another weapon in her enemies' hands when she acknowledged herself a slave, and tried to revenge herself in the manner of a slave. By 1763 the Whiteboys had spread over all the land, and the outbreaks of riot and robbery, murder and arson, became more frequent.

In 1763 the Earl of Northumberland succeeded Halifax. His vice-regality was marked by a prodigal hospitality; the Castle became a kind of club where men of all parties met, and naturally it was the centre of social life.

In August, 1764, the Fifth marched into Dublin,

---

[1] Fifth Regiment of Foot: H.M.'s bounty to non-commissioned officers and men privates reduced or discharged with an allowance of 30s. in lieu of their swords, £209 2s. 4d. (Papers of Sir D. W. Smith).
[2] See " History of Ireland " (Lecky).

after ten years' absence. They found the same "ill-built, filthy, and badly policed city," though the new town was fast springing up, and already contained " houses as elegant as any in the Metropolis." The barracks were built on a small hill near the river; they consisted of four courts, " the largest and most complete buildings of their kind in Europe "; they could accommodate 3,000 foot and 1,000 horse. Parliament House was a quarter of a century old; the Dublin Society flourished; Lord Moira encouraged the fine arts. Trinity College provided cheap education and the originators of many riots. The fashions were those of London and Paris, though naturally they somewhat lagged in their coming. Provisions were plentiful, and living was cheap, and an English shilling was worth thirteen pence; better still, the redcoats were welcome in every house.

Early in September one of the officers' wives had a horrible experience. Mrs. John Smith had been with others of the regiment at a party, but feeling unwell had left early, and returned to her house, the Brick House in Queen Street, opposite to Oxmantown Greengate. She had scarcely entered her door when she heard a most dreadful and piteous cry of " Murder!" which sounded very near. She opened the door, and found outside a dying man, who had been ripped up by a madman. This maniac had sworn to kill the first person he should meet after the clock struck nine. Mrs. Smith passed him as she entered her house, and the clock was striking nine as she closed the door. That night her son was born, David William Smith, who, fifteen years later, joined his father's regiment.[1]

On the 26th September a riot broke out between the butcher-boys and the Liberty Boys; the affray became serious; one Liberty Boy was killed, several injured; the Fifth were called out and fired on the rioters, first with powder, and, this having no effect, with ball; three or four men were killed, the rest dispersed.

The regiment spent the winter in Dublin, and in May of the next year marched to Kilkenny; reduced from

Papers of Sir D. W. Smith.

war strength, they were only 529 strong. Kilkenny could boast of a theatre, several schools, a bishop's palace, and other fine buildings, altogether a healthy and prosperous town.

On the march Captain Bell, commanding the grenadier company, had as his guest a comrade of the German wars, William Medows, late of the 50th Foot, and now a young cavalry major in the 4th Regiment of Horse. George Harris was brought to his notice: " the finest English boy he had ever met," Bell boasted; and so began a friendship between Harris and Medows which was to last many years.

In 1766 from Kilkenny the Fifth marched south. In May they came to Clonmel, and in June were garrisoned in Duncannon Fort on the east coast of Waterford Harbour. The regiment was only 346 strong, but a year later was reported as being " good in every part, well taken care of; the greatest attention both in officers and men; and fit for immediate service. The men very good, very upright, and remarkably well dressed to arms, good and very clean. Hats extremely well cocked, and accoutrements extremely well put on. The exercises performed with the greatest correctness and exactness possible."[1] George Rawson succeeded Marly (possibly deceased) in October of this year, Ross becoming major.

Early in 1767 a system of honorary distinction for long-continued good behaviour was introduced into the Fifth. This distinction consisted of three classes of medals, worn suspended by a ribbon at a button-hole of the left lapel. The first, or lowest, class was of gilt metal, with the motto and badge on one side and on the other " 5th Foot Merit "; this could be won by seven years' good service. Fourteen years entitled a man to a silver medal, also with the badge and motto, and on the reverse, " Reward of fourteen years' military merit." The third was also of silver, but on the reverse was inscribed, " A.B., for twenty-one years' good and faithful

[1] For Inspection Reports quoted in this chapter, see *St. George's Gazette*, September, 1899.

THE ORDER OF MERIT.
From the collection of Mr. Alfred Brewis.

service as a soldier, had received from his commanding officers this honourable testimony of his merit."

Bennet Cuthbertson in his book advocated such a system of reward and encouragement, and the scheme, as adopted by the Fifth, appears to be based on his recommendations.

George Harris had saved enough money to purchase a lieutenancy in 1765, and having got the adjutancy in 1767, the following year asked, and obtained, leave to travel and improve himself in French, riding, and fencing. On rejoining he found himself in a difficult position. From the very first the senior captain had taken a great interest in him, and had treated him like a father; then for some reason Captain Bell's manner changed; Harris could do nothing right. Finally a duel was forced on the young man, and the two officers met, fortunately without damage. Poor Bell afterwards became insane, left the service, and died in London.

Alured Clarke,[1] from the 50th regiment, got Bell's company. Clarke had been gazetted to the 50th in 1759, at the age of fourteen, got his lieutenancy in 1760, and had served through the campaign in Germany. In May, Lieutenant-General Dilkes reported the Fifth "in every respect an excellent Regiment."

In June, 1768, the Fifth were at Limerick; the barracks were at the west end of the city, exceptionally large and well built. The walls that had so long enclosed the city and had seen so many fights were pulled down about this date, and a residential part grew up without the bounds.

In October two companies were sent to Carrick-on-Shannon, " an agreeable town." The barrack there was built for one full company (100 men), but in this year each company only numbered 40, officers, non-commissioned officers, and men. Two more companies were at Banagher; the remainder of the regiment stayed in Limerick. General Hodgson was gazetted to the 4th

[1] Alured Clarke was the son of Charles Clarke, Vice-Chancellor of the Exchequer, and his second wife, Jane, daughter of Major Mullins, of Windersten. He was born about 1745 (D.N.B.).

Foot, and in his place, on November 7th, Hugh, Earl Percy, became colonel of the Fifth.

Lord Percy was then in his twenty-seventh year. Born in 1742, he was not yet seventeen when, on May 1st, 1759, he received his first commission as ensign in the 24th Foot. In August of the same year he exchanged as captain into the 85th, and a short time afterwards was gazetted a captain and lieutenant-colonel in the Grenadier Guards. He served as a volunteer with Ferdinand in Germany, and fought at Bergen and Minden. From 1764 to 1767 he sat in Parliament as Member for Westminster, and in 1767 he and Lord Thomas Clinton fought a famous election with the Wilkes candidates, Lords Mahon and Mountmorris. In 1764 he married a daughter of Lord Bute, the then Prime Minister.

The Fifth in past years had had for colonels men of age and experience, soldiers all their lives, who had, though not lacking interest, worked their way through all the grades of rank; the command had been looked upon as a just reward for long and good service. The senior officers of the regiment cannot have accepted as a compliment the appointment of one who, though high in rank and with unlimited wealth, good ability, and unquestionable courage, yet seemingly owed his appointment to political jobbery.

Junius had something to say on this matter. On February 7th, 1769, he wrote:

" As to his [*i.e.*, Lord Granby, commander-in-chief] servile submission to the reigning ministry . . . did he not betray the just interests of the army in permitting Lord Percy to have a regiment ?"

To which Sir William Draper made reply:

" If this influence at present has done no greater harm than the placing of Earl Percy at the head of a regiment, I do not think that either the rights or the best interests of the army are sacrificed or betrayed, or the nation undone. Let me ask Junius if he knows of any one nobleman in the army who has a regiment by seniority? I feel myself happy in seeing young noblemen of illustrious name, and great property, come among us. . . . Junius needs not to be told that should the time ever come when this nation is to be defended only by those who have nothing more to lose than their arms and their pay its dangers will be great indeed."

To this Junius answered:

" With respect to Lord Percy it means nothing, for he was already in the army. He was aide-de-camp to the King, and had the rank of colonel. A regiment therefore could not make him a more military man, though it made him a richer, and probably at the expense of some brave deserving officer."

However, the deed was done, Lord Percy was colonel, and colonel he meant to be; and shortly after his appointment he joined his regiment in Ireland. With whatever feelings the Fifth received their young colonel they quickly became imbued with that spirit that in after years made them as proud to bear the name of Northumberland as of any of their battle honours. Political job or not, there was a decided advantage in having a colonel who was above the cares of poverty, and who had interest enough in his family to be free from the necessity of paying court to any man. The city of Limerick made him welcome; tales of his father's brilliant hospitality had spread from the capital, the Freedom of the City was presented to him, and the regiment grew in favour every day. The new colonel had a true and real interest not only in military matters but in all regimental detail. It was at this date by their furbishings and pipeclay that the Fifth won their name of the " Shiners."

The country round Limerick, perhaps because less dependent on uncertain harvests, was quieter than the inland counties; the kindly redcoats were not looked on as an alien garrison, but were allowed to drill undisturbed and make their preparations for the " Review."

In England Junius wrote bitterly of the ruin of the army in Ireland. The weak state at which the battalions were kept did not make for efficiency, but a capable commanding officer had material enough to form a highly trained nucleus for the future.

There were other changes in the regiment. Walcot became major *vice* Ross in May, and, in December, George Rawson left—possibly his political duties necessitated this; he was member for Armagh in three successive Parliaments. In his place the young cavalryman William Medows,[1] late major in the 4th Regiment of Horse, became lieutenant-colonel. To him the Fifth were to owe much.

In May, 1770, the Fifth marched to Cork Harbour and the companies scattered for the summer. The next May found the regiment back in Dublin, where the Marquis of Townsend was reigning at the Castle. Light companies were ordered to be raised and added to the Foot, making ten companies to each battalion. Captain Clarke got his majority in the 71st, and George Harris, purchasing a company, became captain,[2] and was sent over to England on a recruiting tour, which lasted nearly a year. In 1772 he stayed at Alnwick with the Duke of Northumberland, and was taken by Lord Percy to Kelso Races. To his cousin, Mrs. Dwyer, he wrote:

" As I flatter myself I prefer friendship to pleasure, I left his Lordship and the bonny Scots lasses to see a brother officer, who has lately gone on half-pay from several good motives. Regret at not seeing merit meet with its reward . . . the care of an old mother, and to pay some debts which, through his openness of disposition, he had incurred. These were his reasons; and, as I knew them, had I not gone to see him when so near,

---

[1] William Medows was the second son of Philip Medows and Lady Frances Pierrepoint. Born December 31st, 1738. Ensign in the 50th in 1756; he fought in Germany in the Seven Years' War. He afterwards exchanged into the 4th Regiment of Horse, then quartered in Ireland.

[2] For purchase money, Harris borrowed £1,100 from his mother, which took him many years of economy to repay.

he would have considered it a slight, and imagine that
I, like the greater part of the world, only worshipped
the rising star."

Harris does not give the name of this officer.
Notwithstanding the undercurrent of disturbance in
the country and the threat of larger troubles in the
world outside, the winter was a gay one, and the regiment became as popular in Dublin as it had been in the
western counties.

The sergeant-major, Hill, left the regiment, going to
the 62nd as adjutant. Benjamin Hill had enlisted in
1759 at Okehampton; as sergeant in the grenadier company he had served in Germany, and in 1769 he had been
made sergeant-major. The year after he left the Fifth
he was able to purchase an ensigncy in the 62nd, and as
ensign and adjutant he served until 1775, when he returned to his old regiment.

In March, 1772, the Fifth were ordered north, three
companies to Gilford, a village in County Down, two to
Lurgan, and one each to Armagh, Hillsborough, Newry,
Castleblane, and Killtleigh (*sic*). The Hearts of Oak
Boys were out in Ulster, and the soldiers were called
upon to do the work of police. Near Gilford the house
of Sir Richard Johnson was attacked, and a Protestant
clergyman, Mr. Merrol, dragged out and murdered.
The murderers escaped for the time, and the presence of
the soldiers quieted the country. The Fifth then went
back to Dublin, but not to free themselves from the
Whiteboy and his tribe. " A set of villains in Dublin
hide themselves in holes near the Barracks, and when
they see a soldier alone hamstring him. Sixteen have
lately been lamed for life." By such means Ireland
tried to revenge herself on servants of the Crown.

The young colonel of the Fifth, who felt some interest
in affairs of state, viewed with consternation the policy
of the Ministry, who were endeavouring to force on the
" Plantations " the same disabilities of trade that to a
large extent were the cause of the Irish troubles. It
was evident that on the other side of the Atlantic the

storm was gathering; the Ministers could not ignore the disquiet of the American colonies; soldiers would be needed to police the recalcitrant people, regiments were warned for service, and one of the first on the rota was the Fifth.

The American station was an unpopular one, and such service promised small reward or honour; but Lord Percy refused to accept the exchange his father offered to procure for him, and chose to stay with his regiment. His soldiers had been his pride and care for six years, the Medal of Merit met with his warmest support, and he had so arranged matters that the medal was given before the annual review instead of later in the year. After the review the regiments went into summer quarters, the companies dividing, " which prevented the men who were entitled to that mark of distinction from receiving it in so publick a manner as his Lordship could wish."[1] He fitted his men out—the first corps so dressed—in white waistcoats and breeches, and with their waistbelts across their shoulder-blades, " the which they were ordered to discontinue, but soon after an order came for the whole army to wear them."[2]

At the end of 1772 Lord Percy purchased the adjutancy and presented it to the regiment, " with the positive orders that on no account whatever it shall be at any time sold for the future."[3]

On July 14th, 1773, the Fifth collected in Dublin, and presently marched away to Kinsale, where, and at Cork, they wintered.[4]

In the spring of the new year the transports collected. In April, 1774, Lord Percy wrote from Kinsale: " Our

[1] Order quoted by Cannon.
[2] Papers of Sir D. W. Smith.   [3] *Ibid.*
[4] August 3rd, 1772, Dublin. Inspection by Major-General Dilkes: 11 English, 19 Irish officers.
Officers: Made a good appearance . . . in general saluted well.
N.C.O.'s: Made a very good appearance; very clean and alert; not one of them deserved punishment since first they enlisted.
Drums and Fifes: Beat and play well.
Men: Steady and attentive. . . .
131 recruits enlisted since last review. The clothing well fitted; the arms very clean and remarkably polished; the main exercises well performed.

orders with regard to our encamping at Boston you know in London full as well if not better than we do; as I find we are to have eight regiments there I fancy security is intended."

On May 7th the Fifth embarked at Monkstown on board the *Symetry*, the *Alicia and Henry*, and the *Father's Goodwill*. The 4th, 38th, and 43rd sailed at the same time. Before the regiment sailed Lord Percy received a letter addressed to the " Colonel of the Fifth." Stubbs, the corporal who eleven years before had deserted as the regiment marched through Bedford, wrote asking " his Lordship's leave to rejoin, the Fifth never having been in his time in action without him." To this reply was made that there was no time for him to join before the transports sailed, neither could any promise of pardon be made to him; but, added the colonel, " the Regiment will be at Boston in two or three months' time if you intend to rejoin." Sure enough, when the ships came into Boston harbour the first man to greet them was Corporal Stubbs. He conducted himself as well as before, and was shortly after made a sergeant, only to lose his life at Bunker's Hill.[1]

The transports had a very bad passage;[2] troopships were never comfortable, often unhealthy, and sometimes unseaworthy. The soldiers were made to sleep in hammocks, which they much disliked, or on the upper deck, where during bad weather they were exposed to cold and damp. Fresh water was none too plentiful, and was still carried in casks stored in the hold. No effective remedy had been found for scurvy and kindred diseases. That the Fifth lost only one officer and no men during their two months' voyage across the Atlantic shows that care must have been exercised and good discipline maintained.

" I do certify that H.M.'s 5th Regiment of Foot embarked on board the *Symetry, Alicia and Henry*, and

[1] Papers of Sir D. W. Smith.
[2] On May 8th, Lord Percy wrote to the Rev. T. Percy: " I am so cold I can scarce hold the pen. Messrs. Baker, Palmer, Gale, etc., who are on board with me, beg their compliments."

Father's Goodwill, transports on May 7th last at the town of Cork, complete according to the establishment excepting Lieutenant Francia Lord Rawdon and Ensign Henry King, ordered to join but not then joined . . . and disembarked this evening at Boston in North America, complete, wanting the above officers and Lieutenant and Quarter-Master Robert Palmer, who died in the passage. June 9th, 1774."[1]

George Harris wrote to his cousin, August 4th: " My mother has no doubt told you of the loss I have sustained in my friend Lieutenant Palmer's death, which, as well as his illness, added inconceivably to the disagreeableness of the voyage. He chose me, poor fellow ! to assist him in making his peace with a God he had scarce ever offended, I believe, even in thought. . . . Never did man make a better end, or (after acknowledging his weaknesses) go to meet his Saviour and his God with a greater confidence in their mercy. He had more in his favour and less against him than any man I know."

The Fifth disembarked 422 men and 99 officers and women.[2]

[1] American Letters of Hugh, Earl Percy, p. 27.
[2] Ten companies—2 sergeants, 3 corporals, 1 drummer, 36 privates to each company; 2 fifes to the grenadier company (Papers of Sir D. W. Smith).

CHAPTER XIV

1774-1775

GEORGE III., 1760-1820

AMERICA; BOSTON

LORD PERCY

THE Treaty of Paris was signed in February, 1763, and for twelve years there was peace, but the spirit of unrest was abroad. England, outwardly prosperous, had suffered five changes of dynasty in the last century and a quarter. The Stewarts had succeeded to the splendour of the Tudors, and to the last the glamour of Divine Right had surrounded them. The bloodless revolution of 1688 had fostered, not killed, that sentiment, for William imposed his kingship on the English people, who at first merely accepted him as a protection against Rome. The loyalty of the people could not but suffer in 1714 when they learned how easy was the art of making kings. They accepted with very little protest the banishment of the Stewarts, and acknowledged without comment the Hanoverian Succession; but for a time the loyalty rendered by Englishmen, colonist, exile, or home dweller, to the person of the king was dead.

In their fathers' time the throne had been won by force of arms, now the crown went by favour of political faction. Men began to live by their wits, not by their courage; the longest purse promised more than the longest sword.

In 1774 London and the provinces were disgraced by riots and processions vilifying the name of the Dowager Princess of Wales and the hated Bute. The King's mother could not leave her house without being mobbed. The unfortunate marriages of the King's uncles, and the lack of dignity attending the Court, contributed to lower royal authority in the eyes of the people.

Although the degradation of politics during the three last reigns could not fail to influence the country at large there was still a disinterested enthusiasm which would not be stifled, and this, detached from the Royal family, found expression in a local patriotism. This feeling was highly developed in the Colonies—each plantation possessed independent forms of government; each sought to develop their trade regardless of the general good; each, when danger threatened, demanded the aid of a regiment or despatch of a fleet; each, when danger was removed, grumbled when a contribution to State expenses was asked.

Of the Ministry, Pitt alone could see the vision of an Empire beyond the seas; to the others—North, Townshend, Germaine—England was England, and beyond the seas were the plantations, a refuge for the discontented, an exile for political or religious offenders, a dumping-ground for convicts—plantations that must be protected lest they fell into the hands of France or Spain, and must pay for that protection; plantations that must trade when and how England should dictate, must receive, recognize, and obey Governors sent by the Crown, and continue to model themselves on the home counties.

After 1760 the colonists in America were secure from the menace of France. To their thinking England had only fought a common enemy, choosing her battle-ground across the Atlantic rather than in Europe. The Provincial troops had of late years maintained the war without help from the regulars; the spirit of their forefathers led them to overrate their military powers and to undervalue the trained soldier.

Attempts to make the Trade laws other than nominal everywhere met with violence, and injudicious politicians in London by their speeches gave every encouragement to the rioters.

In 1771 fear of a Spanish war caused a reaction, but, this danger being removed, the unrest quickly developed. An attempt to prevent smuggling met with violence, which had the sanction of the civil authorities; then, in December of 1773, the tea went overboard into Boston Harbour.

In 1774 Governor Hutchinson was succeeded by General Gage. The general had long commanded the troops in Massachusetts; his wife was an American, and his appointment was popular. Unfortunately, he lacked firmness, and his conciliatory methods, which alternated with attempts to enforce the letter of the law, only gave encouragement to the rebels. In any case, it was beyond the power of an individual to delay the contest.

On July 5th the little force outside Boston was augmented by the arrival of the Fifth and 38th, and further reinforcements were daily expected from Halifax and New York. An officer wrote: " With this force we have no very great apprehensions from the very great numbers in this Province should they ever come to extremities, as they sometimes affect to insinuate; for, though upon paper they are the bravest fellows in the world, yet in reality I believe there does not exist so great a set of rascals and poltroons."[1] Lord Percy wrote a month after his arrival: " The people here are a set of sly, artful, hypocritical rascals. I must own that I cannot help but despise them compleately."

The soldiers were in a false position, and they knew it. Nominally they were garrisoned among a loyal people for their protection from a handful of malcontents, and to assist in the enforcement of laws passed with the consent of the country. The reality was far different: the British uniform was treated with insolence, provisions could only be had at enormous prices, and the troops suffered daily annoyance by the wilful destruction of stores and equipment, and also from the incessant efforts

[1] William Glanville Evelyn, captain in the 4th Foot; served in Germany. A friend of Lord Rawdon's, to whom he left his servant in his will. Killed in attack on Fort Lee, November 30th, 1776, " much regretted as a gallant officer."

to induce desertion. The civil powers made no attempt to arrest or punish the evil-doers.[1]

If the military agreed in their estimation of the American character they were unanimous in their admiration of the scenery and climate. The soldiers were in good health and spirits; " the beautiful country, lovely trees, and park-like demesnes " were noted by Lord Percy, and the abundance of " fine apples, Madeira, and turtles," by a younger officer.

On his arrival the colonel of the Fifth provided large tents for the women of the regiment, one for each company. For himself he slept in camp, but rented a house[2] near, which he used as a private mess, and each day officers of the line and the loyal country gentry were asked to dine. Lord Percy found the entertaining of some twelve people a day a considerable expense, but he earned the sincere gratitude of the junior officers. It was the custom for two or more officers to live together and share expenses, but a general mess was seldom practicable.

Fortunately for the troops the weather continued fine until late in the autumn, for, wrote Evelyn: " The good people of this place are doing all in their power to prevent our getting quarters and to distress us by forbidding all labourers and artisans to work for us; by hindering the merchants to supply us with blankets, tools, or materials of any kind; by burning the straw provided in the country for the troops, and threatening to stop all provisions coming to the market; but money (for which these Holy men would sell the Kingdom of Heaven) defeats their charitable intentions."[3]

Lord Percy wrote anxiously, emphasizing the danger —in case of open revolt—of the law obliging every man to carry and use a firearm. In the first cold winds he

[1] August 21st: "Desertion greatly decreased, only one man for upwards of a fortnight, but frequent parties and patrols sent out at present. The weather is hot but healthy, no one dead in camp since we arrived" (Lord Percy).

[2] Probably an old-fashioned wood house in a pleasant garden, situated at the north corner of Winter and Tremont.

[3] "Never did I see treason and rebellion more naked and unashamed" (Evelyn, October 31st, 1774).

showed his solicitude for his men by insisting that they should wear next their skin a dress of a new fabric called "flannell." This was accomplished with some difficulty, as there was hardly enough flannel in the town for a whole regiment.

On July 15th, by General Gage's orders, a guard had been placed across Boston Neck; this very necessary precaution against espionage and desertion was looked upon as a preliminary to the storming of the town. Gage took the opportunity of a general muster of the militia to deprive them of ammunition and stores. As an answer, the governor's own company of cadets suddenly disbanded themselves and returned their standard. Gage then resolved to fortify Boston Neck and build barracks; but in this he was frustrated by bands of rioters. During these autumn months not a shot had been fired. At this critical time an unhappy incident in the Fifth regiment gave an opportunity to the provincial press.

The following reprimand from the commander-in-chief was sent to the adjutant: "The Commander-in-Chief has to his great astonishment read an article in a paper called the *Massachusetts Spy*, relative to a Court-Martial held in the Fifth Regiment of Foot, subservient to all military order and discipline, and in every situation fatal to the service, but in times like the present, when officers and men should naturally exert themselves to show a ready obedience to their superiors, and keep up harmony among themselves, and vie with each other in doing their duty to their King and Country, the General cannot look on the said publication without abhorrence. It is his order that the commanding officer of the Fifth does his utmost to discover the author of the said publication, that his name and crime be transmitted to the King at the first opportunity."

The court-martial referred to sat on September 5th; Captain Jackson was president, and Lieutenants Cox and Croker and Ensigns Patrick and King were members. They were ordered to try William Fanthrop, of the grenadier company, who had been confined by Captain Harris for being drunk on picquet, and had also attempted to take his arms from Corporal Cheen, who had been ordered to disarm him and take him prisoner to the quarter guard. The charges appear to have been fully and clearly proved by the evidence of Captain Harris, Lieutenant Benjamin Baker, and Corporal Cheen. The sentence was passed as follows: " The Court-Martial having taken the matter into consideration are of opinion that the Prisoner is guilty of a breach of the 5th Article of the 2nd Section and of the 5th Article of the 4th Section of the Articles of War, and do therefore order him to receive 200 lashes in the usual manner by the drummers of the Regiment."

The commanding officer deeming the punishment to be inadequate to the offence, ordered the proceedings to be quashed, and here the matter should have ended, but apparently some misguided young officer of the Fifth sent an account of the proceedings to the *Massachusetts Spy*, ending: " How are military gentlemen nowadays to act, their honour slighted, and their characters injured by tyrannical commanders ? Can officers do their duty with that spirit becoming their character when treated in such an infamous manner ? Were it not for the present unsettled state of the country and serving their King, what officer would serve in a regiment to be thus scandalously abused."[1]

A month later, on October 10th, Lord Percy wrote: " One would really think that the spirit of the inhabitants had got amongst the officers, for there is almost every day some complaint or other from the different commanding officers, owing to a certain unwillingness which the young men in general discover to proper obedience and discipline."[2] Although as commanding

[1] Papers of Sir D. W. Smith.
[2] It would appear that Lieutenant-Colonel Walcott was not altogether a tactful commanding officer; doubtless he had some intemperate young sparks to deal with. In April, 1775, a General Court-Martial was held for the trial of Lieutenant-Colonel Walcott and Ensign Patrick of the Fifth Regiment for " quarrelling." The said court-martial being approved and dissolved, " the 2nd Brigade was ordered under arms, in order that the Brigadier commanding might reprimand the Lieutenant-Colonel, according to the sentence

HUGH, LORD PERCY,
AFTERWARDS SECOND DUKE OF NORTHUMBERLAND, K.G.

officer he permitted himself this general criticism in the case of his own regiments, it is not confirmed by other authorities. The Fifth had a reputation for admirable discipline; no officer was allowed to evade duty; the men were treated with consideration, and, except under sentence, were not allowed to be struck.

This was not the time for laxity; openly the malcontents collected stores and munitions, openly the young men were drilling, openly the soldiers were seduced and the loyalists intimidated. Massachusetts raised 12,000 men; other colonies joined with their quota. Gage wrote in October: "If force is to be used it must be a considerable one, for to begin with small numbers will only enrage, encourage resistance, and not terrify." Then came the news that the King's Fort and cannon in Newport Harbour had been seized by insurgents.

In November Gage withdrew the troops into the town, and there, surrounded by spies and enemies, they spent the winter waiting eagerly for news from England. Lord Percy complained that his papers arrived a month late because sent to coffee-houses to await the sailing of ships, " Whereas if they were sent on the first Wednesday in any month to the General Post Office, they would come quicker and safer by the packet that sails from Falmouth;" and he asks for books, among them Mantes' " History of the French and Indian Wars."

In the new year he wrote: " Both parties are waiting

---

of the Court-Martial. Which was accordingly done, mildly and literally." "However, three days afterwards the Commander-in-Chief was pleased to take off the suspension which the Court-Martial had also imposed on the Lt.-Col., adding, that it appeared through the course of time that Ensign Patrick did behave disrespectfully to his commanding officer, but it had not been inserted in his crime, the court did not proceed upon it, and Lieutenant-Colonel Walcott now excuses it, and will not bring it to trial; but the Commander-in-Chief thinks proper to warn Ensign Patrick that he behaves with more respect for the future to his commanding Officer " (D. W. S.).

By sentence of the court-martial Walcott was suspended from pay and allowance for six months, and Ensign Patrick was ordered to draw his hand across the face of the lieutenant-colonel before the whole garrison (see also " American Letters of Hugh, Earl Percy," edited by Chas. K. Bolton; published Boston, 1902).

impatiently for the determination on your side of the Atlantic. If Great Britain relaxes in the least to the Colonies they will be lost for ever."

In England the Government refused to put the army on a war footing, refused to comply with Gage's request for a large force, and weakly played with dreams of conciliation.

Gage spent an anxious winter locked up in Boston, while the country round seethed with rebellion.

On December 5th the Duke of Northumberland obtained a permit from General Gage to send Lord Percy to England, but the colonel of the Fifth refused to leave his regiment.

CHAPTER XV

1775

GEORGE III., 1760-1820

LEXINGTON—BUNKER'S HILL

Strength, Dec., 1775–Feb., 1776: 33 Officers, 415 N.C.O.'s and Men.

LORD PERCY

January 19th, 1775.

"In Boston at this time, under General Gage, are the 4th, 5th, 10th, 23rd, 38th, 43rd, 47th, 52nd, and 65th regiments. Two regiments of Marines, two Companies of Artillery, and the 64th Foot at Castle William. . . . In the whole fourteen regiments exclusive of Artillery, add to these almost the whole of the Tories in Massachusetts Bay. . . . ' My House shall be called the House of Prayer, but ye have made it a den of thieves !' To complete all the town is surrounded by ships of War !"—*Cutting from a Provincial Newspaper.*

GAGE's position was not an enviable one. The Home Government refused to give him definite orders, and every day without action increased the forces against him.

In April he resolved to make a surprise attempt against Concord, where the Americans had accumulated large stores of arms and ammunition. On the 18th all egress was forbidden from Boston town, the flank companies alone marched out with secret orders, Colonel Smith of the 10th Foot in command.

The people crowded into the streets to watch them pass. "They will miss their aim !" said a citizen. "What aim ?" asked Lord Percy, standing by. "Why, the cannon at Concord !" was the answer. Percy went at once to Gage to tell him how well the secret had been kept. He received orders to command a supporting force, and, fearing disaster to Smith's party, he hurried matters on, and early on the morning of the 19th marched away to the sound of distant guns.

Meanwhile Colonel Smith's party were rowed silently across the harbour to the mouth of the Charles River and up the stream for some distance, then landed and marched across country. Concord is some twenty miles from Boston, and two men were riding hard by different ways to warn the garrison of the coming of the English.

The sound of the alarm gun told Smith that the Americans were warned, and that the militia would not yield as peaceably as they might have done to a surprise attack. Smith detached Major Pitcairne of the Marines with six companies to secure the bridges west of Concord. This detachment marched into Lexington at five in the morning and found the militia drilling on the green. Pitcairne ordered them to disperse; as they filed off some shots were fired from the houses and behind a wall; one soldier was wounded and Pitcairne's horse hit. The soldiers replied by a volley; eighteen Americans were killed or wounded, the remainder dispersed. Smith's party came up, and the force marched on to Concord, meeting no resistance. The light infantry held the bridges while the Grenadiers destroyed such stores as had not been hidden or removed. While this was going on, the militia, reinforced to some 400 men, attacked one of the bridges and forced the light infantry back on Concord. Smith saw the danger of delaying the retirement, and began to withdraw his troops. This was no easy task, for the firing of the first shot had roused the whole country—every wall, every tree concealed an armed man, and twenty miles of difficult country lay between Smith's little army and the Boston lines.

The day was very hot, the men desperately tired, the retreat had become a rout, almost a surrender, when their fighting instincts were renewed by seeing a few of the dead and wounded scalped by some rough Americans. They fought their way through to Lexington, and there the party of 1,400 under Lord Percy awaited them. Percy formed a hollow square, and the survivors of Smith's force flung themselves exhausted on the ground. Food and drink were given them, then, surrounded on all sides by fire, like a moving circle, fighting every inch of the fifteen miles, Percy ably and boldly conducted his retreat, the grenadier company of the Fifth, under Harris, acting as rearguard.

At sunset the diminished and weary force came into Boston, having expended every cartridge. The casualties amounted to 19 officers and 250 men killed and wounded;[1] the Americans, fighting under cover, did not lose above 90. The drill-book had suffered from contact with the tactics of irregular infantry, but the discipline of the English soldiers had saved them from what might easily have been a disaster. As it was the effects were serious enough; some faint returns to loyalty were checked, and the defeat was the signal for demonstrations of independence in every State.

"After two or three such instances you good people will find out that five or six thousand men are not sufficient to reduce a country fifteen thousand miles in extent, fortified by nature, and where every man from fifteen to fifty is either a volunteer or compelled to carry arms," wrote a young soldier.

Lord Percy said much the same: "Whoever looks upon them as an irregular mob will find himself much mistaken. They have men among them who know very much what they are about. . . . Nor are several of them devoid of a spirit of enthusiasm, as we experienced yesterday, for many of them concealed themselves in houses and endeavoured within ten yards to fire at me and other officers, though they were morally certain of being put to death themselves in an instant."

In a very few days Boston was securely blockaded by 20,000 men. New England resolved more boldly to make a stroke for Canada, and an expedition under

---

[1] The grenadiers of the Fifth suffered severely; Lieutenant Baker was wounded, and Harris wrote that half his company were casualties.

Benedict Arnold achieved some success. The Home Government gradually realized the gravity of the rebellion; and, late in May, the first reinforcements arrived in Boston.

With the reinforcements came three general officers, William Howe, Henry Clinton, and John Burgoyne. They had all seen service—Burgoyne in Portugal, Clinton in Germany as aide-de-camp to the Hereditary Prince of Brunswick during the Seven Years' War, and Howe had led the forlorn hope up the cliffs at the attack on Quebec.

The American army was now assuming a definite shape, and veterans of the French and Indian wars were appointed to responsible posts. Of necessity and habit the men were, for the greater part, excellent marksmen, and their habits of independence and self-reliance lessened some of the difficulties of supply and transport; but even in these early days the causes that had led them to take up arms nearly brought about their undoing. The lack of any centralized authority led to military stores being diverted from their true objective, and any petty quarrel was made the opportunity for wholesale desertion. Nevertheless, their officers had enough military instinct to see that while England held command of the sea and could reinforce and provision the town at will, a real blockade was impossible. To drive the English from Boston was their one thought, and to do this a position must be held that could command the town.

The Americans were established on a semicircle of heights, north, west, and south, but at too great a distance for their cannon to damage the town. Boston Neck was fortified,[1] and the fleet, holding the surrounding sea, commanded the low lands. There were only

[1] Harris, by his own account, was planner, director, and executor of a section of the fortifications (*vide* a letter to his cousin written May 5th, 1775): " As often taking the spade as telling others where to employ it, which is attended with these good effects—exercise to myself and encouragement to the men, who, you will be pleased to hear, fly to execute that for me which for others would be done with a very bad grace, because I set them a good example in not being afraid of work. I had three approving generals in favour of my work, with one of whom I dine to-morrow; that, perhaps, will

two vulnerable points, the high ground on the Charlestown peninsula to the north, and Dorchester Heights, covering the town from the south.

Gage foresaw the danger from the north, and resolved to forestall it. He reckoned without the Boston spies, and the Americans made good use of their forewarning.

On June 16th, in the evening, an American force with entrenching tools quietly marched across the narrow neck, and, passing over Bunker's Hill, securely entrenched themselves on Breed's Hill, nearer Boston on the south-east. They threw up a strong redoubt on the hill-top, and carried the trench line north to the sea. The work was done quietly and swiftly; no alarm came from the anchored men-of-war, not a shot was fired, and when day came Gage found the Americans had taken the very position planned for his redcoats.

Whether or no the Americans were sufficient soldiers to realize the impossibility of holding their position, they must have been well satisfied with their game of bluff when they saw a landing-party making for the eastern point. Under the fire of the fleet they continued their work, and their position was so strong that the English officers reconnoitring asked for further battalions before attempting the assault.

For some reason, possibly faulty staff work, the British troops carried three days' provisions; this, with knapsack, cartouche, ammunition, and firelock made up a weight of 125 pounds. Except in the inhabited parts Charlestown peninsula was overgrown with long grass, at this time of year knee high, and the ground was made more difficult by small enclosures, walls, and fences. Not yet was the day when the soldier rejoiced in such good cover, for it sadly interfered with drill-book formation and shock action tactics, and necessitated frequent halts under fire to dress line and keep proper alignment.

The day was very hot; the landing-party were drawn

---

be all my recompense, and, indeed, all I expect, as I act from a conviction that every officer in our present situation should not merely do his duty, but by his example encourage others to exert themselves, etc."

up in three lines; the massed grenadiers, Fifth, and 52nd, forming the left wing, commanded by Howe; the light infantry companies, 38th, and 43rd, the right wing, under Pigot. A sharp cannonade from eight field pieces and howitzers opened the attack, but did little harm to the redoubt or entrenchment; then the infantry advanced, and at the same time deployed. The English, with the hope of drawing the enemy, began firing at too great a range, but the Americans stood like veterans, and waited until the redcoats were within fifty yards, then poured in a withering volley. Chosen marksmen were told off to pick out the officers, and they were kept supplied by relays of loaded muskets. Harris, leading the grenadiers, flung up his hands and fell back; Rawdon, his subaltern, caught him and laid him down, then ran on to take the lead, head up, and sword in hand.

Harris was shot through the head, but still lived; four of his grenadiers stayed by him and carried him to the beach. Three were hit on the journey—a rough one. Coming to, Harris prayed. " For God's sake, let me die in peace !" but he lived through the agony and was brought into Boston.[1]

[1] Harris's account is recorded by his biographer: "The hope of preserving my life induced Lord Rawdon to order four soldiers to take me up and carry me to a place of safety. Three of them were wounded while performing this office (one afterwards died of his wounds), but they succeeded in placing me under some trees out of the reach of the balls. A retreat having been sounded, poor Holmes [his servant] was running about, like a madman, in search of me, and luckily came to the place where I lay just in time to prevent my being left behind; for when they brought me to the water's edge, the last boat was put off, the men calling out they 'would take no more.' On Holmes hallooing out, ' It is Captain Harris,' they put back and took me in. I was very weak and faint, and seized with a severe shivering; our blankets had been flung away during the engagement; luckily there was one belonging to a man in the boat, in which wrapping me up, and laying me in the bottom, they conveyed me safely to my quarters. The surgeons did not at first apprehend danger from the contusion, notwithstanding the extreme pain I felt, which increased very much if I attempted to lie down. A worthy woman, seeing this, lent me an easy chair, but this being full of bugs, only added to my sufferings. My agonies increasing . . . the surgeons . . . performed the operation of trepanning, from which time the pain abated, and I began to recover."
It was some time before Harris was fit for duty, and in the autumn he was induced to return to England with a recruiting party. His leave of absence lasted from October, 1775, to August, 1776.

The fire was so terrible that the English, after a gallant attempt to reload, fell back out of range. The left wing also suffered from rebel sympathizers in Charlestown, who kept up an intermittent fire on their flank until a battery in Boston opened on the village and set fire to some of the houses; but then the thick hot smoke was blown across the face of the English, greatly adding to their discomfort and confusion.

The men rallied and re-formed, and again Howe led them up the hill, passed the little heaps of dead and wounded, up to the trenches. All his staff fell under another fierce burst of fire, and again the redcoats were driven back.

Like his brother, Howe could say that he did not know fear, and was not yet beaten, and for the sullen exhausted troops there was no turning back. By their general's orders they threw down their packs, drew and fixed their bayonets, and waited ready at a word to climb the hill once more.

Meanwhile, the 47th and a marine regiment had landed, and Clinton, observing the confusion incidental to loss of officers, came hurrying across the water and rallied two battalions who had suffered heavily.

The men lined up for a third advance; Howe concentrated all his force on the redoubt and breastwork; without firing a shot the soldiers climbed the hill, and, as before, the Americans held their fire not alone from choice, but from lack of ammunition. All the long day neither men nor powder had been sent to aid them, and, gallantly as they had fought, they were not brave nor disciplined enough to stand and wait for the line of cold steel coming over the brow of the hill. After one irregular volley the Americans, save a few gallant men, broke and ran, and in their retreat suffered heavily from the guns of the fleet. There was no pursuit: enough work for the exhausted men to have carried the position after three desperate assaults.

The English losses were very heavy, and of the Fifth it was said, " The Fifth Regiment has behaved the best and suffered the most;" and Lord Percy wrote: " My regiment, being one of the first to enter the redoubt, is almost entirely cut to pieces: there are but nine men left in my company, and not above five in one of the others."

The regiment went into action commanded by Lieutenant-Colonel Walcott 400 strong, and lost 158 killed and wounded. Of the officers, Captain Harris of the grenadier company, and Captains Jackson, Downes, and Marsden, and Lieutenants M'Clintock and Croker, and Ensigns Charleton and Balaquire, were wounded. Young Lord Rawdon won his spurs leading the grenadier company when Harris fell. " Lord Rawdon behaved to a charm; his name is established for life." Captain Benjamin Baker claimed the distinction of having killed Dr. Warren, " a famous dissenting minister who was preaching to the rebels in their trenches." Possibly, like William III., he considered no punishment too severe for civilians on the battlefield. The Americans, on the contrary, lamented the loss of Dr. Warren as a famous physician and general who fell commanding the redoubt, whose talents and virtues they highly extolled. Howe gave young Thomas Harris[1] an ensigncy in the Fifth out of regard for his brother's gallantry.

Lord Percy took no part in the action; he and General Howe were not the best of friends, and Percy did not conceal his disapproval of Howe's strategy. Though he had not fought with them he now did all in his power to alleviate the sufferings of his men. It was said of him that his humanity to the sick and wounded and his generosity to their families was unparalleled. He gave to the widows of every fallen man in the regiment seven dollars, paid their passage home, and gave them five guineas on landing in England.

After the action of Bunker's Hill the two armies were able to take stock of each other. Howe had learned

---

[1] Thomas Harris, born 1754, was intended for a business career, and was placed " in a London merchant's counting-house," much to his distaste. He was overjoyed when his brother wrote from America offering him an ensigncy in the Fifth.

at bitter cost that the provincials were not to be despised, and the Americans, though defeated, now knew that they could hold their own against a disciplined army, not only in irregular warfare but in the method taught in Flanders. The fight had great influence on the civilian population, and materially assisted in consolidating the revolutionary party. Two days before, on June 15th, George Washington had been chosen commander-in-chief of the " Continental Army," and on July 2nd he arrived before Boston to take command. Contingents from Maryland, Virginia, and Pennsylvania marched in to serve under him.

The Home Government maintained their right to direct the military strategy; and crippled by insufficient numbers, the generals in the field were not anxious to take the initiative. Howe, who later in the year by the recall of Gage was left in command, set forth a plan of campaign by which the army, co-operating on the line of the Hudson with a force to be landed in Canada, would isolate the New England provinces and at the same time act as a shield to Canada. Unfortunately, Howe received little support; a part of the troops sent to him were diverted to the southern States to rally the Loyalists, and when Gage went home in September the situation looked very black. As Adjutant-General Harvey said, " America is an ugly job. . . . A damned affair indeed."

Howe, helpless in Boston, could only watch his enemy's army daily increasing and was forced to turn a deaf ear to calls for aid from scattered Loyalists.

In August fresh provisions came in, but later in the year the ships could not keep the seas, and the distress in the town became very great. The church pews were burned to provide fuel, horseflesh was eaten in the town, and the army lived on salt pork and pease, with the result of an outbreak of scurvy and kindred diseases. A raid was made on some islands, and 2,990 sheep were captured and given to the sick and wounded. Some of these wounds received in skirmishes were bad to heal; the provincials were running short of ammunition, and rusty nails, jagged bullets, and wire were used to load their muskets.

The ladies of the garrison, some of the Loyalists' wives, and all the disabled men were sent home. The Light Dragoons and other moneyed men could afford to buy provisions, but for officers of the Foot, mutton and bad butter at 1s. 6d. a lb., 12s. for a goose or bushel of potatoes, and 6s. for a chicken, were serious matters. More than ever subalterns of the line welcomed the hospitality of the colonel of the Fifth.

In July brave young Rawdon[1] left the regiment, purchasing his company in the 63rd; never again would he lead the grenadiers; the Fifth lost a good officer. "He is very distinguished here, and a very promising young man in the military line," wrote Lord Percy. He made a present of his lieutenancy to Benjamin Hill, who was with his regiment in England, and who at once took his passage to America, only to fall prisoner to a privateer.[2]

Patrick Downes died of his wounds, and Captain-Lieutenant John Smith got his company on August 1st. Gair, the doctor, was very ill, and his colonel, expressing his sorrow at the fear of losing him, said, "A perfectly bred gentleman, and holds a very high rank in his profession, and is in great esteem among all military persons here."

The weather broke wet and disagreeable, and, to their annoyance, the English had to watch the rebels building stout barracks for themselves.

However, Washington was in no very good plight; he came to command an army, but found a rabble of men who would only serve at their own time and on their own terms. Desertion and malingering became more frequent and re-enlistment rarer every week.

[1] Francis, afterwards first Marquis of Hastings, son of John, first Earl of Moira, and his wife Elizabeth, *suo jure* Baroness Hastings; born December 9th, 1754; married July 12th, 1804, Flora Muir, Countess of Loudoun in her own right. Lord Hastings was at one time Governor-General of India. He was a general officer in the army, and colonel of the 27th Regiment. He died November 28th, 1826.

[2] Liberated in January, 1777, joined his regiment at Rhode Island (see his "Journal," published in "Military Library," 1800).

Howe has been blamed for not attacking Washington at this time, but it should be remembered that Howe had small means of moving his army, that the Americans could easily disperse, and the English blow fall on empty air; and that in face of a hostile populace, in winter, with inadequate transport, pursuit would be impossible. Howe also had far too small a number of men to hold the perimeter of the outer works.

Howe realized that his position was untenable, and that his army had lost its power with its mobility, and he only waited for the spring to bring the transports that he might evacuate the town.

CHAPTER XVI

1776–1778

GEORGE III., 1760-1820

BRANDYWINE—GERMANTOWN

Lord Percy

For two months the little army received no news from England, and they thought themselves deserted. American privateers held the seas and captured the storeships sent over without convoy. However, the garrison kept up their spirits, the theatre flourished and brought forth some " very capital performers " among the officers and ladies. General Burgoyne wrote a play, " The Blockade of Boston," taking off the figures and manners of the Yankee soldier—" a very laughable affair "—but turned to something more serious by the booming of real cannon and the sudden call to arms. Possibly the rebels had got wind of the matter, for the attack proved only a feint. In January General Clinton with six battalions left Boston for Virginia. Clinton was to command the troops sent from England to reinforce the Loyalist opposition. In his absence Lord Percy had the inspection of the garrison.[1]

Thanks to the activity of the American privateers and the complaisance of neutral countries, Washington had now collected sufficient stores to take the offensive; a violent bombardment opened on March 2nd, and under cover of the guns the Americans occupied Dor-

---

[1] February 23rd, the Fifth was returned at 33 officers, 415 non-commissioned officers and men. Captain Harris, 2 sergeants, 2 corporals, 2 drummers, and a private away recruiting.

chester Heights. The enemy batteries commanded the British entrenchments on Boston Neck, the town was no longer tenable. Howe resolved on instant evacuation. The utmost secrecy was observed; the officers of the Fifth slept with their men. Not only had the twenty battalions of foot and marines, artillery and dragoons to be provided for, but also the unhappy Loyalists, who urged that they should not be left to the mercy of the rebels. The embarkation resembled the emigration of a nation; 150 ships were crowded to their utmost, and beyond the point of safety considering the probable danger of the passage to Halifax. There was no room for the guns, and the work of destruction was very imperfectly done.

On the 17th the great fleet stood out, though it was some days before they cleared the harbour. It was bitter to the soldiers to hear the triumphant drums of Washington's men and the bells ringing as the American army marched through Boston.

The transports had a good passage, and came safe to Halifax on April 2nd. The troops quickly disembarked, and orders were issued for training and exercising the battalions. A few days later the Fifth were served out axes to cut fuel for themselves. Captains John Smith and Benjamin Baker were made brigade-majors; and for brigade training the Fifth became the left-hand regiment of the first line of the 2nd Brigade under Major-General Pigot.[1]

Carleton having taken the offensive in Canada, by the end of June succeeded in driving the rebels out of the country. The Canadians, on the whole, remained loyal, and the English generals were not handicapped by any policy of conciliation.

On June 10th Howe and his army sailed from Halifax. The battalion companies of the Fifth were on board the *Amity's Admonition*, 410 tons, and the *Experiment*, 202 tons, stated, somewhat optimistically, to accommodate 355 men. On the 29th, convoyed by the frigates *Greyhound* and *Chatham*, the transports reached Sandy-

[1] 2nd Brigade: Fifth, 28th, 35th, and 49th.

hook. Howe learnt that strong batteries were posted to command the North and East Rivers, and he decided to land at once on Staten Island.[1] On July 2nd and 3rd he disembarked; on July 4th America declared her independence; on the same day the Fifth received permission from the commander-in-chief to " complete from the inhabitants of the Island for home service only, to be discharged at the end of the rebelling."

More troops came from England, and a squadron under Vice-Admiral Lord Howe, brother of the commander-in-chief, and that same " Black Dick " the Fifth had known at Rochefort, St. Malo, and St. Cas. Outwardly stern, he was as warm-hearted as his brother, though the family good nature had not with him degenerated into " an indolent good humour fatal to his military efficiency." Lord Howe came with the authority of the Government to open negotiations with the rebels; for fighting them he and his brother had little heart. The correspondence with Washington only emphasized the hopelessness of the quarrel.

At last Clinton returned from his abortive southern raid, and Howe could reckon his army at 25,000. The grenadiers and light infantry[2] of all the regiments were massed together; the Fifth remained in the 2nd Brigade. Washington had about 18,000; 5,000 distributed for the defence of New York and the forts on the North River, and 9,000 or 10,000 on Brooklyn Heights covering the approach from Long Island.

The Fifth were sent on board the *Nancy Brig* to land camp equipment. On the 22nd a first division of the British landed on Long Island at Gravesend Bay; the American advance parties retired to a ring of wooded hills which barred the approach to the Brooklyn lines. As they withdrew they burned all houses and barns. Cornwallis, with the Light Infantry, Grenadiers, 33rd

---

[1] The Fifth were cantoned as follows: Light infantry from the Dutch Church to Richmond; Grenadiers at Richmond, and the battalion companies at Blazing Star (D. W. S.).

[2] Brigadier-General Leslie commanded the light infantry— 2 battalions—and Lieutenant-Colonel Medows the Grenadiers.

and 42nd, pushed on to Flatbush, and the rest of the army encamped.

George Harris rejoined in time for these operations, and was once more with the grenadier company. He wrote: " I am happy to say that I was never better in my life. Marching all day under a scorching sun, and laying my length at night with only a blanket to cover me, instead of spoiling, improves my appearance. As for Tom, he looked very well when I saw him about a week ago, since when our corps has been moving so quick that I have not been able to hear of him. We have had what some call a battle, but if it deserves that name, it was the pleasantest I ever heard of, as we had not received a dozen shots from the enemy when they ran away with the utmost precipitation. . . . Colonel Medows is my commanding officer, and this I consider one of the pleasantest things that ever happened to me. We sleep together in a soldier's tent, which, when well littered down with straw, we consider a luxury. He led us on to action in the most gallant manner."

Medows was, of course, the same officer who had served with the Fifth in Ireland, afterwards exchanging into the cavalry, and later into the 55th Foot.

Three roads led to Brooklyn; Stirling[1] guarded the west road, General Sullivan lay right across the middle one, but the third, the Jamaica road, was to the east of Sullivan and beyond his reach, and this led to Bedford village in his rear. Clinton was sent along this road; his force included the light infantry and grenadier companies of the Fifth. He marched off at nine o'clock in the evening, and learning from a captured patrol that the pass was unguarded he sent a battalion on to occupy it. In support of Clinton, close on his heels, followed Percy with the Guards, 2nd, 3rd, and 5th Brigades, and halted close behind him an hour before dawn. The army baggage was sent down the same road. The two divisions waited while the frontal attack developed. Stirling, on the west, was awakened by a

[1] General Stirling, a New Jersey man, who claimed the title of Earl of Stirling.

cannonade from Grant's guns, and at daybreak Sullivan saw the dreaded German mercenaries marching down the Flatbush road. Von Heyster and his Hessians did not press the attack—merely keeping the enemy engaged—until Clinton could complete his turning movement. Sullivan slowly retired to find himself attacked in the rear by Clinton's men; the light infantry had outstripped the others and were for a time hard pressed, but the Guards came up, the Hessians pushed forward and Sullivan's men broke. Stirling made a stand until he, too, found his position turned; then his men fled, and he himself was taken prisoner. The victory was not pressed, though Clinton had some difficulty in preventing his division from storming the lines.[1] The Americans were allowed to rally undisturbed; they were joined by Washington and reinforcements from New York.

Howe then seems to have contemplated a surprise attack by water. On the 28th orders were issued to prevent " the soldiers huzzahing when getting in or out of the boats." This was abandoned, and Howe broke ground for a siege of the entrenchments in form; but Washington, fearing the men-of-war would enter the channel with a fair wind and cut off his retreat, determined to escape while the way was still open; this, owing to his skill and Howe's neglect, he was able to accomplish without loss, transferring his men and stores across the mile of water to New York. Although this reverse caused the provincials to desert in large numbers, yet the bulk of the army remained intact, and Congress rejected with scorn the overtures of peace. Against the advice of Washington it was decided to try and hold New York; entrenchments were hurriedly dug, and 14,000 men were stationed in the town and Kingsbridge. The entrenchments were useless against the men-of-war's guns, and under cover of the fleet the British landed at Kip's Bay. Washington withdrew unmolested to Haarlem Heights; New York was recovered September 15th, and

---

[1] Howe lost 531 killed, wounded, and missing. Washington, 673 killed and wounded, and 400 prisoners. The Fifth had no casualties—only the flank companies engaged.

some 67 guns and 300 prisoners taken. Washington's army, still unbeaten, was in a very formidable position. Howe contented himself with a skirmish, then waited, hoping the Americans would either attack or that their army would automatically dissolve. To the annoyance of the British the town was set on fire by enemy incendiaries, and much damage was done. Entrenchments were dug on Macgowan's Hill to protect New York.

The Fifth were employed making fascines and pickets, and on the 21st a working-party of 400 men were ordered up Macgowan's Hill with an engineer officer in attendance. Three days later they were set to work cartridge making, for, the entrenchments being complete, Howe had resolved to leave Lord Percy[1] with three brigades to hold the lines while he himself advanced and threatened Washington's communications and his rear.

In October the sick and wounded were ordered on board the *Peace and Plenty*. Howe embarked his men in boats and landed at Pell's Point, and from there marched inland about six miles to New Rochelle. To meet this movement Washington changed front, and now faced east, extending from Kingsbridge to Whiteplains along a deep river, the Bronx. Whiteplains, the base on the east bank, was entrenched, the encampment facing south; all the fords were guarded by powerful works. The Fifth were with Howe, and by the 25th were within four miles of Whiteplains. On Sunday the 27th the King's gracious order was read relative to widows and the loss of eye or limb in action ! With this to cheer them the attack was begun on the next day. Notwithstanding the slow advance of the royal army the Americans were taken by surprise, tents were left standing, and the call to arms caused much confusion. Washington's main army was very strongly posted, but on the west bank of the Bronx Colonel Spencer, with 4,000 men, held an isolated position. Rahl, of the Hessians, seeing that Spencer had neglected to occupy a hill which commanded his flank, sent a battalion

---

[1] Lord Percy was promoted lieutenant-general with local rank of general in 1776.

across the river to seize it. At the same time Howe ordered two other battalions of Hessians and the 2nd Brigade against the front of Spencer's division. A simultaneous attack on the main position was ordered, but for some reason this did not take place. The 2nd Brigade and the Hessians gallantly advanced and crossed the river with the Fifth and 49th, who showed the same zeal, in support; they stormed and carried the position, though with heavy loss.[1] The inactivity of the rest of the army nullified their victory, and Washington remained undisturbed.

Fresh troops were sent by Lord Percy, and, though heavy rains prevented another attack, Washington found it best to retreat across the Crotton. Howe saw his opportunity and summoned Fort Washington, which summons was treated with contempt. On November 16th the guns of the Kingsbridge redoubt and of H.M.'s ships opened fire. The American general deemed the place impregnable, but an attack was delivered by four columns, and, though the resistance was stubborn, the outer lines were captured and the fort surrendered. The Fifth were not engaged, but the light infantry and grenadier companies fought in the column under General Matthews.

Two days later Cornwallis with a flying column crossed the Hudson. His design was betrayed by a deserter, but with small loss Fort Lee fell, and the campaign came to an end. The armies went into winter quarters.

New York was then a town of less than 3,000 buildings, a mile in length, and half a mile in breadth; the streets were irregular, paved with round pebbles, but clean; and the houses were well built of brick, many of them having tiled roofs. There were two churches where worship was held in the Dutch language, and also two for Episcopalian service—Trinity Church, built

[1] British lost 214 killed and wounded; Hessians, 99 killed and wounded; Americans, 140 killed (Fortescue). The Fifth lost two men killed, and Lieutenant-Colonel Walcott was slightly wounded (Cannon). The grenadier and light infantry companies were not engaged.

in 1696, and the other dedicated to St. George, " a very neat edifice," only twenty years old. Beef, pork, poultry, butter, fish, roots, venison, and herbs were to be had in abundance; and oysters were a considerable article in the diet of the poor. Unfortunately, except for the flank companies, the winter quarters of the Fifth fell in no such pleasant place; they were soon ordered off to New Jersey, where " the weather was particularly severe, the duty unremitting and hard, the enemy watchful, and provisions and forage not to be obtained without repeated skirmishes. Nevertheless, the soldiers endured with a fortitude that did them infinite honour."[1] Stringent orders against marauding had been issued, and, with the success of the army, the loyalty of the inhabitants increased. For the better protection of the Loyalists the chain of outposts was extended from Newark to New Brunswick, and on to Trenton and Bordenton. Unfortunately, the borderland was garrisoned by the foreign troops, who, brave and disciplined as they were in battle, had been brought up to live on a conquered country, and their plunderings alienated the weaker spirits. In contrast the men under Generals Clinton and Percy maintained a high standard of conduct.

Trenton was garrisoned by 1,300 Hessians under Colonel Rahl, and Bordenton by 2,000 under Von Donop. Despite orders, Rahl had neglected to throw up redoubts, and Washington was quickly aware of the omission. He chose Christmas-tide to attack the lax garrison. Von Donop was drawn south by a feint, half Rahl's men were away plundering, Rahl himself fell early in the fight, and the remainder surrendered.

The news came to New York just as Cornwallis was leaving for England; but he was quickly at Princeton, and on January 2nd marched against Trenton, which Washington, after depositing his 1,000 prisoners in Philadelphia, had reoccupied. With Cornwallis marched the grenadiers of the Fifth; they were much harassed by skirmishers on the march, and the light was failing when they reached Trenton. Washington was in a

[1] Stedman.

strong position, and, after a sharp cannonade, Cornwallis decided to send for reinforcements and wait for morning. Washington left his fires burning and stole away, intending to surprise and capture Princeton and all its stores. On his way he fell in with the reinforcing column under Colonel Mawhood. The British first took Washington's men for Hessians, but, quickly discovering the mistake, thought that the Americans must be retreating before Cornwallis. The little force boldly engaged, but were soon driven back by superior numbers; Cornwallis came hurrying back; Princeton was safe, but the outposts were lost.[1] The moral effect of the late campaign was diminished, and many " Loyalists " joined the enemy. On the other hand, Loyalist regiments were raised in New York, and promises of help came from Pennsylvania. From beyond the seas, Howe and his army could look for no encouragement; France had proclaimed her policy, " to meddle adroitly in the affairs of the British Colonies, to give to insurgent colonists the means of obtaining supplies of war, while maintaining the strictest neutrality."[2] Spain and Holland pursued similar tactics, and from the Home Government there came vacillating orders that only added to the difficulties of the commanders in the field. It suffices to say that Germaine endeavoured from London to dictate to the military, with the result that Burgoyne and Carleton, operating from Canada, and General Howe at New York received contradictory orders, and found themselves, against their better judgment, committed to various campaigns with hopelessly inadequate forces.

The American General Lee, now a prisoner at New York, turned traitor, and confirmed the report that the Loyalists in Pennsylvania would rise for the King if the Royal army would come to their support.

[1] Harris wrote to his cousin: " You would have felt too much to be able to express your feelings on seeing what a warmth of friendship our children, as we call the light infantry, welcomed us, one and all crying, ' Let them all come! Lead us to them, we are sure of being supported.' "
The flank companies were afterwards quartered at Brunswick, where Cornwallis retired after the action.
[2] Mahan, " Influence of Sea Power upon History," p. 337.

Howe made his report to Germaine, and asked for a further 8,000 men. Hardly had the packet sailed when the disaster at Trenton occurred, and Howe realized that the situation was entirely changed. The commander-in-chief and Percy were no better friends, and there went with Howe's despatch a letter from Percy asking for his recall. Early in 1777 the colonel of the Fifth sailed for England, much regretted by Loyalists and Englishmen, and especially by his regiment. In London his constituents hailed him as the Patriot Hero; in his honour dinners were given and verses sung.[1] In April Lieutenant-Colonel Walcott, on Howe's behalf, wrote very strongly to Washington, declaring that the Americans had not fulfilled their part of a treaty in that though the rebel prisoners had been released the Englishmen were still detained. Washington defended his conduct by alleging that the American prisoners were returned neglected and starved. With the preliminary letters Walcott's share ceased, but he showed himself no mean scribe, and Howe evidently held him in esteem. Harris was employed to carry these letters.

On May 8th Howe received Germaine's letters of March 3rd approving his original project for the invasion of Pennsylvania, and on the 24th fresh drafts arrived from England, bringing his force up to 27,000 men. Washington, with 8,000 men, was at Middlebrook, but on Howe's advance declined battle and retired to the hills. It was Howe's intention to invade Pennsylvania from the sea, and on June 30th the embarkation began.

Clinton, with 9,000 men, was left to hold New York, and Howe, with 15,500, sailed for Philadelphia. Washington was outwitted. He had certain news from

[1] One verse shall suffice:
"To Heaven our voices raise
For Percy's length of days,
Britain's true friend.
Praise him for actions past,
Praise him at this repast,
Praise him from first to last,
And without end!"
TRIONYMUS.

Montreal of Burgoyne's advance down the Hudson, and he naturally supposed that Howe would try to effect a juncture. He would not credit the rumours of an attack on Philadelphia. On August 22nd he learned that Howe was in Chesapeake Bay, and immediately he marched south to Wilmington.

Howe landed August 25th, and slowly, and with great care, marched north-west.[1] His men were not yet recovered from the hot crowded voyage. By September 3rd the reserve had landed, and advance parties of both armies came into collision. Medows, commanding the grenadiers, sent the Fifth company forward to cover the advance of the battalion guns, and Captain Harris was again wounded, shot through the leg. The Americans fell back across the Brandywine, a creek which runs into the Delaware at Wilmington, covering the way to Philadelphia. At Chad's Ford batteries were erected and the position entrenched. The woods afforded good cover, and the depth of the stream and steepness of the ravine protected the American left.

Howe was marching in two columns, Knyphausen commanding the left and Cornwallis the right. The Fifth were with Knyphausen, a German general; the flank companies were with Cornwallis. On the 10th Howe encamped at Kennet Square, four miles from Chad's Ford; his force was rather under 15,000, and Washington's was slightly superior in numbers though inferior in armament and discipline.

At daybreak on the 11th Knyphausen took the direct road eastward for Chad's Ford, while Cornwallis filed away to the left, making for the upper forks of the Brandywine. Knyphausen opened a cannonade and skilfully engaged the enemy's attention, using his cavalry and light infantry to prevent the discovery of Cornwallis's turning movement, but about midday some hint of this danger reached the enemy. Washington took the initiative, and sent 2,000 men across the creek to attack Knyphausen, who repulsed them with ease,

---

[1] August 24th, regiment 565 strong; in 1st Brigade, under Major-General Grant.

and shortly afterward Washington realized that the turning movement was no threat but an accomplished fact. At four in the afternoon Cornwallis finished his eighteen-mile march and deployed with a front of eight battalions, seven in support, and four in reserve. Medows distinguished himself greatly, charging on horseback with his grenadiers until he fell badly wounded, shot through elbow and back, his collar-bone broken. Sullivan swung to the right to oppose Cornwallis, but his men would not stand and were driven back to Dilworth. Knyphausen now attacked in good earnest; the 4th, followed by the Fifth, plunged into the ford, swept up the slope, stormed the entrenchment, and captured four guns. Chad's Ford was won. In the woods Washington endeavoured to make a stand, when, from the rear, two battalions of redcoats came blundering through. Some of Cornwallis's men who had lost their way in the woods by mistake fell upon the American centre, and so completed the victory. In the darkness Washington was able to withdraw a large part of his army in good order; the British were too weary for pursuit. Howe bivouacked on the field. Detachments were sent to Chester and Concord. The Americans evacuated Wilmington, and Howe established a hospital there.[1] Captain Harris, on account of his wounds, was in a chaise with the baggage when the action began, but he could not allow his grenadiers to go into battle without him; seizing a horse he rode barebacked into the fight; he was the first to find Medows lying senseless on the ground. Together they were sent to sick quarters at Wilmington.

A brilliant little action by Grey[2] cleared the way to Philadelphia, and on September 25th the British marched in.

Before evacuation the Americans had rendered the river unnavigable, and Howe's first task was to capture

[1] Ensign Andrews, 1 sergeant, and 12 men wounded (Cannon).
[2] Charles Grey, afterwards first Earl Grey; son of Sir Henry Grey, of Howick, first Baronet; born 1729; ensign in 6th Foot, 1746; served at St. Malo, in Germany, North America, and the West Indies; died November 14th, 1807.

a fort on Mud Island and a redoubt on Red Bank, and then to remove the obstacles sunk in the river. Until this was done the British were dependent on an overland route to Chesapeake for supplies. Three thousand men were detached to guard this route; of the remaining 9,000 the greater number were encamped at Germantown, a few miles from Philadelphia. Washington, at Skippack Creek, reinforced to 8,000 regulars and 4,000 militia, resolved on a surprise attack on Germantown, a long straggling village extending for two miles along the Philadelphia-Skippack Creek road. About the middle of the village was a four-cross-way—the Limekiln road from the north, and the Old School lane from the Schuylkill River on the south, crossed the main road. Knyphausen was encamped along the Old School lane, with Grey on his left and Grant[1] on his right, along the Limekiln road. Howe had full notice of the impending attack; the inhabitants were eager to give all help and information to the British and to withhold it from the Americans. He therefore pushed forward his advanced posts and enjoined special vigilance on all patrols.

Very early in the morning of October 4th shots were heard—Sullivan had come in contact with the outposts; the British stood to arms. Sullivan, with five brigades, was advancing down the main road against Howe's left and centre, while two militia brigades made a feint attack on the Old School lane. Greene[2] was ordered with three brigades down the Limekiln road. The two battalions which formed the British advanced post made so stubborn a resistance that Sullivan's whole division was held up. The militia attacked the troops in the Old School lane, but were easily beaten off. With the sun a thick fog came on, and when Washington

[1] James Grant, of Ballindalloch (1720-1806). First studied law; entered the army as cornet in 1741; captain in Royal Scots 1744; acted as brigadier during American War; major-general, 1782; general, 1796. He was far from thin in his latter years, being a "liker of good living" (D.N.B.).

[2] Nathaniel Greene, one of the bravest and most skilful of the American generals.

ordered Sullivan's division forward the mist caused some confusion, and the troops deployed both sides of the road instead of to the right only. By this time Greene was in position, and was pressing his attack with some vigour, but, not realizing Sullivan's error, his battalions on the right overlapped the centre and were deployed in rear of their comrades, who presently finding themselves between two fires broke and ran.

The Fifth now came into action from their place in the British right centre; Colonel Grant led them and the 55th upon Sullivan's left flank, and Grey, from the extreme left, completed the panic by wheeling up a regiment against Sullivan's right. The sound of guns brought Cornwallis from Philadelphia, but the Americans were in full retreat. The dutch courage of the officers had quickly evaporated, and the task set them was too high for the untrained men.

Howe lost 517 killed and wounded, and 14 prisoners. Washington, 673 killed and wounded, and 400 prisoners. The Fifth had 4 officers wounded and 52 men killed and wounded.[1]

Fiery but generous Colonel Walcott was mortally wounded, shot through the body; at first hopes were entertained of his recovery, and he survived the fight six weeks, but died November 16th. On October 10th, Howe wrote of him from Germantown,[2] "His behaviour on this occasion reflects upon him infinite honour."

The fleet anchored in the Delaware below Newcastle. The task of clearing the river was a hard one, and was not completed until November 15th. Howe then offered battle to Washington, who declined, and the armies went into winter quarters. Howe wrote to Germaine that the next campaign would require at least a further 10,000 men, and, since his requests for reinforcements were ignored, he proffered his resignation.

Philadelphia was a friendly town, and a pleasant

---

[1] One drummer, 9 men killed; 5 sergeants, 37 men wounded. The wounded officers were: Lieutenant-Colonel Walcott, Captain Charlton, Ensigns Thomas and Stewart (Cannon).

[2] October 7th, Captain George Harris to be major *vice* Mitchell promoted.

place for winter quarters. Howe in his genial way encouraged hospitality and gaiety of all sorts, to the great detriment of discipline, especially of the younger officers, who shocked the provincial gentry by their licence. The young gallants imposed, not unsuccessfully, their robust ideas of fashionable life, and held the old-fashioned and gentler provincial in open scorn. Naturally the noisy crew attracted a large following, but they alienated the people of worth and standing. Fortunately for the Fifth, Major Harris kept them well in hand until their new commanding officer (and old friend), Lieutenant-Colonel Medows from the 55th Regiment, was appointed early in the new year. " Colonel Medows is perfectly recovered from his wound, and is, as ever, the pleasantest and best man I know," wrote Harris. Medows[1] was first and foremost a soldier, and he had lately distinguished himself in command of the grenadiers at Brandywine. He was a generous and sweet-tempered man, who had earned the affection with which his soldiers regarded him; but, with all his good nature, he was strict in discipline, and he had the courage to remonstrate with the commander-in-chief himself for the licence that prevailed.

Then came the news of Saratoga,[2] and the story of how New England had risen to crush Burgoyne and his forsaken army.

When this tale of disaster reached England the Opposition hailed it with shouts of triumph, though the Government refused to own defeat. France openly rejoiced, and Spain and Holland gathered courage and pressed their demand to sail the seas unchallenged.

General Howe was not the man to turn away when things looked black, but in April he heard that his resignation had been accepted, and that Clinton was to come from New York to take command. He therefore sailed for England on May 8th. The day before his

[1] In 1773 Medows left the Fifth to command the 12th Light Dragoons; but on the outbreak of the American War he exchanged into the 55th Foot in the hopes of seeing active service.

[2] Saratoga, the surrender of Burgoyne and his army, October 17th, 1777.

departure a wonderful entertainment, called a "Mischionza," took place.

A new factor now appeared in the war, a frigate came in with the news that France and England were at war, and that the French Admiral D'Estaing[1] with a large fleet had sailed from Toulon on April 13th.

Clinton had been told to evacuate Philadelphia, which, in the face of Washington and 20,000 men, would at all times have been difficult, and now his communications by the Delaware were threatened. Lord Howe's ships were scattered, and greatly inferior to D'Estaing's squadron, and there was no news of Admiral Byron[2] and his reinforcing squadron. Clinton decided to march overland, but the supplies had to be sent by sea. Fortunately, Howe the Admiral had retained the good qualities of Howe the young Commodore.

On July 5th the French fleet sailed up and anchored in Delaware Bay; but they were too late, Howe had slipped out and had reached New York in safety.

Meanwhile, Clinton had marched out of Philadelphia, on June 18th, and, thanks to Howe's admirable dispositions, crossed the Delaware with celerity. With him went 3,000 refugees and an enormous train of baggage. His soldiers numbered about 15,000. Undoubtedly discipline had suffered in the winter months; the army moved slowly, a single colomn nearly twelve miles long, the Fifth regiment acting as rearguard.

Washington speedily sent a large force of light troops to harry them, and small parties to break down bridges and cut up the single road. Clinton at first intended to march by Amboy, but, hearing that Gates, with his division, was approaching by rapid marches, and being threatened by Washington with an army equal in strength and unencumbered, he deflected his route to Sandyhook, and, sending Knyphausen with ten battalions forward with the baggage, he turned at bay on the heights of Freehold. Knyphausen moved off at dawn,

[1] D'Estaing, 12 two-deckers (eight ·74, three ·64) and 3 frigates; Howe, 6 sail of the line, none exceeding ·64.
[2] Admiral Byron, "foul weather Jack," a gallant but unlucky officer; a survivor of the wreck of the *Wager* (1723-1786).

the rear division at eight o'clock; the battalion companies of the Fifth marched away from the enemy and the sound of guns, for before ten o'clock Lee had come up and opened with cannon on Clinton's rearguard. The 16th Light Dragoons drove back the American Horse, but Lee pressed on. Clinton sent the Guards and Grenadiers against him; Lee gave way, and the British pursued until they came in contact with the main army, when they in turn were forced to retire. Darkness put an end to the fight. The losses on both sides were about equal, but besides 358 killed and wounded, Clinton lost 600 men, mostly Germans, who returned to other attractions in Philadelphia.

Captain Gore of the grenadier company of the Fifth was among the killed.

Washington abandoned the pursuit and returned to his old encampment on Whiteplains. Clinton met Howe at Sandyhook and embarked his troops, reaching New York on July 5th, the same day that D'Estaing arrived off the Virginia coast.

Six days later, when the French ships came in sight, the greatest enthusiasm prevailed. The soldiers, though still weary from their long march, were eager for a fight against their hereditary foe, and 1,000 men volunteered to man the fleet. Howe so skilfully disposed himself to guard New York that D'Estaing would not face him, but, on the 21st, bore away to the south, to the great chagrin of Howe and all his men.

The army divided between Rhode Island and New York contented itself with minor operations. In one of these — the expedition to Little Egg Harbour — the Fifth took part. This harbour, in Flat Bay Sound, on the coast of New Jersey, was a noted rendezvous for privateers. Washington had detachments at Old and New Tapaan, but these were skilfully seized by General Grey, and operations against the harbour begun. Some ships were sent, but the alarm had been given, and four of the privateers escaped. The troops were landed, and destroyed ten prize vessels, the salt works, and some stores. A detachment under Captain

Ferguson[1] of the 70th regiment surprised and cut to pieces part of a legion under the Polish Count Pulaski. Captain Ferguson in his despatch of October 10th states: " It is but justice to inform you that the officers and men, both British and Provincial, behaved on this occasion in a manner to do themselves honnour. To the conduct and spirit of Captain Cox, Lieutenant Littleton, and Ensign Cotten of the Fifth Regiment, and Captain Peter Campbell of the 3rd Jersey Vol., this little enterprise owes much of its success."[2]

This was the last exploit of the regiment in America during the War of Independence. On October 24th the Fifth, with other battallions, were concentrated in Staten Island under General Grant.[3] Drafts for the 10th, 45th, and 52nd regiments were made over to them, and once again the transports lay ready. On November 4th Major-General Grant and 5,000 men sailed for the West Indies, escorted by Commodore Hotham and six ships. The same day D'Estaing slipped out of Boston Harbour and headed for Martinique.[4]

[1] Major Patrick Ferguson, killed at King's Mountain, October 8th, 1780.
[2] Captain William Cox; ensign, 1768; lieutenant, 1771; captain, 1777. Lieutenant Thomas Littleton, or Lyttleton; lieutenant, 1777; captain, 1781. Ensign Edward Cotton or Cotter; ensign, 1777; lieutenant, 1778.
[3] Captains John Smith and Benjamin Baker were attached to the staff as brigade-majors.
[4] First Brigade: Brigadier-General Robert Prescott, 15th, 28th, 46th, 54th.
Second Brigade: Brigadier-General Sir H. Calder, 27th, 35th, 40th, 54th.
Third Brigade (or Reserve): Brigadier-General W. Medows, Fifth, Grenadiers, and Light Infantry.

CHAPTER XVII
1778–1780

GEORGE III., 1760-1820

ST. LUCIA

Lord Percy

WHILE the French ships were gathering in Toulon and Rochelle, and all southern England waited the signal to flee inland, Chatham spoke for the last time, called on his countrymen to fight Europe or the whole world rather than yield one inch of empire, and then fell, to die a few weeks later. The British navy at this date numbered some 223 ships of the line, frigates, corvettes, and sloops, but to guard the Plantations the fleet was naturally much dispersed, and it was quite easy for France to send an overwhelming naval and military force against any British outpost before her garrison or guardships could be reinforced. Above all the British West Indian Islands were vulnerable points, therefore D'Estaing, foiled by Howe, evaded Byron's weather-worn ships and sailed for Martinique.

The British West Indian Islands divide themselves into two groups, the Leeward and Windward, and their strategic value was in those days governed by the trade wind. This wind blowing three-quarters of the year from the south-east made it a matter of months for a ship to beat up from leeward, while a fleet could sail from Barbadoes to Jamaica in as many days. For three months in the year, August to November, the station was untenable by the hurricanes, and then the island garrisons had to defend themselves against pirates and insurrections without hope of assistance. In 1778, besides England, France, Holland, Spain, and Denmark had possessions, and their trade had much profited by the American War. Not only foreigners but also Englishmen had made large fortunes by supplying the enemy with contraband. The smaller islands were nests of pirates of all nationalities, but with sympathies entirely anti-British.

To windward England held a slight advantage over France in the possession of the Barbadoes, but the usefulness of these islands was partly lost for want of a safe harbour. St. Vincent and Grenada could supply no dockyard, and the nearest port of refit was at Antigua. France had three admirable harbours in St. Lucia, Martinique, and Guadeloupe.

In September Admiral Barrington[1] with a small fleet lay at Barbadoes waiting reinforcements, the French Admiral de Bouille garrisoned Martinique against surprise, and swept down upon Dominica and forced the small garrison to surrender; then, for fear of Barrington, he retired to Fort Royal.

Meanwhile, Hotham was on his way from New York with his fifty-nine transports, his sailors and soldiers all eager for a fight. Some of the soldiers were on board the men-of-war; the *Preston* made signal for a lieutenant, sergeant, corporal, and fifty men of the Fifth to go on board the *Centurion*. The transport with the Fifth on board was ordered to hoist a Jack to guide the ship's boats. Hotham made good time; he looked after his transports in a fatherly manner, and on December 10th brought them safe to the Barbadoes, only one missing—a transport with the field officers' horses on board had parted company soon after leaving New York and had been lost sight of.

Barrington had his plans ready; not a man was allowed to disembark. Grant promised co-operation. Hotham vowed that D'Estaing was safe, blockaded in Boston harbour.

[1] Samuel Barrington, fourth son of John Shute, first Viscount Barrington.

On the 12th they came to St. Lucia and anchored in Cul-de-Sac Bay. The Grenadier and Light Infantry battalions and the Fifth were immediately landed,[1] Medows in command, and with another brigade forced the heights to the north. The next day the remainder of the force landed. Strict orders against marauding were issued; culprits were threatened with immediate execution. Protection was promised to the inhabitants; many French sick had been left behind and all humanity was shown them. The resistance was slight; Morne Fortuné, commanding the southern side of the harbour, was quickly captured; George Harris,[2] in command of the massed Grenadiers, charged up the slope to find no enemy. By evening the harbour, with fifty-four guns, the forts, batteries and magazines, and also Vigie Point to the north, were in British possession.

But ill-rumour flies apace, and already the news was being whispered that D'Estaing had escaped from Boston; if so, he would be hard on Hotham's heels, when the little army would be in a very awkward situation, and could only hope that Byron in his turn might be hunting D'Estaing.

As the last French flag fluttered down in Cul-de-Sac Bay the first white sails appeared from the north. All doubt was at an end, and almost all hope too, for here was D'Estaing with his transports and victual ships and all his men-of-war. Barrington cleared for action, and swung his ships across the mouth of the harbour under the guns of the forts. The redcoats, some of them very sick from eating green oranges, crowded together to see the great ships come up so close that the Frenchmen on deck could be counted. The situation, though

[1] Brigade Orders, December 13th, 1778: "From the active gallantry of the Light Infantry, the determined bravery of the Grenadiers, and the confirmed discipline of the Fifth Regiment, every success is to be expected. The troops are desired to remember that clemency should go hand in hand with bravery; that an enemy in our power is an enemy no more, and the glorious characteristic of a British soldier is to conquer and to spare" (Medows).

[2] Harris wrote, October 30th: "I am on the tip-top of Fortune's wheel. . . . Major Harris, Commander of the Grenadiers, second in command under Brigadier-General Medows."

interesting, was sufficiently perilous. D'Estaing was justified in thinking the recapture of St. Lucia an easy task with his fleet and army of more than double strength. There was no sign of Byron, and Barrington was left to fight the odds alone. When Grant sent an officer of the 46th on board the flagship, he found the admiral sleeping in a hammock amidships, who said, " Young man, I cannot write to the General at present, but tell him that I hope he is as much at ease on shore as I am on board." And so determined was Barrington's aspect that the French ships declined to enter the harbour. First, at eleven in the morning of the 15th, ten ships came up to force their way past four British sail of the line; the Frenchmen would not have it but backed out again, to come back later twelve strong. Even then they could not get past Barrington and the forts. D'Estaing then beat to windward, and landed his troops in the Anse de Choc, and sent back to Martinique for more men. The French troops were to drive out the British from the landward side, and then, when the forts were once again in French hands, Barrington would be forced to put to sea, and would fall an easy victim to D'Estaing.

Grant realized the situation, and did the best he could with his inadequate little army. Calder and four battalions were left to cover Cul-de-Sac Bay, five more battalions covered Morne Fortuné, and the Reserve occupied the peninsula of Vigie.

The peninsula of Vigie, with its narrow neck, offered an admirable position for defence, but Medows, realizing he would be of little use if the French were able to " bottle " his troops, stationed an advance-guard on the mainland. This outpost was so close to the French lines that a grenadier of the 46th was ordered to be punished for taking a pinch of snuff from a Frenchman, and though, owing to his previous good conduct, Major Harris pardoned him, the men were cautioned not to let such a thing occur again.

At right angles to Medows, and only two miles away, lay the main French army. A deserter came into Vigie on the night of the 17th, and from him Medows learned that D'Estaing and 12,000 men were coming to make an end of him and his little brigade before they turned their attention to Cul-de-Sac Bay. Medows was not dismayed; his army of 1,400 men was for the most part composed of veterans; his own regiment, the Fifth, he could depend on, officers and men alike, and the Grenadier and Light Infantry battalions were the pick of eight regiments. "At that moment they were probably without any exception the finest troops in the world."[1] They had need to be, for the conditions were depressing. It had hardly ceased to rain from the moment they landed, they were without tents, and all the December night it rained so that the men were wet through.

Early on the 18th, Medows, with Harris and Sir James Murray, who commanded the Light Infantry battalion, went down to inspect the advanced posts held by five companies of the Light Infantry, Downing of the 55th in command. The Fifth and Grenadiers went to their stations on the higher ground of the neck. To their dismay they saw a long line of French troops advancing, threatening not only to overwhelm the Light Infantry but to capture the general himself. Hastily they consulted whether to charge down to the rescue when back rode Medows, cool and quiet, saying, "The Light Infantry can take care of themselves; as for you, stand fast"—and the Grenadiers watched the drill-book go down before the lore learnt in the backwoods.

Two battalions, one whitecoated, the other a Blue Regiment of Martinique, swung up in parade order, and poured in two tremendous volleys on flank and centre; the Light Infantry answered by a straggling fire, every man behind his own stick of cover. On came the French against an invisible enemy; "But they retired and they advanced, they broke and they rallied, and when we no longer saw a single man we received a heavy fire in every direction." It was too much for drill-book tactics; first one battalion and then the second broke pursued by the victorious five companies. The Fifth

[1] Fortescue, "History of British Army," vol. iii., p. 268.

and the Grenadiers then saw the main army advancing
and the danger the pursuers ran; they cried out to their
comrades to retire; the sound could not reach the Light
Infantry, but discipline sent them back to their posts,
and, with skill, they made good their retreat through the
thick brushwood.

The outpost gone, the French were able to press the
attack, and from the cover of the trees they poured in
a deadly fire. Men in the close ranks began to fall fast
as the big battalions moved nearer. Medows had some
captured guns with him, and, the Light Infantry safe,
he was able to open fire, and with two twelve-pounders
he silenced the enemy's lighter guns. One grenadier
company (the 4th) had made a redoubt for themselves,
and suffered less than the others. Shortly after the
cannon opened the Grenadiers and the Fifth began to
fire steady volleys, with no haste or hesitation but with
determination that every bullet should find its mark,
and they knew they had only thirty rounds apiece.
Medows, hoping for fresh supplies, sent boats to Morne
Fortuné. When they came, Hill[1] hauled up a box from
the water-side, two men staggering after him with another
of like size. Quickly Harris and Hill knocked the lids
off, and as they handled them the cartridges fell to dust
through rottenness. Hill turned away without a word
and went back to his company. The Grenadiers had
just three rounds left.[2]

The French columns had changed direction again and
again to escape the steady fire. One battalion broke
twice and twice rallied, but they could do no more, and
they were too hard driven to realize that the silence
from the hillocks meant want of powder and shot. By
Medow's orders Harris had silenced the Grenadiers; with
fixed bayonets they stood waiting the word. It was
now nearly eleven, and the first shots had been fired
before eight. Two hours earlier Medows had been shot

[1] Benjamin Hill had been liberated in January, 1777, and had rejoined the Fifth at Rhode Island as lieutenant of the grenadier company. He was brother-in-law to George Harris, a very tall man, and of great strength.
[2] Fortescue, "History of British Army," vol. iii., p. 270.

through the arm, but nothing could make him relinquish the command; the pain of the wound, the want of ammunition, and the odds against him failed to ruffle his temper. He placed himself at the head of his regiment and the survivors of the Light Infantry, determined to fight to the last. Harris was ordered to wait until the French advanced within distance, then with the bayonet to sweep them off his flank, rally to the general, and join in one last charge.

The French recovered themselves in the brief lull and came on again. The Grenadiers, standing like rocks, waited for them; the two last shots from the twelve-pounders made the columns waver, the head of one turned, Harris seized the moment and bade his men concentrate their last powder on the wavering line. Medows restrained his men; there was no need for that last heroic charge, for slowly and deliberately the enemy were retiring, in good order, but with no looking back. As Barrington's four ships had held up D'Estaing's fleet, so three battalions of redcoats had stood up to ten times their numbers, and in both cases the bigger dog had turned away.

By eleven the action was over,[1] and the men could get the taste of cartridge out of their mouths, and had time to curse their flints, which, being supplied by contractors, were very bad, although their powder was said to be better than the French stuff. The Fifth swarmed down from the little hills they had so gallantly held, and from the caps of the dead French soldiers they pulled out the white plumes. There were 400 French dead on the field, enough to fit out the whole regiment with their new feather. This they were allowed to keep, and for many years the Fifth flaunted a white plume to remind other regiments that they had held the heights of Vigie

[1] Killed, wounded, and missing, 171. Grenadiers, 90; Light Infantry, 60. Fifth: 2 men killed and 20 wounded; and Lieutenant-Colonel Medows and Lieutenants Pratt and T. Harris wounded. Medows visited every wounded officer and man before he would permit a surgeon to attend to him (H. B. A., iii. 271). Thomas Harris died of his wounds and exertions; George Harris wrote to his mother: "Queens might behold you with envy, mourning as a Mother for such a son."

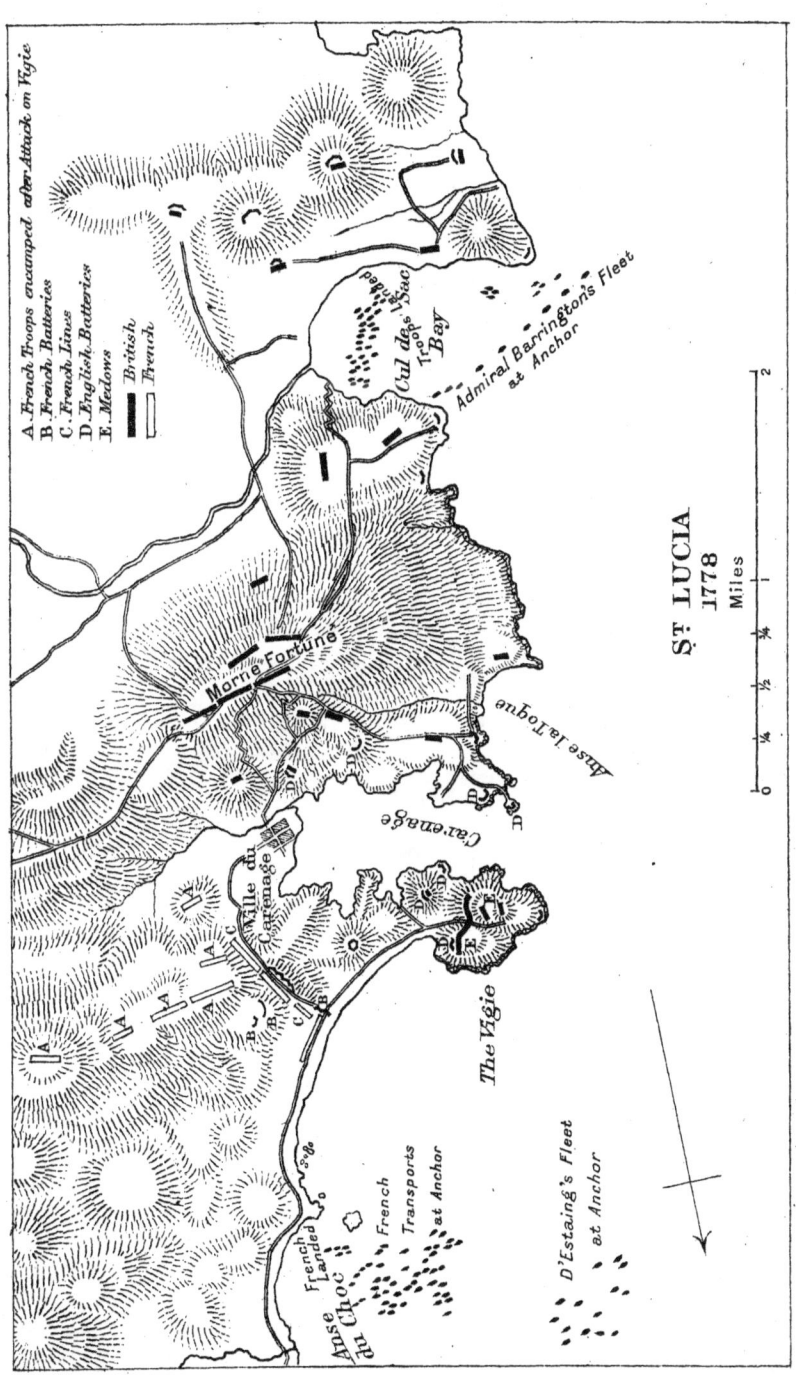

against ten times their number. The wounded were looked after, and a flag was sent for the exchange of prisoners. The soldiers of the two nations quickly fraternized, and D'Estaing added his compliments to those of Grant, who wrote: " Sir, I cannot express how much I feel myself obliged to you, and the troops under your command, for repulsing with so much spirit and bravery so great a body of the enemy: I own it was just what I expected from you and them."

In case of another attack redoubts were added to that of the 4th Grenadier company and the place entrenched, and the little army spent an anxious week of rumours and alarms. A great attack was expected on Christmas Day; orders to the Reserve were made, December 25th, 1778: " As soon as our gallant and generous enemy are seen to advance in great numbers, the troops are to receive them with three huzzas, and then be perfectly silent and obedient to their officers. Whilst they are cool by day and alert by night they have nothing to fear. If the enemy want our arms let them come and take them. During the attack the drums and fifes are to assemble round the colours of the Fifth Regiment and beat the Grenadiers' March." But D'Estaing had no wish to renew the fight, and sailed away to Martinique, leaving St. Lucia elated but still somewhat anxious, having no news of Byron and his ships; the tale went round that all the fleet had been lost in the great hurricane, but at last Byron appeared with only his usual ill-luck to explain his late coming.

The Fifth now heard how they had been so fortunate as not to fall in with D'Estaing on their voyage from New York. The lost transport had fallen into French hands, and her commander, Mr. Thomas Middleton, was closely questioned as to the appointed rendezvous. He had, on losing sight of the convoy, read and destroyed his instructions, but refused to make any answer to all persuasions. Finally, they threatened to put him in irons, and thinking they might by accident hit on the truth, he spoke: " Since they must know it, Antigua." D'Estaing turned from his direct course to Martinique to find himself hoaxed, and Grant and Barrington gained many priceless hours.

When, six days after the New Year, Byron brought this fleet in, he was too late to cut off D'Estaing's retreat, but in time to blockade him securely in Fort Royal. The sight of more ships was very welcome to Grant and his little army, who were fighting a worse enemy than France or Spain. " Without bark we should not have a man fit for duty," but the hospital at New York could not spare much from their scanty store. The return of February 5th gives 850 sick in the preceding week. Byron's sailors were in no better case, and he applied to Grant for men to serve on board the fleet. Grant, with true instinct into the strategic position, realized that the offensive lay with the navy, and lent willing help, refusing to obey counsels from England and divide his small force among the other islands. He kept St. Lucia well defended, and gave all the men he could spare to the fleet. The Fifth and 40th were warned for this service until " the seamen should recover or the fleet leave this coast."

The headquarters of the Fifth were on Morne Fortuné. By the end of January the regiment's baggage was ordered on board certain ships, and a detachment was sent on board the *Trident*, 64, Captain A. J. P. Molloy.

In March the Reserve was found to be encamped on unhealthy ground. The Grenadiers and Light Infantry were allowed to join their regiments but not to disband. The Fifth were ordered to take up ground near the redoubt on the Vigie, where they remained until a packet came in with orders to repair on board H.M.'s ships.

The Fifth were sent on board the *Elizabeth*, a 74, Captain Truscott. The women were left on shore, with orders to draw their provisions from the Commissary. When any sick were landed they were to be sent to the hospital at Gros Islet. There was also a convalescent ship, the *Elizabeth and Isabella*. The soldiers found that D'Estaing could not be provoked to come out and fight, and that they were to sail down to St. Kitts to quiet the fears of the planters, themselves a source of sedition and danger but now loyal through abject fear.

No sooner were Byron's sails out of sight than De Grasse slipped into Martinique and joined D'Estaing with large reinforcements. Admiral Rowly joined Byron, but the odds were still in favour of the French, and, though the news had not yet reached the Indies, Spain had declared war on June 16th. Byron gave way to the demands of the traders and left with most of his fleet to escort a large convoy of merchantmen through the danger zone. D'Estaing swooped down on St. Vincent, which made no resistance, and, landing a sufficient force to hold the island, sailed against Granada. Byron, hearing that St. Vincent was threatened, came hurrying back, and on July 5th came within sight only to find the Lilies flying from the fort. His second in command, the energetic Barrington, was after D'Estaing without losing a moment, and arrived off St. George's harbour on the 6th. Granada had fallen on the 4th, after a gallant resistance. D'Estaing, knowing that Byron was close on his heels, was lying at the mouth of the harbour, and at sight of the English ships turned to fly. Barrington made signal for general chase, and twenty-five ships fled before twenty-one, of whom the greater number were not within shot. Barrington's vanguard attempted to hold the enemy and force a general engagement. The *Grafton, Cornwall,* and *Lion* sustained the whole fire of the French as they passed, and Fanshaw in the *Monmouth* threw himself desperately, singlehanded, across their van. The action was undecisive; D'Estaing escaped; and if the English had the glory they also suffered the greatest damage. The *Lion* and the *Monmouth* fell in with each other, and, being both much disfigured, failed to recognize a friend, and were accordingly, with great eagerness, bringing up to fight when they discovered their mistake. The British losses were 188 killed and 346 wounded, of whom 74 officers and men were military. Byron spoke of the soldiers' exemplary conduct: "The troops behaved as brave soldiers." Barrington was among the wounded. Grant and Medows saw the action from on board the *Sybella* victualler.

A few weeks later Byron struck his flag, and both he and Barrington returned to England, leaving Hyde Parker in command pending the arrival of Rodney. Grant also resigned and went home, leaving Brigadier-General Calder at St. Lucia and Major-General Prescott at St. Kitts. In December Major-General Vaughan was appointed commander-in-chief in Grant's place, and sailed with reinforcements.

Had it been possible to continue the happy co-operation of navy and army as under Byron, Barrington, and Grant, the war in the West Indies might have been an easier and more successful task. " The Fleet and the Army act with the greatest unanimity," wrote James Grant. " It is a pleasure to serve with Admiral Barrington, Commodore Hotham, and the gentlemen of the navy in general." His successors were not strong enough to withstand the importunities of Burt and the other governors, and with the division of the small army came demoralization and sometimes disaster. Grant knew the Islands when he said that to divide the troops was to lose all semblance of soldierly feeling among them.

Life at sea had its drawbacks. The Fifth were ordered to land their sick at Sandy Point, and on July 21st 290—more than half the regiment—were returned as non-effective. Captain Cox was in charge of the convalescents. The headquarters of the regiment were at Sandy Point, but during the autumn part of the regiment remained on board the *Elizabeth*, and in September returns were made from on board ship in Sandy Bay. In December the *Elizabeth* sailed to Antigua, probably to refit; the two brigade-majors were sent, Baker to St. Lucia and Smith to St. Kitts, where Governor Burt made his task no easy one. The little island contained as unpleasant a company as could well be found. Shortly after his arrival General Prescott was forced to take strong measures, and the following order was made: " In consequence of the interference of Governor Burt, Brigadier-General Prescott informs the officers that Brigade-Major Smith is the only officer authorized to give orders either verbally or in writing."

D'Estaing had also left the West Indies, and his successor, De la Motte Piquet, was inferior in strength to Hyde Parker, and could do little to protect the French trade, which suffered severely.

In February, Vaughan arrived at Barbadoes, and Hyde Parker met him with sixteen sail; and shortly after victorious Rodney came from the Mediterranean with four more ships. France, too, had sent reinforcements, and De Guiche to take command. Rodney tried to provoke an engagement, but De Guiche lay safe in Fort Royal until Rodney's back was turned. Then, when the English sailed for St. Lucia, he, with twenty-three sail of the line and a number of frigates, slipped out in the darkness. Rodney had left fast vessels to bring him word of any movement of the enemy, and he was quickly on their heels, and by the 17th had not only caught up with them but with great skill brought them to action. The flagship showed the way, forced three ships to quit the line, and, unsupported, engaged the *Couronne* and two others until the French admiral bore away. To Rodney's disgust some of the English ships stood off, and without proper support from his captains he was forced to break off the engagement. A misread signal caused him to forgo an almost certain victory. The *Elizabeth*, now commanded by Captain Maitland, lost 9 men killed and 15 and an officer—Lieutenant Heriot of the Marines—wounded. It does not appear that any of the Fifth were wounded.

The English garrison had suffered terribly through the winter.[1] The return of the Fifth in February gives 371 as non-effective.

The regimental returns were sent from on board ship, but the headquarters remained at Gros Islet Bay, and on May 2nd a General Court-Martial was held there, and Ensign——[2] of the Fifth was cashiered for using insult-

---

[1] On May 31st, 882 out of 2,086 men in the army were on the sick list.
[2] Papers of Sir D. W. Smith. No name given.

ing, provoking, and disrespectful language to Brigadier-General Sir H. Calder when in the execution of his duty.

On May 6th Rodney heard the French were trying to get back to Martinique, and off he went on the hunt. On the 10th they were in sight, but declined action. The English van outsailed their rear, and for three days a running fight went on. Each day the advantage lay with Rodney. At last the French crowded on all sail and stood away to the north, Rodney went back to Barbadoes to refit, and De Guiche managed to slip into Martinique. A detachment of the Fifth fought on board the *Albion*, 74, Captain George Bowyer. Among the killed on the 15th was Ensign Currey of the Fifth. Rodney reported that " the *Albion* and the *Conqueror* suffered much in the last action."

Alarm spread through the island, for word came that a great Spanish fleet, with transports, cannon, and twelve ships of the line, had sailed from Cadiz in April. Rodney had his ships put in repair, and hoped to bring the Spaniards to action before they could join forces with the French. Don Salano would not venture to Martinique, but kept to the north, and from Guadeloupe sent messages to De Guiche to join him. This was done, and panic seized Jamaica and the Windward Islands. Fortunately, the Spaniards were in no condition to take the offensive; the sick rate was so appalling on board the crowded transports that the men were finally disembarked at Martinique. Disagreements arose between the two admirals; the fleets separated; the English breathed again; the planters once more sent the soldiers to the devil, and continued to supply the enemy with contraband at a very considerable profit. The Fifth became landsmen, and to their joy were ordered home.

By the end of June they were on board the *Dorothy and Catherine* transport, called at St. Kitts in July, and then sailed for England and so escaped the hurricane that later raged over the islands.

The war in America had prospered; Charlestown had surrendered, and the Americans had suffered defeat at Camden; Spain was rebuffed for the moment, and

Gibraltar had a short breathing-space; but in India Hyder Ali made war on the English, while close at hand Paul Jones brought the American War to the English coast. The whole country was involved in the general unrest; mobs, exploited by party politicians, stormed through London streets; 20,000 troops were sent for to keep order. No victories could make the American War a popular one, and the news of Yorktown brought many petitions to Parliament and the King.

"Your Majesty's Fleets have lost their wonted superiority, your armies have been captured, your dominions have been lost, and your Majesty's faithful subjects have been loaded with a burden of taxes, which, even if our victories had been as splendid as our defeats have been disgraceful . . . could not in itself be considered but as a great and grievous calamity."

The Fifth were not allowed to land in England, but were sent forthwith to Ireland in the *Two Brothers* transport.[1]

Medows, as a just reward, was made colonel of the 89th. Able and brave, cheerful and sweet-tempered, his time of command had been all too short, though long enough to prove him zealous and unselfish, and to show that an officer by such qualities could earn the enduring devotion of his men. Fortunately the Fifth did not lack good officers. Major Harris, by special request of the colonel, succeeded Medows in command, Gaspard Battier got his majority, and John Smith became senior captain. George Harris had obtained leave late in 1779 and had sailed for home, only to be captured by a French privateer and carried off to St. Malo. By the courtesy of Comte D'Ossume he was released on parole and allowed to proceed to Dover. From Dover post-horses carried him safely to Bath, and there he married Anne Carteret, daughter and heiress of Charles Dixon of the town. His misfortunes were not yet over, for on proceeding in December to join his regiment, now at Cork, his ship was wrecked on the way, and he and

[1] Benjamin Hill. Cannon states that the Fifth landed at Portsmouth September 16th, and re-embarked in December for Ireland.

his wife had to endure much discomfort and some loss. The transport was commanded by an incompetent captain, who lost all authority over his crew. They declared they would obey no orders save those of Colonel Harris, and it was said that only Harris's energy and coolness saved the ship from being dashed to pieces on the Old Head of Kinsale.

The late General Sir William Medows, K.B.

CHAPTER XVIII

1781-1787

GEORGE III.—1760-1820

IRELAND

LORD PERCY—MAJOR GENERAL HONOURABLE EDWARD STOPFORD

THE attention of Westminster had several times of late been drawn to Ireland. The King was much concerned at the poverty and distress in the country.[1] The old trade restrictions still obtained, and Irish politicians hoped to allay the discontent by the promise of free trade and a free nation. The French declaration of war had called forth a tremendous outburst of loyalty. The possible invasion of the island indicated an outlet, for the regular garrison was seriously depleted, and quite insufficient. The youth of the country with one accord volunteered their services to repel all invaders. In the first panic they were hurriedly armed by the Lieutenants of the Counties and hailed as the saviours of the kingdom; but when the danger grew less the English Government viewed with a rather natural alarm the presence at such a time of discontent and revolt of this large number of armed men, under no official authority.

In 1780 Lord Carlisle, who was of the school of Fox, became Lord-Lieutenant. His leader carried through Parliament the repeal of one of the trade restriction acts; but conciliation came too late—" Liberty with England—but—at all events, Liberty!" was the cry.[2]

[1] " In this and last year about 20,000 manufacturers in this metropolis have been reduced to beggery for want of trade " (Hutchinson, 1779).
[2] Grattan.

"The Irish were no longer afraid of the French or any other nation or minister," and the various parties interpreted Liberty to their own ends; some to bribe and some to oppress, some to open revolt, and some to black doings for business or pleasure; the days were better than the nights, for the Whiteboys and Captain Firebrand and the ghosts of the old Rapparees kept the roads after sundown.

The commander-in-chief of the Forces in Ireland was Sir John Irwin. Twenty years had passed since he had served with his old regiment, and during those years many things had happened. Irwin had been governor of Gibraltar 1766–68, and there his second wife had died. He had sat in four Parliaments, travelled a little, and spent much time in society. Since 1775 he had been in Ireland, and his house in Dublin was a byword for lavish hospitality. Shortly after the Fifth landed Irwin gave a banquet to Lord Carlisle, and had a great centre-piece of barley-sugar made, representing the siege of Gibraltar, which " conceit " was reported to have cost him some £1,500. Sir John's appointment came to an end with the downfall of the North ministry, and he returned to London to his house in Piccadilly.[1]

It may be taken as a compliment to the Fifth that they were sent to assist to keep order in Ireland, that they did not need the Mutiny Act to keep them to their duty, and that their officers could show a high standard of conduct.

On January 5th, 1781, the regiment landed at Cork and marched to Kilkenny, where they stayed until September, then on to Limerick by Youghal. From Limerick the Fifth went to sea again in two small vessels to Kilrush, to protect some stranded Portuguese vessels from the peasantry. " Lieutenants Henry Darly and George Hill, with a few men from Limerick, apprehended

---

[1] Sir John Irwin became a full general in 1783, but his military career was ended, and his reckless extravagance forced him to leave London and cross the Channel. He set up house in Parma, where the Duke of Parma and his wife became his very dear friends, and there he showed hospitality to every Englishman that came his way. He married a third time, and died in 1788, aged sixty years (D.N.B.).

some deserters at Horsfield under very difficult and trying circumstances."[1] Another officer of the Fifth involved himself in a more unpleasant affair. Lieutenant Hickson of the Fifth and Major Brereton of the Yeomanry Cavalry were playing hazard in a gambling house. Brereton insulted Hickson, refusing to take his money, whereupon Hickson challenged him, and a duel was arranged for the next morning. Brereton continued to taunt the young lieutenant, vowing he would forget the meeting, until at last Hickson drew his sword. Then in the crowded room the fight began. The other men present tried to separate the duellists, throwing chairs between them; but gradually Brereton with his heavy sword forced Hickson back against the wall; the door swung open, and the Major's sword caught in it as he cut at his enemy, and Hickson ran him through. Hickson was tried for murder at Cork, but honourably acquitted April, 1782.[2]

The Fifth spent the winter at Limerick and Kilkenny, and when, in July, they marched away to Carlow the mayor and citizens of Kilkenny petitioned the Lord-Lieutenant and General Burgoyne (who had succeeded Irwin as commander-in-chief) that the regiment should return for the following winter. This was a grateful testimony to their good conduct.

This year " Captain Firebrand " was caught and hung; he had been responsible for the attack on Sir F. Johnson's house in 1772, when the Fifth had been sent north to keep order.

In 1783 Carlisle was recalled and the Earl of Northington sent in his place. The policy of conciliation was continued, though the means adopted were hardly adequate. The King created a new knighthood— " St. Patrick "—which the patriots not unnaturally regarded as a fresh chain to be hung round their necks.[3]

[1] Papers of Sir D. W. Smith.   [2] *Ibid.*
[3] " George sends his stars and garters to our land:
    We send him ropes to hang his pensioned band—
And, having made this crew disgorge their pelf,
    He then may, if he pleases, hang himself."

The first installation, on March 17th, was attended with much splendour; the grenadier company of the Fifth furnished the guard of honour to St. Patrick's Cathedral.

The Fifth always found themselves well received by the Volunteers, and the officers were much complimented by the salutes given them, until it was discovered that they owed them, not to their past reputation and their present tact, but to the " V " on their buttons, which closely resembled the Volunteer "V." Collisions between the regulars and Volunteers were sometimes inevitable, and two detachments under Major Battier were sent to Carlow in April in support of a regiment of Fencibles who had been insulted by some young hotheads. John Butler of Kilkenny Castle executed steady and judicious control, and no lives were lost. The Fencible, or Militia, regiments were often the cause of trouble; the majority were in a very corrupt state, and later were to prove themselves worse than useless; and their swaggering sins of the moment were terribly requited in after years.

The officers of the Fifth had other matters to worry them. Under the Special Recruiting Acts of 1778 and 1779, large numbers of men had been enlisted for three years' service; the moment peace was concluded orders for immediate reduction were issued, and these short-service men were allowed to take their discharge without waiting to complete their time. A bounty of a guinea and a half was offered to good men who would re-enlist, but this was of no effect. The following apocryphal story of the Fifth appears to date from this period.

" General Burgoyne, while at Cork, saw one day a very corpulent soldier among the spectators on the parade whom he addressed as follows: ' Who are you, sir ? You must be drilled twice a day to bring down your corporation. Who are you, sir ?' ' Please, your honour, I am the skeleton of the Fifth Regiment of Foot, who have just marched over from America !' "[1]

[1] This incident may have happened in 1780, when Benjamin Hill was sent home from the West Indies to recruit.

A NEW COLONEL

Matters were not really so bad with the regiment; the recently enlisted men were induced by promise of increased bounty and future discharge again to take up arms. Other Regiments were not so fortunate; the Royal Scots lost 500 of their 700 men. As well as the loss of the short-service men there was the almost daily drain of desertions. Sheltered by the magistrates, and abetted by the country-folk a man could, and often did, earn half a dozen bounties in as many weeks. It was calculated that a sixth of the forces in Ireland was lost each year by desertion.

In 1784 the Fifth lost the colonel who had done so much for them—Lord Percy was gazetted to the Horse Guards. His old regiment had paid him the highest compliment in their power: they solicited and obtained permission to be called the Northumberland Regiment.[1] From Alnwick, taking leave of the Fifth, Percy wrote:

ALNWICK,
November 5th, 1784.

" SIR,

"His Majesty having been pleased to appoint me Colonel of the Second Troop of Horse Grenadier Guards, in succession to His Royal Highness Prince Frederick, I take the earliest opportunity of acquainting you with it; and although this new appointment is a very flattering mark of His Majesty's approbation of my services, yet I cannot help feeling the greatest regret at quitting the Fifth regiment of Foot, which I have had the pleasure of commanding for sixteen years with great pleasure, satisfaction to myself, and I trust with some advantage to the corps. The very uncommon attention which I have always met with, both from the officers and men of the Fifth, will ever be remembered by me with the greatest pleasure, and however changed my situation may be with respect to them, my regard, esteem, and affection for them will

[1] The Fifth apparently became the Northumberland Regiment in 1782. On August 31st of that year they were recommended to enlist in that county as much as possible.

ever continue the same, and I shall always be happy in having an opportunity of convincing them of it.
"I am, with the greatest regard,
"Yours most sincerely,
"Percy,
"Officer commanding the Fifth Foot."

Major-General the Honourable Edward Stopford[1] succeeded Lord Percy, and was gazetted colonel of the Fifth on November 1st.

In March a riot had broken out in Dublin when the Fifth were on guard, and to them it fell to arrest the ringleaders. This work was quietly and efficiently accomplished. For summer quarters four companies were sent to Drogheda and four companies to Dundalk; the summer over, the Fifth went into garrison at Belfast. During the winter they were called upon to extinguish a big fire, and owing to their exertions a great deal of property was saved. Mr. Blackwell, at whose house a great many of the officers lodged, strained himself moving a barrel of gunpowder, and died in consequence. The Mayor of Belfast sent his grateful thanks to the commanding officer of the Fifth for their help.[2]

On May 20th Major-General Luttrell reported the regiment as "good." "The internal economy of this regiment very much attended to; the Regimental Standing Orders well digested and properly established by Lord Percy."

On St. George's Day in the parish church new colours were presented, to be carried in place of the old ones, all battle-stained and torn; in the evening the men dined by companies as guests of Lord Percy.

Captain Benjamin Hill left the regiment this year, and the Fifth lost a good officer. Some time before

[1] Honble. Edward Stopford, second son of James, first Earl of Courtown; born 1732; married 1783, Letitia, daughter of William Blacker, of Carrick Blacker, Co. Armagh. Ensign 29th Foot 1750; lieutenant-colonel 66th Foot 1766; major-general 1782. Died October 22nd, 1794.
[2] Papers of Sir D. W. Smith.

he had married a sister of George Harris, and the expense of the constant removals of his family forced him to this step. He sold his company, receiving only £1,800 in lieu of the 1,800 guineas he had paid in 1779. Two years later his old brother officer Sir Ralph Abercromby got him the adjutancy of the 75th, and Hill went with his regiment to India. In 1795, after eight years, he obtained leave to visit his family, and came back to England as a lieutenant in the 75th. The next year he went on half-pay, and his old colonel, now Duke of Northumberland, made him adjutant to the 1st Northumberland Militia.

The Fifth remained garrisoned at Belfast, with summer quarters at Coleraine, Mullingar, Carrick, and Banagher. When they could get leave the officers went down to Dublin, the gayest capital in Europe. In 1784 Charles, fourth Duke of Rutland, had been made Lord-Lieutenant. He was a young man of thirty who had attracted attention by a chivalrous speech on Irish affairs; the Ministry trusted his appointment would be agreeable to the Irish Leaders. He was the son of brave Lord Granby of the German campaign; his young wife was a daughter of the Duke of Beaufort, and they were reckoned the handsomest couple in the kingdom. Rutland came to the Castle with the highest hopes and ideals to find himself surrounded by a mob of toadies and schemers. " The aristocracy crowded round the government as to the emporium of their profits and their honours." He quickly lost heart, and resigned himself to reigning over a court more luxurious than the King's, but accompanied by a laxity of decorum that marked a new epoch in Irish society. The manners of the Regency found ready though more graceful exponents in Dublin. The trickle of claret that had distressed Chesterfield had grown to a mighty fine river.

David Smith was hoping for his captaincy. He stood next for purchase, was a son of the eldest captain, and a popular young officer. Captain Hawkshaw, a married man, had long talked of selling, and, in

December, sent in his papers. Rutland gave General Stopford to understand that Lieutenant Smith should have his company, and on the strength of this Lieutenant Smith ordered his new regimentals and was chaired by Hawkshaw's men. Unfortunately, Sir Henry Calder and his aide-de-camp, Joseph Bunbury, went to dine at Dublin Castle, and there Bunbury and the Lord-Lieutenant " happened to get drunk together," and Rutland promised his cheerful companion the next vacant company. David Smith's commission was as yet unsigned, his name was quickly scratched out and Bunbury's written in. Smith never forgot this injury; he gave up all thoughts of a soldier's career, and remained in the regiment only waiting for a good moment to sell.[1] A pity, for—*vide* General Lord Luttrell— " This regiment is in very good order, ever well attended to by its officers."

Marching orders came in 1787—the Fifth were ordered to Canada, a land of promise, where some of the officers hoped to make their fortunes and settle for life. Lieutenant-Colonel Harris had made up his mind to sell, go out with his old regiment, and live in the new world, when a letter came from Medows, just appointed to the Bombay command, who much wished to have Harris on his staff. The East Indies certainly promised wealth, but life was uncertain, and Harris was a poor man with a growing family. Medows decided for him by insuring Harris's life for the benefit of his family for £4,000. So, after twenty-five years, George Harris left the Fifth to add to his laurels and to practise in a wider field the lessons he had learned with the old regiment. And to the Fifth it had meant a great deal to have had such a man as George Harris in command during these difficult years. His unaffected bearing, kindly disposition, and simple manners had set a fine example, and withal he was a disciplinarian and an excellent officer.[2]

[1] Papers of Sir D. W. Smith.
[2] In after years, when Harris was asked to name the title he had won, he would only say that the 5th Foot was the only home he had known for twenty-five years.

LIEUT.-GENERAL LORD HARRIS.

Lord Henry Fitzgerald,[1] from half-pay of the 85th, was gazetted lieutenant-colonel *vice* Harris; but apparently Fitzgerald did not sail with his regiment, and another lieutenant-colonel was appointed in September, 1788.

Captain William Cox resigned his commission and settled at Coolcliff in Wexford, becoming captain of the Taghmon Yeomanry Cavalry. In the worst days of the Irish Rebellion—1798-1799—he suffered a horrible death—his house was surrounded by rebels; in a small boat he tried to make his escape down the river to the sea and in the shallow water his boat grounded. Cox cried to a priest for mercy, but the sins of other men had to be expiated, and the pikemen swarmed down upon him and cut him to pieces.[2]

Richard Talbot, from half-pay of the 85th, became captain *vice* Cox. Battier[3] left, and John Smith succeeded him as major, Benjamin Baker becoming eldest captain.

The Fifth marched south, and in March were quartered in Cork and the surrounding villages. One company found itself at Brandon, the Protestant town; on the principal gate were the words:

" Traveller, beware !
Jew, Turk, or Atheist
May enter here,
But not a Papist."

And under a Catholic had added:

" These lines have been indited well,
No Papist enters at the Gate of Hell."

---

[1] Lord Henry Fitzgerald, fourth son of the first Duke of Leinster, and brother of Lord Edward Fitzgerald; born 1761, died 1829; married Charlotte, Baroness de Ros.
[2] Papers of Sir D. W. Smith.
[3] John Gaspard Battier died in his house in North Cumberland Street, Dublin, August 15th, 1817, in the sixty-eighth year of his age. " He was a man of strictest integrity, pious resignation, and charitable without ostentation " (*The Times*). His son, Cornet Battier, late of the 10th Hussars, was a victim of one of the earliest " ragging " cases. The colonel and officers resented his appointment direct from the Horse Guards, and forced Battier to resign his commission in 1824 (D. W. S.).

Lieutenant Darling with a detachment marched from Roscommon to Athlone for "subsistance," and returned the same day in good order—"this being a great march."

On May 24th the Fifth embarked at Monkstown, close to Cork, Major Smith, thirteen officers, and four non-commissioned officers on board the *Lord Mulgrave ;* Captain Stephenson, nine officers, and three non-commissioned officers on board the *Lord Leighton ;* and Captain Charlton, three officers, and one non-commissioned officer on board the *General Elliot.*[1]

[1] Papers of Sir D. W. Smith.

CHAPTER XIX
1787-1797

CANADA

HONBLE. EDWARD STOPFORD—SIR ALURED CLARKE

THE Fifth sailed away to the New World from a Europe full of unrest, for the nice adjustment of power was a difficult task. The Emperor had repudiated the Barrier Treaty; France and Holland were closely allied, and Pitt had just completed a secret treaty with Prussia. Canada was free from such intrigue; but the late war had disclosed the vulnerable points, and had shown that invasion and even conquest was possible. The French settlers had, for the most part, stood loyally by the English, raising among themselves a militia to repel the invaders. In 1783, when peace was made, many Loyalists—10,000 it is said—emigrated to Upper or Western Canada, where large grants of land were made to them. Although the division of the Canadas was not made until 1790, already a sharp line was drawn, not only by natural boundaries, but by racial qualities. The French Canadians inhabited Eastern or Lower Canada, while the English settlers and American refugees made their homes in the west. The French, under the Quebec Act, 1774, had revived their ancient civil legislation, which remained in force until 1792, when the first Representative Assembly was called.

The Anglo-American colony, with its ill-defined boundary, possessed no adequate form of government until 1792. Collisions on the debatable borderland were frequent, and the settlers also suffered from raids and depredations by dispossessed Indians.

Lord Dorchester, formerly Carleton[1] of the American War, had been appointed governor of Quebec in 1786. This was the third time he had held the post, and his wise administration commanded respect, though his pride lost him popularity. His brother, Thomas Carleton, was from 1788 to 1794 lieutenant-colonel of the Fifth, but it is probable that he did not serve much with the regiment. He was also governor of New Brunswick, and his duties and domestic interests kept him fully occupied. He had seen much service in Canada, and was a resourceful officer.

The King's soldiers in Canada[2] had to maintain the law, written and unwritten; keep the peace between two or more nations, or between a man and his own family; fight if necessary on lake, or land, or sea, against red men or white; camp in virgin forests, and explore unknown rivers; keep themselves smart and soldierly for the honour of their country, and their powder dry for the safety of their skins.

The buffeting of the Atlantic caused one of the transports, never the newest of ships, to spring a leak. Fortunately they were then within sight of land, and the *General Elliot* was able to put into Louisberg. On July 5th the two others came to anchor in Cape Broglie harbour, Newfoundland; on the 10th they sailed again, and entered the great mouth of the St. Lawrence. Close to the river banks, more especially on the southern side, the little old French settlements were grouped. The houses, built mostly of logs, were small and close together, and round each village the land had been cleared and the trees cut away. Scalping parties were too recent a danger to allow of cover

[1] Christopher Carleton of Newry, Down; married Catherine, daughter of Henry Ball; his second and third sons were, respectively, Sir Guy Carleton, afterwards first Baron Dorchester, three times Governor of Quebec; and Thomas, Lieutenant-Governor of New Brunswick and lieutenant-colonel of the Fifth 1788-1794.

[2] Regiments in Canada in 1788: 4th, 5th, 6th, 26th, 37th, 42nd, 53rd, 54th, 57th, 1/60th, 2/60th, 65th, and one battery of artillery. The IFoot were in three brigades in seniority of regiment.

near the hamlets; and all along the coast huge churches reared themselves, and the sound of their bells carried across the water.

On the 26th they came to Quebec, the fortress towering above the landing quay. Beneath the sheer precipice, crowded on the rock, were huddled the miserable houses of the lower town, intersected by noisome dark alleys and endless flights of dripping steps.

The Fifth disembarked on July 28th. The old Jesuit college within the fortress was used as a barrack, and on their way thither the regiment passed by the wooden figure of Wolfe in scarlet broad-skirted coat with slashed sleeves, standing at the corner of St. John's Street, which led to the gate of St. Louis.

The upper town had many fine buildings, but the men were given little time for sightseeing. On the 30th the regiment was inspected by Brigadier-General Hope and then dismissed to summer quarters. Four companies marched to Old Loretto, an Indian village, where a small party of Hurons had lived for many years. There were about 250 of them, living in square houses divided by yards, and wearing their Indian clothes. The French had built a fine church for them, but it was falling into decay. The rest of the Fifth went, two companies to St. Foix and one to Lorrimer. By this time the *General Elliot* had got under way and come into Quebec, and the eighth company was sent to St. Foix.

On August 14th Major John Smith made an order: " The regiment to parade to-morrow evening at sunset before Major Smith's windows, dressed as for review, to fire a Feu-de-joie in honour of H.R.H. Prince William Henry."[1]

This young prince was the third son of George III., a post-captain of twenty-two, in command of H.M.S. *Pegasus*, of 28 guns. For a year he had been stationed in the West Indies, where the friendship and example of young Captain Nelson had kept him to his duty. In June Nelson went home, and Prince William sailed

[1] Papers of Sir D. W. Smith.

off to Jamaica, without waiting for orders, ran through the Gulf of Florida, and sailed for Halifax. He was ordered to report at Quebec, and, with somewhat ill grace, he obeyed, not looking forward to a winter of exile in the frozen St. Lawrence.

On the 29th the Fifth were ordered to the Plains of Abraham, there to be reviewed by the Prince; a regimental poet wrote:

> " When children cry,
> They know not why,
> The nurse adopts a rattle;
> This Prince to please,
> And us to teaze,
> We've had a rare sham battle !"[1]

Then, this excitement over, the regiment embarked at Wolfe's Cove in " bateaux," and, crossing the St. Lawrence, entered the Sorel River, easy of navigation, and a highway to the States.

In September the Fifth were inspected by Post-Captain Prince William, who did Major Smith the honour to breakfast with him, and the little town at the juncture of the two rivers was christened William Henry. Then the Prince tired of soldiering, took French leave, and escaped down the St. Lawrence before the winter ice froze him in. After an adventurous journey he came to the Cove of Cork. He hoped his friend Rutland would intercede for him, but the young Viceroy was six weeks in his grave, and the Prince had to make his own peace, and to judge if the walls of Plymouth Dockyard were more amusing than the Plains of Quebec.

The Fifth, having done with inspections, had snow-shoes served out, and were ordered to practise marching with them. They had leave to recruit, and by the end of the year the regiment was complete.

During their first winter the Fifth remained on the Sorel, and learned how to kill sufficient meat and poultry in November to last until the spring came. In May, 1788, from Chambre Test they marched to Montreal,

[1] Papers of Sir D. W. Smith.

arriving there on June 19th–20th, the grenadier company joining on the 24th.

The roads of Lower Canada, though few, were kept in fair order. The holes routed up by the hogs were carefully filled in. In winter the snows were well beaten down, and fir bushes planted to mark the track. Round Montreal and Quebec stood the old country-houses of the French seigneurie, some long and low, in the colonial fashion, others castellated and designed for defence. The Fifth passed other buildings on their march, convents and hospitals, and once or twice a priests' seminary. From every side came the sound of bells; the church peals never stopped ringing, and spring brought out the calêches, their harness all hung with bells. From every township, with its company of soldiers, came the beating of drums—" A very noisy country!" remarked a traveller a few years later.

The French settlers had retained the simplicity of a past age and a capacity for work. Their naïve admiration for the redcoat found expression in sincere imitation of words and ways; strangers met with civility, and could travel the country without extortion or interference. Montreal, on its island, showed like an Old Country seaport, with long ranges of walls and storehouses, and with a great high embankment to serve as quay. The soldiers were made welcome by the inhabitants; all the children, and some of the older folks, ran out to the sound of fife and drum. Major Smith was made commander of the district and remained in Montreal; five companies of the Fifth remained with him; two were sent to Kingston, late Fort Frontenac, one to Oswego, and one to Quinchien.

In the spring of 1790 they embarked and crossed the lakes to Detroit, a flourishing village of about 200 houses, with a fort and military works. Two companies were sent on to Michilinakimac.

Surgeon Holmes fell out with one of the captains of the 60th, and the gentlemen met to decide their quarrel with pistols. They fired on the word, and the surgeon fell. Fortunately the pistols had been lightly charged, and the ball, glancing off one of the doctor's brace buttons, fell into his fob; his mortal wound resolved itself into a bruise. The ball had impressed on it the pattern of the Russian sheeting that covered the button.

After the surgeon's fight came a plague of caterpillars, and the Fifth were called upon for service. They dug trenches and laid ambuscades, and were responsible for killing a very large number.

In June Lieutenant-Colonel Buckridge inspected the regiment, and reported them as fit for service, the men in general young, strong, and remarkably healthy.

Major Smith had gone to Detroit with the Fifth, and, in the absence of his lieutenant-colonel, was in command of the district as well as the regiment. His position was a difficult one; the American boundary was still a matter for local dispute; the Indians took advantage of the bad feeling, and the Loyalist settlers lacked the simplicity and pliability of the French.

General St. Clair, with 6,000 Americans and artillery, pursued some delinquent Indians over the border-line. The Indians appealed for protection, declaring themselves, then as always, allies of Great Britain; the Loyalists urged that the invaders should be shot down— it was not customary to pursue Indians with artillery. To Smith, General St. Clair sent two of his officers, who, in a menacing style, desired that no protection should be granted to the Indians. Very little was needed to start the war again, but Smith managed the affair with great skill. He calmed the Loyalists, quieted the Indians, and earned the thanks of the American President. Captain Stephenson[1] was sent as envoy to General Washington, and acquitted himself with distinction. The Fifth were in every way ready for war, but the tact and firmness of their officers saved the necessity.

Captain Benjamin Baker left the regiment this year after thirty-five years' service.

[1] Papers of Sir D. W. Smith.

The Fifth remained at Detroit for two years. In
1791 Augustus Fitzgerald joined as captain, and J.
Ussher as ensign; and Lieutenant Johnson[1] of His
Majesty's Fifth Foot benefited by the will of an old
miser, who died in Ireland, leaving " My only pair of
white stockings and my old scarlet great coat to
Lieutenant Johnson of His Majesty's Fifth Regiment."

In 1792 the regiment moved down country and
garrisoned the fort at Niagara; the village and the
French-built fort were at the entrance to Lake Ontario,
about fifteen miles below the Fall. In 1791 General
Simcoe,[2] who had proved his capacity in the American
War, was appointed governor of Upper Canada, and
in July of 1792 he arrived from England to take up his
post. He chose Niagara as his first capital, and there
fixed his headquarters, and devoted himself to many
" extremely useful and well-managed schemes " for
improving the province. Simcoe was, above all, a
keen soldier, with a true conception of the duties of
light infantry. Captain Stephenson of the Fifth acted
as his quartermaster-general.

From Niagara Lieutenant Henry Darling, with small
parties of men, made several excursions into United
States territory; by these scouting expeditions he was
able to obtain much useful information, and his success
brought him to the general's notice. Another officer,
Lieutenant Sheaffe, was sent with a detachment along
the coast of Lake Ontario to protect the American
settlements during the suspended execution of the first
American Treaty.[3]

Simcoe was a man of energetic character and strong
will, and he and Dorchester did not always see eye to
eye; but in the governor-general's absence his lieutenant, Sir Alured Clarke, late of the Fifth, and a very

[1] Lieutenant Robert Johnstone, who joined March 23rd, 1781 (?).
[2] John Graves Simcoe, 1752-1806. In 1793 he raised a Canadian
regiment, afterwards the famous Queen's Rangers; their uniform
was green faced with blue. In 1794 he went to the newly captured
St. Domingo as Governor.
[3] Cannon.

good friend of Simcoe, acted with discretion and judgment and allowed the general a free hand.

Mrs. Simcoe was a very charming woman, clever and artistic and hospitable; she soon made Navy Hall the centre of the garrison society. Besides Navy Hall the only other house of note was that of Major Smith, " made of joiners'-work, but in the best style, with a good garden and court, surrounded by railings, and painted as elegantly as in England."[1] Major Smith had also a large kitchen-garden, kept in good order, possibly with the help of soldier labour, for officers were allowed to employ their men at 9d. a day.

General and Mrs. Simcoe were hardly settled before their first guest, Prince Edward, the young Duke of Kent, arrived from Quebec, where he was quartered with his regiment (7th Foot). At 6.30 a.m. on August 23rd he and Major-General Simcoe reviewed the Fifth, and so pleased was the Duke with their appearance that he demanded some of the men for his regiment. Accordingly, all over 5 feet 9 inches were ordered to parade, cautioned to be perfectly clean, and any who wished to do so were invited to join the 7th Foot.

A month later the Assembly of Upper Canada was called, and the first Session was opened; the sloops in the little harbour were dressed with flags, and their guns thundered a salute; the guns of the Fort echoed, and the Jack flew from the old bastion. The green-clad Rangers and the scarlet-coated Fifth lined the streets, and a subaltern's guard of the Fifth made an escort for the lieutenant-governor at the Freemasons' Hall. The untamed forest fringed the little town, and from the wild lands groups of feathered Indians came in to watch the ceremony.

After this the garrison settled down to the making of roads and fortifications. For the men there were few diversions; sometimes life was so dreary that rum was the only consolation. English regiments were apt to deteriorate, for vacancies were filled from the provincial

[1] Papers of Sir D. W. Smith.

FORT NIAGARA IN 1794.

From a water-colour sketch belonging to the late Sir David William Smith.

militias recruited from the later Loyalists, often idle and profligate men. Desertion was very common; for this offence one of the Fifth paid the death penalty. Charles Grisler deserted while acting as night sentry over a few bateaux on Lake Erie; he was captured, court-martialled, and, standing by his coffin, was shot, October 29th, 1793.

In the early spring Simcoe made an official tour of his western domain. Besides his staff he took with him David Smith of the Fifth. They drove in sleighs, leading a trapper's life, and meeting with many adventures. The party returned to Niagara May 13th, and four days later the three Commissioners from the United States arrived at Navy Hall as General Simcoe's guests. They stayed a month, but could come to no terms.

Before they left Mrs. Simcoe gave them a ball, an immense excitement for the garrison. Twenty well-dressed ladies and sixty gentlemen danced with great spirit from 7 until 11 p.m. Everything was conducted with propriety; the music and the dancing were good, and the supper excellent and " in pretty taste."

All the autumn and winter the American clamour for war grew louder. Much to Simcoe's credit and to the honour of the isolated garrisons an honourable peace was maintained.

In 1794 General Stopford died, and was succeeded by Sir Alured Clarke,[1] who had left his company in the Fifth in 1771 to become major of the 54th. In 1775 he had commanded the 54th, and served through the American War; from 1782 to 1790 he was lieutenant-governor of Jamaica; and from the West Indies he came to Quebec; a full colonel in 1781, he was promoted major-general in 1790. From 1791 to 1793 Lord Dorchester was in England, and the government of the province devolved on Sir Alured. On Dorchester's return Sir Alured was given the Fifth regiment, but very soon

[1] Clarke, lieutenant-general East Indies 1796; colonel of the 7th 1801; general 1802, afterwards field-marshal. On September 16th, 1832, he died at Llangollen Rectory, the home of his niece, Mrs. Egerton.

afterwards he left Canada, and went on an expedition to harry the Dutch at the Cape.

In July Carleton had resigned, and John Smith became officially what he had long been in fact, lieutenant-colonel and commanding officer of the regiment. Stephenson got his majority, and Robert Pratt, after twenty years' service, became eldest captain.

In August Lieutenant Sheaffe with one officer and seven men was sent to Sodius as a protest against an American settlement in Ontario. The party went unarmed in evidence of their peaceable intentions.

This year De la Rochefoucauld stayed with General Simcoe, and put on record his amazement at the elaborate style of hair-dressing worn by the Fifth in the virgin forest. He tells how they plastered their hair " with a thick white mortar, which they laid on with a brush and afterwards raked, like a garden bed, with an iron comb, and then fastening on their heads a piece of wood, as large as the palm of the hand and shaped like the bottom of an artichoke, to make a ' cadogan,' which they filled with the same white mortar, and raked in the same manner as the rest of their head-dress."

John Smith held his hard-earned commission little more than a year, dying in harness November 19th, 1795. He was buried with full military honours on the Canadian side of Niagara River. His son, David William Smith, left the regiment and settled in Upper Canada, took to law, and eventually became Speaker of the Assembly. Stephenson succeeded Smith, and Pratt got his majority.

In 1796 Fort Niagara was handed over to the United States, and the Fifth went by lake, river, and road to Quebec with its vine-clad houses, gay gardens, and sound of calèche bells.

Simcoe returned to England at the end of 1795; Dorchester had gone a month or two before, and General Prescott, a man of seventy-one, was left to govern Lower Canada and as commander-in-chief of the Forces. His reign was a short and stormy one. England and France were at war; an outbreak with the United States was still possible; the greater number of Canadians were of enemy origin, and the royal troops were a negligible quantity. Prescott involved himself in a dispute with his Executive Council on a question of land tenure, and the discontent became so acute and widespread that the military had to be called out to disperse the rioters and malcontents. The Fifth were turned out in the depths of winter, and were sent across the St. Lawrence, which was frozen over, to Point Levi, where the insurgents had collected. As there is no record of any casualties it would appear that the Fifth were able to disperse the mob without loss.

In 1797 orders came for home; the men were to be drafted into the 24th regiment, the officers and non-commissioned officers only to return. This drafting order was in accordance with custom, but did not add to the popularity of the army or the efficiency of individual regiments. Many, however, of the Fifth had, during their stay in Canada, been recruited from among the countrymen, and it was advisable to transfer these to regiments garrisoned in Canada.

The Fifth had maintained a very high standard through many difficult years. The regimental officers had worked hard for the benefit of the service, and also, without doubt, for the well-being of their men. At a time when field officers were being rebuked in orders for their display of ignorance and indifference, even to the sending in of casualties without giving the names of the privates, one at least of the company officers of the Fifth had a neat memorandum for his own satisfaction of the officers, non-commissioned officers, and drummers of each company. Later, when the ill-advised order releasing the short-service men was issued, the Fifth had no great difficulty in maintaining their proper establishment. In Ireland and in Canada both tact and discipline were needed, and the Fifth came triumphantly through the ordeal. After years brought to Rawdon, Medows, and Harris a greater brilliance and wider fame; but they, with others more obscure, both gave and owed much to the regiment. Of the men who gave long years and all their ambitions to the Fifth, Baker left a captain after thirty-five years' service, and John Smith spent nearly forty years from volunteer to lieutenant-colonel, while Robert Pratt got his majority after twenty-five years. There were many others of lesser but still lengthy service. Some of the younger men, having learned their lesson in this fine school, earned their laurels in other company. Henry Darling[1] left the Fifth before 1797 to command a company of the 68th Foot. General Simcoe had a great regard for him, and attached him to his staff. In after years Simcoe was to have gone to India, and Darling with him, as quartermaster-general, but Simcoe died before his appointment took effect. Sheaffe eventually commanded the 48th Foot, and acted as governor of Fort St. George. Against his severe discipline the troops mutinied, and seven were shot. He was allowed to retain his command, and under milder rule discipline improved. In later years, at Brinston Hill, he showed he was lacking in the qualities essential for a leader.

Not all the officers returned to England. For some the call of the New World was too strong, and they had formed ties which could not be broken. The Smiths, as has been said, had bought land; Lieutenant Ross-Lewin[2] married a lady of Quebec; Prideaux Selby,[3]

[1] Henry Darling was the second son of Henry Darling of Berwick and Ann Gradon his wife, which Henry was the son of Henry Darling of Embleton and Jane Proctor his wife. Henry Darling of the Fifth was baptized at Berwick, April 24th, 1755; admitted to the freedom of Berwick, February 19th, 1781, by patrimony; a major-general in the army in 1821; died in September, 1835, and buried at Embleton on the 15th of that month.

[2] Ralph Ross Lewin, fifth son of Harrison Ross Lewin of Fortfergus, Co. Clare, and his wife Hannah Westropp. Married Archange, daughter of M. Baubie of Quebec, and died s.p.

[3] Prideaux Selby, son of George Selby of Alnwick, attorney; baptized at Alnwick, December 21st, 1747; is stated to have died at Toronto May 12th, 1813. He was the great-grandfather of the late Mr. Beauchamp Selby of Pawston.

too, turned his back on Northumberland, and lived and died in Toronto.

Many years later David Smith came to England, and his old colonel appointed him commissioner of the Percy estates. At his house in Alnwick, Sir David Smith, who had been created a baronet for his services to the Canadian Assembly, entertained such of his old comrades as came that way. Major-General Henry Darling and Sir Roger Hale Sheaffe were constant visitors, and in October, 1828, Thomas Talbot, once his lieutenant-colonel, came from Canada for a brief visit.

His Majesty's Fifth Foot were indeed becoming the Northumberland Regiment.

CHAPTER XX
1793-1798

AFFAIRS AT HOME AND ABROAD

In 1797 the Fifth came home to find the French Revolution an accomplished fact, and the Tricolor triumphant on land. When, in 1795, France had invaded the new Belgic Provinces and threatened Holland, England had sent help to her old ally, and at Neuwinden the Duke of York had defeated the French. Austria and Prussia lent their aid, but the after campaigns proved disastrous, and the Allies quarrelled. In 1796 York evacuated Belgium. Holland, not without reason, thought her old ally a broken reed, and made a separate peace with France, and with her new ally turned on England, only to find the British Navy still triumphant, and to lose her Cape colonies and nearly all her East Indian possessions. Then Spain, hoping to retrieve some of her old glory, turned on England, but the White Ensign ruled the seas, and Jervis off St. Vincent made this clear to the Spaniards.

When the Empress Catherine died England lost another ally, for her successor withdrew Russia from the Alliance and made a separate treaty with triumphant France. In Ireland, rebellion, long brewing, was hastened by the recall of Fitzwilliam; enemies of England were welcomed, and only a storm prevented a French landing in Bantry Bay.

Two years' bad harvests and the continued dislocation of trade had brought much misery to England. Pitt was blamed for every misfortune—bad harvests, bad trade, negro or Irish risings—only his high courage carried him on; he did not swerve from his conception of a stateman's policy in spite of his countrymen who hoped to adjust matters by gentle repression and a speedy peace.

In February of 1797 French ships sailed up the Irish Channel and raided Fishguard. In the English army there was talk of treason, and the navy broke into open mutiny. For the Mutiny at the Nore and the disaffection at Woolwich and other garrisons Pitt must take the responsibility. The men who lived so miserably and died so bravely for England were paid the merest pittance. Caprice and fortune had been responsible for any amelioration of their lot, though it is true that since 1781 investigations into public departments had been made, and, in 1784, the Pay Office was reorganized. Some of the colonels made objection to the loss of their "stock-purse" and the curtailment of their initiative; but good officers continued to exert themselves for the well-being of their men, while the neglect, or eccentricities, of extravagant colonels was diminished.

In the eighteenth century the standard of living was raised throughout the country, but the soldier's pay remained the same, and out of the surplus he was expected to keep himself in blackball and powder and other odds and ends. Very few could, like Corporal Trim, honour their father and mother by "Allowing them, an't please your honour, three half-pence a day out of my pay when they grow old."[1]

A new warrant in 1793 slightly bettered conditions and left the soldier 18s. 10½d. a year to call his own after all deductions for food and clothing had been made.[2]

In one matter the Fifth had been fortunate, in that so much of their time had been spent in Ireland or the Plantations, and they had escaped the billeting evils of the home garrisons. In the inns the private

[1] In 1797 the Mutiny at the Nore enforced the just demands of the services on the Government. The army obtained a few benefits. Subalterns' pay was increased by 1s. per diem, and the deductions for poundage, hospitals, etc., were allowed to lapse.

[2] See table on p. 216.

soldiers and poorer subalterns were not welcome guests, for they could contribute little to the good of the house. The men were crowded in garrets with broken floors and ceilings, or in noisome, unfurnished outhouses. If the company officer lacked experience he found himself confronted with a bill for liquor which his men had drunk and for which they could not possibly pay. In well-regulated regiments like the Fifth the men were not allowed credit. For a sound man the life was hard enough, but for a sick one it was unalleviated misery. With the relaxed discipline of the late eighteenth century field officers seldom did duty with their regiments, and their subalterns took advantage of their absence to shirk their duties and kill the long hours by gaming, drinking, and other sports. It was possible for a private, failing a friend as poor as himself, to die in his garret without a soul near him. Again, unless the billets were regularly visited, strict cleanliness could not be ensured; "to appear twice a day on parade was no guarantee of cleanliness when billeted all over a town." Each regiment had a surgeon appointed, and many of these men did their duty by their country; but with scattered companies their

---

1798. *Stoppages per annum for necessaries.* (7th Fus.)

	s.	d.
2 pairs of black cloth gaiters at 4s.	8	0
2 pair of breeches	6	6
1 hair leather	0	2½
2 pair of shoes at 6s.	12	0
Mending do.	4	0
1 pair of stockings or 2 pairs of socks	1	6
A foraging cap	2	3
Knapsack at 6s. once in six years	1	0
Pipe clay and whiting	4	4
Clothes brush at 1s. in two years	0	6
3 shoe brushes at 5d.	1	3
Black ball	2	0
Worsted mitts	0	9
A powdering bag and puff every three years 1s. 6d.	0	6
2 combs at 6d. each	1	0
Grease and powder for the hair	3	0
Washing at 4d. a week	17	4

£3 6 11½

work was made very difficult.[1] In some regiments the sick fund was very small—only £30, of which £9 2s. 0d. was earmarked for the nurses' wages. The hospital diet was meagre, and all extras had to be supplied from the sick fund.[2]

When a young man found himself gazetted to an ensigncy his first business was to write to the regimental agent, and to find out, through him, where his regiment was stationed and all particulars as to uniform. He had then to discover if his uniform could be made up at the regimental headquarters, and if the quartermaster was likely to have all the necessary accoutrements. When these preliminaries had been arranged, and he had joined his regiment, the young officer was given the standing orders of his battalion to study, and was put to learn his drill. It was the adjutant's duty to teach him the sword salute, and he was advised to accustom himself to long marches. He was recommended to study the nineteen manœuvres by the aid of wooden blocks, a recent invention to elucidate the drill-book of David Dundas. Should the young officer wish to purchase his way he was advised to pay some attention to the price of commissions, the money for which he must deposit with the agent. No officer could sell without the King's permission, and when leave was obtained the matter was left in the agent's hands. Those officers who, through merit or interest,

---

[1] It is indicative of the customs of the time that a regimental surgeon, writing in 1794, should speak very strongly of the dangers of excessive drinking by surgeons. He also proffers good advice that they should avoid too great an intimacy with the younger officers, in case they became too deeply involved in gaming and sports to attend to their work (see Robert Hamilton, "The Duties of a Regimental Surgeon").

[2] FULL DIET.

Breakfast.	Dinner.	Supper.
1 pint of oatmeal or rice gruel.	1 lb. bread, 1 lb. meat, 1 quart of small beer.	1 pint broth.

HALF DIET.

As before.	As before, ½ lb. meat only.	As before.

Those on milk diet were given 1 pint of milk for breakfast and supper, and 1 pint of broth and 1 lb. of bread for dinner (see "The Duties of a Regimental Surgeon").

had obtained their commissions without purchase could only "look to the King for permission to retire from the service by disposing of their appointments." Their chances of promotion were almost too small to be taken into account, and often they had to content themselves with subaltern rank.

Drill and tactics were in a somewhat transitory state: the old school of Flanders and the Prussian grenadier viewed with the utmost contempt the new theories enjoined by the veterans of the American wars. They agreed that advance of column in line would fail of its object in the backwoods, but they argued that to attempt Indian methods in open ground against European armies was to court destruction. The one school advocated the training of the individual, the other placed all its hopes on a disciplined but massed force. Colonel David Dundas, of the Dublin Headquarter Staff, was a stanch advocate of the Prussian method; his drill-book was received with much approval, and became, after 1792, the official textbook. At the same time a new school of young officers was springing up, and the lessons of the American War were not allowed to be forgotten.

The last half of the century modified but brought few real changes to the clothing of the Foot. White gaiters, always damp with fresh pipeclay, were changed for black linen in 1767, and in 1784 the linen was changed for wool. The three-cornered hat lost one of its corners, and became the cocked hat, looped back and front, and affording no protection from sun or rain. The hair was still well greased and powdered and clubbed, and much valuable time and some of the soldiers' scanty pence were thus wasted. The new American tactics necessitated means for quicker firing; the waistbelt was transferred to the right shoulder, so as to carry a second cartridge pouch; the number of rounds in the two pouches was raised to fifty-six; the light infantry, who had hitherto carried powder-horn and bullet-bag, were now given cartridge and priming horn.[1]

[1] Fortescue, "History of British Army," vol. iii., p. 542.

In 1791 the first difference was made in the dress of regimental officers—those of field rank were ordered to wear epaulettes; embroidered on the epaulette of grenadier officers was a grenade, and on that of the light infantry a hunting-horn.

When, in 1793, war with France was inevitable, Parliament voted an increase of 25,000 men. The army was dangerously weak, the service unpopular, and the majority of officers disinclined for duty. The Ministry tried to complete by drafts from independent companies, and found themselves with a number of indifferent recruits, a long list of half-pay officers, and many discontented regulars, who objected to seeing young subalterns of never a day's service promoted over their heads for recruiting the official number of men. The campaign in Holland showed the weakness of the army; both men and officers were alike in their ignorance; the men neither disciplined or capable of independent action, and the officers lacking every virtue save courage. " While the shameful traffic of the army brokers and the raising of endless new regiments continued, every officer who could command money or interest was sure of obtaining advancement at home without the knowledge of his chief in the field, and had, therefore, not only no encouragement to do his duty, but an actual reason for avoiding it."[1]

In 1795 the Duke of York, to the very great advantage of the army in general, succeeded Lord Amherst as commander-in-chief. He was not a clever man, rather slow, and at times impatient; but he was honest and courageous, and very just in his dealings; without fear or favour he devoted himself, within his limits, to much needed reform.

The difficulties to be faced were enormous, both for army and Ministry, for the vagaries of Henry Dundas had caused the already reduced army to be further dissipated. Besides the regiments in Canada and other garrisons, and the expeditionary force in Holland, a little army had been sent to the Cape to

[1] Fortescue, " History of British Army," vol. iv., p. 297.

take the Dutch colonies; and, having accomplished this, was ordered with fresh battalions to capture Ceylon and Pondicherry. The game of grab in the West Indies necessitated frequent reinforcements, and there were other raids in the Mediterranean and against the coast of France.

The Fifth came home to an England filled with unrest. There were starving men and women in the country and in the towns. In those days the Methodists collected many followers; many were driven to pray aloud in the streets, and prophesy; the country squires sought to uphold the throne by suppressing the poor ; education was blamed for the horrible things done across the Channel; progress was set back a dozen years when they watched for the French ships in the Channel and looked on redcapped liberty as the Anti-Christ.

The Fifth were probably more annoyed by the militia officers, who swaggered up and down and aped the manners of Carlton House.

In October the Emperor made peace with France, ostensibly ceding Belgium in exchange for Venice and lands on either side the Adriatic; secretly he gave to France the left bank of the Rhine.

In the fight with France England stood alone, Holland and Spain against her, and those nearer enemies in the sister island.

CHAPTER XXI

1797-1799

GEORGE III.

HOLLAND

Sir Alured Clarke

WHEN the officers of the Fifth arrived in England they were at once ordered to Grantham, in Lincolnshire, to recruit. Flags were flying for Duncan and Camperdown. Events in Europe had moved swiftly; the enemies of England were concentrated in one man, Napoleon Bonaparte, not yet First Consul, but sufficiently master of the situation to use the armies of France at his will. In the camp at Boulogne vast quantities of men and stores were collected; preparations went on all through the winter of 1797.

In 1798, from the fight at Kilcullen, in May, to Castlebar, in September, the long-expected rebellion in Ireland raged, until the rebels were scattered and their French auxiliaries taken or killed.

Had Bonaparte seized this opportunity and sent a sufficient force to help the rebels, or himself led a real invasion, he could hardly have failed to achieve some success; instead, the fatal east lured him away. Switzerland and Italy were invaded; the true object of attack, Egypt, and through Egypt the Indies, was kept secret. Russia and Turkey became alarmed, and Austria viewed the movements in the Mediterranean with suspicion; the three nations opened negotiations with England. In June the French captured Malta, but the English fleet was after them, and on August 1st the Battle of the Nile gave check to Bonaparte.

The temporary loss of Malta roused the Tsar Paul, and he resolved to make war on France. On January 5th England joined the Russo-Turkish alliance; negotiations were opened with Prussia, who refused to entertain them, but Austria, though evading the conditions England wished to exact, joined herself to the coalition. Prussia remained neutral, leaving England, Russia, Austria, and Turkey to make war against France, Italy, Switzerland, Spain, and Holland.

The majority of the French allies were conquered countries, and were regarded by the coalition as unwilling victims; while Austria and Russia attacked Italy, England and Russia resolved, as a preliminary task, to rescue Holland. England pledged herself to provide 30,000 men and to pay for 18,000 Russian troops.

A great wave of enthusiasm swept over the country and many militiamen volunteered to serve with the regulars. This was fortunate, as otherwise Pitt could not have fulfilled his promise, for there were scarcely 10,000 regular troops available for service. The militiamen were allowed to choose their own corps, guaranteed against drafting, given a bounty of £10, and packed off to the camp on Barham Downs.

The Fifth spent the year of 1798 peacefully in Lincolnshire recruiting among the country lads. At Boston they made themselves so popular that when, a few months later, they were again quartered in the town—by particular request of the inhabitants—the population turned out to receive them; the volunteers lined the streets, and a great ball was given to the officers.[1]

From Boston they were hurriedly sent to Norman Cross, where disturbances had broken out amongst the French prisoners.

Five miles from Peterborough, the prison stood on high ground above the flats and fens; the Great North

[1] Cannon.

Road ran past the gates, but from Boston the Fifth probably went by canal. In 1798 the "mighty casernes, with their blank blind walls," were less than a year old, and did not yet hold their full complement of French and Dutch. However, there were always enough for ferment and threatened riot, and it was as well to have a seasoning of regular troops to help the militia keep order. The duties of the garrison were monotonous rather than arduous, while the barracks were scarcely more comfortable than the prison.

In the summer of 1799 rumours of the Holland expedition were in the air; the Fifth were divided into two battalions, with Major-General George Hewett as colonel commandant. Both battalions marched away to the great camp at Barham Downs, and there completed with militiamen.

The Ministry, Grenville and Pitt, were gambling on the chance that Prussia would join the coalition, and they believed and preached that the Dutch were only waiting the arrival of the English to rise and turn against the French invaders. Brave old Sir Ralph Abercromby, "that very good-natured lion," who was in command at Barham Downs, gave his opinion that no landing should be attempted until the arrival of the Russian troops. Intelligence of the enemy's movements was deficient, and each minister and every naval and military officer had a fresh scheme to propose.

On August 13th Abercromby sailed with the first contingent, and on the 27th, after many misadventures, and with great difficulty, he disembarked on the Helder. The landing had to be forced in face of considerable opposition, but on the 28th Abercromby was able to occupy the town and fortress; and to Admiral Mitchell the Dutch yielded their fleet without a shot being fired.

In England the news was received with a storm of applause; Pitt and Henry Dundas hurried down from London to inspect the remaining troops in the camp. All day, and every day, militiamen came posting down with little left of their £10 bounty but the memory of a brief and glorious debauch. The ministers were pleased with the feu-de-joie, though but a quarter of the men were able to fire; but the march past had to be abandoned, as, of the whole camp, only some 500 men had kept sober. The militiamen were good honest country lads, and, their dissipation over, were amenable to discipline, but of drill they knew little, and of musketry and manœuvres even less. They had chosen their regiments, but their facings and militia uniform betrayed them; there was no time for the tailors to alter this, and a motley crew straggled along and called themselves by the titles of some of the King's proudest regiments of foot.

In accordance with custom the light infantry and grenadier companies of all battalions were massed together, and so from already weak regiments the best men were taken away.[1]

In September embarkation orders were received, for the Duke of York was going with the remainder of the troops to reinforce Abercromby, and to take supreme command. The two battalions of the Fifth found themselves brigaded with the two battalions of the 35th, under Prince William Frederick of Gloucester,[2] a young man of twenty-three, who as a commanding officer showed no trace of military virtue, other than courage and good temper.

The campaign was expected to be brief and victorious; the men were ordered to embark in light marching order, and all surplus kit was left behind. Many of the militia boys came with large stores from careful homes, and their fine-worked shirts were packed and sealed in barrels to await their return, few ever

[1] The light infantry were under command of Colonel Sharpe of the 9th, " an experienced and gallant veteran " (Surtees). It should be noted that this was the last campaign in which the Fifth fought unsupported by the grenadier company.
[2] Son of the first Duke and his wife Maria, Countess of Waldegrave. Born in Rome, in 1776, he was educated at Cambridge, and in 1794 was made a colonel. His intellectual powers were not very high, but his private life was blameless, and much of his income was spent in charity !

saw their possessions again. They embarked at Deal, where the sea appeared covered with ships; the voyage sobered the last of the bounty men, for it lasted seven days, and this allowed the men to become acquainted with their officers.

In the meantime Abercromby had taken up a strong position right across the peninsula, from Putten on the North Sea to Oude Sluis on the Zuider Zee, his front covered by the Zype Canal. There he waited, for, even with the addition of two brigades, which had arrived on the 29th, his force, though not greatly inferior in numbers, was not of the quality to drive a skilful enemy from a strong position.

General Brune held supreme command in Holland. The ex-printer, friend of Camille Desmoulins, and member of the Cordeliers, was not a soldier to be despised. He called up every man from the eastern provinces, summoned the national guard, arranged for the defence of Amsterdam, and resolved to attack the English before reinforcements arrived. He joined General Daendels, and the French and Dutch troops made a concerted attack, which Abercromby succeeded in repulsing at every point. Brune then retreated and took up a position from Bergen on the west to Oudkarspiel. The villages north of Bergen—Groet, Kamp, and Schoorl—were fortified and entrenched, and all bridges and roads along the French front were destroyed and barricaded. The village of Schoorldam on the great northern canal was strongly fortified, and barred one of the ways south. Brune had not sufficient troops to prolong his line beyond Oudskarpel, but by breaking the dykes the country could be inundated in a very short time.

Abercromby was very well pleased when two divisions of Russians marched into camp and the fleet of transports appeared. By September 18th all battalions were landed, and the Expeditionary Force was complete.[1] The Duke of York was in command, chiefly

[1] The 35th Foot signalized their landing by cropping each other's hair, an evidence of good sense, if not of discipline.

because there was no other man of suitable rank to control the allied armies ; his late unfortunate campaign had undermined the confidence of the Ministry as well as of the military, and the Government had appointed a Council of War to control his movements. The council consisted of David Dundas of the drill-book, Abercromby, Pulteney, and that Lord Chatham who afterwards showed his incapacity in the Walcheren Expedition. General Herman, the Russian commander-in-chief, was also a member of the council. The army totalled about 48,000, three-quarters being English.

The Dutch nation showed no inclination to hoist the Orange Flag and acclaim England as their saviour. The Prince of Orange, attached to Abercromby's staff, had with difficulty and many bribes collected some 3,000 volunteers, deserters, and riff-raff, whom he expected the English general to provide with arms, clothing, and pay. The bulk of the nation remained quiescent, though somewhat resentful of the interference, but a large number were actively hostile, allying themselves with their French conquerors.

The redcoats were certainly very unwelcome, and they found themselves in a cold and unfriendly country. It rained; the roads were bottomless; and always and everywhere were the great dykes, which at night looked so like roads that the men marched boldly into the water. On the first disembarkation it was difficult to find lodgings for them all, and some, to their amazement, were billeted in churches. To the whole army their allies the Russians were a continual source of interest. One of the soldiers wrote: " The Russians is people that as has not the fear of God before their eyes, for I saw some of them with cheeses and butter, and all badly wounded; and in particular one man had an eit days clock on his back, and fiting all the time, which made me for to conclude and say ' all his vanity and vexation.' "[1]

The Russians wore great high boots and long green

[1] *U. S. J.*, February, 1836.

coats, the grenadiers distinguished by enormous hats covered with brass. Many wore medals commemorating battles and campaigns. Rather undersized, but healthy and strong, their two divisions raised great hopes until it was seen how they lacked discipline.

The English transport and staff arrangements quickly proved themselves inadequate; by embarking in light marching order many necessities had been left behind. The men were served out a blanket apiece, but without orders or instructions; a few were rolled up on the knapsacks; some were worn as great-coats; many were "lost." There were no storehouses for the accumulation of stores, and no sutlers had gone with the army, therefore the men could obtain no spirit, which was a very necessary article in the low damp country. Abercromby had 1,600 men sick from the miserable conditions caused by the wild wet weather. Some Dutch men-of-war and East Indiamen were turned into hospital-ships, and proved adequate; the proportion of deaths to wounded was very small.

Of the first days the Fifth spent in the Texel a letter from an unknown soldier gives a graphic picture: "The 17th we saw the land of the Texel, and landed that nit, and it rained very hard, and dismal was the nit indeed, but I began for to see my folly, but I had not anyone but myself to blame, being diferent than if I had been pressed into the sarvice. The next day we marched again, and as we marched along the sand-hills I saw several dead bodies, which seemed somewhat strange to me." The militia recruits straggled badly on those first marches, and wished themselves safe home again.

The Council of War resolved to attack the French position forthwith. They had nothing to gain by waiting, and the French and Dutch were outnumbered by nearly two to one. The country was a difficult one; the causeways running by the bigger dykes were the only means of communication; it was decided to attack by column the fortified villages guarding these highways.[1] The first column was to drive the French from the sand-dunes of Bergen on their left; the second column was to force the positions of Warmenhuizen and Schoorldam; the third column was to carry Oudkarspel; and a fourth column was to march to the extreme left and attack Hoorn on the Zuider Zee, and from there envelop the enemy's right flank and rear.

On the evening of the 18th Abercromby marched off, and after a tiring twenty miles of bad roads found Hoorn sleeping. Without a shot the small garrison fell. The fourth column were too exhausted for further work, and Abercromby stayed at Hoorn waiting for news of the main attack.

Very early on the morning of the 19th two impatient battalions of Russians in the first column began the attack, and Herman, though realizing the attack was premature, went forward in support. Before dawn the enemy's first two lines had been carried; but many Russians had fallen, the troops were out of hand, and Herman, whose one soldierly virtue was courage, was not the man to restrain them. The first column was in hopeless confusion, and the French, hastily reinforced from the right, poured in a deadly fire. The Russians fell back, the retreat becoming a rout. Herman was left a prisoner, and General Essen succeeded him in command of the Russians.

News of the total defeat of the first column came to the triumphant Fifth, breathless from the storming of Schoorldam. With the second column they had moved off at daybreak; ahead of them on the right they could hear the spattering irregular fire of the Russians; but Dundas was not to be hurried; slowly and methodi-

[1] *First Column.*—General Herman and the Russians, 9th Brigade (Manners), and the 7th Light Dragoons.
 Second Column.—General David Dundas: 1st Brigade (D'Oyley), 2nd Brigade (Burrard), 8th Brigade (Prince William), and two squadrons of 11th Light Dragoons.
 Third Column.—Pulteney: 3rd Brigade (Coote), 5th Brigade (Don).
 Fourth Column.—General Abercromby: 4th Brigade (Moore), 7th Brigade (Chatham), 6th Brigade (Lord Cavan), Reserve (Macdonald).—" H. B. A.," iv., 671.

cally the low meadow country was cleared; flying bridges had to be made to cross the dykes, but by six o'clock Warmenhuizen was in sight. The village was held in some strength, but the 1st Brigade of Guards entered from one side and Sedmoratsky's Russians from the other, and carried it in good style. Dundas detached the 2nd Fifth and the 3rd Guards to keep up communications with the third column, and then with the rest of his force marched on to Schoorldam. The roads were so broken up and damaged that they were compelled to strike across country, while the three gunboats in support made their way down the great canal; by nine o'clock they came to the village, which the 1st Fifth helped to storm and carry, losing both officers and men. Lieutenant-Colonel Stephenson fell, severely wounded, and the command devolved on Lieutenant-Colonel Bligh. The Duke of York had accompanied the second column, and on the news of the Russian defeat he ordered up the troops left in reserve—Manners' brigade to attack Schoorl, and Prince William with the 35th Foot to cover Essen's retreat. Dundas detached two battalions of Russians in support of Manners, who found Schoorl deserted and on fire, having been first plundered. Manners then found himself in danger of attack; the Russians defied all attempts to rally them, and streamed away a drunken and defiant mob. More battalions were detached from the second column, and Dundas was left in a precarious position. For many hours he held Schoorldam under a heavy fire, but his position was made untenable by the rout of the first column, and at length he withdrew, his retreat covered by the gunboats in the canal.[1] This was accomplished in good

[1] Surgeon Fergusson wrote: " I verily believe that if the apparition of a French rifleman had risen up amongst our new troops, so stupified and confounded, as well as slaughtered, in a six hours' combat had they been, they would have fled like frightened children. This was a terrible state of things for the old Fifth. . . . It was found that the newly joined militia-men had never fired a ball-cartridge in their lives. . . . Through the indefatigable exertions of the old officers, in a few days they were made better " ("Notes and Recollections," p. 31).

order, and with little loss, for David Dundas was brave, and careful, and well skilled—a good soldier for all his crabbed austere character and the nineteen manœuvres which hampered his soldier's soul.

The third column, Pulteney's, had met with some success, but by the failure of the other columns this advantage had to be thrown away. The whole army retreated to its former position on the Zype. Certainly the victory lay with France, and the Allies lost confidence in their commander and in themselves. The Dutch were more openly hostile after the plunder of their villages.[1].

The Duke of York was not the man to command an army in the field; he was of fair understanding, but slow wits; of cool courage, but lacking that active bravery to seize the psychological moment; his good qualities were nullified by one indiscretion; as Bunbury said, " He was too apt to talk when drunk." His scathing comments on the behaviour of the Russians in general, and Essen in particular, naturally added to the discord between the Allies.

It rained without ceasing, and heavy gales blew from the south-west and delayed operations. The soldiers, still in light marching order, suffered severely. Private benevolence came to the rescue of the Government, and the good people in England sent out flannel shirts and strong shoes to the shivering men, and so saved many lives.

The Council of War discussed various plans of attack, and finally decided to repeat the operations of September 19th, and again advance in column, but with English troops, not Russian, in the place of honour. The French still held the same line; Warmenhuizen had been abandoned, but Schoorl and Koedyck, three miles

---

[1] Allies' losses: English, 6 officers and 127 men killed, and 44 officers and 397 men wounded, about 800 missing; Russian, total casualties between 2,000 and 3,000. The French and Dutch lost about the same, with the addition of 3,000 prisoners and 16 guns (Fortescue, H. B. A., iv., 680).

The Fifth lost Lieutenant Harris and 5 men killed, and Lieutenant-Colonel Stephenson and 4 men wounded, and 4 men missing (Cannon).

south-east, had been strengthened. To protect the French right the fenland round Oudkarspel had been flooded, making impossible any outflanking movement. The advance was ordered for October 2nd.

Abercromby was given command of the first column, about 8,000 infantry, which included the Reserve, composed of the massed grenadiers and light infantry, under Macdonald. A troop of Honourable Artillery and nine squadrons of cavalry were also attached, and the column was ordered to march by the coast over the sand-dunes, round the French left, and carry Egmont aan Zee in the rear. The second and third columns were ordered to co-operate with Abercromby and march upon Schoorl and Bergen, and Ketten and Schoorldam. Prince William's brigade was transferred to the fourth column under Pulteney, and was ordered to protect the English left and threaten the French right. Pulteney was not hampered by orders, but was bidden to seize any opportunity of attack. He was a man of ability and some scientific attainments, good tempered, cool in action, and utterly indifferent to danger; but, on the other hand, he was dreamy and undecided, and from his awkward manner and grotesque appearance failed to inspire his men. However, during this battle his column had no opportunity for action, though his judicious dispositions prevented any movement of the French right. The Fifth lay at Schagen.

The grenadier and light infantry companies marched off from Petten with the first column. The rain had ceased, the day broke fine and warm; by six the division was on its way; the French picket at Camperdown fell back before them. Coote's brigade of the third column swung off to the east, and Macdonald and the Reserve bore westward to cover Abercromby's flank. Macdonald, "a very wild warrior," quickly became entangled in a battle of his own; the sand-hills southwest of Groet sheltered small parties of French skirmishers; and Macdonald, engrossed in sweeping the little valleys and clearing hillock after hillock, lost himself among the dunes and left Abercromby in the air. All day the first column strove against the French attack, and at sundown, weary and exhausted, were still a mile or more from Egmont, with no word of Macdonald or the other columns. Coote had joined the second column; Groet and Schoorl had been taken; but at midday, after Sedmoratsky's Russians had helped to take Schoorldam, Essen halted the Russians and refused to march farther. The weakened columns of the English moved forward alone; and Coote, on the extreme right, suddenly found Macdonald and his lost battalion struggling through the sand. The Reserve joined in line, and a general advance drove the enemy before them and cut the direct communication between Bergen and the French troops in the dunes. The exhausted and weary men could do no more, and nightfall rendered the sand-hills an impossible battlefield.

Abercromby and Dundas bivouacked where they stood; Macdonald brought his men into Abercromby's lines. The Fifth would have disowned their flank companies, their clothes all filth and dust, mouths black from biting cartridges, and faces and shoulders bruised from the kick of the muskets. The water-bottles had been emptied at midday, and the salt air and sand caused a misery of thirst. Fresh water there was none, until the rain, for once welcome, came teeming down, then the men soaked their clothes and wrung the drops into their mouths. Of the 1,500 odd casualties the Reserve lost 300. The French losses were probably much the same as those of the Allies, with the addition of seven guns and a few hundred prisoners.

Brune quietly withdrew in the night, and took up a strong position from Wyk aan Zee to Beverwyck on the Hetz, carrying his line on to Purmerende. While the Duke's army dwindled away the French army increased, and, with further reinforcements, Brune covered his front with three lines of outposts. The English were suffering from lack of food—indeed, of supplies of all sorts—delay was impossible, so on October 6th the Allies again advanced. Essen on this occasion exceeded his orders and advanced beyond his supporting columns; at one moment he was threatened with total destruction, then a handful of English cavalry changed the fortune of the day. When night fell both armies retired to their former lines. The flank companies of the Fifth were again engaged, and in this action and that of the 2nd they lost several men killed and wounded. On the 2nd Captain Pratt of the second Battalion, and on the 9th Lieutenant Hamilton of the first Battalion, were wounded.[1] The detachment fought well, and received the particular thanks of the officer commanding.

The third of these costly attacks decided the Council that further advance was impossible. The Duke of York agreed that an immediate evacuation was desirable—ultimately it would become inevitable—and the longer the delay the greater the demoralization and weakening of the troops and the wider the breach between the Allies.

On October 7th began the melancholy pilgrimage north; the roads were bottomless; the country bare of all supplies; the wounded had to be left for want of waggons. The recruits, veterans by powder, but innocent of discipline, straggled all over the country. "Keep your places!" cried the adjutant. "Form two deep." "We're too deep already," answered the floundering men. About 300 camp followers, mostly women and children, fell into the enemies' hands, and were kept prisoners for three days at Amsterdam. Brune treated them most generously, and when they were sent back the children had all been fitted out with new clothes.

The battalion companies of the Fifth were far away out of all this clam-jam-fray. Pulteney's division[2] still held the line to the Zuider Zee, Prince William's brigade lying at Hoorn, on the extreme left. Facing them, Daendals commanded the French line, and when the retreat began he made a bold attempt to turn Pulteney's left.

[1] Cannon.   [2] Pulteney's Division, 5th, 8th, and 9th Brigades.

On the 10th both battalions of the Fifth, acting as rearguard, held the little village of Winkel, commanding the Winkel Canal; on them fell the full force of the French attack. It was a trying moment for young troops disheartened by retreat and conscious of their isolated position and the overwhelming force to their front. Bligh of the first Battalion kept his men well in hand, planted the colours of the regiment on the top of the dyke, and held his ground until he had news that the brigade was no longer in danger of being cut off. Then, while the enemy were attempting to cross the canal, he fell on them and drove them back in confusion.

Surgeon Fergusson described the action: " There was a good deal of firing in the advance, whence wounded men were being brought in; and we were waiting for orders in the cover of a village, when a staff officer galloped up, directing us to advance, for the enemy were turning our left, and we were to drive them back. We advanced accordingly along a broad sandy road in a column of companies, until a well-directed dropping fire (which struck down several men) came upon us from an invisible enemy out of an extensive beanfield on our left in front. The battalion was halted, and street firing was ordered into the bean-field. . . . This was accordingly begun, but as some could not be made to understand the order, others mistook it, calling out that retreat had been ordered, and many would not obey, firing from where they stood; so in a very short time we became as complete a medley as ever was seen. The enemy, for a moment, seemed puzzled (for the firing did not increase) at the strange performance that was being enacted before them; but indecision was none of their habits. They rose from their cover with loud cries, the beanstalks seemed instantaneously to be converted into armed men, and we were evidently on the brink of something very serious. Our commander, the Honourable Edward Bligh, a man of most chivalrous courage, had lately joined from the Guards, and had never, I believe, seen any service beyond the parade in St. James's Park. He proved himself, however, equal to the occasion. Two very young lads carried the Colours. He instantly seized upon one, and giving the other to our trusty veteran adjutant, called upon all to follow. The rush was made with all the goodwill of British soldiers, and the foe did not stand a moment; they were driven in the way I have above described."[1]

Talbot and the second Battalion were in reserve, and, in their turn, covered the orderly retirement of the first Battalion.

From Oude Sluys Prince William issued a general order: "Prince William desires Colonel Bligh and the first Battalion Fifth Regiment will accept his thanks for the gallant manner in which they attacked the enemy when he was passing through the canal opposite Winkel, and Lieutenant-Colonel Talbot and Lindsay of the 2nd Fifth for their exertion on the 10th instant."

After this repulse the Allies were allowed to retreat undisturbed, and by October 12th were safe within their former lines. The re-embarkation of the troops presented many difficulties, and Abercromby for one doubted very much if half the army would get safely away. Fortunately Brune did not know that only three days' supply of bread remained to the Allies, and an armistice was arranged and terms agreed upon —singularly easy ones for the Allies, in that they comprised the evacuation of the Helder, already decided, and the return of the 8,000 prisoners taken, whose removal would have presented serious difficulties.

Before the end of October the troops were all on their way to England; the weather was very stormy, and the transports overcrowded. The Fifth landed, a dirty, unkempt crew, very different from the gay parti-coloured battalions who had set out.[2] If they did not come back with fresh honours, at least no discredit was attached to them. The little victory

---

[1] "Notes and Recollections," pp. 31, 32.
[2] See Appendix for the Return of Great Coats and accoutrements lost by the 2nd Battalion in this campaign.

at Warmenhuizen was not a real test, for to attack is not hard to young troops; afterwards, in Pulteney's division, there was little fighting to be had until the day at Winkel; there veterans and militia boys stood fast and were proud to act as rearguard, and to be among the last to retreat. The flank companies saw more fighting, but under Macdonald the actions of October 2nd and 6th were too confused to prove or disprove any claim for especial merit.

As a whole, the Expeditionary Force behaved well; there was little or no crime, and there was all the material for a fine army if only the men had had some knowledge of drill, some acquaintance with their officers, some clothing, and a little food.

The Russian troops came over to England, and, after scandalizing the people of Yarmouth by drinking the oil out of the street lamps, were sent off to garrison Jersey and Guernsey.

The Fifth marched to Silver Hill Barracks, near Battle Abbey, where they were inspected by Major-General White, who found the regiment "a very good body of men, but needing two months to fit them for service."[1]

[1] In November of this year, Garnet Joseph Wolseley was gazetted lieutenant, shortly afterwards exchanging into the 25th Foot. He was the father of Field-Marshal Viscount Wolseley, and also of Surgeon-General Richard Wolseley, who joined the second Fifth in 1867, and who died at Meerut in 1886, leaving many devoted friends in the regiment.

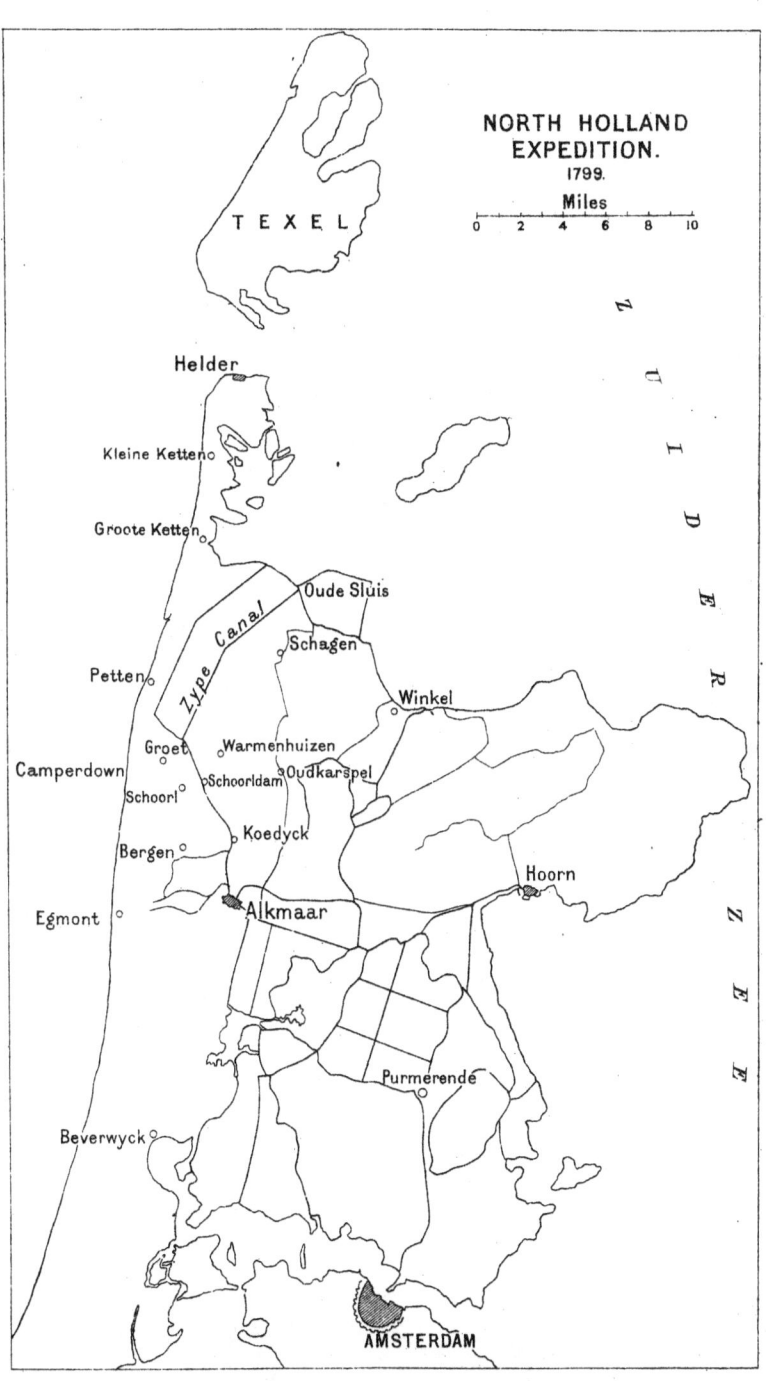

CHAPTER XXII

1799-1806

GEORGE III.

GIBRALTAR—GUERNSEY—HANOVER

Sir Alured Clarke—Richard England

On Christmas Eve, 1799, Napoleon became First Consul, and immediately set about to reorganize the disordered economy of France. The campaigns of the past year had ended in the disruption of the Allies, with Russia and Austria at loggerheads, and bad feeling, bred by the Helder expedition, between Russia and England. Prussia remained obstinately neutral, and only Austria agreed to fight on. England promised active co-operation in the Mediterranean, and on May 5th Sir Ralph Abercromby was appointed commander-in-chief of all the forces in the Mediterranean.

Both battalions of the Fifth had spent the winter at Silver Hill; other regiments, less fortunate, had been scattered all over the country, with the greater part of their officers away on leave. The high character borne by the senior officers of the Fifth leads one to hope that they were not so indifferent to matters of discipline as their contemporaries.

Early in 1800 the regiment was ordered to Gibraltar for garrison duty, and on April 12th the two battalions embarked at Torbay. The transports had come round from Deal with part of the Mediterranean Expeditionary Force on board, and there followed overland an unhappy regiment of women and children. Orders had come just before the sailing that no women or children were to accompany the army; hearing the fleet was at Torbay they made their way there in hopes of reprieve, but the order stood, and the women were left behind.

The officers were ordered on board on the 23rd, and the next day the fleet sailed, Commodore Page in the *Inflexible* commanding the escorting squadron. The first day out the convoy hailed a sloop-of-war, but she ran up Dutch colours and dashed all hopes of a sea-fight. The next day, in stormy weather, a strange sail was sighted, and two of the fastest ships were sent in chase; disappointment again, for she was found to be a friend. On Sunday the 27th the sea went down and the soldiers paraded on deck, the men in high spirits. One day the commodore made signal for great gun practice, and big guns were slid out and thundered defiance to the indifferent coast. The redcoats, not to be outdone, fired their small arms.

Three days later the transports with the Fifth on board and the *Serapis*, store-ship, parted company and came to Gibraltar, where the 28th Foot was in garrison.

More than seventy years had passed since the Fifth had left the fortress; in many ways the place had undergone little improvement. It was notorious for filth, deficient even in common sewers; the streets were unpaved and without effective scavenging arrangements. The drinking-water, supplied entirely from cisterns, was sometimes very scarce, always stale, and often bad. On the other hand, wine was cheap and plentiful, and wine-house licences were a recognized governor's perquisite. Under General O'Hara, governor since 1793, the fortress was garrisoned by a mob of " Bacchanalians dressed in scarlet as a mark of rejoicing!" Every soldier coming off a working-party was given 8d. to buy his drink of " blackstrap." Food was confined to one meal a day, called " The King's own," mess beef, or pork and pease-pudding. The sight of soldiers and sailors lying drunk in the filthy streets was too common to excite comment. " It was the mark of spirit and good fellowship among the officers to go to bed every night 'glorious,' and with them also it was only limited by the means."[1] In war-time the fortress was like a prison, no intercourse with the Spaniards was allowed; there were no amusements, and no ways of killing time other than by gambling or drinking.[2] No morning parade was held, only an evening one at the most lucid interval of the day, about 6 p.m. A garrison library had been recently started for the officers, each of whom on arrival gave one week's pay as subscription. The town had been almost destroyed during the great siege, and the new buildings were neither large nor beautiful.

General O'Hara was a brave man, an excellent linguist, and capable officer, and though under his governorship the discipline of the troops suffered very seriously yet he allowed no laxity to the garrison guard. The sentries were kept on the alert by frequent visits from the general himself. To distinguish mounted officers at a distance they all wore different feathers—general officers, black; colonels, blue; lieutenant-colonels, red; and so on.

In June Abercromby arrived, and learnt how Napoleon had crossed the Alps and was threatening to overwhelm the Austrians; on the 22nd he sailed for Mahon and Genoa, leaving the Fifth fretting at inaction. Marengo forced Austria to terms, the English attempt on Ferrol came to nothing, and the Mediterranean operations resolved themselves into the project of annihilating the French army in Egypt.

The Fifth had to possess their souls in patience; all the summer transports came in and sailed again, their late generals, Pulteney and Dundas, came and went. In October Abercromby put in for the last time before the old lion set out for his last fight. The 28th went with him, but not the Fifth. In November a fire burned down the Royal battery and gave them brief employment, but the winter was uneventful.

[1] Lieutenant-Colonel Wilkie, *U. S. J.*, iii., 1843.
[2] During General O'Hara's term of office he increased his income through the sale of wine-shop licences by some £7,000 a year. No cricket match or foot race could take place without wagering in wine.

The New Year opened auspiciously for Napoleon—Austria accepted terms; Naples turned from England to make peace; the Rhine was once more the boundary of eastern France; Prussia stood aloof; and the Tsar Paul was meditating a descent on British India. Spain agreed to declare war on Portugal if she did not desert her old ally. With the whole of Europe behind him Napoleon waited to crush England, an England weakened by the loss of Pitt, who resigned office in February.

Then the tide turned. In March Abercromby inflicted a decisive defeat, and in April Nelson at Copenhagen enforced the command of the seas. Russia was paralyzed by the assassination of Paul, and the new Tsar showed little inclination to remain the friend of France. Spain, however, stood by her contract, and, by purchase or hire, Napoleon secured six sail of the line from Cadiz; in addition, the Spanish fleet agreed to put to sea and attack Lisbon.

Then began exciting times. In June the enemy fleets were known to be at sea. On July 1st the French ships were first seen; Dundas, in the *Calpé*, sent a messenger to Admiral Sir James Saumarez, who with his squadron was blockading Cadiz. Soon after another despatch-vessel was sent off with the news that the French Admiral Linois, with three sail of the line and gunboats, had put into Algeciras. Sir James had hard work to bring his ships round from Cadiz; they tacked off shore; the *Cæsar* made signal for battle, and ordered the fleet to keep together; but the wind dropped, and the ships lay becalmed, drifting in the current. At last they were in sight, and in the early morning of July 6th came up line ahead—Hood in the *Venerable* leading, after him the *Pompée*, *Audacious*, *Cæsar*, *Spencer*, and *Hannibal*. Round Caprita Point the *Venerable* made signal that she saw the French ships, which lay close up under the Spanish batteries. The faint breeze gave the *Pompée*, *Venerable*, and *Audacious* the advantage, and they anchored close to the French ships. At nine in the morning the battle began; at ten, the *Hannibal* was ordered to support the *Pompée;* she cut her cables and tacked for the *Formidable,* whom the French admiral was trying to warp inshore; then she grounded, and with her signal halliards shot away lay under fire from ship and fort. The French ships cut their cables and ran aground, Saumarez making signal to his captains to pursue; but the wind had died away, and the Frenchmen escaped. The *Pompée* had suffered severely, and was towed off by the boats of the fleet, and was brought alongside the Mole at Gibraltar. All attempts to get the *Hannibal* off had failed, and at two in the afternoon she had been forced to haul down her colours. The rest of the battered ships came into Gibraltar, and all available hands set to work to repair the damage. Respite was brief; in the evening of the 9th the *Paisly,* brig, came crowding into the bay with the signal for an enemy flying, and the news that the French and Spanish fleet had escaped from Cadiz, and were on their way to join Linois. At three o'clock, while the enemy squadron were hauling round Caprita Point, the *Superb,* who had escaped the late fight, and the *Thames,* frigate, anchored in Gibraltar Bay. The *Cæsar* lay in the Mole, so shattered from her battle that the admiral had changed his flag to the *Audacious.* The *Pompée* was for the time being a wreck, and her crew was distributed among the fleet, and Saumarez decided to draft the *Cæsar's* crew as well. Her captain and the crew prayed to be allowed to remain on board as long as possible, and day and night the work of repair went on, the redcoats lending a willing hand. On the 12th, when the enemy began to move, the *Cæsar* was taking in stores and almost ready for sea.

This July day was a Sunday, the weather fine and very clear; by midday the enemy ships were well under way, and the towering white sails came steadily over the blue water. The entire population of the Rock came out to witness the fight; the Lime-walk, Mole-head, and batteries were crowded to the Ragged Staff. At one o'clock the *Cæsar* warped out, the bands playing "Come, cheer up, my lads, 'tis to glory we steer," the soldiers cheered them, and the garrison band replied with "Britons, strike home." At three o'clock the *Cæsar* passed under the stern of the *Audacious* and rehoisted the admiral's flag. Then signal was made to weigh and prepare for action. The English squadron was quickly at sea and sailing after the enemy, who were seeking refuge rather than battle. The pageant was over, the soldiers disappointed of their show. West went the great *Real Carlos* and *Hernenegildo*, each of 112 guns, and eight other sail of the line, and after them the *Cæsar* and her sister ships; darkness fell before the low booming of the guns again lined the walls. Afterwards the soldiers learned how the *Hannibal* had been avenged—the *Real Carlos* and the *Hernenegildo* set on fire and destroyed, and the *St. Antoine* captured; the other ships of the combined squadron making good their escape. If the Fifth had none of the glory, at least they, as dockyard maties, did their share of the work.[1]

The garrison of the Rock was each month reinforced by victorious sailors and soldiers, full of prize money, and anxious to begin the spending. Then General O'Hara died, and was buried in the garrison cemetery, and with him died many of the old infamous privileges. A young prince, the Duke of Kent, was appointed to succeed him, and from the outset he refused to make money by the degradation of the men who worked and fought for England. The Fifth did not benefit by his administration, for they were ordered to England early in 1802.

[1] BRITISH.	SPANISH.	FRENCH.
Cæsar, 80.	*Real Carlos*, 112 (blown up).	*Formidable*, 80.
Venerable, 74.	*Hernenegildo*, 112 (blown up).	*Indomptable*, 80.
Superb, 74.	*San Fernando*, 96.	*Saint Antoine*, 7 (taken).
Spencer, 74.	*Argonauta*, 80.	*Desaix*, 74.
Audacious, 74.	*San Augustina*, 74.	*Libre* (frigate).
Thames (frigate).	*Sabina* (frigate).	*Muiron* (frigate).
Calpé (sloop).		

In the previous October preliminary peace negotiations had been discussed, and in March a definite treaty was signed at Amiens. The terms of this treaty made it improbable that it would be a lasting one; France had both too much and too little to rest content, and the menace to the Central Powers was unaltered. England, ever timid in statecraft, again threw away much that her soldiers had won for her, for the Ministry had not the courage to withstand the tradesman clamour for peace, neither had they the courage to uphold that peace by maintaining the Services at proper strength.

Immediate reduction was ordered, and the brief life of the second Battalion came to an end. On landing, they marched to Winchester, and there disbanded.

In 1801 Sir Alured Clarke had been made colonel of the 7th Foot; Major-General Sir Richard England, colonel-commandant of the second Battalion, succeeded him as colonel of the Fifth, August 21st, 1801. England had entered the service as ensign in 1766, and had served seventeen years in the 47th; in 1783 he went to the 24th as lieutenant-colonel, and in 1796 he became major-general. He was a man of considerable bulk, very tall, and proportionately broad. On his return from abroad he attended the Duke of York's levee; as soon as he had turned his back and was out of hearing, the Duke exclaimed, " England ! England ! Great Britain, by God !" In August, 1803, he became governor of Portsmouth.

The Fifth were not allowed to remain long in England, but were sent off to Guernsey, the Russians having returned to their own country. In war-time garrisons in the Channel Islands were kept on the alert, for a raid was certain to take place sooner or later. In peace-time the resources of Guernsey were quickly exhausted; fortunately the climate was good, the land productive, and the cider excellent. The little island proved a good training-ground, and Stephenson made the most of his time.

Early in the year England was at war again; doubt of the good faith of France, and the fear of Napoleon's designs in the East, brought about the rupture. On May 16th England declared war. In the East and the West Indies the peace had received scant recognition; France had allowed her fleet to grow dangerously weak, and one by one the French and Dutch possessions were taken. Napoleon retaliated by invading Hanover, and kept that kingdom as hostage, closing the Elbe and Weser to English trade, and using his conquest as a threat to Prussia. He then ordered Spain to declare herself his ally, sent an army to Italy, and prepared to invade England. Addison's Ministry hurriedly tried to counterplot; Militia Bills and Volunteer Acts followed each other in hopeless confusion.

Charles Stephenson[1] left the Fifth after twenty-five years' service to command a new regiment; he was a brave and skilful officer, a man of tact and resource, and had justly earned General Doyle's praise for the discipline he maintained. William Cockell became lieutenant-colonel. Captain George Hill, commanding at Vale Castle, was sent home to recruit; he went to Boston in Lincolnshire, and over the old recruiting ground. While in England he heard from Stephenson, who wrote to offer him the first majority in his new regiment. Hill, a married man with a large family, standing second on the captains' list, accepted Stephenson's offer. Events in Europe put an end to West African philanthropic schemes, and Stephenson's regiment was never raised; he himself was appointed adjutant-general under the Duke of Gloucester, his late brigadier, who was commanding the London District. Hill eventually joined the 85th, and as major in that regiment was killed in the Walcheren Expedition. " . . . Whose conduct as an officer, whose zeal as a soldier, and whose integrity as a man endeared him to all the honourable men of his profession, who sincerely regret his loss."[2]

[1] Stephenson was gazetted colonel to a regiment to be forthwith raised, composed of West Africans, and called "The York Rangers," to be employed in the abolition of the slave trade.
[2] *Morning Post.*

In the spring of 1804 a young recruit was drafted to a reserve regiment garrisoned at Guernsey with the Fifth. In his ill-fitting uniform, learning an endless drill with others as awkward as himself, he gazed across the barracks with envious eyes. There lay the Fifth regiment, as he afterwards wrote:[1] "Whose neat appearance, personal cleanliness, long white feathers waving in the wind, their bright breastplates, and powdered patrician dressed heads (volunteering too), presented so many attractions as, taken together, were irresistible." And so Stephen Morley and two others left the hated Reserve and volunteered to serve with the Fifth, attesting June 4th.

Morley had an eye for dress, and describes the uniform that so took his fancy: "A long-tailed coat, white pantaloons, and Hessian boots, with hair tied and powdered, and a cocked hat. This was the dress of the officers, to which the staff-sergeants wore an affinity in the hat, with silver laced coats. The men's dress was perfectly white, except the stocks, queues, and shoes, when on fatigue; but when dressed for parade their coats were froglaced, with facings of gosling green, white breeches and gaiters, and hair tied and powdered or (may I acknowledge it?) well whitened with flour."

Another young man to be noted also joined at this time, Ensign John Bent, from the Devon Militia.

In May Pitt returned to power, and at once instituted a bold scheme for raising recruits for the regulars, and from these the Fifth filled up ranks. There was still a leaven of old soldiers, called "Americans," from having served in the American War. Captain Pratt of the grenadier company, Lieutenant and Adjutant Clark, Quartermaster Creighton Irwin, Sergeant Bruce,[2] Sergeant Bennett,[3] Drummer Adam Brand, and Drum-

---

[1] See "Memoirs of a Sergeant of the Fifth Regiment" (Stephen Morley).

[2] Bruce, afterwards an ensign in a Veteran battalion (Morley).

[3] Sergeant-Major John Hall was made adjutant to the Reserve, and Bennett became sergeant-major in his place. In 1824 Hall was made a captain in the 21st regiment (Morley).

Major Thomas Armstrong had served upwards of twenty years, and were regarded by the recruits with veneration. Of the remainder a considerable number had joined the regiment at Barham Downs in 1799, and had served with the Fifth in Holland and at Gibraltar.

One morning on parade a letter was handed to Lieutenant-Colonel Cockell, who immediately informed his officers that a second battalion was to be raised forthwith, that he was gazetted a brigadier, and that Humphry Davie, major since July, 1796, was to succeed him in command of the first Battalion. Captain Pratt became major of the second Battalion. On August 4th, Captain the Hon. Henry King,[1] from the 43rd regiment, was gazetted major to the first Battalion; he was a man of twenty-eight who had seen much service and had the reputation of being a good soldier.

In December the Fifth left the " pleasant and delightful " island of Guernsey for Haslar Barracks, and from there marched to Colchester, " where we found Sir James Craig, Sir James Pulteney, Sir David Baird, general officers, besides General Sherbrooke. In those capacious barracks were, besides our own regiment, the 34th, the 3rd, 2nd, and 3rd Royal Lancashire Militia."

" There we had plenty of drills, and nearly every day were under arms from four or five in the morning till twelve, one, or two o'clock in the day. It was often said that the skins of Generals Craig and Pulteney were insensible, for after they and ourselves had been for hours complêtely drenched, they would raise their hats, and, with perfect nonchalance, exclaim, ' I think it rains.' "[2] John Bent went off to his own country

---

[1] Henry King, born July, 1776; fourth son of the second Earl of Kingston. He was educated at Eton and Harrow, and Exeter College, Oxford. In 1794 he joined the 47th as ensign; lieutenant 1795; and captain in the 56th in 1796. Captain King served at St. Domingo and in the Holland campaign of 1799, when, on September 19th, he had been severely wounded in both legs. From this wound he never really recovered. From the 56th King went to the 1st Foot Guards with sick leave (December, 1799), and to the 43rd regiment in 1802.

[2] Morley.

and recruited for the Fifth at Crediton in Devon, securing 200 fine young men from his old militia.

In December Spain had declared war on England; Portugal dared not assist her old ally; Holland and the Republic of Italy were practically French provinces; Austria, exhausted by the late war, lay quiescent; and Prussia waited to make sure of the winning side. Pitt opened negotiations with Russia, and Alexander was not unwilling; together, by promises of support and subsidy, they induced Austria to join the Alliance.

In May, 1805, a treaty was signed at Petersburg; the evacuation of Italy, Hanover, and North Germany by the French, the independence of Holland and Switzerland, and the security of the Kingdom of Naples and the re-establishment of the Kingdom of Sardinia were the principal objects.[1]

Napoleon was perfectly aware of the coalition against him. Using the Boulogne Camp as a blind he made plans for a campaign in Austria. The attempts of the Allies to recover Naples ended in failure, and when the Austrians retreated before the French armies Naples turned on the Allies.

Pitt still dreamt of the invasion of Holland and the recovery of Hanover. Many refugees, the King's subjects, had fled to England, and the King's German Legion grew daily in strength. The senior officers urged a descent on Hanover, and, with the co-operation of the Russian armies, an attack on Holland from the east. Gustavus IV., the mad king of Sweden, joined the coalition and promised help. Frederick William was asked to guarantee the Allies a passage through Prussia, but the vacillating King refused to make any promises. The Hanoverians urged immediate action; the season was late, the rivers might close at any time; the presence of a large force might induce Prussia to defy France.

After many delays Van de Decken of the German Legion sailed in advance to make arrangements for the wintering of the force, which was to enter the

[1] Fortescue, " History of British Army," vol. v., p. 243.

Elbe, disembark at Gluckstadt, occupy and fortify Stade, and establish magazines at Cuxhaven and Bremenlade.

Van de Decken arrived on November 8th, and reported that Russian and Swedish troops were advancing from the west, a Prussian contingent was in Hanover on the Ems, and a French corps of observation was concentrated at Nienburg, and Hameln on the Weser.

Major-General Don arrived on the 17th, and found the King of Sweden on the field and the Russian commander-in-chief, Tolstoy, absent. Gustavus considered himself slighted and refused to move forward; Tolstoy arrived, and wished to besiege Hameln. Frederick William was nibbling at the Allies' bait, and while one minister haggled at St. James's another, Haugnitz, was sent with an ultimatum to Napoleon. He arrived in an inauspicious moment: the Austrians had suffered defeat; Ulm had fallen (October 20th): the Russians had retreated; the French occupied Brunn; and Napoleon had entered Vienna. Haugnitz came to him there, heartened by the news of Trafalgar; but before the interview Austerlitz was fought, and Austria lay in the dust. The ultimatum was changed to a letter of congratulation, and Prussia agreed that the Allies should not be allowed passage through Prussia into Holland.

Lord Cathcart had been sent from England with further troops, with orders to disembark in the Weser and take command of the Anglo-Hanoverian force; and, before Pitt was notified of Prussia's decision, more regiments had been despatched from England, among them the 1st Fifth.[1] The regiment had been warned for service, and was on its way to embark at Ramsgate. Early in November they were at Canterbury, and there

---

[1] Troops of the Second Division which arrived in the Weser on or before January 1st, 1806:
    First Brigade (Sir Arthur Wellesley).
    Second Brigade (Major-General Fraser).
    Third Brigade (Major-General Sherbrooke): 1st Fifth (5 companies only, 480 strong), 2/27th (6 companies only, 251 strong), 2/34th (402 strong).

Lieutenant-Colonel Davie and Captain P—— fell out. On Sunday, November 17th, at 8 o'clock in the morning, the two met in the brickfields behind the barracks. They fought with pistols, at ten paces. P—— fell, shot in the right breast.

The weather was very rough and stormy, foul winds delayed the news of Austerlitz, and it was not until December 29th that the Ministry learnt of the disaster. Cathcart, who had heard the news on arrival at Cuxhaven, had wisely retained his transports, seeing that the project was at an end. Austria was forced to terms; Prussia could not be trusted; the Swedes refused to move; Alexander had placed the Russian troops under Frederick William, the tool of France. France opened negotiations with England, and on January 21st Cathcart was ordered to withdraw. By February 13th all was ready, and on the 15th the transports sailed with a fair wind and came safe back to England.

Though this campaign had proved a bloodless one, yet the Fifth had temporarily lost half the first Battalion. Recruited to full strength from militia regiments, they had embarked at Ramsgate on December 9th in the *Brunswick* and the *Helder*.[1] The *Brunswick* arrived safely in the Weser, but the *Helder*, a large armed transport, formerly a Dutch brig-of-war, suffered shipwreck. Escorted by the *Leopard*, 64, she had sailed from the Downs on the 22nd, and in the night parted

[1] Return of officers and men embarked on board the *Helder* December, 1805, left wing:

	Officers.	Sergeants.	Drummers.	Rank and File.
Fifth	24	25	9	413
3rd (Buffs)	2	1	0	45

Officers of the Fifth Regiment.—Major: Henry King. Captains: Charles Broke, Gregory Way, Nicholas Hamilton,* Thomas Emes, Martin Armstrong. Lieutenants: John Simcockes, John Hamilton,* John Spearman, Fred. W. Hutchinson, Robert Dobson, Wm. Hamilton,* Patrick Bishop, David E. Johnson, Robert Bateman, John Crosdaile, C. E. Bird, R. M. Bates. Ensigns: Henry Green, Michael Doyle, Richard Croker, H. L. Hopkins. Paymaster: John Hamilton.* Assistant-Surgeon: W. MacKish.

* John Hamilton and his three sons were all serving with the Fifth at the same time. Nicholas lost a leg at Flushing, and William died of Walcheren fever.

company with her escort; fortunately, the next day she fell in with a fleet from the Nore, escorted by the *Regulus*, and proceeded in company. The weather was fine, wind fair and moderate, but, running close to the Dutch coast, the transport grounded at about ten o'clock in the night. She was bumping badly, and, at first, the deck was crowded with men and women, who ran from side to side fearing each moment she would capsize. Major King was on board, and he managed to restore order. Many of the convoy saw their distress, but stood off, fearing themselves to run aground. Every moment the *Helder* drove further on to the bank, and threatened to break up. Her guns of distress brought no answering signal from the convoy; no boat was sent to them; the transport had 600 men on board, and was greatly overcrowded; but all night the troops behaved with the utmost order and obedience to their officers. The morning of the 24th was very foggy; the Jack was hoisted upside down at the mizzen peak, and the crew set to work to make a raft. An ensign of the Buffs had escaped in the jolly boat when the ship first struck; and the gig had been sent away to ask help from the commodore; after all attempts to get the ship off failed the launch and the cutter were hoisted out. The launch came back with the news that land was in sight, and once more the *Helder* fired her guns. This time they were answered by musketry. At 1.30 p.m. the captain of the Dutch admiral's ship came on board with a flag of truce, and Major King agreed to surrender as prisoners. The fog lifted, and just as the Dutch boats came alongside the boats from the commodore's ship were seen in the offing. The water was too shallow for the *Regulus* to approach, and seeing the Dutchmen, the English boats returned. Under a flag of truce word was sent by the lieutenant of the *Regulus* of the loss of the *Helder* and the safety of her passengers and crew. A sergeant and private of the Fifth were drowned; their bodies washed ashore a few days later. The prisoners remained on board the Dutch men-of-war until December 30th, when they were sent to the town of Enkhuysen on parole. They had been treated not unkindly by their captors, but were suffering much discomfort for want of clothes. The *Helder* broke up shortly after the taking off of the men, and the swell had prevented the removal of the baggage.

Enkhuysen was a large, though decayed, town. At first the English were left alone, but after a few days a company of Dutch soldiers marched in as guard. The officers were required to report each day at the Stadt House; later this formality was dispensed with. They received nothing but politeness from the Dutch, who displayed no animosity towards the English nor affection towards the French.

On January 21st Major King was informed that he and twelve other officers would be sent to England on parole. That night he dined with the admiral on board his yacht, and the next day sailed for England, where, after a rough voyage, he landed at Sheerness February 2nd.

The rank and file were interned for some time longer, with an ever-present fear of being sent as prisoners into the interior of France. They were herded together in prison ships, old hulks, damp and full of disease.

When, late in the summer, news came that the right wing had landed in England, Nicholas Hamilton was sent off with a small escort to Chelmsford, where he met the ragged filthy companies, weakened by starvation and sickness. Hamilton drew a hundred pounds on the agents and bought clothing and necessaries. Plenty of beer and kindness put new life into the men, and they set off for Rye. On their way they met a jolly crew; a troop of Life Guards came flashing down the road; then a train of waggons, manned by singing sailors, treasure from Buenos Ayres, captured Spanish hoards. A league from Rye the grenadier company awaited them with the drummers and fifes, and to the old tune the lost half battalion at last came marching in.

The right wing had found Pladen Barracks near Rye a very pleasant place; Sunday evenings were a kind of gala, the band played from parade to sunset, and numbers of the well-dressed people strolled in the barrack-yard. While at Rye Sir Arthur Wellesley came down to review the regiment, and Morley, with his eye for colour, remarked on the shade of the staff's pantaloons, something between scarlet and crimson.

Major-General Sherbrooke reported the men " stout and healthy," but the officers and sergeants not so smart or correct as before the Hanover expedition.

The Fifth had been again warned for service, and this inspection was a preliminary to marching orders.

CHAPTER XXIII

1806-1807

GEORGE III.

BUENOS AYRES

RICHARD ENGLAND

NAPOLEON found himself in the New Year with half Europe at his feet. Austria, after Austerlitz, had acceded to all his demands; he was King of Italy, and arbiter of the fate of Naples; the Holy Roman Empire was at an end. Holland was no longer a republic, but a prospective kingdom, ruled by a Bonaparte as his brother's vassal.

The English Ministry declined to discuss terms of peace unless such terms were agreed to by her late ally, Russia. England was the only obstacle between Napoleon and the command of the Mediterranean and road to the East. The Russian army were cajoled into accepting terms; and Napoleon then turned to England, bereft of her last ally, and offered her Hanover if she would evacuate Sicily and withdraw from the Mediterranean.

In the midst of these negotiations newsletters reached England from Commodore Sir Hume Popham and Colonel Beresford asking that reinforcements should be sent immediately to South America; for, without orders, the commodore had planned and initiated an attack on the Spanish colonies of the River Plate. Popham wrote enthusiastically of the ease of the task and the treasure to be won; he did not confine his predictions to the Ministry, but spread among the merchants and city tradesmen an advertisement of his scheme.

The idea itself was not a new one, but had before found favour with adventurers. In August, 1805, Popham had sailed, with Sir David Baird, to the Cape against the Dutch colonies, and the expedition had been entirely successful. The commodore, who had led a " miscellanous sort of life," was in his element with transports and landing-parties. His restless, adventurous soul was not content; an American merchant's tale of the unrest in the Spanish colonies set him on fire, and away he sailed, with one regiment, six light dragoons, no ammunition or battering train, one sapper subaltern, but no miners or military artificers, and few entrenching tools. With something under a thousand men Popham set out to conquer a country half as large as Europe, and defended by an entirely unknown force. He was joined at St. Helena by a detachment of troops with artillery, and about May 15th the transports came to the mouth of the River Plate. The commanding officers did not waste time; the lighter transports made their way up the river; Beresford and his little force landed eight miles from Buenos Ayres, scattered the outer line of defence and summoned the town to surrender. His terms were agreed to, and at the cost of one man killed and a few wounded Beresford obtained possession of a town of 70,000 inhabitants, defended by eighty-six guns. Popham wrote even more enthusiastic newsletters of the captured El Dorado, but before they could arrive, or Baird send reinforcements, the game of bluff was over. Led by Liniers, a French colonel in the Spanish service, the people rose, and, after a desperate fight, Beresford and his men were forced to surrender. Then the threatened revolution took place; the Spanish viceroy fled, and a new republic arose, united against a common enemy in the English. Beresford and his army were carried prisoners into the interior. Popham maintained a blockade of the mouth of the river pending the arrival of reinforcements. Baird sent him two regiments, and, after an abortive attempt to batter down Monte Video, he took possession of the Island of Goretto and wintered there. The first reinforcements sailed from England on October 9th, with Sir Samuel Auchmuty in command; at the same time other regiments were sent on board the transports to await sailing orders. The first Fifth marched to Portsmouth September 25th, and embarked there, 836 strong; then proceeded to Spithead, where they lay in company with four other regiments—Robert Crauford, a very junior colonel, in command of the brigade.

Auchmuty reached Goretto, after a long voyage, on January 5th. Two days later Popham was superseded and sent home, forced to pay his own passage in a merchant brig, with the certainty of a court-martial before him, and many indignant and mulcted tradesmen to conciliate.

Auchmuty, too weak to attempt Buenos Ayres, turned to Monte Video, and on February 3rd the town was stormed and carried. All hope that the Republic might turn to England as an ally was dissipated by the report of Beresford, who escaped from the interior and made his way to Monte Video. He assured the general that the interference of Great Britain was even more unpopular than the rule of Spain. Liniers had been installed as governor in the capital, with the Spanish viceroy a prisoner in his hands.

Meanwhile, Crauford and his army, forty transports and four sail of the line, had left England with orders to circumnavigate the globe, land on the west coast of South America, march 900 miles across an unknown continent and over the Andes, to take the revolutionaries in the rear. The soldiers mixed with the sailors, sharing their work; each morning, to cheer them, the bandsmen assembled on the poop. In the Bay the winds blew, and for fourteen days raw recruit and seasoned veteran wished himself safe on land again. Bandsmen and instruments rolled in a headlong race over the decks, and the pork and pease in the galleys. Then, with a fair wind, they came to Madeira, where some of the transports put in for a store of wine. At Cape Verde Islands they anchored in Porto Praga harbour, where they stayed a month waiting for Admiral Murray and his squadron. The days passed pleasantly enough: fine weather—" Hot in December !" exclaims Morley—abundance of game and fishing, and for greater excitement the adventures of King in the Carabineers, who went ashore with a sack in which to stuff the Portuguese governor and sell him to a slaver lying in the harbour. The governor's pistol missed fire and saved a tragical ending.

In January Crauford vowed he would wait no longer for Murray. Persuading Admiral Stopford to act as escort he sailed again, and on February 23rd came to Table Bay, some of the bad sailors among the transports not arriving until two or three weeks later. Morley says his transport, the *Atlas*, arrived March 31st,[1] and adds: " We were most liberally supplied with fresh meat and vegetables by our officers, and from them received every kindness and every comfort which humanity could bestow. Never were there such officers and such men together !"

A rumour went round the fleet that orders had been changed, and gradually the news of the recapture of Buenos Ayres and the surrender of Beresford became known. Murray was waiting for Crauford at the Cape: a fast frigate came with orders from England, and, as soon as the transports were victualled, they put to sea again, making for St. Helena, with a fair wind. A week at St. Helena and then across the Atlantic, and the nearer to America the more adverse blew the wind. The sea-stock failed, and the soldiers were reduced to Government ration, " as tough as shoe-leather, which was swallowed in sober silence by the long faces assembled round the dinner-table."[2] Symptoms

---

[1] This may be in error, possibly the date was earlier. Morley's account of this expedition and of the attack on Buenos Ayres is confused, and was probably written many years afterwards. Major King's account has been used in preference to Sergeant Morley's.
[2] Tom Plunket, *U. S. J.*, 1842.

of scurvy began to appear, and when at last the fleet came in sight of the mouth of the Plate, their troubles were not over, for a storm blew up, cables parted, and the old hulks drove all night before the gale. By morning the fleet was scattered, and it was some days before the water-logged hulks beat their weary way back to Monte Video. They came dropping in one by one; it was the middle of June before all the troops were landed.

On May 10th Lieutenant-General John Whitelocke had arrived in a frigate, sent out to supersede Auchmuty and take the supreme command. At St. Domingo, in 1794, Whitelocke had won a certain reputation, perhaps not altogether an enviable one: he had blustered himself into favour with the Duke of York, and had the reputation of being a smart officer and great martinet. He was the terror of all subaltern officers, whom he disciplined with contempt, and the laughing-stock of the soldiers, whom he flattered by a knowledge of their nicknames and barrack-room slang.

Auchmuty had already won golden opinions from his men, and regret at his supersession was ill-concealed. Whitelocke, jealous at once, held this a grievance throughout the whole campaign.

With the arrival of Crauford's force Whitelocke began his advance. The army was divided into four brigades, Sir Samuel Auchmuty in command of the first, which included 1st Fifth, 38th, and 87th. Of the 38th, two companies, although in good order, were left with other battalions to garrison Monte Video.

The Fifth had no sooner landed than they were once more ordered on board ship; in light-draught vessels, " packed like herrings in a barrel," when one lay down another must stand up, they sailed up the river. In the smooth waters it was not unpleasant. The fleet called at Colonia for Auchmuty's outpost, and then crossed the river to Ensenada de Barragon, where, June 28th, the disembarkation began. On shore lay the corpse of a freshly killed tiger, shot by a Spaniard the night before. The ghost of that tiger kept the sentries particularly alert.

Buenos Ayres was thirty miles away, no foe was in sight, the landing met with no obstruction. Leveson Gower, second in command of the expedition, was sent on to occupy some rising ground four miles away; with him went Crauford's brigade and two battalions from Auchmuty, leaving Sir Samuel with only the Fifth. On both sides of the river the low marshy land extended from two to four miles inland. Beyond the swamp the ground rose gently to a height of twelve to fifteen feet, and this higher ground extended as far as Reduction, a village nine miles from Buenos Ayres. Between Reduction and the capital was another stretch of swampy ground, reaching far inland and crossed by several streams.

The next day the main army began their march. Like Gower, they quickly found that between the shore and the heights lay a bog covered with water two feet or more in depth. The Fifth had been cheered on their landing by the capture of the first prisoner, a large pig, which was quickly killed, roasted, and eaten; and now they needed all their good spirits, for they were called on to help to pull the artillery through the bog. There were tracks across where the mud and water were only knee-deep, but to deviate one inch meant to plunge up to the shoulders. The army was in good spirits, and even when the guns stuck fast the footsoldiers, Fifth and others, only paused in their efforts to thrust in a dirty arm and fish for a lost shoe or rusted musket; they could raise a halloo, too, at sight of snipe or ostrich, or vow they saw a tiger in the reeds.

At last they floundered on to the higher ground, and halted for the night, having advanced barely six miles. A few mounted skirmishers appeared but remained at a discreet distance. Food was none too plentiful; the swamp had devoured the major part of the biscuit and spirit landed; much that the soldiers carried had been spoilt by the liquid mud; and, by faulty staff-work some of the battalions failed to receive the three days' rations ordered to be carried. "If a general himself does not attend to the supply of his troops, sir, they will often want provisions," coldly said the Fifth's brigadier in reply to General Whitelocke. Fortunately great droves of cattle wandered over the treeless region, and, with farmhouse poultry and an odd bullock or two, the army managed to ration itself. Whitelocke's arrangements were altogether inadequate. Reduction was two days' march distant; nothing could be hoped for from the country between, so with a small portion of biscuit salved from the bog, and a commandeered flock of sheep, the army moved forward. The 38th and 87th were returned to Auchmuty, and his brigade led the way; and when at sunset on the 30th the main body halted, the Fifth, with the remainder of the brigade, the 95th, and cavalry, were sent forward some four or five miles. The next day the army reached Reduction, and were able to provision from the fleet. The weather had broken, and the first torrents of the rainy season fell.

Very early on the morning of July 2nd Whitelocke ordered Gower forward; he was to cross the Chuelo, which lay between Reduction and Buenos Ayres, and then march round and threaten the north of the city. The Fifth, with the main body, encamped in the village and rejoiced at the thought of a peaceful day; the sight of bullock carcases in the market-place gave them hopes of a good feed at last. Suddenly orders came to leave the meat and the uncooked dinner and march at once. At ten in the morning the starving army set out, Gower an hour's march ahead with Crauford's and Lumley's brigades, Crauford leading. They managed to cross the Chuelo at the Paso Chico. Had Gower pressed on with decision the town might have fallen, for Liniers was completely taken by surprise; his guns and a large body of troops were guarding the bridge on the main road, and the column sent to watch the Chico ford arrived after Gower had crossed in safety.

The main army for some time kept Gower in sight, but on reaching the river Whitelocke bore to the left to avoid the Paso Chico, not realizing that it was practically unguarded, and that the advance column had been able to cross unmolested. By the river the army wandered along, all trace of Gower lost, and after sundown there was little chance of finding a ford. In the darkness, and still on the wrong side of the river, Whitelocke halted for the night. He was not man enough to carry his exhausted troops on to the sound of guns that came from the capital.

Before daylight the army was on the road, and by one o'clock had crossed the river, which was running so high that it was with great difficulty the men got their ammunition safely over. " How a young gentleman, Ensign Hopkins, got over," Morley never learnt; " he was a mere boy, and very short." Whitelocke marched on to the capital and joined Gower, whose summons to surrender Liniers had treated with scorn. The rain was falling in torrents, and the troops were ordered to shelter in the houses of the suburbs for the night. A council of war was ordered for the next morning.

The streets of Buenos Ayres run east and west and south and north with the greatest regularity, and divide the town like a chess-board. The proposed plan of attack was very simple: the army, divided into thirteen columns, was to advance along as many streets; part of the force was eventually to concentrate on the Plaza de Toros—an open space at the north-east corner of the town, where the artillery barracks, arsenal, and amphitheatre stood—the remaining columns were to capture the line of houses along the river and to form up on the roofs. The attack was ordered for noon, but, by Auchmuty's protests, was delayed a day to allow of a brief reconnaissance of the ground.

Before dawn on July 5th the army took up its position; Auchmuty's brigade was placed on the left, to attack the northern end of the town—the 38th and 87th in two wings, Auchmuty accompanying the right wing; then the Fifth, also in two wings, Major King commanding the left and Colonel Davie the right. On the right, south of the Fifth, came Lumley's brigade, the 36th being the left-hand regiment; south of Lumley were the Light Brigades, under Pack and Crauford.[1]

[1] This included the light infantry company of the Fifth, commanded by Captain G. B. Way.

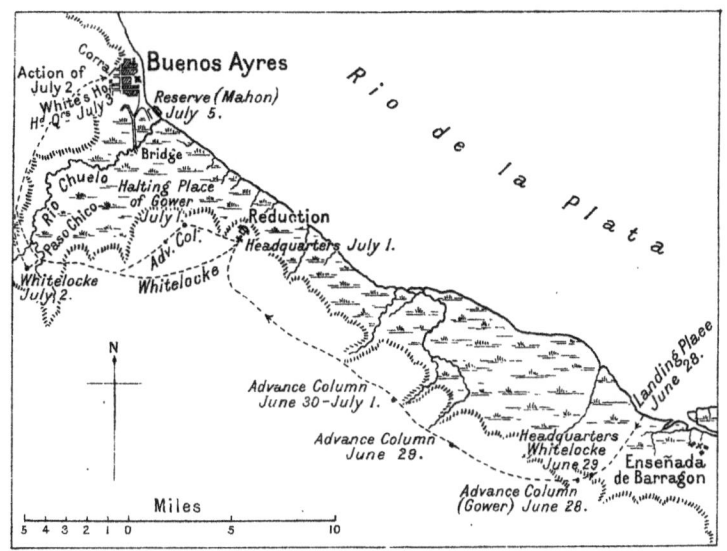

THE ATTACK ON BUENOS AYRES

The enemy had recovered from their shock of the 2nd, when Crauford had come headlong to the town. Liniers would not hear of surrender; the houses were particularly well adapted for resistance—substantially built, and with bars fixed to the lower windows, and flat roofs guarded by parapets. Cannon were stationed in the streets, and every man, woman, and child resolved to do their utmost to keep their liberty.

Auchmuty discussed the attack with his battalion and wing commanders, and gave them verbal instructions as to the roads to be followed.

The signal for attack was made; Lieutenant-Colonel Davie and the right wing of the Fifth marched straight down their appointed route without encountering any opposition; by seven o'clock they occupied the church of St. Catalina, and the King's Colours flaunted on the tower.

Major King led the left wing; they entered the town in quick time. On their left the 87th were already engaged, and they could hear the rallying shouts of the company officers. From a side street four Spanish guns appeared; retiring before the 87th they swung round and opened on the Fifth, and at the same time an irregular volley came from the roofs. King gave the order, and the left wing charged the guns, the front rank of the leading section with fixed bayonets. The enemy fled, and King's men pursued their triumphant way to the river. There was another burst of firing on the left, and two officers of the 87th, both badly wounded, came up with a tale of strong opposition and heavy losses. King decided on his headquarters. With entrenching tools a house was broken open; there was no waste of powder and shot, the house and roof were quickly cleared with the bayonet, and on the top was planted the Regimental Colours. King stationed a large party on the roof, and bade them keep under cover of the parapet; even then some were hit by stray bullets. The lower rooms were turned into a dressing-station, and Assistant-Surgeon Bone was kept well occupied. Barely was this house garrisoned than a heavy fire opened from the right, and a storming-party was sent to clear other houses in the neighbourhood; again the bayonet came into play. About nine o'clock the left wing saw the King's Colours on St. Catalina Tower, and the right and the left wings cheered each other thinking the battle must be nearly won. The firing from the Plaza de Toros had ceased; the 38th and 87th had forced the surrender; many prisoners were brought in to Major King, who now determined to move to the right and attack a house where a French colour was still flying. There was no further danger from the left; a sergeant and twelve men were put in charge of the wounded and prisoners, and the remainder of the left wing were formed up outside the house, and then, Colours in front, marched up the street to the right.

Major King wrote in his Journal: "On advancing some distance I received a heavy fire from the tops of the houses, etc., and in consequence broke open a house on the opposite side of the street to the one we intended to attack, about 150 paces from it, and where it was my intention to retreat should we fail in our attempt. On breaking the door, we entered the courtyard, and, the men being formed, sallied up the street, but received so heavy a fire, and sustained such loss, that I returned to the above house, and had the wounded brought in. I sent Captain Phillips to take the wounded to the first house, where Mr. Bone was, and to go to the church to Lieutenant-Colonel Davie, to request him to send me a reinforcement. I then formed my men again in the yard, having had in the above attempt three or four killed, and a good many wounded; however, my men wishing it, I again determined to attempt to get into the house where the French colour was displayed."

Morley describes the little assembly in the yard: "We had a sergeant with us, George Golland, who I verily believe would have sabred the first man showing symptoms of what he never felt—fear. Such was our confidence in our leader, that when, sword in hand, he exclaimed, 'Now, my brave fellows, death or victory!' onward we went."

The second attack met with no more success; so many men were hit that to proceed with the assault was impossible; King himself was struck on the head by a spent ball and slightly wounded in the arm. From the shelter of the courtyard the wounded were sent back to Assistant-Surgeon Bone. There was no question of another attack, for the enemy were endeavouring to surround the little force, and two guns loaded with grape were sweeping the street. King, fearing to be cut off, made his way to the right.

" I left some killed behind me, and Drummer Downie, mortally wounded, in the courtyard of the last house. I, however, previous to retreating, got off all the wounded. A short time before, I got a message from General Lumley not to retreat on any account as I covered his left (36th Foot). I, however, exercised that discretionary power which in my opinion every officer in danger has a right to do. . . . I preferred proceeding to where I could more advantageously annoy the enemy without risking the certain and total destruction of the few gallant fellows with me. . . . A party of the 36th occupied a corner house of the street we entered. I was here joined by some men, and Captain Ridge soon after informed me that a party of the enemy were advancing up the street, and wished to charge them; on which the Fifth were formed, and advanced up the street, each section extending across it, the front rank of the leading one at the charge."

Then a curious incident took place, for the enemy, with a considerable number of mounted troops, came forward waving their hands and displaying a white flag, in token, the Fifth thought, of surrender. Major King made signs to them to lay down their arms; his orders were not obeyed, and seizing two or three muskets from them he flung them down; one of the Spaniards promptly aimed at King, who parried the musket with his sword. One of the soldiers thrust at the Spanish officer, who leapt back, saving his life, but tearing his clothes. With difficulty King restrained his men. The Spaniards were each moment reinforced; they filled the road and far outnumbered the five companies. King was a tall man; holding his great sabre in his hand, with a handkerchief round his arm and another round his head, he stood out in front of his men, half divining the enemy's purpose and half suspecting treachery. Behind him the five companies stood ready; that they were being asked to surrender never entered their heads; their only sentiments were those of regret that the enemy should have given in so soon. Redmond O'Connel, of Ridge's company, gently raised his musket. " To surrender, is it ? then I'll be just after giving them an easy touch." Then, to their amazement, the Spaniards were upon them, calling them prisoners. The officer had seized King's wrist, and was demanding his sword; proudly and defiantly it was refused; King's sabre pressed the Spaniard's chest, and it was the Spaniard who gave up his sword. There was a cry from Ensign Harvey that they were trying to seize the colours; off went Redmond's musket, and a dozen others, and King gave the order to charge. The enemy fled, with the loss of twelve killed and some wounded.

The left wing now received orders to join the right wing, and to retreat together to the Plaza de Toros. This was done, and at about three o'clock in the afternoon the Fifth found themselves with the rest of the brigade and their general. Shortly after, General Lumley and the 36th joined them; part of Lumley's brigade was missing. Whitelocke had remained all day at headquarters without news of any of the columns. About three o'clock one of his staff, Captain Whittinghame, managed to make his way through to the Plaza de Toros and to consult with Auchmuty, who was urgent that the general should shift his headquarters and join him. This Whitelocke declined, remaining where he was for the night. The Fifth took up their quarters in the Plaza for the night; sniping continued notwithstanding a flag of truce which had been sent in. A church was converted into a hospital; Bone and the wounded of the Fifth were taken there and left, protected by a sergeant's guard, under Sergeant Prior and Corporal Byron. A wine-store close by proved too much for some of the tired men; two, from want of food and excitement, were quickly overcome, and were shot as they tried to rejoin. The sergeant placed a sentry over the door of the wine-house, but he, too, was shot; then the sergeant himself fell. The church where the wounded lay was some way from the Plaza de Toros; one of the few remaining guard was sent to ask for reinforcement. Lots were drawn, and Morley was chosen for messenger. He did not much like his errand, for it was dark, and friend was as dangerous as foe. With loaded musket and fixed bayonet Morley made his way through the streets, and at last found his regiment. Colonel Davie refused to send a relief. " It is too late, the guard is disposed of; join your company." This Morley did, and then had leisure to hear the news of the other columns, of how Crauford was a prisoner with the Light Brigade, and of how the 88th had been captured.

Corporal John Byron, with his six remaining guard, stuck to his post, though eventually he was forced to surrender to overwhelming odds.

About midday on the 6th Whitelocke joined Auchmuty. Liniers had sent through a letter offering to restore all the English prisoners if Whitelocke would withdraw; he and Auchmuty and Gower consulted together. On the one hand, they had captured 1,000 prisoners and over thirty guns, and held a strong position in the town; but on the other hand, the casualties had been very heavy.[1] The generals now realized that the capture of the town did not entail the subjugation of the province; the determined resistance had disillusioned the most sanguine.

On the 7th terms were agreed: the restoration of all prisoners (for good faith three hostages were demanded, and one of the three volunteers was Hamilton of the Fifth), and the evacuation of the province within ten days, with the exception of Monte Video, which might be retained for a month, but was then to be restored intact. The soldiers scribbled all over the walls, " General Whitelocke is a traitor or coward, or both." Later, the court-martial in England somewhat endorsed

[1] 401 killed, 649 wounded, and 1,924 prisoners. The Fifth lost 14 killed, including Sergeant Prior and Drummer Downie; 47 wounded, including Major King and Captain Ridge slightly; 24 missing—of these 6 were the hospital guard, probably the remainder belonged to the light company.

this view. The man of " confident carriage and boastful mode of talk " was declared " totally unfit and unworthy to serve His Majesty in any capacity whatever."[1]

In light boats the Fifth sailed down the river with the rest of the melancholy army. At Monte Video a hungry crowd of merchants waited for them—come out to the new El Dorado and expecting to find the province in English hands. The embarkation was hurried forward, but it was some time before all the troops could be got on board and the ships provisioned. During the two months the Fifth stayed in Monte Video Sergeant Bruce was given a commission in a Veteran Battalion, and Dubordieu was made captain.

The prisoners returned, among them Corporal Byron and the six remaining men of the guard. Byron, for his gallant defence of his post, received a silver medal from Colonel Davie and was made sergeant. Towards the end of August the Fifth embarked; Major King had preceded them, and was on his way home, where he arrived in November. The regiment neither touched nor saw land from the time of sailing till they came to the Cove of Cork December 19th, and from there marched to the barracks at Kinsale. So ended for the Fifth this disastrous expedition. Morley says the last word: " That the country was disappointed is well known, although no blame it is understood attached to us. The British soldier, fortunately for himself, is a dunce in politics ! it is a subject which he heartily despises. To keep his arms in serviceable condition, as well as clothing and appointments; to be patient under privations; cool and steady in danger; brave and daring in action; to be obedient to orders, and have an honest, cheerful heart, form the perfection of his character."

[1] Medows, who once commanded the Fifth, was president of this court-martial, which included another of the Northumberland regiment in General Harris. The other officers were: Lake, Moore, Cathcart, David Dundas, and Henry Fox. The trial lasted thirty one days.

CHAPTER XXIV

PORTUGAL, 1808

GEORGE III.

ROLIÇA—VIMEIRO

RICHARD ENGLAND: 1ST FIFTH

THE position in Europe had changed during the Fifth's year of absence. Napoleon's campaign in the west had ended in the Treaty of Tilsit. With Russia an ally and Prussia a slave, France was free to turn attention to England and her two remaining friends Sweden and Portugal. The Regent of Portugal vowed the House of Braganza would emigrate to the Brazils rather than, at the command of France, close their ports and sequestrate English property. Then the unhappy tale of Buenos Ayres made the weak Regent falter in his purpose; a French army was on its way through Spain; by November Prince John was ready to sign anything; Junot was at Ciudad Rodrigo, and hastening to Lisbon.

Not only in Portugal, but in Spain as well, Napoleon had stationed his armies. The domestic quarrels of the Spanish Bourbons gave Napoleon his opportunity; Murat was appointed vice-regent, and occupied the capital with a large force. King Charles abdicated, then repented of his abdication; Ferdinand proclaimed himself king, and appealed to Napoleon to uphold his throne. The Emperor inveigled both Charles and Ferdinand to France, and then declared the reign of the Bourbons to be at an end, and named Joseph Bonaparte King of Spain. To this King Charles and his son meekly submitted; but not so the nation—Joseph Bonaparte entered Spain to find the whole country in revolt.

A riot in Madrid gave the signal; then the province of Asturias declared war on Napoleon and appealed to England for help. Arragon, Valencia, Murcia, and Andalusia followed suit. England at once decided to send aid. Sir Arthur Wellesley was chosen to command the expeditionary force, and from the latter half of June preparations went forward, the general looking into every detail.

Fired by the Spanish patriots the Portuguese also rose, and Junot was forced to abandon the north and south and content himself with holding Lisbon. The English Ministry therefore decided to make Portugal the first object, and on July 13th the expedition sailed from Cork, 444 officers and 10,284 men, among them the 1st Fifth.

Lieutenant-Colonel Davie had left, and Lieutenant-Colonel Mackenzie from the second Battalion was gazetted in his place. Mackenzie, a strict disciplinarian was in the early forties. Morley remarked on a certain commanding expression in his eye which, once seen was never forgotten. From December, 1807, to July 1808, both battalions had been quartered near each other in Kinsale, Cork, and Fermoy. Major Prat went to the second Battalion as lieutenant-colonel and about this time Lieutenant Simcockes got his company. Morley tells the following story:

"At Charles' Fort, about two miles from Kinsale, lay Captain Brodie's company, still commanded by Lieutenant Simcockes. We had a bugle-man named Patric Ganley, who was considered a splice of a wit. One morning, being employed about the mess-room, he accidentally heard something about Lieutenant Simcockes. Pat quickly hastened to the road by which the Lieutenant had to pass; when making the military salute he said, ' Good luck to your honour, Captain and may you soon wear two epaulettes.' ' Than you, Ganley,' replied the Captain, whose promotion had not appeared in orders, ' here's something for you to drink.' This was exactly what Pat had been contriving for."

The battalion was made up to full strength[1] by volunteers from the Irish Militias, and the first Battalion left Cork 1,107 strong.

Sir Arthur Wellesley had sailed in advance to learn definitely the state of affairs. At Corunna he heard of the defeat of the Galician army at Medina de Rio; from there he sailed to Oporto, where he conferred with the Supreme Junta, and decided to land in Mondego Bay. This was not a favourable spot, several boats were upset in the heavy surf and some lives were lost. Here the original force was joined by Spencer's division, and the landing of the two armies occupied eight days. The fleet was to act as base, and the men left their packs on board and carried only greatcoats, shirt, a pair of shoes, and four days' bread. The redcoats were very welcome; the peasants came forward with bread, and Morley and his fellows congratulated themselves when they discovered that wine was plentiful and cheap. Afterwards they found it "sour weak stuff," and altogether unworthy of the British soldier.

Before the Fifth disembarked Mackenzie made the following order from the *Norfolk* transport, July 24th:

"The Fifth Regiment being about to disembark and be employed in a glorious and arduous service, Lieutenant-Colonel Mackenzie is extremely happy to think that its courage is so well known that little is left for him to recommend, but that little the Lieutenant-Colonel most anxiously requests that the officers will take care to impress well on the minds of the soldiers of the different companies.

"(1) The most profound silence in getting into and out of the boats, and upon all occasions in the Ranks.

[1] 46 officers and 1,061 men (Fortescue). Oman and Norman give the strength as 990. The *Lord Cathcart* had on board one detachment—16 officers, 16 sergeants, 16 corporals, 334 privates, 30 women, and 13 children. Orders were made that hammocks were to be brought up at seven o'clock in the morning and packed neatly; the men to wash, comb, and plait their hair; parade and inspection, 8.45; the officer of the day to be present at the issue of all provisions, mixing of the grog, etc., and to inspect the coppers; the cooks were ordered to appear clean at evening parade; shirts to be washed Mondays and Fridays, and clean linen put on on Thursdays and Sundays.

" (2) Attention and obedience to words of command, and, above all, to the word or signal of 'Cease Firing.'

" (3) The C.O. will himself be all eye and ear to the Commands of his Superior in Rank, and trusts and hopes that every Officer and Soldier in the Battalion will pay the same attention to his."

On August 10th the army began their march to Lisbon, following the coast road, which ran through Leira, Alcobaça, Obidos, and Torres Vedras. The weather was very hot; deep sand covered the road; the first day's march, twelve miles, produced much straggling. The army was formed into six brigades, the Fifth, with the 9th and the 38th, in the first brigade, under Major-General Hill.[1] At Leira the Portuguese general, Freire, met them; but he did not agree with the chosen route, and withdrew his troops with the exception of 1,400 infantry and 200 or 300 cavalry. The army reached Calvano on the 12th, Alcobaça, where they first came in contact with the French, on the 14th, and Caldas on the 15th. Here the French outposts were driven in, and here Wellesley halted his army for a day. He was aware that two French armies were operating from Lisbon—before him Delaborde, with probably some 6,000 men; while Loison, with much the same number, had been last heard of two days before at Santarem, and might be expected to take part in the coming action. From Obidos, Wellesley saw Delaborde's army in position on a little hill just north of Roliça. With his superior numbers he determined to envelop the enemy. Ferguson, with two brigades, some cavalry and artillery, was sent away to the left, while Trant, with the Portuguese, was sent to the extreme right. Next to Trant's brigade came the Fifth, the right-hand regiment of Hill's brigade; between Hill and Ferguson were the brigades of Nightingale, Crauford, and Fane. The

---

[1] Rowland, first Viscount Hill; son of Sir John Hill, third baronet; born 1772; for his services in Peninsular War was given G.C.B. and created Baron Hill of Almarez and Hawkstone, Co. Salop; commander-in-chief 1828-1842; died, unmarried, December 10th, 1842.

English came on in magnificent order, Hill's brigade in line of battalion columns. At intervals the line was halted to correct the gaps caused by the rough ground. Delaborde saw his peril, and, under cover of his skirmishers, withdrew to a second position at the foot of a hill, where his front—only three-quarters of a mile long—and both flanks were covered by a stream in a deep gorge. Wellesley advanced again in the same order, but Ferguson's division lost its way, and was slow in completing the turning movement. Before the left flank was in position the 29th Foot had rushed impetuously forward and begun the attack. Hill's brigade at once deployed against Delaborde's left front, the Fifth attacking the extreme left. The hills on which the enemy were posted were high and too steep for direct ascent; but the Fifth plunged down into the gorge, and, led by their officers, made their way up some narrow gulleys. Mackenzie turned his horse adrift and ran on foot before his men. On the hillside above the gorge were vineyards full of skirmishers, and behind these the enemy edged away. Nothing daunted by the thick cover the Fifth swept aside the skirmishers and formed up to charge. Delaborde was in full retreat, but by no means broken; and, by skilful use of the ground, he withdrew his battalions.[1] There was no immediate pursuit, for Wellesley had first to arrange for the safe disembarkation of two brigades just arrived off the coast. Of the 487 casualties, the Fifth lost 3 men killed and 41 wounded, and 2 officers, Major Emes and Lieutenant Doyle, wounded.[2] They encamped on the battlefield in high spirits at the success of their first encounter with Junot's invincibles. Although the total English force was greatly superior, only a number about equal to the enemy was actually engaged.

In order to cover the landing of the reinforcements Wellesley marched to Vimeiro; and, as soon as the

---

[1] Delaborde had 4,000 infantry, 250 light cavalry, and 100 artillery with 5 guns. His losses amounted to 600.
[2] Cannon.

greater part were on shore, issued orders for an advance against Torres Vedras, where he expected to find the main force of the enemy. However, Sir Harry Burrard had arrived off the coast in a frigate, and, after interviewing Wellesley on board, forbade an advance until Moore's division had arrived. Junot, not realizing that the English had merely halted to collect reinforcements, underrated his enemy, and resolved to attack forthwith and drive the English into the sea; this he hoped to do with 13,000 men.

Wellesley had thought of attack rather than defence, and his army was placed with more regard to convenience than battle. In front of the village of Vimeiro was a little broad, low hill; while behind ran a high ridge, sharply divided north of the village by a deep gorge. On the 20th the greater part of the troops were stationed on the western ridge, but when the alarm was given the troops on the east were strengthened and the little Vimeiro hill was occupied. Hill's brigade remained on the west, and Wellesley seems to have thought that the main attack would fall on his right centre. As things turned out the assault was delivered against the eastern ridge and Vimeiro hill, and the Fifth never fired a shot all day.

The first warning of Junot's approach was given soon after midnight, but it seemed incredible that he should risk so much. The troops to the east and south were roused by the rumble of the artillery wheels, but Hill's brigade passed a peaceful night, and the Fifth, after early morning parade, set to the usual avocations of soldiers at rest.

Morley was washing his clothes when the drums beat " To arms "; but the wet linen was quickly thrust away, and in very few moments the Fifth were in line and accoutred. There on the side of the hill they stood, chafing at being mere spectators. Some of the officers could not bear it, and ran off and plunged into the thick smoke; and the remainder plotted eagerly to draw the regiment into action. Suddenly a cry went up, " The colonel's shot !" and, from behind the lines, his distraught wife came rushing down the slope. Some of the men followed after her, and only returned when threatened by the fire of the brigade's pickets. This was all a ruse to get into the fight: the colonel was untouched!

The action began about eight in the morning, and by noon the French were beaten at every point, and were in full retreat. General Burrard had come ashore about nine o'clock, but had refused to take command. The battle over, Wellesley could no longer enforce his wishes, and Burrard, to his chagrin, refused to allow him to follow up the victory and annihilate the French army.

The next day Sir Hew Dalrymple landed and took over supreme command.[1] On the 22nd Junot made overtures and asked for terms. The Convention of Cintra was signed August 31st, and the French agreed to evacuate Portugal, bag and baggage. Ten days later the British troops marched into Lisbon, and the campaign of Portugal came to an end.

The Fifth marched to Abrantes, where they spent the next two months.

[1] The Ministry would have been content to leave Wellesley in command if this had not entailed the supersession of Sir John Moore. Though this was their object yet they had not the courage to proceed directly. Having failed in their efforts to induce Moore to resign, they appointed two officers, both senior to Moore and Wellesley, to proceed to Portugal. The Fifth discussed the vexed question of their general's supersession over their biscuits and rum; and, with the rest of the army, were emphatic in expressing their disgust.

CHAPTER XXV
1808–1809

CORUNNA

1st Fifth

THE Convention of Cintra roused a storm of protest in England; Dalrymple and Wellesley were recalled. Help had been promised to Spain, and many tales were told of the loyalty and enthusiasm of the Spaniards and the great armies that local patriotism had raised. At the same time it was certain that the French armies had been reinforced, and that at least 70,000 French troops were in the country. Orders were given that Sir John Moore was to advance into Spain to co-operate with the Spanish generals; a further force under Sir David Baird was being sent out to join him.

Sir Harry Burrard gave his junior every assistance in his power. The order arrived October 7th, and by the 18th the first regiments had begun their march. Moore decided to go overland; Baird was to disembark at Corunna, and it was hoped that the armies would effect a juncture at Salamanca.

Means of transport were very difficult to obtain, and, to add to Moore's troubles, he had no money at his command. The army marched by three roads, of which the general knew nothing save that they were unfit for artillery; the guns therefore were sent by a fourth road. The brigades of Hill and Bentinck marched together by Abrantes, Castello Branco, and Guarda.[1]

[1] 1st Fifth (833). 1/32nd, Hill's. Bentinck, 1/4th, 1/28th, 1/42nd.

The Fifth were still at Abrantes, which saved them a day's march. Some of the men were suffering from dysentery—grapes were too plentiful in the pleasant vineyards.

From the warm valley the country rose steep, rocky, and desolate. It grew suddenly much colder, and in the hills the rain turned to hail. The men were marching in their thin white fatigue jackets, their regimental coats and great-coats in their packs. Each day it rained and hailed, and many fell out from weakness, to be jeered at as shirkers and militiamen. On the evening of November 4th they came into Guarda. Major Emes was sent back for stragglers; some he brought in, but five lay dead by the roadside. Guarda was a dreary little town. One company was billeted in a barn without a fire, till someone set the whole place ablaze, then a whisper of a powder store under the roof cleared the ruin in three minutes.

From Guarda they marched to Ciudad Rodrigo. The country people were glad to see them, but language was a barrier to good understanding; however, the soldiers behaved excellently, there was no straggling, and few complaints.

Moore left Lisbon on October 27th with the last of the troops. He followed Hill's brigade, and was three days behind the Fifth at Guarda. His army was in high spirits, but not so the general. The news from Spain was vague and unsatisfactory; there was no generalissimo, and the different armies were acting without plan or coherence. On November 13th he reached Salamanca, and the next day he learned that the French had occupied Burgos, and that Blake and his Galician army had been defeated. While he waited he heard news of another disaster—Castanos and the Andalusian army had been routed. Moore then made all his plans for retreat, waiting only for Hope and the slow-moving guns to come safely in. Baird halted on his way from Corunna for definite orders.

Every day, almost every hour, conflicting intelligence arrived. Moore's common sense told him that the

Spanish resistance was broken, and that, alone, the little English army could do nothing; at the same time he was urged by the British Ambassador and the agents of the Government to advance boldly, since it was certain that the country would rally round him. The French force was asserted to be anything from 60,000 to 150,000 and the reputed numbers of the existing Spanish armies varied to the same extent. The Supreme Junta, who had fled to Badajos, implored that help might be sent to Madrid menaced by the invaders. Confirmation came from the British Ambassador— Madrid was holding out, and would hold out till death; so Moore gave the order to advance, sent word to Baird, and set out to save the capital.

Sir John did not know, and did not learn for some days, that Napoleon had arrived before Madrid on December 2nd, and that the town, unfortified and indefensible, had surrendered two days later. The Galician army, twice defeated, had practically ceased to exist (November 13th); Soult had crushed Belvedere (November 13th); Laurens had defeated Castanos (November 23rd); Moore, with a divided army of 30,000 men, was advancing to attack over 200,000 victorious French.

Not that Moore's army were in the least alarmed— they did not, of course, realize the situation; and, if the enemy were victorious so were they, for were they not the first soldiers who had beaten " Boney's invincibles " ? They had driven the conquerors of Europe from Portugal, and were now going to sweep them out of Spain. In high spirits the army prepared to march; then came the news that Madrid had fallen. It was obvious there must be a large force round Madrid. Moore set off for Valladolid, determined to strike a blow at the French communications; Sir John Hope,[1] with Hill and three other brigades, making for Tordesillas. At Alaejos they were halted and swung north, for a despatch

---

[1] Sir John Hope, second son of John, second Earl of Hopetoun; born 1765; colonel 42nd Foot; for his services in Peninsular War received the G.C.B., and was created Baron Niddry, 1814; succeeded his half-brother as fourth Earl of Hopetoun 1817; died 1823.

had fallen into Moore's hands, and he had learnt of his danger. Napoleon was at Madrid; with him Ney and four divisions; south-west lay the Imperial Guard; between Talavera and Madrid a further two divisions of infantry and a cavalry brigade; north-east, one infantry division; further north, Junot, with three divisions; north-west, Soult, with two divisions and cavalry. Napoleon was concerting plans to march into Portugal with 40,000 troops; the Spanish rebellion was crushed; the English, he had been told, were in full flight for the frontier, the road was clear. Four days later he learned that the English cavalry, foot-soldiers and guns were at Salamanca, and were advancing, not running away. Orders followed quickly; the armies were to close in, Ney to push forward; but by then the English had swung north, and on the very day that Ney set out the two armies, Moore and Baird, met at Mayorga.

The united army made up three divisions and a reserve. Sir John Hope commanded the second division of Leith, Catlin Crauford, and Hill's brigades, and to Hill's brigade were added the 2nd Foot and the 2/14th. The sick were sent off under convoy; there remained about 26,000 men, in good spirits and under excellent discipline, a little confused by the sudden turn north away from the enemy, but a brilliant cavalry action on December 21st made them believe more than ever that they were equal to any number of the foe. From the intercepted despatch Moore had discovered the isolation of Soult's force between Carrion and Saldana. Napoleon was apparently quiescent, and Moore hoped to have time to defeat Soult before the hounds were let loose. The infantry marched to Sahagun on the 21st, and there rested for forty-eight hours, with orders to march at dark on the 23rd and attack Carrion at dawn.

That night Moore learnt that the French were across the Guadarrama, and were hastening to overwhelm him. The orders were countermanded, the leading divisions halted and turned back, and at dawn on the 24th the retreat began in good earnest. Hope and Fraser led the way, and before night had reached Mayorga. Moore was bent on saving his army—the British army, picked troops, for a time irreplaceable; and, it should be remembered, the only army in Europe left to face Napoleon.

The hounds were in full cry, Ney in the centre, Soult and Junot on either flank, while over the Sierra, in the teeth of a blizzard, came the Emperor at the head of his guards.

The weather was cold and stormy, the roads half frozen, and sometimes deep with snow; but this had been of no account until the troops had turned away at Sahagun. The blizzard thawed the frozen roads to knee-deep clay. Eight hours on the march, four hours to rest, then eight hours march again, the men struggled along in sullen discontent. Doubtless the Fifth went neither better nor worse than their fellows; they had a good general, an excellent brigadier, and Mackenzie, their colonel, had drilled them and taught them to fight, though perhaps he may have failed to impose a higher discipline. The young officers who had left their companies to plunge into the fight at Vimeiro were not of the stamp to keep their men together in a retreat. Very soon there was hardly a pair of shoes left in the regiment, and dysentery broke out again.

There was barely a man of the 26,000 who was not cursing John Moore for running away from the French. The senior officers did not disguise their sentiments, and the private men were not discouraged in their condemnation. The political relationship between the nations offered a fine encouragement for adventurers; it was as popular to cry that the English were deserting their brave allies, as to say that the Spaniards had broken faith. The soldiers inclined to the latter view, and chose to attribute the disgrace they were suffering to the disloyalty of the men who had asked for help. It should not be forgotten that the Fifth and other regiments were fresh from the Buenos Ayres disaster, where, landing to help, they had remained to be defeated by the very nation for whom they were now fighting. Already on the road to Benavento disgraceful scenes of plunder and pillage had taken place. Hope's division did not escape censure, and Moore issued a stern general order.

The enemy were forcing the pace. On the 27th there was a cavalry skirmish. Hope's division marched into Astorga on the 29th, where the one remaining Spanish army waited for Moore's coming. Ragged, starving, without arms, and suffering from typhus, Romanos' men crowded the town. When Hope's brigades, already insubordinate, marched in the men broke away from all control. It was impossible to make a proper distribution of stores; the army plundered and destroyed and a drunken rabble lay about the streets. In less than a week sheer ill-temper had turned a fine army into a plundering mob.

Here on the 31st the army divided, and Crauford's division turned west for Vigo. Moore marched on by Bembibre to Caçabelos, a ragged trail of stragglers following each division. Many men left the road intent on plunder, and in the vast wine cellars at Bembibre some 1,000 men were left, too drunk to march.

At Caçabelos Hope halted for the division to close up, and while they waited in the snow they saw Moore coming. They formed a square, and the general rode into the middle and looked round at them, and told them how he'd "rather be a shoeblack" than their general. The troops, thinking they had another Whitelocke to deal with, filed sullenly away.

Napoleon halted at Astorga; his net had failed to catch the little army; the ferocity of pursuit slackened, but Soult and Ney were sent on to drive the English into the sea.

At Villa Francia there was a great depot loaded with stores. For want of transport much of these had to be destroyed. The men broke from the ranks and seized what they could from the flames; if they might not fight, at least they would eat and drink; neither threat nor order could hold them. Then for fifty miles the road ran through desolate country. Many good soldiers were lost in the forced marches; numb with cold, weighed down by their heavy load and ill-fitting knapsack with its constricting straps, great-coat, and heavy old musket, they plodded along more like beasts of burden than men; when they fell from fatigue they could not rise without help. It was not only the drunken and faint-hearted who fell away; many good soldiers, sick and half frozen, laid down and died in the snow. And with them went the women and children. On a wild night, in the bleak hills, the wife of William Ashton of the band gave birth to a son.

The French cavalry clung to the retreating army, their infantry ten miles behind, in what force the English did not know. The road ran over the hills, dropping suddenly into deep gorges, rising as precipitously; snow made foothold treacherous; the men had to sling their muskets round their necks and cling with their hands; the last of the oxen gave out, and the sick had to be left in the deserted waggons. And always, here and there by the roadside, were little companies of women and children, broken by the long marches, huddled together waiting for death. Past them went the regiments, mutiny in their hearts; and still Moore drove them on.

On January 5th a rear-guard action was fought at Constantino; but Hope was well on his way to Lugo, where Moore, rumour ran quickly through the army, was at last to turn at bay. Discipline at once improved; companies lately reduced to a dozen men paraded three-quarters strong; stern orders were issued, and regiments took on some semblance of themselves and their former pride. Moore offered battle; Soult declined, preferring to wait for reinforcements. Moore, with only one day's bread, could not delay; watch-fires were left burning, and in the night the troops moved silently away.

Moore's well-planned scheme was worsted by the weather. In the wild night many battalions lost their way, and the army made little progress. Hope's division reached Guitiriz on the 9th, with the rear-guard at Astariz; and again discipline broke down—self-preservation obsessed both officers and men. Five hundred prisoners fell to the enemy, among them some of the Fifth. The sight of a building near the road with smoke coming from the chimney was too much for the tired men; they were near breaking-point. Morley crawled into the barn. "It was . . . full of our men who had made a fire," and then he went to sleep, waking at nightfall to find the army had marched on. Tired and stiff the men cooked themselves some food, then slept again, until a shot through the windows brought them to their feet and they found themselves surrounded by French cavalry. "We were seven men and a drummer who was unable to move, and we resolved to defend ourselves. . . . The French, observing the poverty of our numbers, galloped up to us," and the fight was quickly over. Morley shot his man, and was himself wounded in the arm; then, their cartridges expended, they were forced to surrender, and were ordered to destroy their arms. One of the other prisoners offered to break Morley's firelock for him. "This was too much! It had travelled with me from Guernsey, had been my companion in all my troubles, and was like an old friend," so with one hand Morley seized the stock and broke it against a stone. Then one of the Frenchmen tied up his wounded arm and gave him a drink. The prisoners were sent back to Lugo.[1]

Stumbling over the hills Moore's army came to Betanzos on the 10th. There before them shone the sea and the sails of good English ships. The road ran down into a fresh warm country, where everything was bursting into spring. Checked by the destruction of the bridge across the Minho, pursuit had slackened, but on the 11th Soult was over the river and on Moore's heels, and more stragglers were caught. That day Moore marched into Corunna—the Guards proudly, drums beating, and not a man lagging behind; the other regiments as best they could; few with much reason for pride, except those of the Reserve who had borne the brunt of the rear-guard fighting.

[1] Wm. Harwood of the band, Lintwhite of the grenadier company, John Barber, and others, in all about twenty (Morley).

There were few ships in harbour, and foul winds kept the fleet of transports from entering. The sick were embarked, and Moore hoped Soult would delay until the wind changed. On the 13th El Burgo was occupied; the transports came in on the 14th, and, to cover the embarkation, Moore took up a position to defend the town.

A high ridge of hills lay between Corunna and the French, but Moore had too few men to hold the heights, and contented himself with a chain of outposts. For his main position he occupied a small hill, Monte Mero, with his left covered by the estuary of the Burgo. His right was in the air, but safeguarded by divisions held in reserve. Hill's brigade was on the extreme left of the line, with probably the Fifth as the left-hand regiment; the heights of Palavea directly to their front was held by their pickets. Rest and good feeding had done wonders for the men, and the prospect of a fight did still more. The arsenal provided new muskets to replace the rusty veterans.

All the 14th Soult delayed, waiting till his guns were in position and his men ready; then on the evening of the 15th he ordered a general advance, and the English pickets found themselves in a precarious position. On Palavea the Fifth disputed every inch of the way, General Merle's advance-guard, three companies of voltigeurs, pressing them hotly. The Fifth having done with retreats, sent back for reinforcements, and would not give ground. Mackenzie himself rode out to their support with thirty men and Lieutenant Clerke of the Light company. From behind a wall the voltigeurs fired a volley, which brought down the colonel's horse and checked his men. Mounting a second horse he went forward, the men following him. Before they could win the wall another volley crashed out; Mackenzie fell, mortally wounded. About this time word was passed along to withdraw; this was done in good order, and with no further loss. Clerke brought in the body of his dying colonel, who was carried into the town. Major Emes took over command of the regiment, and the Fifth waited eagerly for the morrow to avenge their colonel's fall.

The morning came bright and sunny, and other regiments won the glory; the battle swept round the centre and right wing and the Fifth were hardly menaced. The faint-hearted attack on the left flank was easily repelled and fell away, and the Fifth apparently lost no men. After Sir John Moore had fallen and a shot had shattered Baird's arm, the command devolved on Sir John Hope. Neither side could claim a victory, but the French attack had been successfully repulsed, the enemy flung back; and the English, diminished but undaunted were allowed to embark in peace.

The brigades of Hill and Beresford acted as a rearguard, and covered the embarkation, Hill's men embarking at two o'clock in the afternoon, under the Citadel. For a short time the troubles of the Fifth were at an end. Colonel Mackenzie died at midnight on the 15th, and was buried on the left hand of Sir John Moore.[1]

No return was made of the losses in the action of January 15th.[2] Cannon states that when the regiment landed in February 132 (1 sergeant, 2 corporals, 3 drummers, 126 privates) were found to be missing. These figures are not borne out by Professor Oman, who gives the strength of the regiment on October 15th as 893, on December 19th as 833 (excluding those in hospital or on command), and the disembarkation return as 654. This shows a total loss of 239, and a loss between December 19th and January 17th of 179. Another return puts the Fifth at 833; and we know from Morley that several men died, and it is certain others had to be left in hospital before the Fifth reached Salamanca.[3] Taking the more favourable figures, if the number of missing is any evidence of the behaviour of the troops

[1] Hamilton's Diary.
[2] Captain G. Clerke was wounded in the head on the 15th, and Captain Martin Armstrong died of fatigue after landing in England (Hamilton and Culley).
[3] Hamilton's return of July 16th, 1809, gives 3 officers and 123 rank and file in Portugal, and 138 rank and file in Spain.

the Fifth cannot claim to rank with the few regiments who maintained real order.[1] It should be remembered their ranks had been lately recruited from Irish militias; a notorious source of indiscipline.

In time the Fifth learnt to be proud of Corunna on their colours, but with a pride that should never allow them to forget that the honour was won by their dead general; while they, with most of their comrades, had barely saved themselves from shame.

[1] Professor Oman treats the return of the troops as an index to their conduct on the march. Mr. Fortescue (H. B. A., vol. vi., pp. 413, 414) combats the figures, and does not agree with the deductions.

CHAPTER XXVI

1809

WALCHEREN

"His Majesty could have wished that the information upon which the practicability of this expedition has been finally decided had not been so imperfect" (H.M. to Lord Castlereagh, June 22nd, 1809).

1st Fifth

BEARDED, filthy, ragged, and cramped from the crowded transports, the British army landed in England. The kind-hearted people of the seaports were eager to feed and welcome the men; but throughout the country there was much discontent and bitter feeling at the downfall of English hopes. Fortunately criticism of Moore soon gave way to more attractive gossip, and the great affair of Colonel Wardle, the Duke of York, and Mrs. Mary Ann Clark usurped the attention of the man in the street.

The little army was given six months to recover itself, recruit, equip, and drill. The Fifth, at Steyning Barracks, in Sussex, spent their time well, and were soon at full strength, in good health and fine spirits. They were inspected May 8th, and reported to be "as forward as could be expected considering the sickness (after Corunna) and the number of militia recruits. This is a steady, well-conducted Battalion, and very clean; great pains are bestowed on the interior economy, as the regularity and order of the soldiers' barrack-rooms clearly show."

Charles Pratt, from the 2nd Fifth, succeeded Mackenzie, and Henry King, to his great joy, got the command of the second Battalion.

In Europe, Prussia was fretting at her humiliation, and her patriot statesmen were in communication with the English Ministry. Russia, tired of the French Alliance, opened negotiations with Austria. In April the Austrians invaded Italy, and began a campaign of varying fortune. To assist the Austrians and hearten the Prussians, Castlereagh decided on a diversion in the north. The Scheldt was to be attacked, and, if possible the French fleet blockaded or destroyed. Lord Chatham was chosen to command the land forces, with Sir Robert Strachan admiral of the fleet. The expeditionary force was to number 40,000.

A vast quantity of transports were required; it was July before the fleet was ready and the embarkation begun. It was the largest force that had ever left England; the Deal and Downs road was crowded like a fair, and the Downs so full of shipping that the masts were like a forest of trees.[1] The weather had been wet and cold, but in the last week of July the sun shone; everyone was in good spirits; the bands played on board the ships, and fine folks in fine clothes thronged the beach.

The Fifth were in wonderful order, England and Picton inspected on July 8th, and had nothing but good to say.

At last the Blue Peter was hoisted and the officers were called on board; Lord Chatham and his staff came posting down; the great secret expedition got under way, July 28th, and sailed for the mouth of the Scheldt.

The island of Walcheren divides the river mouth, the eastern channel leading to Wilhelmstadt, the western being the high water-way to Antwerp. The island was defended by batteries; the western channel was covered by the cannon of Flushing and the batteries on the Katzand. Flushing was strongly fortified, and unlikely to surrender without a regular siege. Chatham intended to invest the town with part of his force, and with the remainder advance against Antwerp.

[1] 352 transports and 264 men-of-war.

At Flushing there were in garrison some 4,000 regulars, not of the best quality, under Monet, and on Katzand another 2,000. Reinforcements were not far away, and the original 6,000 defenders were afterwards trebled.

The Fifth were brigaded in the 4th Division of the left wing, commanded by Major-General Thomas Graham; and, with the other battalions of that division, embarked on board men-of-war[1]—the Fifth, 939 strong, in H.M.S. *Bellona*.

A fair wind brought the great navy across in a very short time, but the surf was too heavy for a night landing. The next morning, July 30th, signal was made, but so strong a sea was running that the ships' boats could not pull ashore. At four o'clock in the afternoon the 1st Division succeeded in landing at Breezand, and Fort Ten Haak was secured. Next, Graham's division, with the Fifth in Hay's[2] brigade, disembarked; the men had to wade ashore, up to their middles in water. Veere was invested, and the landing went on, the Fifth remaining under arms and very wet all night. But the next day all were on shore, the army redistributed, and the advance began.[3]

The Fifth in Graham's column marched on the extreme right by East Kapelle to Meliskerke, the advance posts reaching Zouteland.

The Fifth marched along a flat road, the country like Lincolnshire. It was very hot, and the salt pork and biscuit ration was a nuisance to carry and unpleasant

[1] *Field Off. Capts. Lieuts. Staff. Sergts. Crpls. Drs. Ptes.*

	Field Off.	Capts.	Lieuts.	Staff.	Sergts.	Crpls.	Drs.	Ptes.
1st Fifth	2	10	26	6	40	39	16	900
Sick in England..	–	–	–	–	3	3	1	50
Recruiting and Staff..	2	–	4	–	4	–	–	3
Portugal ..	1	–	2	–	6	4	1	112
Spain ..	–	–	–	–	1	2	3	132

(Hamilton's Diary.)

[2] Brigadier-General Sir Andrew Hay, served in Peninsular War.

[3] The centre under Lord Paget, the left under Fraser, and the right under Major-General Graham. The right column consisted of artillery, two battalions of light infantry, and an infantry brigade under Colonel Day (Hay ?), 3/1st, 1/5th, 2/35th and thirty men of the staff corps (H. B. A., vii., 70).

to eat. There was plenty of water, streams and rivers everywhere, and great dykes and sea-walls. The peasants came out to see the redcoats passing, and were evidently pleased at sight of them, while the soldiers exclaimed at the queer Dutch dress and the extreme cleanliness of the little Dutch houses. The small boys, dressed in the fashions of Queen Anne, each with a miniature pipe, amused them considerably. As they neared Zouteland they had their first brush with the enemy. The English were taking the sea batteries in the rear, but the French would not surrender without a struggle. Graham's advance-guard, the flank companies of the Fifth and the 3/1st, under Major Emes, finally drove them out, but the Fifth lost 4 men killed, 3 sergeants and 16 men wounded, and 10 men missing.[1]

Among the enemy prisoners were found some English soldiers captured in Spain, and deported to garrison Holland.

Gradually the columns closed in on Flushing; Graham halted with his right on the dyke at Nolle and his left on the West Souburg road; Paget was at West Souburg, the Reserve at East Souburg, and Fraser on the south was investing the Rammekens Fort on the Veeregat. When the weather allowed the fleet was to enter the Sound and complete the investment.

In the meantime Hope with his division had landed on South Beveland, and with little or no opposition reached Bat, the easternmost point; from there he reported the French fleet fled to Antwerp.

While the besiegers waited for the heavy guns they made for themselves huts of sods and green bushes, and lived pleasantly, cantoned in rich meadows and beautiful gardens, where fruit grew in abundance; the weather was fine and very hot. Sniping was, of course, continuous, and between August 2nd and the 6th, the Fifth, advance-guard of the column, lost one man killed and forty wounded, some of whom died of their wounds.[2] On the 3rd Rammekens Fort surrendered, but the fleet

---

[1] Hamilton.
[2] Hamilton.

could not enter the channel; and on three separate occasions Flushing was reinforced from the Katzand. The garrison made a sortie on the evening of the 7th, and fell on the pickets of Graham's division; fortunately he was a general of " unremitting vigilance and ability," and, with the aid of his fine infantry, the French were driven back with considerable loss. General Graham spoke warmly of the conduct and gallantry of his troops; the Light Infantry and the Fifth bore the brunt. Brevet-Major Bird was surrounded and taken prisoner; Captain Nicholas Hamilton,[1] of the Light Infantry company, who commanded an outpost, was dangerously wounded; shot through the thigh, he was carried to the rear by four seamen, to whose care and courage he owed his life. Lieutenant Bird and Ensigns Galbraith and Walton were slightly wounded. Walton's life was saved by his great-coat, which, rolled up and slung on his back, broke the force of the bullet. Hamilton's wound caused him much suffering, and eventually his leg had to be amputated. A sergeant and 4 men were killed, 47 men wounded, and 2 missing, 59 casualties in all—113 since landing.

Now appeared a new enemy; the water in the dykes began to rise; there had been some rain, but not enough to account for the flood; and it was rumoured that the dykes had been cut by Napoleon's orders. From the swamped meadow-lands thick mists rose at night; the soldiers began to complain of rheumatism and queer pains. On parade, men fell suddenly in the ranks; and these illnesses too often ended in death. At first the surgeons blamed the stagnant water and the abundance of fruit; but the evil was deeper rooted, and they could find no remedy. Sentries were relieved twice in the night, and the dead men buried by candlelight to keep depression from the troops.

[1] Lieutenant-General Sir Nicholas Hamilton, K.H.; joined Fifth as ensign 1796; lieutenant December, 1796; captain 1803; major 1812; brevet lieutenant-colonel 1825; colonel 1838; major-general 1851; lieutenant-general 1858; colonel of 82nd 1856. The son of Paymaster Hamilton; born 1781; married Frances Anne, daughter of the Rev. S. Beamish; died in Dublin 1859. " Amiable, courtly and gentle,"

At last, on the 13th, the big guns came up, sailors from the fleet lending a willing hand; the batteries opened fire, and the garrison vigorously responded; at night rockets were fired into the town, and set it ablaze in several places. The next day the fleet bore up; and the great battleships, the light breeze filling their sails, went past the town, pouring in a broadside as they went. By two in the afternoon no answer came from the enemy guns; but still Monet refused to surrender, until, in the night, one of the advance works was carried by storm, and the garrison capitulated. They marched out, bands playing, eagles flying; then, drawn up in ranks, laid down their arms—close on 6,000 prisoners of war, not including 1,800 already taken and 1,000 sick and wounded.

On the 16th the British marched in. Part of the town was still on fire; many of the houses were without roofs; few had escaped damage. The terrific bombardment had not made the English very welcome to the natives, who preferred their conquerors to their deliverers. Few houses could be found in which to billet the troops, and the generals were hard put to it to find accommodation for the ever-increasing sick.

Between August 8th and 15th the Fifth lost Captain Talbot and 2 men killed, and 1 drummer and 10 men wounded.[1]

A general advance on Antwerp was ordered; Graham's division, one of the last to leave, embarked at Rammekens, and sailed up the river to join the main army on South Beveland. Chatham had moved his headquarters to Bat, and there the Fifth arrived on the 24th; and there the expedition was destined to end. Friction between the general and the admiral, and the spread of low fever, numbed all enterprise. On the 20th, 1,600 men were sick; on the 27th, 3,400; the next day, 4,000; and each day men died. It was hopeless to attempt Antwerp with this ever-dwindling force; it might even prove difficult to hold what was already won. Part of the army was sent back to England; the

[1] Hamilton.

remaining unhappy troops were left to garrison the graveyards of Walcheren.

By September 5th South Beveland was evacuated, and two days later the more fortunate troops sailed for home, leaving, under command of Sir Eyre Coote, a garrison of 19,000, of whom 6,000 were in hospital. By October 1st the sick had increased to 9,000, with one thousand deaths in the past three weeks. The battered houses in Flushing were no cover to the men in the cold wet weather; Middleburg was quickly overcrowded; there was small chance for the sick men lying two in a bed in a crowded room. The plague was so unexpected and unforeseen that the surgeons could not cope with it, and help from England proved of little avail. The Fifth had at one time 600 men on the sick list, and a bare half-dozen officers fit for duty. Captains Philips, and William Hamilton, and Lieutenants Brown, Cary, and MacDonough died, and many men, especially the wounded.

There was no court of justice in Walcheren, and while the island remained under British protection the people expressed a wish for English law. A Provisional Court was established at Middleburg, and there Brigadier-General Rothenburgh and Major Emes of the Fifth acted as judges, and tried all cases of civil appeal.

On October 27th Coote handed over the command to General Don, who at once asked for transports to send 6,000 invalids home.

In November the garrison numbered 4,500 fit for duty and 4,900 sick, and there seemed every prospect of a French counter-attack. Don was ordered quietly to destroy the naval defences; preparations for evacuation were willingly made; and on December 9th the embarkation began. A storm delayed matters, but at last, one by one, the transports with their meagre load of haggard men weighed anchor, and Walcheren was left to the wardenship of the great army of the dead.

CHAPTER XXVII

1804–1810

GEORGE III.

DOURO—TALAVERA—BUSACO

RESERVE COMPANY OF 1ST FIFTH, 1809, AND 2ND FIFTH, 1804–1810

WHEN first raised the majority of second battalions were regarded as second-line troops and not as separate units. The officers were interchangeable; the second battalion remained on home service and was expected to supply the service battalion with drafts of men. However, in the first decade of the nineteenth century England found herself involved in a Continental war of such magnitude that her standing army proved hopelessly inadequate, and the new battalions were sent into the battle-line. In the spring of 1809 the 2nd Fifth were under orders to embark for the Peninsula.

The Battalion dated from 1804, when it was embodied at Horsham, in Sussex, under Lieutenant-Colonel Edward Baynes. After a year at Chichester the 2nd Fifth was sent, in February, 1806, to Guernsey. On May 9th they were inspected by Lieutenant-General Doyle, who reported: "This small battalion is very well composed, a good body of men, well appointed, and very forward in discipline." In August they were sent to Alderney, and were there inspected by Brigadier-General Robertson, who found the clothing, arms, and accoutrements in very good order, but regretted that any of Bonaparte's men had been allowed to recruit. The number of courts-martial had increased, possibly owing to the greater facilities for getting drunk. The establishment then numbered 570.

From Alderney they were sent to Ireland, where they landed at Cork, December 3rd, in time to welcome their first Battalion home from South America.[1] From Kinsale they marched to Fermoy, and the next spring to Coloony; and in June to Cork, where the transports lay waiting.

The five-years-old Battalion had seen five commanding officers: John Baldwin succeeded Edward Baynes[2] in May, 1805, followed by John Mackenzie in May, 1806. Mackenzie had been second in command since the first raising, but on Davie's retirement he went to command the first Battalion, and was in his turn succeeded by Charles Pratt, March, 1808.

Pratt, "that old American," was a good soldier, and had learnt his trade in a hundred wars. Mackenzie fell at Corunna, and Pratt went to command the 1st Fifth. The two senior majors were with the first Battalion—Copson with the reserve company at Lisbon, and Emes with the regiment in Walcheren; fortunately another good soldier was close at hand.

Henry King had left the regiment on his promotion in January, 1808. As lieutenant-colonel he had been appointed inspecting field officer of militia in Nova Scotia, but an accident kept him in England; his wound of the Holland campaign broke out afresh, and when this healed he still lingered, hoping for active service. The command of the 2nd Fifth was vacant, and at his earnest solicitation, and to the satisfaction of the whole corps, Henry King was gazetted lieutenant-colonel January 16th, 1809.

When Moore marched into Spain a mere handful of men was left to defend Portugal. Burrard returned to

[1] Roll Book, begun 1800 (at Depôt)—first entry: "Timothy Tongres, enlisted at Niagara, America, June 18th, 1800, age 7; height, 3 foot 7 inches; discharged 1837 as drummer; character very good; service, 29 years, 91 days." If these dates are correct, Tongres must have been drafted to a battalion of the Fifth in 1808, aged fifteen.

[2] Edward Baynes, afterwards Adjutant-General North America.

England, and Sir John Cradock took command. As
generous as Burrard, he divested himself of every spare
man, and sent what reinforcements he could into Spain.
When he learnt of the Corunna retreat he realized
Portugal's defenceless position. The Regency was at
its wits' end for money and arms; the Portuguese army
had ceased to exist, and the armed mob in Lisbon was
only an additional danger to the English. Moore had
left his sick in Lisbon, and the men who had fallen out
on the road to Salamanca had been sent back under
convoy. These men, now convalescent, Cradock
organized in two battalions, afterwards reinforced by
some of the sick and stragglers from the Corunna retreat
to about 3,000 men. Some of these men were drafted
back to their own regiments. In May these two
battalions numbered respectively 900 and 980. The
second battalion of Detachments contained a considerable number of the Fifth, and was commanded by Major
Copson, who had not marched with his regiment into
Spain. He was given brevet rank as lieutenant-colonel,
but his command was not an enviable one; sick men
may be good soldiers, but stragglers are not, and in
a composite regiment there is little to hold the men
together.

Cradock could muster some 11,000 men; with these
he covered Lisbon. Moore's retreat diverted the
French offensive and gave him a brief respite. Ney had
plenty to occupy him in Galicia; but, from Corunna,
Soult was ordered to invade Portugal. His task was
not made easy by the cloud of peasants who clung to his
army, cut off stragglers, and worried his supplies; but
he drove his way on, and, March 29th, carried Oporto
by assault. At the same time danger threatened
Cradock from the east, for Victor appeared at Merida.

Castlereagh meant to keep his hold on Portugal;
reinforcements were sent out, Wellesley once more
in supreme command, and Beresford to general the
Portuguese.

Soult lay at Oporto; Lapisse stormed and sacked
Alcantara, and joined Victor at Merida. Cradock had

his little army at Abidos, Caldas, and Rio Major, but dared not advance farther. On April 24th Wellesley arrived at Lisbon. Wellesley divided his army, about 50,000 English and Portuguese; and leaving Mackenzie with 12,000 to hold the line of the Tagus, he advanced with the remainder to Coimbra. Before Victor and Lapisse were offered battle Soult was to be driven from Oporto across the frontier.

With Beresford on the right and Hill on the left the main column marched on. Copson's battalion was brigaded with a Portuguese battalion, the 97th, and a company of the 5/60th, under Brigadier-General Sontag, in Sherbrook's division.

On May 10th the van came in contact with the enemy, who resisted strongly, but had to give way. Sherbrook's division was ten miles in the rear, and did not come under fire; and, throughout the operations of the next two days the second Battalion Detachments remained in reserve. On the 12th they seem to have debouched from the main road and followed Beresford, for it was near Vizeu that Stephen Morley rejoined. His adventures as a prisoner are too long to be quoted. Through the kindly help of a Spaniard he and Michael Wall of the 52nd made their escape, and, travelling at night and by hidden ways, found their way into Portugal. Once over the border they marched along without concealment, for had they not driven every Frenchman out of the country? At Chaves, Morley fell sick, and Wall went on alone. Recovering, Morley set out for Oporto, never dreaming that Soult was in possession. To his surprise, near Lamego, he fell in with an advance-guard of the 52nd (first Battalion Detachments); he learnt from them of the French invasion, and also that some of the old Fifth were close at hand.

The little company of the 1st Fifth received him gladly. Once more he had a regimental home, received arms and accoutrements, and was made first acting corporal, and then, to his infinite pride, sergeant and clerk. His first day as sergeant was nearly his last, for the unaccustomed sword entangled itself between his legs, and pride had many a fall.

The little detachment of the Fifth had no heroic part to play in the great crossing of the Douro; they were still on the dusty road when the venture was made, though part of their division crossed with Sherbrook by the ferry. Sufficient for them that they had in four days covered eighty miles of difficult country. On the right Beresford beat Lorison, who fell back with Soult, abandoning transport and sick, cannon and plunder. After a day's rest the troops set off in pursuit, but never came up with the French in their headlong flight. At the cost of 500 casualties Oporto was recovered, and Soult driven across the frontier with the loss of 4,000 men.

By the second week in June the troops were back at Abrantes and ready to deal with Victor.[1] The conduct of some of the regiments on the return march had been bad, and Wellesley issued stern orders. Charles Stewart wrote to Castlereagh on June 15th: " I wish these Detachment Battalions were replaced. I am sure they are the cause of great disorder; no *esprit de corps* for their interior economy among them, though they will all fight. They are careless of all else, and the officers do not look to their temporary Field Officers and superiors, . . . as in an established Regiment. I see much of their indiscipline."[2]

The first brief campaign had taught Wellesley some of the defects of his army—the lack of transport, inefficiency of the commissariat, and want of good regimental officers. He had yet to learn the difficulties of campaigning with his Spanish allies.

With the help of Cuesta and Vinegas he hoped to catch Victor; but the Maréchal, failing news of Soult, and short of provisions, had evacuated Estremadura and retreated to the Alberche, where his right rested on Talavera. Beresford, with the Portuguese troops,

---

[1] Lieutenant Read was left, sick of ague, at Oporto, June 2nd, 1809.
[2] " History of British Army," vol. vii., p. 234.

was left as an observation corps on the northern frontier, and Wellesley set out after Victor with 23,000 men. Ney and Soult, he thought, were safely occupied in Galicia; but, unknown to him, they lay, the one at Astorga and the other at Benavente.

Sontag had been sent home, and Copson's battalion was now in Colonel Kemmis's brigade in the 4th Division, commanded by Alexander Campbell. The army marched from Abrantes on the 27th; crossed the frontier July 3rd; and July 9th entered Plascencia. The weather was glorious and the late campaign had altered public opinion; the redcoats for once were welcome in the land of shrines and bells and yellow petticoats. The Fifth found that lemonade at midday and hot chocolate at night were excellent drinks.

King Joseph and Victor were in complete ignorance of Wellesley's movements; and not until July 24th did Victor realize that he had the English army, and not a party of Portuguese raiders, to fight.

On July 27th the two armies faced each other; and after a preliminary skirmish, in which the British advance-guard was severely handled and thrust back, Wellesley took up his chosen position on the heights of Talavera. Campbell's division was in the centre, with the Spaniards on the right, Kemmis's brigade in the second line.

So a little company of the Fifth fought at Talavera, not in the place of honour nor in the front line, but waiting in reserve while the battle swept past. The fighting went on till the sun went down; and in the morning began again, while the yellow stubble turned black with the trampling and the heat, and the parched grass broke into flames. The first evening Copson's men heard a great volley from the Spaniards on their right, and then saw a motley crew rush past to the rear; Wellesley was with their general, and rode up to see the gap in his line. The next day the fighting came nearer, and their comrades, the 97th, were called into the battle-line; and the reserve brigade on their left marched away, Mackenzie leading his men into the thick smoke. The French were pressing hotly, the second line was moved up, and Copson lost twenty of his men; then suddenly, their force expended, the French fell back, and for the English right the battle was over. The 2nd Detachments went into the fight 625 strong, and lost 7 men killed, 13 wounded, and 1 missing. For the day's work Copson got his Talavera medal. A contemporary criticism says: " Some lieutenant-colonels (one in particular, who commanded a corps of Detachments, and who, it is said, found it difficult to get his name inserted among distinguished men) received this badge,"[1] much to the disgust of hard-fighting majors and captains, to whom it had fallen to lead regiments in the battle.

This criticism must apply to either Colonel Bunbury of the 1st Detachments or Lieutenant-Colonel Copson. The 1st Detachments fought hard, if somewhat incoherently, and had 274 casualties in the two days. Bunbury was mentioned with credit in Wellesley's despatch, but this does not necessarily mean that he was a good officer. On the other hand, the 2nd Detachments were persistently kept in reserve in the Oporto and Talavera campaigns, from which it would appear that the battalion was not one to be relied on.

After the battle Wellesley remained on the field, his troops had won the day on half rations and a spoilt dinner, and needed rest. On the 30th he learnt of the danger that threatened him. The pass at Banos had been left unguarded, and through the defiles Soult and Mortier were making their way to cut him off. Warned in time, he crossed the Tagus, and made good his retreat to Badajos.

The 2nd Fifth landed at Lisbon in July, and with the 2/58th were at once sent to join Beresford, who, with his half-made Portuguese army, was guarding the frontier near Ciudad Rodrigo. As Wellesley retreated the French advanced, and Beresford was ordered to make south, with headquarters at Zarza, covering the Castello

---

[1] See " A History of the Campaigns in Spain and Portugal," vol. iv., p. 439, published in 1813.

Branco road; there, in September, the 2nd Fifth rejoined their brigade, under General Lightbourne, an officer of no distinction, who failed to find favour with the commander-in-chief—Lord Wellington since Talavera. Five companies from the 2nd Detachments joined the 2nd Fifth; and Copson, with the remaining companies, paymaster, and clerk, returned to England.

Political and strategic reasons caused Wellington to bring his whole army into Portugal. The Allies were scattered, and in some part demoralized; the French united and strengthened. Wellington foresaw, and prepared for, a French offensive, and the possible invasion of Portugal. In December he moved his headquarters from Badajos to Vizeu, and cantoned his army along the Mondego; then he had a short breathing-space to reorganize his force, men, officers, and corps commanders. The last twenty years of grand warfare debased in petty operations had failed to breed good generals. Wellington had first to fashion his weapon before he could strike.

He had an army of 30,000, weakened by the late campaign, and some 40,000 allies of doubtful value; a country all frontier to be defended; no means of transport, and indifferent supplies. In Spain, France had eight army corps, the greater part veteran troops, under tried generals, ready for invasion—200,000 men against 70,000.

Lightbourne's brigade, with Mackinnon, and one Portuguese brigade, made up the Third Division, and in January Thomas Picton[1] arrived from England to take command. After a brief rest at Abrantes the 2nd Fifth were sent off to Trancosa, on the high road between Almeida and Vizeu. The Third Division held the line between Trancosa and Celorica, Trant and his Portuguese covering their left, and the 4th Division their right. In front of them Crauford and the Light Division held the

---

[1] Sir Thomas Picton, K.C.B., born at Poyston, in Pembrokeshire, August, 1758; entered 12th Foot as ensign November 14th, 1771; brigadier-general 1801; major-general 1808; lieutenant-general 1813; killed at Waterloo.

outposts, extending along the Agueda from Ciudad Rodrigo to the Douro. Trancosa in the depths of winter was a cheerless spot, high up in the clouds, and buried in snow and fog; but King kept his men in good spirits, and Majors Broke and Ridge ably seconded him.

In March the French began their forward movement: Astorga was besieged, Ciudad Rodrigo threatened; Picton's men moved east, the 2nd Fifth near to headquarters at Pinhel; and the Third Division was ordered to support Crauford if need be. The Agueda had many fords; the French were strong in cavalry, and outnumbered the Light Division by six to one, but never a man got through. Picton, rough and ready in speech and temper, did not much like being at the call of a brigadier, and there was some friction between the two generals.

There was a strange friendship between high-minded, chivalrous King and his rough general; the lieutenant-colonel of the 2nd Fifth discerned in his chief those magnificent qualities of courage, coolness, and daring which later campaigns brought to light; and they had this in common, both placed discipline and obedience first among soldierly virtues; both knew that a regiment that behaved well would fight well; both demanded of their subordinates that attention to detail and care for the men that is the foundation of every good army, or regiment, or platoon.

In April Masséna was appointed commander-in-chief of the army of Portugal. On the 22nd Astorga surrendered; and in May, Ney appeared before Rodrigo with his whole corps, and set about the investment of the town.

King was like a chained dog straining for action; the sound of the cannon reached Pinhel, and off he rode to see what was doing. On June 22nd, with one of the lieutenants, Shadwell Clerke of the Light company, he made his way down the rocky road, crossed the Coa, and came to Almeida, where they stayed the night with Cox, the English governor. The next day they went on to

RETREAT FROM THE FRONTIER

Rodrigo, and examined the whole fortress; then rode towards the enemy camp to get a nearer view of a Frenchman, for King was rather short-sighted. Naturally enough, the French pickets opened fire, and one of the horses was hit. After this hint they retired, first taking off their hats and bowing, the Frenchmen answering, " Bon soir, messieurs; allez vous en !"

A week later Ney bridged the Aguedo and cut off the town; and, after a gallant resistance the Spaniards surrendered July 10th. Eleven days later the French advance began in good earnest.

The siege of Almeida began August 15th, and the town fell twelve days later. Wellington had drawn back his line; and while Masséna lingered trying to collect transport the English army began its retreat. The country was laid waste, the people told to flee to Lisbon, and destroy what they could not carry.

Covered by Crauford, the 1st, Third, and 4th Divisions went slowly down the Coimbra road, and soon discovered that the French were not following on their heels, but had marched west, and were converging on Vizeu.

The English soldiers did not approve the order to retreat, but discipline had improved, and, with few exceptions, the regiments behaved well. They had faith in their general, and behind them lay, not the sea, but those mysterious lines of which they had talked and guessed so much.

Masséna's advance from Vizeu gave Wellington hope of crushing his enemy in a pitched battle; for, barring the way to Coimbra, ran the heights of Busaco, a single continuous line, joining another range on the left, and dropping suddenly to the River Mondego on the right. The position was certainly nine miles long, and crossed by four roads, and the heather and furze with the granite outcrops made the movement of troops none too easy; but the western slope gave admirable cover, with a country road traversing the whole length.

On September 24th the main army turned off the highway to the right, crossed the Mondego, and took up a position on the heights. Lightbourne's brigade came to the river, and the leading regiments fell out and began to strip before entering the broad, rapid stream. Then up swung the Fifth, the Light company leading; King quietly turned on his horse, and said, " You know what to do," and the battalion, without a moment's pause, entered the river in column of sections, marched through waist-deep and out the other side without a break in the line, and without a musket splashed or grain of wet powder.

Skirmishing soon began with the French advance-guard; but the main army was slow in coming up, and Wellington had ample time to collect his divisions. For the next forty-eight hours King barely rested or slept; the Third Division held the centre, Lightbourne's the left-hand brigade. On the left the hill rose abruptly, and on this inaccessible ground were the Guards and Cameron's men. On Picton's right were stationed a Portuguese brigade and Leith's division. The 2nd Fifth numbered 31 officers and 464 men.

From the ridge the French movements were very plain; the armies came toiling on, and great bivouac fires burned all the night of the 26th; but on the hill-top the redcoats lay dark and silent, no fires, all very quiet and still. Masséna, victor of Austerlitz, and yet to meet the English; he only knew of them as the men who could win if they were three against one, who had fled to Corunna and retreated after Talavera, and who had now run before him, leaving two besieged towns to their fate. He determined to march boldly up the hill and drive through any resistance he might meet. Ney was ordered to attack the right centre, while Reynier was sent against the left.

Reynier started at dawn; there was a heavy ground mist, but his skirmishers made their way forward, and Merle's division was sent to the right against Lightbourne's brigade. At the foot of the slope, all along the front lay the light companies, and the first spattering shots brought the British to arms. The mist began to clear. King had his men along the hill-top; on their right ran a combe, and at the head, a little receded, stood the

88th, of Mackinnon's brigade, sent by Picton to support this weak place in the line. Merle's men swung up the hill, their officers urging them on. Clerke and the Light company came running back, and shots from the French skirmishers began to take effect in the close ranks of the waiting men. Wellington came galloping up from the left wing and bade King withdraw his men under cover of the crest, promising them that when the time came they should charge. King fixed bayonets and dressed his ranks. Merle's big battalions were clambering up, alignment somewhat lost, but formidable, nevertheless; short-sighted King, peering forward, thought his time had come, and joyfully the Fifth sprang forward. " Too soon, King ! " cried Brent Spencer, motioning them back; " too soon ! " and at the order King halted his men. Then came a roar from their right, and down the combe and over the crest came the 88th, while half the 45th swept, cheering, on the flank. Merle's columns rolled back, broken and lost. Never another Frenchman came up that hill.

Not a man moved in the ranks of the Fifth till night-capped Picton rode by to say the day was won; they stood as ordered with their virgin colours, and still untried; but King was proud and confident of his men.

That day the English lost 632 men, their allies much the same, while Masséna had learnt his lesson at the cost of 4,498. The 2nd Fifth had only one man killed, and a sergeant and four men wounded.[1]

Before Masséna could outflank him, Wellington slipped away and retreated by Fornos and Coimbra. Junot and his army entered Coimbra on October 1st, hard on their heels; but the plunder of that well-provisioned town put the French army out of action for the time being. On October 10th Wellington was safe within the lines of Torres Vedras. The regiments of the Third Division came in for some censure for their conduct on the march; it was a great temptation to the hungry men to leave the deserted towns to the French

[1] *Gazette*, October 4th, 1809.

marauders, but the 2nd Fifth appear to have upheld their reputation for good conduct.

The famous lines stretched across the peninsula from the Tagus to the Atlantic, garrisoned by 20,000 second-line troops. To support the garrisons between Torres Vedras and the sea, a twelve mile-stretch, the Third Division was cantoned. The wet weather began on October 8th, and the temporary huts proved poor protection, and the heather thatching let the rain in. The officers used their cloaks to line the walls.

Outside the lines Masséna stayed a month, unwilling to batter himself against such defences; then, suffering greatly from want of food and the bad weather, he withdrew to Santarem.

King's health gave way; his old wounds, always troublesome, broke out again; and a bad attack of fever forced him to apply for sick leave.

By December 1st Wellington's army was in winter quarters, the Third Division at the western end of the lines. Lightbourne was sent home; and Colville,[1] an officer of good reputation, who had seen service in the West Indies, took over the command. The brigade numbered 122 officers, and 1,533 men, excluding sick and detached.[2]

[1] Honble. Sir Charles Colville, G.C.B., etc., third son of John, eighth Lord Colville of Culross; born 1770; served with distinction in Peninsular War; wounded at taking of Badajos; a general in the army, and afterwards colonel of the Fifth Foot; Governor of Bombay 1819-1825; and of Mauritius 1828-1833; died 1843.
[2] According to Fortescue ("History of British Army," vii., 419), Dunlop superseded Lightbourne, sent home September 10th; but Oman (iii., Appendix) gives Colville in command of the brigade in November, 1809.

CHAPTER XXVIII

1811

GEORGE III.

REDINHA, March 12th—SABUGAL, April 3rd—FUENTES DE ONORO, May 5th—BADAJOS, May 30th–June 17th—EL BODEN, September 25th

THE DIVISIONS IN THE PENINSULA.

The 1st, Gentlemen of the Guards.
The 2nd, Corps of observation, not seen but heard of.
The 3rd is *The Fighting Division*.
The 4th, Will fight if asked.
The 5th, Comes to the towns after they are taken.
The 6th is always scattered about.
The 7th is always trying to collect them together, and
The Light Division is The Division.

U. S. J., 1833.

RICHARD ENGLAND: 2ND FIFTH

WELLINGTON'S men were none too well fed or comfortable; but behind them was the open sea, a highway for the King's ships. Masséna at Santarem was in a far worse case—reduced to living on the country, cut off from all communications, his army dwindling by starvation and disease. Wellington was content to wait; the French must either retreat or attack, and for either course he was prepared. Beresford was sent across the Tagus to bar the south, the other troops remained in their old quarters.

Brevet-Lieutenant-Colonel James Bathurst of the Quartermaster-General's staff was gazetted major in the 2nd Fifth *vice* Broke, who exchanged February 16th. In King's absence Ridge commanded the battalion.

News came that Soult had left Cadiz and was marching

into Estremadura with 2,000 men. Olivenza fell January 23rd, and Badajos was besieged. Masséna could hear the guns, but dared not cross the Tagus in face of Beresford. When the sound of cannon ceased, and no news of Soult came through, Masséna in despair turned north on March 6th. He concealed his movements well, and it was two days before Wellington discovered the birds had flown. The Light Division was sent in pursuit, Picton in support. The troops were slow in getting under way, but the trail was an easy one; the whole country lay desolate, and the sight of the murdered peasants and pillaged homes roused the Englishmen, and spurred on men who at no time needed any urging for a fight. Alcobaça, Pombal, and Leira were in flames.

The Third Division[1] reached Permes on the 9th, the Light Division ahead of them, and the 5th Division a day behind. The Fifth had done with retreats and blockades, the hunt was begun. They were at Leira on the 10th; from there the whole division was hurried forward; and the next day, after a hard march, came up with the van. In front of them, across a little river, was Pombal, held by the French rear-guard under Ney's command. Picton was ordered to the left to ford the stream as best he could and cut off the rear, while some of the light troops rushed the bridge and took the town. This much was done, but Picton had Ney to deal with, and did not get his men round quick enough; the Fifth hurried on only to see the French corps' orderly retreat. Five miles down the road Ney turned again, and, dividing his army, left Mermet on the high ground south of the valley of the Ancos, while Marchand crossed the stream and posted himself on the hills behind Redinha, covering the Coimbra road.

By 5 o'clock on the morning of the 12th the vanguard was on the march, Picton on the right, Pack, with a Portuguese brigade, in the centre, the Light Division on the left. Mermet had first to be driven from his woods; in this the Light company of the Fifth took

[1] British, 4,500; Portuguese, 1,550.

part, and it was probably here that Lieutenant Clerke[1] was so severely wounded that his leg had to be amputated. The first position carried, the troops were formed up with great accuracy and celerity, Picton in the centre, his division in two lines. Between them and the enemy was the river, crossed by one narrow bridge with a ford close by, both commanded by cannon. Picton fought his way over, and the other troops followed; the heights were quickly won, and the rearguard driven back upon the main army at Condeixa.[2]

Trant, with a few irregulars, was holding Coimbra; so Masséna turned east down the Celorico road; leaving Ney to hold Condeixa, from which he was skilfully manœuvred by the vanguard. His hurried retreat somewhat inconvenienced Masséna.

Wellington pressed on; these were days of hard marching; a fight was a rest to the weary troops, who had far outdistanced their transport, and had only the leavings of Masséna's army for subsistence.

At Casal Nova on the 13th the Light Division involved themselves in a hard fight, and Picton had to go to their rescue. The Fifth had eight men wounded.[3]

On the 15th at Foz d'Arouce Ney turned once more, or perhaps he was caught napping, for half his troops were left on the west bank of the Ceira, and no very good watch was kept. It was a thick foggy morning, and the English started late; but Wellington ordered the attack to go forward, and sent Picton to the right and Pack to the left, with Crauford between. The sudden assault broke the Frenchmen, who lost 250 men and, more important, some baggage and food, for the redcoats had hardly a biscuit between them. The Fifth lost one man killed and seven wounded.[4]

After a day's rest the army divided, and the Third

[1] Lieutenant T. H. S. Clerke received £100 per annum pension for loss of leg, March 12th, 1812.
[2] British losses, 12 officers, 193 men; French, 14 officers, 213 men. The Fifth lost 1 officer wounded, 3 men killed and 5 wounded (Oman). Colville, their brigadier, was mentioned in Wellington's despatch.
[3] Oman.   [4] Oman.

Division, with the 1st and 5th, was sent along a parallel road to the retreating army. Picton crossed the Alva on the 18th; by the 20th the whole army was across and halted, while the cavalry, Third and Light Divisions were given what food there was left, and sent on; but Masséna kept his lead, and made his way to Celorico.

Picton's men had but one bread ration to last them four days when from their crannies and hidden caves the peasants brought down pitiful gifts of food from their little store. They thought to catch the French at Celorico, but the cavalry rode in to find a deserted town; Masséna had gone south. This meant more work for the Fifth; Picton was sent round by Prados, and, directly the main army came up, Wellington started for Guardo. Without any waste of powder and shot the French were turned out of Guardo and forced across the Coa; there Masséna, though he attempted to guard a twenty-mile line, was in a very strong position, for the Coa was difficult to ford, and the ground rose on the eastern bank.

Opposite the main position lay the Light Division, with the Third on their left, and the 5th Division beyond the Third. Erskine (in temporary command of the Light Division) was ordered to turn the French left, while Picton and Dunlop (in temporary command of the 5th Division) contained the enemy. The morning of April 3rd was so foggy that Picton and Dunlop refused to move, but impetuous Erskine rushed forward and committed his troops; he was, of course, greatly out-numbered, his brigades making a gallant fight against the French divisions. It began to rain, and the fog lifted a little; Wellington, seeing the Light Division struggling with three times its strength, sent Picton across the Coa. The general rode past his troops, his stick over his arm, and gave them a word of good advice "Steady, don't throw away your fire." The Light companies and Colville's brigade led the way, and the hard-pressed riflemen on the hill heard a volley, and looking to their left, saw the Fifth coming up at a tremendous pace, bayonets fixed, and cheering as they came. Merle had swung south to meet the first attack, and the Fifth caught his troops on the flank and rolled them up. The rest of Picton's men came along and joined in the pursuit. The rain turned to a storm of hail; nothing could be seen, the troops were therefore halted and ordered to bivouac where they stood. The Fifth had two officers, Lieutenant Sinclair and Ensign Williams, severely wounded, and one sergeant and five men; they were mentioned in Divisional Orders; " The 2/5, commanded by Major Ridge, is entitled to, and deserving of, great credit for its steadiness and gallantry in repulsing the enemy's column at the passage of the Coa near Sabugal."

Masséna fell back, April 5th; and, with the French across the frontier, Wellington could rest content. The Third and the Light Divisions had borne the brunt of the long pursuit : " the Light Division had the fighting as well as the fag, the Third had only the fag," said one of the riflemen; but the Fifth certainly had done their share of the fighting. Picton's division had won a name, and of that division the Fifth was the senior regiment, and could justly claim the place of honour. Ridge had done well; and King, on his way out to rejoin, had every reason to be proud of his young soldiers.[1]

Without siege train Wellington could not attempt Ciudad Rodrigo, so contented himself by a blockade; leaving Spencer in command, he went off to Beresford at Badajos on April 12th. A fortnight later Masséna came to life again; and, with his army rested and reinforced, appeared before Rodrigo and crossed the Agueda. That same day Wellington returned, and at once decided to hold his ground. His chosen line ran from the old fort at Aldea on his left to Fuentes de Onoro on the right; in front was the Dos Casas, formidable on the left, but easy of passage farther west. The greater part of the army was massed behind the little town; here were the 1st and Third, with the 7th and Light Divisions in support; the high-walled town itself was held by the

[1] Masséna's army in September, 1810, numbered 65,050; in March, 1811, 44,407; and in April, 39,546.

Light companies, twenty-eight in all, of the 1st and Third Divisions. The 2/83rd was in support. The Light company of the 2nd Fifth[1] was in the battalion commanded by Lieutenant-Colonel Williams of the 5/60th.

The roads were black with French troops, and early in the afternoon of May 3rd the attack began. Masséna demonstrated against the whole line, and Colville's brigade was moved to the left to fill up a gap between the Third and 6th Divisions, but the main attack fell on the devoted Light companies in their little stronghold. Here fierce fighting went on all the afternoon with varying fortune, but the French could not break through. The Fifth had four men wounded. All the next day the two armies stayed as they were, bickering only in Fuentes de Onoro; Crauford rejoined, and also King, in time for the next day's fighting. Masséna had his cavalry out, and they soon discovered that Wellington's right flank was unprotected. This Wellington knew very well, and the 7th Division was moved out to lengthen the line; the Light companies came back to their regiments, and fresh battalions were sent to hold the town. Colville's brigade was back with the Third Division, and the Fifth could see the French cavalry moving across the plain against the little 7th Division. Crauford was sent to the rescue; and, to meet the enemy, Wellington swung back his whole right *en potence*, Mackinnon touching Fuentes, with Colville on his right. Towards them retired the 7th and Crauford's men in pretty order, forming square and repulsing the charging enemy. In Fuentes the battle raged again; the pickets of the Third Division were called in, and again the Light companies were sent to reinforce the garrison. The soldiers were worn out by eight hours' fighting in the dust and heat; but at two in the afternoon Mackinnon's brigade, more fortunate than Colville's, charged down and swept the French out for the last time. The worst of the fighting was over; Masséna would not risk his men against that stubborn line that stood waiting. The

---

[1] Strength at Fuentes de Onoro, 28 officers, 476 men (Oman).

Allies lost 1,452 and the French 2,192; the Fifth, seven wounded in the two days.[1] Masséna had had enough, and, abandoning Almeida, he retreated. For a time there was nothing to be feared in the north, so Wellington, knowing that Beresford must soon try conclusions with Soult, immediately after the battle sent him reinforcements. The Third and the 7th Divisions marched south on May 14th by way of Castello Branco, now familiar ground to the 2nd Fifth. They marched well and eagerly, but were too late for Albuera, fought on the 16th; not till a week later did they come to Campo Mayor. Soult had retreated, and once more Badajos was to be besieged. Wellington left Spencer in the north and arrived to take command. On the 27th the Third Division crossed the Guadiana, and took up position before the great fortress. There, having a rest from battles and marches, the 2nd Fifth took to trench-digging. At dusk on the 30th the first parallel was begun. They were only 800 yards from the castle, but, uninterrupted, they worked all night, and by morning had a trench three feet deep, with a three-foot parapet, 1,100 yards long. Next the guns were got into position, curious old brass cannon of the wars a century old. The enemy's guns were more effective; and the men in the trenches found that a shell, at a distance a pretty sight, was far from pleasant near at hand. One fell in the middle of a working-party, who bolted for the traverses, and Trench of the 74th was knocked headlong into a party of sappers with gabions, in one of which he stuck fast. "Well," said King, "I often saw a gabion in a trench, but this is the first time I ever saw a Trench in a gabion."

Across the Guadiana, in front of Fort San Cristoval,

[1] Eighteen regiments bear Fuentes de Onoro on their colours, but not the Fifth. There seems no adequate reason why they should be left out. The light companies were certainly engaged, and though the casualties were small, those of the 45th and 51st were even less. If it be maintained that the regiment as a whole was not engaged, this would apply equally to Busaco, and with greater reason to Vimeiro.

lay the 7th Division, and to them were entrusted the assaults of June 6th and 9th, both valiant failures. Without adequate artillery or engineers the task was hopeless; moreover, Marmont, who had superseded Masséna, was moving south to join Soult, and the Allies had no wish to be caught in the trenches. Wellington withdrew his guns and stores, and then his infantry, and ordered Spencer south. The Fifth crossed the Guadiana on June 17th; and, with the rest of the Third Division, retired to the left of the allied line, between Ougella and Campo Mayor. They had not come out unscathed; between May 30th and June 5th Lieutenant Sedgewick and three men had been killed,[1] and four men wounded; and an unhealthy fever, bred in the low river lands, had broken out in the army.

Soult and Marmont met and exchanged compliments, but accomplished little. Badajos was provisioned; but Wellington they dared not attack, and presently Soult went south. Wellington sent his men back to the highlands, the Third Division to Castello Branco. Reinforcements came from England, including the 77th Foot for Colville's brigade.

After a short rest the Third and 7th Divisions were ordered north again; though the attempt at Badajos had failed, there might still be time to take Rodrigo before Marmont could go to the rescue. The 2nd Fifth marched the first week in August, without their Colonel, for King had again broken down, and Ridge was in command. The Light Division led the way, followed by the Third, and these two divisions cut off Rodrigo from the east and established a blockade. The Fifth lay at Fuente Guinaldo, about fifteen miles south of the fortress, where Wellington made his headquarters; and there, for close on six weeks, the general's bodyguard kept watch and ward—for, on August 11th, Pakenham had written to Colville: " Sir, His Excellency having ordered a British Regiment of the Third Division to be stationed at Head Quarters at Guinaldo, from the uniformly exemplary conduct of the Fifth Regiment,

[1] Cannon.

From a miniature in the possession of the Officers' Mess
First Battalion Northumberland Fusiliers.

To face page 312.

Major-General Picton desires it may be ordered for that duty."

Ciudad Rodrigo was well provisioned, and Marmont was not roused to action until he learnt of a siege train on its way from Lisbon; then he hurried north. On August 22nd Wellington had news of his approach, and Crauford and Picton were ordered to call in their troops, leaving the Salamanca road open; outposts from the Third Division occupied the plateau south of Rodrigo.

The next day French cavalry appeared in the plains. Colville, at headquarters, was ordered to send the Fifth north; apparently it was by Wellington's express desire that the Fifth were sent,[1] and the order was given to the officer commanding, and by him notified to General Colville. They marched away, Major Grey in command, on the evening of the 24th to support two batteries covering a main road running south from Rodrigo, at a position not far from the village of El Boden. Pickets were placed, and all made safe against surprise; but the night was an anxious one, for there was only a thin cavalry screen between Marmont's main army and the scattered outposts. Early next morning that screen was pierced, and vast bodies of enemy horse moved across the plain. Colville was anxious about his detached and well-loved little battalion, and at daybreak rode forward to see how they fared. He found the Fifth on a little height, covering the two Portuguese batteries, with a gully to cover their right, and five squadrons of German hussars in support. One company posted in advance was under cover of a stone wall on the hill slope.

The enemy were seen to divide into three columns, one evidently making for the El Boden road. Colville hurried back to his brigade and ordered the 77th forward to support their comrades. Ridge, who had been absent when the battalion marched, came hurrying up.

Down the road came a French cavalry brigade, while a battery took position on a confronting hill. The Portuguese guns opened; and at that moment Welling-

[1] See *U. S. J.*, 1831, i. 98.

ton rode up and bade the infantry hold their ground, promising to send cavalry to their support.[1] He had scarcely moved to the rear before the enemy charged and cut their way through to the Portuguese guns, the artillerymen disputing every inch of the ground, but overborne and ridden down. Ridge did not hesitate a moment; boldly he called on his men; and down from their place of vantage they moved, steadily and with precision. Three times they halted, fired, reloaded, and marched on; the third volley broke the French dragoons; and, with a cheer, the Fifth fixed bayonets and charged. A single battalion of infantry in line charged half a cavalry brigade. The Portuguese gunners ran back to their batteries and fired a parting shot. By this time the 77th had arrived, but the fight was not yet over; again and again the enemy came on and tried to break a way through, until, at last, the leading squadrons refused to dash themselves again against the iron wall of the two devoted regiments. Then the French tried to find a way through between the contested hill and El Boden village, now deserted of its English troops. All the Third Division had been called in, and the Fifth were in danger of being cut off; the guns and cavalry, and a lately arrived Portuguese regiment were sent to the rear; and then, covered by two squadrons, the Fifth and the 77th made their way south. The two small battalions made but a single square.[2] In the flat country, unbroken by cover, they were caught by the enemy. On three sides at once came the charging squadrons. The square waited in grim silence until, at thirty yards, they poured in such

---

[1] An account of this action in the *U. S. J.*, 1829, p. 352, apparently written by Major John Grey, has been used for detail concerning the movements of the Fifth. This account was somewhat severely criticized in the *U. S. J.*, 1830, p. 871, by a late member of General Colville's staff. Both writers mention the presence of Wellington, but do not imply that he gave any direct orders, except to artillery, beyond general instructions to Colville before going to the rear. This he appears to have done before the arrival of the 77th. The staff officer gives high praise to Major Ridge. The correspondence is continued in *U. S. J.*, 1831, pp. 98 and 254 (see Appendix).

[2] 2nd Fifth, 550; 77th, 450.

a fire that the dragoons recoiled; and then, broken and beaten, were charged by the German hussars. One French officer had his horse shot under him and lay on the ground as if dead; a hussar cut at him, and he sprang up and defended himself with his sword. Up galloped another hussar, but the Frenchman would not surrender. Young Canch,[1] anxious to save a gallant enemy, ran out from the square, but before he could reach him the baffled Germans had pistolled, and, to the great regret of the Fifth, killed the Frenchman.

The French squadrons then kept their distance, and the Fifth joined the long column of the retreating Third Division. " For six miles across a perfect flat, without the slightest protection from any incident of ground, without their artillery, and almost without cavalry (for what are five squadrons against twenty or thirty ?), did the Third Division continue its march. During the whole time the French cavalry never quitted them; six guns were taking the division in flank and rear, pouring in a shower of round shot, grape, and canister. This was a trying and pitiable situation for troops to be placed in, but it in no way shook their courage or confidence; so far from being dispirited or cast down the men were cheerful and gay." Picton, cool and unconcerned, rode along the side of the column and kept his troops moving as if on parade. There was one last flourish from Montbrun's cavalry, and a mounted officer called out, " Had we not better form square ?" " No," answered Picton, shading his eyes from the sun; " it's only a ruse to frighten us, and it *won't do*."[2] And in safety they came into camp at Fuente Guinaldo.

The total loss to the Allies was 149; of these the Fifth had 5 killed, and 1 officer and 13 men wounded— not a big price to pay for their good work. Wellington

[1] Ensign Thomas Canch, joined Fifth 1809, having probably first served with them as a volunteer or in the ranks. He served in the Peninsula, August, 1808, to December, 1812, and October, 1813, to end of war. He lived to receive the Peninsular medal with twelve clasps. In February, 1840, he was appointed Fort-Major of Edinburgh Castle; sup. pay £83 13s. 4d. per annum.
[2] " Memoirs of Grattan of the 88th," p. 116.

said of them: " I cannot conclude this report . . . without expressing . . . my admiration of the conduct of the troops engaged in the affair of the 25th inst. . . . The conduct of the 2/5, commanded by Major Ridge, in particular, affords a memorable example of what the steadiness and discipline of the troops and their confidence in their officers can effect in the most trying and difficult situations. The conduct of the 77th regiment, under Lieutenant-Colonel Bromhead, was equally good;[1] and I have never seen a more determined attack made by the whole of the enemy's cavalry, with every advantage of assistance by superior artillery, and repulsed by these two weak battalions."

With his Third Division safe Wellington was ready for the enemy, but Marmont declined to face him, and turned back to his winter quarters in New Castile and the long campaign came to an end. Wellington kept the Third, 4th, and Light Divisions on the Spanish frontier, to maintain a mild blockade of Rodrigo.

[1] Colville commended the " more perfect instruction and discipline of the 2nd Fifth as superior to the more recently enlisted 77th, especially noting the perfect silence and attention in officers and men."

CHAPTER XXIX
GEORGE III.

CIUDAD RODRIGO, January, 1812—BADAJOS, April, 1812-June, 1812

RICHARD ENGLAND: 2ND FIFTH

IT must not be forgotten that Wellington's campaigns were only a part of the great war, although they were the deciding factors in the struggle. In Spain the Spanish armies were fighting hard in most adverse circumstances, and their digressions were of great value. In Catalonia, Aragon, and Andalusia the war went on, and after the defeat of Blake the triumphant French invaded Valencia. Napoleon had heard that the English, after many defeats, were reduced to a mere handful of starving men, therefore Marmont could well spare a third of his army, and he ordered him to despatch Montbrun and 15,000 men to Valencia.

That autumn and winter of 1811 Wellington had watched like a cat for his opportunity, for at last his siege train was ready; and when Marmont weakened his force, he judged the time had come. In snow and storm the British divisions were moved up to the Agueda, the Third to Martiago and Zamora.

In Rodrigo, Governor-General Barrié commanded a garrison of 1,600 infantry, two companies of artillery, and a detachment of engineers. He had ammunition in plenty, and 153 heavy guns, but there was a scarcity of gunners.

Wellington began to cross the river on January 6th; the sleet had stopped, and a light frost set in; luckily for them the Third Division were already on the left bank, and escaped a freezing. By the 8th the trap had closed; that day the Light Division seized the new redoubt on Great Teson, and the first parallel was begun. The divisions spent twenty-four hours in the trenches, and then rested in camp; the Fifth had their first turn from midnight on the 11th to midnight on the 12th, and helped to make platforms for the guns; and there was always the damage done in the daytime by the enemy's guns to be repaired. The Light Division followed the Third, and nearly completed the batteries; and the next night the 1st Division began the second parallel. Santa Cruz, a fortified convent outside the walls, was stormed and carried. This the enemy presently retook; but on the 14th the batteries opened fire and the convent was stormed once more, and remained in English hands. The walls soon began to show signs of wear, and the cannon concentrated on the weak places. The Fifth spent the night of the 15th–16th in the trenches, but met with no adventures. For three days more the guns pounded away; the walls were breached in two places, and some of the French cannon were destroyed. Barrie refusing to surrender, Wellington judged the time had come for an assault.

The Third Division was ordered to storm the great breach, while the Light Division attacked the lesser one. The chosen hour was seven o'clock on January 19th, when it would be dark enough to conceal the movement of troops and yet too early to allow the French to repair the walls. The officers commanding brigades and regiments assembled together and set their watches that there might be no error in time. Brigade orders were issued, the 2/83rd were to line the second parallel, while the 2nd Fifth, the 77th, and 94th assembled behind the captured convent. From there Ridge was told to turn to the right and make for a place under the castle, where the counterscarp, covering the north front, joined the body of the fortress. The 2nd Fifth were to break down the gates, jump into the ditch, scale the fausse-braye, and from there make their way east to the great breach, where they would support the Forlorn Hope. They were to carry twelve ladders twenty-five feet long, and sacks stuffed with heather to break the fall.[1]

The 94th were to strike in half-way between the castle and the breach, the 77th to remain in reserve.

The little force assembled behind the convent in good time; Dunkin, Colonel of the 77th, was the senior officer; and, much disappointed at being left in reserve, gave orders with grim voice and set face. The Fifth were in great spirits. Macdougal had that very day rejoined from the staff, and his fine moustaches were much quizzed. Just before the hour Picton came galloping up on his cob to wish them " God speed "; " the Fifth," he knew, " could not be daunted, and he was confident the 77th would behave as well." Colville, too, came up to wish his little battalion good luck—he was temporarily commanding the 4th Division, and could not go with his men. Then the regiments moved off in column of sections, the Fifth leading; Colville walking along by Ridge's side, reluctant to let his brigade go into action without him. At a given place a staff officer and some engineers waited for them; then in perfect silence the men moved on. The moon rose, and they saw, barely three hundred yards away, the towering castle walls. There was a whispered word from the rear that Colonel Campbell of the 94th, temporarily commanding the brigade, wished to speak to Ridge; he looked at his watch, and saw there was little time to spare; Dubordieu with the grenadiers was ordered to go slowly on, and Ridge hurried away. He was soon

[1] Brigade Orders: " The Fifth Regiment will attack the entrance of the ditch at the junction of the counterscarp with the main wall of the place. Major Sturgeon will show them the point of attack. They must issue from the right of the convent of Santa Cruz. They must have 12 axes, in order to cut down the gate by which the ditch is entered at the junction of the counterscarp with the body of the place. The Fifth Regiment is likewise to have 12 scaling ladders, 25 feet long, and immediately on entering the ditch are to scale the Fausse Braye in order to clear it of the enemy's parties on their left towards the principal breach. It will throw over any guns it may meet with, and will proceed along the Fausse Braye to the breach in the Fausse Braye, where it will wait until Major-General Mackinnon's column has passed on to the main attack, when it will follow in the rear."

back at the head of the battalion, and they came right under the high walls without being seen or heard by the enemy. The engineers began to hack down the gates; then came the challenge, " Qui va là ? Sacrés Anglais !" The alarm was too late, there were few troops that side of the town, and the gates were down before a musket could be fired. Up went the ladders; the first broke with the press; Ridge then ordered an officer to stand at the foot of each and keep the men back; mounting one, he called on Ensign Canch, who carried the Colours, to show the way.

The enemy were completely surprised; for a few moments, infinitely precious, there was no opposition; and when the storm of musket-shots and hand-grenades poured down, the Fifth were firmly established on the fausse-braye, and were making their way rapidly to the breach. At the double they went forward, and were soon picking their way over the mass of rubble and broken rock. McKinnon's brigade had not yet arrived; only the leading companies of the 94th clambering the counterscarp were in sight. The garrison manned the breach, and the little force was swept by a hail of grape and musketry. Some of the Fifth knelt down to reply. Dubordieu exclaimed, " Major, it is as well to die in the breach as in the ditch, for here we cannot live !" " Up, brave men !" cried Ridge; and without a moment's pause the two regiments struggled up the heap of stones and rubbish and knee-deep soil. At the mouth Ridge called out to them to swerve right and left, for no man could stand against that deadly fire. At that moment he fell, but was up again in an instant; and, with his orderly sergeant, made his way across a forgotten plank over the ramparts and into Rodrigo. Here a handful of men, some thirty in all, joined him, and Colonel Campbell and six men of the 94th. They were in a narrow, dark street; close by they could hear the awful struggle in the breach, until there was a loud explosion, and afterwards silence. " I fear all is lost, and we are prisoners," said Campbell; then, through the quiet, they heard an English cheer—the Light Division had carried the lesser breach. Firing began again. Campbell formed the little party in two divisions two deep, ready to wheel right or left. Shortly after steps were heard; and, receiving no answer to their challenge, the left file fired a volley to which there was no reply. The firing died away, the advance-guard of the Light Division came through the street, and Ridge learnt that the ramparts were won.

The real storming-party had arrived at the great breach to find the Fifth and 94th in possession, with the 77th treading on their heels; all together they tumbled up under an awful fire. Twice the head of the column was shot away; then some of the Fifth and 88th managed to cross the ditch, storm the parapet, and kill the gunners. The garrison retreated, blowing up a great mine, which killed many men.

Sergeant-Major Golland came along and reported to Ridge, who thereupon made his way back to the breach with some difficulty, for his ankle had been hurt when he fell. Fitzgerald, with a great number of men, lay wounded; among them Canch, with his Colours firmly clasped, St. George and the Dragon nearly shot away.

Then Ridge set off to find the Governor. Here he was forestalled; but, with other officers, he billeted himself in the Governor's house, unkennelled the butler from the body of an old chaise, and, later, the Governor's cook slid down the chimney and gave himself up. Ridge secured a very handsome crimson and gold saddle-cloth, and a jewelled gun. He offered his spoils to Picton, but the general refused to take them. The drummers of the Fifth were completed with French drums.

In the town 7,000 excited and victorious soldiers were scattered from their regiments, some turned to plunder and some to feast. Many of the unhurt officers and steady men looked after the wounded, and endeavoured to keep order. Pillage was to some extent licensed, but there was more noise and confusion than actual violence. Ridge could say, " It was, even here, glorious to see Britons incapable of slaying unarmed men, though their lives became forfeit by awaiting the assault with two practical breaches." By morning most of the men were under control before Picton rode storming through the town. " Give us a cheer, your honour !" cried the grinning men. " Here, then, you drunken set of rascals, Hurrah, we'll soon be in Badajos !"

Ridge was too lame to move in the morning, but sent his orderly sergeant to the breach. Most of the wounded had been taken away, but the dead lay in heaps, and many wore the uniform with the gosling green; and there lay poor Macdougal, dead, stripped of his clothes, never more to flaunt his moustaches and staff finery. One sergeant and thirty-four men were killed; Major Grey, the second in command, Dubordieu[1] of the Grenadiers, and Lieutenants Wylde, McKenzie, D. E. Johnson, Fitzgerald, Fairtlough, and Ensigns Ashford and Canch, Volunteer Hillyard, three sergeants and fifty-five men were wounded. Lieutenant Pennyman,[2] of Number One company, had been wounded in the trenches just before the assault, but he would not go to the rear; and in the breach, was close up to the Grenadiers.

Ciudad Rodrigo had fallen in twelve days, and all the train and heavy guns of the army of Portugal were captured.[3]

[1] Dubordieu received a year's pay on account of his wounds, and later a pension of £100 per annum.
[2] Lieutenant Pennyman, or Pennington, afterwards paymaster of the 48th.
[3] In the controversy between the Fifth and 94th Foot, both regiments and their partisans claim to have been the first to ascend the breach and enter Rodrigo. Ridge's account implies that the 94th were there, or at least in sight, when the 2nd Fifth arrived at the breach. Other accounts distinctly state that the 2nd Fifth were the first arrivals. In any case, the leading companies of both regiments seem to have joined and made the ascent together, with the 77th close behind and mingled with the Fifth. Dunkin gave his orders a liberal interpretation and, under the circumstances, he was justified. Ridge and his orderly sergeant, Jones, were under the impression that they were actually the first to enter Rodrigo, and there were many in the army who thought the Gurwood-Mackie dispute would have a satisfactory conclusion in both parties acknow ledging that only an accident prevented Ridge from receiving the Governor's sword.

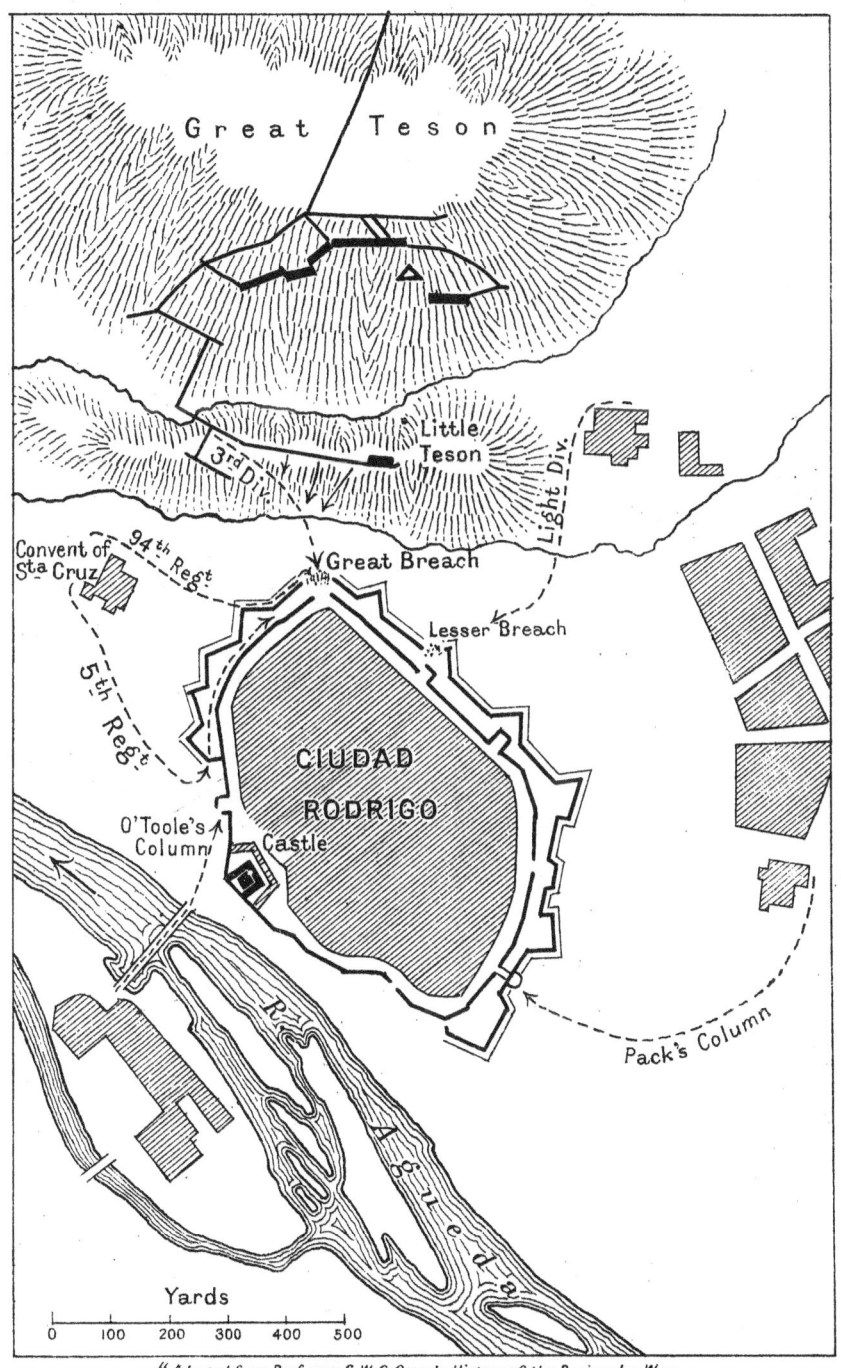

"Adapted from Professor C. W. C. Oman's History of the Peninsular War, by permission of the Clarendon Press."

Lieutenant-General Picton, in his Divisional Order from Zamorra, January 20th, 1812, said:

" By the gallant manner in which the breach was last night carried by storm, the Third Division has added much credit to its military reputation and has rendered itself the most conspicuous corps in the British Army. The breach was first entered by the Fifth, 77th, and 94th regiments, most ably supported by the flank companies, Major-General McKinnon's brigade, the 45th as well as other regiments of the Division. . . . Lieutenant-Colonel Campbell, commanding the Right Brigade and 94th, Lieutenant-Colonel Dunkin, commanding the 77th, and Major Ridge the 2nd Fifth, are peculiarly entitled to the thanks of the Lieutenant-General as having led and carried the breach."

Marmont only knew of the siege on the 14th; Madrid did not know until the town had been six days in English hands. Marmont heard of the fall on the 21st; he was then at Salamanca, and only 15,000 of his scattered force were within reach. Guessing that Wellington would next advance against Badajos, he left Rodrigo to its fate, and placed himself in the valleys of the Tagus and Douro.

Wellington repaired the walls and placed Rodrigo in a state of defence; and, on February 15th, a Spanish garrison was installed. Then, one by one, the British divisions made their way south, the Third from Zamora by the upper Agueda. They met with no opposition, for Marmont was preparing to invade Portugal. His orders had come from Paris, and, though he knew they were founded on a misconception of the situation, he dared not disobey. Once again he concentrated his army at Salamanca. This left the road clear; Soult's forces were too scattered to be a danger; and, even if Marmont broke into Portugal, he and his men would starve before Lisbon was in sight. Wellington could count on three weeks for the taking of Badajos. By the middle of March the Allies, except the 5th Division, were concentrated at Elvas; and, on the 16th, Beresford, with the Third, 4th, and Light Divisions, invested Badajos, while

Graham and Hill commanded a covering force of the remaining divisions and cavalry.

The fortress had been strengthened since the last siege, Fort San Cristoval improved, and glacis and counterscarp raised, and also a redoubt thrown up on the rising ground to the east. On the southern side many more guns had been mounted and the old breach repaired; the Rivillas stream had been dammed, and in the dry ditch of the Trinidad a narrow gully had been cut. The three bastions on the west had been mined, but this was betrayed by a deserter and they were left alone. Governor Phillipon commanded a garrison of picked troops, some 4,700 in all, who from experience knew every inch of the town.

No time was wasted, the night of the 17th was dark and wet, and, unmolested, the English started work. San Cristoval and the castle were left alone, but the first parallels were begun against the Trinidad and Santa Maria bastions. The French opened fire at daybreak; but, under cover of the heavy rain, the work went on. Next day the garrison made a sortie, but were driven off. The rain never ceased; the trenches were knee-deep in water; when at last the batteries were complete, it was four days before the guns could be moved.

At last the cannon were placed and the batteries opened fire. Two days' cannonade met with indifferent success; but on the 25th a covering fort was stormed and carried. The 26th was devoted to repairs. About this time Lieutenant Fairtlough, acting as engineer, was cut in two by a round shot from San Cristoval. All day and every day the bombardment went on, but the stout walls showed little signs of wear. As the parallels advanced they cut into the lower ground, and the water in the trenches rose waist high. The Rivillas flooded the low land, and an attempt to break the dam failed.

On April 3rd two breaches showed in the walls, and by the 4th these were judged practical. There was a rumour that Soult was hurrying to the rescue; it was better not to delay. Phillipon was making a good fight, and the garrison quickly raised an inner wall behind the two gaps. The whole of the 6th April the cannon pounded away, and a third breach, between the two first, was made in the curtain wall. The assault was ordered for half-past seven that night; the Light Division and the 4th were ordered for the storm.

Picton hurried off to Wellington to plead that his division might take part; he volunteered to carry the castle while the attention of the garrison was fixed on the breaches; he vowed it could be done, and had himself marked a spot where the wall was comparatively low. Wellington gave in to his impetuous lieutenant, and two other demonstrations were ordered to take place at the same time as the main assault.

As soon as it was dark a covering party crept forward and lay under the walls, listening to the sentries and their cry, "Alles war wohl ins Badajos."[1] For some reason the attack was postponed until ten o'clock. Picton started before time, and at 9.45 was well under way. His troops leaving the first parallel were seen and caught in a heavy fire, for the French were burning flares by the flooded river; but the men plunged in and crossed by the ruined mill, rushing the palisade on the western side. Here they were sheltered, but as they rushed the steep slope, Kempt's brigade leading, they came under fire from the San Pedro bastion. Picton was hit, and fell, the command devolving on Kempt. Six ladders were placed against the walls, but the fire was so heavy no man could gain a foothold; all the officers were shot down; Kempt's men fell back. Next came the two brigades of Portuguese, to fall back in their turn.

Campbell's brigade, the 2nd Fifth leading, came running up, and placed their ladders a little to the right of Kempt's. The ladders were heavy, and the breathless men fumbled as they raised them. Ridge sprang on one and called to Canch to mount another,

[1] From which it would appear that the garrison included German mercenary or auxiliary troops (see also " History of British Army," vii., 395).

and again lead the Fifth. Canch started up, but was hauled down by the engineer officer, who wished to make it fast. Ridge, smarting at the delay, once more called out, " Canch, won't you lead the Fifth ? " This was too much, and Canch broke away and sprang up, the men crowding after him. Next to them, little L'Estrange, leading his men, found his ladder too short by ten yards or more; but he had not done his schooling at St. Malo for nothing, and hailing the sentry, was hauled up by a French musket, saving his life and gaining a foothold in the fortress, where, side by side with Ridge and Canch, he held the parapet until some fifteen or twenty men could join them. Then the little band pushed on, driving the enemy before them. The first excitement over they could hear the uproar from the breach; Picton came hobbling up and relieved Kempt, who also had been wounded. Inch by inch the garrison defended the keep, but the Third Division were not to be denied, and by midnight the castle was securely held. It was meant as a last refuge for the garrison, and the main entrances had been blocked, leaving only one small postern gate.

The castle theirs, Picton's men set out to capture the town. The Fifth led the way, and outside the postern were met by a reserve regiment, who refused to surrender. At the first volley Ridge fell, as he would have wished, at the head of his men, in the heart of a conquered city, leaving not only his own little battalion nor Colville's brigade, but the whole army, to mourn his loss. The soul of truth and honour, a soldier son of a soldier family, brave with a courage that knew restraint, the Fifth paid dearly for Badajos when Ridge died.

For the town was won—the awful carnage at the breach had done its work; a brigade of the 5th Division had entered the town almost unobserved, and the castle, with all its reserves of ammunition and food, was in Picton's hands. Phillipon fled into San Cristoval, and surrendered at dawn.

All night and all the next day plunder and pillage went on. " I believe it has always been understood that

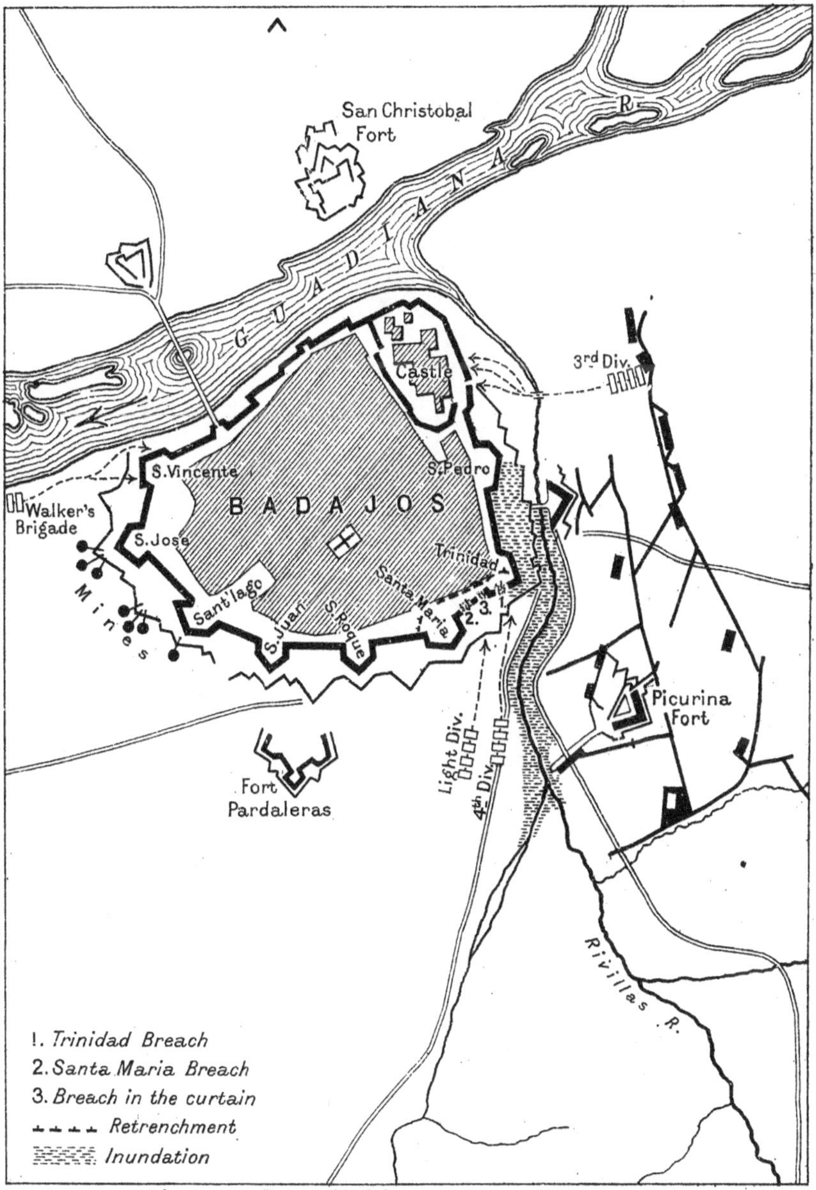

1. *Trinidad Breach*
2. *Santa Maria Breach*
3. *Breach in the curtain*
- - - *Retrenchment*
▒▒▒ *Inundation*

"*Adapted from Professor C.W.C. Oman's History of the Peninsular War, by permission of the Clarendon Press.*"

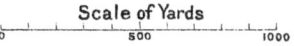
Scale of Yards
0   500   1000

the defenders of a fortress stormed have no claim to quarter," wrote Wellington in after years; and in Badajos they received none. The Fifth had Ridge to avenge, and the men of the Light Division swore the town should pay for their comrades' lives.

The following General Order was made on the 7th: " It is now full time that the plunder of Badajos should cease; an officer and six steady men will be sent from each regiment, British and Portuguese, of the Third, 4th, 5th, and Light Divisions into the town at 5 a.m. to-morrow morning, to bring away any men still straggling there."[1]

After Badajos, the 2nd Fifth had little time to bury their dead; Marmont was threatening Ciudad Rodrigo, and Wellington promptly turned north to the rescue. The Light Division and the Third led the way.

The army of Portugal had arrived before Rodrigo on March 30th, but without artillery (for all had been captured with the fortress) the siege promised little success. Leaving a containing division, Marmont set out to raid Portugal. He marched by Sabugal, ravaging the country; and, on April 14th, surprised and seized Guarda, driving out Trant and his Portuguese. The next day he heard of the fall of Badajos, and began to retreat.

The Third Division marched by Arronches and Portalegre, crossing the Tagus by the Villa Velha Bridge. On the 17th they occupied Castello Branco. By the 21st the cavalry were at Sabugal, the Light Division and Third close behind. The army of Portugal, ignorant of their approach, lay at Fuente Guinaldo, with the Agueda in full flood barring their retreat.

Then, just when an overwhelming victory appeared

[1] The 3rd Division (eight battalions) lost 521 men; the 2nd Fifth, 1 officer and 11 men killed, and 3 officers and 28 men wounded (Oman).

Cannon gives—Killed: Ridge and Fairtlough, and 17 men; wounded: Captains Bennet (aide-de-camp to Kempt) and Doyle, Lieutenant Pennington, and Ensign Hopkins, and 30 men. This includes casualties during the siege, but possibly Captain Bennet, on the staff, is not given in Professor Oman's return.

certain, the river fell, and Marmont escaped through the fords. Wellington carried the pursuit no farther; his army badly needed rest; and for six weeks he remained near Rodrigo resting his troops and collecting supplies. This was a difficult matter, for he had no money, and the Home Government was embarrassed by the immediate prospect of an American war. Nevertheless, reinforcements were ordered to Spain; and, among other Walcheren regiments, the 1st Fifth were sent to Cork to embark for the Peninsula.

King rejoined early in May, and resumed command; and, on June 1st, the 2nd Fifth were inspected, and were reported, " In every respect in as high order as could possibly be expected. The Regiment has distinguished itself on all occasions, and has been as conspicuous for its regularity and discipline as for its irresistible gallantry in the field."[1]

[1] This and the preceding reports are to be found in *St. George's Gazette* for 1899.

CHAPTER XXX

April–December, 1812

GEORGE III.

SALAMANCA CAMPAIGN

RICHARD ENGLAND: 1ST FIFTH AND 2ND FIFTH

THE 1st Fifth, or, rather, the remnant that returned from Walcheren, had been sent to Bexhill in Sussex. There, in March, 1810, Morley rejoined from Spain. At the different stages of his journey he divested himself of his temporary rank; setting out as sergeant, he first reduced himself to corporal; then, on arrival at Bexhill, to private, though it was not very long before he again won promotion.

In May the Fifth marched to Lewes to relieve the 82nd, and were there inspected by Major-General Houston, who reported that the discipline and system of the Battalion were excellent, that the officers were well-instructed and attentive, and appeared to have a proper knowledge of their men, and that the non-commissioned officers were good. The Battalion promised well, but was still very weak, and suffering from want of practice. Many of the men had the fever in them, and the recruits were young and sickly.

In the autumn they were again reviewed on Brighton Downs by the Regent and the Duke of Clarence (that same Prince William Henry who had once reviewed them on the banks of the Sorel). They were much commended for their appearance and discipline, and forthwith despatched to Ireland, where they spent the next year.

Early in 1812 the welcome route came, and Colonel

Pratt and his men marched from Fermoy to Cove to embark for Spain. An unhappy accident marred this departure. One young ensign lodged with his father in Cove; some of his friends came to see him off, and rowed with him out to the transport. As he went over the side his hand slipped, and, letting go of the man-ropes, he fell into the sea and was drowned.[1]

The 1st Fifth, a thousand strong, landed at Lisbon on June 24th; and, after a short rest in barracks, were sent off to join Wellington's army. They marched by Castello Branco and Ciudad Rodrigo. Wellington had crossed the Agueda three weeks before, and it was the middle of July before the 1st Fifth found him at Salamanca. They there joined the younger battalion in Campbell's brigade.

Wellington had invaded Spain with 48,000 men on June 13th. Naval raids kept many of the French troops pinned to the coast; and farther south the Spaniards had been stirred up to occupy Soult; Wellington hoped to catch Marmont at a disadvantage. The Allies marched in three columns; Picton commanded the left, made up of the Third Division, Le Marchant's cavalry, and Pack's and Bradford's Portuguese. Picton, still suffering from his Badajos wound, was laid low by an attack of fever; and on June 28th Pakenham, Wellington's brother-in-law, took over his command.

The army of Portugal was widely dispersed; Marmont had hurriedly to withdraw from Salamanca and retreat to give his army time to concentrate. Three forts, commanding the town from the south-west, were garrisoned and left to contain the English. This they did rather effectually, for Wellington had advanced without adequate artillery, and was forced to wait for both cannon and ammunition. The whole city turned out to welcome the Allies, but it was some days before the ·forts fell. Once the 2nd Fifth were called out and took position with the rest of the Third Division. Marmont was advancing to relieve the forts; but, after some

---

[1] *Vide* Morley, who gives the name as Ensign Pratt. He wa probably of the colonel's family, and may have been a volunteer.

FIRST BATTALION JOINS THE SECOND

thirty-six hours of looking and longing, he thought better of it, and did not venture to attack. After this the Third Division was sent to cover the left flank and hold the fords at the junction of the Douro and the Trabancos. Here the 1st Fifth joined them, and for a short time the two battalions marched and watched and fought side by side.

Marmont, too, had received reinforcements, and grew bolder. He watched Wellington as a cat watches a mouse, hoping to take him unawares, turn his flank, and cut him off from Rodrigo. For a week or more the two armies manœuvred. On July 20th Wellington was offered battle, but declined. The men were beginning to grumble; their feelings had been highly tried, for they had seen, marching parallel with them, within gunshot, the whole of Marmont's army. They were not allowed a shot, even when some cannon-balls came bowling in amongst them. Stern orders were passed along that no stand was to be made. That night Wellington bivouacked on the heights south-west of the town. The Third Division was still on the left, and lay across the Tormes, with headquarters at Cabrerezos. From there the line extended south to Arapile, with a front of about three miles.

By this time Marmont was contemptuous of his foe, and was certain he need fear no attack. Early the next day he began to lengthen his line, moving troops to his left, preparing to march round the British right and cut off the army from its base. Wellington had his troops well behind cover, where, unseen, he could prolong his line to meet the threatened attack. A messenger was also sent to Pakenham with orders to cross the river and march south, thus bringing the Third Division to the rear and right of the British line, where they would be able to act as circumstances should direct. Except for the bickering of skirmishes in front of the British centre, there was little action; and, as the day wore on, Marmont congratulated himself that he had so well judged his enemy, and he still further lengthened his line.

Pakenham got his orders at midday, and at once

set out. His column crossed by the town bridge and clattered through Salamanca. It was Sunday; in the open spaces people were praying for victory, while some of the Spaniards cursed the English for running away. Part of the baggage had been sent along the Rodrigo road, and now it seemed that Pakenham's men were following hard after it. One officer of the Fifth did indeed slip away, ostensibly for a glass of rum. " We shall be engaged to-day; the captain knows it, and, depend upon it, has taken French leave," observed Sergeant McNeil to Sergeant Morley. It would be charitable to suppose that he was really ill, for he appeared no more.

About two o'clock in the afternoon the column reached Aldea Tejada, where they halted for a short rest. They could make out, on the western heights, some of the English brigades; but all was quiet. Then, about half-past two, a roar of cannon broke out; and, at the same time, a horseman came galloping down the Arapiles road—Wellington himself, all alone, far out-distancing his staff. He rode up to Pakenham. " Edward, move on with the Third Division; take those heights in your front, and drive everything before you." " I will, my lord, by God ! " cheerfully answered Pakenham; and Wellington returned to the main army to order a general advance.

The Third Division set out, marching across the rough country, all hill and wooded valley. Wallace's brigade led the way, followed by the Portuguese, with Campbell in the rear. On the right rode two cavalry brigades. Out of sight, but only two miles away, the leading regiments of Thomières' division were heading straight for them. The cavalry saw the French first, and, charging, caught the head of the column as it came over the crest of a hill and flung it back broken and disabled. Then Thomières coming up found he had infantry as well as horse to deal with; Wallace was less than a thousand yards away. Hastily skirmishers were flung out to give the unwieldy brigades time to come into position, but Wallace, swinging into line from open column, poured in a volley at two hundred and fifty yards.

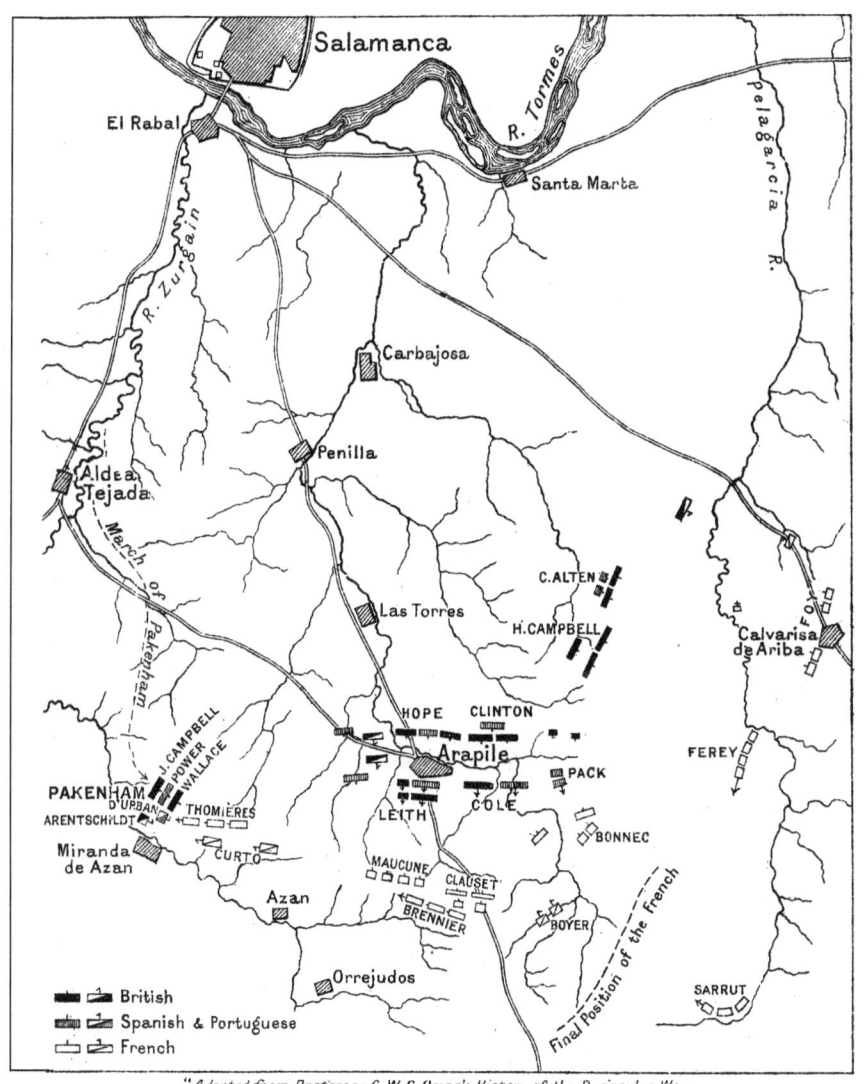

The French were bunched together, and, as Campbell's brigade came within range, his regiments deployed and swung into line, far outflanking them. Slowly the English advanced up the hill, coming under a furious fire. The French cavalry rode up and charged the right flank, the 1st Fifth as right-hand regiment, bearing the brunt. Three companies were drawn back *en potence* and the enemy beaten off, until Arentschildt's Horse could come to the rescue. Just at this time the fire from the hill-crest was so deadly that the Fifth staggered and fell back, retiring slowly a hundred paces.[1] Pakenham rode up to them. " Re-form !" he ordered quietly; then, a moment later, " Advance !" adding, " there they are, my lads; let them feel the temper of your bayonets," and on the Fifth went, everyone making up his mind for mischief. Keeping their order, they moved slowly until at last the bugles rang out " Charge !" then, with a rush the whole division swept over the crest and rolled the French column back. Thomières was killed, and all his divisional batteries taken, and his men scattered to the four winds. The Third Division did not lose 500 men.

Pakenham pressed on, driving the flying men back on the fugitives from the main front. Joining with the 5th Division, he swept back Maucune and Brennier, breaking through their rear-guard. Altogether on this day the French lost over 14,000 men, while the Allies lost under 5,000. The 1st Fifth had 10 men killed, and 6 officers and 110 men wounded. The 2nd Fifth lost 1 man killed, and 2 officers and 21 men wounded.[2]

---

[1] Oman implies that the charge of the French cavalry was the cause of the Fifth's retirement, and that they were at that time still part of the reserve brigade. Morley distinctly states that they fell back from the galling fire of the French infantry, and that they were then in line with the leading regiments, and advancing with them to clear the heights.

Cannon says the cavalry charge was repulsed by the three companies *en potence*, and in the excitement of the moment Morley may not have noticed this episode, for he, with other sergeants, had been called into the centre of the line and were grouped round the Colours.

[2] Captain Simcockes, Lieutenants Bird, McPherson, O'Dell, Gunn, J. B. Hamilton, who carried the Colours, Hillyard, and Ensign Pratt (Cannon).

During part of the day, King assumed command of the brigade in succession to Campbell, and the command of the 2nd Fifth devolved on Captain Bishop.

James Grant, of the second Battalion, deserves notice. He was a bandsman, and as such had his proper place in the rear. This did not please him when there was fighting to be done; and at Salamanca, as at other battles, he escaped from his station, and being a tall man placed himself on the right of the grenadiers. Wherever the 2nd Fifth had fought James Grant had been in the thick of the fighting; and from it all he escaped without a scratch; many years later, as Sergeant-Major, he died of an accident at Malta (1835).

The next day Wellington carried on the pursuit, and drove the French across the Douro. The pace slackened on the 25th, for the troops were exhausted by hard marchings. Leaving Clinton with the 6th Division to guard the Douro, Wellington made his slow triumphant way to Madrid.

The 2nd Fifth were under orders for home, so weakened were they by their hard service, and the following order was made from Arcala, July 27th, 1812:

" The Commander of the Forces cannot part with the officers and non-commissioned officers of the 2nd Fifth without again requesting them to accept his thanks for their uniform good conduct and brilliant and important services since they have been under his command."

The 2nd Fifth marched with the army to Madrid, and shared in the triumphant entry on August 12th. King Joseph had fled the day before. The road was crowded with people carrying laurels for the victors, and fruit, flowers, and wine; all the bells rang, and everyone shouted and sang. The army was overwhelmed with kindness; and at last the men had to be confined to quarters to save them from their hospitable Allies.

The 1st Fifth was left, with the other Walcheren battalions, with Clinton on the Douro.[1] They had all proved unfit for hard work; but after a short rest the

[1] On August 4th, 1812, the Adjutant-General notified the officer commanding the Fifth (in company with the 4th, 38th, 42nd, and 82nd) that the unhealthy state of the corps, owing to want of blankets, would oblige him to send the regiment to the rear.

SECOND BATTALION ORDERED HOME

first Battalion arrived in Madrid in time to take over all effective privates from the second Battalion, and to bid them God-speed.

On September 3rd the crippled remnant of Wellington's Bodyguard marched away with their skeleton ranks and tattered colours. The little ever-fighting, never-failing Fifth embarked at Lisbon in November, landing at Plymouth December 1st, having gained nothing but glory in Portugal and Spain.

A month later Wellington ordered a general offensive, and with the main Anglo-Portuguese army advanced against Burgos. The fortress proved unexpectedly strong, defying assault after assault, and fever attacked the weakened troops. A siege was impossible, for the ineffectiveness of the Spanish operations had permitted the French armies to concentrate. Soult evacuated Andalusia and joined King Joseph. Wellington retreated just in time, Soult in hot pursuit.

The Third Division had remained in Madrid, but were ordered to fall back with the main army. They had not suffered the same loss and frustration, and it is to be hoped that they did not share in the general ill-conduct of the troops. The commissariat and hospital staffs failed; the sick were neglected; the sound were doled out two rations in five days. Surly and hungry the men tramped back in ankle-deep clay and water, the worst dispositioned wreaking a mean revenge on the defenceless peasantry.

Soult clung to their heels, but no serious engagement took place. In December the Allies were across the frontier and safe in winter quarters, the Third Division lying about Castello Branco. The headquarters of the 1st Fifth were in the village of Ferrerina.

Morley, probably one of many, was down with typhus, and nearly died. All the winter he was ill, and the next spring was sent to the rear and to England as only fit for home service. On board the transport he met his old-time comrade Bishop, now ensign and adjutant in the 2nd Fifth, and " quite at his ease in conversation with the officers." The two joined the 2nd Fifth at Windsor.

CHAPTER XXXI

1813–1814

GEORGE III.

VITTORIA—NIVELLE—ORTHES—TOULOUSE

WILLIAM WYNYARD: 1ST FIFTH

INCESSANT rains delayed the opening of the new campaign, but Wellington made good use of his time. The whole army was reorganized and the Spaniards heartened for fresh fight.

Colville was back with his brigade, and one day there was a general stir all along the lines of the Third Division; word passed from mouth to mouth; little groups of men fell in, then whole battalions, then the three brigades, and they cheered themselves hoarse; for Picton had come back to his fighting men, and all was well!

About the middle of May, Wellington concentrated on the Douro, the Spanish armies preparing to co-operate. The moment was well chosen, for the Russian war was sapping the strength of France; and King Joseph, generalissimo in Spain, was not a strategist to be feared. Before he could determine where the blow threatened he found his flank turned and the English between him and the sea.

On June 2nd the Allies crossed the Esla. Five days later they were over the Carion, and were near enough to hear the roar of a great explosion: the French, in abandoning Burgos, had blown up the castle. Driving the enemy before him, Wellington marched on, toiling for six weary days over the wild hills. He came up with them in the valley of the Zadora. Vittoria lay six miles in their rear.

Seven bridges spanned the river which covered the French front. Graham was ordered to the left, Hill to the right; Picton commanded the centre. At daybreak on June 21st Wellington broke camp. It was wet, and there was a mist in the valley. Under cover of the mist they left the hills. Some of Hill's troops were first in action, and the 4th and Light Divisions were pressed well forward. The centre grew impatient under the bickering of the light troops, " Damn it !" exclaimed Picton, " Lord Wellington must have forgotten us !"

The day cleared, the development of the action could be seen, and the division began to suffer from shell-fire. Presently an aide-de-camp came galloping up with an order for the 7th Division to commence attack on the Mendoza Bridge in the left centre, with the 4th and 6th in support. This was too much for Picton. " You may tell Lord Wellington from me, sir, that the Third Division under my command shall, in less than ten minutes, attack the bridge and carry it. And the 4th and 6th Divisions may support if they choose." Then he shouted:

" Come on, ye rascals ! Come on, ye fighting villains !" and forward leapt the men. Wallace's brigade swarmed over the bridge; Colville turned to the left and plunged into the river, the 7th Division in support. They fought their way up the bank and pierced the French centre. Forward went Picton at the double, his division in echelon of battalion. The rest of the army crossed after him, but Picton kept well ahead, forcing the enemy back. A mile in front of Vittoria, on a little hill, the French made their last stand. Behind them the roads were blocked with a hapless crowd of fugitives, camp-followers, and sick. The Third Division, swinging into line, charged the hill; but with the courage of desperation the French resisted; then the 4th Division came up on the flank, the battle was over, and the cavalry took up the pursuit.

The whole of the artillery, vast treasure, and over 1,000 prisoners were taken, and, besides, the enemy lost some 6,000 killed and wounded. Wellington lost over 4,000.

The 1st Fifth had 4 officers killed and 4 wounded,[1] and 22 men killed and 133 wounded.

Colville's brigade was specially mentioned in the despatch: " Major-General the Honourable Sir Charles Colville's Brigade of the Third Division was seriously attacked in its advance by a very superior force, well formed, which it drove in, supported by Major-General Inglis's Brigade of the 7th Division, commanded by Colonel Grant of the 82nd. These officers, and the troops under their command, distinguished themselves."

Graham, with two divisions, was detached to reduce San Sebastian, but the main army went on in pursuit of King Joseph. Harried by the Light Division, the fugitives from Vittoria fled to the Pyrenees, and retreated behind the fortress of Pampeluna. The victorious redcoats hunted them through the rocky valleys; Picton, out on the right, drove Clauzel back, and the Fifth had a skirmish near the Horte del Reigen.

Then the tide turned. Soult superseded Joseph; San Sebastian and Pampeluna defied assault and menaced Wellington's rear; and in the valley of Roncesvalles Soult turned, outflanked and drove back the scattered pursuers. For eight days the battle went on —desperate fighting in the entangling hills. Picton was brought back to cover the retreat. Over against the Third Division lay D'Erlon, but he would not give battle. Then Wellington extricated his army and drove Soult back, but would not press the pursuit while the fortresses remained intact.

San Sebastian fell on August 31st, but Pampeluna held out against a Spanish force until the end of October. This considerably delayed the advance. And always there was political vacillation; no money, very little food, and insufficient clothing for the troops.

When the army advanced in November Picton was again absent, and Colville commanded the Third Division.

On the evening of November 9th Wellington's troops

---

[1] Captain Adams, Lieutenant Higgins, Ensign Bolton, Volunteer Reed killed; Captain Bateman, Lieutenants Welch, Galbraith, and Arthur Johnson wounded (Cannon).

climbed the last ridge and bivouacked on the heights. They had crossed the Pyrenees; below them lay the sea-like plains of France; on their left was the Atlantic, with ships little and big crowding together, and every ship flew the Jack.

Soult had gathered his men in the plain. Covered and flanked by the twisting Nivelle, they had entrenched themselves, raising great outworks and bastions. They did not expect the English so soon, and some of these were unfinished.

As the sun rose on a glorious day, the signal-gun spoke from the heights, and the Light Division sprang up and raced down the steep slopes. The Third Division advanced more slowly; but about nine o'clock they came into action with the 7th on their left. They were sent against the right centre, where the enemy were established in a bend on the left bank of the river.

Colville quickly seized some unfinished works covering the Amotz bridge. Then the bridge itself was rushed, the defenders driven back, and the general killed. The flank secured, the Third Division then turned on a strong redoubt, " Louis XIV.," in the centre; and after a hard fight, and with the help of the 4th and 7th Divisions, this too was won. Everywhere the French were driven across the river. All day the fight went on; at dusk the British centre was firmly established, and Wellington's army bivouacked in France.

The Fifth had 2 officers wounded and 1 taken prisoner,[1] 15 men killed and 109 wounded. The whole brigade suffered severely in this battle, losing over 450 men.

Soult made no further defence, but fell back behind the Nive. The clouds fought for him; the rain fell in torrents, and turned the valleys to bogs of clay. Horse and foot could struggle along, but the guns could not move. A month later Wellington advanced and forced the passage of the Nive. The Third Division were at Urdains, out on the right, containing D'Erlon, and took no part in the hard fighting. After the battle the

[1] Captain Clarke and Lieutenant Bird wounded; Captain John Hamilton prisoner (Cannon and Norman).

division was posted near Urçuray—the 1st Fifth at Hasparen, thirteen miles from Bayonne.

They were billeted in houses which at first seemed very quiet and still. Then they discovered that there were no children to be seen—all the babies had been hidden away, for it was well known that " the English were cannibals." In a very short time this was all changed and every redcoat had a pack of little " froggies " at his heels.

Not all the army behaved well. The temptations of this land of plenty were too much for some; but stern orders and a few hangings restored discipline.

The new year brought fresh allies; many Bourbon adventurers came flocking to the southern ports; but Soult had still to be conquered, and Bayonne and Bordeaux held out for Napoleon. Wellington seriously considered the advisability of retreat. He was many miles from his base. His only line of retreat lay over the snow-wrapped mountains. Some of his regiments were useless for lack of clothing; all were hungry, for they might not steal, and they had no money; they were like rats in a trap.

At last the rain stopped and frost made the roads passable. Wellington made his preparations for crossing the Adour and bringing Soult to battle. On February 24th the Third Division was sent by Osserain to the bridgehead at Sauveterre, there to make a feint of crossing the Gave d'Oleron. Picton brought his troops down to the river and, opening a cannonade, ordered the Light companies of Colville's brigade to make a diversion. Captain Culley[1] of the Fifth was in command of the detachment. They plunged into the swirling river, and, under a heavy fire, made their way across. The landing was hotly contested, and they were driven back by overwhelming numbers; some were taken prisoners, some were drowned.

Meanwhile Picton had developed his attack. There was no nonsense of a feint. His guns pounded away and his men fought, the French fell back before so much

[1] James Culley, joined the Fifth as captain, 1805; collected notes for history of regiment; a friend of Sir David William Smith.

determination, and the passage was won. Captain
Culley and Lieutenant Pennington were wounded, and
the Fifth lost 7 men killed and 13 prisoners.[1]

Soult fell back and covered Orthes, Wellington following him. The Third Division were sent five miles below
the town; and on February 27th Picton was ordered to
cross the Gave de Pau by the broken Berenx bridge;
then, with the 6th Division, to carry the heights on his
right. Here the French were massed very strongly on a
narrow front, and their fire swept the English as they
toiled up the hill.

John Bent[2] led the Fifth, and fell at their head—but
it was only a clump of heather that brought him down,
and he was quickly up again. One raw recruit was
wounded in the hand, and prayed not to be sent to the
rear. " Though I can't dra me ramrod, I can shove
with me bagginet." And so well did the Third Division
shove that the French were driven out, the guns brought
up, and the retreat turned to a rout. The enemy " who
had fought like lions then ran like hares." Orthes
cost Wellington over 2,000 men, but Soult lost 14,000.
Lieutenant Hopkins of the 1st Fifth was killed, and
11 men; 33 were wounded.[3]

Again Wellington delayed. Bordeaux was occupied
and abandoned. The Bourbon flag and the Tricolour
flaunted in turn. Soult reorganized his army and
threatened a counter-attack; but, giving way before
Picton, retired behind the Garonne and covered
Toulouse. And there, on April 10th, the last battle of
the long war was fought and won.

The French troops, behind outworks, guarded
Toulouse on three sides. Wellington made his main
attack from the east, and Picton was detached against

---

[1] Cannon.

[2] Major John Bent was a dapper little man. He commanded the
grenadier company, who were all over six feet. One day he caught
the men smiling on parade, whereat he sternly said that he was far
from pleased with them as they had not dusted their hat-tops that
day! He retired in 1831 on succeeding to some property, but he
never lost his love for his old regiment (*St. George's Gazette*, November, 1896).

[3] Cannon. Norman gives 1 officer and 5 men killed, and 31
wounded.

the north front with orders to make a feint attack on the Ninimes bridge. To prevent any misconception he was allowed no supports.

This made no difference to Picton; the Third Division were there to fight, not to play; so he swung aside from the Ninimes bridge and attacked that of Jumeaux. Brave men can fight other brave men, but stones and mortar defy rifles and bayonets, and so the Fifth found. The Third Division struggled in vain, and finally the French sallied out and drove them back. The outworks were won, but not by Picton.

Soult retreated into the town, and Wellington prepared for a siege. That night Picton rode round his outposts, and was stopped by John Bent, who reported that the French were evacuating the town. Picton hurried off and returned with Wellington, and together the three stood under the walls of Toulouse and listened to the rumble of transport wheels.

Wellington entered the town in triumph on the 12th. He knew by then of Napoleon's abdication. The Fifth were cantoned near Toulouse for a month, and soon made friends among the conscripts returning to their homes. Ragged redcoat and ragged blue marched together, lending a helping hand and sharing their small rations. Then the 1st Fifth were sent to Bordeaux and there billeted; but so unaccustomed were they to beds that, for choice, they slept on the floor.

One war was over, but another was still going on. By the end of the month the Fifth were on board ship, and on May 31st they sailed for Canada.[1]

[1] Officers of the Fifth who lived to receive the Peninsular Medal:

Thomas Canch, Fort-Major, Edinburgh Castle	12 clasps.
Chris. Hilliard	10 ,,
John Spearman	9 ,,
D. E. Johnson	8 ,,
M. T. Doyle	6 ,,
H. Henstock (quartermaster and sergeant)	7 ,,
J. T. Watson (quartermaster)	6 ,,
W. R. Hopkins	4 ,,
Wm. Tiller (sergeant)	4 ,,
M. G. Hamer	3 ,,

321 men claimed the medal. All the above, with the exception of Colonel Johnson, had left the Fifth (1847).

CHAPTER XXXII

1st Fifth, America, 1814–1815—Occupation of France, 1815–1818
2nd Fifth, Disbandment, 1816

GEORGE III.

William Wynyard

The United States Congress declared war on England June 18th, 1812; American privateers harried English merchantmen, and American troops crossed the frontier and invaded Canada. There were some 4,000 troops in the Dominion, about four men to every mile of frontier, but the loyalty of the habitants did not falter, and the Indians proved useful allies. Sir George Prevost was appointed governor-general, and, for two years, with the very small force at his disposal, he managed to confine the war to the frontier and the sea.

When the close of the Peninsular War set free a large number of troops, reinforcements were sent to Sir George with orders that the war must be carried into the enemy's country and pressed forward at all points. One brigade, under Ross, landed in the Patuxent River and invaded Virginia; while other regiments, among them the 1st Fifth, reinforced the Canadian army. The Fifth landed at Sorel on August 7th, and from there marched to Chambly. They were brigaded with the 3rd, 27th, and 28th, under Sir Manly Power.

In the south Ross won the battle of Bladensburg August 24th, and captured Washington. In the north, Prevost, with 12,000 men, drove back the last lingering raiders and invaded the State of New York. His advance along the shores of Lake Champlain brought him to Plattsburg; there he halted on September 6th, waiting for the fleet to come up.

The little town, a handful of wooden houses round the dockyard, lay where the Saranac entered the lake. On the landward side were three redoubts and other defences. In the lake and river the enemy fleet was anchored—a brig, a schooner, a sloop, and ten gunboats —eighty-three cannon in all.

Wellington's veterans were very eager to fight; at a word from their general they would have stormed and carried the town; but Prevost, worn out by the weary months of anxiety, would take no risks.

At last Sea-captain Downie hove in sight with his laggard fleet, his ships just out of harbour and crews fresh on board. At the first sight of the white sails the soldiers stood to arms ; Plattsburg would be child's play after Badajos. Up came the fleet—a brig, two sloops, twelve gunboats—ninety-one guns in all, and Downie gallantly thrust them into battle; but no word came to the soldiers.

The unskilled sailor-men did their best. Suffering from the fire of the town as well as from the enemy fleet they still fought on until their ships sank under them. And still Prevost held in his men. At last, when the little navy had battered itself to death, the order was given, and 12,000 men turned away without firing a shot.

The officers broke their swords; the men broke ranks and turned into the woods; nearly a thousand good soldiers deserted from sheer anger.

Thus for the Fifth began and ended the American campaign. In the southern operations, Ross was killed in an attack on Baltimore; and a few days later the southern force re-embarked. The Canadian army was split up in detachments, and garrisoned the borderlands; the Fifth spent the winter in Montreal and Côteau du Lac. Early in the new year they moved to Upper Canada, and were cantoned along the St. Lawrence, billeted in farmers' houses. There was no renewal of the war; the peace terms of Ghent were ratified, and in the early summer the 1st Fifth were ordered home.

Then came the news that Napoleon had escaped from Elba; France was in arms; the whole war was to begin again, and England had need of all her veterans. While the Fifth were at sea Waterloo was fought and won; this they learnt at Portsmouth, where they did not land, being hurried on to France. They landed at Ostend July 11th, five days after the surrender of Paris and final abdication of the Emperor. They went by canal to Ghent, and from there marched to Paris, where they joined the victorious army at St. Denis on August 24th. Once more they formed part of the Third Division, its fighting days past, but its glories not forgotten. Their late brigadier, Colville, was in command *vice* Picton, killed at Waterloo.

This was a strange and new world. The Bois was full of English troops, guarding Frenchmen's houses, and keeping Frenchmen's roads. In Paris they had made a new king, and white cockades were again the fashion. Prussian and Austrian soldiers filled the city, earning plenty of curses. An English sentry stood by the Bridge of Jena to protect it from Blucher and his men. Two emperors and two kings held court; and in the Conciergérie their old and gallant enemy, Maréchal Ney, lay waiting his trial.

The Fifth were too late for the great review on July 24th; but in September all the Russians, 160,000 men and 540 guns, made a fine show, prophetic symbol of the Holy Alliance and new era of peace! Many English came flocking over, and the narrow streets were crowded with cabriolets and gigs. There was plenty to amuse the redcoats; they strolled about in little parties, buying lemonade and looking at caricatures of themselves. They soon made friends with their involuntary hosts, and were allowed to help with the harvest. The men might make their own terms, but all applications had to be made through the commanding officer; and it was strictly enjoined that every officer should know where his men were employed.

In October an order was issued by the commander-in-chief: "Before the troops go into barracks or cantonments, an officer of each troop or company is to visit the barracks or cantonments which the soldiers are to occupy, and to ascertain the state they are in." The officers were also ordered to make a note of the name of any householder where soldiers were billeted, and particularly to inquire into any complaints that should be made against the men. Officers were warned against shooting over country without permission from the proprietors, and they were reminded that the country was not yet at peace, therefore ammunition must be strictly guarded; and in case of a riot, they were authorized to take strong measures.

By the terms of the Treaty of Paris a certain number of the allied troops, under the Duke of Wellington, were to remain in occupation for a definite period; the British contingent numbered 39,000. The 1st, 2nd, and Third Divisions of infantry were chosen; the 1st Fifth was brigaded with the 9th and 21st, in the 5th Brigade. The Fifth was well above strength, numbering 37 officers, 1,152 men, and 49 horses. The English troops were distributed among the northern frontier fortresses, with headquarters at Cambrai; early in January they marched from Paris, the Fifth and 21st proceeding to Valenciennes, where they found their old comrades, the 81st and 88th.

Hounds were brought from England, and sport encouraged, but there was no relaxation of discipline; drill and musketry were kept up to the mark, the regiments behaving as if on active service in a friendly country but with an enemy close at hand. The riots in southern France were sufficient warning.

The soldiers continued to behave excellently, and quickly made friends with the peasantry; but the richer bourgeois and small gentry gave trouble. Wellington wrote, December 11th: "There are constant broils between individuals of the middling and better classes and officers of the Army, particularly in Valenciennes. We can get no justice from the authorities of the

5th. FOOT OFFICER (BATTALION COY.) 1814

5th. FOOT 1768 GRENADIER

country." On the whole the French people bore their humiliating position with dignity. In July the officers of the Fifth gave a grand entertainment to the mayor and townsfolk in honour of the Prince Regent's birthday.

In the autumn, manœuvres on a large scale were arranged near Demain—26,000 troops taking part in a sham fight and attack on Valenciennes. On the whole the troops were healthy except for an outbreak of ophthalmia, which dated from the occupation of Paris, and proved infectious and recurrent.

In the autumn of 1818 the Sovereigns of the Quadruple Alliance met at Aix-la-Chapelle and agreed that France should now be left to manage her own affairs. With her own money fortresses had been raised to defend the frontier she had violated; part of her spoils had been reft from her; the work of the army of occupation was done. A great review was held at Villars-en-Couchies; and then, after being thanked for their discipline and good conduct, the British troops marched away for Calais and home. The 1st Fifth left France on October 31st, landing at Dover the next day. From Dover they marched to Winchester, taking ten days on the road.

Europe was at peace, the Millennium had begun. England was the victor, yet there were few joy-bells for the home-coming of her soldiers. There was a reaction against the discipline of the late struggle; riots and disturbances followed, and the soldiers were called on for police duty; while among the rioters were many men who had fought for England and been wounded in her service. The reduction of the navy and disbandment of the second battalions had begun.

The 2nd Fifth had landed in England December 1st, 1812, and had joined their depot at Kingsbridge, going in January to Exeter. From Exeter they were sent to Chelmsford, being then nearly at full strength. They were at Windsor from December, 1813, until October, 1815 (except during the Corn Law troubles, when they slept in wooden sheds in Hyde Park), when they were ordered to Gosport; there they remained until the end came, hoping against hope. In June, 1816, appeared in the Gazette:

"Orders have been issued for the reduction of the 2nd battalion of the Fifth regiment at Gosport on the 24th instant."

The author of " Humphrey Ravelin " wrote:

"I assure you, Humphrey, it was bitter work, though we tried to make light of it, and had been long expecting it. They gave us but short warning, too, at last. When we were met on parade, after the Colonel had told us the contents of the order, we all endeavoured to laugh the thing off; but every joke fell desperately flat, and only made the thing worse. It was very little better at mess; though the soul of good humour and cheer, old D——, in capacity of treasurer, insisted upon the necessity of our finishing the remains of a pipe before the evil day; because, as he said, it would be beneath our dignity and reputation for good fellowship to bargain with the wine-merchant about taking back any remnant, anything less than untouched pipes. So it was resolved to get through it, but the wine had not its usual flavour with us. The next days, when the boys had had more time to think of it, faces grew blanker. What worse evil, . . . Humphrey, can stare a man in countenance who has not a sixpence of his own, and has passed his life in a regiment, than the penury of half-pay and the separation from every friend he has in the world? . . . Poor S——! his pride and irritability grew stronger as the day approached. It seemed as if he looked upon the question as an insult if you asked him where he meant to settle. He had, and perhaps wished to have, no other home than the regiment—you know, he had never left it since he joined in 'ninety-eight'; it was literally turning him out on the wide world, and yet he swore he would never join another corps. . . . But the worst of the business was the farewell visits to the married people. I shall never forget the scene at R——'s lodgings. I went in to shake hands with Mrs. R—— before she set off. She

DISBANDING OF THE SECOND FIFTH

was looking agitated and careworn, and wretchedly ill, yet obliged to exert herself, with an aching heart, in preparation for the journey. Amidst all the confusion of packing there were the children, fretful and troublesome, and ever in the way. R—— himself was walking about the room, with his hands in his pockets, labouring to put a cheerful air upon what was inevitable; now whistling ' Erin-go-bragh,' now talking, while every expression of his countenance belied him of the satisfaction of retiring to ' a nate little box in the County Carlow.' . . . But how did the men receive the news ? Why, variously; most were pleased, for you know novelty is everything to a soldier, and joy at freedom was the first feeling, particularly with those entitled to pensions; but, to do them justice, they were all striving to show some little additional token of respect to their officers, as the time drew nearer. . . .

" At last the day of our fate arrived; we were disbanded in the barrack square, and our second Battalion was extinct. We had resolved, however, to close the scene by dining together after the ceremony. . . . The walls were covered for the last time with blazonry of the memorable days of our Peninsular services. At the head hung those colours, in tatters, which we had received in 1804. . . . Opposite to them, Humphrey, hung the new colours which we received on our landing from Spain. We had hoped they too would have lost their freshness, like the old ones. There was no servility now in forcing the Colonel into the chair, and he felt the compliment justly. As we moved into the room for the last time, and the band struck up our regimental march, a chord of sympathy was touched within us. . . . The cloth was removed, and the first toast, standing and in silence, was, ' The memory of the second Battalion.' . . . Old D—— cried like a child. ' Can't help it, boys, can't help it,' was all his apology. We were a parcel of old fools, Ravelin, for there were few dry eyes among us."[1]

[1] " Lucubrations of Humphrey Ravelin," by an Officer of the Fifth.

When his health had permitted, Colonel King had served with his old corps. At the reduction General Wynyard,[1] then Colonel of the Fifth, and commanding the Yorkshire district, wrote to him from Acomb, near York, June 15th:

" MY DEAR COLONEL,
" I have to thank you for your letter of the 18th inst. Captain Bent informs me of your having left Gosport, and, therefore, I shall desire he will send the old colours to the agents, with the new ones, that I may have the pleasure of offering them to you, as one of those gallant fellows who have witnessed the exploits of the second Battalion upon so many and brilliant occasions."[2]

Henry King afterwards entered Parliament as one of the Members for Sligo; he was appointed colonel of the 1st Royal Veteran Battalion in 1823, became a major-general in 1825, and lieutenant-general in 1838. For many years he suffered from ill-health and his old wounds, dying at the age of sixty-three at his house near Windsor. The tattered Colours of his old battalion covered his pall.

[1] Lieutenant-General William Wynyard succeeded General England as colonel of the Fifth Foot in November, 1812. He joined the 64th Foot as lieutenant in 1777, afterwards going to the 2nd Foot Guards. Major-general 1809; lieutenant-general, 1814. Deputy Adjutant-General to the Forces from 1799 to 1814, afterwards commanding the Yorkshire District. He died July 10th, 1819.
[2] The regimental Colour-pole is now in the possession of the first battalion, having been presented to them, in 1886, by Mrs. King, daughter-in-law of Sir Henry King, widow of Captain John W. King, late of the Fifth.

CHAPTER XXXIII

1817–1856

GEORGE III.—GEORGE IV.—WILLIAM IV.—VICTORIA

ENGLAND—WEST INDIES—IRELAND—GIBRALTAR—MALTA—CORFU AND IONIAN ISLANDS—GIBRALTAR—IRELAND—MAURITIUS

SIR HENRY JOHNSON—SIR CHARLES COLVILLE—SIR JASPER NICHOLS—SIR JOHN GREY

FORTY-TWO years of peace lay before the Fifth regiment; the glamour of the Napoleonic era quickly faded; the great age of utility began; machinery, commerce, education, the world moved more quickly. The army was looked upon as a nuisance, though, with regard to the unsettled state of Europe, an indispensable one. It was reduced as much as possible, and the remaining battalions divided. Six companies, called service companies, were held ready for foreign duty, while the remaining companies formed a reserve, or depot. In the event of war the reserve could, with the existing half-pay officers, form the nucleus of a new battalion.

The morale, too, of the army began to change. The regiments who fought at Waterloo were in essentials very little different from the regiments which had fought at Fontenoy. The men, disciplined by the lash, dependent on the caprice or good-will of their officers, were, even in the best regiments, regarded as so many fighting units. Very early in the new century the great flogging campaign was started; and the news journals, whenever short of interest, added fresh zest to the discussion. Corporal punishment was greatly modified in 1817, and from that date records of inflictions were kept. Later, in 1835–36, a commission sat to inquire into matters of discipline, and in the final report it was advocated that flogging should be retained but used with discretion. There was also held a general inquiry into the comfort and instruction of the men; regimental libraries and savings-banks were encouraged, and the instruction given to recruits was supplemented.

In 1829 gratuities for good service were added to the pensions given to non-commissioned officers and men; and in 1830 a " Good Service " medal was granted, followed by one in 1845 for " Meritorious Service."

In 1836 good-conduct badges or stripes were instituted.

The Fifth were far ahead of their day; their " Order of Merit " was half a century old, and to them belongs the credit of being the first to encourage and not to drive. Even though they lost the regimental order in 1856, the credit should still remain.[1]

The health of the army also became a matter of concern; the men were well fed, clean, and well clothed, and were attended by an excellent medical staff. Yet a foot-soldier was an old man at fifty, and sometimes crippled and worn-out at forty. Rheumatism was partially traced to the white summer trousers, kept clean with pipeclay, and worn before they were dry; the general debility, to the ill-ventilated barracks, with never-opened windows and never-empty rooms. For even if there was no sick there were always women and

---

[1] Among men of the Fifth who obtained commissions from the ranks are the following:

Henry Bishop, ensign and adjutant 1813; lieutenant 1825.
Colour-Sergeant Kysh. (An Ensign F. W. Kysh was in the Fifth in 1819.)
Sergeant-Major Charles Carter.
Sergeant-Major Mackay Robertson.
Sergeant-Major Donald Munro.
Sergeant-Major Pelham Aldrich, ensign and adjutant in Fifth 1829.
Wm. Colls, or Coles, quartermaster 2nd Fifth 1811; adjutant 1812.

children. Life was hard for these poor creatures. There were schools for the children, and the officers and their ladies took a kindly interest in them; but for the soldiers' wives there was no privacy, and when they or their children fell ill they were turned out of the barracks; then the soldier on his shilling and penny a day had to find them food and lodging.

The Army Council gave a considerable amount of attention to details of uniform; some of the most useful lessons of the Peninsular War were forgotten; once again the foot-soldier was made a beast of burden. Blanket was piled on knapsack, and a greatcoat on blanket; collars and waistbelts were tightened, and head-dresses made heavier.

The Fifth became a fusilier regiment in 1836, and the busby took the place of the shako. Their coatee collars were embroidered with gold grenades (white worsted for the men) and epaulettes and fringes took the place of wings. Eight years later, when the busby was changed for the Albert shako, the Fifth were allowed to wear a red-and-white ball to retain their old St. Lucia distinction. In 1855 the coatee disappeared and a double-breasted tunic took its place.

The old flint-lock gave way to percussion caps in 1843, but with the first musket rifles, 1853–54, began a revolution in musketry. Already, in 1843, officers had recommended that drills should be simplified and more time given to making the soldier a good shot; but the long years between Waterloo and the Crimea were dedicated to the goose-step, and to preparations for the yearly inspection, conducted by some old major-general who had earned his position by a campaign on somebody's staff. In 1836 all companies had been ordered to practise light infantry tactics, but regimental officers looked for distinction on the parade ground and not in field work.

On February 4th, 1819, the Fifth left Portsmouth for the West Indies, landing in April in Carlisle Bay, Barbadoes. Major and Brevet-Lieutenant-Colonel

Emes[1] was in command; Colonel Pratt did not go with his regiment. After being reviewed by Lieutenant-General Lord Combermere on April 4th the companies separated and sailed, five to Antigua, four to St. Kitts, and one to Montserrat. Antigua was pleasantly like England, and St. Kitts comparatively dry and healthy, but the West Indian station was a bad and unpopular one; the vast number of slaves and the cheapness of labour bred enervating habits; there was every encouragement for vice and drunkenness, and little or nothing to do. The religious revival, bred by the Holy Alliance in Europe, found few converts and disciples among the planters.

Emes made St. Kitts his headquarters, living at Brimston Hill until March, 1821, when the stations were changed, and the Fifth were sent, five companies to St. Vincent, two to St. Lucia, and three to Dominica. His departure caused much regret in St. Kitts, and, at a meeting of the Council and House of Assembly held at the Court-house in the town of Basseterre, it was unanimously resolved, " That the thanks of the Board of Council and House of Assembly of St. Christopher be presented to Lieutenant-Colonel Emes, the officers, N.C.O.'s, and privates, of the detachment of that distinguished regiment the Fifth Foot, for the faithful and honourable discharge of their respective duties as soldiers and citizens, while under command of Colonel Emes, in the garrison of Brimston Hill." This resolution, signed " Thos. Harper," was conveyed to Emes by the President, Stedman Rawlins, and the Speaker, W. W. Rawlins, who said: " Sir, we have the honour to transmit to you the resolution of the Council and Assembly of St. Christopher, expressive of their high sense of the conduct of yourself and that of the officers, N.C.O.'s, and privates who served under your command

---

[1] Thomas Emes, born in Derbyshire, April 28th, 1770; joined 1s Dragoon Guards in 1794, exchanging into the 10th Foot the next year; captain in Fifth 1802. In 1804-05 he served on the staff as major of brigade, in Guernsey. Commanded 1st battalion a Corunna.

in this Island, and we assure you that we derive much satisfaction in thus discharging our public duty, to find it so strictly in accordance with our private feelings."

To which Emes replied from Dominica:

" Gentlemen, I have the honour to acknowledge the receipt of your letter enclosing a resolution of the Board of Council and House of Assembly of St. Christopher, and beg to return my warmest thanks, with those of the detachment there under my command, for the very handsome and kind manner that the Houses have signified their approval of our conduct during our residence with you, and although we only did our duty as soldiers, it is, and ever will be, a pleasing reflection to us to know that the duty was carried on in a way to satisfy so respectable a colony. As an individual I again thank you, and believe me sincere in saying I can never forget the kindness and hospitality I received in St. Christopher. . . ."[1]

In this year the regiment was reduced to eight companies.

Half the regiment was garrisoned in beautiful St. Lucia, in the barracks on Morne Fortuné. The swamps made this island unhealthy, and it was difficult to keep the soldiers from " white rum," a spirit most detrimental to their health and morals.

In Dominica, Emes made his headquarters at Morne Brune, which should have proved healthier than St. Kitts; but in November of the following year a dreadful fever broke out. The Fifth in the island numbered 137 all told, and of these, 3 officers,[2] 1 sergeant, 2 corporals, 56 privates, and 4 women died.

In 1824 Lieutenant-Colonel Emes was attacked by this same fever, and died November 2nd. The Fifth, officers and men, mourned his loss as a fine soldier and a good man. For all his tact, mild manners, and gentle

---

[1] See *U. S. J.*, 1827, ii. 363.
[2] Major Bishop, Lieutenant Armstrong, and Lieutenant Equino.

ways, he never allowed discipline to relax. They raised a monument to his memory.

> LOST AND LAMENTED FOR EVER.
> TO PERPETUATE THE MEMORY OF THEIR BELOVED
> AND GALLANT COMRADE, LT.-COL. THOMAS EMES,
> OF THE 5TH REGIMENT,
> WHO DIED IN THIS ISLAND
> ON THE 2ND DAY OF NOV., 1824,
> IN THE 55TH YEAR OF HIS AGE.

In 1825 the Fifth was again raised to ten companies; and in May Sir Charles Pratt, promoted major-general, ceased to command. He was succeeded by Lieutenant-Colonel William Sutherland, of the 2nd West Indian Regiment. Before Sir Charles Pratt left the regiment he applied for leave to continue in the Fifth the distinguishing mark won at Vigie in 1779. On July 2nd, 1824, Torrens, the Adjutant-General replied: " Sir, I have the honour to receive and submit to the Commander-in-Chief your letter of the 28 ultimo, and enclosure, and in reply am directed to signify to you, that under the circumstances therein stated, H.R.H. has been pleased to approve of the White Feather, which for a long series of years has been worn as a mark of distinction by the Fifth Regiment of Foot, being continued to be used by that Corps."

In 1826 the Fifth were ordered home; they embarked in March in three transports, and landed at Portsmouth on April 12th and 22nd and June 3rd. From Portsmouth they marched to Weedon, in Northamptonshire, where they were joined by the depot from Tynemouth Castle, 4 captains, 4 subalterns, a surgeon, 1 sergeant, and 69 rank and file. Recruiting parties were sent out and 156 men brought in. Even after the West Indies England was a very unpleasant place. Machinery, " that invention of the devil to rob a poor man of his wage," had come to stay, though not without protest and riot. There was trouble, too, between Spain and Portugal, and a British force was landed at Lisbon. For the moment it seemed that England was to be once more involved in a Continental war. The Guards were brought back from Lancashire, and the Fifth and other regiments ordered north. Again they marched in three divisions, January 1st, 3rd, and 4th, arriving at Hull ten days later; sending one company to Bradford, one to Halifax, and, later, one to Brigg. They were there to keep order, overawe malcontents, protect property, and gain recruits. At Hull 124 men enlisted. Yorkshire was fairly quiet; subscriptions had been raised and a bazaar held at York for the relief of the starving poor. In April the Fifth were sent to Lancashire, where, in desperation, the out-of-work weavers were making their protest. Fortunately the Fifth were not needed for reprisals. They gained another seventy-seven recruits, and then, being at full strength, were sent to Ireland. They marched from Bolton to Liverpool, and there embarked in two new steam-vessels, the *Britannia* and the *Birmingham*, and landed at Dublin the next day.

The winter was spent in the Royal Barracks. Sir John Byng commanded the Forces, and Lord Wellesley was at the Castle making an honest effort to hold the balance between the " fantastic violence of the Catholic Association and the domineering bravado of the Orange leaders."

Dublin had not suffered like the country districts, where wages were at their lowest, and where the authority of the law had almost ceased to exist; but beneath all the traditional gay hospitality of the capital an undercurrent of unrest was felt.

The 2nd Dragoons were also in Dublin, and a report was very widely spread of a riot and affray between this regiment and the Fifth. Sutherland wrote to the *Morning Post* giving a direct denial and contradiction of the story, so it may be concluded there was no truth in it.

The English regiments were used to garrison the most disturbed districts and assist the constabulary. In the spring the Fifth were sent to Athlone, with companies at Shannon Bridge, Ballymahone, and Roscommon, and detachments at Tullamore, Baltinacarrig, Abbeyshrule, and Strokestown.

Early in 1829 the Fifth received new colours. These were consecrated in St. Peter's church in Athlone, and afterwards presented on parade by Major-General Sir Thomas Arbuthnot, commanding the Connaught District. The General spoke a few words commending the uniform good conduct of the Fifth in the field and in quarters.

From Athlone they marched to Castlebar, with companies and detachments at Westport, Foxford, Dunmore, Ballaghadareen, and Ballinasloe. This was in April, and on the 13th of that month the Catholic Emancipation Act was passed. This garrisoning of little Irish villages was dull, harassing work, but the Fifth kept to their old traditions, and managed to make friends wherever they went. They spent the winter in Galway, at Oughterard, Tuam, Ballinasloe, Mount Shannon, and Kinavara.

A general election followed upon the death of George IV. in June, 1830; the contest in Galway was a keen one, but the Fifth acquitted themselves so well that the several candidates and their supporters passed the following resolution: " That having witnessed the prompt, active, and efficient exertions of Lieutenant-Colonel Sutherland, the officers, non-commissioned officers, and privates of the Fifth regiment in preserving peace and good order during the late contested election . . . we deem it an act of justice thus to put on record the high value we entertain of their services. . . ."

From Galway the regiment was sent to Buttevant, and from there, during the Clare elections, March, 1831, headquarters and four companies were sent to Clare Castle to keep order. Detachments were also posted in the villages round. Headquarters then moved on to Ennis, and in May back to Buttevant, leaving eight companies to patrol Clare, which county was on the point of rebellion. Arbuthnot had no easy task, and the Fifth did not keep order without loss. On May 8th Colour-Sergeant James Robinson, in command of seven soldiers and seven police, was sent on special service. In disguise, and armed only with pistols, they set out for Ballynacally. As they went they were recognized and attacked by a mob armed with scythes and guns. The little party retreated slowly, fighting hard until their ammunition was done, then ran for their lives. Two soldiers and a policeman were wounded, and Robinson was killed. To his memory his officers and comrades raised a tombstone in Ennis, " to record their regret for the soldier and esteem for the man."

In June, when Sir Richard Hussey Vivian succeeded Byng in the Irish Command, the latter wrote: " The Lieutenant-General cannot forget that the troops, more especially at the out-stations, have been frequently called to exercise those qualities on which subordination and good order mainly depend, under circumstances of peculiar difficulty and excitement, and he wishes to mark in the strongest manner, by this public acknowledgment, to Major-Generals Sir George Bingham and Sir Thomas Arbuthnot, his sense, not only of the individual services of those officers but of the forbearance and exemplary conduct which have characterized the behaviour of all under their orders." General Hussey Vivian, in an order, expressed his hope that the behaviour, temper, and discretion of the troops would continue to be observed.

And upon the temper of the army much depended. The magistrates in Clare and Galway declined to act, and Major Tovey and Captains McDonald and Spencer of the Fifth were selected as gentlemen upon whose firmness, prudence, and discretion, the Government could rely. They received Commissions of Peace for the two counties and did their work well and thoroughly. Sutherland was a disciplinarian, a hard man to serve under, but officers and men did credit to his training. They realized that the regiment was his pride, and how sacred to him was every detail that could aid present efficiency or recall the glories of the past.

In September, from Ennis, Arbuthnot signified to Colonel Sutherland, " the very great pleasure he feels in having to assure you that both officers and men of the Fifth Regiment performed their duty, under most trying circumstances, during the disturbances in this country, to his perfect satisfaction in every respect."

Ten days later the service companies received orders to hold themselves in readiness to proceed to Gibraltar, where there seemed every probability of seeing active service. These years, 1829–1832, were full of agitation and unrest. England was in the throes of the Reform and Catholic Emancipation Bills; Belgium had broken the hated ties that bound her to the Netherlands; in France the Bourbons once more were dethroned and Louis Philippe had won a precarious kingdom. The Czar of the Holy Alliance had not lived to see his high hopes shattered; his successor was at war with Turkey and Poland. There was an insurrection in Portugal and a threat of war with Spain. To add to the miseries of an unhappy Europe a terrible cholera outbreak spread through every land.

Before its departure the regiment was reviewed by Generals Vivian and Bingham, both officers expressing their approbation. The Reserve was left in Ireland and sent to Fermoy, and the service companies marched to Cork, recently depleted of its naval establishment, and there embarked on board the *Marquis of Huntly*, the *William Harris*, and the *Sylvia*. They did not sail until after Christmas, arriving at Gibraltar, after a rough, quick passage, on January 9th, 10th, and 12th.

Gibraltar had improved since 1800. There was now a tolerably efficient system of drainage, and the town had ceased to be notorious for its filth. For the soldiers the Duke of Kent's drastic reforms still held good; the canteens and wine-shops were under proper control, and drunkenness was no longer officially encouraged.

At the inspection held just before leaving Ireland the regimental medal had attracted attention, and Sutherland was now called upon to give an account and explanation of the Order. This proved satisfactory, and the King was pleased to give his Royal sanction for the confirmation and continuance of the badge.

In April of the following year the mess-room and Sutherland's quarters were burnt down, and, among other losses, the regimental Colours were destroyed; these, presented at Athlone in 1829, were of no historical interest; but with them disappeared the third Colour, traditional relic of Wilhelmstahl, never to be borne again at the head of the regiment among the drummers of the Fifth.

Cannon says this third Colour was a small banner of green silk, inscribed with the badge, motto, number, and designation of the corps. At a review at Colchester in 1805, the Duke of York had noticed the banner, and inquired into, and approved, the claim of the Fifth. Now, after much correspondence, this claim was disallowed, and the regiment had to content themselves with grenadier caps, with the King's cypher " W. R. IV." in front and the regimental badge at the back (July 31st, 1835). A year later, on May 4th, 1836, when the Fifth were made Fusiliers, the word "Wilhelmstahl" was ordered to be borne on the colours and appointments.

In the summer of 1834 cholera attacked the garrison, and 1 officer, 2 sergeants, 1 drummer, 41 privates, 3 women, and 4 children died. That autumn they were sent to Malta. Before they left, General Houston made the following order, October 14th:

" His Excellency, the Lieutenant-General Commander, cannot suffer the Fifth Regiment to embark from hence without expressing his approval of the general conduct of this corps during the period it has been under his command in this garrison, and he desires to offer his thanks to the officers, non-commissioned officers, and privates of this regiment, and more particularly he begs to acknowledge his sense of the zealous and constant exertions of Lieutenant-Colonel Sutherland, which have so essentially contributed to maintain the discipline and good order of the corps under his command!"

The Fifth owed a great deal to William Sutherland; he commanded the regiment at a difficult period. After the strain of continued active service discipline had relaxed; there had been a corresponding deterioration amongst officers. Militarism was to a certain extent still the fashion, but in many regiments it found its expression in a petty swaggering and neglect of duty for the more showy vices.

On October 15th the Fifth embarked on board H.M.S. *Romney* and sailed for Malta, anchored in Valetta harbour on the 26th, and landed the next day. Malta was a new experience for the regiment. After the barren Rock, they appreciated the picturesque country and the hospitality of the inhabitants. Here they spent two and a half uneventful years.

In March, 1835, Sir Harry Johnson[1] died, and to the gratification of the whole regiment their old brigadier, Sir Charles Colville, became their colonel. Once more he commanded, if not his old " favourite little Battalion," at least the elder brother, and one of the same name and tradition.

In May, 1836, the regiment was, as has been said, equipped as Fusiliers, and from this date became the Fifth, or Northumberland Fusiliers. On December 14th the Governor of Malta, Sir Henry Bouverie, presented the new Colours which had been sent from England.

The regiment was drawn up in review order on the Florian Parade; after the display of the Colours the men formed three sides of a square, and the Chaplain, Mr. le Mesurier, solemnly read the consecration service. A little company of boys and girls, soldiers' children, with new clothes and shining faces, repeated the responses; then the new Colours were handed to the Lieutenants, and Sir Henry Bouverie addressed the troops :

" Officers and soldiers of the Fifth Fusiliers, I am happy that it has fallen to my lot to present to you these Colours. I do it in the full confidence that they will never be disgraced by insubordination, by loss of discipline, or misconduct in garrison or in the field. . . . I trust I shall never have occasion to alter the high

---

[1] Sir Henry Johnson, first baronet; created 1818; born 1748; a general and Governor of Ross Castle; commanded at Battle of New Ross 1798; died 1835. His grandson, Henry Franks Frederick Johnson, born 1819, afterwards third baronet, served in the Fifth for many years.

opinion I have formed of you, not only here, but in scenes on service of which I was myself a witness." Then followed an inspection and review of various field exercises, of which the Governor expressed his unqualified approbation. That evening the officers gave a great dinner to Sir Henry, Vice-Admiral Rokeby, and the captains of his squadron, and others.

The next year the Fifth sailed east for Corfu, March 28th. In 1814 England had assumed the protection of the Ionian Islands, and since that date an English garrison had been maintained. An English High Commissioner presided over the Senates ruling in the different islands. One of the first acts of the British occupation had been the disarming of the inhabitants, a very necessary precaution, for the degenerate Ionians were quick-tempered men, and pistols and daggers were in frequent use. Corfu was a rendezvous for Greek and Russian political agents, and all manner of scamps and intriguers. The town itself was a labyrinth, partly Oriental, partly Greek, with fortifications dating from the various occupations of Venice, Turkey, and France. The 53rd and the 1st and 2nd battalions of the 60th were also in garrison. The Fifth did not stay in Corfu but were detached to the different islands, with headquarters at Cephalonia, the largest and most important. In 1839 Sir Howard Douglas, the Commissioner, made a tour of the islands, and at Cephalonia stayed the night with Colonel Sutherland. Sir Howard desired to inspect the regiment, and for that purpose they were fallen in on the parade ground, but without their Colours. These were kept in Sutherland's study, and there Sir Howard had gone to write his letters, and, being rather deaf, he failed to hear the orderly's repeated knock. The Colour-party grew impatient, and no answer coming from within, Gresham, the orderly, ventured to open the door and creep in. Just as he grasped the Colours the Commissioner turned and saw him. He was a quick-tempered man, and would hear no explanation, and sending for Sutherland, he desired him to order his servant off to parade for entering the room without knocking. Mrs. Sutherland then intervened, and pointed out, no servant then no dinner, and Private Gresham was allowed to return to his work.

In December, 1841, the Fifth were relieved at Cephalonia by the 47th, and, with the 38th, occupied the citadel of Corfu. News of the birth of a Prince of Wales was brought by H.M.S. *Hedea*, December 2nd. All the yachts in the harbour were decked with flags, and the mess-rooms of the artillery and the two regiments were thrown open to 200 guests, and dinner lasted until breakfast-time.

About December 24th certain disturbances took place. A zealous American Mission had roused the jealousy of the Greek Church. The Fifth were called upon to clear the streets; three days later a soldier of the Fifth was stabbed, and a mêlée ensued in which more soldiers were hurt. Small pickets were pelted with stones, and finally a corporal's party fired and dispelled the mob. The garrison were confined to barracks, various restrictions placed on the inhabitants, and an order made to the troops appealing to their discipline and good-will. An inquiry was held, and the original attack—of which the man died—declared to have been without provocation, and the soldiers of the Fifth were found to have behaved with patience and discretion.

Early in 1842 Prince George of Cambridge visited the Ionian Islands. The Fifth impressed him as a very fine regiment. Sutherland he described, in after years, as a hard man, but very smart officer, with a human heart. Then the regiment went back to Gibraltar, the left wing sailing on February 15th, followed a month later by the right wing and headquarters. The 48th and 79th were at Gibraltar. The Fifth spent a year on the Rock, and it may have been about this time that General Fox saw written up in the regimental canteen, " The Old and Bold," and commented, " Old enough," scratching his elbow, " but as for bold, I've run away three times with them myself!" In September Captain Ward died, and Dubourdieu got his company after fourteen years' service.

From Gibraltar they returned to Ireland and rejoined

the Depot companies, who, with a brief interval in England, had been stationed at various places in Ireland. Ireland was in much the same state, except that the increase of English troops amounted to a military occupation; a quarter of the standing British Army garrisoned the country; a military demonstration was thought to be a daily necessity. The unrest in the country was perhaps more apparent than real, and the affection frequently inspired by regimental officers was able to divert danger from isolated detachments. The Fifth were stationed successively at Fermoy, Birr, Dublin, Belfast, Enniskillen, and Templemore.

In December of this year an old soldier called at the barracks one day—George Cowden—who had served in the Fifth when Lord Percy was colonel. He had his discharge papers, dated 1784, and had walked many miles to visit his old corps. The soldiers crowded round him, fêted and feasted him, and before he left raised a subscription of over £11—chiefly from their own pockets. Ten pounds of this money was sent to the clergyman of Killila parish in County Down, where the old man hailed from, and he was requested to see that Cowden—late of the Fifth—should lack nothing. He was a Devonshire man, but had long settled in Ireland.

In May[1] they were ordered to complete to establishment—800 rank and file—540 service companies, and 260 to the Depot. In this year Sir Charles Colville died, and was succeeded by Sir Jasper Nichols.[2]

The Fifth went to England in 1846, three companies going to Plymouth; and headquarters and seven companies to Devonport. Lieutenant-Colonel Sutherland was promoted major-general this year, and David Eng-

---
[1] One of the captains serving at this time deserves notice—Malcolm Macgregor, gazetted from half-pay, unattached. In 1847 he had seen forty-five years' service, including the Battles of Calabria and Maida and the capture of Catrone. He fought at Alexandria, Rosetta, and the actions at El Hamet; and was five months a prisoner in Cairo. He served in Holland 1814-15. Brevet-major in July, 1830.
[2] Sir Jasper Nichols, served in Mahratta War, Hanover (1805), and South America (1806-07), Corunna campaign, Walcheren, Nepaul War (1815), and Pindarree War.

land Johnson,[1] after forty-two years' service, got command of the regiment.

In 1847 there were riots in Devon and Cornwall, the troops displayed great forbearance, and Major-General Murray, commanding the district, expressed his great satisfaction at the efficiency and discipline of the Battalion.

In July the six service companies, under Lieutenant-Colonel Johnson, embarked for Mauritius, followed in September by the reserve companies, who formed a reserve battalion. The Depot remained in England. It was the first time the regiment had been so far east, and the voyage round the Cape seemed very long. They disembarked in November, and the men cheered on leaving the ship. "Damn you boys!" said the Colonel; " cheer when you go home ! "

Mauritius was a pleasant island, picturesque and healthy. Port Louis was a neat town, well laid out. Two infantry regiments besides artillery were in garrison, and the officers received an island allowance in addition to their pay. In 1848 Captain Milman, by a gallant deed, won the Royal Humane Society's gold medal. He, with five others, were fishing in a small boat off the south coast when a sudden squall upset the boat. She floated bottom up, and the whole party managed to find a precarious lodgment. Finally, after drifting for two hours she grounded on a shoal. Milman set out in the dusk through the shark-infested waters to swim ashore and secure help. This he accomplished after an hour's struggle in a rough sea, and the whole party was saved with the exception of the creole boatman, who had also gallantly set out for the shore but had been drowned.

General Nichols died in 1849, and Sir John Grey,[2]

---

[1] David England Johnson, joined 2nd Fifth in 1804, aged sixteen, born at Bettysville, Co. Limerick, January, 1788; adjutant 1808; major 1837; *vice* Lieutenant-Colonel Wellesley, promoted to unattached list. His son, Arthur England Johnson, born 1828, exchanged from the 60th to the Fifth in December, 1846, and fell at Lucknow.

[2] Sir John Grey, K.C.B., of Morwick, Northumberland; a lieutenant-general, and sometime Governor of Bombay; born 1782; served in the Fifth in Peninsular War; wounded at Ciudad Rodrigo; d.s.p. 1856.

UNIFORM OF FIFTH NORTHUMBERLAND FUSILIERS, 1846.
From a print by A. M. Hayes. Published by G. Spooner, 1846.

To face page 366.

a Northumbrian, and late of the regiment, became colonel, which appointment pleased the regiment.

In 1850 Colonel Johnson retired by sale, and Lieutenant-Colonel Schonswar, commanding the Reserve Battalion, succeeded him. An old friend of the Fifth's was governor of the island, Major-General William Sutherland, and in 1851 he was called on to present new Colours to them, the third presentation in which he had been an actor.

The Russian war began in March, 1854. The Fifth were increased to twelve companies, and the regiment applied to be sent to the Crimea. Sutherland was asked to present the petition, and he was as anxious as the youngest ensign that his regiment should win fresh laurels; but no orders came for the Fifth.

Schonswar died in 1855, and Lieutenant-Colonel Guy of the Reserve Battalion succeeded him. Guy had joined as ensign in 1824.

In 1856, under the new regulations, the " Order of Merit " was abolished. The new Enfield rifle was served out, and Major Simmons,[1] a good officer who had seen service before he joined the Fifth, qualified as instructor, and put the whole regiment through a course, a training for which they were shortly very grateful.

The 33rd arrived at Port Louis in 1857 to relieve the Fifth, who were under orders for Hong-Kong, where they hoped to see service in China.

The first detachment, 735 strong, embarked in H.M.S. *Simoon* on May 22nd. The men came straggling down to the harbour in no sort of order. The departure of the regiment caused universal regret, and it was hard for the men to part with their hospitable friend. The troopship was very crowded. A third of the men had to sleep on deck. Before leaving, the officers of a Russian frigate in the harbour were entertained, and proved charming guests.

H.M.S. *Simoon* arrived at Singapore on June 19th. There the Fifth received orders changing their destination to Calcutta: their help was needed to quell a sepoy rising.

[1] Captain Simmons, served in Afghanistan with 2nd Foot in 1839. He joined the Fifth as captain February, 1843; promoted major January, 1856.

CHAPTER XXXIV
1857

THE INDIAN MUTINY

Lovelace Walton

EARLY in 1857 the new Enfield rifle was served out in India, and arrangements made for instruction in the new arm. The Indian peoples, deprived under British rule of their natural warrior outlet, had long waited " for an occasion and a pretext; the Russian War was the occasion, greased cartridges the pretext."

The first warnings came from Barrackpore, only sixteen miles from Calcutta. In March the unrest broke into an open mutiny. The 84th Foot was hurriedly sent from Rangoon and the disaffected native regiments disbanded. In April the officer commanding was able to report everything quiet and to recommend that the 84th be returned to their station.

One month later the native troops at Meerut mutinied, murdered their officers, looted the town, and set out for Delhi. The heroic defence of a handful of Englishmen failed to save the city.

The commander-in-chief in India, General Anson, was at Simla; within reach he had three English regiments, very little train, and no heavy guns. The disbanded regiments had joined the rebels, and at once there were some 30,000 trained and tried Sepoys in arms against English rule.

Benares rose, and the mutiny spread through Bengal. Oudh was the next: this province had only been annexed in February of the preceding year. Henry Lawrence, the new Administrator, had just taken up his residence at Lucknow when the cartridge trouble was made the excuse for the general discontent; and when the news came of the fall of Delhi, Lucknow broke out into open mutiny. Fifty miles away lay Cawnpore, where, from June 6th to 20th, a little English garrison held out. On the 20th they capitulated, claiming the protection of Nana Sahib. The well at Cawnpore became a lasting memorial of that trust. Heartened by murder, the mutineers closed round Lucknow; the Presidency was invested June 30th, and on July 1st the siege began. Havelock[1] was sent to their rescue; with a small column he left Calcutta and marched and fought his way into Cawnpore July 17th, his brigade reduced by casualties and disease to less than a thousand men.

The Fifth landed at Chinsurah on July 5th, and were at once fitted out for field service. On the 14th, Nos. 1 and 2 companies, under Captain L'Estrange, started up the Ganges, on flats towed by steamers, to reinforce the Lucknow relief column. Major Simmons, with Nos. 3 and 5 companies, followed on the 18th, and headquarters on the 19th. The wives and families, with Ensign Cubitt, were sent to Dum Dum. It was urgent that the regiment should proceed with all possible speed. Boat after boat, each with its pitiful load of fugitives, floated past them down the river, and it was difficult to turn a deaf ear to the prayers for protection that assailed them at every landing-stage. At Bhaugalpore 100 men, under Captain Masters, were landed to protect the station from the 5th Irregular Cavalry. Colonel Guy asked permission to disarm this regiment: this was refused by the civil authorities, and the troopers afterwards joined the mutineers.

Six hundred miles by river from Calcutta was Dinapore, headquarters of one of the great military divisions of the Bengal army. Here was stationed the only British regiment between Calcutta and Cawnpore. A veteran, General Lloyd, was in command, who proved

[1] Major-General Sir Henry Havelock, 1795-1857, at this time a brigadier.

unequal to the emergency. Patna, the ancient Hindu
capital, lay twelve miles to the south, and it was of
vital importance to the loyalty of Bengal that mutiny
and sedition should not spread there. The civil
authorities petitioned Canning that the Fifth might
be landed at Dinapore, but this was left to the discretion of Lloyd, who was told only to delay the regiment
in case of urgent necessity. Nos. 1 and 2 companies
reached Dinapore July 22nd, and were allowed to
proceed. Two days later Lloyd sought to render the
Sepoys harmless by calling in all percussion caps. This
caused the latent mutiny to break out into open rebellion;
the three native regiments fired on their officers, then
fled from Dinapore to ravage the surrounding country
and fan the flame.

Lloyd was removed, and, on his arrival, Colonel Guy[1]
placed in temporary command. A hundred of the Fifth
were sent to Patna and fifty to Monghy. On the arrival
of Nos. 9 and 10 companies the remainder of the
regiment proceeded up the river, Major Simmons in
command.[2]

At Ghauzerpore, Simmons was asked to land and
disarm the 65th Native Infantry. This was done;
these men afterwards joined the mutineers at Lucknow.

At Mirzapore the residents were in great alarm; a
large force of rebels was in the neighbourhood, and they
implored the Fifth to disperse them. Simmons con-
sented to halt for a day, because, apart from any
sympathy with the residents, he was reluctant to leave
a large enemy force so near to his lines of communication.
The rebels proved elusive; a nine-mile march led to no
result; one man died of heat apoplexy. Simmons
reluctantly stayed another day, and after a long weary
march through thick jungle at last found the enemy,
who immediately fled. Only one Sepoy was captured,
and promptly hung.

At last, on August 25th, the five companies disem-

---

[1] Colonel Guy remained at Dinapore until November, when he
joined Outram's force, and was given command of a brigade.

[2] 3, 6, 8, 9, and 10 companies.

barked at Allahabad, where they spent ten days in comfort.

Meanwhile Nos. 1 and 2 companies had passed through Dinapore before the outbreak, but they had seen the flames of the burning cantonments and villages. Vincent Eyre of the Bengal Artillery—and of Cabul—must have passed them with the news that Arrah was in danger, for he had landed a battery at Dinapore on July 25th; then, finding pursuit useless, had hurried on to Buxar, and from there to Ghauzerpore. On the night of the 29th he was back at Buxar collecting a relief force, and L'Estrange needed little persuasion to join him.

Arrah was a picturesque old town, headquarters of the district, lying between the Ganges and the Soane, about twenty-four miles from Dinapore. The residents had long realized their precarious position, for, should the troops at Dinapore mutiny, Arrah lay open and unprotected. In June the women and children had been sent to safety; but eight men decided to remain in the town and hold the judge's house. This they put in a state of defence; and later a few loyal natives joined the garrison, which numbered 9 Europeans, 6 Eurasians, 1 native, and 60 Sikh police. On Sunday, July 26th, a sowar came galloping in with the news that the Sepoys were coming from Dinapore. Next day they swarmed in, looted the town, released the prisoners in the jail, and besieged the blockhouse. They were quickly reinforced by Koer Singh, a lord of the Rajput, and his men.

Very early on July 30th the two companies of the Fifth and the guns were landed at Buxar, and the field force organized under command of Major Eyre—150 of the Fifth, 40 artillerymen, 14 Buxar Mounted Volunteers and 12 officers. A little after 5 in the afternoon Eyre and his army set out to relieve a blockhouse thirty miles away, besieged by three regiments and numberless armed men.

All night they marched. The bullocks, fresh from the plough, were very slow, the men were out of condition, and suffered much from their feet, the grass was long, and the going heavy. In the day they rested, marching again at 4 o'clock in the afternoon, the Fifth in desperate haste lest Arrah should be relieved before they could arrive. A bright moon helped them, and L'Estrange's men sang as they marched. By morning they had reached the villge of Shahpoor. Here they heard of the disaster that had overtaken a relief force sent from Dinapore. This did not discourage the Fifth, but gave them a new fear that Arrah might fall before they could march in. The train was started early in the afternoon, and four miles from Shahpoor the column met their first opposition—the villagers were trying to destroy a bridge. They were soon scattered and the road repaired. Eyre, fearing an ambush, halted for the night at the village of Gujrajegunge, sending a detachment of the Fifth to guard a bridge leading to the village. The roads were very bad, and thick jungle on either side gave good cover to lurking rebels. That night a man died of cholera.

The 2nd of August was a Sunday. Almost at daybreak Eyre was on the road. Half a mile from the village the jungle closed in, and faintly through the groves the Fifth heard the " assembly " sounded by the mutineers. And then the Sepoys began to show themselves more freely, and to contest the way. Eyre swung his guns on to open ground and began to shell the groves; skirmishers were sent forward, and for the first time the men whom Simmons had trained showed what use they could make of the new rifle. The Sepoys gave way and were gradually driven back.

Under cover of the skirmishers the guns and train moved forward and pushed safely through the wood. Then they found their way barred by a gully; the bridge had been broken down; it was impossible to get the guns across.

About a mile away, on the right, ran the new railway, a direct road to Arrah; but to reach the embankment a way had to be found through soft rice-fields, swamps, and woods, with the jungle on the flank. Slowly and heavily the guns plodded on, the skirmishers still holding the Sepoys back. Near the embankment the groves

THE RELIEF OF ARRAH

thickened and the angle was strongly held. The drivers and elephants bolted at the first rebel fire; the second volley brought down many men. Eyre's guns answered; but the Sepoys were firing from cover and his force was in the open. Koer Singh's followers closed up in the rear; the column was almost surrounded. Twice the Sepoys charged the guns, twice grape drove them back. Then Hastings of the Stud rode up to Eyre. " The Fusiliers are losing ground." " Go and tell L'Estrange to charge," commanded Eyre, and in his own words: " Promptly and gallantly he (L'Estrange) obeyed the order; the skirmishers on the right turned their flank; the guns with grape and shrapnel drove in the centre, and the troops, advancing on all sides, drove the enemy panic-stricken in all directions." Two thousand five hundred men flying before a hundred and fifty ! With a clear road before them the column turned down the embankment and marched for Arrah. There were four more weary miles to be covered, but not a rebel was to be seen. At 4 o'clock they came to a nullah with another broken bridge, and, tired though the men were, they at once set to work to bridge the stream, sixty feet wide, and deep and rapid. They were heartened by a message, " All's well in Arrah "; and the mounted volunteers crossing the stream rode forward, the infantry staying to see the guns safely across. A few hours later the relief column marched in. They had saved Arrah from the fate of Kotah and Futtelepore; and, if the strategic value of what they had accomplished was small, the moral effect was beyond all price. On the very day of the relief Canning had written: " The disastrous result which has followed the attempt to relieve Arrah . . . has very seriously diminished the hope of preserving the peace of the Lower Provinces." And now a handful of heroic men had reasserted the ascendancy of Britain. The losses were small; of the Fifth one man had died and Ensign Oldfield and eight men were wounded. Captains L'Estrange and Scott and Ensigns Oldfield, Lewis, and Mason were deservedly mentioned in despatches; and the regiment gained a recruit in one of the Buxar Volunteers, Mr. C. Kelly, who attached himself to the Fifth throughout the mutiny, and was identified with them in their labour and their reward.

The sick and wounded were sent to Dinapore under charge of one of the garrison, Assistant-Surgeon Hale, who afterwards wrote an account of the defence, in which he speaks of Eyre, Hastings, and L'Estrange as "that glorious band of fearless and true-hearted men."

Koer Singh and his men had fled to his castle at Jugdeespoor, and there Eyre was determined to follow him. Captain L'Estrange made official report: "The difficulty attending the enterprise was, by universal report, very great. The roads were represented as being (at that season of the year) almost impassable, and the position of Koer Singh and his followers was deemed by all who had any knowledge of the country surrounding him as being inaccessible . . . a feeling of doubt . . . might easily have persuaded troops less confident than ours were in the judgment, talent, and courage of our leader." It could not be regarded otherwise than as a forlorn hope, and many men made their wills before setting out.

Eyre had been reinforced by 200 of the 10th Foot and 100 Sikhs; and, with 140 of the Fifth, he started at 2 p.m., August 11th. The column passed the scene of the Dinapore ambush, halted in the open plain, and camped for the night. They set out again at daybreak, and about 10 in the morning came on a party of the enemy in a village. These were driven out by skirmishers, but Eyre was convinced that there was a large force close at hand. A round of grape on a patch of cover drove the Sepoys into the open, to be charged, broken, and driven back by the 10th. On the right the Fifth were holding Koer Singh in check, and presently the artillery scattered this force, and they fled with the Sepoys. Another stand a mile or two back was no more successful, and an hour after noon the stronghold was won. The palace and town were destroyed, and Eyre would have followed up his success had he not received an urgent message from Outram recalling the force.

Back to Buxar went Eyre and the Fifth. On August 24th they embarked in the steamer carrying Outram and his staff, and received at first hand his compliments on their " glorious little campaign."

On September 1st Major-General James Outram arrived at Allahabad to take command of the Dinapore and Cawnpore Divisions. His first object was the relief of Lucknow, and, incidentally, the reinforcing of Havelock's army, now reduced to 700 men. Outram's division was small enough, the Fifth and 90th, much reduced by detachments, and together less than 1,000 men, with artillery and some Gurkhas—in all, under 2,000. The great province of Oudh was Outram's own country. He had left only a short time before the outbreak, and his recall had brought him back post-haste. The little dark man with slow hesitating manner had all the qualities of decision, chivalry, and courage that the moment called for.

The guns and a detachment of troops, consisting of the Fifth and a few men of the 64th and 84th, started September 5th on their march to Cawnpore. Outram and the 90th followed close behind. Three marches from Cawnpore, on the 12th, Outram learnt that a party of 400 rebels, advance-guard of a large force, was threatening his communications. He at once detached his right flank—Eyre, with two guns, and 100 men of the Fifth, under Captain Johnson and Lieutenant Brown (Nos. 6 and 8 companies), and 50 men of the 64th, all mounted on elephants—to cut off the van. All night the elephants plodded along, and at daybreak came upon the rebels not far from the Ganges. The cavalry at once engaged them, and drove them back to the river. The infantry hurried up and opened fire. Brown was ordered to charge. The Fifth came along at the double, and the rebels took to their boats; but these had been made fast to the side, and they could not cast off. Brown emptied his revolver, then took his sword and laid about him till that broke in his hand. A big Sepoy came at him with his hilmar, but a sergeant of the Fifth struck him down. Then Brown seized a rifle from one of the men and got to work again. The Sepoys tried to save themselves by jumping overboard, but Brown and one or two of the men went after them and swam back with some draggled prisoners. The infantry then drew back, the guns came up and opened with grape, and few of the rebels escaped.

Outram met with no further molestation, and two days later marched into Cawnpore. The Fifth had thought themselves veterans until they saw the haggard remnant of the devoted regiments who had struggled so desperately to save Lucknow. Havelock was ready to surrender his command, but Outram would not ask it of him, and for the next eleven days the general served as a volunteer in Havelock's army.

The force was divided into two brigades, Hamilton commanding the second and Neil[1] the first, consisting of the Fifth, the 84th and 64th, and the Madras Fusiliers. Havelock began his second advance on September 18th. A floating bridge was laid across the Ganges, and the whole army crossed to the Oudh bank. At daybreak on the 21st, in a deluge of rain, the actual march began. They entered a wild land seething with rebellion. The fall of Delhi weighed on them, and the memory of desolated homes and murder and torture was always with them as they marched on to rescue the women of Lucknow from the fate of their sisters at Cawnpore.

Across the road at Mungulwar the enemy had built a barrier and mounted six guns. His right rested on the village, the barrier protected his left, and the great cornfields gave him ample cover. Eyre's guns, drawn by elephants, were coming up the road when the battery opened; one elephant was hit by a lucky shot, swung round in pain, and not a step further could they get the elephants to go. For a moment there was some confusion; then, covered by the Fifth, the guns were

---

[1] Lieutenant-Colonel J. G. Neil of the 1st Madras Fusiliers, a soldier of extraordinary activity and daring, who had seen service in Burmah and the Crimea.

man-handled on and across the road, and opened fire. Havelock allowed the enemy no time to think. The village was cleared by his cavalry. The main force advanced, and the Sepoys broke. Outram, armed with his malacca-cane, galloped in pursuit. The cavalry captured two guns and a colour, and the enemy suffered considerable loss. An eyewitness, Major North, speaks of the Fifth, lately arrived from Mauritius, who displayed the most perfect training."

The Sepoys had neglected to destroy the bridge over the Sye, and Havelock reached Bunnee on the 22nd. It was still raining, and the men had to rest as best they could, with a swamp for bed, downpour for cover, and scanty rations. Lucknow was only sixteen miles away, and the guns thundered a message; but the wind was the wrong way, and the besieged failed to hear it.

At 8 the next morning they broke camp. The floods were out in vast sheets; there was not a Sepoy to be seen. A ten-mile march brought them to the Alum Bagh the Prince of Oudh's garden palace, walled for defence; and there 12,000 men barred the way. Sepoy cannon commanded the road. The first shot smote the head of the column; three officers of the 90th went down. The troops could not deploy in the marshy ground, they had to go straight ahead. The 1st Brigade halted for the 2nd to come up in support. Simmons bade his men lie down. In the very act of dismounting, Haigh, the adjutant, had his right arm carried away. Of this wound he afterwards died—the first break in that band of brothers—regretted by officers and men.[1]

The column went forward, the 2nd Brigade leading. On the left, across a ditch, there seemed to be a stretch of drier ground; and here, in front of the enemy, the troops deployed, forming with Neil in the centre and Hamilton on the left. Olphert's battery came racing up, swung off to the left and into and through the ditch, and formed up beyond the 2nd Brigade, Neil's men

[1] One man at least could vouch how tender a nurse Haigh had been when his men were sick with cholera in Allahabad.

cheering them as they thundered past. Then the infantry advanced under cover of Olphert and Eyre's heavy guns. The Fifth were on the right, pivoting, while Hamilton turned the enemy's flank. The Sepoys broke, only the Alum Bagh held out. When the right wing of the Fifth got the welcome order, they dashed forward most gallantly and cleared the gardens and enclosure, while the 78th entered the main gate and completed the rout. Alum Bagh was won.

All night it rained. Through the storm they could hear the cannon in Lucknow; and, to cheer them, they heard a report of the capture of Delhi. This, however, was premature: Delhi did not fall until September 25th.

Havelock decided to rest his men. They had far outpaced his train; and for three days had marched and fought in a downpour. The general risked too much to throw away men's lives; so the next day, while the generals matured their plans, the men lay about in lazy content. A reconnoitring party, under Lieutenant Brown, was sent to ascertain the depths of a nullah on their front. With them went Lieutenant Havelock, aide-de-camp, impetuous as ever, riding far ahead, the infantry advancing in skirmishing order to cover him. He quickly discovered the stream to be impassable, and, as he turned back, a heavy fire broke out, and Sepoys closed in on the little party. Havelock galloped back, ordering the companies to retire at the double. Brown hurriedly gave a counter-order, halted the men, and the retreat was made in good order without confusion. One of the men had his leg carried away by a cannon-ball. Brown ran back to him, followed by Corporal Grant; under a heavy fire they brought him safely in to the Alum Bagh. For this deed Corporal Grant received the Victoria Cross.

A garrison of 6 officers and 300 men, including Lieutenant Oldfield and 70 of the Fifth, most of them too footsore to march, was left in the Alum Bagh, together with the sick and wounded, ammunition train and baggage. At 8 on the morning of the 25th the remainder of the column moved off.

The morning was dull and grey, the country a sea of mud, but there was a light in the men's eyes and a look on their faces which gave their general a serene confidence whatever the odds might prove to be.

Neil's brigade led the army, and two companies of the Fifth led Neil's brigade. Following them came Maude's battery, with Outram—malacca-cane and all—riding alongside. They had advanced barely two hundred yards down the road when the enemy opened fire and a sergeant and five men were hit; but they pushed on until a murderous fire poured out from some houses and garden walls abutting the road. The column was ordered to halt; the Fifth took cover in the ditches, and Maude's guns opened, the men at the batteries falling fast. Outram was wounded. One by one the gunners dropped; some of the Fifth sprang up and took their places. Here Captain L'Estrange was hit by grape and mortally wounded. Then at last the order to advance came, and the Fifth and some of the 84th rushed the enclosure on the right, while the 84th and 64th cleared the left, and the army marched on.[1]

Half a mile farther they were checked again. The canal was barely two hundred yards away, and a strong battery and breastwork defended the Char Bagh bridge. The battery was covered by high loopholed houses. The blue-capped Madras Fusiliers were sent forward to hold the bank, while Outram and the Fifth turned to the right and cleared the Char Bagh enclosure. While they were still fighting their way through, the 84th and the Madras Fusiliers carried the bridge and captured the guns. The houses near were then captured, and the way cleared for the main column. To the disgust of the Fifth, the 78th were at first ahead of them, but Simmons soon put that right.

Across the bridge the army turned to their right and

[1] In Division Orders, dated from the Lucknow Residency September 26th, Outram especially noted " the behaviour of the Fifth Fusiliers and Captain Maude's battery, who led the column on the 25th instant under a most murderous fire."

followed the canal for some way, then advanced into the city, meeting with no serious opposition until they came to the Moti Mahal. In the Hasratganj the Fifth were fired on from a house, which was promptly stormed and carried, and the garrison, mutineers of the 5th Native Infantry, killed. Their colours were taken, and were offered to Havelock and Outram, but were returned to the Fifth, who carried this trophy through the Mutiny.[1]

The enemy were strongly posted in the Moti Mahal, and the column halted for the rear-guard to come up; then the wounded were left in a walled passage with a small guard, and Havelock pushed on. So near his goal, he was determined to fight through; and fight through he did, and reached the Residency that night with the 2nd Brigade, the 1st halted without the walls. Worn out, the men lay down. Then up came Quartermaster Drake with his camel loaded with rum. He had been separated from his regiment in the advance, but had stuck to his camel and his rum, and the Fifth were the only regiment to get a drink that night.

The Fifth had won their way in, but at a heavy cost; their brigadier, brave, gallant Neil, was dead, the idol of his regiment, and the hero of the whole brigade; L'Estrange was dying, and they had lost David Johnson, son of their old colonel, and a true son of the regiment. " He possessed all the elements that constitute a true soldier. . . . On many occasions he performed far more than what mere duty required, till at length, in the pride and flower of manhood, he died as became a soldier."[2]

Early on the 26th Major Simmons, with two hundred and fifty of the Fifth, was sent out to reinforce the little guard who had been left with the wounded and

---

[1] If the Fifth gained a new trophy they also suffered a much regretted loss—a drum-major's stick, captured from a French regiment during the Peninsular War (at Ciudad Rodrigo ?) was stolen during the second relief operations, and never recovered.
[2] Major North, " Journal of an English Officer in India," p. 211.

supply near the Moti Mahal. Simmons made his way as best he could, but soon came under a heavy fire, and lost some men. When he had accomplished two-thirds of the way he found himself in a cul-de-sac, unable either to advance or retreat. The rebels swarmed round him. It was all he could do to hold his own. A hundred and fifty of the 78th and small parties of Sikhs reinforced him from time to time, but until nightfall he could not move. Then, under cover of darkness, he pushed on to the Moti Mahal, and the work of drawing off the guns and removing the wounded was begun. They had still to fight their way back to the Residency, and many gallant deeds were done before the guns were brought safely in. Some of the wounded in the dhoolies were carried by another route, which led through the very square where Neil had fallen two days before. Again a tremendous fire poured from the houses, most of the dhooly bearers dropped their burdens and fled. Some of the wounded were hacked to pieces, one or two were carried into safety. A small party of nine sound men, two wounded officers, and three wounded soldiers, fled into a little house, where they quickly found themselves besieged.

On the steps outside the door, sheltered behind a small pillar, Private M'Manus of the Fifth took his stand. Quietly and coolly he fired, picking his men. At the end of half an hour many had fallen to him, and he had only to raise his rifle and all the Sepoys ducked for cover. At last one of the native leaders called out that there were only three men in the house, but in answer the fourteen men—wounded, dying, and whole—raised a great cheer, and the Sepoys would not come on.

In revenge they began to fire on the deserted dhoolies. Private Ryan of the Madras Fusiliers could not bear to see his officer done to death, and he and M'Manus, who had himself been wounded, ran out, and under a hail of fire tried to move the dhooly. The weight was beyond their strength, so, stooping, they lifted the lieutenant out and carried him into the house, escaping themselves in a miraculous way. Next, a private, mortally wounded, was carried in; but with only six sound men left the little party could do no more. The Sepoys started new tactics. They brought up a great metal screen on wheels and rolled it to the door, and, from behind this cover, set the house on fire. Gathering up the three most helpless, the sound men fled out by a back door and across the square to a shed on the farther side; and there, till darkness fell, the survivors, with desperate courage, kept the enemy at bay. When the sun went down the firing ceased, but all night the Sepoys paced the roof, watching that none should escape. Very early in the morning heavy firing was heard, but it died away, and the men had lost heart when dawn came. Suddenly firing broke out again, very close. "That's our chaps!" great-hearted Ryan cried, and once more wounded and dying raised a cheer. It was a rear-guard of the 90th who rescued and brought them safely in to the Residency. Peter M'Manus received the Victoria Cross.

In the fighting between the 25th and 27th the Fifth lost nearly a third in killed and wounded. Corporals Curran and Phelan were taken prisoner, possibly during the first entry, when details were easily separated from their regiments. They, unhappy men, were forced to work in chains until the English advance in the following March, when they, with other prisoners, were put to death.

The day after the entry Outram took over command. He quickly realized that the garrison, though reinforced, was not relieved, for it was impossible to evacuate the Residency, with its company of women and children, sick and wounded, and to cover the retreat with his small army. The troops were ordered to occupy the palaces abutting the Residency along the river. The Fifth took the Chuttar Manzil. Rumour had it that the vaults were full of powder, and that they were to be blown sky high. One of the men volunteered to make sure, and was lowered into the vaults, which he found innocent of powder but full of water from the Goomptee. On the 28th, a small party of the Fifth and 90th were detached to clear the palace buildings in the direction of the Khas Bazaar; and Lieutenant Creagh with a few men found and destroyed a party of lurking Sepoys in the walled garden. Lieutenants Carter and Adair were wounded.

The next day three sorties were made simultaneously to drive the enemy back. One of these, 200 strong, including 90 men of the Fifth, commanded by Major Simmons, with a reserve of 150 under Captain M'Cabe, was ordered to destroy the guns in front of the Cawnpore battery.

At daybreak they started from the brigade mess, marching in single file, clambering over the ruins of houses that had been blown up during the siege. Clear of the houses confronting them was an eighteen-pounder gun, and from behind a breastwork the Sepoys fired two rounds before the red wave could break over the battery. The Cawnpore road was not yet in sight, the alarm had been given, and from the street houses came a deadly fire. M'Cabe turned to the left and drove his way into a garrisoned house, falling mortally wounded before it was won. Simmons left a picket and pushed on; two more buildings blocked this way, and they had to be carried before the Cawnpore guns could be attacked. On the threshold of the first house Simmons fell, shot in the mouth. Seven of his men leapt forward under a hail of fire to save him or recover his body, and then the little company could not be gainsaid, but swept through the house, cutting the garrison in pieces. The gun was in sight, but promised to be dearly bought, for from all sides it was covered by walls and garrisons. Outram would risk no more, and sent word ordering a retreat. The captured house was demolished and two guns destroyed, and the little party, without further loss, reached the Residency at 9 a.m. But Simmons was dead, and his loss was irreparable; Outram could justly say of him that he was " most deeply regretted by the whole army; a gallant, brave, accomplished officer." Six men were wounded.[1]

It will be remembered that Havelock had left his sick and wounded at the Alum Bagh. This detachment was being hard pressed, and was in urgent need of provisions. Outram determined to relieve them by the Cawnpore road, fighting his way from house to house, capturing each in turn. First the battery and house that Simmons had failed to take had to be seized. A column was formed of detachments of the Fifth and other regiments, Major Halliburton of the 78th in command, under the direction of Major Napier of the staff. The contingent from the Fifth consisted of 100 men and 4 officers, Lieutenants Meara, Brown, and Creagh, and Ensign Mason.

The right flank had been cleared by Simmons' operations, and Napier's column succeeded, on the night of October 1st, in seizing some of the left-hand houses before a stubborn resistance put a stop to their operations. In the morning, under cover of artillery, the troops advanced; but from behind a barricade the Sepoys kept up a tremendous fire. The Madras Fusiliers doubled down the Cawnpore road and came up in the rear; while Captain Shute of the 64th and Lieutenant Brown of the Fifth led the troops through a break in the stockade and drove the enemy from their cover, to find the guns had been skilfully withdrawn. Phillip's House was quickly taken, and from there the guns could

---

[1] There appears to be some discrepancy with regard to the dates of the losses of officers of the Fifth. The Regimental Record states that Captain Scott was wounded October 6th, and implies that Captains Johnson and L'Estrange and Lieutenant Carter died after that date. A note on the L'Estranges in *St. George's Gazette* states that Captain L'Estrange was killed September 25th. Another account gives September 29th, while Danvers says that by September 27th the Fifth had lost, out of 13 officers, 2 killed (Haigh and Simmons), 2 died of wounds (Johnson and L'Estrange), and 3 wounded (Scott and Oldfield), one of whom (Carter) was dying from want of nourishment. After October 6th Lieutenant Meara was left in command of the regiment, "a good and brave officer, but too junior to bring the regiment to proper notice." Ensign R. W. Danvers was attached to the regiment as interpreter, and served throughout the Mutiny (see his account in *St. George's Gazette*, 1893-1894).

be seen at the end of the garden and adjoining street. The Sepoys defended with grape and musket shot; but, without waiting for orders, Pat M'Hale of the Fifth, six-foot-two of him, fair-faced and sandy-haired, ran down the road, followed by the rest, and charged the guns. The hand-to-hand fight lasted only a minute, and the battery was won and the guns turned on the flying rebels.

The next few days the work went on, the column taking house by house, destroying as they went, until, on the 6th, they were checked by a mosque, strongly fortified and garrisoned, which effectually blocked the way. Without reinforcements they could advance no further, and no men could be spared. After destroying all the houses round the column withdrew to Phillip's House.

Outram was endeavouring to hold a very much larger perimeter than Lawrence[1] had attempted. This was necessary, both to keep back the enemy and in the interests of health, but the strain on his army was very great. The Sepoys, in revenge for the loss of Phillip's House, counter-attacked by mining operations and assaults. On the 6th they blew up a picket overlooking the Cheena and Khas Bazaars, and in the confusion penetrated into the palace. They were driven out with considerable loss, but in comparison the garrison suffered more severely; three men were killed, many injured, and Captain Scott of the Fifth was severely wounded. This was only one of many such attempts, and Outram finally abandoned the offensive and contented himself with defending the Residency and the position he had won. Some of the privates were employed as engineers, and one of them, Private Boylam of the Fifth, was recommended in orders for gallantry during mining operations. There was much sickness, food had to be carefully husbanded, and only short rations were

[1] Sir Henry Lawrence had died of wounds July 4th; Colonel John Inglis then commanded the garrison until Outram's arrival.

allowed.¹ There were no comforts for the sick and wounded, and barely sufficient clothing. Fortunately Outram was no longer anxious for the Alum Bagh, for small reinforcements and supplies had made their way in, and the place was manfully holding out.

And so was the Residency, for on the 22nd a message was received from Colin Campbell, the new commander-in-chief, that he, with every available man, was hurrying to the rescue of the little garrison, of whom Outram said, " Never could there have been a force more free from grumbles, more cheerful, more willing, or more earnest."

---

¹ Havelock wrote: " We eat a reduced ration of artillery bullock beef, chupatties and rice, but tea, coffee, sugar, soap, and candles are unknown luxuries."

CHAPTER XXXV

1857–1860

THE INDIAN MUTINY

LOVELACE WALTON

No. 4 company sailed from Mauritius July 19th. In the Straits of Malacca the transport was struck by a gale and driven on to the sands, but by good fortune escaped shipwreck. The men landed safely at Calcutta August 15th. Major Bryan Milman was in command.[1]

He was ordered to proceed immediately to Cawnpore and join the relief force collecting there. The company had to be fitted out for field service, and the bullock train proved somewhat slow; it was the end of September before they reached Cawnpore. They were there joined by No. 7 company, which had been detached from the regiment on landing, and sent as garrison to Bhaugulpore, but had now been relieved and also attached to the relief column. Small detachments of troops kept coming in, and on October 26th Brigadier-General Hope Grant arrived with a column from Delhi; pending the arrival of the commander-in-chief, he took command at Cawnpore. On October 30th he crossed the Ganges and advanced into Oudh, with the intention of withdrawing the sick and wounded from the Alum Bagh. This was safely accomplished by November 6th; and, incidentally, a village was cleared of the enemy and a brass gun captured.

[1] He dined with Lord Canning, the Governor-General, the evening after his arrival, and there met the new commander-in-chief, Sir Colin Campbell, very amiable and cheerful, and full of talk.

Campbell arrived at Cawnpore on the morning of November 3rd. Grant was then encamped about ten miles from the Alum Bagh. Not only was the whole of Oudh in rebellion, but a strong army—the Gwalior contingent—was threatening the communications with Allahabad. Nevertheless, Campbell did not hesitate; leaving General Wyndham with a small force to hold Cawnpore, he pushed on with every available man and a month's provisions.

On the evening of the 9th, after a forced march, Campbell joined Grant at Buntara. The next morning two Sikhs came in from an out picket escorting a ragged, weary man, with his face and body streaked with dirt: Kavanagh[1] had made his way from Lucknow to lead the relief force in.

Campbell, with 4,500 men, set himself to defeat an enemy 60,000 strong, drive them from their chosen position, rescue above 600 sick, wounded, and helpless creatures, and, with these in his keeping, return swiftly to Cawnpore, lest Wyndham should be attacked and fail to hold his own. The commander-in-chief was sixty-five years old; his slight, upright figure was still compact of force and energy. Before breaking camp he reviewed his army, the Naval Brigade and Bengal Artillery, the 9th Lancers, some faithful Punjaub Infantry, the 8th, 75th, and 93rd, and the battalion of Detachments. He spoke to Milman and the two companies of the Fifth. He had known the Fifth in the Mediterranean many years before, and then the regiment was noted for cleanliness and discipline; he was very glad to see them again. The men vowed that Sir Colin had the same pair of overalls that had gone through the Russian War.

At break of day on the 12th the army set out, and that night camped near the Alum Bagh. The garrison was changed, the details were drafted into two pro-

---

[1] T. H. Kavanagh, a clerk in a government office, who served through the siege as an assistant field engineer. He escaped in disguise from the Residency to lead the relief force in, and for this deed received the first civilian V.C.

visional battalions, and the 75th left in their place. The remaining infantry was divided into three brigades, under Grant, Greathed, and Russel. The second brigade under Colonel E. H. Greathed of the 8th Regiment was made up of the 8th, 2nd Punjaub Infantry, and the battalion of Detachments.

The army set out from the Alum Bagh at 9 on the morning of the 14th, Greathed's brigade acting as rear-guard to protect the left flank, for Sir Colin did not follow Havelock's route, but turned to the right, marching east for the Goomptee River. Three miles down the road the column was met by fire from the park wall of the Dilkoosha Palace. Part of Greathed's brigade came hurrying up and reinforced the leading brigade. The battalion of Detachments assisted in driving the Sepoys from the palace into the Martinière, the cavalry completing the rout. The Lancers, carrying the pursuit too far, came under a heavy fire; but, under cover of the guns, the infantry swept on; by noon Palace and Orphanage were occupied and secure. Here, with Grant's brigade on the right flank and Russel's on the left, the troops bivouacked for the night, the commander-in-chief visiting every sick and wounded man before he rested. Just before nightfall the enemy made two attacks, but were beaten off.

All the next day the troops rested, waiting for ammunition and provisions to come up. Reconnaissances were made and the ground examined. At noon a fierce attack was beaten off, and all day long the guns and mortars kept up their fire. As evening fell a signal was made from the Martinière to the Residency, "Advance to-morrow!" and a great bonfire blazed all night. The two companies of the Fifth (and many others) had their night made hideous by Peel's infernal rocket car. Young Fitzroy[1] rebuked the serene sailor for frightening his picket; one of the Fifth was even wounded by a missfire.

[1] Sir William Peel, captain R.N., commanded the Naval Brigade in the Crimea and in India. Philip Fitzroy joined as ensign in 1854, and lived to command the Fifth in 1885.

At eight the next morning the van started, Greathed following as rear-guard at noon. The canal was crossed without difficulty; it was nearly dry, and the column had struck a point where the banks sloped gently, and where even the guns were got across with comparative ease. Keeping close to the river, the army hurried on, until the Secunda Bagh came in view. This garden, a hundred yards square, high-walled and bastioned, was a formidable obstacle. The glory of its storming belongs to the 53rd and the 93rd, and the 4th Punjaub, but the battalion of Detachments arrived in time to act in support, and the two companies of the Fifth could claim to have helped in the work. Two thousand Sepoys perished before the garden was won.

Next the Shah Nujjeef blocked the way, a mosque surrounded by jungle and mud cottages. Here the sailors and Highlanders fought desperately, and the losses were so terrible that Campbell had all but turned away when it was found that the Sepoys had given up heart and fled. The mosque became headquarters, and the army bivouacked for the night. An alarm just before dawn brought them standing to arms, but the Sepoys held off. The Colours of the 93rd were hoisted on the Shah Nujjeef, and were answered from the Chuttar Manzil—for the garrison had broken out of the Residency and stormed the first line; only the Moti Mahal and the Mess separated Outram and Campbell.

The naval guns were quickly at work, and the mess-house bombarded, then stormed. The Moti Mahal was rushed, and the rebels driven from room to room. Only five hundred yards of open ground separated rescuers and besieged; but across that space, from the Kaisar Bagh on the left, and from across the river on the right, the Sepoys poured in a desperate fire. It was some time before the generals could join hands. At last they met on the lawn of the mess-house—Havelock, a grey and white shadow of a man, but still erect until broken by the cheers of the soldiers who had risked so much to save him; Outram cool and quiet; and

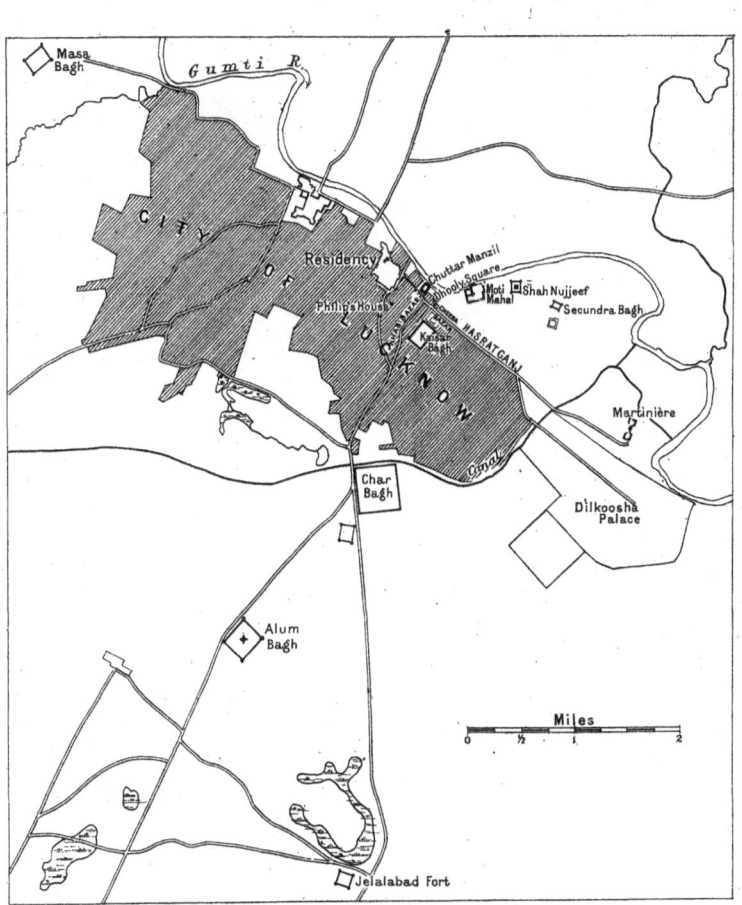

Campbell outwardly unmoved. Together they stood and counted the cost.

A few of the relief force ran the gauntlet and entered the Residency. They found the garrison too weary to be glad, grimed with smoke and dirt, and weak from their long fast. The Fifth were together again, their company sadly reduced, no longer the " shiners," but more than ever the " ever-fighting, never-failing Fifth."

Sir Colin held to his decision to evacuate the Residency with the utmost speed. He had no intention of tying up his field army in a hopeless attempt to reduce the great city. Making a show of an attack on the Kaisar Bagh, the withdrawal began. The women and children were sent off, and the whole of the treasure and provisions destroyed. Then, on the 22nd, the garrison fell in just before midnight. A fire broke out, and a red glare lit up the battered courts of the Residency. Breathlessly they waited, but no alarm came from the city. Then they marched out, past Outram and past Inglis, who had claimed the right to be the last to leave and to close the gates. Not a shot came from the rebels until the garrison was safely through Campbell's lines; then, as Hope's brigade fell back, a storm of musketry and grape came from the Kaisar Bagh. Peel promptly answered with a shower of his much-abused rockets, and the firing ceased. Before dawn every soldier had left the city, and the army was again in position round the Dilkoosha and the Martinière. The evacuation had been accomplished, in the face of an enemy 50,000 strong, without the loss of a single man.

Havelock died, his work done, on November 24th, and his soldiers buried him in the gardens of the Alum Bagh.

Campbell divided his army; leaving Outram with a division to hold the Alum Bagh, he returned with the remainder to Cawnpore to reinforce Wyndham and defeat the Gwalior force.

The Fifth were in Outram's division, which, less than 4,000 strong, was expected to hold in check Lucknow, with its huge army and its 70,000 turbulent rebels. The Alum Bagh itself could only accommodate a small garrison. The main force was encamped about a mile in the rear, across the Cawnpore road. The right was covered by the Jelalabad Fort, and the whole was protected by batteries, abatis, and swamps. The advance posts and pickets extended as far as the city outposts.

The Fifth were in the third brigade under Hamilton, lieutenant-colonel of the 78th (Fifth, 64th, 78th). Colonel Guy took over the garrison at the Alum Bagh on November 13th; and here the Fifth lost another officer, Lieutenant Brown, who fell from his horse and broke his leg, afterwards dying of lockjaw. He had done well in the late campaign, and could be ill spared.

Outram had chosen his position well, and his defences were skilful; but the commander-in-chief hardly gave him credit for the magnitude of the task with the small army at his disposal. The strain on the troops was very great. The continual skirmishing between outposts occasionally developed into serious attacks, and the necessity of escorting convoys and maintaining communications added to the difficulties.

In December, Outram learnt from his spies that the enemy intended to surround him and cut off the Cawnpore road. A large force was already at Guilee, three miles to the south-east, and in a strong position, flanked by the Dilkoosha walls. The force was reported 4,000 strong, with 4 guns. Outram at once detached 1,200 infantry, 190 cavalry, and Maude and Olpherts with 6 guns. Between four and five on the morning of the 21st the Fifth paraded, 400 strong, under command of Colonel Guy, who was to lead the left-hand column; and before dawn they started, heading for Jelalabad, No. 8 company leading, under Captain Bigge.

An hour's march brought them to a village, where a vedette challenged and galloped off. Before the column lay an open plain, with a patch of mango groves in the distance. In the groves they could see the enemy position. It was just beginning to get light. Guy continued his advance, and gave the order to deploy.

At that instant the rebels opened with grape; the Fifth hung together a moment; there was some confusion. Guy turned, halted the movement, and bade them begin again; this time it went as if on parade. The Fifth advanced in line, captains on the right of their companies. When within distance they charged, racing for the guns. Cubitt, the subaltern of No. 8 company, ran forward, but Bigge was easily first. The Sepoys did not wait for their coming, but fled, leaving a gun for the Fifth.

Guy then re-formed his men, and, covered by skirmishers, pushed on to Guilee village. Here the enemy made another stand, with a gun posted to command the street. The Fifth came on swiftly and silently, the skirmishers falling back. Then, regardless of grape and musket shot, Pat M'Hale sprang forward and led the charge. Untouched he reached the gun, killed the gunners, and turned their own weapon on the flying Sepoys.

The right-hand column had met with equal success, and had turned the enemy out of their entrenchments; but the third column, with the train, had tried to cut off the retreat to the city, and were in difficulties. Reinforcements had come to the rebels from Lucknow, and the third column were barely holding their own. Part of the Fifth were detached and sent to the rescue. With the help of Olpherts' guns the rebels were driven off and their guns captured, two more falling to the Fifth.

All was over by eleven o'clock, and the men were back in time for a late breakfast, with the loss of only three killed and seven wounded. Lieutenant Danvers, attached to the Fifth, was slightly wounded by grape, but otherwise the regiment escaped. For his conduct on this and other occasions, Pat M'Hale received the Victoria Cross. He was a fine soldier, worthy of England in those great days. Never absent from duty, he served throughout the campaign without a scratch. In 1859 he survived an attack of cholera, refusing treatment, and walking the wards all night—one of the very few who recovered. M'Hale died at Shorncliffe,

October, 1866, having earned, besides the Mutiny medal with the Lucknow clasps and the Victoria Cross, both the medals for Merit and Good Conduct.

When the regiment had been sent up country, Major Chapman, with 70 men (30 of No. 10 company, 40 of No. 7 company), had been left at the base. In December he was ordered to Purneeah in Lower Bengal, to protect the district from the 11th Irregular Cavalry. With the help of the Calcutta Volunteer Naval Brigade the mutineers were hunted down and brought to action. Thirty-five Sepoys were killed and twenty taken prisoner, the rest escaping in the fog. Sir George Yule wrote of the Fifth: " You have no idea how well the men behaved. There never was a complaint against them. They never grumbled, though they had no liquor for weeks together, and not one of them was ill all the time, though we had to camp in the most horrid places in the forest." Commissioner Yule did his best to keep the men in spirits; and, once, at least, took Chapman and his men tiger hunting on elephants. There is no reco d of the bag.

To return to Outram. The defeat at Guilee did not daunt the enemy; early in January they made their first general attack on the encampment. The Fifth, from their position on the right of the line, were swung round to protect the Jelalabad Fort. In this they were completely successful, turning the enemy's right, and forcing them under Maude's guns. The attack lasted from dawn until five in the evening, and was everywhere driven off. Four days later, like a tide, the Sepoys came surging back, this time fighting into the night, but still Outram held his own. Then peace for a month, until, in February, the assaults began again, first on the 16th, again on the 21st; then —with the Queen-Regent, her son, and all the Court as spectators—a great and final attempt on the 25th. Thirty regiments, 1,000 cavalry, and 8 guns, came out against Outram and his 3,000 men. The British Cavalry won the honours of the day, but the Fifth, who held the left-hand pickets under Major Chester

Master, were mentioned by their general, and praised for the warm reception they gave to the enemy when, late in the afternoon, he shot his last bolt and hurled himself against the palisades. When night fell the rebels withdrew, leaving two guns in English hands.

For twelve weeks Outram had held out, and his personality had much to do with his success—"a kind, considerate man, well liked by officers and men," wrote Danvers. No general was ever better served; few have had a harder task; within the camp uncomfortable quarters, poor and scanty fare, constant alarms, and sickness that lingered and spread; while beyond the pickets and feeble barricades were nearly 100,000 men, drunk with blood.

Now the worst was over. On the last day of February the commander-in-chief rode in to confer with Outram and inform him of his plan of campaign. Then, on March 2nd, a cloud of dust was seen on the Cawnpore road; Campbell and his men were coming to storm Lucknow. The army passed left of the Alum Bagh, and halted a mile from Jelalabad, cavalry, Horse Artillery, the guns of the *Shannon*, and the 2nd Division of infantry. Campbell marched east, and Outram followed him; but, to their sorrow, the Fifth and 78th were left to garrison the Alum Bagh. Guy was appointed to command the 3rd Infantry Brigade, and Chester Master was left to command the Fifth.

For a week or more the cannon thundered; men came back with news how place after place was won. By the 15th the Kaisar Bagh had fallen, and the next day the Residency once more flew the British flag. In revenge the Sepoys attacked the Alum Bagh, but were beaten off. Three days later the Fifth were relieved, and sent to occupy the Masa Bagh palace, north of the city. Their march occupied two days, and was not accomplished without opposition. Lieutenant Cubitt and three men were wounded. In the Mess at the present day are two tables made of marble slabs found in the Masa Bagh.

Although Delhi, Cawnpore, and Lucknow had fallen and the Gwalior field force been defeated, there were still vast provinces and kingdoms where the British rule had been obliterated; and there were thousands of men in arms to whom that authority must be taught anew. Oudh, as has been said, was a very recent annexation, and the fall of Lucknow did not greatly affect the spirit of the feudal chiefs. Koer Singh kept the rebel flag flying in northern Bengal; central India was alive with sedition, and the wild lands of Rohilcund were full of treason. It was Canning's wish that Campbell should at once invade Rohilcund to hearten the loyal Hindus and quell the Mussulmans. The commander-in-chief therefore left a permanent garrison in Lucknow, and marched north with 10,000 men. The Fifth, worn out and much reduced in numbers, were sent to Cawnpore, where they remained in garrison for two months. Drafts from England arrived; Guy broke down in health, and went home, Lieutenant-Colonel Kennedy succeeding him; but shortly after he too fell ill, and the command devolved on Major Chester Master. The regiment was served out with tunics and trousers of thin cotton, dyed a new colour, called " khaki."

Early in June the Fifth marched to Calpee. On the 14th the Rohilcund campaign came to an end, with the complete subjugation of the province. The commander-in-chief then made Allahabad his headquarters, and there the Fifth joined their division a month later.

Oudh was the next business. In September and October the destruction of forts and the clearing of the country began; but before the real campaign opened the old " John Company " was dead and Lord Canning had come to Allahabad with the Queen's message to the people and native princes.

On November 1st, through a double line of infantry, the new Viceroy, with the commander-in-chief, now Lord Clyde, rode to a dais in front of the Fort. There the Proclamation was read.

Only half the Fifth were present; the left wing was already on its way north, advance-guard of an expeditionary force against the Rajah of Amethee, one of the most powerful of the old feudal rulers. The left wing marched October 28th, crossed the Sai and occupied Loolee. The main army followed November 7th and 8th. The Fifth were brigaded with the 54th, a battalion of Sikhs and a regiment of Oudh police, under Brigadier-General Pinckney.

From Loolee the roads were narrow and bad, and the bordering cornfields quickly became plains of trampled mud. This made heavy going, and when Pinckney halted, three miles from Amethee, his men were tired out. The army had marched in three columns, and was now in position, enclosing the town on three sides. The frightened Rajah tried to make terms; Clyde demanded an unconditional surrender; that night the Rajah fled to the English camp, and the next day Clyde entered a deserted city, for the rebels had escaped, and the hunt must begin again. A detachment was left to hold Amethee, and the three columns turned west, heading for Shunkerpore, the stronghold of the Rajput Chief, Beni Mahdo, whose flag the Amethee army had joined. Shunkerpore had an eight-mile perimeter, and Clyde's army was insufficient to complete the investment. The Rajah was sternly summoned to surrender; he replied that the fort was his own, therefore he would yield it, but that his body was his king's. In the night the place was evacuated; the English marched in, but Beni Mahdo and his army had vanished. Eveleigh's brigade was detached and sent in pursuit, and, two days later, came in touch with him at Roy Bareilly. All night and all day Clyde marched, the Fifth toiling with him, and came up with Eveleigh on the evening of the 19th, but Beni Mahdo had not waited for his coming.

From all points of the compass came certain news of this Indian De Wet. Clyde regretted that he had not thirty-two columns to aid him. Eveleigh was sent west, and the headquarters column moved north-west at one on the morning of the 21st. By noon Buchraon was reached, and there Clyde heard that the Rajah was west of them, at Doun de Khara, twenty-eight miles south of Cawnpore. Eveleigh was watching the rebels, a precarious position for his little force. Clyde was on the march before sunrise. By 8 o'clock his army was crossing the Sai, for the fourth time since the column had left Allahabad. The river bottom was sandy and treacherous, and there was much difficulty in getting the horses and elephants across. Clyde made his infantry strip, and the Fifth muttered, " they knew he'd have them Highlanders before he'd finished with them." Six precious hours were wasted, but again the next day Clyde set out before dawn, and this time did not halt until he had led his men into Eveleigh's lines.

Beni Mahdo was standing his ground. On the 24th Clyde advanced to give battle. " We should fight damned well," said the men, too stiff and footsore to run away. Clyde rode at the head, his infantry in two divisions, with artillery between and on either flank, and cavalry on the wings. A line of skirmishers, led by Major Milman, covered the advance, and drove their way through the jungle and fields. They were swept by grape, but did not waver for an instant. The artillery opened on the barricades, and the skirmishers charged the village. To their great disgust the rebels broke and ran, the cavalry after them in hot pursuit. Four guns were captured, one by Major Milman; but Beni Mahdo and most of his men escaped.

Two other columns were on the hunt, and met the flying rebel and headed him north across the frontier. Clyde and the headquarters column returned to Allahabad, the work done, though not as thoroughly as they could wish.

A few days later the Fifth were attached to Brigadier Eveleigh, and sent out to capture and destroy the fort of Oomeriah in the Lucknow road. They met with sharp resistance, and the Fifth lost twenty men before the place was won. Again Milman led the skirmishers, and Eveleigh reported that " his coolness and courage under fire was the remark of all who witnessed it." Three days were spent in levelling the fort.

Eveleigh was then ordered north to Gonda, for Beni Mahdo was again on the war-path, and threatened to cross the Goghra river. The Fifth were left at Gonda, in reserve for a month, while the northern country was cleared of rebels. This work done the regiment returned to Allahabad and went into cantonments. Here ended the campaign as far as the Fifth were concerned. Clyde's wonderful organization had done its work, but the general could not have succeeded without the patient endurance, self-sacrifice, and insolent daring of the British infantryman.

The Fifth suffered from two outbreaks of cholera, losing forty-six men in April, and twenty-four men in August. In March, 1860, they sailed from Calcutta, Chester Master in command.

Lucknow may well be on the Colours, for, through the Mutiny years of horror and glory, pity, and revenge, every man of the Fifth had upheld and added to the honour of the old regiment.

CHAPTER XXXVI

1857–1899

2ND FIFTH

ALL the time of the Mutiny drafts were being sent out from England to the old regiment; altogether 16 officers, 3 sergeants, 1 drummer, 10 corporals, and 633 privates went from the depot. In addition, Lieutenant-Colonel J. A. Vesey Kirkland[1] was, on October 26th, 1857, authorized to raise a second battalion at Newcastle-upon-Tyne. The men of the north were of the same blood as the garrison of Lucknow, and in less than two months Vesey Kirkland could report that 1,000 men had come forward; and on December 26th he was gazetted lieutenant-colonel of the new 2nd Fifth.

In February the Battalion moved to Aldershot, and their training was so far forward that in August they were embarked for Mauritius for garrison duty. They landed in November, and on the following St. George's Day were presented with their new Colours by Mrs. Stevenson, the wife of the governor. The 2nd Fifth were welcomed for the sake of the first Battalion, and they quickly made friends. Vesey Kirkland was an excellent commanding officer. He insisted that his subalterns should know their men, and he allowed no relaxation in the perfecting of their drill. The second Battalion was to be worthy of the First and in all things as perfectly trained.

After four years in Mauritius the Battalion was sent to South Africa, one wing to Port Natal, the other to

[1] John A. Vesey Kirkland, served as staff officer in the Crimea; commanded 2nd Fifth 1858-1869.

East London. Light was just beginning to flicker in the Dark Continent. Livingstone had set out on his second journey; Speke, Grant, and Du Chaillu were at work; for a time the Boers were content with a peaceful antagonism; the troublesome Kaffir War was in abeyance; Natal, an independent and prosperous colony, had only Bishop Colenso to disturb her tranquillity.

Port Natal, or D'Urban, was a flourishing little town, surrounded by trees, and very healthy. In the spring of 1864 both wings united at East London, the half Battalion from D'Urban coming by sea in H.M.S. *Valorous*. The redcoats did not take kindly to the very strict discipline on board, and there was considerable friction.

From East London the Fifth went to King Williamstown, forty miles up the Buffalo, the military headquarters. A house for the colonel was provided, but no quarters for the other officers, who lived in little houses standing in pleasant gardens by the river. The town was clean and well cared for, especially the neat tenements in the German quarter. There were also several stores, well filled with American goods. Everyone rode or travelled in bullock-carts, for there were no roads. Twice a year the little town was crowded for the races.

After a year in King Williamstown the regiment trekked south to Grahamstown—forty waggons, each with its dozen oxen, laden with the tents, luggage, women, and children; with them went droves of sheep and herds. The cavalcade set out across the veldt October 13th, 1865, not a bridge nor metalled road in the country. They encountered duststorms, and thunderstorms, and great heat; but five days later, after a halt to smarten up and place their plumes in their shakos, they marched into Grahamstown. Here the country was treeless and barren, the town large and straggling, almost entirely English in its population, and military in its interests.

The next year the Battalion was ordered home, calling at St. Helena for three companies which had been sent there in 1866.

The 2nd Fifth landed at Dover July 9th, 1867, and were

quartered in the barracks until the following spring, when they were sent to Aldershot. They were there put through some hard work in very hot weather; under arms from 5 a.m. to 2 p.m., with the thermometer at 80° F. in the shade. In 1869, Lieutenant-Colonel Bartley[1] succeeded Vesey Kirkland in command.

From Aldershot the Battalion went north; for the first time the Fifth crossed the Border. They were quartered in Glasgow and Ayr; and when the route came, in 1871, the Corporation of Glasgow gave a banquet to the regiment, so popular had they become.

From Glasgow the 2nd Fifth went to Dublin, distributed between Ship Street, the Royal Barracks, and Linen Hall. They had grumbled at the dirt, and fog, and smell of Glasgow until the hospitality of the inhabitants had reconciled them, but now they were in an unfriendly town, quartered in the worst barracks in Europe, dirty, gloomy, tumbledown, wfth plenty of hard, unpleasant work. The Curragh was no better, for the huts were falling to bits. Later, the 2nd Fifth were sent to Waterford and Kilkenny, and conditions improved. In this year Lieutenant-Colonel Carden[2] succeeded Bartley in command.

The Battalion left Ireland in 1874, spending the next four years in Jersey, at Aldershot, Woolwich, and Chatham. Three years then followed in this stronghold of engineers and marines. One thing, Buckly Hall, a new-fangled notion, canteen and recreation-room for the men, excited their interest and admiration; but the Chatham atmosphere was not altogether congenial.

In 1880 the Battalion, Lieutenant-Colonel Bigge[3] in command, sailed for India, and, eight years later, had their first taste of active service.[4]

[1] John Cowell Bartley, served in Crimea with 4th Foot; major in Fifth, October, 1857; died a major-general.
[2] George Carden, joined Fifth as captain in September, 1856, after serving in Crimea with 77th Foot; major 1864.
[3] Thomas Scovell Bigge, served in Crimea with 23rd Foot; joined Fifth as captain September, 1856; major 1864; died a major-general.
[4] John Granville Harkness, served with 55th Foot in Crimea; joined Fifth as captain in 1857; major 1877; commanded 2nd Fifth 1885-1886. Frederick Pocklington, served with 28th Foot in Crimea; captain in Fifth, October, 1877; major 1877; commanded 2nd Fifth 1886-1888.

1888] THE BLACK MOUNTAIN CAMPAIGN 403

In the farthest northern corner of the Punjaub, between Kashmir and Afghanistan, is a frontier valley, backed by the Black Mountains, inhabited by a number of tribes of Afghan race, whose depredations for many years had annoyed the civil authorities. A punitive expedition in 1868 had proved too lenient, and the raids and murders became more daring, culminating on June 18th, 1888, with an attack on a party of British troops in British territory, and the murder of the officers.

At this moment the 2nd Fifth were at Kuldana, in the Murree Hills. They got their orders in September, and 600 picked men, dressed in khaki, their belts and pouches washed in mud, set out for Dilbori, Lieutenant-Colonel Vincent[1] in command. Major-General M'Queen commanded the Field Force, which numbered 8,000, in two brigades of two columns. Brigadier-General Channer, V.C., commanded the 1st Brigade, and Colonel Sym, of the 5th Gurkhas, the 1st Column.[2] Brevet-Major Money, of the 2nd Fifth, acted as D.A.Q.M.G. to General Channer. The Fifth, on arrival at Dilbori, were instructed, both officers and men, in first aid; they were also initiated into the art of hill warfare, and told to forget all their drillbook knowledge.

The advance was made on October 4th by the four columns, working independently, but co-operating with each other. The 1st Column made for the Mana Ka Dana ridge, the 2nd Fifth ahead, acting as pioneers, and screening the advance of the mountain guns. The men were strictly enjoined not to commit themselves to an engagement. The Pathans did their best, calling out: " Come on, Lords ! Come on !" But the " lords " were told to keep under cover and hold their fire; so the Pathans grew bolder, and the Fifth suffered until the guns were in position, when the first round scattered the hillmen. That night the column bivouacked on the hill they had won, though not undisturbed, for sniping went on all night, and one private was mortally wounded.

[1] John Love Vincent, ensign in Fifth 1861; lieutenant 1865; captain 1876; major 1881; commanded 2nd Fifth 1888-1892.
[2] First column: 2nd Fifth, 5th Gurkhas, 3rd Sikhs, and detachment of engineers.

404 THE SECOND BATTALION, 1857–1899 [CHAP. XXXVI

The next day they marched on against Chittabut. G and H companies, under Major Cherry, were sent to occupy a ridge until the baggage-train had been got up the steep, rough road. The hillmen hovered round; one of the rear-guard was wounded, but the Pathans were driven back.

On the 6th, Colonel Vincent, with C and E companies, and three companies of Sikhs, advanced on Doda Hill and village, where he was met with stubborn resistance. Some Sikhs and C company, under Lieutenant Tuite, were charged by the enemy. A steady fire checked the hillmen, and then Tuite counter-charged, and the enemy ran. The bandmaster of the Fifth, Wallace, acting subaltern, showed conspicuous gallantry.

The other columns were driving along with equal success. Gradually the hills were cleared, and the tribes retreated into the wild lands. M'Queen offered generous terms of submission, but these were refused, and the expeditionary force proceeded to sterner measures. Maidan was destroyed by the second brigade, and on the 16th C and E companies helped to burn the village of Saidara, where they met with slight resistance. A week later the commander-in-chief, Sir Frederick, afterwards Lord, Roberts, paid a visit to the Field Force. On the 25th he inspected the 1st Column and to the Fifth he said:

" Fifth Fusiliers, I am very glad to hear from General M'Queen such a good account of the regiment. He tells me that there has not been a single case of insubordination since the regiment came on service, and that you have made light of any hardship and difficulty, and behaved as I knew the regiment always would. I congratulate Colonel Vincent on having such a fine body of men under him. There is not a better regiment in Her Majesty's service than the Northumberland Fusiliers."

'Before M'Queen could properly harry the enemy's country he had to possess himself of the high lands. On November 1st the Fifth marched as advance-guard, and came in for some sharp fighting before the Ghoraphir Pass and Chaila Ridge were won. Hidden in the scrub, from a high crag the enemy kept up a heavy fire. The

Fusiliers clambered up the hill-face on hands and knees, with the Khyberees racing alongside, to the accompaniment of pipes and tom-toms. Rocks came hurtling down on them, and the never-ceasing snipers' fire. Pushing and pulling they made their way, Houston, the fighting doctor, leading the Fifth; and at last the ridge was theirs.

That night they bivouacked without baggage, 10,000 feet above sea-level, huddling round the fire, half frozen, half scorched, and wholly hungry. From the high lands M'Queen could command the situation, and the destruction of the recalcitrants' property was continued. When the burning of the crops began the tribes made overtures. This was the beginning of the end, though guerrilla warfare went on for some months. A large force was no longer necessary, and Channer's brigade was withdrawn.

When the column advanced the Fifth were in the van, and now they guarded the rear. The Pathans hung about the column, and the Fifth had plenty to do before Maidan was reached. Surgeon Houston rescued a man under heavy fire, and, with the help of two privates, carried him to safety. The column reached Abbottabad on November 17th, and on the 19th were inspected by the General Officer Commanding, who said to the Fifth:

" With regard to your behaviour before the enemy, I myself saw you advance against that almost impregnable position at the Chaila Crag. Nothing could have been better done, and the way you behaved that day adds fresh laurels to the already glorious record of your distinguished regiment."

Lieutenant J. F. Riddell,[1] Sergeant Thompson, Corporal Coyne, and Private T. Hamilton were mentioned in despatches, and Vincent was promoted full colonel. Again the regiment was praised, not only for its courage, but for its cheeriness, good conduct, and discipline.

[1] Brigadier-General James F. Riddell, joined 2nd Fifth in 1880; afterwards commanded the 3rd battalion, raised during the South African War, until its disbandment in 1907; colonel in command Northumberland Infantry Brigade (Territorials) July, 1911; killed second battle of Ypres, 1915, leading his brigade.

The Battalion spent six more years in India, in 1891 acting as reserve to the Black Mountain troops, and for the greater part of the time they were stationed not far from the unrestful border.[1] In February, 1895, they sailed from Bombay to Singapore, landing March 16th. They spent eighteen months there, then embarked for Gibraltar and home.[2]

The first Battalion arrived at Gibraltar in October, the second in December, nearly a hundred years since last the two Battalions had been together on the Rock; 500 privates were transferred to the first Battalion, and the second sailed on to Southampton, arriving January 6th, 1897.[3]

The 2nd Fifth was now forty years old; thirty-six years had been spent on foreign service; it was high time the North Country should again see the regiment they had raised.[4] In the spring of 1898, Riddell, now a captain, was sent with 200 men to Newcastle-on-Tyne. The Tynesiders showed their welcome; the Mayor received them, and a service was held in the Cathedral.

From Newcastle the detachment marched to Tynemouth; from there to Morpeth, then Alnwick, Rothbury, Cambo, and Hexham; and everywhere the people turned out to cheer them. Volunteer bands met them at each town, except at Alnwick, where the third Battalion played them in. The detachment did the Fifth credit.

There was no doubt that they belonged to " the best regiment in Her Majesty's service."

The 2nd Fifth moved to Portsmouth in September, 1899, and two months later followed the first Battalion to South Africa.

[1] Wilfred Fitzallan Way, commanded 2nd Fifth 1892-1896; joined as ensign 1864; lieutenant 1868; captain 1878; major 1883.

[2] George Hart Dyke succeeded Way; ensign in Fifth 1865; lieutenant 1870; captain 1880; major 1883; commanded 2nd Fifth 1896-1898.

[3] Under the Cardwell system battalions on foreign service were kept at full strength by drafts of long service men from the battalion at home.

[4] In 1898 Richard Lionel Pennington succeeded Hart Dyke; he had joined as lieutenant in 1876.

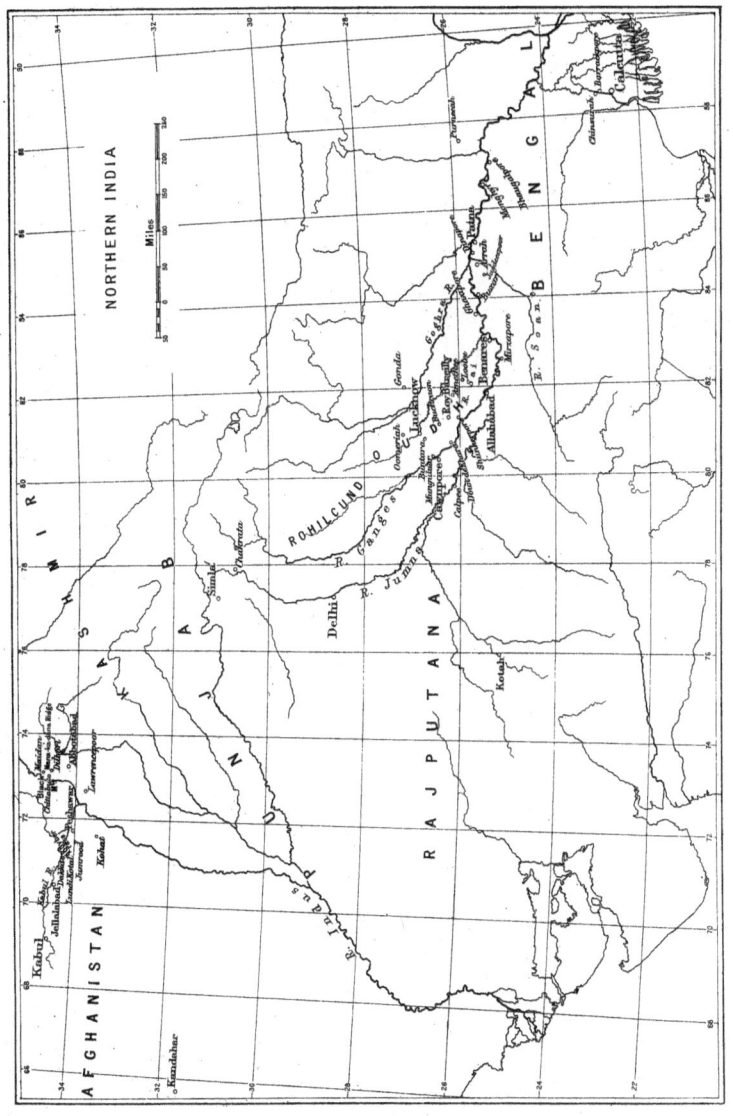

CHAPTER XXXVII

1862–1899

1st Fifth

2ND AFGHAN WAR, 1878–1879—3RD AFGHAN WAR, 1879–1880—
EGYPT, 1898—CRETE, 1898–99

LOVELACE WALTON, 1856–1865—WILLIAM DAMES, 1865–1868—EDWARD ROWLEY HILL, 1868–1878—LORD LONGFORD, 1878–1887—J. H. LAYE, 1887–1899

WHEN the 1st Fifth returned from India they were stationed in Portsea Barracks; Colonel Guy went to Colchester, and Chester Master[1] succeeded to the command of the regiment.

The summer of 1862 was spent at Aldershot, all clean new yellow brick, and there, under the eye of the commander-in-chief, the Duke of Cambridge, the Fifth manœuvred and marched. They won commendation. " Colonel Master, your regiment is one of the finest in the Service, and I hope that the other regiments will all take the Fifth Fusiliers for an example for steadiness in marching and general soldierlike bearing."

In the sixties certain abuses in the army were ventilated; the early social reformers found a mouthpiece in Charles Dickens, and in different periodicals some of the worst disabilities were pilloried. The men were still treated as machines; their day's work done, they had no resources save the beershops and one or two

---

[1] William Chester Master, C.B., joined Fifth as 2nd lieutenant in 1839, lieutenant 1841; captain 1846; major 1857; second in command 1858; succeeded to command 1861; and retired by sale 1866.

deplorable music-halls. And the day's work was a strenuous one, made the harder by the regulation uniform —thick, close fitting, and heavy; high stiff stock, and weighty hat. Manœuvres on the dusty hills under the burning sun cost the army many useful lives. Although the standard of living was being raised in the country, in the Services there was no improvement. Two women in each company were allowed to follow their husbands to Aldershot camp, the rest had to shift for themselves: their only certain support was the 3d. a day, and 1½d. per child lately allowed by the Government. Those married without leave could only hope for such support as their husbands could spare out of 4d. a day. The camp had no accommodation for women and children. The wife still had to live in her husband's crowded hut, shared with nineteen other men, her only privacy a blanket slung curtainwise round her bed.

From Aldershot the Fifth went to Shorncliffe, 1863, and from there to the Tower, where, on July 13th, 1864, they were presented with new Colours by the Duke of Cambridge, who could recall the Fifth as the very fine regiment he had known in Corfu in 1842, and who could justly say that they had maintained their reputation for good conduct and soldierly bearing.

In the autumn the Fifth went to Woolwich, and while there a terrible explosion happened at Erith which destroyed the embankment. Fortunately it was low tide. Every man in garrison was quickly hurried to the marshes, where they worked twenty-four hours without rest to remake the river wall and save the lowlands from the flood tide. The Fifth never got any compensation for their spoilt clothes.

From Woolwich, in 1865 they were sent to Ireland on board H.M.S. *Urgent*, and were stationed at the Curragh, Birr, and Athlone. Ireland was very unrestful; American agitators were at work, and garrison duty was far from easy. Somehow the Fifth made themselves popular. After two months' stay in Parsonstown Colonel Master received an address from the Town Commissioners, who had learned, to their great regret, that the regiment was leaving. After thanking him for every kindness, and praising the conduct of the men, the address concluded: " We shall, therefore, bid you only a temporary farewell; and we need not say how anxiously we look forward to, and how heartily we shall welcome, your return."

Less than two months later, on July 8th, Lieutenant Clutterbuck, while out shooting, was murdered by a man called King, who was afterwards caught, tried, and hung for the crime.

In August, 1866, the Fifth were under orders for India. Colonel Master exchanged with Colonel Roberts[1] of the 28th; and, under Roberts' command, the regiment embarked in two old sailing transports, the *Sussex* and *Essex*. They landed early in 1867, and were sent north to one of the frontier garrisons, Ferozepore.

The next year the King's crest was sanctioned in lieu of the Imperial Crown. Each year the uniform changed in some small degree: steel scabbards replaced the black leather and gilt (1866); blue braided patrol jackets succeeded blue frock-coats (1867); slashed cuffs were changed for pointed cuffs (1868); and the bearskin hat was revived. In 1870 there was a more important and far-reaching change in the regulations, for " purchase " was abolished by Royal Warrant.

In India the northern borderlands were always unrestful; the wild hillmen cared little for England; civil war had raged in Afghanistan since the death of the late Ameer, in 1863. The Indian Government remained strictly neutral, but when Sher Ali won back his inheritance, in 1868, he was approached as a possible and valuable ally. An important one, too, for the cloud of Russian menace overhung India, and the Slav advance had assumed formidable shape. Sher Ali played his hand well, holding out for the best terms he could get; he preferred England for friend, but she must pay his price. The haggling went on; Russians occupied Khiva. When

---

[1] William Roberts, served in Crimea and Mutiny in 28th Foot; exchanged with Chester Master March, 1866; commanded 1st Fifth for fourteen years, died a lieutenant-general.

Turkey and Russia went to war in 1877, it appeared almost certain that England would be involved; her reserves were called out, and Indian troops were sent to Malta. Fortunately the Eastern Question was settled for a time by the Treaty of Berlin, and Europe quietened down. While the congress was still sitting a Russian mission was wending its way to Kabul; and when Lytton would have countered, his delegates were stopped at the frontier. Russia had won the first round.

Diplomacy having failed, the Afghans had next to be made allies by force of arms. On November 21st the advance against Kandahar, Kuram, and the Khyber Pass began.

The 1st Fifth had spent the last ten years at various hill stations. In the spring of 1878 they moved from Allahabad to Chakrata; and while there, on October 8th, they were warned by telegraph for service against Afghanistan.[1]

Ten days later they marched, 800 strong, under Lieutenant-Colonel T. Rowland,[2] officers and men in fine condition; and, November 2nd, they came into Lawrencepore, joining the 2nd Brigade, commanded by Brigadier-General Doran, of the 2nd Division Peshawar Valley Field Force. The Division, under command of Lieutenant-General Maude, V.C. (whom the Fifth had known in Mutiny days), proceeded to Nawshera, arriving November 20th.

The main offensive was carried on by three columns, commanded by Sir Samuel Browne, Sir Frederick Roberts, and Donald Stewart. Browne's column at once occupied the Khyber Pass. Before the New Year Roberts had captured the Peiwar Khotal, while Stewart menaced Kandahar. The Peshawar Valley Field Force remained in reserve, and for three months they guarded the supplies that travelled up the mountains.

A forced march was made to Peshawar December 2nd

[1] Strength, 30 officers, 88 N.C.O.'s, and 780 men.
[2] Thomas Rowland, C.B., joined as major in 1866; served in Crimea with " Royals." In the absence of Colonel Roberts he was in command of 1st Fifth during first and second Afghan Wars. He succeeded Roberts in 1880.

(twenty-eight miles); and on the 13th the Battalion was sent to garrison Jumrood—a rough stony fort, nine miles west, at the entrance of the Pass. There they spent Christmas, and there they found life very monotonous, all the worry and none of the fun.

To clear the country of raiders and protect convoys, 350 of the Fifth, under Brevet-Major Creagh, were sent into the Bazaar Valley, where they destroyed some villages and small forts, returning a week later without casualty.

By the end of the year Sher Ali was hardly pressed; the Russians had promised to withdraw; the Sultan had refused to countenance a " Holy War." The Afghans were tired of a struggle so little profitable. All the same, the war dragged on; and in January another expedition was sent against the Bazaar Valley. Major Creagh again commanded the detachment of the Fifth (B, C, D, E, and H companies). With them went half a battalion of native infantry, three guns, and some cavalry, the whole under General Doran. The first expedition had been a mere reconnaissance. Doran's column went up the rocky way into the heart of the valley; and, while flanking parties swept the country and destroyed the villages, the main force marched on to Wallai. They met with some opposition; Creagh, commanding the rear-guard, had one man mortally wounded. The Fifth were very skilfully handled, and though under fire for three-quarters of an hour had no other casualties beyond a few slight scratches. In good health and spirits the men returned to Jumrood, much envied by the less fortunate garrison.

Sher Ali died February 21st, and his son Yakub Khan succeeded him, and presently opened negotiations with England. By the peace terms, signed at Gundamuk on May 26th, part of the occupied country was retained, and also the control of the Khyber Pass. A British resident, escorted by a small escort, set out for Kabul. The troops began to move south.

The Fifth left Jumrood in March, passing through Lundi Khotal to Basawal, finding the country quiet From Basawal raids were made, hillmen rounded up, and villages burned; there was also always convoy duty to be done. In June they began their return march, spending the hot weather at Changi, close to Abbottabad; in August they got their orders for home, and preparations went forward until, one September day, the news flashed over India that the Embassy at Kabul had been sacked, and Cavagnari and his staff murdered by a wild mob of fanatics, a thousand and more to each heroic Englishman.[1]

A Field Force was at once set in motion; Stewart was ordered to reoccupy Kandahar, and Roberts to hold the lines of communication. The Fifth had their sailing orders cancelled; but once again they were kept in reserve, while the luckier 72nd and 92nd marched and fought and won their way to Kabul.

December saw the whole country aflame, a " Holy War " spreading along the borderland, the governor of Maidan was murdered, everywhere unrest. To subdue the country Afghanistan had first to be conquered: this was impossible without guns and supplies. A great road was made between Peshawar and Kabul; and a chain of forts, barracks, and telegraph stations sprang up between Jelalabad and the frontier. These posts required garrisons, and the garrisons depended on convoys; so the Fifth, denied the greater glory, was split up in companies, and left to hold the forts, guard the road, and bear with cheerfulness the trials of hill warfare with none of the compensations of a good fight.

Creagh, with B and C companies, garrisoned Kohat from October to January; E company guarded a convoy to Lundi Khotal; F and H companies followed. They were then allowed a brief expedition to drive some rebel Mohammedans across the Kabul River. By the end of January the other companies had reached Lundi Khotal.

In February an officer and 100 men were detached to escort four guns from Dakka to Jumrood. A thunder-

[1] Major, afterwards Field-Marshal, Sir George White, wrote from India at this date : " There are a few fine regiments still left out here—the 92nd, 72nd, Fifth Fusiliers, 17th, and others that I have not heard so much of " (" Life of Sir G. White," vol. i., p. 178).

storm caught them in the hills, and they hurriedly camped. Under cover of the storm the hillmen crept down and looted the camp, leaving the aforesaid officer with only a blanket and helmet to continue his march.

The force was in general well supplied with clothing, and the sick-list was small. Strips of cashmere, called puttees, were worn as protection to the legs, and became speedily popular.

From Lundi Khotal the Fifth marched in April by Dakka to Basawal, and then to Jelalabad. The roadside was marked by the bodies and skeletons of the camels and bullocks which had perished as the army pushed on. The kites were always hovering overhead, and from every defile came the same awful stench. The loss in camels and baggage animals along this road was reckoned at 70,000, and the work was only half begun.

From Jelalabad, on May 8th, Rowland was sent against a party of raiders and cattle thieves, who naturally evaded battle, but one of the Fifth was killed by a sniper's bullet. Then 2,000 Safees rose at Besud, and a force from Jelalabad was sent to deal with them. Doran commanded, taking with him the headquarters of the Fifth, some guns, a detachment of native infantry, and 160 cavalry.

Doran crossed the Kabul River May 20th, and found the Safees holding a ruin and enclosure; from this they were quickly driven out, and fled, except for twenty-two men, who were cut off from the hills and retreated into a bastion. The mountain guns were brought up and opened fire; out charged three of the Afghans; Rowland and Kilgour were ready, and cut them down; then, with Colour-Sergeant Wood, Private Openshaw, and a private of the 12th, the little fort was rushed, and the hillmen slain. Rowland was hit twice, but only slightly wounded; two men of the Fifth were severely wounded. Doran's total casualties only amounted to ten wounded men, while the enemy lost fifty killed. Doran spoke very highly of the courage of the Fifth. Woods won the medal for distinguished conduct in the field. The force then marched on to Fort Abdul Khan and blew it up; and the next day a detachment under Rowland surprised and destroyed

Fort Benares Khan, and took the garrison prisoners. Doran then returned to Jelalabad.

The Indian Government had found a successor to the treacherous Yakub Khan; but the prospective Ameer, a nephew of Sher Ali, was not very eager to assume the government as an ally of Britain. He was a pensioner of the Czar, and a defeated enemy of Yakub Khan; therefore with reluctance he yielded to *force majeure*. In July British troops occupied Kurram, Kabul, and Kandahar. The new Ameer was proclaimed, and in August entered his capital.

The Fifth marched back to Peshawar, and from there to Lawrencepore; and again, in September, they received orders for home, this time not to be countermanded. So they turned their backs on the tragedy of Maiwand, and the glories of that final march from Kabul, and the victorious end.

For their services, Rowland was made C.B. and Kilgour brevet-major.

The 1st Fifth embarked at Bombay in November, and landed at Portsmouth a month later; they were quartered in the Anglesey and Cambridge Barracks.[1]

The new year saw England involved in another war. The Transvaal had been annexed in 1877, and for more than three years the storm had been brewing. Open warfare began in December, and in January fourteen men of the Fifth volunteered to serve with the mounted infantry, and sailed with a regiment of detachments for South Africa. These men rejoined a year later, a very favourable report being made of their conduct. They had not been called on for active service, for the disastrous war came to an end in April. The peace terms led to much after bitterness and trouble.

In this year, the Territorial system being introduced, the Foot by Royal Warrant lost their ancient numbers. On July 1st the old regiment ceased officially to be the Fifth, and became the Northumberland Fusiliers; the

---

[1] Lord Longford had succeeded General Hill as colonel of the regiment in 1878; he was a veteran of the Crimean War, " of medium height and courtly demeanour." He had served as Adjutant-General in India during the Mutiny.

facings were changed from " bright green "[1] to white; later in the month the Depot was moved from Berwick-on-Tweed to the new barracks at Newcastle-upon-Tyne, and became the headquarters of the Fifth Regimental District.

In January, 1882, the strength of the regiment was 586 rank and file, with an average age of twenty-nine, and an average of ten years' service. On the 19th the Fifth were sent to Ireland, sailing from Holyhead to Mullingar, where they remained two years. Here the *St. George's Gazette*, first and best of regimental papers, came into being; the first number was published January 31st, 1883.

The next year the Fifth moved to Dublin, where they were inspected by Lord Clarina, who made a very favourable report.[2]

From Dublin, in 1886, the regiment marched north by companies. Headquarters to Newry, with detachments at Downpatrick and Belfast. In June a riot broke out in Belfast docks between some workmen and dock-labourers, and the two companies of the Fifth were called out to aid the civil powers. Two days later they were called out again; streets had been pulled up, the police barracks wrecked, and the town flooded with a dangerous mob. For fourteen hours the troops were very actively employed. The disturbances went on for two months, and on one occasion at least the soldiers had to fix bayonets to clear the streets. At all times their steadiness and good conduct won the highest praise.

The next year, 1887, was Jubilee year. The 1st Fifth left Newry July 1st for the Grand Review at Aldershot, where they joined the Fusilier Brigade commanded by Colonel Philip Fitzroy,[3] and marched and manœuvred in Queen's weather.

[1] The " gosling " green facings had been changed to " bright " green in 1836; the original facings were restored in 1900.
[2] 1884: Average age, 25·9; service, 7 years; 596 N.C.O.'s and men. 1885: Average age, 23·87; service, 5 years; 544 N.C.O.'s and men.
[3] Philip Fitzroy, born March, 1837; ensign October, 1854; commanded 1st Fifth 1886-1888; retired on full pay 1888; died January 15th, 1892; the " regiment's best and staunchest friend."

The Fifth spent the years 1887–1893[1] between Colchester and Woolwich, proceeding to Dover in July, 1891, after the Aldershot manœuvres. In this year an old friend marched with the Battalion from Clapham Junction to Aldershot. Franklin, born in the regiment at Paris in 1816, served off and on, and always retained his affection for the Fifth. Part of his life he spent in Australia, where on public occasions he made a point of wearing his scarlet coat, black trousers, and cap.

In the summer manœuvres of 1894 the Fifth furnished a guard of honour to the Queen and also to the German Emperor. From these old field days with additional borrowings from the Prussian model, grew the wider training schemes of recent years. Four years were spent at Dover, then the Fifth were sent to Portsmouth, where the old Duke of Cambridge made his last inspection. In November a detachment, a sergeant and twenty-four men, under Captain W. H. Sitwell,[2] went to Aldershot to join a composite battalion for service in Ashanti. The Field Force left England in December, and returned in February, after the capture of Kumassi. In October, 1896, the 1st Fifth, 500 strong, were sent to Gibraltar, and there the two Battalions met, for the second was homeward bound from India.

After a year on the Rock, the 1st Fifth received orders for Egypt; they embarked January 17th, and landed in time to take a small part in the last act of the tragedy of the Sudan.

The first Mahdi rising of 1882 had culminated in the death of Gordon; and, even after Wolseley's punitive march, in the practical evacuation of the country. In the years of waiting the young Anglo-Egyptian army grew steadily, and the Sirdar[3] conceived a new plan of

---

[1] Charles Hackett, commanded the 1st Fifth 1888-1892; joined as ensign in 1864, lieutenant 1867; adjutant 1868; captain 1878; major 1883. He was succeeded by Henry Aitkin Cherry (1892-1897), who joined as ensign 1865; lieutenant 1869; adjutant 1872; captain 1880; major 1883.

[2] Brigadier-General William Henry Sitwell, C.B., D.S.O., p.s.c.; served in Afghan War, Ashanti, Nile Expedition, South Africa; commanded 4th battalion, raised during South African War; commanded 34th Infantry Brigade at Suvla Bay, August, 1915.

[3] Sir Herbert, afterwards Lord, Kitchener.

conquest when his weapon should be ready. The Sudan railway became a fact, and struck out across the desert for Abu Hammad and Khartoum. The first campaign established Egyptian authority as far as the Fourth Cataract. The campaign of 1897 ended in the taking of Abu Hammad and occupation of Berber. Greater things were planned for 1898, and the aid of British troops demanded. The Fifth arrived in January, and were garrisoned in Cairo; the more fortunate 6th, 10th, 72nd, and 79th going up country and taking part in the spring campaign which ended with the defeat of a Dervish force at Atbara.

The Sirdar waited for the Nile to rise, for Osman's whole army defended Omdurman, and reinforcements were needed before he could advance. A second brigade was on its way. On August 3rd the right half battalion of "Colonel Money's[1] fine-looking Northumberland Fusiliers, most smart and soldierlike,"[2] left Cairo, followed three days later by the left half. They travelled by rail to Luxor, seventeen hours in a sweltering box, with the dust everywhere. Then from Luxor to Assuan by the narrow-gauge military line; and from there by steamer, stern-wheeled, with four packed barges lashed alongside, they came at last to "windy, green tree'd Halfa." After three days at Halfa the Fifth were sent on to Atbara. Thus far had the army dragged the line.

Atbara was the starting-point of the campaign. The Sirdar was there; Hunter,[3] with his Egyptian division; tireless Gatacre, with the English troops, and his brigadiers, Wauchope with his seasoned men; and Lyttelton,[4] newly arrived. The first brigade were veterans of the Atbara campaign, and were not very eager

[1] Charles Gilbert Colvin Money, C.B.; born 1852; lieutenant 1872; captain 1882; major commanding 1st Fifth November 1897; commanded 1st Fifth 1897-1901; 24th Regimental District, 1902-1905; colonel in charge of Military Records, Warwick, 1905-1907.
[2] *The Times*, August, 1898.
[3] General Sir Archibald Hunter; Major-General Sir William Gatacre, died 1906; Major-General Andrew Wauchope, killed at Magersfontein, December 11th, 1899.
[4] General the Honble. Sir Neville Lyttelton; served in Canada, Egypt, South Africa, etc.

to welcome troops travelling by Cook's tour in time for the last battle. The Rifles were the first to arrive, then the Guards, both coming in for some criticism. Then came the right wing of the Fifth, played in by the Guards' band, and, to quote an onlooker, they made a very fine entry: " The men were not tall, but they were big round the chest, and averaged nearly six years' service. They swung up in a column of dust, with their stride long, heads up, shoulders squared, soldiers all over. The officers were long limbed, firmly knit, straight as lances. There are not many more pleasing sights in the world than the young British subaltern marching alongside his company, his long legs moderating their pace to the pace of the laden men, his wide blue eyes looking steadily forward, curious of the untried future, confident in the traditions of his service and his race. From the look of the Fifth Fusiliers you might guess with safety that the young soldier's confidence was not likely to be abashed."[1]

The three battalions of the 2nd Brigade camped a little south of Atbara; the Fifth had leisure to gain some experience of a Sudan thirst.

" . . . The Northumberland men were working away at their ammunition all the next morning, Tommy lugging at the camel's head-rope, and adjuring him to, ' Come on, ol' man !' and the old man, unaccustomed to friendly language, only snarling the more devilishly, and tipping his load on to the sand."[2]

The second half Battalion arrived on August 13th; and on the 16th the cavalry and camel corps marched south; the infantry followed by river, the Fifth leaving on the 18th. On the 22nd the force again concentrated at Wadi Hamed, just below the Sixth Cataract. They marched again on the 25th, heading for Khartoum. One officer of the Fifth remained behind, Lieutenant C. Wood, who set out with Major Stuart Wortley to follow the right bank in company with some " friendlies."

The British Division marched into Gebel Royan on

[1] G. W. Steevens, " With Kitchener to Khartum," p. 210.
[2] G. W. Steevens, " With Kitchener to Khartum," p. 211.

the 28th, welcomed by the massed black bands of the Sudanese, who had preceded them. The Rifles and Northumberland Fusiliers were commended for smartness in marching, but the division had taken four days to cover twenty miles. The going was exceptionally bad. On the 30th Stuart Wortley's "friendlies" captured some spies and a barge laden with wheat. They had an exciting journey, but, fortunately, met with little opposition, for the friendlies were inclined to bolt; and on one occasion, when attacked by twenty-five Baggara horsemen, Lieutenant Wood narrowly escaped with his life.

Three more marches brought the Sirdar's army within sight of Omdurman, a vast tract of mud houses, dominated by the Mahdi's tomb. Without the walls spread the white tents, and in front, again, a long thick black line, a solid wall of troops five miles in length.

The Sirdar's army was encamped at Agaiga, September 1st. A reconnoitring party of cavalry was pursued by a Dervish force, and the troops stood to arms all night. With their backs to the Nile they formed a half-circle, covering the village. Lyttelton's brigade held the left of the line, touching the river on the south, the Fifth and Grenadiers on his right, and joining them the regiments of the 1st Brigade.

With the first light the troops made ready for the advance, but the Sirdar gave no order; then, as they waited, they heard far away the tom-toms and war cries. The Faithful were coming out to give battle.

The Khalifa divided his army into three corps, and one devoted force hurled itself on the Sirdar's troops. A wave of Dervish swept down on the zariba, to be met by shrapnel, maxim, and rifle fire. Each section of infantry fired as one man, and swept away whole ranks of the enemy. Another wave broke, and another, only to be spent before half the way was won. Then they came by twos and threes, never a man reaching the zariba. At last there was only a white carpet where the Khalifa's men had died, and for half an hour there was silence.

The advance was sounded, and, the 2nd Brigade leading, the Sirdar marched on Omdurman. As they marched the two other armies fell on them, but were driven back. The 2nd Brigade were out of the fighting and well on their way to the capital; it was only eleven o'clock, but men and horses were thirsty from the morning's work, and thankful for the thick muddy waters of the Klor. The troops marched through the city with the Sirdar riding ahead, the Egyptian flag and the conquered flag of Mahdism held before him. The Fifth bivouacked clear of the town, cheerful enough, though without food or drinkable water and perhaps somewhat disappointed in their day. For them the artillery had shot too well; they could have wished a closer touch with the enemy; they had only three casualties to show for Omdurman.

On Sunday, September 4th, Colonel Money and fifty men made their way by steamer to Khartoum. There the Union Jack and the Khedive's flag were hoisted, and there, on the threshold of his ruined house, a service was held to Gordon's memory. The campaign was over, the troops went north, the Fifth to Alexandria, and there they paid the price of victory, for two officers[1] and thirty-four men died of enteric—the Sudan's revenge![2]

The Russian menace of the "seventies" had been succeeded by the French scare in the "nineties." There was every prospect of the regiment being engaged in a more serious war. The reconquest of the Sudan had to some extent cleared the air, but a sudden Mohammedan outbreak at Crete threatened to reopen the eternal Eastern Question. Crete was at this time policed by British and Turkish troops, and in Candia, within the British zone, the little English garrison of Highland Light Infantry and a handful of bluejackets was roughly handled, and forced to take refuge on board the *Hazard*. Then fanaticism broke loose and the mob looted and

---

[1] 2nd Lieutenants Lonsdale-Hale and H. V. Tyson.
[2] For services Colonel Money received the C.B., Major Lambton the D.S.O., Major Sitwell and Brevet-Major Keith-Falconer became brevet-lieutenant-colonels, Captain Ray was promoted major, Captain Henry and Lieutenant C. M. A. Wood mentioned in despatches. Colour-Sergeant T. Burdett, Sergeant-Drummer J. Cordeal, and Sergeant A. Bannerman received the D.C.M.

burned and murdered at will until the *Illustrious, Revenge,* and *Camperdown* came steaming up and covered Candia with their guns.

Reinforcing troops were quickly sent—the Rifles and the 1st Fifth from Egypt. After a bad landing, October 3rd, the Fifth found themselves garrisoning a Turkish fort; it rained and it blew, tents were almost useless, the task of rounding up the Bashi-Bazouk both difficult and dangerous. The apathetic Turkish soldiers were a hindrance rather than a help, and finally it was decided that the English should be left alone to restore order. The Turks were in no hurry to leave, but it was useless to stand on ceremony. Major Dashwood,[1] with E, F, and H companies, urged the departure of the last 600—the aged colonel, under a military escort, the men much pleased at his likeness to " Old Kruger," lately made famous by the Jameson Raid. Five of the captured Bashi-Bazouks were hung for the murdered Highland Light Infantrymen, others were transported with their families.

After the departure of the Turks the Christian population began to return to the town, where the British soldier was doing his utmost in his own way to restore confidence. Football was, of course, in full swing, and a golf course was in the making. The returning Christians, men, women, and children, showed their joy by emptying rifles into the air or not into the air, as it pleased them. To stop the eternal fusillade all firearms were called in, and in one district alone between 3,000 and 4,000 were collected. The island was portioned out into districts; and in these British officers restored order and taught the first elements of progress. The subalterns of the Fifth, living on goat, brown bread, and onions, quietly, and without any disturbances, ruled their remote and wild villages, earning no medals or decorations, and little thanks.

The other great nations came to claim their share, and it was decided by International conference that the island should be ruled by a neutral. Prince George of Greece,

---

[1] Colonel Dashwood commanded 2nd Fifth 1905; colonel commanding Depôt, Newcastle-on-Tyne, August, 1914-1919.

the new Governor, landed from a French cruiser in January, 1899, and a few weeks later the British troops were withdrawn.

The headquarters of the Fifth left in April, followed in May by the other half-battalion. The summer was spent at Aldershot and on Salisbury Plain, and in the autumn the regiment was ordered to the West Indies.

These orders were cancelled in September, and on the 16th the 1st Fifth embarked at Southampton for South Africa. Of 900 men only one failed to pass the medical test.

Lieutenant-General Bryan Milman[1] went down to Southampton to see his old battalion sail, for in May he had been appointed colonel of the regiment he had joined as ensign sixty years before.

[1] Lieutenant-General Sir Bryan Milman, K.C.B., became colonel of the regiment on the death of General J. H. Laye, C.B. (born 1816; entered army 1834; lieutenant-colonel 1854; lieutenant-general 1877; served with 58th regiment in New Zealand; colonel of Fifth 1887-1899).

CHAPTER XXXVIII

1899

VICTORIA

BELMONT—GRASPAN—MODDER RIVER—MAGERSFONTEIN—STORMBERG

Sir Bryan Milman

The South African War of 1899-1902 was the natural outcome of the British system of colonization. The Cape, seized by force during the Napoleonic Wars, was afterwards restored to Holland, from whom the colony and station were bought in 1815, with the primary idea of forming a British naval base. By purchase, therefore, the original Dutch settlers came under British rule and protection. Very soon friction began. The Cape Hollanders were a stubborn, narrow race, contemptuous of progress, and resentful of interference, especially with regard to their treatment of native tribes. The Society for the Abolition of Slavery found no converts among the old settlers. Misguided zeal on the part of missionaries and the want of judgment of those in authority gave cause for discontent; and the Great Trek of 1836-37 was the first attempt of the Boers to break away from the English yoke and establish themselves as a nation.

The Home Government did not regard the matter seriously, and, in spite of recommendations and appeals from British subjects, who soon far outnumbered the original settlers, no determined attempt was made nor a definite policy employed to induce the Boers to return to their allegiance.

In 1852 Great Britain sanctioned the declaration of the Transvaal to be an independent republic. The Orange River Sovereignty, a flourishing colony established in 1848 under British rule, was also, in spite of the protests of the inhabitants, declared a Free State. Certain conditions were made, and a High Commissioner appointed to watch over the interests of British subjects and to protect native tribes; but the subsequent work of the High Commissioners was to a great extent nullified by the indifference and lack of support of the Home Government.

The geographical isolation of the Republics accentuated the natural Boer characteristics. The government fell into corrupt and degenerate hands, and in twenty years' time progress was at a standstill and the States practically bankrupt. The Orange River Free State openly advocated return to the British flag, and they were supported by a handful of enlightened Transvaalers under President Burgers. Negotiations were opened; in 1876 the threat of a Zulu rising hastened matters, and on April 12th, 1877, the Transvaal was formally annexed. Amidst great enthusiasm the Union Jack was hoisted in the market-place at Pretoria.

If Great Britain had risen to her opportunity there would have been no war of 1899, for the immediate result of the annexation, which, it should always be remembered, was made not only with the consent but at the request of the inhabitants, was a burst of prosperity. English gold paid the interest on the national debt and the long-outstanding official salaries; English soldiers secured the country from native invasion; English trade brought an influx of wealth—the revenue doubled itself. On the other hand certain promises made on behalf of the Home Government were not kept; the African colonies were left to themselves, and the Boers could see that British subjects were neither controlled in schemes of aggression nor supported in schemes of development. The disaster of Isandhlwana bred distrust and contempt of British arms. There arose a party in the Transvaal who preached " Africa for the Afrikander," and who hated all things British. This party, having found a fitting leader in Paul Kruger, proclaimed a Republic on December 15th, 1880, invaded Natal, and ambushed and shot down a company of British soldiers.

An attempt at reconquest was made with the few troops in the country, but Majuba was fought and lost February 27th, 1881; then, frightened by the loss of half a regiment, Gladstone sued for peace. The Republics were recognized, loyalists and natives abandoned, and the Union Jack buried.

Other countries were less shortsighted; Germany promptly annexed the Damaraland coast, and began intriguing with the Boers.

Had it not been for the discovery of the goldfields in 1886 the second Republic would have become bankrupt even sooner than the first. The opening out of the country and the large influx of immigrants saved Kruger's Government. Enormous sums were extorted in taxes from the Uitlanders, who, though contributing over 90 per cent. of the revenue, were denied all rights of citizenship. Under Kruger no British subject—and they constituted half the population of the Transvaal could have any voice in the government of the country. Even justice was denied them, for at threat of a native rising British subjects were commandeered, and imprisoned when they refused to fight. British statesmen were imbued with long-standing indifference to colonial affairs; appeals for protection and redress met with no response.

The misguided Jameson Raid was a protest against the supineness of the Home Government. Jameson hoped by a *coup d'état* to overthrow Kruger and, with the help of the loyalists and opposition " Reform " party, once more unite the South African colonies. The affair failed miserably, and Kruger, whose corrupt rule had alienated many of his former adherents, enjoyed a return of popularity. Opposition was stifled, the enlightened Reform party banished or imprisoned, Uitlanders treated with greater contempt, and all their protests ignored. Germany openly showed her hand; the famous Kaiser telegram was followed by an attempt to smuggle German marines through Portuguese territory. It was fortunate for England that Joseph Chamberlain had become Colonial Secretary in 1895. At last a strong policy was declared. It was first made plain that England would brook no interference from any foreign Power; then the attention of the Boer Government was called to the terms of the Convention, agreed in 1881, ensuring the rights of British subjects.

Kruger, indulging in dreams of a great South African Republic, had induced the Orange Free State, under President Steyn, to join unreservedly in union with the Transvaal. Lord Salisbury's Government, though conciliatory, was firm; but the stubborn old Boer had lost all faith and fear of England, and had no belief in her authority or will to protect her people.

England then had to pay for her long years of neglect and indifference; she had to decide in 1899 whether to use force of arms to uphold the rights of her loyal subjects, or whether to withdraw, abandon the British in the Transvaal, and suffer the Boer Republics to become a German protectorate.

There were enlightened Afrikanders in the Transvaal who, deprecating the idea of war, would have welcomed a closer alliance with England, but the unfortunate raid had debarred many of these from public life, and Kruger and his following were in sole power. It was soon evident that hostilities were inevitable, Dutch and German arms and ammunition poured into the country, and many volunteers came from Europe, where Britain at this time had few friends and no allies. The Republics refused to recognize International Law, and all September and October there was a great exodus of Uitlanders: more than half the population, trekking south, fled to the Cape.

England faced the prospect of war with a light heart; there was a general indifference to the main points at issue, which were merely regarded as subject-matter for party politicians. Some of the newspapers, those with Jingo leanings, painted the Boer in a most unfavourable light. The Little Englander party dwindled in numbers, and the ardent youth of the country were anxious to force a treacherous and cowardly foe to acknowledge the power of the British Empire. The recent conquest of the Sudan, and the successful outcome of many little wars, gave promise of easy victory.

The authorities in South Africa did not regard the situation with the same cheerful indifference. They knew that there were under 10,000 regulars in the country with which to protect Natal, the Cape, and Bechuanaland; and that the two Republics could put in the field nearly 40,000 men, trained to warfare from their cradles, an army mobile and self-contained.

There were also military advisers in England who said plainly that the army had much to learn; that too much of the men's time was wasted in looking after their costly and cumbersome uniform, and that they were, in consequence, deficient in practical training and very indifferent shots. The Staff College was only just beginning to fulfil its true mission; and the Intelligence Department, numbering seventeen officers, was somewhat inadequate for modern requirements. With regard to South Africa, there was an almost total ignorance among regimental officers of the nature of the country and the tactics to be met.

The 1st Fifth, Money in command, landed at Capetown October 7th, amid great enthusiasm. They marched out to Stellenbosch for equipment, and there formed a mounted infantry company of 5 officers[1] and 118 non-commissioned officers and men, about half of whom had already gone through a special course in England.[2]

On October 10th the 1st Fifth was hurried to De Aar; two days later war was declared, and the invasion of Natal began. The Boer plan of campaign was simple enough: Dundee, Ladysmith, and eventually Durban, were to be seized; while on the west the rooineks were

[1] Captain and Brevet-Lieutenant-Colonel Keith-Falconer, Lieutenants Crispin, Bevan, Toppin, and Hall.
[2] A scheme for the regular training of detachments from infantry battalions in mounted infantry work was drawn up in 1888 by Major, afterwards General, Sir E. T. H. Hutton.

to be swept from the frontier; then Cronje and his men would march south, join the rebel Dutch, and drive the English into the sea. Someone always seems to wish to sweep the English into the sea.

The English plan was even simpler: they were going to march to Pretoria and end the war.

Sir Redvers Buller, with the First Army Corps, arrived in Capetown October 31st, to find Sir George White and his field army shut up in Ladysmith, Kimberley besieged, the Cape invasion just begun, and rebellion spreading. Proceeding to Natal, he ordered Lord Methuen, the general officer commanding the 1st Division, to move up the west line to the relief of Kimberley. The Fifth were at Orange River using the station waiting-room as headquarters. With them were the 9th Lancers, under Colonel Bloomfield Gough, and some artillery.

On November 9th Gough, as senior officer, ordered a reconnaissance. Two squadrons of the 9th and the mounted infantry of the 1st Fifth rode out to Belmont, which was drawn blank. After a night at a friendly farm they searched the country to the east, and quickly got in touch with what proved to be a commando, 350 strong, with guns. The Lancers dismounted, and with the artillery held the enemy while the mounted infantry were ordered to outflank the position and discover the Boer lager. The Boers were ready for this, and had a few men out to protect their right; these poured in a heavy fire on the mounted infantry. The men took cover as they had been taught, but Bevan fell, shot through the thigh. Keith Falconer started to his rescue, and was instantly brought down. Hall and his men fired steadily, and held the Boers back when they would have cut off the little party. Hall also was wounded in the thigh. Finally Gough withdrew, having somewhat singed his wings. Keith Falconer was a great loss; brave and skilful, sportsman and gentleman, his early experience in the British South African Police would have been invaluable, not only to his regiment, but to the whole army. Major Ray then took command of the mounted infantry company.

This unfortunate reconnaissance was not without good results, for sword-belts and other distinctions were abandoned, and the officer became less conspicuous.

Methuen brought to Orange River the 1st Brigade (Guards) and the remainder of the 9th Brigade,[1] in which the 1st Fifth were incorporated. He had the 9th Lancers, Rimington's Guides, and three companies of mounted infantry for cavalry. General Featherstonehaugh commanded the 9th Brigade. Methuen wasted no time. At dawn on the 21st the column set out, each man carrying great-coat, field cap, a spare shirt, socks, shoes, and many other " necessities," but otherwise the general did not try his men too high, and contented himself with a ten-mile march. They reached Belmont on the 22nd, where the enemy was found to be in force, holding a line of hills east of the railway. A hurried reconnaissance decided Methuen on a night attack. With only a rough sketch to guide him he made his plans. A steep kopje, Mount Blanc, was the main position, covered by Gun Hill on the south and Table Mountain on the north-west. The 9th Brigade was ordered to outflank the enemy and seize Table Mountain, while the Guards carried Gun Hill.

The column broke camp and marched at two in the morning; the 9th Brigade followed the railway for some distance and then deployed, with the Fifth on the extreme left (A and B companies in reserve). Already the first grey light was showing, but not a sound came from the right. The clear atmosphere had misled the staff, and the Guards were behind time. The Fifth were in a fierce mood, for they were breakfastless, and anxious to get the work done. A staff officer prancing before them roused their wrath: " Dom thee ! get thee to hell, and let's fire !"[2] Then at last came the spatter of rifles, and the 9th Brigade advanced. The Boers could see the dim figures, and the Fifth and Yorkshire Light Infantry

---

[1] 9th Brigade: 1st Fifth, 2/58th (Northamptons), 2/105th (K.O.Y.L.I.), 1/47th (Loyal North Lancashires). At this time two brigades of infantry, with artillery, comprised a division.
[2] See " The Great Boer War," by Sir A. Conan Doyle, p. 133.

came under a heavy fire. The Boers had a flanking-party on a small kopje, and the Fifth had to clear this before they could make headway. The Northamptons and Yorkshires were able to push on, and the Guards carried Gun Hill. Ten minutes later the 9th Brigade swept over Table Mountain. Featherstonehaugh was wounded, and the command of the brigade devolved on Colonel Money. The Fifth then set themselves to clear the northern slopes while the Guards attacked Mount Blanc. The Boers clung to their position, but after a fierce fight they were driven out and the hills were won. The battle was over by 7.30 a.m., but the fruits of victory were lost for want of cavalry.

The Fifth lost heavily. Captain Eagar was killed while tending a wounded man; Lieutenant Brine was also shot dead; and Major Dashwood, Captain Sapte, Lieutenants Fishbourne and Festing were wounded; 12 men were killed and 33 wounded.[1]

Methuen rested a day, and then, November 25th, marched on. The Boers had retreated north, and from the hills above Graspan covered the railway. The 9th Brigade, led by the newly joined Naval Brigade, was detached to drive them out, the 1st Brigade following in reserve. The Boer position was a strong one, a two-mile front, steep faced, and both right and left wing *en potence*. The Naval Brigade and part of the 9th were sent against the eastern angle, while the Fifth and Northampton-shires contained the front and the mounted infantry tried to outflank the right. Colonel Money still commanded the 9th Brigade. The desperate courage of the Naval Brigade and its supports carried the day. The Fifth only lost two men wounded.

Methuen then advanced on Enslin.

The first enthusiasm of the Boers was nearly dead, but De la 'Rey rallied his men. On the 27th Cronje joined him with a part of the Mafeking force. The Boers concentrated at Modder River Station, and for defence changed their tactics, utilizing the river-bed instead of

---

[1] British losses: 4 officers and 71 men killed; 21 officers and 199 men wounded. Boer losses: 100 killed and wounded, 40 prisoners.

1899] MODDER RIVER—MAGERSFONTEIN 431

a line of kopjes farther north. Although Methuen knew there was a river to his front, he was ignorant of its course. Beyond the plain he could see the Magersfontein hills, where he was convinced De la Rey would make his final stand. On swung his infantry, well pleased with themselves. They had had some good fighting, and had twice driven the Boer from his chosen position. In a day or two they would march into Kimberley; another month should see the end of the campaign. They were marching in extended order, but that did not stop their songs and jokes. The 1st Fifth had the Coldstreams on their right and the Yorkshire Light Infantry on their left, and they were very close to the green-edged river, when suddenly, on a four-mile front, they were enveloped in a ring of fire. The Modder and the Riet twisted and turned, and from the willow-clad banks the Boers had the English at their mercy. The men flung themselves down, seeking cover behind tussock or stone. They could not go forward, but they would not go back. As they lay in the hot sun some of the men slept. At last the British guns got to work. The Boers could not stand the shell fire, and, led by Pole Carew,[1] the Lancashires, Highlanders, and some of the Fifth crept to the river and made their way across the slippery rocks and through the shallow water. The Boers, finding their flank turned, began to retreat. Pole Carew pushed on and occupied Rosmead. The handful of the Fifth returned to the Battalion and recrossed next morning with the rest of the brigade. The Boers retired undisturbed to the slopes of Magersfontein, where they entrenched themselves. The 1st Fifth lost 11 men killed and 32 wounded; the long hours on the rack left its mark on many of the others.

Methuen halted at Modder River on the 29th. Reinforcements (Wauchope and the Highland Brigade) were coming up, and his own troops needed rest. Many of them had gone twenty hours without food. The general himself had been wounded in the late fight.

[1] Major-General, afterwards Lieutenant-General, Sir Reginald Pole Carew, Coldstream Guards; served in Afghanistan, Egypt, and Burmah; afterwards commanded 11th Division in South Africa.

One of the Fifth won promotion on patrol duty on December 3rd. When his lance-corporal was wounded Lieutenant Crispin rode back under fire, gave up his horse to the man, and walked back, carrying the man's rifle; he was recommended for the Victoria Cross, and afterwards received a brevet-majority.

Then, on December 11th, came the tragedy of Magersfontein. Methuen attempted to force the Boer position. While the Highlanders suffered, the Fifth, with the 9th Brigade, Pole Carew in command, were away on the left, making a safe but ineffective demonstration. On the right the mounted infantry and cavalry did their best to retrieve the disaster. All day long they gallantly fought; in the evening they retired, but Ray returned for a wounded man and so lost his life, and the Fifth a much-loved officer they could ill spare.

Methuen accepted the defeat with two-thirds of his troops untried. The army retreated to the Modder River, where they settled down to daily bombardment and frequent sandstorms. Water was scarce, and had to be boiled, and it was hard to get it cooled again. Always the red dust and sand swirled through the tents. Enteric broke out.

Seven weeks after the first Battalion the second embarked, 1,000 strong, Major G. Frend in command. They landed at East London November 26th, and immediately went north to Putter's Kraal. General Gatacre, nominally in command of the 3rd Division, had the defence of the north-eastern border country, his right guarded by the native territories, while, far away on his left, Sir John French formed a frail link with the Orange River–De Aar communications. Stormberg had unfortunately been evacuated early in the month, and the general made his headquarters at Putter's Kraal, where, until the arrival of the 2nd Fifth, he had, of all his division, only one battalion of infantry, 300 mounted infantry, and about 1,000 irregular cavalry. With this small force the country, seething with disloyalty, could be only lightly held; and the Boers, realizing this, became aggressive. They occupied Stormberg, camping

on the hills covering the junction and the Rosmead line.
The first Battalion could have told the second something
of Gatacre's tireless energy. By feint and by bluff he
held the Boers, and when the 2nd Fifth were followed
by the 1st Royal Scots he determined to take the
initiative and recover Stormberg. Molteno, farther up
the line, was still in English hands, and was chosen for
the starting-point of a night attack.

On December 9th the 2nd Fifth, the Irish Rifles, four
companies mounted infantry, engineers, and two batteries, altogether 2,600 men, were detailed for the attacking column. At four in the morning the infantry began
to entrain, and all day long the weary men hung about.
The staff, recruited haphazard, were unequal to their
task; the last tired company did not reach Molteno
until half-past eight in the evening. Less than an hour
later the column set out on the night march. The staff
maps were worse than useless, the position was unre-
connoitred, and it was rumoured that the main position
was not only entrenched but also guarded by a wire
entanglement. Gatacre altered his original plan of a
direct advance along the railway, and thought by
skirting to the left to avoid the wire and outflank the
position. For guides he had two or three Cape Police,
who asserted they knew every inch of the way. Misfortune dogged the column. Two hours late in starting,
they next lost their field ambulance and ammunition
train, which turned down the wrong road, and all but fell
into Boer hands. For some reason the infantry were
ordered to march with fixed bayonets. This was useless
and irritating, and added to their fatigue. Three hours'
march brought them to a railway. Gatacre realized
they were too much to the east, and questioned the
guides, who again declared they knew the way. The
column rested at a farm for an hour, then set out along
a rough stony path. Again they crossed the railway,
the staff hopelessly confused. The path led between
rising ground, and presently they came to a steep donga.
The misty hills began to show on the right; day was
just breaking. Suddenly a sleepy sentry saw the

approaching army and gave the alarm. Shots rang out,
and the startled Boers blazed away at the huddled men.
For a moment they hung in the valley crowded like
sheep. Then the Irish Rifles swung to the left and seized
a kopje to the north of the pass; while the Fifth, without
waiting for orders, opened out and charged up the hillside,
determined to carry all before them. Half-way they
checked, for the hill face rose sheer, and only here and
there could the men struggle higher. Their first ardour
spent, they lay down to await developments. Very
soon the word to retire was passed along. They withdrew
in fair order, taking it in turns to cover, but some
of the men were completely worn out, and it was
difficult to hold them. A third of the Battalion never
got the order and stayed where they were; a few had
crept to the summit; a few were sleeping; a few stayed
for choice, but two-thirds came dribbling down to the
donga. Here the Boer fire caught them and they fell
back behind the western hills. Gatacre had no one in
reserve. The Irish Rifles and mounted infantry were
holding their own on the left; but the right had frittered
its strength away, and was in no condition to go forward.
Then on the west appeared more Boers. A commando,
returning from a raid, threatened to take the English
on the flank. Gatacre gave the order to retire. Covered
by the mounted infantry and the guns, the hill was
evacuated; and by skill and good luck the little force
managed to extricate itself. The batteries, firing tail
to tail, kept the Boers at bay. On the slopes, forgotten
and overlooked, were still the men of the Fifth and Irish
Rifles who had not retreated. The column straggled
away; Gatacre, with the rear-guard, held the men together;
few fell into Boer hands. But of the men left
behind 634 gave themselves up without firing a shot

The weary, disheartened little force marched into
Molteno at eleven in the morning. The 2nd Fifth had
lost 12 men killed, and 6 officers and 349 men were among
the missing.[1]

[1] British losses: 28 killed, 10 officers and 651 men missing. Boer
losses: 8 killed, 26 wounded.

The Battalion had been highly tried in their first fight with the Boers.[1] The weary journey between Putter's Kraal and Molteno had diminished their enthusiasm; the miseries of the night march taught them to distrust the staff. The Boer, whom they had once despised, they now overrated, and tales of ghastly traps and barbed wire paralyzed their initiative. They had every excuse for failure, but still they had failed. The action did as little credit to the enemy. If they had followed up their advantage not a man could have escaped; as it was, they failed to reap any real benefit, for Gatacre retained the initiative, and, establishing his headquarters at Sterkstroom, a little to the north of Putter's Kraal, returned to his old tactics of bluff.

The 2nd Fifth were sent down to East London to recruit and reorganize, and there they remained until the end of January.

[1] 2nd Fifth mentioned in despatches: 2nd Lieutenant Duncombe Shafto, Band-Sergeant J. Stone, Colour-Sergeant A. Landen, Private G. Benson.
Prisoners of war: Major Sturges, Captains Fletcher and Morley, 2nd Lieutenants L. B. Cookson, G. R. Wake, and Lieutenant Radcliffe, attached.

CHAPTER XXXIX

DECEMBER, 1899—OCTOBER, 1900.

VICTORIA

THE MARCH TO PRETORIA—SANNAH'S POST—REDDERSBURG—
FIRST DE WET HUNT

SIR BRYAN MILMAN

BLACK WEEK ended the campaign of 1899: Stormberg, Magersfontein, Colenso, and the fate of Mafeking, Kimberley, and Ladysmith hung in the balance. In Europe the other nations looked to see the end of an empire.

Then magnificently from overseas the Colonies gave of their best. More home troops were sent, and with them Lord Roberts came to take supreme command. Pending his arrival the armies in Natal and the Colony were forbidden to commit themselves to any action. The 1st Division remained at Modder River, the veldt taking its toll of good men.

Roberts knew the necessity of strategical mobility, and, in spite of the lack of topographical knowledge and the encumbrance of a necessarily enormous transport, he conceived and executed the great flank march which carried his army to Bloemfontein, and eventually to Pretoria. Part of Methuen's army marched with him on February 11th, but the 1st Division were left on the Modder to contain Cronje during the execution of the flank movement; so the 1st Fifth had to see their more fortunate companions march away.

Besides two divisions of infantry, Roberts took with

him Sir John French's cavalry division, with Alderson[1] in command of the mounted infantry brigade. The mounted infantry company of the 1st Fifth was incorporated in the 3rd Battalion mounted infantry, commanded by Lieutenant-Colonel Pilcher,[2] late of the Fifth, who had already shown himself a capable leader.

The 3rd mounted infantry covered the early movements on the southern flank. In the wonderful charge at Klip Drift on the 15th, their brigade was in reserve, bringing up the rear with the guns. That same night the cavalry rode into Kimberley, and the next day French started off with two cavalry brigades and Alderson's mounted infantry, hoping to cut off the retreating Boers before they could remove their siege guns.

Near Macfarlane Siding a handful of men held out. The cavalry were ordered to envelop them while the mounted infantry pressed the attack; but the wearied horses could hardly move, and the Boers escaped. Colonel Pilcher was left at Macfarlane, men and horses completely exhausted, and suffering from lack of water.

The 1st Fifth mounted infantry missed the battle of Paardeberg, only arriving, with the rest of Alderson's brigade, on the 21st, when the cordon was tightening. Six days later Cronje, with 4,000 men, surrendered, and they had leisure to inspect the wonderful dugouts and deep narrow trenches by which the Boers had escaped the bombardment. The next day, February 28th, Ladysmith was relieved, and the war took on a different aspect.

Roberts gave his men a week's rest while supplies were being collected, then began his advance on Bloemfontein. The 3rd mounted infantry had little to do at Poplar Grove and Driefontein, where the Boers were manœuvred out of their chosen position and the way cleared to Bloemfontein. On March 12th Roberts marched in, to

[1] Lieutenant-General Sir E. A. H. Alderson, K.C.B., A.D.C.; born 1859; served in European War 1914.
[2] Major-General Thomas David Pilcher, C.B.; born 1858; lieutenant in Fifth 1881; captain 1886; afterwards served in 1/W.A.F.F.; brevet-lieutenant-colonel for services; commanded 17th Division 1914-1916.

be welcomed by a cheering crowd thronging the decorated streets. Once more the Union Jack flew over the town.

In the meantime the 2nd Fifth, now commanded by Lambton from the first Battalion, had rejoined Gatacre at Sterkstroom and had raised two companies of mounted infantry, one commanded by Captain F. G. Casson, the other by Captain M. O'Brien. Colonel Brabant had arrived in command of the Colonial Division, and to him Gatacre's mounted infantry were attached.

Roberts's plan of campaign included a simultaneous advance by the columns operating in the Colony. On February 17th Brabant was able to occupy Dordrecht, but from lack of transport could not advance farther. A week later Gatacre lost a very valuable officer in Captain Montmorency of the Scouts, who, with two of his men, was killed; Sergeant Howe, of the 2nd Fifth, had been left at the foot of the kopje with the horses, and he escaped.

Shortly afterwards Stormberg was found to be evacuated, and Gatacre marched in. Three companies of the 2nd Fifth proceeded to Dordrecht as reserve to the Colonial Division. Bethulie was occupied on March 15th; the retreating Boers had blown up the great bridge over the Riet, and the 2nd Fifth were employed in diverting traffic and reconstructing the line.

Rumours of peace were in the air. The Boers had been driven from Natal and from the Cape, and the Free State occupied.

On the west Methuen moved his headquarters to Kimberley. He had lost Pole Carew and the Guards, who had followed Roberts to Bloemfontein. The 9th Brigade, now commanded by General Douglas,[1] was chiefly employed in guarding the supplies and transport, though later, as the main operations developed, small expeditions became possible. On March 16th the 1st Fifth and a battery occupied Warrenton, commanding the south bank of the Vaal, and protecting the railway. The Boers also had guns, and the troops suffered some-

[1] General Sir C. W. H. Douglas, G.C.B., A.D.C., Gordon Highlanders; born 1850; died 1914.

what from shell fire, but managed to hold on to the position.

Early in May a flying column was organized for the relief of Mafeking; the 1st Fifth remaining in garrison in the Boshop district, going from there to Kroonstadt on the 28th.

From Bloemfontein patrols were sent out with propaganda for the country districts, and detachments occupied outposts to overawe malcontents and protect loyalists. Gradually the Boers were recovering from their first demoralization consequent on Cronje's surrender, and the English were soon made to realize that schemes of settlement were premature.

Pilcher's regiment was at Thaba N'chu in March with Broadwood's[1] Brigade (1,800). Bloemfontein was thirty-seven miles away, and threatening Broadwood was Olivier with a large commando some 5,000 strong. The general wisely decided to fall back on Sannah's Post, where a small detachment was guarding the Bloemfontein waterworks. All loyalists who wished were allowed to accompany the convoy; and at noon on March 30th, escorted by Pilcher's mounted infantry, the long train of waggons set out.

Unknown to the English, another Boer commando was in the vicinity; Piet and Christian De Wet, with 1,600 men, were making for Sannah's Post, intending to seize the waterworks, and cut off Broadwood. While Piet prepared to attack the Post his brother, with 400 men, made to the rear and lay in ambush, where the Bloemfontein road ran through a drift in the Koorn Spruit. Then De Wet found that the whole of Broadwood's force was retreating, marching straight into the trap. With quiet confidence Piet watched the last man across the Modder and camp near Sannah's Post for the remaining hours of night. At six in the morning of the 31st he opened fire.

Broadwood thought Olivier was upon him, and quickly got his convoy under way and despatched along the

[1] Major-General Broadwood, C.B., 12th Lancers; born 1862; died 1916.

Bloemfontein road, while the mounted infantry were left as rear-guard to prevent the Boers crossing the Modder.

Down the road went the convoy and two batteries, with Roberts's Horse for escort, and down into the drift where the Boers lay waiting them.

Meanwhile the mounted infantry were being hard pressed. Pilcher's men were holding the drifts north of the waterworks in the centre of the line. More and more Boers came from the north and east and threatened to envelop the left flank, while from the rear they could hear the guns as the convoy struggled in the ambushed drift. Some of the waggons were at last extricated and sent on a southern road; then Broadwood, fearing his mounted infantry would be reduced to their last cartridge, gave the order to retreat.

The mounted infantry fell back by companies. From north and east and west the Boers came surging down, but there was no hurry nor confusion; guns and horse retired in good order, the enemy with equal gallantry pressing them hard. Pilcher turned back to pick up a wounded man and set him on his horse; and Captain Booth, fearing some of his company had been cut off, waited on a hillock in the hope of rescue. With him stayed two of his men and his subalterns, Hall and Toppin. They had a maxim gun, and for a short time held the enemy; then Booth was killed and one of the men, Hall and the other man wounded; then, their ammunition exhausted, the three survivors surrendered. Lord Roberts wrote of Booth that " he fell like a gallant soldier," and the Fifth mourned a much-beloved friend and officer.

Conan Doyle wrote: "Among many brave men who died, none was a greater loss to the Service than Major Booth of the Northumberland Fusiliers, serving with the mounted infantry. With four comrades he held a position to cover the retreat, and refused to leave it."

Broadwood managed to save the remainder of his force, having lost 12 guns, 92 waggons, and some 600 men.[1] Two officers and 40 men, the survivors of the 1st Fifth mounted infantry, rode into Bloemfontein at dusk.

Three days later disaster overtook the mounted infantry of the 2nd Fifth. On March 28th Casson was sent with his company to patrol to the north-east. At Dewetsdorp he joined a detachment of the Irish Rifles (three companies foot and one company mounted infantry). Captain McWhinnie of the Irish Rifles, as senior officer took command of the little force. The disaster at Sannah's Post had taught the staff a lesson, and orders were sent to Gatacre urging the recall of any detachments. This order reached McWhinnie late on the evening of April 1st, but he had no warning that victorious De Wet was on the hunt. De Wet swept down on Dewetsdorp, and finding that McWhinnie had retreated, he followed the trail, keeping on a parallel course, and waiting his opportunity. Early on the 3rd he was reinforced; then, hurrying his men on, he came up with the English close to Reddersburg. McWhinnie hastily took position on a little horseshoe ridge, his mounted infantry on the west and his foot-soldiers on the east, with the 2nd Fifth mounted infantry on his right.

Up came De Wet with his 2,000 men and three guns, and demanded a surrender. McWhinnie refused; the guns opened fire, while the Boers formed a cordon round. Young Barclay of the 2nd Fifth had been sent out to parley, and on his return he was ordered, with six men, to occupy a little kopje in advance of the eastern flank. This proved untenable; Barclay was instantly killed, and Casson forced to shorten his line. Very soon afterwards Dimsdale of the Irish Rifles fell; Casson went at once to his assistance, and while helping him to cover was himself killed. This left 2nd Lieutenant Butler in command of the 2nd Fifth company. In the afternoon

[1] 159 killed and wounded, 421 prisoners. The 1st Fifth lost 1 officer and 2 men killed, 1 officer and 6 men wounded, 1 officer and 24 men prisoners. The majority of the prisoners were sick men captured with the convoy. The Records give Booth's party as 32 men and 3 officers, and state that the horses stampeded. The accounts apparently all differ.

the Boer fire slackened and McWhinnie sent off a messenger begging for help; ammunition was running short, they had no water. All night the thirsty, weary men stood to arms; the attack did not come till dawn; then, with gun and rifle fire, the enemy carried the western flank, and McWhinnie surrendered. The relief column heard the last shots fired. Too late to save the detachment they occupied Reddersburg. Later in the month Dewetsdorp was garrisoned by the 3rd Division; the 2nd Fifth remained there until June, when they were sent to Bloemfontein. Gatacre was relieved of his command, and was succeeded by Major-General Chernside.

At Bloemfontein the army had been rehorsed, revictualled, and reshod; and on May 3rd the great march on Pretoria began. The mounted infantry company of the 1st Fifth went forward with the army. Early in April the corps had been reorganized, and the 1st Brigade[1] put under command of Major-General Hutton.

On May 3rd the mounted infantry Brigade was sent forward at daybreak to cut the line north of Brandfort, where De la Rey and some 2,500 Boers waited to oppose them. Hutton's men were soon skirmishing with the western outposts, but the Boers would not stand before the great enveloping army. The 3rd Battalion, now under Captain Anley of the Essex Regiment, drove them from their last point. Roberts halted at Grandfort on the 4th that the railway might be repaired, but Hutton and another column were sent forward to the Vet River to secure the drifts and cut the line.

The drift by which Hutton intended to cross was very strongly held; but finding a disused ford to the west part of the force was sent round to outflank the Boer right; and, under cover of this surprise, Anley, without

[1] The 1st Brigade of mounted infantry, two corps, was composed of Alderson's original corps with the addition of Colonial troops, General Hutton commanding, was the pioneer of mounted infantry tactics. Colonel Alderson retained command of the 1st Corps (four battalions), and Colonel Pilcher was given command of the 3rd Corps (Queensland, New Zealand, New South Wales, and the 3rd battalion mounted infantry).

waiting for orders, led his men through a drift to the east and came galloping down in extended order, rolling up the Boer left. This brilliant little action won the high ground on the north; the Boers evacuated their position, retreating to the Zand. Hutton would have harried them, but Roberts feared to involve his horse without the support of the slow-moving infantry.

Roberts advanced on the 10th, and on the 12th Kroonstadt was occupied and the Boers in full flight.

Again the army halted for supplies; Hutton made a reconnaissance west to Bothaville, Pilcher and Alderson riding along parallel roads. Between them they captured a quantity of arms and horses, and some prisoners. Methuen was ordered to close in from the west and occupy Kroonstadt, while the main army continued its advance. They met with little opposition, and crossed the frontier on the 26th. Pilcher was temporarily attached to the baggage of French's column, and did not come into action again until the 28th, when Roberts began to close in on the Boer position on the hills covering Johannesburg. The marshy Klip River ran along their front. At various points the cavalry and mounted infantry forced a crossing—Pilcher at Potchefstroom—but failed to gain a foothold on the hills. At night French withdrew south of the river, Pilcher alone holding his drift. In the morning French again crossed, and supported Ian Hamilton's infantry division; the hills were carried. A party of the enemy were seen escaping to the north; after them went Pilcher and G Battery with him. They were rewarded by the capture of a 3-inch gun and ammunition waggon, and fifty-four prisoners of the German Legion.

Then Johannesburg surrendered, and Roberts marched in. The Boer Government hurriedly left Pretoria and no serious attempt was made to protect the capital. On June 5th the British occupied the town.

Meanwhile the 1st Fifth had reached Kroonstadt on May 29th, and from there had been sent post-haste to Lindley, where an advance-guard of yeomanry had got themselves into difficulties. Methuen was too late for rescue, and the Fifth were employed guarding the railway and communications between Heilbron, Lindley, and Kroonstadt. Many Boers had escaped through the meshes of the northern advance; the De Wets and De la Rey were a very real danger to the long lines of communication linking Capetown and Pretoria; and with the vanishing of the big battalions the new-found loyalty also disappeared, and many a man who had surrendered his rifle and sworn allegiance found arms and opportunity to make war again. The thousand-mile line could of necessity be only lightly held, and Methuen's " Salvation Army " were hurried from point to point where danger threatened. The 20th Brigade was left to hold Lindley, while Methuen turned the 9th into a flying column. Between May 14th and June 13th the 1st Fifth marched over three hundred miles, often on half rations, and sometimes without boots.

A little to the south-west, the 2nd Fifth guarded communications near Bloemfontein. The fall of Pretoria had released some prisoners, and the 350 unfortunates of Stormberg were able to rejoin their regiment.

De Wet's success in the south rekindled Boer patriotism. Botha collected an army and offered battle sixteen miles east of Pretoria. There, on June 12th, Diamond Hill was fought, and Pilcher's mounted infantry, back from an abortive attempt to raid the Delagoa Line, came into action on the left wing. Once again the Boers were out-manœuvred, but unbeaten.

Before securing the Delagoa communications Roberts decided to round up the scattered commandos. In July Buller invaded the Transvaal from the east, Baden-Powell and Hunter from the west. The scattered brigades along the line began to draw in; four flying columns swept the country, and the driven commandos took refuge in the Brandwater Basin. Unfortunately one of the Boers heard the closing of the trap; and on the evening of July 18th De Wet and his column, with President Steyn, broke out, making good their escape. Twelve days later Prinsloo and 4,000 men surrendered.

While the main army was besieging the Brandwater

Basin, Botha on the east and De la Rey on the west had to be kept at bay. Pilcher was given little rest. From June 23rd to July 12th there were daily skirmishes, and in one of these—Rietfontein, June 24th—Captain Crispin was wounded. Then, on July 11th, there was a simultaneous Boer rising. Pilcher was hurriedly recalled to Pretoria and Methuen ordered to move north.

The 1st Division left Kroonstadt on the 15th for Rustenberg to arrest the advance of De la Rey. They found Olifant's Nek strongly held, and the 1st Fifth were called on to clear the pass. This was done with the loss of one killed and two wounded.

On the east Hamilton and Hutton drove Botha back, and Roberts moved forward. The mounted infantry came in for some sharp fighting crossing the Eland's River, and on the 26th the Boers had to be driven off before Middleburg could be occupied.

Here for a time the eastern advance ended, and Pilcher's corps was recalled to Pretoria to take part in the first De Wet hunt.

De Wet had fled from Brandwater, pursued by Little and Broadwood, and had taken refuge at Rhenostenpoort on the Vaal River. Very soon the net began to close round him. The 2nd Fifth were sent from Bloemfontein and temporarily attached to Broadwood, at Wilgebosch-drift south of the Vaal. In August Methuen moved down from Rustenburg, and was assigned the task of watching the twelve crossings of the river. The 1st Fifth held the most western, Scandinavian Drift on the Potchefstroom road. De Wet was expected to break away to the south, and Colonel Money, with three companies and some yeomanry, was detached to reinforce the Colonial division on the Rhenoster. This diminished still further the 9th Brigade, already weakened by hard work, and, unfortunately, one drift on the Vaal was left unguarded. De Wet, seizing his opportunity, crossed the river on the 6th. Methuen was quickly on his heels, two companies of the Fifth with him, and at Tygerfontein, on the 7th, they came up with the enemy and drove him from ridge to ridge, but failed to hold him. The other five companies rejoined, and the pursuit went on.

The 2nd Fifth had been transferred to Hart's[1] column, and were sent along a parallel road south of the river. It was still thought that the Boers would make for the Free State, and Hart hoped to cut off the Lindgue Drift. There, on the 9th, he caught sight of the enemy and shelled his rear-guard, but De Wet was not to be stopped. He had shaken off Methuen for the moment, and now he swung north and was lost in the hills. After him pounded the columns, over burnt veldt and dusty road, footsore, and with bloodshot eyes, choked with dust, and thirsty in a waterless land.

North of Buffelsdorp De Wet crossed the Gatsrand on the 10th, Methuen arriving in time to see the tail of the convoy disappearing through the gap. Then De Wet slipped through Smith-Dorrien's men, and crossing the railway made for Ventersdorp. The British columns toiled after him, the worn-out infantry keeping in good spirits as they followed the trail of deserted waggons and dead beasts.

Then Methuen discarded the tired foot-soldiers, and with yeomanry and the Colonial Division managed to catch up the Boers and head them north, where their only escape lay through Olifant's Nek, which Hamilton had been ordered to hold. But there were no British troops there, and the 9th Brigade came up on the 15th, after a sixty-mile march from Friedrichstadt station, to learn that their prey had escaped.

Methuen doggedly turned west and crossed by the Magoto Nek, which was held in some force. The Fifth had one man wounded in fighting their way through. Then Hamilton took over the pursuit, and Methuen was sent to Mafeking, where his column had a well-earned rest.

When the pursuit ceased the 2nd Fifth halted at Reitfontein on the Krugersdorp–Zeerust road, and from there marched to Pretoria. The Battalion had covered 133 miles in eight days, and, like all units, had shown

---

[1] General Sir Reginald Hart, V.C., late R.E.

pluck, energy, and determination. Many of the men were in rags, with boots hardly hanging to their feet. They had far outdistanced their baggage, and had been often without food or water. One of them wrote: " We are like greyhounds . . . our coats no longer fit us . . . but flap idly against our sides like a sail about a mast." As hardbitten and tatterdemalion a crew as ever Ridge led marched into Pretoria August 29th.[1]

So ended the first drive.

Then Roberts continued his advance along the Delagoa railway. The 3rd mounted infantry were sent to Middleburg to join French and link up Pretoria with the Natal column. On that day, September 1st, the Transvaal was annexed by Proclamation; three weeks later Pole Carew reached the Portuguese border, and the British gained command of the Delagoa line. The Boers were completely isolated from the outside world; the conflict lost its International interest; Kruger fled, and the foreigners left. Lord Roberts handed over the command to Kitchener. Lord Milner was appointed administrator of the new colonies. The Household Cavalry returned home. The war was over—but not the fighting.

[1] August 8th to the 22nd, 234½ miles.

CHAPTER XL

September, 1900—May 31st, 1902

VICTORIA—EDWARD VII.

NOOITGEDACHT—DEFENCE OF LINDLEY—TWEEBOSCH

Sir Bryan Milman

Towards the end of September De Wet slipped back across the Vaal and roused the Free State to revolt. Trains were captured and burnt, culverts destroyed, and sections of the line blown up. The British infantry marched about and the elusive Boer disappeared at their approach. Methuen, in the far west, with his limited numbers had a difficult task to subdue the country and hunt De la Rey and Steyn. His battalions, the 1st Fifth included, had to be everywhere at once, trekking from Lichtenburg to Ottosdorp, and Rustenburg to Zeerust.

The 2nd Fifth, in the 22nd Brigade, joined Clements's[1] column and operated west of Pretoria, linking up with Methuen at Rustenburg. In October they were employed destroying crops and clearing the Magaliesberg hills of live stock. This led to lively skirmishing; and once a big sweep, in conjunction with other columns, resulted in a bag of 38 prisoners and 200 waggons. In November the column moved south to Krugersdorp, but in December Clements was ordered north again to patrol the Hekpoort valley on the south of the Magaliesberg. The column reached Nooitgedacht on the 8th, and camped at the foot of the Nek. Clements was somewhat

[1] Major-General Ralph A. P. Clements, D.S.O., A.D.C.; born 1855; died 1908.

uneasy, for he had only 1,500 men all told, and De la Rey was close at hand with an unknown force. Five days before, only a few miles away, a British convoy had been captured.

Above the camp the hills rose sheer; a cliff, a thousand feet high, cut through by the Nek with its narrow path. From the cliff communications by heliograph were maintained with Broadwood's column, operating north of the range. The heights were picketed by 300 men of the 2nd Fifth, under command of Captain Yatman. The position had been chosen by Colonel Lambton, and covered both sides of the Nek, two miles in all. In the event of an attack the four companies were practically isolated, for the path leading to the camp could be commanded from the west. The camp itself was picketed by yeomanry and mounted infantry, and a kopje to the east was held in some force.

Very early on the 13th the camp was attacked. Kitchener's Horse and the mounted infantry gallantly held their own, and De la Rey drew back, waiting for Beyers's men, who were not yet in position. The shots below had hardly died away when the pickets on the height saw a large commando riding towards them. The first volley from the Fifth scattered the Boers, who took refuge in a kloof, there left their ponies, and advanced on foot, 1,000 or more against 300. Using the cover of the rough stony ground with great skill the Boers came on, and leaving a few men to contain the eastern pickets they worked their way up to the western section held by H and G companies, under Captain Somerville. Then they rushed boldly forward, shouting as they charged.

The two small companies were overwhelmed, outnumbered six to one, ammunition failing, and no hope of support. They fought like lions; some were taken, but many refused to surrender; and the signaller, flashing to Broadwood, died at his post.

Then the Boers swept round and took Yatman and E and F companies in the rear. Again the Fifth fought desperately; again ammunition failed. They were fighting back to back, with the enemy all round them,

29

when at last, with a third of their force killed and wounded, the survivors surrendered and the Nek was lost.

Already from the western heights the Boers were firing into the camp below, and now they came surging down the narrow pass, where a handful of yeomanry tried to block the way. A company of Yorkshire Light Infantry and half a company of the Fifth, under Lieutenant Woods were sent to the rescue, but the Boers overran them and cut them off. Woods and his men and half the Yorkshire Light Infantry surrendered.

The position was untenable, for at any moment De la Rey might resume his attack, and the pass was in Beyers's hands. Clements therefore re-formed his men, and slowly and in good order fell back to Yeomanry hill, the kopje on the east. Some of the transport was saved, though half the natives had bolted, and many of the teams were shot down. The great 4·7 gun was under so fierce a fire that the oxen could not be inspanned, but the escort of the Fifth came to the rescue and man-handled it to safety. Before nine the whole remaining force was in the new position, and only the abandoned camp with the deserted waggons fell into Boer hands. Beyers's men sang hymns as they looted and burned.

Then De la Rey attacked again, opening fire with two guns; but Clements held his own, and for four hours kept the Boers at bay. Beyers had had enough from the Fifth; his men would not fight again. A little after three Clements began his retreat and brought his force into Rietfontein. The 2nd Fifth lost 23 men killed, 5 officers[1] and 80 men wounded. The majority of these were among the 8 officers and 333 men missing. The prisoners were shortly afterwards released.

While the 2nd Fifth were fighting so desperately at Nooitgedacht the first Battalion, a hundred miles to the west, was marching from Kaffirpan to Lichtenburg. Lemmer and his commando continually harassed Colonel

[1] Wounded: Captain Somerville, Lieutenant Jones, 2nd Lieutenants H. J. Stanton (died of wounds), Westmacott, and Isaac. General Beyers afterwards told General Clements that the Fifth fought like lions, and would not surrender though outnumbered six to one (Regimental Records).

Money's column. On December 9th Lemmer was killed in a rear-guard action. The 1st Fifth then garrisoned Lichtenburg, a pretty little town, with trees growing among the houses and streams bordering the streets. Two companies, under Captain Percival, were detached and marched with Lord Methuen, who visited his garrisons in turn. Gradually the spirit of offence died down. De la Rey found it hard to rouse the burghers to leave their homes. January passed quietly enough, and February; then suddenly, on the night of March 2nd, the Boers came down on Lichtenburg, surrounded the town, and even penetrated the streets.

Methuen was far away, the nearest reinforcements seventy miles distant. De la Rey had 1,200 men and a gun, Money 620 officers and men all told.[1] His main force held the market-place, while a ring of lightly held pickets encircled the town. These pickets, owing to trees and undergrowth, commanded a poor field of fire, and, for the same reason, although entrenched, were difficult to defend. Very early on the 3rd the alarm rang out. Shots were coming from three sides and from the town itself, with its company of malcontents and Boer sympathizers.

At once the market-place was manned, and a small reinforcement sent to the outposts, which were held by two companies. After that all communication with the pickets was lost; they were completely isolated. Creeping through the trees, the Boers surrounded them with overwhelming numbers. From behind their trenches and sangars the Fifth kept up a steady fire, saving ammunition and defending themselves with the utmost determination. Without food or water, Lieutenants James, De H. Larpent, Nelson, and Wreford Brown held on to their posts, and many gallant and heroic deeds were done that day. Late in the afternoon firing ceased for two hours, and dead and wounded were withdrawn. Then the attack began again, but the Boers were disheartened, and displayed no great eagerness. Before morning De la Rey had gone, having lost 14 killed and

[1] Six companies 1st Fifth, 100 yeomanry, two New Zealand guns.

38 wounded. The defenders lost 18 killed and 24 wounded. Of these the Fifth had 2 officers—Major E. W. Fletcher and 2nd Lieutenant H. D. Hull—and 14 men killed, and 18 men wounded.

After this the trees and undergrowth were cleared away, for only the gallantry of the pickets had saved the town.

In May Methuen returned, and A and E companies were exchanged for B and C, the companies in turn going on trek or remaining in garrison. Backwards and forwards the columns toiled. Farther east the 2nd Fifth were stationed in blockhouses and outposts on the Ladybrand–Bloemfontein road.

In October A and F companies of the 1st Fifth came in for some fighting. They were attached to Von Donop's[1] column, and were near to Kleinfontein on the 24th when De la Rey and Kemp attacked the rear-guard. The column,[2] quite unsuspicious, was trundling along the worst road in the Transvaal, fringed with bush and overhung with wooded heights. Patrols were out on either flank, but the nature of the country made effective scouting by yeomanry impossible. And the Boers chose their moment well.

A spattering shot or two held up the head of the column; then three lines of Boers, 500 in all, charged down on the convoy, shot the native drivers, hauled the waggons round, and turned on the rear-guard, having cut the column in half. The gunners were cut to pieces; half Girdwood's little company were shot down, but they and the yeomanry put up a splendid fight, and held on for two hours until Von Donop was able to come to their rescue. The Boers captured 12 waggons at the cost of 60 killed and wounded. Von Donop had 84 casualties; of these the Fifth had 7 killed, and Captain Girdwood and 18 men wounded, of whom 5 died of wounds. Sergeants Bailey and Miller displayed exceptional gallantry.

In the Eastern Transvaal the mounted infantry were

[1] Major-General Sir Stanley Von Donop, K.C.B., Master-General of Ordnance 1913-1916.
[2] One squadron Imperial Yeomanry, one section R.F.A., F company of the 1st Fifth, commanded by Captain Girdwood.

both harrying and being harried. They were at first attached to Smith-Dorrien's column; in January they hunted Beyers and Kemp; in February Botha attacked the camp at Lake Chrissie, but was beaten off. Then the 3rd mounted infantry were transferred to General Douglas, and all the winter months the columns continued their drives.

Botha returned to the Eastern Transvaal in October, where he found his countrymen subdued and awed by one little column under Colonel Benson, who in a series of brilliant raids had captured many prisoners. Benson had just gone to Middleburg to refit and reorganize his column. The 3rd mounted infantry were transferred to him, and on the 20th he again set out.[1]

At Klippoortge a night raid brought in thirty-seven prisoners, but farther south Benson found the country all aflame. The return of Botha had roused the sleeping commandos. Benson still rode on, clearing the country by day and parking his train securely at night. By the 29th he had collected fifty prisoners and many non-combatants. Then supplies began to run low, and seeing small opportunity for any really effective raid, the column turned north from Zuakfontein, heading for the railway. The morning of the 30th was misty and threatening. The 3rd mounted infantry acted as advance and flank guard to the main column, and almost as soon as the force began to move the Boers came down and hung about the flanks. The roads were very heavy, and the mist turned to rain. About one o'clock two waggons got bogged, and the rear-guard halted, while the convoy moved on and parked four miles north. The 1st Fifth company went on with the convoy and so missed the terrible and gallant fight on Gun Hill, where Benson and his heroic men died so bravely that Botha's men dared not storm the camp. The convoy entrenched themselves and held out until November 1st, when two columns marched in to their rescue, and Wools-Sampson

[1] 3rd Mounted Infantry (350), commanded by Major Anley; 25th Mounted Infantry (350); 2nd Scottish Horse (250); 2nd Buffs (650); four guns, two pompoms, 350 waggons and carts.

took the remnant of Benson's column back to Brugspruit.

In January Methuen, called to Vryburg for administrative work, handed his column over to Von Donop, with orders to occupy Wolmaransstadt, a hundred miles east of Vryburg, and use it as a base of operations. This little place was isolated, and all supplies had to come from Klerksdorp, fifty miles north-east. The first convoy met with no adventure; the second, leaving February 23rd, escorted by 700 men, under Colonel Anderson of the 5th I.Y.,[1] marched straight into an ambuscade only thirteen miles from Klerksdorp. So well had the Boers concealed their movements that Paget's Horse had been allowed to ride on into the town on the evening of the 24th.

At 4.30 the next morning, when it was still dark, the convoy started. The waggons were empty, but there were three carts loaded with small arm ammunition, and these three carts had brought De la Rey and his lieutenants hot-foot on the hunt.

A mile or so on the way to Klerksdorp the road ran down to the Jagd Spruit with its border of thick bush. Suddenly through the dim morning the thicket blazed from end to end, and bullets at twenty yards range swept the guard and transport. Then Kemp rode down on the centre and Celliers came up in the rear. The guns were hastily turned on the bush, and for a moment the Boers fell back. The rear waggons were extricated with difficulty, and Anderson ordered the convoy to move forward, cross the spruit and make for Klerksdorp, while the escort held up the enemy. Off went the drivers, pell-mell down the road, waggon running into waggon, and all collapsing in the spruit. On came the Boers, charging and firing from the saddle, and sweeping over men and guns. Here and there a gallant handful held out, but the day was lost, and before the sun rose, convoy, guns, men, and half a million rounds of ammunition were in De la Rey's hands.

[1] Imperial Yeomanry (230), Fifth (225), Paget's Horse, details, and guns.

Captain F. R. Coates, Lieutenant Quin, and 30 of the Fifth were killed; Major S. H. Enderby, 2nd Lieutenant Gibson, Sergeant-Major M'Donald, and 62 men wounded; and 2nd Lieutenant R. G. Raw and 105 men captured. The prisoners were taken to Kraaipan and then released.
Methuen, on hearing of the disaster, was on fire for action. Having learnt that De la Rey was heading north-west he set out from Vryburg on March 2nd with the Kimberley Column, commanded by Major Paris, strengthened by 200 of the 1st Fifth under Captain Montague. They marched through a barren land. It was hard work to find water for the oxen, and they were burdened with seventy waggons. Progress was slow, and a skirmish on the 6th showed the weakness of the mounted troops.[1]

Methuen made an early start on the 7th, and had reached Klip Drift on the Great Hart River when De la Rey attacked the rear of his unwieldy column. The ox convoy was ordered to halt, the drivers were already under the waggons, and the convoy closed up. The pressure on the rear continued, and the attack developed on both flanks. More and more Boers pressed on, reckless of shell fire, and contemptuous of the wild shooting of the half-trained horse. Then De la Rey boldly charged, his men firing from the saddle, and broke through the weak cavalry screen. Almost the whole of the mounted troops fled;[2] the unprotected gunners were shot down, while round the waggons the handful of infantry stood at bay. Coolly and slowly they fired, but the odds were too much; surrounded on three sides they were shot down one by one; the last battery was silent, the general badly wounded; the reserve ammunition waggon had stampeded; nothing more could be done. By 8.30 the fight was over, and Methuen, with his little bodyguard, prisoners of De la Rey, who then, as always, showed great kindness and chivalry. At Tweebosch Methuen lost 4 officers and 64 men killed, 10 officers and

---

[1] 900 irregulars of ten different corps.
[2] Some of the horse were rallied, and held out on an isolated hill until after the surrender of the infantry.

111 men wounded. The 1st Fifth had 3 men killed, and Lieutenant D. B. Mitford and 15 men wounded.

After these two disasters three more columns were directed to the west, and the final struggle with De la Rey began. The mounted infantry company was transferred to the 20th Brigade, under Colonel Dawkins and attached to Rawlinson's[1] column. In April Ian Hamilton was sent to take command, and Roodewal, the last action of importance, was fought on the 11th, Rawlinson's column coming up in time to harry the retreating Boers.

The remnant of the 1st Fifth were garrisoning the chain of blockhouses from Vryburg along the Kimberley-Mafeking road; the 2nd Fifth were still round Ladybrand. In May Bruce Hamilton's last drive brought in Mannie Botha and 200 prisoners; and in a night raid, Captain Warwick, of the 2nd Fifth, with twenty of his men and some mounted infantry, captured Andries Delport, the chief of Keen's scouts, and a troublesome cattle raider.

A week later the Peace Delegates met again; Botha was for settlement, De Wet for resistance, and De la Rey, that " old lion of the Western Transvaal," for peace. Terms were finally agreed May 31st. That very day Private Sloan of B Company was wounded while on sentry duty at Modderpoort. So the Fifth saw the war from beginning to end.

They had fought a clean fight with a foe they could respect. They had been beaten in fair fight by straight shooting and quicker wits; they had been the victors when discipline and courage could win the game. The first Battalion had lost 9 officers and 85 men in battle and 35 of disease; 15 officers and 189 men had been wounded. They could be proud of their record: Belmont, Graspan, Modder River; that first drive after De Wet which so nearly ended in victory for Methuen's men; the defence of Lichtenburg; the rear-guard fight at Kleinfontein, and the despairing courage that held out at Yzer Spruit and Tweebosch. Methuen wrote: " I do not suppose there

[1] General Sir Henry Rawlinson, G.C.B., etc.

is a battalion possessing a body of officers of a higher or more manly tone than those of the Fifth Fusiliers. . . . There never was a cheerier battalion, and the men have been with me from the beginning for better or for worse."

Misfortune dogged the second Battalion: Stormberg and Reddersburg, and the redeeming heroism of Nooitgedacht, and all the long weary months of blockhouse and outpost duty. Three officers and 37 men were killed; 6 officers and 103 men wounded; 9 officers and 628 men prisoners; while 28 died of disease. In comparison with other regiments the Fifth lost very few men from sickness, much to the credit of the internal economy of the Battalions and the physique of the men.

It has become the fashion to discredit the great South African War. The abuses which led to hostilities are forgotten, and the German menace ignored; all that Englishmen remember is that a great and powerful nation fought a small and isolated people, and paid dearly for victory by three long years of war. The failures of once-famous generals, the early defeats, the humiliating surrenders, are all remembered: the difficulties are ignored and the final achievement unrealized.

It should be remembered that the end in view was not the military conquest of the Transvaal—as was well understood by Lord Roberts, who endeavoured by every means to manœuvre the Boers into submission. Kitchener, by more ruthless and military methods, would have ended the war in a fraction of the time, but a conquered people would never have rallied to defend the Empire in 1914.

Few wars have been fought with less bitterness. Isolated instances of treachery certainly occurred, but the early efforts to rouse race-hatred soon gave place to frank admiration of the skill, courage, and chivalry the Boers so often displayed. They had refused to recognize the International Law of warfare, but no Uitlander women need have fled from the Republics, and with very few exceptions prisoners were treated with chivalry.

One of the many difficulties the British and Boer leaders had to face was the disinclination of their men to take the war seriously. When outmanœuvred the men surrendered, not so much from fear of losing their lives, but in tacit recognition that the enemy had won that move of the game. In the few instances where small numbers of men held out and fought to a finish they had some definite object to defend or were inspired by some heroic leader. Again, more military tactics would have shortened the war but lengthened the years needed in which to forgive and forget.

The Fifth should be proud of the Honour on their Colours, " South Africa, 1899–1902." They should be proud, not only of the price paid by hard fighting, but for that record of good conduct they share with other regiments. The kindly chivalry of the British soldier then made it afterwards possible for their late enemy to become their comrade-in-arms.

With the close of the war, this history must end. The second Battalion sailed for England in 1903, the first Battalion remaining to garrison South Africa for three more years.

The total casualties amounted to 13 officers and 240 N.C.O.'s and men killed or died of wounds or disease; and 21 officers and 292 N.C.O.'s and men wounded.

The Distinguished Conduct Medal was won by the following: Q.M. Sergeant M. White; Colour-Sergeants F. Poulter, C. W. Honnor, A. Landen, G. J. Taylor; Band-Sergeant J. Stone; Sergeants J. Hutton, J. Railton, W. Smith; Lance-Sergeant G. P. Wymer; Corporals W. G. Down, F. Lincoln, H. G. Seager; Lance-Corporals J. Davis, W. Brown, R. M. Delaney, W. W. Raynham; Privates W. Cooper, H. Earle, J. East, A. Harris, G. Metcalfe, T. O'Donnell, J. Rea, J. Slater, J. Smalley, J. Snowdon, J. Tracy, G. Black, A. Naylor, and S. Symons.

APPENDICES

I.—EXTRACTS FROM ARMY LISTS.
II.—PHŒBE HESSEL.
III.—HOLLAND CAMPAIGN, 1799.
IV.—"THE AFFAIR OF EL BODON, SEPTEMBER 25, 1811."
V.—LETTER WRITTEN AFTER THE CAPTURE OF CIUDAD RODRIGO BY LIEUT.-COLONEL RIDGE.
VI.—AN EXTRACT FROM "CAMP AND QUARTERS" (1840).

BIBLIOGRAPHY.

APPENDIX I

I.—EXTRACTS FROM ARMY LISTS.

ABREVIATIONS.

O.R. = out of regiment.
O.B. = out before.
C.R. = commission renewed.
S. = serving.

Lt. = Lieutenant.
Capt. = Captain.
Lt.-Col. = Lieutenant-Colonel.

K. = killed.
Res. = resigned.
Excd. = exchanged.
Dd. = deceased.

CHAPTER III.

1688. Twelve Companies. Dalton's "English Army Lists," vol. ii., p. 227.

COLONEL.
Thomas Talmash, March 24, 1688.

LT.-COLONEL.
Godefreid Loidd.[1]

MAJOR.
Edward Loidd.[2]

CAPTAINS.
William Persons.
Remwald or Renovard, David. O.B. 1692.
Willem Thaylor. O.B. 1692.

Sacharias Curteis. O.B. 1692.
William Lowther (Lawers, Lomour,) vice Bernardi, March 29, 1688.
Thomas Handisides,[3] vice Saxby, April 20, 1688.
Robert Jackson,[4] vice Barnewall, Jan. 26, 1688.
Robert Cicile, vice Du Puy, April 21, 1688.
Thomas Borroughs, vice Wilson, March 31, 1688. S. as Major 1692; O.R. 1693.

CHAPTER IV.

1693. ("English Army Lists.")

COLONEL.
Edward Lloyd,[5] May 1, 1689.

LT.-COLONEL.
Thomas Brudenell,[6] W'Hall, Oct. 1, 1692.

MAJOR.
Thomas Burroughs.[7]

CAPTAINS.
William Parsons.[8]
William Lowther,[9] March 29, 1688.

---

[1] Son of Sir G. Loidd, "a stout choleric Welshman," who served under the Prince of Orange. A former Capt. in 1st Foot Guards. Col. of late Duke of Bolton's Foot in West Indies Sept. 24, 1692. Held the command until Jan. 1, 1695. His son, Godfrey Lloyd, gazetted Capt. in Fifth March 16, 1695.

[2] Probably of same family. Served many years in Fifth. Appointed Col. May 1, 1689. Died Aug. 25, 1694.

[3] Capt. of Grenadier Company, April, 1692. Major of Col. Gibson's Foot March 16, 1694. Col. of 22nd Foot Jan. 20, 1702. Died 1712.

[4] Lt.-Col. of Ford Cardross' new regiment of Scots Dragoons 1690; afterwards Lt.-Col. of Earl of Argyle's Foot. Killed by a random shot from cannon-ball at Nieuport in Flanders Jan. 10, 1693.

[5] See *ante*.

[6] As Thomas Prudenell, Capt. in Earl of Pembroke's Regt. of Foot, eldest son of Richard Brudenell and Eliz., daughter of Sir Walter Lyttleton, Knt. Lt.-Col. of Foulke's Regt. of Foot Sept., 1689. Lt.-Col. Fifth 1692. Col. of Regt. of Foot, vice Henry Rowe, March, 1695. Was at Battle of Boyne. Served in Portugal. Maj.-Genl. June 1, 1706. Dd. Gibraltar, 1707.

[7] O.R. Dec., 1693.

[8] Or Persons. Major Dec. 10, 1693. Lt.-Col. March 16, 1695. (Capt. in Royal Regt. of Foot Guards Oct. 1684?)

[9] Or Lawers. Major March 16, 1695. Petition in Treas. Papers, Oct. 10, 1694, from Barbara, wife of Wm. Lawers, for allowance of arrears of pay due to her husband.

CAPTAINS (*continued*).
Thomas Handiside,[1] Grenadier Company, April 20, 1688.
Corns. Nanningh,[2] Senr., Loo, April 2, 1692.
Peter Godby,[3] Loo, April 2, 1692. Ashpool.[4]
Edward Johnson.[5]
Mark Ashley.[6]
Peter Atcherley.[7]
William Lloyd.[8]
Thomas Kynaston.[9]
William Elrington,[10] Captain-Lieutenant, Loo, April 2, 1692.

LIEUTENANTS.
John Tichborne,[11] 1st, Lieutenant, of Gren., Loo, April 2, 1692.
Anthony Sheppard,[12] 2nd Lieutenant of Gren., Loo, April 2, 1692,
Ralph Johnson,[13] Loo, April 2, 1692.

John Worthington.[14]
Brockwell Lloyd.[15]
Joseph Fletcher,[16] W'Hall, Nov. 30, 1693.

ENSIGNS.
Corns. Nanningh, Junr.,[17] Loo, April 2, 1692.
Griffith Drisdale,[18] Loo, April 2, 1692.
Daniel Whittingham.[19]
Thomas Boys,[20] Nov. 10, 1692.
Thomas Worchester,[21] Kensington, Dec. 29, 1692.
William Low,[22] W'Hall, April 12, 1693.
William Howell,[23] W'Hall, April 12, 1693.
Thomas Wolhouse,[24] Dec. 4, 1693.

CHAPLAIN.
Edward Griffiths, May 31, 1693.

QUARTER-MASTER.
John Pepper,[25] May 31, 1693.

---

[1] Capt. in " Talmash's," *vice* Wm. Saxby, April, 1688. O.R. Dec., 1693. Major of Col. Gibson's Foot March, 1694. Bt.-Col. June 28, 1701. S. in Spain and Flanders. Col. of 22nd Foot 1702. The family of Handysyde, or Handiside, of Harehaugh, in the chapelry of Holystone, near Rothbury, Northumberland, were a military family. Thomas Handiside became Major-General and Governor of Jamaica. He died March 20, 1729, aged 84. His son Roger was Colonel of the 22nd Foot and Governor of Berwick, etc. [2] O.R. 1695.
[3] Capt. April, 1692. Major's commission not forthcoming. Served at Battle of Caya. At Gibraltar, 1712. Bt.-Lt.-Col. April 5, 1707. Lt.-Col. May 10, 1708. The will of a certain Peter Godby proved at Dublin, 1735.
[4] Dd. before Oct. 31, 1693.
[5] Senior Capt. 1702. Serving as Major 1709. O.B. 1715.
[6] O.R. 1695. [7] O.R. Feb. 16, 1694. [8] O.B. 1702. [9] O.B. 1702.
[10] Capt. Feb. 16, 1694. Bt.-Major June 12, 1708. Major Fifth Sept. 28, 1715. Commandant at Gibraltar 1719-1720. Lt.-Col. Aug. 25, 1722. S. in Ireland 1728. Not in any subsequent list. Possibly of the family of Elrington of Elrington and Espershields in the chapelry of Haydon, Northumberland. (See " History of Northumberland," vol. vi., p. 209 *et seq.*)
[11] Fourth son of Sir William Tichborne, of Beaulieu, co. Louth. Bt.-Capt. Gren. Co. Dec., 1693. Called Col. Tichborne in Burke's "Extinct Peerage," and said to have been Governor of Athlone. Major before 1715. Sold his commission to William Elrington. Appointed Governor of Charlemont, Ireland. Dd. 1745. [12] Capt. March 18, 1695. O.R. 1696.
[13] C.R. 1702. O.B. 1715. [14] Capt. Oct. 31, 1693. Dd. Feb., 1698.
[15] Late Capt. in Col. John Hale's Regt. of Foot. Capt. Nov. 1, 1693, of Major Burrow's late Co. O.B. 1715.
[16] Capt. Jan. 1, 1696. C.R. 1702. S. 1705. O.B. 1715.
[17] Lt. before 1694. O.R. 1702. [18] O.R. 1694.
[19] Lt. Jan. 1, 1695. C.R. 1702. O.B. 1715.
[20] C.R. 1702. S. as Lt. 1706.
[21] S. 1694. O.R. 1702. [22] O.R. 1694.
[23] Lt. March, 1694. O.B. 1695.
[24] Lt. March 1, 1694. S. as Lt. 1705. O.B. 1715. [25] Ens. 1705.

APPENDIX I

CHAPTER V.

1702; on the Irish Establishment. ("English Army Lists.")

COLONEL.
Thomas Fairfax,[1] Nov. 6, 1694.

LT.-COLONEL.
William Parsons,[2] March 16, 1695.

MAJOR.
William Lowther,[3] March 16, 1695.

CAPTAINS.
Edward Johnson.[4]
Peter Godby,[5] April 2, 1692.
Brockwell Lloyd,[6] Nov. 1, 1693.
John Tichborne,[7] (Gren. Co.), Dec. 29, 1693.
William Elrington,[8] 1694.
Godfrey Lloyd,[9] March 16, 1695.
Jos. Fletcher, Jan. 1, 1696.
Daniel Sherrard,[10] Feb. 25, 1698.
Edward Spagg.
Robert Oulds,[11] Captain-Lieutenant, March 1, 1694.

LIEUTENANTS.
Timothy Banks,[12] Gren., March 1, 1694.

Robert Brudenall,[13] April 10, 1694.
David Lloyd,[14] April 10, 1694.
George Leicester,[15] April 10, 1695.
Daniel Whittingham,[16] June 1, 1695.
Thomas Giles.[17]
Benjamin Garraway,[18] March 1, 1696.
Richard Hanmer,[19] before 1696.
Ralph Bethell,[20] Hague, Dec. 1, 1698.
Nicholas Fenwick.[21]
Theo. Warren.[22]
R. Johnson.

ENSIGNS.
Thos. Boys,[23] Nov. 10, 1692.
Thos. Wolhouse,[24] Dec. 4, 1693.
L. van Riell, Senr.,[25] June 1, 1695.
Henry Owens,[26] June 1, 1695.
Job Elrington,[27] March 21, 1696.
Charles Fermore,[28] March 26, 1696.

---

[1] Lt.-Col. of Visct. Castleton's Regt. of Foot March 8,1 689. Bt.-Col. of Foot April 25, 1689.
[2] See *ante*.   [3] See *ante*.   [4] See *ante*.   [5] See *ante*.
[6] See *ante*.   [7] See *ante*.   [8] See *ante*.
[9] Son of Godfrey Lloyd, late Lt.-Col. Ens. in his father's Regt. Nov. 26, 1692. O.R. April 28, 1709.
[10] Served in Defence of Londonderry, 1689. Engineer in Flanders train of Art. 1693, at 10s. per diem. Eng. of bridgemen and tin boat men 1693; afterwards Eng. of brass ordnance for Sea Service. Lt. in Sir Mat. Bridge's Regt. Oct. 1, 1696. Capt. in Fifth 1698. C.R. 1702. O.R. 1705.
[11] O.R. 1706.   [12] O.B. 1715.
[13] Capt. before 1706. Adjt. July 1, 1698. S. in Portugal 1708.
[14] Ens. in Carne's Regt. of Foot 1688; disbanded 1689. C.R. 1702. S. 1706.
[15] Ens. Ffoulke's Regt. of Foot Oct. 24, 1690. O.B. 1715.
[16] O.R. 1706.
[17] Capt. Jan. 28, 1708. O.R. April 17, 1709.
[18] O.R. 1705.   [19] Capt. March 26, 1707. O.R. 1727.
[20] C.R. 1702. Living in 1724, in which year he petitioned Sir R. Walpole for some reward due to him for service connected with the rebellion of 1715.
[21] Capt. March 25, 1707. O.B. 1723.
[22] O.B. 1715.   [23] See *ante*.   [24] See *ante*.
[25] Lt. April 30, 1707. S. 1715. O.B. 1723.
[26] S. as Lt. 1706. Capt.-Lt. 1709. Capt. Aug. 26, 1717, *vice* "Morrice," resd. O.B. 1723.
[27] Ens. in Fairfax's Foot March 1, 1696. 2nd Lt. Grens. March 14, 1705. S. at Gib. 1715. S. Port. and Spain and Gib. Capt. May 24, 1723.
[28] O.B. 1715.

1702 AND 1715

ENSIGNS (*continued*).
Francis Pyle,[1] Hague, April 28, 1697.
James Steenblock.[2]
Trevor Lloyd.[3]
S. Jones.[4]
Mathew Chambers.[5]

CHAPLAIN.
Edward Griffiths.

SURGEON.
J. Heath,[6] Hague, Jan. 10, 1699.

MATE.
J. Pepper.

The following men in the Fifth between 1695 and 1702, not in Army List of 1702:

Carey Godby,[7] Ens. to Capt. P. Godby, Hague, May 8, 1696.
Bernard Dequilhern,[8] Ens. to Capt. B. Lloyd, Attre, Aug. 3, 1696.

Martin Bladen,[9] Ens. Capt. P. Godby, Kens., Dec. 12, 1697.
Gilbert Abbot,[10] Lt. to Capt. P. Godby, Kens., May 14, 1698.
Charles Ashfield,[11] Ens. Capt. Ed. Johnson, Kens., March 4, 1700.

CHAPTER VI.
1715. ("George I.'s Army.")

COLONEL.
Brig.-Genl. Thomas Pearce, Feb. 5, 1704.

LT.-COLONEL.
Peter Godby,[12] May 10, 1708.

MAJOR.
John Titchborne,[13] Jan. 28, 1708.

CAPTAINS.
William Elrington,[14] Feb. 16, 1694.

Richard Hanmer,[15] March 26, 1707.
Thomas Giles,[16] Jan. 28, 1708.
William Vatchell,[17] April 28, 1709.
Bacon Morris,[18] Aug. 17, 1710.
John Morrice,[19] June 24, 1713.
Charles Pearce.[20]
Richard Bickerstaff.[21]
Thomas Morris.[22]
Henry Owen,[23] Captain-Lieutenant, 1709.

---

[1] Ens. in Fairfax's 1697; Lt. 1705. S. at Gib. 1715. Left regt. 1717, when he succeeded his father, Sir Seymour Pyle, as Bart. of Compton. Beauchamp, Berks.
[2] C.R. 1715. [3] O.B. 1715. [4] O.B. 1715. [5] O.B. 1715.
[6] *Vice* Jno. Houles (Houlez, Surg. in De Belcastel's Foot 1694), apt. July 7, 1696, Gemblours. C.R. 1702. S.R. 1706.
[7] A child. Out of regt. April 28, 1697. Rec. Com. as Ens. May 17, 1709. S. Gib. 1715. [8] O.R. 1702.
[9] Capt. in Sir Charles Hotham's Foot March 23, 1705. S. in Spain. A.D.C. to Earl of Galway, Bt.-Col. Editor of " Cæsar's Commentaries." Of Aldborough Hutch, Essex. Comptroller of the Mint, and a Lord of Trade.
[10] Late Lt. in Col. John Gibson's Foot; trans. to Major Lower's Coy. Mar. 4, 1700. Lt. in Visct. Mountjoy's Foot June 28, 1701. Maj. in Col. Charles Hobby's newly raised Regt. Foot in New England April 1, 1707.
[11] Cornet in Princess Anne of Denmark's Regt. of Dragoons 1692. Lt. March 1, 1694. Ens. in Tidcombe's Foot 1698.
[12] *Ante*. [13] *Ante*. [14] *Ante*. [15] *Ante*. [16] *Ante*.
[17] Capt. and Lt.-Col. of Coldstream Gds. May, 1720. Excd. to half-pay of Magny's Dragoons May 1, 1728. Drawing half-pay Sept., 1740, then aged 58. Possibly a son of William Vatchell, Col. of 6th Foot.
[18] Lt. in Brig.-Genl. Jos. Wrightman's Regt. Foot 1708. Lt.-Gov. of Landguard Fort May, 1718. Gov. of do. Sept., 1719. Dd. as Gov. 1744.
[19] One of this name S. in Duke of Schomberg's Horse 1693. Res. Aug. 1717?
[20] Charles William Pearce, son of Brig.-Genl. Thomas Pearce, adjt. about July, 1717. Major Aug. 25, 1722. Lt.-Col. Jan. 1, 1738. S. 1751.
[21] Dd. March 10, 1716.
[22] Res. 1717? A Lt. of this name S. with train of Art. 1693. [23] *Ante*.

APPENDIX I

LIEUTENANTS.

Job Elrington,[1] May 14, 1705.
Fras. Pyle,[2] 2nd Lt. Grenadiers, June 5, 1705.
Lambert van Riel, Senr.,[3] April 30, 1707.
John Napper,[4] May 21, 1707.
John Parry,[5] Aug. 15, 1707.
John Elrington, May 21, 1708.
Christopher Alcock,[6] Dec. 17, 1701.
Paul Pepper,[7] Dec. 1, 1711.
William Wynne,[8] May 26, 1712.
John Durrant Brenall, Nov. 10, 1713.
Phil Barry.[9]

ENSIGNS.

Fras. O'Farel,[10] Sept. 20, 1707.
Edward Hayes,[11] March 1, 1708.
Thomas Browne, Oct. 12, 1708.
Butler Chauncey, Nov. 9, 1708.
Peter Burnevale,[12] Jan. 24, 1710.
Augustus Erle,[13] March 29, 1711.
Henry Vatchell,[14] Dec. 1, 1711.
Gilbert Keene,[15] March 7, 1713.
Robert Claxton, Nov. 10, 1713.
Peter Beakes.[16]
Carey Godby,[17] May 17, 1719.

CHAPLAIN.

Samuel King.

SURGEON.

Robert Hill.

1723. ("George I.'s Army.")

COLONEL.

Brig.-Genl. Thomas Pearce, Feb. 5, 1704.

LT.-COLONEL.

William Elrington,[18] Aug. 25, 1722.

MAJOR.

Charles William Pearce,[19] Aug. 25, 1722.

CAPTAINS.

Thomas Giles,[20] Jan. 28, 1708.
John Napper or Napier,[21] May 28, 1720.
James Paterson,[22] July 28, 1720.
John Horseman,[23] May 20, 1721.
Daniel Pecqueur,[24] June 9, 1721.
John Elrington,[25] April 24, 1722.
Christopher Alcock,[26] May 9, 1723.

---

[1] *Ante.* [2] *Ante.* [3] *Ante.*
[4] Quarter-Master Aug. 15, 1707. Capt.-Lt. Aug. 26, 1717, *vice* Henry Owen, preferred. Dd. March, 1725. His widow was drawing a pension of £26 per annum in 1734. [5] O.R. 1717.
[6] Capt. May, 1723. S. 1724. O.B. 1740. [7] Half-pay 1722.
[8] Capt.-Lt. May 20, 1720. Capt. 1739. [9] Parry—adjt.; res. 1717.
[10] Taken prisoner in Portugal at Battle of Caya. O.R. 1727.
[11] Probably Capt. Ed. Hayes, appointed Lt.-Gov. of Landguard Fort before 1730. Dd. 1753, aged 61.
[12] Lt. July, 1720. Capt. March, 1732. Senior Capt. 1746. O.B. 1752.
[13] O.R. 1727. Drawing half-pay as Lt.-Col. 1740.
[14] Or Vachell. Ens. Coldstream Gds. Jan., 1718. Res. April, 1722.
[15] Lt. 1722. Capt. 1739. S. 1740. Res. 1754. Dd. 1764. Will proved at Dublin in same year.
[16] Res. April 16, 1717.
[17] Son of Lt.-Col. Peter Godby. 1st Lt. of Gren. Co. 1722. S. as Lt. 1740. O.B. 1752.
[18] *Ante.* [19] *Ante.* [20] *Ante.* [21] *Ante.*
[22] Lt. May 6, 1719. Capt. 1720. Major Jan., 1736. Lt.-Col. 7 Marines (Cornwallis) Jan., 1741. Col. of New Regt. of Marines Dec., 1755. Lt.-Genl. Jan., 1761. Dd. Richmond, 1771.
[23] Lt. Gren. Gds., Brig.-Gen. Wheeler's Co. Oct., 1719. Capt. of Invalids March, 1723. Excd. Will's Regt., 1723. Major 1739. Dd. 1740.
[24] From half-pay. S. in late reign in Barrymore's Foot (13th), Major in Fifth Feb., 1741. S. 1748.
[25] O.B. 1740. [26] Adjt. Nov. 24, 1722. Dd. 1732.

1723

CAPTAINS (continued).
Job Elrington,[1] May 24, 1723.
William Wynne,[2] Aug. 25, 1723.
James Ormsby,[3] Capt.-Lieut., May 24, 1723.
James Holmes,[4] Capt.-Lieut., Oct. 13, 1723.

LIEUTENANTS.
Augustus Earle,[5] Nov. 1, 1718.
Henry Coltopp, Nov. 1, 1718.
Andrew Peterson,[6] Feb. 18, 1719.
Charles Vachell,[7] May 29, 1720.
Peter Bruneval,[8] July 28, 1720.
John Coultrone,[9] March 29, 1721.
Gilbert Keene,[10] April 24, 1722.
William Heele,[11] April 24, 1722.
James Stratton,[12] May 9, 1722.
Walter Devereux,[13] Aug. 11, 1722.
Andrew Crewe,[14] Aug. 22, 1722.
Carey Godby,[15] 1st Lt. Gren. Co., Aug. 25, 1722.
Ralph Urwin,[16] Nov. 24, 1722.

John Knyvet,[17] March 9, 1723.
William Pyle,[18] May 24, 1723.
Robert Napper or Napier,[19] Oct. 13, 1723.

ENSIGNS.
Bullock, Nov. 1, 1718.
Hercules Ogilvy,[20] July 28, 1720.
William Maxwell,[21] March 29, 1721.
Henry Houghton,[22] June 5, 1721.
Nicholas Skinner,[23] April 11, 1722.
James Bennett,[24] April 24, 1722.
Robert Napier,[25] May 9, 1722.
Robert Cuthbertson,[26] May 31, 1722.
Scipio Olyphant,[27] July 13, 1722.
John Murray,[28] July 19, 1722.
Michael Mitchell,[29] Aug. 25, 1722.
Lambert Vanriel, Junr.,[30] Nov. 24, 1722.
John Fenwick,[31] Oct. 13, 1723.

SURGEON.
W. Ellis, Oct. 1718.

---

[1] *Ante.*   [2] *Ante.*   [3] O.B. 1735.
[4] S. as Capt. 1737. O.B. 1740.   [5] *Ante.*
[6] Ens. in Paston's Regt. Sept., 1706. Lt. Aug., 1907. Half-pay 1712 Lt. in R. Lucas's Regt. before 1715. Lt. in Fifth 1719. O.B. 1728.
[7] Ens. Fifth Jan. 3, 1718. Lt. in 4th Foot June, 1724. S. 1730. Drawing half-pay 1759. Belonged to a Berkshire family of this name.
[8] *Ante.*
[9] Ens. May 28, 1720. Capt. Jan. 1, 1736. S. 1740. O.B. 1752.
[10] *Ante.*
[11] Hale in subsequent Lists. Capt.-Lt. 1736. S. 1740.
[12] Lt. May 9, 1722. Capt. Earl of Orkney's Regt. Dec., 1726. O.B. 1740.
[13] Capt.-Lt. in Handysyde's Regt. (16th) Jan., 1740.
[14] Capt. 1741. Major to Lt.-Col. Rawson 1751. Dd. at Piddle Hinton, Dorset, 1759.   [15] *Ante.*
[16] Ens. Nov. 1, 1718. O.B. 1752.
[17] S. as Lt. 1737. O.B. 1740.
[18] Son of Francis Pyle ? Capt. in Morton's Marines Nov., 1739. S. at Cartagena 1741. Dd. April, 1741, from fever.   [19] O.R. 1741.
[20] O.R. in Oct., 1723.   [21] O.B. 1727.   [22] O.B. 1727.
[23] Lt. in 15th Foot 1723. S. 1730. Dd. before 1735. His widow, Barbara Skinner, was drawing a pension of £20 p.a. in that year.
[24] O.B. 1736. Possibly a son of James Bennett, Quarter-master of 1st Foot Gds. May, 1696. O.R. 1705.   [25] O.B. 1736.
[26] Lt. March 11, 1732. Capt.-Lt. May, 1739. Probably father of Bennett Cuthbertson, whom see.   [27] (Oliphant) O.B. 1736.
[28] S. 1730. Dd. before 1735 in which year his widow was drawing a pension of £16 p.a.
[29] Lt. Jan. 1, 1736. Capt. June, 1749. Res. Oct., 1755.
[30] Lt. May, 1739. S. of former Lt. May, 1742.
[31] S. as Sen. Ens. 1740. 2nd Lt. of Gren. 1742.

APPENDIX I

Commissions after 1723.

William Ellis,[1] Ensign, Jan. 24, 1724.
John Purcell,[2] Lieutenant, June 1, 1724.
Benjamin Gregg,[3] Capt., *vice* (Jno.) Napier, dd. March 20, 1725.

Charles D'Avenant,[4] Ensign, May 10, 1726.
Roland Johnson,[5] Chaplain, Aug. 26, 1726.
Richard Johnston,[6] Ensign, Jan. 18, 1727.

CHAPTER VII.

1737. (Record Office.)

COLONEL.
Sir John Cope.

LT.-COLONEL.
Francis Ligonière, July 8, 1737.

MAJORS.
William Peirce,[7] Aug. 25, 1722.
James Pattinson,[8] Jan. 1, 1736.
Paul Malide,[9] July 12, 1737.

CAPTAINS.
John Eltrington,[10] April 22, 1722.
Arthur Balfour,[11] Nov. 22, 1723.
James Holmes,[12] May 11, 1728.
George Lestanguate,[13] June 1, 1733.
Charles Fitzroy,[14] June 20, 1735.
Peter Bruneval,[15] Jan. 1, 1736.

William Humphreys, June 12, 1737.
William Hele,[16] Captain-Lieut., Jan. 1, 1736.

LIEUTENANTS.
John Coltrane,[17] March 29, 1721.
Gilbert Keene,[18] April 24, 1722.
Andrew Crewe,[19] Aug. 22, 1722.
Carey Godby,[20] Aug. 25, 1722.
Ralf Urwin,[21] Nov. 24, 1722.
John Knyvet,[22] March 9, 1723.
William Pyle,[23] May 24, 1723.
John Purcele, March 7, 1724.
Robert Cuthbertson,[24] March 11, 1732.
George Crawfaurd,[25] July 26, 1735.
Michael Mitchell,[26] Jan. 17, 1736.
Sir William Gorsturch, July 12, 1737.

---

[1] Son of Surg. William Ellis. O.B. 1737.
[2] From Ens. in Regt. of Invalids. Capt. in Fifth, 1740.
[3] Ens. in 16th Foot March, 1705. Fought at Malplaquet. Capt. in R.I. Regt. April, 1712. Half-pay 1713. Major in Robinson's Marines Dec., 1739. Cartagena 1741. Probably dd. West Indies same year.
[4] Ens. Major-Gen. Newton's Regt. Oct. 12, 1711. Bt.-Capt. and Town Adjt. at Portsmouth before 1757. Dd. as Town Major of said garrison, 1773.
[5] O.B. 1728.   [6] S. June 1728. O.B. 1737.
[7] William Charles Pearce. See *ante*.   [8] See *ante*.
[9] O.B. 1740.   [10] Elrington. See *ante*.
[11] Dd. May 7, 1742.
[12] See *ante*. Ret. half-pay 1738.
[13] Major in 2nd July, 1742.
[14] Lt.-Col. in 1st Regt. Foot Gds. from half-pay March, 1741.
[15] See *ante*.   [16] See *ante* "William Heele."
[17] See *ante*.   [18] See *ante*.   [19] See *ante*.   [20] See *ante*.
[21] See *ante*.   [22] Capt. Ind. Coy. Jan., 1738.
[23] See *ante*.   [24] See *ante*.
[25] Capt. June, 1739. Major Fifth, 1746. Major in Otway's Regt. May 2, 1750.
[26] See *ante*.

1737 AND 1746

ENSIGNS.
George Lovell,[1] Oct. 28, 1721.
Lambert Vanriel,[2] Nov. 24, 1722.
John Fenwick,[3] Oct. 13, 1723.
Richard Johnston,[4] Jan. 18, 1727,
Joceline Robinson,[5] March 11, 1731.

Robert Scott,[6] May 10, 1732.
Jeremiah Hicks, Dec. 21, 1733.
George Hollwalf,[7] Jan. 19, 1734.
Samuel Horsey, Aug. 23, 1735.
Stanhope, Jan. 1, 1736.
James Smollet,[8] Jan. 31, 1736.

1746. (Record Office.)

COLONEL.
Alexander Irwin,[9] Jan. 22, 1737.

LT.-COLONEL.
Charles William Pearce,[10] Jan. 1, 1736.

MAJORS.
Daniel Pequire,[11] Feb. 1741.
George Crawford,[12] Feb. 1746.

CAPTAINS.
Peter Bruneval,[13] Jan. 1, 1736.
Gilbert Keene,[14] June 1739.
Andrew Crewe,[15] Feb. 1741.
George Fowke,[16] March 1741.
John Corneille,[17] May 1742.

Denny Cuffes,[18] July 1742.
Carey Godby,[19] Captain-Lieut., May 1742.

LIEUTENANTS.
Ralph Urwin,[20] Nov. 24, 1722.
John Parcell (Purcell),[21] June 1724.
Robert Cuthbertson,[22] March 1732.
Michael Mitchell,[23] Jan. 1736.
John Irwin,[24] Jan. 1737.
Lambert Van Riel,[25] May 1739.
George Lovell,[26] June 1739.
John Fenwick,[27] Jan. 1739.
James Reid,[28] June 1741.
John Edgworth,[29] May 1742.
Henry Bourne,[30] May 1742.

---

[1] Lt. June, 1739. [2] See *ante*.
[3] See *ante*. [4] Resigned.
[5] Cornet in Wynn's in 1737.
[6] Lt. June, 1741. 2nd Lt. (Gren.) May, 1742.
[7] Hollway, Lt. May, 1742. O.B. 1746.
[8] Gazetted to "Cope's," but afterwards transferred to "Lanoes." Commission probably did not take effect.
[9] Ens. in 2/1st Foot Oct., 1689. Adjt. to 2nd Batt. May 22, 1694. Capt. Aug. 1695. Major Aug. 1704. W. at Schellenburgh. Dd. a Major-General.
[10] *Ante.* [11] From half-pay? See list of 1723.
[12] *Ante.* [13] *Ante.* [14] *Ante.*
[15] *Ante.* [16] O.B. 1752.
[17] Possibly a son of Rodolph Corneille an Engineer Officer in Ireland, 1692. Capt. in Hanmer's Foot 1695. Half-pay 1698. O.B. 1752.
[18] Of Battlerans. 2nd son of Agmondisham Cuffes and Anne, daughter of Sir John Otway. Married 1715, Grace, daughter and heiress of Ebenezer Wright, Sheriff of Kilkenny. O.B. 1752. Dd. 1754, leaving a son, Joseph.
[19] *Ante.* [20] *Ante.* [21] O.B. 1752.
[22] *Ante.* [23] *Ante.*
[24] Captain's com. not forthcoming. Major, Feb., 1751. Lt.-Col. 1752. Col. of 74th Foot in Jamaica, March, 1761. Commander-in-Chief in Ireland. Dd. a Lt.-General.
[25] *Ante.* [26] O.B. 1752. [27] *Ante.*
[28] O.B. 1752. [29] O.B. 1752.
[30] Adjt. and Lt. May, 1742. Exd. Jan., 1755. Quarter-master James Bromhead from half-pay in Hansons.

468   APPENDIX I

SECOND-LIEUTENANTS.
Mead Vanlewen,[1] May 10, 1742
Lewis Nicolo,[2] May 11, 1742.
William Wilkinson,[3] May 12, 1742.
Henry Troughear,[4] May 13, 1742.
Chudleigh Dering,[5] May 14, 1742.
Thomas M. Leroth,[6] May 15, 1742.
Luke Gardiner,[7] May 16, 1742.
John Chappell,[8] May 17, 1742.
William Oxford,[9] May 18, 1742.

ENSIGNS.
Henry Reddish,[10] May 19, 1742.
William Hamilton,[11] May 20, 1742.
Anthony Nicholson,[12] May 21, 1742.
John Norris,[13] May 22, 1742.
Baston Bindon,[14] May 23, 1742.
John Corneille,[15] May 24, 1742.
Charles Edmonstone,[16] May 25, 1742.
John Wise,[17] May 26, 1742.
David Maitland,[18] May 27, 1742.

Additional.

James Tynte Chaigneau,[19] Nov. 6, 1745.
William Cashell,[20] Nov. 6, 1745.

Ulysses Fitzmaurice,[21] Nov. 6, 1745.
Joseph Preston.[22]

CHAPTER VIII.

1752. (Record Office.)

COLONEL.
Alexander Irwin.[23]

LT.-COLONEL.
Charles Whitfourd,[24] Sept. 1751.

MAJOR.
John Irwin,[25] Feb. 1751.

CAPTAINS.
Gilbert Keene,[26] June 1739.
Chudleigh Dering,[27] April 1749.
Michael Mitchell,[28] June 1749.
William Eustace,[29] Jan. 1750,
Theophilus Clements,[30] June 1750.
George Rawson,[31] Jan. 1750?

---

[1] Lt. July 1745.   Capt.-Lt. 1756.   Capt. in 21st Foot May 8, 1758.
[2] Lt. Oct. 1745.   Fort Major Kinsale Sept., 1754.
[3] O.B. 1752.   [4] O.B. 1752.
[5] Capt. April, 1749.   Res. March, 1756.
[6] O.B. 1752.   [7] O.B. 1752.   [8] O.B. 1752.   [9] O.B. 1752.
[10] O.B. 1752.   Capt. in Fifth from half-pay Invalids Oct., 10, 1755.
[11] O.B. 1752.   [12] O.B. 1752.   [13] O.B. 1752.   [14] O.B. 1752.
[15] Possibly son of Capt. John Corneille.   O.B. 1752.
[16] O.B. 1752.
[17] 2nd Lt. Jan., 1746.   Exd. Jan., 1755.
[18] O.B. 1752.   [19] O.B. 1752.   [20] O.B. 1752.
[21] Lt. Feb. 1751.   Capt. 2nd Batt. 36th Foot Aug., 1756; with John Irwin in 74th Foot the same year.
[22] O.B. 1752.
[23] *Ante.*
[24] Whitefourd, Col. Nov. 1752.
[25] See *ante.*   [26] See *ante.*   [27] See *ante.*   [28] See *ante.*
[29] Ens. May, 1744.   Lt. Oct., 7145.   Capt.-Major Nov. 17, 1757.   Lt.-Col. Oct. 13, 1761.
[30] Ens. May, 1742.   Lt. Oct., 1745.   Res. 1756.   Capt. 83rd Foot Feb. 1762.
[31] Of Belmont House, co. Wicklow.   Member for Armagh in three successive Parliaments.   Married Mary, daughter of John Bowes Benson, Esq.   Ens. July, 1745.   Lt. April, 1749.   Capt. Feb. 9, 1751.   Major May, 1762.   Lt.-Col. Oct., 1766.

1752 AND 1761

CAPTAINS (continued).
James Nugent,[1] Jan. 1752.
Robert Cuthbertson,[2] Captain-Lieut., May 1739.

LIEUTENANTS.
Lambert Vanriel,[3] May 1739.
Henry Bourne,[4] May 1742.
Meade Vanlewen,[5] July 1745.
Lewis Nicola,[6] Oct. 1745.
John Gifford Craven,[7] April 1749.
Thomas Pearce,[8] June 1749.
Edward Duval,[9] Jan. 1750.
Charles Heathcote,[10] Jan. 1751.
Ulysses Fitzmaurice,[11] Feb. 1751.
Edward Barry, Jan. 24, 1752.
John Wyse,[12] 2nd Lieut., Jan. 1746.

ENSIGNS.
Peter McLaughlin,[13] Oct. 1745.
James Smith,[14] Nov. 1745.

Isaac Bickerstaff,[15] Nov. 1746.
Bennett Cuthbertson,[16] April 1749.
Bernard Higgons,[17] June 1749.
Whitshed Keene,[18] June 1750.
William Reade,[19] Feb. 1751.
Percival Purcel,[20] Jan. 1752.

CHAPLAIN.
Abraham Sandys,[21] April 1750.

ADJUTANT.
Lambert Vanriel, April 1749.

SURGEON.
Hans Bernard Montgomery, Nov. 1747.

QUARTER-MASTER.
James Smith, May 1755.

CHAPTER XII.
1761.

COLONEL.
Studholm Hodgson, May 30, 1756.

LT.-COLONEL.
Thomas Marley,[22] March 24, 1761.

MAJOR.
William Eustace,[23] Nov. 17, 1757.

CAPTAINS.
George Rawson,[24] Feb. 9, 1751.
James Nugent,[25] Jan. 24, 1752.
William Langton,[26] Oct. 1755.

---

[1] Ens. April, 1749. Lt. June, 1750. Capt. Jan. 24, 1752.
[2] See *ante*. [3] See *ante*. [4] See *ante*. [5] See *ante*. [6] See *ante*.
[7] Capt. 2nd Batt. 37th Foot Aug., 1756. Ens. Dec., 1745.
[8] Ens. Oct., 1745. Capt. 130th Coy. of Marines April, 1757.
[9] Oct. 1745. Capt. March, 1756.
[10] Ens. Oct., 1745. Capt. March, 1754. Major 94th Foot (Vaughan) May 1, 1760. S. in America.
[11] See *ante*. [12] Or Wise. See *ante*.
[13] Ens. Ind. Coy. Bristol Nov., 1755.
[14] Ret. May, 1756.
[15] Res. and placed on Ensign's half-pay Aug., 1755.
[16] Lt. Oct., 1755. Adjt. Aug., 1755. Capt.-Lt. Oct., 1766. Capt. Sept., 1767.
[17] Lt. March, 1757. Capt.-Lt. May, 1758.
[18] Lt. Oct., 1755. Capt. March, 1756. Ret. April, 1768. Born in Ireland. Married Hon. Eliza. Legge, daughter of Vis. Lewisham and sister to 2nd Earl of Dartmouth. M.P. from 1768 to 1818. Father of House of Commons, 1780. Surveyor-General of Board of Works, 1782. One of Lords of Admiralty, etc., etc. Dd. April, 1822, at Hawthorn Hill, Berks.
[19] Lt. in Ind. Coy. Bristol Oct., 1755.
[20] Lt. Sept., 1754. [21] Dd. June, 1757.
[22] Capt. in 23rd Foot April 25, 1751. Major in 23rd Foot Sept., 1756. Dd. 1766(?).
[23] *Ante*. [24] *Ante*. [25] *Ante*.
[26] Ens. Sept. 3, 1734. O.R. 1762.

LIEUTENANTS (*continued*).
J. G. Battier,[1] Dec. 1769.
J. Gore,[2] Aug. 1770.

ENSIGNS.
John Cox, Oct. 1766.
William Battier,[3] Feb. 1767.
Thomas Baker,[4] Sept. 1767.
William Cox,[5] Oct. 1768.

Henry Hickman, May 1769.
Robert Pratt,[6] Aug. 1770.
Benson Lawton, Aug. 1770.

CHAPLAIN.
John Russ,[7] July 1762.

SURGEON.
Richard Procter, 1761.

For Chapter XVI. see following page.

CHAPTER XVIII.
1781.

COLONEL.
Lord Percy, Nov. 7, 1768.

LT.-COLONEL.
George Harris,[8] Nov. 29, 1780.

MAJOR.
John Gaspard Battier,[9] Nov. 29, 1780.

CAPTAINS.
John Smith, May 25, 1772.
Benjamin Baker,[10] June 25, 1775.
Anthony Haslam,[11] Aug. 15, 1775.
Thomas Baker,[12] Nov. 22, 1775.
John Westroppe, May 24, 1776.

William Cox, Oct. 7, 1777.
Thomas Hawkshaw,[13] Nov. 8, 1777.
Charles Stephenson,[14] Oct. 28, 1778.
Benjamin Hill,[15] Jan. 21, 1779.
Richard Croker,[16] Captain-Lt., Nov. 29, 1780.

LIEUTENANTS.
Robert Pratt,[17] March 16, 1774.
Joshua Paul Minchin,[18] June 25, 1775.
Henry King,[19] April 15, 1776.
Thomas Bassett,[20] May 31, 1777.
Thomas Lyttleton,[21] Oct. 7, 1777.

---

[1] Ens. Aug., 1765. Lt. Dec., 1769. Capt. Nov. 28, 1771. Major Nov. 20, 1780.
[2] Ens. April, 1767. Lt. Aug., 1770. Capt. March 14, 1772.
[3] Ens. 1767. Lt. July 25, 1771. Capt. 1774.
[4] Ens. 1767. Lt. Sept. 1, 1771. Capt. Nov. 22, 1775.
[5] Ens Oct., 1768. Lt. Nov. 28, 1771. Capt. Oct. 7, 1777.
[6] Ens. Aug., 1770. Lt. March 16, 1774. Capt.-Lt. April 16, 1783. Capt.-Major Sept. 1, 1795. Father of C. Pratt ?
[7] S. of John Russ of Evercreech, Somerset ; of Oriel Coll., Oxford. Matriculated May 13, 1740, aged 18. B.A., Corpus Christi Coll., 1744. M.A. 1749.
[8] See *ante*.   [9] See *ante*.   [10] See *ante*.
[11] From half-pay 83rd Foot. Bt.-Major July 23, 1772. Bt.-Lt.-Col. Aug. 29, 1777
[12] Married Miss Harriet Middleton in 1770. See *ante*.
[13] Lt. Nov. 28, 1771. Capt. Nov. 8, 1777.
[14] Capt. Oct. 28, 1778. Major July 16, 1794. Lt.-Col. Sept. 1, 1795. Col. of York Rangers Sept. 25, 1803. Major.-Genl. July 25, 1810. Lt.-Genl. Jan. 4, 1814. Dd. June 22, 1828, in London.
[15] Lt. July 12, 1775. Adjt. Nov. 11, 1775. O.R. 1785.
[16] Lt. April 1, 1773. Capt.-Lt. Nov., 1780. Half-pay, 1783.
[17] See *ante*.   [18] Ens. March, 1772. Lt. June 25, 1775.
[19] Capt.-Lt. July, 1794. Dd. at Bridgenorth Jan., 1829. Served 31 years in 5th Regt. Son of Henry King, of Belleek, co. Mayo, who married daughter of P. A. Gore, nephew of 1st Earl of Kingston.
[20] Ens. June, 1775. Lt. May, 1777. Capt. 1787. Major Dec., 1800.
[21] Lt. Oct., 1777. Capt. Sept. 1, 1781.

CAPTAIN JOHN SMITH'S COMPANY LIST

March 2nd, 1778.

Companies.	Ensigns.	Sergeants and Corporals.	Drummers.
Lord Percy	Capt.-Lieut. Hawkshaw Ensign Cotter	Herbert Heelas Guy	Stacy Moncroft Jackson	Dowran.
Lieut.-Col. W. Medows	Lieut. Hill Ensign Sutherland	Cowper Leslie Rapenuis	Barker Elridge Woosey	Cooper. Leslie.
Major Harris	Lieut. England Ensign Thomas	Garnock Cramer Hartshorn	Hickey Clarke Tayler	Lindsey. Burn.
Capt. J. Gore (Grenadiers)	Lieut. Pratt Lieut. Minchin	Kirk Allen Crookshanks	Kirby Richardson Bennett	M'Carron. Brand. Bennet.
Capt. J. Battier (Light Infantry)	Lieut. Wilson Lieut. Basset	Lamb Canfield Martin.	Benniman Rowbinson Large.	Barnes.
Capt. J. Smith	Lieut. Patrick Ensign Hickson	Smith Ramsey Cheene	Steevens Needham Allen	Ramsey. Cheene.
Capt. W. Battier	Lieut. T. Harris Ensign Charlton	Story Hughes Howard	Babington Milward Hamilton	Duggan. Phillips.
Capt. B. Baker	Lieut. Croker Ensign Burnett	Garnock Pearce Banks	Hawthorn Markett Markett	Buckley.
Capt. Westropp	Lieut. Littleton Ensign Currey	Green Scott Eustace	Spencer Cole Power	D. W. Durward. P. W. Durward.
Capt. Coxe	Lieut. Andrewes Ensign Comb	Crome Cranley Frazer	James Cadder Criswil	Hogan.

The original of this list, apparently written by Captain John Smith, is among the papers of Sir David William Smith.

474   APPENDIX I

LIEUTENANTS (*continued*).
Edward Cotton,[1] Oct. 29, 1778.
Edward Charleton,[2] Jan. 21, 1779.
Henry Sutherland,[3] Feb. 6, 1779.
William Thomas, Feb. 19, 1779.
Robert Hickson,[4] Aug. 26, 1780.
John Hamilton,[5] Sept. 8, 1780.
Wingfield Halton,[6] Nov. 29, 1780.
Roger Hall Sheaffe,[7] Dec. 27, 1780.

ENSIGNS.
Thomas Nilsbit,[8] Dec. 27, 1778.
Zach. Scrope Shrapmel,[9] June 21, 1779.
Robert Hill,[10] Feb. 8, 1779.
King Combe,[11] March 3, 1779.

David William Smith,[12] Sept. 8, 1779.
William Meredith,[13] May 20, 1780.
Henry Darling,[14] July 8, 1780.
Edward Aldgood,[15] Aug. 26, 1780.
Stephen Watson,[16] Nov. 29, 1780.
Thomas Allison,[17] Dec. 27, 1780.

CHAPLAIN.
John Russ, July 1762.

ADJUTANT.
George Hill,[18] Oct. 25, 1780.

SURGEON.
St. John Neill, Nov. 22, 1780.

QUARTER-MASTER.
Green.

CHAPTER XIX.
1794.

COLONEL.
Alured Clarke,[19] Oct. 1794.

LT.-COLONEL.
John Smith,[20] July 1794.

MAJOR.
Charles Stephenson,[21] July 1794.

CAPTAINS.
Robert Pratt,[22] April 1783.
Edward Charlton,[23] July 1783.

---

[1] Or Cotter. Ens. Jan., 1777. Lt. Oct., 1778.
[2] Ens. July, 1777. Capt. July, 1783. Major 1795. Half-pay 111th Foot 1797.
[3] Or Hugh. Ens. Oct. 6, 1776.   [4] Ens. Nov., 1776.
[5] Ens. Aug. 31, 1776. Lt. Sept., 1780. Capt. Oct. 18, 1793. O.B. 1799.   [6] Ens. Dec. 5, 1778.
[7] Ens. May 1, 1778. Lt. Dec., 1780. Capt. May 6, 1795. O.B. 1799.
[8] Or Nesbitt. Ens. Dec., 1778. Lt. July 16, 1781.
[9] Ens. Jan. 21, 1779. Lt. July, 1781.
[10] Robert George Hill? Ens. Feb. 6, 1779. Lt. Oct. 26, 1786.
[11] James King Combe? March 3, 1779. Lt. Sept 1, 1781.
[12] Ens. Sept., 1779. Lt. Dec. 29, 1781. Capt. Sept. 2, 1795.
[13] Ens. May., 1780.
[14] Ens. July, 1780. Lt. Sept., 1783.   [15] Ens. Aug., 1780.
[16] Ens. Nov., 1780. Lt. Dec., 1783.
[17] Ens. Dec., 1780. Lt. Aug. 11, 1783. Capt. Sept. 3, 1795.
[18] This officer d. in Holland, Walcheren Exp., Nov. 30, 1809. "We . . . have to regret the loss of the late Major George Hill of 85th Regt. His . . . zeal as a soldier and integrity as a man endeared him to all honourable men of his profession. . . . He served his King and Country for 38 years, and fought in all parts of the globe," etc. (*Morning Post*).
[19] Ens. 50th Regt. 1755. Lt. 1760. Capt. in 5th 1776. Major in 54th 1771. Lt.-Col. 7th 1777. Col. 1781. Major-Genl. 1790. Col. of 5th 1794. Took Cape of Good Hope 1795. Acting Lt.-Gen. East Indies 1796. Col. of 7th 1861. General 1802. Dd. Field-Marshal, Sept., 1832.
[20] See *ante*. Dd. as Com. of Fort Niagara Nov. 19, 1795.
[21] See *ante*.   [22] See *ante*.   [23] See *ante*.

CAPTAINS (continued).
Walter Partridge,[1] Nov. 1785.
Joseph Bunburby,[2] Dec. 1785.
Thomas Bassett,[3] Feb. 1787.
Augustus Fitzgerald, July 1791.
John Hamilton,[4] Oct. 1793.
Henry King,[5] Capt.-Lieutenant, July 1794.

LIEUTENANTS.
R. H. Sheaffe,[6] Dec. 1780.
D. W. Smith,[7] Dec. 1781.
Thomas Allison,[8] Aug. 1783.
Henry Darling,[9] Sept. 1783.
R. Ross Lewin,[10] May 1784.
Prideaux Selby,[11] Feb. 1785.
George Hill,[12] Oct. 1786.
Benjamin Roche, July 1789.
P. Falkiner,[13] Oct. 1789.
J. M. R. D. Mason,[14] Oct. 1793.
J. Matthew Hamilton,[15] July 1794.

ENSIGNS.
W. Gainfort,[16] May 1790.
T. Oushen,[17] July 1791.
P. Bellew,[18] Jan. 1794.
C. Pratt,[19] April 1794.
W. Bernard, June 1794.
Abraham Aug. Nunn,[20] July 1794.
Robert Bennitt,[21] Oct. 1794.

CHAPLAIN.
G. Blacker, June 1793.

ADJUTANT.
G. Hill, Oct. 1780.

QUARTER-MASTER.
Daniel Green, Aug. 1780.

SURGEON.
W. Holmes, March 1787.

CHAPTER XXI.
1st Fifth, 1799.[22]

COLONEL.
Sir Alured Clarke.

LT.-COLONELS.
Charles Stephenson,[23] Sept. 1795.
Hon. E. Bligh,[24] Aug. 5, 1799.

MAJORS.
Humphrey Davie,[25] July 1796.
William Partridge,[26] Major.

CAPTAINS.
Thomas Bassett,[27] Feb. 1797.

---

[1] Capt. Nov. 23, 1785. Major Aug. 5, 1799.
[2] Capt. Dec. 24, 1785. O.B. 1799.   [3] See *ante.*
[4] See *ante.*   [5] See *ante.*   [6] See *ante.*   [7] See *ante.*
[8] See *ante.*   [9] See *ante.*
[10] Ens. July 16, 1781. Lt. May, 1784. Capt. Sept. 4, 1795.
[11] Ens. Dec. 21, 1781. Lt. Feb., 1785.   [12] See *ante.*
[13] Ens. Sept. 27, 1783. Lt. July, 1789.
[14] Ens. May 31, 1784. Lt. Oct., 1793. O.B. 1799.
[15] Ens. Oct. 26, 1786. Lt. July, 1794. Dd. Oct., 1799.
[16] Or Gainford. Ens. May 28, 1790. Lt. Sept. 2, 1795. Capt. Aug. 13, 1799.
[17] (John Ussher) Ens. July, 1791. Lt. May 6, 1795.
[18] 5th son of Sir Pat. Bellew, 5th Bart. of Bearmouth? Ens. Jan., 1794. Lt. July, 1795. Capt. Nov. 14, 1796. Major Aug. 5, 1799.
[19] Son of R. Pratt? Ens. April, 1794. Lt. Sept., 1796. Capt. Feb. 28, 1798. Major Aug. 24, 1804. Lt.-Col. March 25, 1808. K.C.B., etc.
[20] Ens. July, 1794. Lt. Sept. 4, 1795.
[21] Ens. Oct., 1794. Lt. Sept. 5, 1795.
[22] "The 5th regiment had not long returned from the Canadas, between 200 and 300 strong; . . . they were speedily filled up to two overflowing battalions by volunteers from the militia; the officers in many instances accompanying the men" ("Notes and Recollections," p. 30).
[23] See *ante.*
[24] From half-pay Lt.-Col. 107th Foot. A.D.C. to King William. Bt.-Col. Jan., 1798. Maj.-Gen. 1805. Lt.-Gen. 1811.
[25] 2nd son of Sir J. Davie, 7th Bart., b. 1775; succeeded his nephew 1824. D.s.p. 1846.   [26] See *ante.*   [27] See *ante.*

APPENDIX I

CAPTAINS (*continued*).
John Guitton,[1] Nov. 1796.
Thomas Jones,[2] March 1798.
George Hill.[3]
R. Featherstonehaugh.
Stewart Henry Drury, Aug. 1799.
Jacob Tonson, Aug. 1799.
M. Alves.
W. Hampton,[4] Captain-Lieutenant, Sept. 1799.

LIEUTENANTS.
Daniel Green,[5] March 19, 1796.
Allan McLean,[6] June 23, 1796.
A. Robertson,[7] Dec. 7, 1796.
Richard Burke Webber, Dec. 14, 1796.
H. Ridge,[8] Jan. 1797.
N. Philips,[9] June 1797.
Fred. Chas. Hamilton, Jan. 1798.
Fras. Plowden, Oct. 1798.
George Clarke,[10] Aug. 1799.
James Stanley Goddard,[11] Aug. 1799.
John McKenzie,[12] Aug. 1799.

Henry Losack,[13] Sept. 1799.
John Hull (Hall?), Oct. 1799.
John Adams,[14] Oct. 1799.
Peter Sanders (Saunders?), Oct. 1799.

ENSIGNS.
Thos. Kenagh.[15]
Edward Burke,[16] Aug. 1799.
J. Gabel, Aug. 1799.
John McPherson,[17] Sept. 1799.
E. Byrne, Oct. 1799.
John Hamilton,[18] Nov. 1799.

QUARTER-MASTER.
John Harrison, June 1799.

SURGEON.
W. Fergusson.[19]

PAY-MASTER.
John Hamilton, March 1798.

AGENT.
Meyrick.

---

[1] Lt. Feb., 1796.
[2] Ens. March, 1796. Lt. Dec., 1796.
[3] See *ante*.
[4] Capt. Sept., 1799.
[5] Ens. Aug., 1795.
[6] John Allan McLean? Ens. Dec., 1795. Lt. June, 1796. (Capt., Aug. 7, 1799, in 2nd Fifth?)
[7] Ens. Dec., 1795. Lt. Dec., 1796. Capt. Aug., 1803. As Captain sent home from Madeira in Buenos Ayres Expedition in consequence of a complaint against him (Morley).
[8] Ens. Jan. 24, 1796. Lt. Jan. 12, 1797. Capt. Oct. 9, 1803. Major March 25, 1808. Bt.-Lt.-Col. 1812. Killed at Badajos 1812.
[9] Capt. Aug., 1804.
[10] Ens. Sept., 1797. Lt. Aug., 1799. Capt. Aug., 1804. Dd. April, 1821, Fort Nevis, Antigua.
[11] Ens. Dec., 1797. Lt. Aug., 1799.
[12] John Davies McKenzie, s. of Lt.-Col. J. McKenzie. Ens. March, 1798. Lt. Aug., 1799. Capt. Aug., 1809.
[13] Capt. Sept., 1804.
[14] Capt. March, 1805.
[15] Lt. 1800. (Kinah?)
[16] Lt. June, 1803. (Theobald Burke, Capt. Aug., 1804.)
[17] Lt. March, 1805. Capt. July, 1812.
[18] Lt. May, 1803. Capt. Feb., 1808.
[19] B. at Ayr 1773. S. in 90th and 67th Foot. Probably joined Fifth in 1799, leaving in 1801 to go as Staff Surgeon with Baltic Expedition. S. in Peninsula; afterwards Ins.-Gen. of Hospitals. Dd. at Windsor 1843. Author of "Notes and Recollections," published 1846.

SECOND FIFTH, 1799

2nd Fifth, 1799.

COLONEL-COMMANDANT.
Sir George Hewitt.

LT.-COLONELS.
Thos. Talbot,[1] Sept. 1795.
John Lindsey, Aug. 6, 1799.

MAJORS.
Wm. Minett, Nov. 1796.
Jos. Bunbury,[2] 1799.

CAPTAINS.
Henry King,[3] July 1794.
Patrick Bellew,[4] Nov. 1796.
Chas. Pratt,[5] Feb. 1798.
Chas. Broke,[6] Feb. 1799.
John McLean,[7] Aug. 1799.
J. N. Hamilton,[8] Aug. 1799.
W. Gainfort,[9] Aug. 1799.
James Tyrill, Sept. 1799.
Hugh Hughes,[10] Nov. 1799.

LIEUTENANTS.
John Wolfe,[11] Dec. 1795.
William Frederick Courteney,[12] June 1796.
John Dennis,[13] June 1796.
Nicholas Hamilton,[14] Dec. 1796.
Boyle Octavius Loane, Dec. 1796.
E. J. R. Green, Oct. 1797.
Fras. D'Arcy Bawn,[15] June 1798.
Daniel Scott, Nov. 1798.
Martin Armstrong,[16] Aug. 1799.
Zobell,[17] Aug. 1799.
John Spearman,[18] Aug. 1799.
David Browne,[19] Aug. 1799.
Chas. Parker, Sept. 1799.
Thos. Conway, 1799.
Ed. O'Bourke, Oct. 1799.
Fras. Nicholas Rossi, Oct. 1799.
John Bridge, Oct. 1799.
Lewis Muller, Oct. 1799.
Dormer Vincent, Oct. 1799.
Henry Lodge, Nov. 1799.

ENSIGNS.
F. A. Clark, Aug. 1799.
C. S. Crawfe.
P. O'Keefe Boulger, Aug. 1799.
H. Worsley.

---

[1] 4th son of Richard Talbot, of Malahide, and Margaret, daughter of James O'Reilly, 1st Baroness Talbot of Malahide. B. before 1776. Dd. Feb. 7, 1853, in Canada. A Colonel in the Army and Member of Assembly of Upper Canada.
[2] See *ante*.
[3] See *ante*.
[4] See *ante*.
[5] See *ante*.
[6] Chas. E. Broke ? Lt. Dec., 1796. Capt. Feb., 1799. Major Feb., 1808.
[7] See John Allan McLean in 1st Fifth, 1799.
[8] See *ante*.
[9] See *ante*.
[10] Temp. rank only.
[11] Cap.-Lt. Dec. 10, 1800.
[12] Ens. Nov., 1795. Lt. June, 1796.
[13] Ens. Dec., 1795. Lt. June, 1796. Capt. 1806 ? In Aug., 1807, Jane, widow of Capt. Dennis, was granted a pension of £40 per annum.
[14] Ens. June, 1796. Lt. Dec., 1796. Capt. June, 1803. Major Jan., 1812. *Vice* Ridge. Dd. a Major-General and K.C.B. 1859.
[15] Capt. July 30, 1800.
[16] Ens. Dec., 1796. Capt. Aug., 1804. Dd. at Steyning Barracks, Feb., 1809, " Much regretted."
[17] Ens. Feb., 1797.
[18] Ens. March, 1798. Capt. April, 1808. Gazette of Jan., 1819. Exchanged with Capt. Johnson, h.p.
[19] Ens. March, 1798.

ENSIGNS (*continued*).
Wm. Bowskill,[1] Aug. 1799.
A. Dubourdieu.[2]
Thos. Lightfoot.[3]
J. Simcocks,[4] Aug. 1799.
Hutchinson,[5] Oct. 1799.
John Vale.
Macdonald, Oct. 1799.
R. Wm. Alexander, Oct. 1799.
W. Swayne, Nov. 1799.

ADJUTANT.
Keen, Sept. 23, 1799.

QUARTER-MASTER.
Barr, Aug. 23, 1799.

PAY MASTER.
Robert Pratt.[6]

SURGEON.
James Curtis, Aug. 23, 1799.

CHAPTER XXIX.
2nd *Fifth*, 1812.

COLONEL.
Richard England, April 1800.

LT.-COLONEL.
Henry King,[7] Jan. 16, 1809.

MAJORS.
Henry Ridge,[8] March 1808.
John Grey,[9] June 1811.

CAPTAINS.
Richard Bishop,[10] April 1808.
John Spearman,[11] April 1808.
Arthur Dubourdieu,[12] June 1808.
Richard Yate, Nov. 1808.
G. D. McKenzie,[13] Aug. 1809.

John Bent,[14] Aug. 1809.
Charles Louis Ramus, Sept. 1809.
Ed. Drury,[15] Oct. 1809.
Michael Doyle,[16] Feb. 1810.
Alexander MacDougal,[17] March 1810.
Richard Carrol, April 1810.
David England Johnson,[18] March 1812.

LIEUTENANTS.
Henry Edward O'Dell,[19] March 1808.
John Masterman Pennington,[20] March, 1808.
John Holland McKenzie,[21] April 1808.

---

[1] Lt. Sept., 1803.
[2] Lt. June, 1803. Capt. June, 1808.
[3] Lt. March 14, 1800.
[4] Lt. April, 1803. Capt. May, 1807. Major Dec., 1824.
[5] Lt. Sept., 1803.
[6] Lt. Nov. 21, 1805. Son of Capt.-Lt. Robert Pratt ?
[7] Joined Fifth as Major Aug., 1804. Lt.-Col. Jan., 1809. H.p. 1816. Lt.-Col. of 44th July, 1819.   [8] *Ante*.
[9] Sir John Grey, K.C.B., of Morwick in Northumberland, eldest son of Charles Grey, of Morwick. B. 1782. Married Rose, daughter and heiress of Capt. Grindall, R.N. Dd. a Lt.-Genl. Feb., 1856.
[10] Ens. Nov., 1803. Lt. Sept., 1805. Capt. April, 1808. Commanded 2nd Fifth after Ridge's death until King rejoined. In temporary command at Salamanca. Bt.-Major 1812.   [11] *Ante*.
[12] B. Annahilt Glebe, co. Down, Dec., 1781. Ens. Dec., 1800. Lt. June, 1803. Ret. as Major 1830. Father of Ens. John D., who joined Fifth 1828.   [13] *Ante*.
[14] Ens. Oct., 1804. Lt. Sept., 1805. See Bateman, 1st Fifth. Captain and Major in 1st Fifth. Left regiment in 1831 on succeeding to a property. His son, Rev. J. O. Bent, was afterwards Hon. Chap. to 5th. See St. G. G. Nov. 1896.
[15] Lt. Aug., 1804.   [16] Ens. July, 1805. Lt. July, 1806.
[17] From Capt. 72nd Foot. K. at Ciudad Rodrigo.
[18] Ens. Feb., 1804. Lt. Dec., 1804. See Spearman, 1799, 2nd Fifth.
[19] Ens. July, 1806. Lt. March, 1808. Capt. Jan., 1822.
[20] Ens. Feb., 1807. Afterwards P.M. of 48th ?   [21] Ens. May, 1807.

1812

LIEUTENANTS (continued).
Samuel Belton,[1] May 1808.
John Newman Wylde, Sept. 1808.
Henry Peistly L'Estrange,[2] Dec. 1808.
James Haggarty, Sept. 1809.
John Pennington, Feb. 1810.
Christopher Hilliard,[3] Feb. 1810.
J. Kershaw, May 1810.
Rowland Pennington, May 1811.
Wm. V. Fitzgerald, Aug. 1811.
John Boyd, Aug. 1811.
Edward Fairtlough, Oct. 1811.
John Dennis,[4] Nov. 1811.

ENSIGNS.
R. Wallace,[5] April 1809.
A. M. Ashford, April 1809.
Thos. Canch,[6] Sept. 1809.

W. Randolph Hopkins,[7] June 1810.
L. Ford,[8] June 1810.
R. Nicholson,[9] Dec. 1810.
J. H. R. Foote,[10] April 1811.

PAY-MASTER.
J. W. Graves,[11] April 1805.

ADJUTANT.
Wm. Coles,[12] Dec. 1812.

SURGEON.
Samuel Scott.

ASS.-SURGEON.
W. B. Lynn.

AGENTS.
Greenwood and Co.

CHAPTER XXX.
1st Fifth, 1812.

COLONEL.
Richard England, Aug. 1801.

LT.-COLONELS.
William Cockill,[13] Oct. 1802.
Sir Charles Pratt,[14] March 1808.

MAJORS.
Edward Copson, March 1805.
Thomas Eames,[15] May 1806.

CAPTAINS.
Nicholas Hamilton,[16] June 1803.
Henry Bird,[17] Sept. 1813.
George Clarke,[18] Aug. 1804.
James Culley,[19] Feb. 24, 1805.
John Adams,[20] March 1805.
Hon. Richard Murray, April 1805.

---

[1] Ens. July, 1806. Lt. May, 1808. Capt. Dec., 1824.
[2] Eldest son of Col. H. P. L'Estrange, of Moystown. Ed. at St. Malo. Joined Fifth as a boy. Resigned his commission on being passed over.
[3] Jan. 1819. Exchanged with Lt. Armstrong, h.p. rec. difference.
[4] Son of John Dennis. Lt. in 1799?
[5] Lt. July, 1812. Gazette of May, 1818. Lt. R. Wallace from h.p. Vice Hamer, exchanged, receiving difference.
[6] Lt. May, 1813. Capt. Nov., 1830. Carried Colours at Ciudad Rodrigo. Adjt. March, 1812.
[7] Lt. Oct., 1813. Carried the Colours at Ciudad Rodrigo. Retired 1816 on account of wounds, his leg having been shattered by grape-shot at Badajos. Dd. at Queenstown 1868, aged 76.
[8] Lt. Oct., 1813.
[9] Lt. Oct., 1813.
[10] (J. H. Rollefoote) Lt. Oct., 1814? [11] Lt. Jan., 1815.
[12] Or Colls. Q.M. Dec. 12, 1811. Promoted from ranks.
[13] Ens. 31st Foot 1782. S. 6 years at Gibraltar. Lt. in 2nd Foot 1792. Captain 95th Foot 1793. Major 105th Foot 1794. Lt.-Col. 1795. A.A.G. in Ireland. Lt.-Col. 46th Foot 1800. Lt.-Col. 5th Foot 1802. Brig.-Gen. in Guernsey 1804. Maj.-Gen. 1810. Lt.-Gen. 1814. [14] Ante.
[15] Ens. 103rd Foot 1793. Lt. 1794. Capt. 1795. 15th Foot 1795. Major 1801. 5th Foot 1805. S. in West Indies at taking of St. Lucia. Bt.-Lt.-Col. 1808. Bt.-Col. 1814. C.B. 1814. [16] Ante.
[17] Lt. 94th Foot 1794. Bt.-Major 1865. Major 5th Foot 1813. Bt.-Lt.-Col. 1812. Major 87th Foot 1816. Half-pay 1820
[18] Ante. [19] Major Jan., 1822.
[20] Ante. Killed Battle of Vittoria Jan. 21, 1813.

APPENDIX I

CAPTAINS (*continued*).
Robert Bateman,[1] March 1807.
J. S. Simcockes,[2] May 1807.
John Hamilton,[3] Feb. 1808.

LIEUTENANTS.
John M'Pherson,[4] March, 1805.
John Leach,[5] March 1805.
John Croasdaille,[6] July 11, 1805.
C. E. Bird,[7] July 1805.
T. S. Girling,[8] Sept. 1805.
Jonas Welch,[9] Sept. 1805.
Smith, Sept. 1805.
Thomas Higgins,[10] Sept. 1805.
Equino,[11] July 1806.
John Gunn, Oct. 1806.
Richard Croker, Jan. 1807.
Lawrence Dundas,[12] March 1807.
Charles Waldron, April 1807.
Henry Louis Hopkins,[13] May 1807.
Arthur England Johnson,[14] Aug. 1809.
William Bennett,[15] Sept. 1809.
Morgan Galbraith,[16] Sept. 1809.
Frederick George Drury,[17] Oct. 1809.

ENSIGNS.
M. G. Hamer,[18] April 1809.
S. H. Wilkinson,[19] April 1809.
W. Williams, April 1809.
J. B. Hamilton,[20] Sept. 1809.
William Pratt,[21] Sept. 1809.
C. E. Bolton,[22] Nov. 1809.
Archibald Campbell,[23] April 1810.
John Evans, May 1811.
William Harding,[24] July 1811.
J. Oughton, Feb. 1812.

PAY-MASTER.
J. Hamilton.

QUARTER-MASTER.
J. Watson,[25] Oct. 1811.

SURGEON.
John Lear, Dec. 1802.

ASS.-SURGEONS.
L. Tate, Aug. 1805.
G. Heathcote, July 1809.

---

[1] Gazette Jan., 1819. Exchanged with Capt. Bent, h.p.
[2] *Ante.*   [3] *Ante.*   [4] *Ante.*
[5] Capt. June 10, 1813.
[6] Ens. Aug., 1804. Lt. July, 1805. Capt. Aug. 5, 1813.
[7] C. Elias Birce?
[8] Capt. Oct., 1814.
[9] Thomas Walsh? Ens. Sept., 1804. Capt. April 19, 1821. *Vice* Clarke dd. Ret. Oct. 4, 1821.
[10] Killed Battle of Vittoria.
[11] Ens. June, 1805. Lt. July, 1806. Dd. West Indies.
[12] Ens. Sept., 1805.
[13] Killed at Orthes.
[14] Ens. Feb., 1807. Dd. Antigua April, 1821.
[15] Ens. Aug., 1807. Exchanged Jan. 1819 with Lt. Pollock, h.p., 43rd.
[16] Ens. Feb., 1808. Lt. Sept., 1809. Capt. April, 1825.
[17] Son of Capt. S. H. Drury? Ens. May, 1808.
[18] Ens. April, 1809.
[19] Ens. April, 1809.
[20] Lt. July 23, 1812.
[21] Lt. May, 1813.
[22] Killed Battle of Vittoria June 21, 1813.
[23] Lt. July, 1813. Fought at Albuera on staff of Portuguese Army (gold medal).
[24] Lt. Nov., 1813.
[25] Gazette May, 1818. Ens. H. Bishop to be Q.M. *Vice* Watson, h.p.

CHAPTER XXXIII.

1841.

COLONEL.
Sir Charles Colville,[1] 1835.

LT.-COLONEL.
William Sutherland,[2] 1825.

MAJORS.
David England Johnson,[3] 1837.
Joshua Simmonds Smith,[4] 1838.

CAPTAINS.
John Spence,[5] 1829.
Charles May, 1831.
Charles Wood, 1831.
Philip M. N. Guy,[6] 1837.
William Prime Jones, 1839.
Augustus Blair, 1839.
Fred. Adolphus Robinson, 1840.
John Woodward, 1840.
Theophilus Jenkins, 1804.
Fra. Rich. Pyner, 1840.

LIEUTENANTS.
John Dubourdieu,[7] 1834.
Charles M. Dawson, 1838.
Charles Durie, 1838.
Thomas Place, 1839.
H. F. F. Johnson,[8] 1839.
Hugh P. Baker, 1839.
William Seymour Scroggs, 1839.
W. H. Kebbel, 1839.

Louis H. Hamilton, 1840.
Charles Danvers Osborn, 1840.
William Woodgate, 1840.
H. W. de la Poer Beresford, 1840.
William John Campbell, 1840.

SECOND LIEUTENANTS.
William Chester Master,[9] 1839.
George Bryan Milman,[10] 1839.
Francis Sutton,[11] 1839.
John Wallace Colquitt, 1840.
J. A. Forrest, 1840.
Piers Geale, 1840.
Robertson Mackay, 1840.
Herbert Venn Stephen, 1840.

PAY-MASTER.
William Clune, 1840.

QUARTER-MASTER.
William Tiller,[12] 1825.

SURGEON.
Duncan Henderson,[13] 1826.

ASS.-SURGEONS.
J. A. D. M'Bean. 1834.
Hugh Mackay, 1837.

---

[1] Peninsular and Waterloo medals, G.C.B., G.C.H.
[2] Served in Ashantee War on Gold Coast in 1824.
[3] Expedition to Hanover 1805 (taken prisoner). Buenos Ayres 1806. Peninsula 1808-Jan. 1809 and June, 1809-1812. Wounded at Sabugal and Ciudad Rodrigo.
[4] Afterwards Major in 1st Dragoon Guards.
[5] Served against Ashantees 1822-25. Joined Fifth as Lieutenant, 1826.
[6] Ens. 1824. Lieut. 1828. Capt. 1837. Major 1847. Lt.-Col. 1850.
[7] Son of Major Dubourdieu, late of the Fifth. Ens. 1828. Lt. 1834. Capt. 1842.
[8] Afterwards 3rd Bart. of Bath and the grandson of Sir Henry Johnson, 1st Bart. and Colonel of the Fifth. B. 1819. Ens. 1836. Lt. 1839. Capt. 1843. Major 1849. Afterwards commanded forces in Jamaica. Dd. 1883.
[9] Lt. 1841. Capt. 1846. Major 1857. Lt.-Col. 1858.
[10] Lt. 1842. Capt. 1847. Major 1857. Bt.-Col. 1865, and placed on half-pay. Major of the Tower 1870. Colonel of Fifth 1899. K.C.B. 1905. B. 1823. Dd. in London Jan. 28, 1915.
[11] Afterwards exchanged into 6th Regt. Dragoons.
[12] Severely wounded Walcheren. Served in Pen. War 1812-14. Vittoria, Orthes, Nivelle, Toulouse.
[13] Served Peninsula, Salamanca and Badajos.

APPENDIX I

CHAPTER XXXIV.
1855.

COLONEL.
Sir John Grey,[1] K.C.B., May 1849.

LT.-COLONEL.
P. M. N. Guy,[2] May 1850.

MAJORS.
H. F. F. Johnson,[3] Oct. 1849.
W. C. Kennedy,[4] May 1850.

CAPTAINS.
J. E Simmons,[5] July 1841.
W. G. Master,[6] Dec 1846.
G. B. Milman,[7] Jan. 1847.
Griffin Nicholas,[8] July 1847.
J. W. Colquitt,[9] July 1847.

F. William L'Estrange,[10] March 1851.
William Lyons,[11] March 1852.
A. W. Palmer,[12] May 1853.
J. S. Hogge,[13] June 1853.
G. S. Home,[14] Oct. 1853.
A. E. Johnson,[15] June 1854.
James Baillie,[16] Oct. 1848.

LIEUTENANTS.
J. H. Chads, May 1844.
F. H. Pender,[17] July 1847.
G. J. Stewart, Aug. 1849.
A. E. Ross,[18] Dec. 1849.
John Flood, May 1850.
William H. P. Meara,[19] Dec. 1851.
J. W. D. Adair,[20] Jan. 1852.
William Leach,[21] May 1853.

---

[1] S. in Peninsula as Major in 2nd Fifth. Also saw service in India. Lt.-Genl. Nov., 1851.
[2] *Ante.*
[3] *Ante.*
[4] Joined Fifth as Captain Jan., 1842, from 2nd W.I. Regt. (Ens. Oct., 1831). Lt.-Col. Aug., 1857. Colonel Dec., 1858.
[5] From 2nd Foot. Served in Afghanistan, etc. Storm and capture of Ghuznee and Khelat. Twice wounded (Ens. Jan., 1832). Killed Lucknow Sept., 1857.
[6] *Ante.*
[7] *Ante.*
[8] Ens. April, 1834. Capt. Dec., 1845. Joined Fifth 1847. Major Oct., 1856. Retd. on full pay. Capt. Gentleman-at-Arms in 1861.
[9] *Ante.*
[10] 2nd Lt. Dec., 1842. Lt. 1846. Capt. 1851. Mortally wounded, Lucknow, Sept., 1857. See family of L'Estrange, of Moystown.
[11] (Ens. 1841.) Joined as Lt. 1843. Capt. 1852. Major 1857. Lt.-Col. 1864. Afterwards A.A.G. in Canada.
[12] 2nd Lt. 1843. Lt. 1846. Capt. 1853.
[13] 2nd Lt. June, 1843. Lt. 1846. Capt. 1853. Major 1854.
[14] 2nd Lt. Feb., 1844. Lt. 1846. Capt. 1853.
[15] 2nd Lt. 1844. Lt. 1846. Capt. 1854. Mortally wounded, Lucknow, Sept., 1857.
[16] 2nd Lt. 1834. Lt. 1839. Capt. 1848. Company in Fifth 1854. Half-pay April, 1859. Major 1860.
[17] 2nd Lt. 1846. Lt. 1847. Capt. 1856. Major of 25th Foot 1866.
[18] Ens. 1846. Lt. 1849. Capt. 1857. Major 1869.
[19] 2nd Lt. 1846. Lt. 1851. Capt. 1857. Bt.-Major for services in Mutiny. Mentioned.
[20] 2nd Lt. 1846. Lt. 1852. Joined Fifth 1853. Adjt. 1854. Capt. 1857. Served in Mutiny, noted for gallantry. Retd. as Major 1862.
[21] 2nd Lt. 1847. Lt. 1853. Capt. 1857. Served in Mutiny Campaign 1858-9. Afterwards exchanged into 46th Foot.

1855 AND 1900 483

LIEUTENANTS (continued).
L. R. Parry,[1] June 1853.
William M. Carter,[2] Oct 1853.
E. R. Simmons,[3] Jan. 1854.
R. H. Hardy,[4] June 1854.
G. H. J. M. Chapman,[5] June 1854.
F. J. Mylius,[6] Aug. 1854.
J. R. Carlisle,[7] Oct. 1854.
Robert Moore,[8] Oct. 1853.
J. C. Brown,[9] Dec. 1853.
John Creagh,[10] April 1854.

ENSIGNS.
G. E. Massy,[11] June 1854.
E. F. Haigh,[12] July 1854.

Oliver Colt, Aug. 1854.
Horatio Walpole,[13] Sept. 1854.
Philip Fitzroy,[14] Oct. 1854.
E. S. Lewis, May 1855.
R. H. Fenessy, June 1855.
J. B. Barker,[15] June 1855.
E. J. Oldfield,[16] Aug. 1855.

PAY-MASTER.
F. B. Forster,[17] Dec. 1851.

QUARTER-MASTER.
Robert Webster, July 1847.

SURGEON.
E. S. Docker, May 1851.

CHAPTER XXXIX.

January, 1900.

1st and 2nd Battalions Northumberland Fusiliers.

* Sailed with 1st Bt. Sept. 16, 1899.
† Sailed with 2nd Bt. Nov. 4, 1899.

LT.-COLONELS.
(1) C. G. C. Money,* C.B., Nov. 1897.
(2) G. L. R. Pennington, Jan. 1898.

MAJORS (2) (Second in Command).
(2) G. Frend,† Jan. 1, 1898; April 22, 1893.

(1) Hon. C. Lambton,* D.S.O., Jan. 21, 1898; Jan. 21, 1895.

MAJORS (6).

d. (2) T. G. L. H. Armstrong, Jan. 27, 1895.
W. E. Sturges,† Jan. 30, 1895.

---

[1] Ens. 1847. Lt. 1853.
[2] 2nd Lt. 1848. Lt. 1853. Mortally wounded, Lucknow, 1857.
[3] 2nd Lt. 1849. Lt. 1854.
[4] 2nd Lt. 1849. Lt. 1854.
[5] 2nd Lt. 1851. Lt. 1854. Capt. 1857. Major 1879.
[6] 2nd Lt. 1853. Lt. 1854. Capt. 1858.
[7] 2nd Lt. 1853. Lt. 1854. Capt. 1858.
[8] Lt. 1855. Capt. 1858.
[9] Lt. 1855. Dd. Alum Bagh 1858. Mentioned for gallantry.
[10] Lt. 1856. Capt. 1860. Ret. as Lt.-Col. Served throughout Mutiny.
[11] Lt. 1856. Capt. 1864. Ret. as Lt.-Col. Served in Mutiny.
[12] Lt. and Adjt. 1857. Killed, Alum Bagh, Sept., 1857.
[13] Lt. 1857. Capt. 1858. Served throughout Mutiny Campaign.
[14] Lt. 1857. Capt. 1858. Major 1880. Lt.-Col. 1885. Served throughout Mutiny.
[15] Lt. 1857. Capt. 1858. Exchanged into 75th Foot. Served with Fifth during Mutiny.
[16] Lt. 1857. Capt. 1859. Major 1880. Retd. as Major-Gen. Served Mutiny 1857-9.
[17] Ens. 1846. Lt. 1848. Hon. Major 1861.

APPENDIX I

(2) D. S. Stewart,† Sept. 23, 1896.
(1) E. W. Dashwood,* Nov. 23, 1897.
W. H. Sitwell, p.s.c., Jan. 21, 1898; (spec. serv. South Africa), Bt.-Lt.-Col., Nov. 16, 1898.
St. G. C. Henry, July 5, 1899; (spec. serv. South Africa, Bt.-Lt.-Col., July 6, 1899.

CAPTAINS (12).

ℓ (2) J. F. Riddell,† Nov. 18, 1889.
(1) C. H. L. James,* June 15, 1891.
s. E. S. Heard, p.s.c., May 11, 1892.
(2) W. A. Wilmott,† May 23, 1892.
(1) D. Sapte,* Oct. 24, 1892.
(2) E. W. Fletcher,† Dec. 15, 1892.
(2) F. G. Casson,† Oct. 17, 1894.
P. S. Wilkinson, p.s.c., Oct. 27, 1894; (West African Front. Force), Bt.-Major, July 8, 1899.
m. G. F. T. Leather (3rd Bt. North. Fus.), Jan. 21, 1895.
A. W. C. Booth,† (Acting Adjutant), Jan. 21, 1895; Bt.-Major, July 8, 1899.
(1) A. F. Dawkins, Jan. 27, 1895.
v. A. E. L. Crofton, (3) Vol. Bt. North. Fus.), May 15, 1895.
(2) Hon. M. O'Brien,† Dec. 20, 1895.
(1) R. H. Isacke,* Jan. 1, 1896.
d. (1) S. H. Enderby, Aug. 25, 1896.
H. S. Ainslie (Malay Pen. States Guides), Aug. 26, 1896.
s.c. (1) F. C. Turner, Jan. 1, 1897.
(2) W. Somervell,† Dec. 7, 1897.
(1) F. C. Ferguson,* Jan. 21, 1898.
(2) C. Yatman, April 9, 1898.
(2) F. B. Morley,† Nov. 16, 1898; Dec. 22, 1897.

LIEUTENANTS (18).

m. H. E. B. Leach (Adjt., 4th Bt. Yorks. Regt.), Feb. 8, 1893.
(2) J. A. C. Somerville,† Oct. 17, 1894.
(1) A. J. B. Percival,* Oct. 27, 1894.
(1) C. E. Fishbourne,* Jan. 21, 1895; Adjt., Oct. 1, 1899.
p.d. S. M. Binny, Jan. 27, 1895.
d. (1) E. M. Moulton Barrett, April 3, 1895.
(2) C. M. A. Wood, May 15, 1895.
(1) H. T. Crispin,* July 21, 1895.
S. S. Flower (serv. with Egyptian Army), Dec. 19, 1895.
(1) C. A. Armstrong,* Dec. 20, 1895.
(1) F. Bevan,* April 10, 1896.
(1) P. T. Buckley,* Aug. 26, 1896.
(1) H. S. Toppin,* Oct. 1, 1896.
(1) H. G. Lynch-Staunton,* Jan. 2, 1897; Aug. 11, 1896.
d. (2) W. H. Wild, March 10, 1897.
(1) R. C. B. Lethbridge,* April 17, 1897.
F. P. Braithwaite, Nov. 27, 1897.
(1) H. C. Hall,* Jan. 12, 1898.
E. E. Williams (West African Front. Force), Jan. 21, 1898.
(1) A. C. Girdwood,* April 22, 1898.
(1) F. L. Festing,* April 8, 1899.
(1) F. R. Coates,* May 1, 1899.
(2) H. J. C. Rostron,† Oct. 22, 1899.
(1) C. W. Wreford Brown,* Nov. 24, 1899.
(2) A. W. Rickman,† Dec. 12, 1899.

SECOND LIEUTENANTS (12).

(2) A. M. Gibbes,† Jan. 5, 1898.
(2) H. R. Sandilands,† Jan. 22, 1898.
(2) A. C. L. H. Jones,† Feb. 16, 1898.

(2) H. B. Warwick,† May 4, 1898.
(2) J. H. Matthews,† Jan. 4, 1899.
(1) St. J. B. Montagu,* Jan. 4, 1899.
(2) H. F. Stobart,† Jan. 18, 1899.
(2) G. R. Wake, April 26, 1899.
(2) L. B. Coulson,† May 20, 1899.
(2) A. Duncombe Shafto,† Oct. 18, 1899.

(2) H. J. S. Stanton,† Oct. 18, 1899.
(2) W. T. Bromfield, Oct. 18, 1899.
(2) C. R. Barclay, Nov. 15, 1899.
(1) G. M. James, Dec. 6, 1899.
A. E. J. Wilson, Dec. 20, 1899.

QUARTER-MASTERS.

(2) J. Thomson,† April 17, 1889; Hon. Capt., April 17, 1899.
(1) J. Betts,* Hon. Lt., July 26, 1893.

NOTE.—This list does not include Bt.-Lt.-Col. Keith Falconer, k. Oct. 25, 1899; Captain Eager, k. Nov. 23, 1899; Lt. Brine, k. Nov. 23, 1899; and Major G. L. S. Ray, k. at Magersfontein.

II.—PHŒBE HESSEL.

PHŒBE SMITH, who was born at Stepney, in London, in 1713, is said to have enlisted in 1728 in the Fifth Foot, then commanded by General Peirce [sic] and under orders for the West Indies.

In 1728 the Fifth returned to Ireland, after twenty-one years' service abroad; they would therefore be quite unfit for garrison duty in the Indies, and it is improbable that such an order was made. Possibly in her old age Phœbe's memory failed, and she confused the Fifth and the 3rd (?) Foot.

She was twice married, first to Corporal Samuel Golding, and secondly to Fisherman Wm. Hessel. She served many years in the army, and fought at Fontenoy.

Phœbe Hessel died at Brighton in December, 1821, aged 108. Her tombstone commemorates her services with the Fifth, but there is no other evidence that she served with the regiment.

III.—HOLLAND CAMPAIGN, 1799.

MR. ALFRED BREWIS has in his possession an original document giving the " Return of Great Coats and Accoutrements lost by the 2nd Battalion of His Majesty's 5th (or) Northumberland Regiment of Foot in the late Expedition." The list is signed by the lieutenant-colonel, Thomas Talbot; it contains the names of 175 N.C.O.'s and men of the battalion, and shows the loss of 80 great-coats, 20 swords, 10 sword belts, 45 plates, 4 sashes, 49 pouches, 49 pouch belts, 40 bayonet belts, 153 slings.

The following is an extract:

HOLLAND CAMPAIGN, 1799.

Name.	Great-Coats.	Swords.	Sword Belts.	Plates.	Sashes.	Pouches.	Pouch Belts.	Plates.	Bayonette Belts.	Slings.	
		Sergts. and Drummers.				Rank and File.					
Sergt. Wm. Bennett	1 D.	1	1	1	—	—	—	—	—	—	Lost in action Oct. 2, great-coat left by order of Col. Bayley, Oct. 1, in a barn and not afterwards found.
Corpl. Norton	1 D.	—	—	—	—	1	1	1	1	1	Wounded Oct. 2. Ditto.
Pte. Thos. Barling	1 D.	—	—	—	—	1	1	1	1	1	Killed Oct. 6. Ditto.
Wm. Barnes	1 D.	—	—	—	—	1	1	1	1	1	Wounded Oct. 6. Ditto.
Joseph Cross	1 D.	—	—	—	—	1	1	1	1	1	Taken prisoner of war Oct. 6. Ditto.
John Dobson	1 D.	—	—	—	—	1	1	—	—	1	Lost in action Oct. 6. Ditto.
Robt. Baker	—	—	—	—	—	—	—	—	—	1	By going sick Oct. 1. D.
Joseph Brandon	—	—	—	—	—	—	—	—	—	1	At Winkle Oct. 10. D.
Saml. Honybald	—	—	—	—	—	—	—	—	—	1	By going sick to Helder Oct. 4. D.
Thos. Stark	—	—	—	—	—	—	—	—	—	1	In action Sept. 19.
Sergt. Singleton	—	1	—	1	—	—	—	—	—	—	At Long Dyke Sept. 19.
Drumr. E. Starr	—	—	—	—	—	—	—	—	—	—	On the retreat from Havinghorn.

IV.—"THE AFFAIR OF EL BODON, SEPTEMBER 25, 1811."

See *U.S.J.*, 1829, p. 352.

SOON after the Battle of Fuentes d'Onoro the French army withdrew from the northern frontier of Portugal, and the Duke of Wellington, with three divisions of the British army and a corps of cavalry, blockaded Ciudad Rodrigo. In September, 1811, Marshal Marmont assembled the army of the North, consisting of 60,000 infantry and 5,000 cavalry, in the neighbourhood of Salamanca, and moved on Rodrigo for the purpose of raising the blockade. On the approach of this force our outposts were withdrawn, and Ciudad Rodrigo was relieved. The headquarters of the Duke of Wellington were at that time established at Fuente Guinaldo, a village three leagues in the rear of Ciudad Rodrigo; and it happened that the second Battalion Fifth regiment, to which I belonged, was doing headquarter duty. On the morning of the 24th of September we received orders to march to the front and occupy a post a league from Rodrigo, where we found two brigades of guns and a squadron of cavalry. About one league to the right of that post is the village of El Bodon, which was occupied by the 3rd Division under Sir Thomas Picton. The Light Division occupied the ground between the village of El Bodon and the River Agueda, on which its right rested; the 4th and only remaining division was in the rear of Fuente Guinaldo, occupying different villages, and not brought into position. In consequence of guns being attached to us I became the senior officer, and having received no orders, whether to retire if attacked (by a superior force) or to defend our post to the last extremity, I thought it prudent, in the first instance, to take the best means in my power to prevent a surprise, and planned the pickets accordingly. Feeling myself in a very responsible situation, I visited the pickets at daybreak, when I discovered large bodies of the enemy's cavalry coming out of Ciudad Rodrigo and crossing the Agueda. There are two roads leading from Ciudad Rodrigo: one to Fuente Guinaldo, the most practicable for guns, was that on our right, which passed through El Bodon; the other led immediately through the post we occupied. It was some time before I could form an opinion whether the enemy meant to advance by El Bodon or by the road which we occupied, the ground being so favourable to mask his movements; in this uncertainty, and still not having received any orders, I directed the guns to be unlimbered and the mules harnessed, ready to move at a moment's warning. I also placed the Fifth regiment in position, occupying an elevated ridge, and its right protected by a deep defile. The approach of the enemy's cavalry left me no longer any doubts as to the object of his attack, and I ordered the guns to commence a fire upon his columns. At this moment the Duke of Wellington came from the right, and after a few minutes passed in reconnoitring, told me he approved of the arrangements I had made, and would order up a brigade of cavalry to our support: but the Duke had hardly time to move to the rear before we were charged by a large body of cavalry, which for a moment succeeded in capturing our guns; however, by a well-directed running fire from the Fifth regiment, followed by a charge of bayonets, the guns were retaken and the enemy repulsed.

Reinforcements now arrived,[1] consisting of two regiments of British infantry and one of Portuguese. This force (now about 1,500 men) maintained the post for the space of about three hours, although frequently charged by the whole of the enemy's cavalry, and exposed to a heavy fire from the guns of a division of infantry which were in reserve; nor was it abandoned until this body of infantry moved forward, when we were forced to retire; and, the ground being very favourable for cavalry to act upon, we retired in squares of regiments, which were repeatedly charged, but from their steady conduct, no impression could be made upon them. During these operations the enemy pushed forward a strong body of infantry, which succeeded in cutting off the Light Division, but by a judicious movement of Major-General Crawfurd, who crossed the Agueda, that division was saved, and effected a retreat. The Duke of Wellington now took up a position in front of Guinaldo with the three divisions above named, from which, not being tenable, he retired on the following day, and posted himself strongly behind the Coa. The enemy only having supplies for ten days was obliged to fall back, when the British army reoccupied nearly the same ground it did previous to this attack.

V.—LETTER WRITTEN AFTER THE CAPTURE OF CIUDAD RODRIGO BY LT.-COL. RIDGE.[2]

MY DEAR ——, *January 24th*, 1812.

I shall first give you a copy of the order under which we acted on the night of the 19th, and then its result:

ORDER.

"The 5th regiment will attack the entrance of the ditch at the junction of the counterscarp with the main wall of the place. Major Sturgeon will show them the point of attack. They must issue from the right of the Convent of Santa Cruz. They must have twelve axes, in order to cut down the gate by which the ditch is entered at the junction of the counterscarp with the body of the place. The 5th regiment is likewise to have twelve scaling ladders, 25 feet long: and immediately on entering the ditch, are to scale the Fausse Braye in order to clear it of the enemy's parties, on their left, towards the principal breach. It will throw over any guns it may meet with, and will proceed along the Fausse Braye to the breach in the Fausse

---

[1] Major-General Colville commanded the troops who came to our support.
[2] *U.S.J.*, 1829, i. 65. See also an account by Sergt. John Jones, late of the Fifth in *U.S.J.*, 1843, i. 272.

Braye, where it will wait until Major-Gen. Mackinnon's column has passed on to the main attack, when it will follow in its rear.
"This regiment will make its attack at 10 minutes before 7 o'clock. The 77th regiment will be in reserve on the right of the Convent of Santa Cruz."

This order was executed to the entire satisfaction of all our superiors—you may suppose not less so to mine. But instead of following into the breach on our arrival at it, Gen. Mackinnon's brigade had not yet arrived—the 94th only, which had also a separate route, came up, and a junction of the two weak regiments was formed, supported by the 17th—one hundred and fifty men! The enemy, on our halting as directed, opened a most destructive fire of shells, grenades, and every kind of combustible devilment he could bring together. This had the effect of deciding the step we must take, as our orders said nothing about going back, and poor Dubourdieu at the moment observing, "Major, it is as well to die in the breach as in the ditch, for here we cannot live," the two regiments, as by one consent, pushed up the breach, almost eating fire. But the "Mounseers" liked fighting best at a distance, and gave us ground; and, taking Gen. Runk with them, neglected to pull away the planks they had thrown over the ditches, cut by them across the ramparts: by which neglect their preparations for defence were rendered ineffectual. Five and ninety-four followed them right and left, at the same time keeping, as well as we could, the centre in check, until the arrival of the intended assailants, when the town and all was ours: the enemy, one and all, throwing away their arms, and flying to their holes, where they endeavoured to conceal themselves until the rage of the British lion had subsided, but they had already taken the most effectual means to obtain mercy—as it was, even here, glorious to see Britons incapable of slaying unarmed men, though their lives became forfeit by awaiting the assault with two practicable breaches.

Besides possession of the fortress, the whole of Massena's battering train had become prize, as well as an immense quantity of light artillery which Marmont brought against us on our retreat after El Bodon. The fortress is so well supplied with warlike stores that not an article of any kind is wanting, notwithstanding the expenditure during the siege. I have been enabled to complete the whole of our drummers present with French brass drums, and more had we wanted them.

The George and Dragon has nearly disappeared from our King's Colour by a shell passing through it, though I trust his spirit is left amongst us.

What will the French and English say now? Ciudad invested—bombarded—and taken in twelve days, which cost Massena fifty-one days, sixteen of which he was bombarding the place. Every part of the proceeding seems to have astonished the garrison, as in erecting works, opening batteries, etc., they were always a day or two out in their calculations.

But I think I hear you ask, "How are all my friends and brother soldiers?" This, my dear friend, is the melancholy part, as our loss has been heavy indeed. Poor M'Dougall killed; Major Grey, Dubourdieu, Johnson, Wylde, M'Kenzie, Fitzgerald, Fairtlough, Ayshford, Canch, and Volunteer Hilliard, wounded; thirty-eight men killed, and sixty-two wounded. This includes our losses during the siege, as well as in the assault.

Your poor Light Bobs have suffered—three killed, and ten badly wounded. The grenadiers are the greatest sufferers.

I got hold of the Governor's crimson and gold saddle-cloth, of which I have entreated the acceptance of our gallant and worthy chief of division. I possess likewise the Governor's French double-barrelled gun. There has been a regular traffic of the plunder, but the brave fellows earned it all.

Your brother was in the thick of the business, and, I rejoice to say, came out unhurt, and slept before the same fire with me after all was over.

VI.—AN EXTRACT FROM "CAMP AND QUARTERS" (1840).

In "Camp and Quarters," published in 1840,[1] Major John Patterson, 50th Foot, wrote: "There is something in the appearance of many corps not easily defined, but which at once gives to the most experienced eye the impression that is usually understood among military men by the term 'crack regiment.' This may be distinguished by an off-handed way of doing things, a smartness of their trim, a neatness and particularity, even to the very polish of their buttons, a sharp, lively step of confidence, a sort of pride in one another, expressed upon their countenance, all of which, both as regards officers and men, informs you, whatever it is, that their *tout ensemble* breathes the very life and essence of a soldier. . . . These regiments seem to be handed down as an heirloom from one clever officer to another. . . . Perhaps none could be said to verify these remarks more strictly than the Old Fifth, or Northumberlands (since made Fusiliers). There was an air of warlike spirit about them, retained from past experience, when, under Ridge, Mackenzie, Eames, Pratt, and many more, they preserved a reputation acquired in other fields.

"There was nothing lively in their uniforms, their facings being a muddy gosling green; but, notwithstanding this, there could not be a cleaner regiment. When I knew them there were three Mackenzies in the corps, one of whom, a colonel, a remarkably fine officer, was killed at Corunna, the others, captain and subaltern of the Light Company, died in the West Indies."

[1] "Camp and Quarters" was reviewed by a late officer of the Fifth in the *U.S.J.*, 1840, i. 410.

BIBLIOGRAPHY

Books directly connected with the Fifth are in italics

Books, etc.
Army Lists and Commission Registers. (C. Dalton, 1892, 6 vols.)
Arrah in 1857. (Chas. Kelly and G. F. T. Leather.)
Battle Honours of the British Army. (C. B. Norman.)
British Military Library. (1799.)
Campaigns of King William and Queen Anne. (Richard Kane, 1745.)
Diary of Sir Nicholas Hamilton. (MSS. in possession of Colonel G. F. T. Leather. Extracts in *St. George's Gazette.*)
Duties of a Regimental Surgeon. (Robert Hamilton, 1794.)
Digest of Service (5th Foot), 1837-1910.
Dictionary of National Biography.
England and the Seven Years' War. (J. S. Corbett, 1907, 2 vols.)
Gibraltar (An Impartial Account of the late famous Siege). (An Officer, 1728.)
Gibraltar, History of. (F. G. Stephens, 1870.)
George I.'s Army. (C. Dalton, 1910, 2 vols.)
Great Boer War. (Conan Doyle.)
Historical Records of Fifth Foot, 1674-1837. (Cannon, 1838.)
History of the British Army, Vols. I.-VIII. (J. W. Fortescue.)
History of England. (Smollett and Hume.)
History of British Standing Army. (Clifford Walton, 1894.)
History of the Campaigns (Peninsular War.) (1812.)
History of England. (Macaulay.)
History of the Coldstream Guards, Vol. II.
Historical Account of British Regiments employed in Defence of Dutch Republic. (1794.)
History of Indian Mutiny. (Forrest.)
Journal of the Late Campaign (St. Malo). (1758.)
Life of John Bernardi. (1729.)
Lives of the Lindsays. (E. of Crauford, 1840.)
Lives of the Admirals. (Campbell.)
Life of Marlborough. (Viscount Wolseley, 2 vols.)
Letters of Lord Chesterfield.
Lucubrations of Humphry Ravelin. (1823.)
Life of Lord Harris. (S. R. Lushington, 1840.)
Military Memoirs of Captain George Carleton. (1729.)
Memoirs of Sir Thomas Picton. (H. B. Robinson, 1836.)
Memoirs of a Sergeant of the Fifth Regiment. (Stephen Morley, 1842.)
Military Sketch Book.

BIBLIOGRAPHY

Memoirs of a Campaign in Holland. (Fras. Maule.)
Notes and Recollections. (Wm. Fergusson, M.D., 1846.)
Northumberland Fusiliers. (Walter Wood, 1901.)
Naval History. (James.)
Narrative of Campaign in North Holland. (Sir H. Bunbury, 1849.)
Northumberland. (*American Letters of Second Duke.*)
Operations of Allied Army. (An Officer, 1764.)
Peninsular War, Vols. I.-V. (Oman.)
Peninsular War. (Napier.)
Regimental Companion. (Captain Chas. James.)
St. George's Gazette. (1883, *et sequa.*)
Stopford Sackville MSS. (Record Office.)
System of Economy of a Battalion. (Bennet Cuthbertson, 1779).
Short Narrative of the Regiment. (An Officer of the 5th, 1873.)
Simcoe (John Graves). (D. C. Scott.)
Siege of Maestricht.
Spain (War of Succession). (Colonel A. Parnell.)
Tom Plunket. (See *U.S.J.*, 1842, *et sequa.*)
Times' History of South African War. (6 vols.)
United Service Journal. (1832, *et sequa.*)
Wars in Ireland. (G. W. Story, 1693.)
With Kitchener to Khartum. (G. W. Steevens, 1898.)
Whitefoord Papers. (Caleb Whitefoord, 1898.)

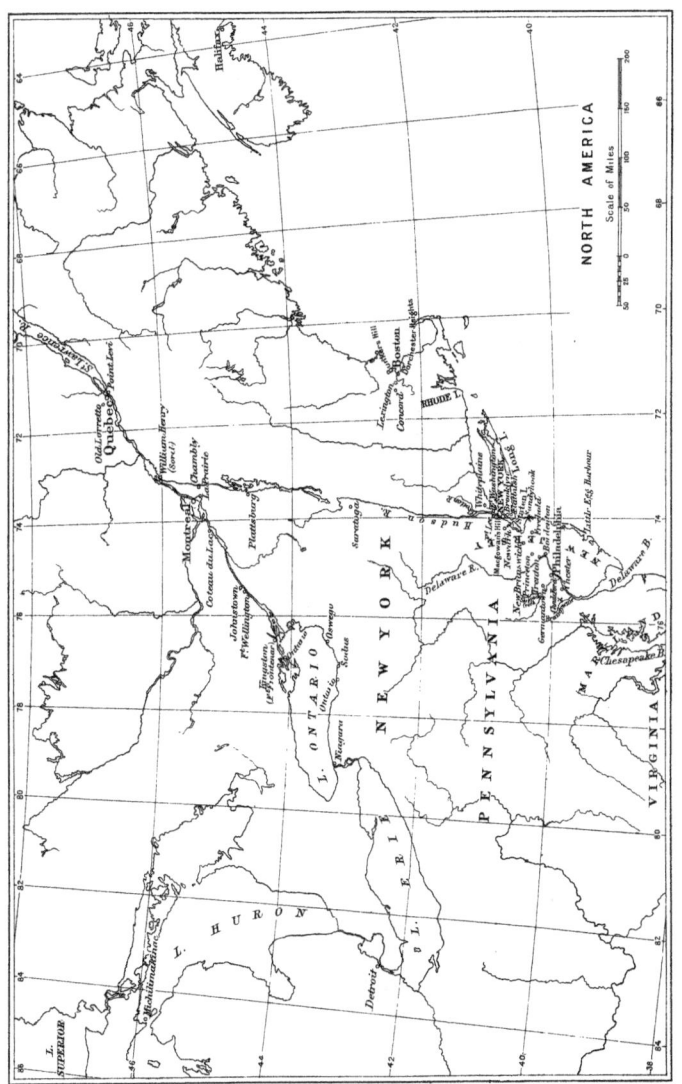

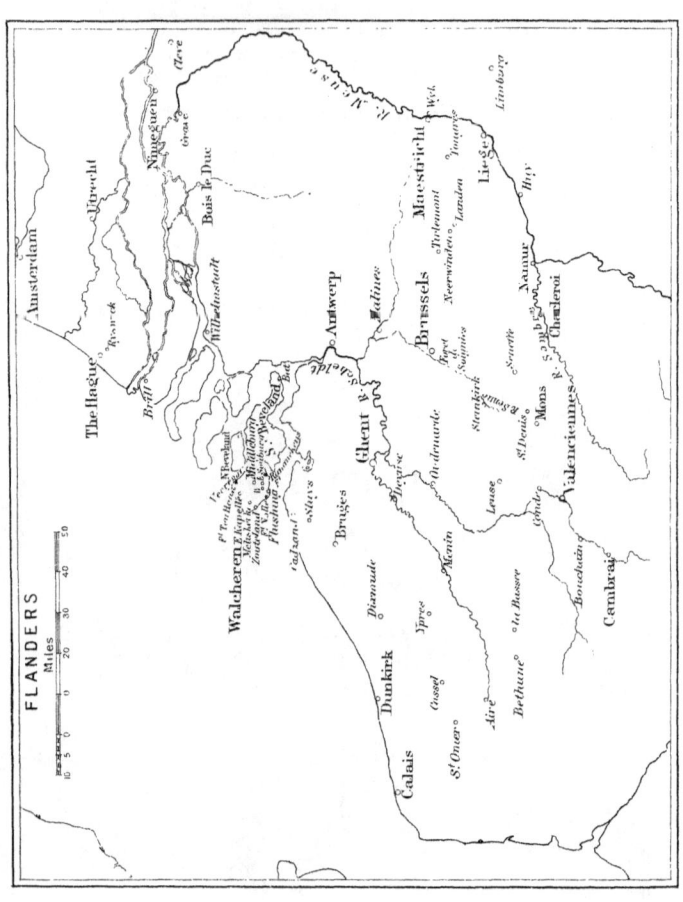

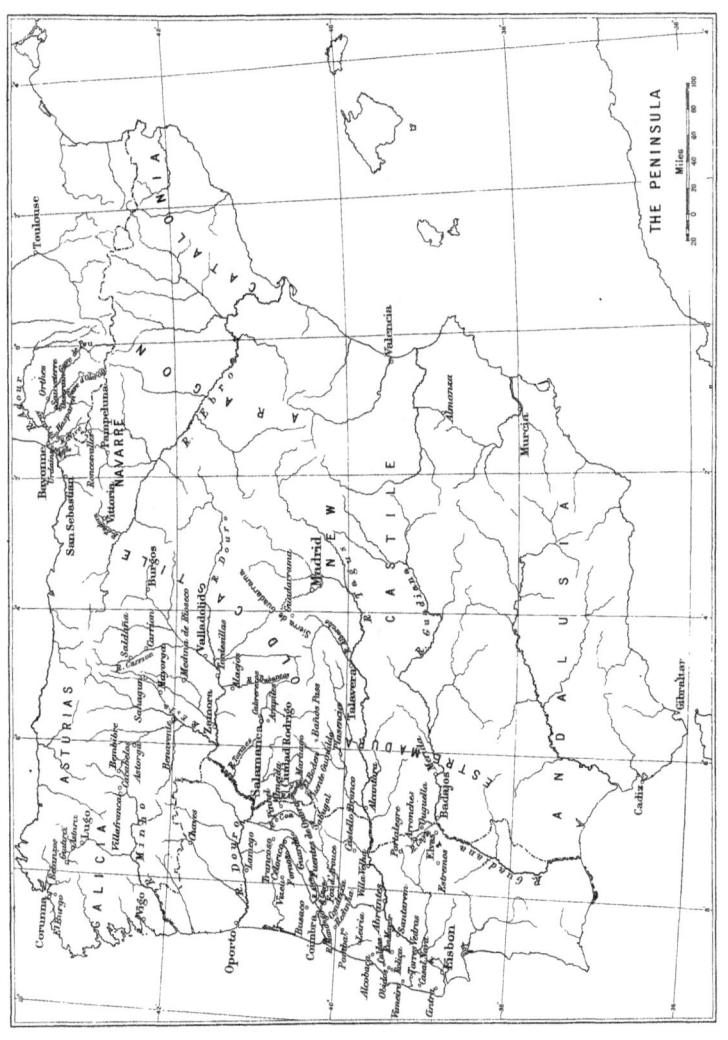

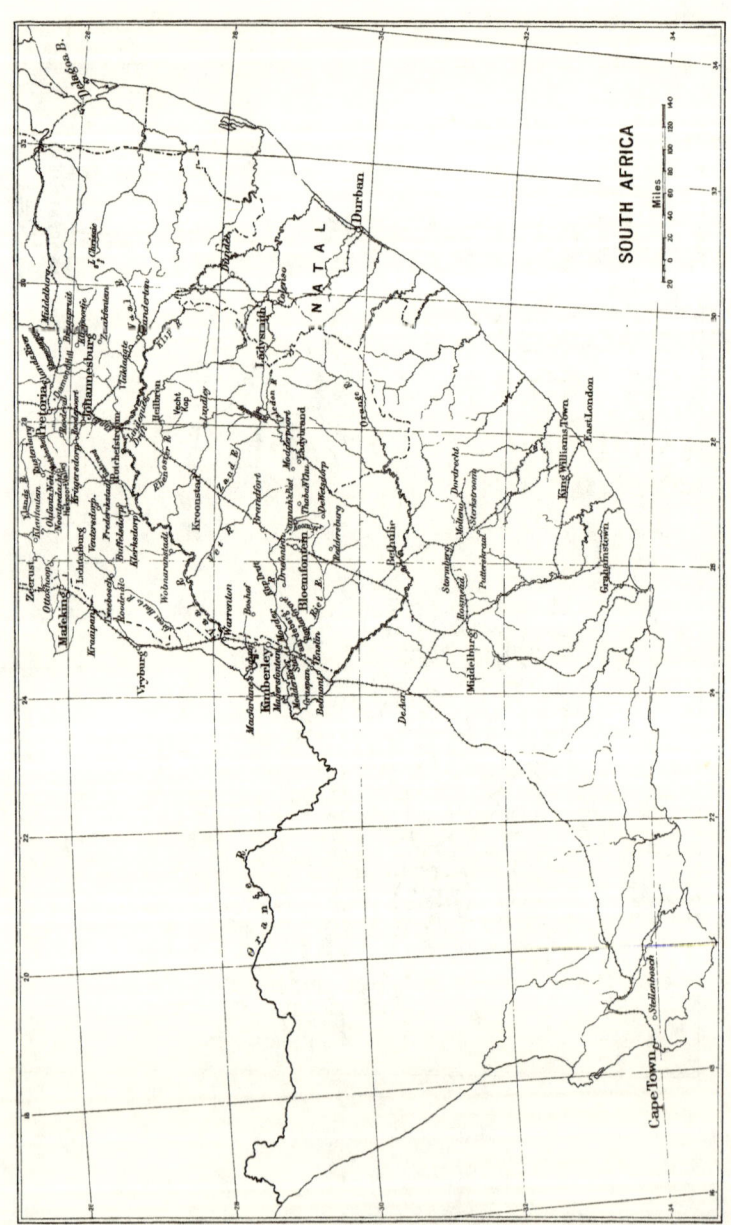

INDEX

ABERCROMBY, Sir Ralph, 223, 225, 228, 235, 237, 239
Abrantes, 1st Fifth at, 273
Adjutant, duties of, 217
Afghanistan, 409
Aldershot, 402, 415, 416
Alderney, 2nd Fifth at, 292
Allahabad, 371, 396, 410
Alnwick, 134, 213, 406
Alum Bagh, 377, 384, 389, 392
" Amen-man," 60
Amöneberg, 123
Arms, 21 note, 50, 151, 218, 353
Arrah, 371, 372, 373
Ashanti, 416
Astorga, 1st Fifth at, 279
Athlone, siege of, 34
Auchmuty, Sir Samuel, 255, 275, 261
Aughrim, battle of, 35

Barham Downs, camp at, 88, 222
Barracks, 63, 81; in Dublin, 129, 352
Bedford, Fifth at, 127
Belfast, Fifth at, 32, 197
Belmont, battle of, 428, 429
Bexhill, 1st Fifth at, 329
Billeting, 81, 87, 215
Black Mountain Campaign, 403
Bordeaux, 1st Fifth at, 342
Boston, 137, 141
Boyne, battle of, 30
Boys, 81
Brandywine, battle of, 168
Brixham Quay, Fifth land, 25
Bruges, Fifth at, 39, 41
Brussels, Fifth at, 20
Buenos Ayres, 254, 260
Bunker's Hill, battle of, 137, 151
Burgoyne, General John, 150, 158, 193, 194
Busaco, battle of, 301-3

Cacabelos, 1st Fifth at, 279
Calder, Brig. Sir H., 175 note, 186, 188
Cambridge, Duke of, 364, 407, 408, 416

Campbell, Colin (Lord Clyde), 386, 388, 391, 396, 397
Campbell, Col. (of the 94th), at Ciudad Rodrigo, 320; at Badajos, 325
Candia, Fifth at, 420, 421
Canada, 1788, 201, 202 and note; 1814, 343; Upper Canada, 201; First Assembly, 208
Cape, South Africa, 256 and note, 423
" Captain Firebrand " hung, 193
Cassel, siege of, 142
Cawnpore, 369, 375
Cephalonia, Fifth at, 363
Chad's Ford. See Brandywine
Chelmsford, Fifth at, 87
Cherbourg, 96
Chester, Fifth at, 43
Chesterfield, Philip Lord, 67 and note, 78 and note, 115
Claverhouse (Graham of), 6, 28, 29
Clayton, Col. Jasper, 57, 59 and note, 60
Clent, Capt. Littleton, 3 and note
Clinton, Sir Henry, 150, 153, 158, 160
Clonmel, Fifth at, 130
Clothing and Uniform, 1706, 49; 1751, 74; 1757, 79; 1751, 82; 1755, 86; 1762, 125; 1772, 136; 1793, 218; 1799, 227, and 230; 1836, 352 and 353; 1860, 408; 409
Collier, David (Lord Portmore), 11; in Portugal, 49; at Gibraltar, 55, 58, 65
Colours, regulated, 79, 113; of 5th N.I. taken, 380
Commissions, children's, 41, 64 note; sale of, 64 and note
Concord, Fifth at, 147
Corfu, 363
Cork, siege of, 32 and note, 60, 63, 136, 199, 293
Côteau du Lac, Fifth at, 344
Courts-martial, 143, 144, 187, 209, 292
Crauford, Robert, 255, 300
Crete, 1st Fifth in, 420
Cumberland, Duke of, 69, 85

494 INDEX

De la Rochefoucauld and the Fifth, 210
Delhi, 368, 378
Desertion, 142, 195, 209
Detachments, 2nd Battalion of, 294; discipline, 296; broken up, 299
Dhooly Square, 381
Dinapore, 369
Discipline, 56, 80, 215; at Gibraltar 239, 278, 352
Divine worship, 83
Division, Third (in the Peninsula), 299, 306 and note, 308, 311, 312, 323, 327, 335, 336, 339, 346
Dogs, 93, 123 note
Dorset, Lionel Duke of, 65, 71, 78
Dover, Fifth at, 42, 416
Drafting, 211, 219, 406 and note
Draper, Sir William, 132
Drill, 50, 217, 353
Drummers, 73, 81, 321; drum-major's stick, 380 note
Dublin, 1690, 33; 1739, 63; 1745, 67; 1763, 128; 1827, 375; 1872, 402
Duels, 17, 131, 193, 205, 249
Dundas, David, 217, 225, 229, 230
Durban, 2nd Fifth in, 401

El Boden, 313 (Appendix IV.)
English Brigade in Flanders, 4, 10, 15, 21, 25
Ensigns, age of, etc., 80, 81
Epaulettes, 219
Erith explosion, 408
Exeter, Fifth at, 26, 104
Eyre, Major Vincent, 371-4, 376, 378

Ferdinand of Brunswick, 97, 105
Fifth Foot: formed, 6; takes rank, 23; Second Battalion raised, 1799, 223; disbanded, 243; raised, 1804, 292; disbanded, 348; raised, 1857, 400
arms, 13 note, 43, 86; loss of, 103; 126 note (Appendix III.)
badge, 8 and note, 80
colours, 196; at Vigie, 183; at Winkel, 234; at Ciudad Rodrigo, 321; of 2nd Fifth, 350 and note, 458
regimental Colours, 261
King's Colours, 86, 261
new Colours, 196, 362, 358, 408
third Colour, won, 123; lost, 361
facings, 8 and note, 79, 80, 415 and note

Fifth Foot (continued)—
Grenadier Company, 103, 108, 112, 113; at Kirchdunckern, 119; at Foorwohle, 120, 160 note, 161, 165; at Freehold, 174; at St. Lucia, 178, 184, 194, 251
inspections, 86, 87, 88, 104, 130, 131, 136 note, 203, 206, 236, 252, 286; 2nd Fifth, 292, 328, 329, 415
Light Infantry Company, 160 note, 161; at St. Lucia, 178, 260 note; at Busaco, 303, 306; at Fuentes de Onoro, 310
losses: Badajos, 312, 327; Brandywine, 169 note; Buenos Ayres, 265 note; Bunker's Hill, 154; Casal Nova, 307; Campaign of 1760, 113; of 1761, 120; the Caya, 48; Ciudad Rodrigo, 322; Corunna, 283 and note; El Boden, 315; Foz D'Arouce, 307; Fuentes de Onoro, 311 and note; Gibraltar, 60; Germantown, 171 and note; Holland, 230 and note; Jagd Spruit, 455; Kirchdunckern, 119; Lichtenberg, 452; Lexington, 149; Modder River, 431; Mons, 37; Noitgedacht, 422; Nivelle, 339; Orthes, 341; Reddersburg, 422; Roliça, 271; Sabugal, 309; St. Cas, 103 and note; St. Lucia, 182 note; Salamanca, 333; Sachsenhausen, 108; Sannah's Post, 441; Stormberg, 434; Sudan, 420; Talavera, 298; Tweebosch, 455; Walcheren, 288-291; Warburg, 111; Whiteplains, 164 note; Wilhelmstahl, 123; Vittoria, 338
Motto, 8 and note
Northumberland Foot, 195 note
Fusiliers, 414
Order or Medal of Merit, established 130, 136; confirmed, 352; abolished, 367
Officers and men (see also Appendix I.)
Adair, Lieut., 383
Adams, Capt., killed, 338 and note
Andrews, Ensign, wounded, 169 note
Anselmne, Lieut.-Col., 4, 6; superseded, 10; death of, 18
Archer, Lieut.-Col., 11, 17; killed, 22
Armsby, Ensign, 22 note

INDEX

Fifth Foot, officers and men (continued)—
Armstrong, Drum-Major, Thomas, 246
Armstrong, Capt. Martin, death of, 283 note
Armstrong, Lieut., death, 355 note
Ashly, Capt., 41
Ashton, Bandsman William, 280
Augeune, Lieut., 22 note
Bagot, Ensign, 127
Baker, Capt. Benjamin, 111,125, 144, 149 note; Bunker's Hill, 154; brig.-major, 159, 175 note, 186, 199; leaves Fifth, 206, 212
Balaquire, Ensign, 154
Baldwin, Lieut.-Col. John, 293
Bannerman, Sergt. A., 420 note
Barclay, 2nd Lieut., killed, 441
Barnewell, Capt. Anthony, 13 and note; killed, 14
Barnewell, Ensign, 22 note
Baron, Ensign, 115
Bartley, Lieut.-Col., 402 and note
Bateman, Capt., wounded, 338 note
Bathurst, Lieut.-Col. James, 305
Battier, Major Gaspard, 189, 184, 199 and note
Baynes, Lieut.-Col. Edward, 293 and note
Bell, Capt., 130, 131
Bennett, Sergt., 245 and note
Bennet, Capt., wounded, 327 note
Benson, Pte. G., 435 note
Bent, Major John, 245; at Orthes, 341 and note; at Toulouse, 342, 350
Bentinck, Lord George, 83 and note, 104
Bernardi, Major John, 3, 5, 15, 17, 21 note
Bevan, Lieut., 427 note, 428
Bigge, Lieut.-Col. T. S., in India, 392, 393; as lieut.-col., 402 and note
Bird, Brevet-Major, prisoner at Walcheren, 289
Bird, Lieut., at Walcheren, 289; Peninsula, wounded, 333 note; wounded, 339 note
Bishop, Major, at Salamanca, 334; death of, 355 note
Bishop, Ensign and Adjt. Henry, 335, 352 note
Bladen, Martin, 42 and note

Fifth Foot, officers and men (continued)—
Bligh, Lieut.-Col. Hon. Edward, 229; at Winkel, 234, 235
Bolton, Ensign, killed, 338 and note
Bone, Assistant Surgeon, at Buenos Ayres, 261, 262, 264
Booth, Capt., killed, 440
Boylam, Pte., Lucknow, 385
Brand, Drummer Adam, 245
Brine, Lieut., killed, 430
Broke, Sir Charles, 300; exchanges, 305
Brown, Lieut., died at Walcheren, 291
Brown, Lieut. Wreford, at Lichtenberg, 451
Bruce, Sergt., 245 and note; commission, 286
Brudenel, Capt. Robert, 48 note
Burdett, Col.-Sergt. T., 420 note
Burroughs, Thos., 39
Burston, Capt. George, 26 and note
Byron, Cpl. John, at Buenos Ayres, 264, 265; medal for bravery, 266
Calcraft, Capt., 93 note
Canch, Major Thos., at El Boden, 315 and note; Ciudad Rodrigo, 320, 322; at Badajos, 325, 342 note
Carden, Lieut.-Col., 402 and note
Carfrae, Ensign, 115
Carleton, George Villiers, 12 and note
Carter, Sergt.-Major Charles, 352 and note
Carter, Lieut., 383, 384 and note
Carey, Lieut., died at Walcheren, 291
Casson, Capt., killed, 441
Caxton, Lieut. Robt., 48 note
Chapman, Major, 394
Charlton, Capt. Edward, 154; wounded, 171 note, 200
Charlton, Capt., killed, 22 and note
Cheen, Cpl., 144
Cherry, Lieut.-Col. H. A., 404, 416 note
Chester-Master, Lieut.-Col., 369, 395, 396, 399, 407 and note, 408, 409
Clare, Viscount, 6 and note, 28
Clarke, Capt. Sir Alured, in Fifth, 131 and note; Lieut.-Governor in Canada, 207; colonel of Fifth, 209 and note; colonel of Seventh Foot, 243

Fifth Foot, officers and men (continued)—
Clark, Capt., 245, 339 note
Clerke, Lieut. Shadwell, at Corunna, 282, 283 note; with King, 300, 301; wounded, 307 and note
Coates, Capt. R. F., killed, 455
Cockell, Lieut.-Col.Wm., 244, 246
Coleman, Capt., 22 note
Colls, Q.M. William, 352 note
Colville, Sir Charles, 304 and note; at Ciudad Rodrigo, 319; at Vittoria, 337, 345; colonel of Fifth, 362; death, 365
Cookson, 2nd Lieut. L. B., 435 note
Cope, Sir John, 65, 68, 70
Copson, Lieut.-Col., 293, 294; at Talavera, 298; returns to England, 299
Cordial, Sergt.-Drummer J., 420 note
Cotter, Ensign, 175 and note
Cowden, Pte. George, 365
Cox, Capt. Wm., 143, 175 and note, 186; death of, 199
Creagh, Brevet-Major, 383, 384, 411
Crispin, Lieut., 427 note, 432, 445
Croker, Lieut., 143, 154
Cubitt, Lieut., 393, 395
Culley, Capt., 340 and note
Curran, Cpl., taken prisoner, 382
Currey, Ensign, killed, 188
Cuthbertson, Capt. Bennet, 80 and note, 131
Cuthbertson, Capt. Robt., 72
Danvers, Ensign R. W., 384 note, 385
Darling, Major-Gen. Henry, 192, 200, 207; leaves Fifth, 212 and note, 213
Dashwood, Col. E. W., 421 and note; wounded, 430
Davie, Lieut.-Col. H., 249; Buenos Ayres, 260, 261; leaves Fifth, 268
Dering, Capt. Chudleigh, 76
Downes, Capt. Patrick, 154; death of, 156
Downie, Drummer, killed, 263
Doyle, Capt., wounded at Roliça, 271; wounded, 327 note, 342 note
Drake, Q.M., 380
Dubourdieu, Capt., 266; at Ciudad Rodrigo, 320; wounded, 322 and note, 364
Du Puy, Capt., 22 note, 24 note

Fifth Foot, officers and men (continued)—
Eager, Capt., killed, 430
Elrington, Lieut.-Col. Job, 48 note, 56, 61
Elrington, Capt. John, 48 note, 61
Elrington, Major Wm., at Gibraltar, 56
Emes, Lieut.-Col. Thos., 275; at Walcheren, 288, 291, 293; in West Indies, 354 and note; death of, 355
Enderby, Major, wounded, 456
England, Sir Richard, 243
Equino, Lieut., death of, 355
Eustace, Major Wm., 77, 78 and note, 125
Fairfax, Col. Thos., 39, 43; death of, 46
Fairtlough, Lieut., wounded, 322; killed, 324
Fanthrop, Pte. Wm., tried by C.M., 143
Fenwick, Sir John, 7, 9, 11; wounded, 13; leaves Fifth, 16, 18, 20; executed, 43, 44
Fenwick, Ensign, 61
Fenwick, Capt. Nicholas, 48 note
Fergusson, Surgeon, 229 note, 234
Festing, Lieut., wounded, 430
Fishbourne, Lieut., wounded, 430
Fitzgerald, Capt. Augustus, 207
Fitzgerald, Lord Henry, 199 and note
Fitzroy, Col. Philip, 389 and note, 415
Fletcher, Major E. W., 435 note; killed, 452
Floyd, Capt., 22 note
Frend, Major G., 432
Gair, Surgeon, illness of, 156
Galbraith, Lieut., at Walcheren, 289; wounded, 338 note
Ganly, Bug. Patrick, 268
Gibson, 2nd Lieut., wounded, 455
Gibson, Dr. Herbert, 76
Giles, Capt. Thos., 48 note, 56, 61
Girdwood, Capt., wounded, 452
Godby, Lieut. Carey, 41, 61
Godby, Lieut.-Col. Peter, 48 note, 56
Golland, Sergt.-Major, bravery at Buenos Ayres, 262; at Ciudad Rodrigo, 321

INDEX

Fifth Foot, officers and men (continued)—
Gore, Capt., killed, 174
Grant, Cpl., 378
Grant, Bandsman James, 334
Grey, Sir John, at El Boden, 313, 314 and note; wounded 322; colonel, 366 and note
Green, Ensign, 48 and note
Gresham, Pte., 363
Griffith, Ensign Edward, 48 note
Grisler, Pte. Chas., a deserter, 209
Gunn, Lieut., wounded, 333 note
Guy, Lieut.-Col., 367, 369; at Dinapore, 370 and note, 392, 395, 407
Hackness, Lieut.-Col., 402 note
Hackett, Lieut.-Col. Chas., 416 note
Haigh, Lieut. and Adjt., 377 and note, 384 note
Hales, Major John, 17 and note, 22 note, 24 note
Hall, Lieut., 427 note, 428, 440
Hamer, Lieut. M. G., 342 note
Hamilton, Lieut. J. B., wounded, 333 note; taken prisoner, 339 note
Hamilton, Lieut. J. M., wounded, 233
Hamilton, Major-Gen. Sir Nicholas, 251; at Walcheren, 289 and note
Hamilton, Capt. Wm., died at Walcheren, 291
Hamilton, Pte. T., 405
Harris, Lieut., killed, 230 note
Harris, Lord, ensign, 126, 127, 130; duel, 131; captain, 134 and note; letter, 138,144, 149 and note, 150 note; wounded at Bunker's Hill, 152 and note; rejoins, 161, 166 note; at Brandywine, 169, 171 note, 172; commands grenadiers, 178 and note; marries, 189; leaves Fifth, 198, 226 note
Harris, Lieut. Thos., 154 and note; death of, 182 note
Harvey, Ensign, at Buenos Ayres, 264
Hart Dyke, Lieut.-Col., 406 note
Hawkshaw, Capt., 197
Heathcote, Capt. Chas., 76 and note; prisoner, 103
Henstock, Q.M. H., 342 note
Henry, Capt., 420 note

Fifth Foot, officers and men (continued)—
Hewett, Major-Gen., 223
Hickson, Lieut., duel, 193
Higgins, Lieut., killed, 338 note
Hill, General Edward Rowly, 414 note
Hill, Capt. Benjamin, 135, 156 and note; at Vigie, 180 and note; leaves Fifth, 196
Hill, Capt. George, 192; leaves Fifth, 244
Hillyard, Lieut., wounded, 333 note, 342 note
Hodgson, General Studholme, 80; colonel of Fifth, 104; at Bellisle 115, 131
Holmes, Surgeon, 205
Holmes, Pte., 152 note
Hopkins, Lieut. H. L., 260; wounded, 327 note; killed, 341
Hopkins, Lieut. W. R., 342 note
Houston, Surgeon, 405
Howe, Sergt., 438
Hull, 2nd Lieut. H. D., killed, 452
Irwin, Major-Gen. Alexander, colonel of Fifth, 65; at Bath, 74; death, 75
Irwin, Lieut.-Gen. Sir John, lieutenant, 65; travels, 67; major, 70, 71; letters from, 75, 78 note, 80, 83, 87; letter, 100 and 103,115; commander-in-chief, Ireland, 192
Isaac, Lieut., wounded, 450 note
Jackson, Capt., 143, 154
James, Lieut., 451
Johnson, Lieut. Arthur, 338 note
Johnson, Lieut.-Col. David England, wounded at Ciudad Rodrigo, 322, 342 and note, 366 and note; commands Fifth, 367
Johnson, Capt. A. E., 366 note; in India, 375; killed Lucknow, 380, 384 note
Johnson, Lieut., 207 and note; Johnson, Sir Henry, 362
Johnstone, Capt. Edward, 48 note
Jones, Lieut., wounded, 450 and note
Keene, Capt. Gilbert, 77 and note
Keith Falconer, Brevet-Lieut.-Col., Egypt, 420; South Africa, 427 note; killed, 428
Kelly, Volunteer C., 374

498 INDEX

Fifth Foot, officers and men (continued)—
Kennedy, Lieut.-Col., 396
Kilgour, Brevet-Major, 413, 414
King, Ensign Henry, 138, 143
King, Col. Honble. Henry, 246 and note, 250; at Buenos Ayres, 260, 262, 263; lieutenant-colonel 2nd Fifth, 285, 293; with Picton, 300, 301, 302; at Busaco, 303, 310; at Badajos, 311, 328; at Salamanca, 334; death, 350
Kirkland, Lieut.-Col. V., 400 and note, 402
Knight, Capt., 18
Kysh, Col.-Sergt., 352 note
Lambton, Col. Honble. Chas. 420 note, 438, 449
Landen, Col.-Sergt. A., 352 note
Larpent, Lieut. de H., at Lichtenberg, 451
Lavallain, Capt. Patrick, 6 and note; a traitor, 7
Lee, Capt. Patrick, 6, 7 and note, 12; killed, 15
L'Estrange, Ensign, at Badajos, 326
L'Estrange, Capt., 369; in India, 371-374; killed, 379, 394 note
Ligonière, Lieut.-Col., 66
Lindsey, Lieut.-Col., 235
Littleton, Lieut., 175 and note
Littlewood, Lieut. Robt., 119
Lloyd, Lieut.-Col. Edward, 29; at Athlone, 35; death, 39
Lloyd, Godfrey, 41
Longford, Lord, 414 note
Lonsdale-Hale, 2nd Lieut., death, 420 note
Macdougal, Capt., 319; killed, 322
M'Clintoch, Lieut., 154
McDonald, Capt., 359
McDonald, Sergt.-Major, wounded, 455
McDonough, Lieut., died Walcheren, 291
McElligot, Col. John, 7 and note, 7
McElligot, Capt. Roger, 6, 7; wounded, 15, 28, 32 note
MacGregor, Capt. Malcolm, 365 note
McHale, Pte. Patrick, 385, 393
McGillicuddy, Capt., 6
MacKenzie, Lieut.-Col., 268; in Portugal, 269; Rolica, 271, 278; mortally wounded at Corunna, 282, 283, 293 (Appendix VI.)

Fifth Foot, officers and men (continued)—
Mackenzie, Mrs., at Vimeira
McKenzie, Lieut., wounded, 322
M'Laughlin, Lieut. Peter, 73 and note
Malide, Major Paul, 66
McManus, Pte., 381, 382
McNeil, Sergt., 332
Marchant, Lieut., 22 note
Marly, Lieut.-Col., 115; at Wilhelmstahl, 123, 125, 130
Marsden, Capt., 154
Mason, Ensign, 384
Meara, Lieut., 384 and note
Medows, Lieut.-Gen. Sir William, 130, 134 and note; commands Grenadier Battalion in North America, 161; at Brandywine, 169; lieut.-col. of Fifth, 172 and note; brig.-gen., 175 note; at St. Lucia, 178 and note; at Vigie, 180; wounded, 182 note; leaves Fifth, 189, 198, 266
Milman, Lieut.-Gen. Sir Bryan, 387; India, 398, 422 note
Mitchell, Capt., 77
Mitford, Lieut. D. B., 456
Monpesson, Major John, 78
Money, Lieut.-Col., 403; in Sudan, 417, 420 and note; in South Africa, 427, 430
Monk, Lieut.-Col. Thos., 5 and note; death, 25
Montague, Capt., 455
Morley, Sergt. Stephen, joins, 245; at Buenos Ayres, 262, 265; at Vimeira, 272; prisoner, 281; escapes, 295; rejoins, 329; Salamanca, 332; illness, 355
Munro, Sergt.-Major Donald, 352 note
Napier, Capt., 61
Nichols, Sir Jasper, 365 and note, 366
Nugent, George James, 78 and note
'O'Connell, Pte. Redmond, at Buenos Ayres, 264
O'Dell, Lieut., wounded, 333
O'Farrell, Ensign, prisoner, 84
Oldfield, Lieut., 378, 384 note
Openshaw, Pte., 413
Owens, Capt.-Lt. Henry, 48 note, 56
Palmer, Lieut. and Q.M. Robt., 115; death, 138
Parry, Lieut. John, 48 note
Parsons, Lieut.-Col. Wm., 39, 41
Paston, Capt. Gaspard, 23

INDEX

499

Fifth Foot, officers and men (continued)—
Patrick, Ensign, 143; court-martial, 144
Pattinson, Major James, 66
Pearce, Lieut.-Col. Chas. Wm., at Gibraltar, 56; lieut.-col., 66, 68
Pearce, Major-Gen. Thos., colonel of Fifth, 46; prisoner, 48 and note; Governor of Limerick, 56, 61; colonel of Fifth Regiment of Horse, 64
Pecquer, Major Daniel, 66
Pelham, Sergt.-Major Aldrich, 352 note
Pennington, Lieut.-Col. R. L., 406 note
Pennyman, Lieut., 322 note
Percivale, Capt., 451
Percy, Lord (2nd Duke of Northumberland), colonel of Fifth, 132, 133; gives adjutancy to regiment, 136; letter from, 141, 142; in North America, 144-147; at Lexington, 149, 153, 154, 158; commands Brigade of Guards, 161; promoted, 165 and note; returns to England, 167; leaves Fifth, 195, 196, 365
Phillips, Capt., at Buenos Ayres, 262; death in Walcheren, 291
Pheelan, Cpl., prisoner, 382
Pinder, Sergt., 12
Plunkett, Capt., 17
Powel, Sergt., 12
Pratt, Major-Gen. Sir Chas., wounded in Holland, 233; 245; major, 246; lieutenant-colonel 2nd Fifth, 268, lieutenant-colonel 1st Fifth 285, 293, 354; promoted, 356
Pratt, Capt. Robt., wounded St. Lucia, 182 note, 210
Pratt, Ensign, drowned, 330 and note
Pratt, Ensign, wounded, 333 note
Prior, Sergt., at Buenos Ayres, 264
Purdon Ensign, 48 note
Quin, Lieut., killed, 455
Rawdon, Lord (1st Earl of Moira), as Ensign, 138, 141 note; at Bunker's Hill, 152, 154; leaves Fifth, 156 and note

Fifth Foot, officers and men (continued—
Raw, 2nd Lieut. R. G., prisoner, 455
Rawson, Lieut.-Col. George, 76, 78, 130, 134
Ray, Major, 420 note, 428; killed, 432
Read, Lieut., at Oporto, 296 note
Reed, Volunteer, killed, 338 note
Ridge, Lieut.-Col., at Buenos Ayres, 263, 300; commands 2nd Fifth, 305; at El Boden, 313, 316; Ciudad Rodrigo, 318, 320, 323; Badajos, 325; killed, 326 (Appendix V.)
Riddell, Brig.-Gen. J. F., 405 and note, 406
Roberts, Lieut.-Col. W. M., 409 and note
Robertson, Sergt.-Major Mackay, 352 note
Robinson, Lieut. Thos., 115, 123
Robinson, Col.-Sergt. Jas., killed, 358
Ross, Major, 111, 130, 134
Ross-Lewin, Lieut., 212 and note
Rowlands, Lieut.-Col. T., 410 and note, 413, 414
Sapte, Capt., wounded, 430
Savage, Capt. Phillip, 5, 14; killed, 17
Saxby, Capt. Wm., 24 note
Schonswar, Lieut.-Col., 367
Scott, Capt., 384 note, 385
Sedgwick, Lieut., killed, 312
Selby, Lieut. Prideaux, 212 and note
Shafto, 2nd Lieut. D., 435 note
Sheaffe, Sir Roger Hale, 207, 210, 213
Sherrard, Capt. Daniel, 43
Shearing, Lieut. Robt., prisoner, 103
Simcocks, Capt., 268; wounded, 333 note
Simmons, Major, 367 and note, 369, 370, 377, 380; killed, 383, 384 and note
Sinclair, Lieut., wounded, 309
Sitwell, Brig.-Gen. W. H., 416 and note, 420 note
Skelton, Capt. John, 24 note
Sloan, Pte., 456
Smollet, Ensign James, 65
Spearman, Capt. J., 384 note
Spencer, Capt., 359

INDEX

Fifth Foot, officers and men (continued)—
Smith, Sir David Wm., 129, 197; in Canada, 209; leaves Fifth, 210, 213
Smith, Lieut.-Col. John, at Warburg, 111, 116, 125; Captain, 156; brig.-major, St. Lucia, 159, 175 note; and Governor Burt, 186, 189; major, 199, 203; commands district in Canada, 206; death, 210, 212
Somerville, Capt., 449; wounded, 450 note
Stanton, 2nd Lieut. H. J., killed, 450 note
Stephenson, Lieut.-Col. Chas., 200; envoy to Washington, 206; Q.M.G. in Canada, 207; Major, 210; wounded, 229; lieut.-col., 243; leaves Fifth, 244 and note
Stewart, Ensign, wounded, 171 note
Stone, Band-Sergt., 435 note
Stopford, Honble. Edward, 196 and note, 209
Stubbs, Cpl., deserts, 127; rejoins, 137
Sturges, Major, 435 note
Sutherland, Major-Gen. Sir Wm., lieutenant-colonel of Fifth, 356; in Ireland, 358, 359; at Gibraltar, 361; Corfu, 363, 364; Governor of Mauritius, 367
Talbot, Lieut.-Col. Thos., 213, 235
Talbot, Capt., killed at Walcheren, 290
Talbot, Capt. Richard, 199
Thompson, Sergt., 405
Thomas, Ensign, wounded, 171 note
Tiller, Sergt., 342 note
Titchborne, Capt., 56
Tollemache, Col. Honble. Thos., 25 and note; colonel of Coldstream Guards, 29, 33, 34; killed, 40
Tongres, Drummer Timothy, 293 note
Toppin, Lieut., 427 note, 440
Tovey, Major, 359
Tyson, 2nd Lieut. H. V., 420 note
Urwin, Ensign Ralph, 56
Ussher, Ensign J., 207
Vanriel, Lieut. Lambert, 61, 72 and note

Fifth Foot, officers and men (continued)—
Vincent, Lieut.-Col., 403 and note, 404, 405
Wake, 2nd Lieut. G. R., 435 note
Walcott, Lieut.-Col. Wm., 134; tried by C.-M., 144 note, 154; wounded, 164 note; death, 171
Walton, Ensign, wounded Walcheren, 289
Ward, Capt., death, 364
Watson, Q.M., 342 note
Way, Capt. G. B., 260 note
Way, Lieut.-Col. W. F., 406 note
Welch, Lieut., wounded, 338
Westmacott, 2nd Lieut., 450 note
Whitefoord, Col. Chas., at Preston Pans, 69; lieut.-col., 70, 71, 72, 74; colonel, 75; death, 76
Williams, Ensign, wounded, 309
Wilson, Major Edward, 22, 24 note
Wisely, Col. Henry; lieutenant-colonel, 9; colonel, 17, 18; drowned, 22
Wood, Lieut. C. M. A., 418, 419, 420 note
Woods, Col.-Sergt., 413
Woods, Lieut., 450
Wolseley, Lieut. G. J., 236 note
Wylde, Lieut., wounded, 322
Wynyard, Gen. Wm., 350 and note
Yatman, Capt., 449
St. George's Day, 196
"The Shiners," 133
Snuff Box, 123 and note
Strength, 1690, 33; 1699, 43; 1713, 54; 1754, 86; 1755, 87; 1758, 92; 1759, 104; 1762, 124 note; 1765, 130; 1768, 131; 1774, 138; at Bunker's Hill, 154; 1776, 158 note; 1805, 249 and note; 1st Fifth at Fuentes de Onoro, 310; 1st Fifth, 1812, 330; 1st Fifth, 1878, 410 note; 1st Fifth, 1882, 415; 1st Fifth, 1899, 422; 2nd Fifth, 1899, 432
"Wellington's Bodyguard," 312
The White Plume, 182, 356
French, Sir John, 432, 437

Gage, General, 141, 143, 145, 151; recalled, 155
Gatacre, Sir William, in Egypt, 417; in South Africa, 432-435, 438

INDEX

George II., 79, 85; death, 113
Germantown, battle of, 170
Ghent, Fifth at, 39
Gibraltar, 49, 53, 237, 360, 364, 406, 416
Glasgow, 2nd Fifth at, 402
Gloucester, Fifth at, 86
Good Conduct Stripes, 352
Good Service Medal, 352
Grahamstown, 2nd Fifth at, 401
Granby, Lord, 109, 110, 117, 119, 126, 132
Grand Fleet, Fifth on board, 38 and note, 93
Grant, Gen. James, 168; at Germantown, 170 and note; West Indies, 175; St. Lucia, 179, 186
Grantham, Fifth at, 221
Graspan, battle of, 430
Grave, Fifth at, 16
Greenwich, Fifth at, 42
Grenadiers, 21, 34, 36, 94, 98, 100, 109, 118, 122, 148, 152, 224 and note
Guernsey, 1st Fifth at, 243; 2nd Fifth at, 292

Halifax (North America), Fifth at, 159
Hanover, Fifth embark for, 248 and note
Hair, 82, 93
Havelock, Sir Henry, 369, 377, 384, 386 note, 390; death, 391
Helder, H.M.T., wreck of, 250
Hexham, 406
Hill, Major-Gen., 270 and note, 274
Hoorn, Fifth at, 233
Hope, Sir John, 276, 283
Hospitals, 35, 82, 93, 125 note
Howe, Admiral Lord, 89, 91, 96, 160, 173
Howe, Gen. Sir Wm., 150, 152; commander-in-chief, 154; at Boston, 157, 162; Pennsylvania, 167; resigns, 172

India, 368, 402, 409
Ireland, 30; 1730, 62; 1761, 128; 1780, 191; 1827, 357; 1844, 365; 1865, 408; 1882, 415
Irish Establishment, 43 and note, 82

Jagd Spruit, 454
Junius, letters of, quoted, 132, 133, 134

Kabul, 411, 412, 414
Kane, Col. Richard, 50, 56
Kent, Edward, Duke of, 208, 242
"Khaki," 396
Khartoum, 417, 420

King Williamstown, 2nd Fifth at 401
Kirchdunckern, battle of, 117
Kitchener, Lord, 416 and note, 447, 457
Kloster Kampen, 113

Lexington, 149
London, Fifth in, 29, 36, 347
Louis XIV., 19, 42, 43, 45, 52
Lichtenberg, 1st Fifth at, 451
Light Infantry, 148, 152, 224 and note
Limerick, siege of, 35; Fifth at, 77, 133, 193
Little Egg Harbour, 174
Lucknow, 369, 395, 399

Mackay, Gen. Hugh, 5; commands English Brigade, 25, 28, 33, 37
Madeira, Fifth at, 256
Madrid, 2nd Fifth at, 334
Malta, 1st Fifth at, 326
Massachusetts' Spy quoted, 143
Mauritius, 1st Fifth at, 366; 2nd Fifth at, 400
Methuen, Lord, 428, 429, 431, 438, 444-446, 451-456
Militia, 105, 194, 209, 220, 224; Devon, 247; Irish, 269, 284
Militia Bill, 85, 127
Modder River, 431
Moore, Sir John, 273 note, 274, 279; death, 283
Montreal, Fifth at, 205
Morpeth, 406
Mutiny Act, 63

Namur, lost, 37; retaken, 40, 41
Neil, Brig.-Gen., 376 and note; killed, 380
New York, 164
Newcastle-upon-Tyne, 400, 406; regimental depot at, 415
Nooitgedacht, 2nd Fifth at, 448-450
Norman Cross, Fifth at, 222
Northumberland, 134, 406
Nottingham, Fifth at, 36
Niagara, Fort, Fifth at, 207; ceded to U.S.A., 210
Nurses, Army, 93

Ochsendorf, 109
O'Hara, Gen., 238, 242
Omdurman, 419
Oudh, 368, 396
Outram, Sir James, 375, 379, 382, 386, 390-394

Palavea, Heights of, 282
Paris, Treaty of, 139; 1st Fifth in, 345

INDEX

Pay, Brig.-Gen., 46; Irish Establishment, 63 note, 215, 408
Pensioners, 53
Peninsula Medal, 342 note
Philadelphia, Fifth at, 169
Picton, Sir Thomas, 286; commands 3rd Division, 299; at Busaco, 303; Pombal, 306; Sabugal, 308; El Boden, 315; Ciudad Rodrigo, 319; Badajos, 325; Vittoria, 336, 340; Toulouse, 342; death, 345
Pikes, 51, 79
Pitt, William, 85, 92, 107, 120, 140
Plattsburg, 344
Plymouth, Fifth at, 29, 335, 365
Point Levi, Fifth at, 211
Portsmouth, Fifth at, 37
Prescott, Gen. Robt., 175 note, 186, 210
Provisions, 217
"Purchase," 217; abolished, 409

Quebec, Fifth at, 203

Recruits, 48; height of, 73, 81, 194, 227, 356
Reddersburg, 2nd Fifth M.I. at, 441
Roberts, Lord, 404, 410, 412, 436, 445, 447, 457
Rolica, 1st Fifth at, 271
Rothbury, 406
Rye, Fifth at, 251

Sachsenhausen, 108
Sackville, Lord George (Germaine), 70 note, 88, 93, 96; at Minden, 97, 115, 140, 166
Salamanca, Fifth at, 332
Salisbury, Fifth at, 86
Sannah's Post, 1st Fifth M.I. at, 439
Say, Clerk Fras., aptd., 23
St. Cas, 100
St. Helena, 2nd Fifth at, 401
St. Kitts, 334
St. Lucia, 177, 354
St. Vincent (island of), 354
Schagen, Fifth at, 231
Schoorldam, storming of, 229 and note
Sick and wounded, in North America, 163; St. Lucia, 184, 186; sick fund, 217; in Holland, 227; Walcheren, 289
Silver Hill Barracks, 236
Simcoe, Gen. John Graves, 207 and note, 208-210, 212

Sluys, Fifth at, 39
Soerst, Fifth at, 116
Steyning Barracks, 285
Stormberg, 2nd Fifth at, 432-434, 438
Sudan, 416
Surgeons, 81, 216
Sutlers, 227

Tactics, 218
Talavera, 297
Tents, 112
Territorial System, 414
Texel, Fifth land, 227
Test Act, 23
Toulouse, 1st Fifth at, 342
Trenton, 165
Tweebosch, 1st Fifth at, 455

Utrecht, Fifth at, 7, 16; Treaty of, 49, 52

Valenciennes, 1st Fifth at, 346
Victoria Cross, 378, 382, 393, 432
Vimeira, 1st Fifth at, 272
Vittoria, 1st Fifth at, 336

Warburg, 109
Warmenhuizen, 229
Washington, George, 155, 156, 158, 162, 173, 206
Waterford, Fifth at, 130
Wellington, Duke of, 252, 269; in Peninsula, 295; Busaco, 303; El Boden, 314; Salamanca, 332; his order to 2nd Fifth, 334; Vittoria, 337, 340; at Toulouse, 342; France, 346
Wesel, Fifth at, 113
Whitelocke, Sir John, 257; withdraws from Buenos Ayres, 265; court-martial, 266 and note
Wight, Isle of, 113
Wilhelmstahl, 121, 361
William III., 2, 9, 24; King of England, 28; in Ireland, 32; death, 44, 154
Windsor, 2nd Fifth at, 347
Winkel, action at, 234
Worcester, Fifth at, 86
Women with the army, 114, 184, 237, 353

York, Duke of, commander-in-chief, 219, 225, 229, 230

Zierenberg, Fifth at, 111

www.ingramcontent.com/pod-product-compliance
Lightning Source LLC
Chambersburg PA
CBHW031128160426
43193CB00008B/70